2007·2008

PUDLO
PARIS

by Gilles Pudlowski

TRANSLATED BY SIMON BEAVER

**Food Translations by
Sophie Brissaud, Phyllis Flick and Lucy Vanel**

The Little Bookroom • New York

Originally published in French by Michel Lafon as
Guide Le Pudlo Paris 2007 by Gilles Pudlowski

With the assistance of Jérôme Berger; Claudine Bordelier, Dominique Brugière,
Didier Chambeau, Sophie Elusse, Jean-Pierre Espiard, Florent Gagnebin de Bons,
Marc Horwitz, Sylvain Knecht, Michèle Maublanc, Albert Nahmias, Alain Neyman,
Jean-Francois Neyroud, Didier Nicolas, Muriel Pragier-Pudlowski, Michaël Pudlowski,
Elisabeth Rocher, Maurice Rougemont, Jean-Daniel Sudres, Philippe Toinard.

Photos: DR
Author Photo: X. Imbert

English edition © 2007 The Little Bookroom
English translation: Simon Beaver
Food Translations: Sophie Brissaud, Phyllis Flick and Lucy Vanel

Book design: Chad Roberts / Louise Fili Ltd

Library of Congress Cataloging-in-Publication Data

Pudlowski, Gilles, 1950-
[Pudlo Paris, 2007-2008. English]
Le pudlo Paris, 2007-2008 / by Gilles Pudlowski ; translated by Simon Beaver.
p. cm.
ISBN-13: 978-1-892145-48-2 (alk. paper)
1. Restaurants--Paris--Directories. I. Title.
TX907.5.F72P375513 2007
647.9544'361--dc22
2007002472

Published by The Little Bookroom
1755 Broadway, 5th floor
New York NY 10019
(212) 293-1643
Fax (212) 333-5374
editorial@littlebookroom.com
www.littlebookroom.com

Distributed by Random House, Random House International,
and in the UK and Ireland by Signature Book Services

PUDLO PARIS 2007-2008
TABLE OF CONTENTS

COULD PLEASURE
BE BACK ON THE MENU?

Queen of inexpensive bistros and fine, creative restaurants; proponent of appealing cafés serving chilled wine as well as more chic establishments, Paris has always been generous, but fickle. This seventeenth edition of the *Pudlo Paris* (yes, already!) is actually the story of a love affair between a group of dedicated gourmets and the French capital.

With his twenty or so professional and amateur researchers, keen rewriters, enthusiastic investigators and epicures hungry for new flavors, the writer of these lines is primarily a conductor, attempting to imprint his rhythm and style on an efficient team. So is the project a success? It would seem so, since more and more readers turn to us for advice each year.

This year, our "Special Favorite" distinction, which is conferred on restaurants that provide good value for money in each district of Paris, has never been so easy to award. From Christophe (in the fifth) to Carte Blanche (ninth), and Hier et Aujourd'hui (seventeenth) to A l'Abordage (eighth), not to mention Dalva (second), Les Ferrandaise (sixth), the spirited Le Châteaubriand (eleventh) and the striking Le Gorille Blanc (seventh), Paris has never provided us with so many new opportunities to celebrate at reasonable prices. Yesterday's musings on the recession are forgotten; worries about the future of the restaurant trade have flown. Great or humble, young or experienced, chefs are becoming increasingly adventurous. Following the example of Senderens at the former Lucas Carton, Christian Constant has turned his Le Violon d'Ingres (seventh) into a chic, gourmet brasserie, and Antoine Westermann, star cook of the Strasbourg Buerehiesel, has restyled Drouant (second) in the same flavorsome, but casual, manner.

The great classics naturally endure, and in a guide that gallantly defends tradition and remains distrustful of untrammeled invention, we have awarded our supreme honor to Bernard Pacaud's L'Ambroisie (fourth), restoring its three Plates, since we felt it was very much at its finest this year. Our Chef of the Year is a woman, Hélène Darroze. She underlines the importance of fine produce, remains true to her Landes roots and is not afraid to stress the delights to be found in recipes from bygone days.

Our other new discoveries and laureates offer reassurance. Showing little interest in "designer cuisine," they refuse to use their customers as guinea pigs and have reintroduced the concept of pleasure. This is true of Géraud Rongier (Chez Géraud in the sixteenth), our Bistro of the Year; Franck Dervin (Hier et Aujourd'hui, seventeenth), our Best Value for Money; and Catherine Delaunay, our finest hostess (La Luna, eighth); not to mention our two international restaurants, run by charming Italian Massimo Mori, who has diverted the Grand Canal through place de la Bourse (Mori Venice Bar, second), and Japanese prodigy Koji Aida, who puts on a one-man show, crafting his outstanding produce with tremendous talent (Aida, seventh).

Then how could we forget Romain Corbière? Our Young Chef of the Year, at Le Relais du Parc in the sixteenth, provides didactic versions (less expensive than the originals) of favorite dishes from two great maestros of our day: Alain Ducasse and Joël Robuchon (perhaps we should mention in passing that Robuchon's Atelier in the seventh collects two Plates this year).

Artisans, an essential feature of this guide, are also brilliantly represented, offering superb bread (like the delicious La Boulangerie par Véronique Mauclerc in the nineteenth) or fresh, light and innovative cakes and pastries (Didier Mathray and Nathalie Robert at Le Pain de Sucre in the third). All provide a subtle mix of pleasure and craft, quality and perfectionism, reliability and warmth.

So do we tend to stray on the side of optimism? Or, on the contrary, are we realistic and visionary? In the past, we have introduced our readers to so many good-quality bistros, subsequently successful (Chez Michel in the tenth, Mon Vieil Ami in the fourth, L'Avant-Goût in the thirteenth and L'Entredgeu in the seventeenth, to name but four), that we hope you will trust us when we say that Paris has never been a better place to eat than in 2006, and we expect to dine even better here in 2007.

Is that so very surprising in a gourmet metropolis that is a legend throughout the world?

GILLES PUDLOWSKI

CHEF OF THE YEAR

● **Hélène Darroze, 6th**

Little Hélène has grown. The one-time rookie from the provinces, former tosser of salads in Monaco for Cousin Ducasse from Castelsarrasin, after years spent at Supdéco business school, is now her own mistress, rallying Paris society to her banner. She has published a large, successful book of sentimental recipes entitled *Personne ne me volera ce que j'ai dansé (No one can take what I danced from me)* and continued her ascent, earning the title of "little princess of the Landes in Paris". Now she stages the cuisine of her day, era, roots and personality in an elegant contemporary setting in red and gold, with shades of carrot, tomato and eggplant. Cry it from the rooftops: the Southwest has acquired another grand culinary temple to stand alongside Alain Dutournier's Carré des Feuillants!

INTERNATIONAL RESTAURANT OF THE YEAR

● **Mori Venice Bar, 2nd**

A Venetian Harry's Bar in Paris! That is the tour de force imagined—and accomplished—by Massimo Mori, the mischievous Mantovan, brilliant maître d' of Armani Caffé. Opposite the Bourse, the former Bon II has metamorphosed into a chic, amusing, enjoyable paneled bar, with kitchen counter, chic dishes, wines by the glass and extra fresh produce. Authentic, elegant, snobbish, good—expensive if you are incautious, reasonable if you take care—the Mori Venice Bar is an event indeed! A petite monkfish soup, shrimp with radicchio, Arrigo Cipriani-style carpaccio, delicate veal tripe, scallops marinated in their shells, salt cod "mantecato" and spaghetti with clams all win our approval, as do the Sicilian wine, Nero d'Avola, and the delicate meringue cake. We predict a bright future for this eatery.

INTERNATIONAL RESTAURANT OF THE YEAR

● **Aida, 7th**

His name is Koji Aida. A young, subtle, discreet native of Tokyo, he has studied oenology in Burgundy and prepares a remarkably elegant "knife cuisine" in his tiny cubbyhole in the heart of the 7th arrondissement. His sushi and sashimi are splendid. The main courses prepared on an iron grill, teppanyaki style, approach perfection. The spinach salad with mushrooms, radish broth with foie gras, miso soup and the tender filet of Limousin beef are devilishly tempting. Looking around, we see a few tables, a bar where we can admire the culinary master sculptor, a small Japanese-style dining room with tatamis and an area to stretch out our legs. In short, an exquisite, exotic establishment whose little lunchtime prix fixe menus are tickets to Tokyo or Kyoto at angelic prices.

YOUNG CHEF OF THE YEAR

● **Le Relais du Parc, 16th**

Now you can taste Robuchon and Ducasse all in one at the Sofitel's Le Relais du Parc restaurant, which has received a modern makeover. In the kitchen, following instructions handed down by the two great traveling, multiple-menu chefs, the young Romain Corbière (formerly at the Louis XV) labors with precision and maturity, preparing the dishes that have made his masters famous. If you have not tasted paté baked in a pastry crust in the style of Lucien Tendret, small pasta shells with truffles and ham, deep-fried whiting, then do so at once: this is the perfect opportunity to indulge your-self (almost) inexpensively! Every dish here not only carries the hallmark of the two great chefs, but also the stamp of a young talent who displays amazing skill and who is undoubt-edly destined for great things. Remember the name!

BISTRO OF THE YEAR

● Chez Géraud, 16th

Once he was the charming bistro owner of Le Val d'Or in avenue Franklin Roosevelt. Now, Géraud Rongier is a restaurateur in a quiet Passy street. He has not given up his Homeric tours of the vineyards though. The proof is in his divine libations, which delight his guests: Mâcon whites, a cheerful red Gevray with a Côtes de Nuits touch and a sumptuous Combier Crozes Hermitage, all accompanying first-rate produce. Scrambled eggs with truffles, truffle-stuffed hen and a magnificent calf's head are painstakingly prepared by the faithful Gérard Vacher. Turning to the desserts, we enjoy the ritual paris-brest, with its airy choux pastry and light praliné butter cream. This is one of the best bistros in Paris, brightened by ceramics inspired by Steinlen.

BEST VALUE
FOR MONEY OF THE YEAR

● **Hier et Aujourd'hui, 17th**

The location is a changing area of Paris by the Périphérique. The restaurant is amusing, modern and inexpensive. Franck Dervin, a chef full of energy who puts on a one-man show in his kitchen behind glass, paid his dues with Guy Savoy and Alain Dutournier. What we like here are his freshness, sharpness and precision, and his amusing way of concocting combinations of flavors that work. The fish and shellfish plunge us into a world of sea spray and flavor. Turning to the meats, lamb layered with mashed potatoes and eggplant and tender beef with cornichons are better than grandmother's! Franck, who does it all on its own, presents a set menu of the day on the blackboard for just 26€. The desserts are splendid (paris-brest with a light praliné butter cream and an airy baba au rhum) and Karin Ouet provides a smiling welcome and prompt service. A fine establishment indeed!

HOSTESS OF THE YEAR

● La Luna, 8th

A restaurant's success does not just depend on its cuisine. The gracious Catherine Delaunay lends credence to this axiom. She runs her dining room with charm and virtuosity, and has refurbished her fine seafood restaurant with a certain discreet elegance, in grey and burgundy. The place has chic and to spare with its banquettes and nooks. The beautiful hostess sets its quietly convivial tone and the cuisine now reflects this ambience. Sea bream, salmon and tuna tartare, langoustine cakes with tender leeks, Noirmoutier sole and giant Zanzibar baba with vanilla cream and artisanal rum all have an easy appeal. The prices take no prisoners, but do reflect the quality.

BAKER OF THE YEAR

● Véronique Mauclerc, 19th

She acquired a master baker's diploma before taking over a local store with great energy. Véronique Mauclerc, who bakes her bread in a wood-fired oven, uses organic flour. Apart from a brilliant crispy light baguette, she also presents splendid varieties with onions and bacon, an Auvergnat brioche with saffron and a licorice roll, not to mention bread with Madagascan pepper and a superb country sourdough loaf. Finally, she offers a first-rate range of fine cakes and pastries: carmelized millefeuille, shortbread lemon custard tart with strawberries, Alsatian brioche with raisins and orange water and finally the "Buttes Chaumont": an almond cookie cake with bitter chocolate and a crème brûlée center. An event, and not only in female terms!

PASTRY CHEFS OF THE YEAR

● **Le Pain de Sucre, 3rd**

They both served as pastry chefs with Pierre Gagnaire before going into business themselves on a modest scale, taking over a narrow baker's store in this gastronomic street. They have painted it a shade of chocolate and now present the cream of today's cakes and pastries there. Didier Mathray and Nathalie Robert's specialty? Taking a fresh look at the classics, lightening and revamping them. Their version of "crumble"-style chocolate eclair, shortbread with red berries, lemon tart, their very fashionable preserves in Mason jars —Zanzibar (pineapple), Mister Tom (green apple), Don Quixote with (apricot)— and their chocolate "shock" or chestnut desserts are well worth purchasing and tasting.

WHAT'S NEW IN 2007

Promoted to ⓒⓒⓒ

L'Ambroisie, 4th arr. `LUX`
Hélène Darroze, 6th arr. `V.COM`

Promoted to ⓒⓒ

L'Atelier de Joël Robuchon, 7th `SIM`

Promoted to ⓒ

Il Cortile, 1st `V.COM`
Mori Venice Bar, 2nd `N COM`
Le Pur'Grill, 2nd `V.COM`
Le 21, 6th `N SIM`
Ze Kitchen Galerie, 6th `SIM`
Aida, 7th `N SIM`
Chez les Anges, 7th `V.COM`
La Cour Jardin, 8th `N V.COM`
La Luna, 8th `V.COM`
La Maison Blanche, 8th `LUX`
Senderens, 8th `N T V.COM`
Les Muses, 9th `LUX`
Romain, 9th `COM`
Le Dôme, 14th `COM`
Le Relais de Sevrès, 15th `V.COM`
Thierry Burlot, 15th `COM`
Conti, 16th `COM`
Chez Géraud, 16th `COM`
Le Relais du Parc, 16th `COM`

Promoted to 🍴

Carré Vlanc, 1st `N SIM`
A Casa Luna, 1st `COM`
Dalva, 2nd `N SIM`
Le Petit Pamphlet, 3rd `N SIM`
Christophe, 5th `N SIM`
Ribouldingue, 5th `N SIM`
Evi Evane, 6th `N SIM`
La Ferrandaise, 6th `N SIM`
Le Gorille Blanc, 7th `N SIM`
A L'Abordage, 8th `N SIM`
Carte Blanche, 9th `N COM`
Le Jardinier, 9th `SIM`
16 Haussmann, 9th `COM`
La Table d'Anvers, 9th `COM`
Aux Zingots, 10th `N SIM`
L'Alchimiste, 12th `SIM`
Le Bambou, 13th `N SIM`
Virgule, 13th `N SIM`
Ban Som Tam, 14th `N SIM`
Millésime 62, 14th `N COM`
Le Casier a Vin, 15th `SIM`

Caïus, 17th `COM`
Hier et Aujourd'hui, 17th `N SIM`
Ripaille, 17th `N SIM`
Les Allobroges, 20th `COM`

Fell from ⓒ to ⓒ

Drouant, 2nd `ⓒ T V.COM`
Le Violon d'Ingres, 7th `ⓒ COM`
La Grande Cascade, 16th `ⓒ T LUX`

Lost their ⓒ

L'Argenteuil, 1st* `🍴 COM`
Jean, 9th `COM`
L'Oulette, 12th `V.COM`
Marius, 16th `COM`
Port-Alma, 16th `V.COM`
Augusta, 17th `V.COM`
Graindorge, 17th `COM`

Lost their 🍴

Pharamond, 1st `T SIM`
Pierre au Palais-Royal, 1st `COM`
Le Press Café, 2nd `SIM`
Le Dôme du Marais, 4th `T COM`
L'AOC, 5th `SIM`
Moissonnier, 5th `T SIM`
Au Gourmand, 6th `SIM`
La Maison du Jardin, 6th `SIM`
La Rôtisserie d'en Face, 6th `SIM`
Le Vin de Soif, 7th `SIM`
L'Oriental, 9th `SIM`
Les Jumeaux, 11th `SIM`
Les Caves Solignac, 14th `T SIM`
La Maison Courtine, 14th `V.COM`
Bistrot d' Hélène, 15th `SIM`
Le Passage, 15th `SIM`
Chez Cédric, 17th `SIM`
Le Zéphyr, 20th** `T SIM`

*Formerly 🍴 **Formerly ⑤

BEST RESTAURANTS

⬭⬭

Le Carré des Feuillants, 1st	LUX
Le Meurice, 1st	V.LUX
L'Ambroisie, 4th	⌂ LUX
La Tour d'Argent, 5th	🍴 V.LUX
Hélène Darroze, 6th	⌂ V.COM
L'Arpège, 7th	V.COM
Les Ambassadeurs, 8th	V.LUX
Le Bristol, 8th	V.LUX
Le Cinq, 8th	V.LUX
Alain Ducasse, 8th	V.LUX
Pierre Gagnaire, 8th	LUX
Taillevent, 8th	V.LUX
Le Pré Catelan, 16th	LUX
Guy Savoy, 17th	LUX

⬭

L'Espadon, 1st	V.LUX
Goumard, 1st	LUX
Le Grand Véfour, 1st	🍴 LUX
Le Relais Louis XIII, 6th	🍴 V.COM
L'Atelier de Joël Robuchon, 7th	⌂ SIM
Le Chamarré, 7th	COM
Le Divellec, 7th	LUX
Le Jules Verne, 7th	LUX
Apicius, 8th	V.LUX
Les Elysées du Vernet, 8th	LUX
Le Jardin, 8th	LUX
Lasserre, 8th	🍴 V.LUX
Laurent, 8th	V.LUX
Ledoyen, 8th	🍴 V.LUX
Stella Maris, 8th	COM
Montparnasse 25, 14th	LUX
L'Astrance, 16th	COM
La Table de Joël Robuchon, 16th	COM

○

Gérard Besson, 1st	LUX
Il Cortile, 1st	⌂ V.COM
Chez Pauline, 1st	🍴 COM
Pinxo, 1st	COM
Chez Vong, 1st	V.COM
Le Céladon, 2nd	LUX
Drouant, 2nd	🍴 V.COM
A la Fontaine Gaillon, 2nd	🍴 V.COM
Aux Lyonnais, 2nd	🍴 SIM
Mori Venice Bar, 2nd	N COM
Le Pur'Grill, 2nd	⌂ V.COM
Le Pamphlet, 3rd	COM
Benoît, 4th	🍴 COM

Mon Vieil Ami, 4th	SIM
Mavrommatis, 5th	COM
Armani Caffè, 6th	SIM
Bastide Odéon, 6th	COM
Jacques Cagna, 6th	V.COM
Le Comptoir du Relais, 6th	🍴 SIM
Fogon, 6th	COM
La Méditerranée, 6th	🍴 V.COM
Le Paris, 6th	V.COM
Le 21, 6th	N SIM
Yugaraj, 6th	COM
Ze Kitchen Galerie, 6th	⌂ SIM
Aïda, 7th	N SIM
Chez les Anges, 7th	⌂ V.COM
Auguste, 7th	COM
Au Bon Accueil, 7th	SIM
Bruno Deligne, 7th	COM
Gaya Rive Gauche par Pierre Gagnaire, 7th	COM
Les Ormes, 7th	COM
Tan Dinh, 7th	COM
Tante Marguerite, 7th	COM
Vin sur Vin, 7th	COM
Le Violon d'Ingres, 7th	COM
L'Angle du Faubourg, 8th	COM
Dominique Bouchet, 8th	COM
Café Faubourg, 8th	COM
Il Carpaccio, 8th	V.COM
Chez Catherine, 8th	V.COM
Chiberta, 8th	V.COM
Citrus Etoile, 8th	COM
Clovis, 8th	V.COM
Le Copenhague, 8th	V.COM
La Cour Jardin, 8th	N V.COM
Garnier, 8th	V.COM
Kinugawa, 8th	COM
La Luna, 8th	⌂ V.COM
La Maison Blanche, 8th	⌂ LUX
Marius et Janette, 8th	COM
Market, 8th	COM
Relais-Plaza, 8th	V.COM
Les Saveurs de Flora, 8th	V.COM
Senderens, 8th	N 🍴 V.COM
Le Stresa, 8th	COM
La Table du Lancaster, 8th	COM
Tante Louise, 8th	🍴 COM
W, 8th	V.COM
Casa Olympe, 9th	SIM
Les Muses, 9th	⌂ LUX
Le Pétrelle, 9th	COM

Romain, 9th	COM
Wally le Saharien, 9th	COM
Chez Michel, 10th	COM
Mansouria, 11th	COM
Le Villaret, 11th	SIM
Le Quincy, 12th	COM
Au Trou Gacon, 12th	COM
Le Dôme, 14th	COM
Le Duc, 14th	V.COM
Le Bélisaire, 15th	SIM
Chen, 15th	V.COM
Le Gastroquet, 15th	COM
Le Relais de Sèvres, 15th	V.COM
Thierry Burlot, 15th	COM
Conti, 16th	COM
Chez Géraud, 16th	COM
La Grande Cascade, 16th	LUX
Hiramatsu, 16th	LUX
Oum El Banine, 16th	COM
Passiflore, 16th	V.COM
Le Pergolèse, 16th	V.COM
Le Relais d'Auteuil, 16th	V.COM
La Table du Baltimore, 16th	V.COM
Tang, 16th	V.COM
Le Relais du Parc, 16th	COM
Les Béatilles, 17th	COM
La Braisière, 17th	COM
Epicure 108, 17th	COM
La Maison de Charly, 17th	V.COM
Paolo Petrini, 17th	COM
Michel Rostang, 17th	LUX
Sormani, 17th	V.COM
Taïra, 17th	COM
A. Beauvilliers, 18th	V.COM
La Cave Gourmande, 19th	SIM

BEST VALUE FOR MONEY

L'Absinthe, 1st	SIM
L'Ardoise, 1st	SIM
L'Argenteuil, 1st	COM
A Casa Luna, 1st	COM
Willi's Wine Bar, 1st	SIM
Dalva, 2nd	SIM
Gallopin, 2nd	COM
Le Mellifère, 2nd	SIM
Chez Pierrot, 2nd	SIM
L'Ambassade d'Auvergne, 3rd	V.COM
Au Bascou, 3rd	SIM
Café des Musées, 3rd	SIM
Chez Nénesse, 3rd	SIM
Le Petit Pamphlet, 3rd	SIM
Napoli Food, 4th	SIM
Au Buisson Ardent, 5th	SIM
Chantairelle, 5th	SIM
Christophe, 5th	SIM
Les Délices d'Aphrodite, 5th	SIM
L'Equitable, 5th	COM
L'Estrapade, 5th	SIM
Les Papilles, 5th	SIM
Ribouldingue, 5th	SIM
La Rôtisserie du Beaujolais, 5th	SIM
Tao, 5th	COM
L'Epi Dupin, 6th	SIM
Evi Evane, 6th	SIM
La Ferrandaise, 6th	SIM
Les Racines, 6th	SIM
Aux Saveurs de Claude, 6th	SIM
Wadja, 6th	SIM
L'Affriolé, 7th	SIM
L'Ami Jean, 7th	SIM
Café Constant, 7th	SIM
Le Clos des Gourmets, 7th	COM
Les Fables de la Fontaine, 7th	SIM
Le Gorille Blanc, 7th	SIM
Le Maupertu, 7th	COM
Nabuchodonosor, 7th	COM
Le P'tit Troquet, 7th	SIM
La Taverna, 7th	COM
A L'Abordage, 8th	SIM
Chez Germain, 8th	SIM
L'Art des Choix, 9th	SIM
La Boule Rouge, 9th	SIM
Carte Blanche, 9th	COM
Fuji-Yaki, 9th	SIM
Georgette, 9th	SIM
Le Jardinier, 9th	SIM
La Petite Sirène de Copenhague, 9th	SIM
Le Pré Cadet, 9th	SIM
16 Haussmann, 9th	COM
Sizin, 9th	SIM
La Table d'Anvers, 9th	COM
Velly, 9th	SIM
Chez Casimir, 10th	SIM
Aux Zingots, 10th	SIM
Astier, 11th	SIM

Le Bistrot Paul Bert, 11th — SIM
Le C'Amelot, 11th — SIM
Le Chateaubriand, 11th — SIM
L'Ecailler du Bistrot, 11th — SIM
Le Marsangy, 11th — SIM
Chez Ramulaud, 11th — SIM
Le Repaire de Cartouche, 11th — COM
Le Temps au Temps, 11th — SIM
Au Vieux Chene, 11th — SIM
L'Alchimiste, 12th — SIM
A La Biche au Bois, 12th — SIM
La Connivence, 12th — SIM
L'Ebauchoir, 12th — SIM
Jean-Pierre Frelet, 12th — SIM
O'Rebelle, 12th — SIM
Les Zygomates, 12th — SIM
L'Anacréon, 13th — SIM
L'Appennino, 13th — SIM
L'Avant-Goût, 13th — SIM
Le Bambou, 13th — SIM
L'Ourcine, 13th — SIM
Virgule, 13th — SIM
L'Amuse-Bouche, 14th — SIM
Ban Som Tam, 14th — SIM
La Cerisaie, 14th — SIM
Les Fils de la Ferme, 14th — SIM
Millésime 62, 14th — COM
Natacha, 14th — SIM

Parnasse 138, 14th — SIM
Les Petites Sorcières, 14th — SIM
La Régalade, 14th — SIM
Le Severo, 14th — SIM
L'Ami Marcel, 15th — SIM
L'Antre Amis, 15th — COM
Arti, 15th — SIM
Le Beurre Noisette, 15th — SIM
Le Casier a Vin, 15th — SIM
Le Pétel, 15th — SIM
Le Restaurant du Marché, 15th — SIM
Stéphane Martin, 15th — SIM
Le Trouqet, 15th — SIM
L'Abadache, 17th — SIM
Baptiste, 17th — COM
Chez Bubume, 17th — SIM
Le Café d'Angel, 17th — SIM
Caïus, 17th — COM
L'Entredgeu, 17th — SIM
Goupil, 17th — SIM
Hier et Auguourd'hui, 17th — SIM
Leclou, 17th — SIM
Ripaille, 17th — SIM
La Rucola, 17th — SIM
Taka, 18th — SIM
Le Village Kabyle, 18th — COM
Les Allobroges, 20th — COM
Le Baratin, 20th — SIM

BEST INTERNATIONAL RESTAURANTS

North African
La Boule Rouge, 9th — SIM
Wally le Saharien, 9th — COM
Mansouria, 11th — COM
Oum El Banine, 16th — COM
La Maison de Charly, 17th — V.COM
Le Village Kabyle, 18th — COM

Asian
Chez Vong, 1st — V.COM
Tao, 5th — COM
Tan Dinh, 7th — COM
Le Bambou, 13th — SIM
Ban Som Tam, 14th — SIM
Chen, 15th — V.COM
Tang, 16th — V.COM

Danish
Le Copenhague, 8th — V.COM
La Petite Sirène de Copenhague, 9th — SIM

Spanish
Fogon, 6th — COM

Greek
Les Délices d'Aphrodite, 5th — SIM
Mavrommatis, 5th — COM
Evi Evane, 6th — SIM

Indian
Yugaraj, 6th — COM
Arti, 15th — SIM

Italian

Il Cortile, 1st	⚑○ V.COM
Mori Venice Bar, 2nd	Ⓝ○ COM
Napoli Food, 4th	🍴 SIM
Armani Caffè, 6th	○ SIM
La Taverna, 7th	🍴 COM
Il Carpaccio, 8th	○ V.COM
Le Stresa, 8th	○ COM
Romain, 9th	⚑○ COM
L'Appennino, 13th	🍴 SIM
Conti, 16th	⚑○ COM
Paolo Petrini, 17th	○ COM
La Rucola, 17th	🍴 SIM
Sormani, 17th	○ V.COM

Japanese

Aïda, 7th	Ⓝ○ SIM
Kinugawa, 8th	○ COM
Fuji-Yaki, 9th	🍴 SIM
Taka, 18th	🍴 SIM

Lebanese

Pavillon Noura, 16th	V.COM

Turkish

Sizin, 9th	⚑🍴 SIM

○	Very good restaurant
ⓒ	Excellent restaurant
ⓒⓒ	One of the best restaurants in Paris
⑤	Disappointing restaurant
🍴	Good value for money
⬤	Meals for less than 30 euros
SIM	Simple
COM	Comfortable
V.COM	Very comfortable
LUX	Luxurious
V.LUX	Very Luxurious

Red indicates a particularly charming establishment

🏛	Historical significance
⚑	Promotion *(higher rating than last year)*
Ⓝ	New to the guide
⬤	Restaurant
▼	Shop
◆	Rendez-vous

1ST ARRONDISSEMENT
THE HEART OF PARIS

People here still talk of Les Halles, the wholesale food market, although it moved from Paris out to Rungis in the suburbs long ago. The memory lives on because many of the fine institutions that inspired Emile Zola's *The Belly of Paris* have survived. You can still do your shopping at Mora's or La Bovida, get a coffee at Le Cochon à l'Oreille, enjoy a plate of charcuterie washed down with Beaujolais at the aptly named Aux Tonneaux (barrels) des Halles and make a point of dining late at the La Tour Montlhéry, just as if nothing had changed since the old days! However, the gastronomic geography of the neighborhood has evolved radically. Stylish bistros have invaded the place du Marché Saint-Honoré, restyled by Bofill (L'Absinthe and Le Point Bar are well worth a visit). Prestige eating establishments (Le Meurice, Le Carré des Feuillants, Le Grand Véfour, L'Espadon) and fashionable eateries (Pinxo, Macéo) lie along the rue de Rivoli, flirting with the place Vendôme and the Palais Royal. Numerically the first arrondissement, this district remains the heart of the capital, the quarter where the stores of skilled tradespersons still breathe their poetry and the Bibliothèque Nationale stands watch over the wine bars (Juvéniles, Aux Bons Crus, Willi's), a symbol of old Paris, where brain and stomach have always been closely related.

● RESTAURANTS

GRAND RESTAURANTS

● Le Carré des Feuillants   ◯◯ LUX
14, rue de Castiglione
Métro: Tuileries, Concorde
Tel. 01 42 86 82 82. Fax 01 42 86 07 71
carre.des.feuillants@wanadoo.fr
www.carredesfeuillants.fr
Closed Saturday, Sunday, August.
Open until 10:30 PM.
Prix fixe: 65€ (lunch), 150€.
A la carte: 140€.
Air cond. Private dining room. Valet parking.

The refined Alberto Bali decor of this gourmet establishment is divided into four interconnecting rooms around an inner courtyard. Behind the scenes, Alain Dutournier, native and champion of the Landes region, beguiles his elegant guests with the cuisine of Southwestern France, fine-tuned to reflect his travels and ideas. He has adopted a philosophy handed down by his mother and grandmother, a "bare minimum" approach that, in his case, results in dishes that are virtual masterpieces. The quality of the ingredients cannot be faulted, and imagination, audacity and unusual permutations do the rest. Diners delight in the foie gras and sweetbreads with crayfish jelly, the baby artichokes cooked with black truffles or, better still, Marennes oysters bathed in seawater jelly, Aquitaine caviar, seaweed tartare and creamy foam or thick slices of John Dory fish with potato, tender cabbage lasagna and an aromatic horseradish mousse or the roasted rack of Pyrénées milk-fed lamb, its leg slowly cooked in a clay pot, paired with lightly curried vegetables. All will conjure sighs of satisfaction from your lips. The journey ends on a sweeter note with wild Andalusian strawberries, rose and litchi macarons, mango and passion fruit ravioli or sweet beignets filled with mango and cardamom or pineapple and coconut. Alain Dutournier has constructed a wine cellar rich in surprises, devoting as much care to choosing the nectars that will match his flavors as he does to devising today's and tomorrow's cuisine.

● L'Espadon   ◯◯ V.LUX
Hotel Ritz, 15, pl Vendôme
Métro: Madeleine, Pyramides
Tel. 01 43 16 30 80. Fax 01 43 16 33 75
food-bev@ritzparis.com
www.ritzparis.com
Open daily until 10:30 PM.
Prix fixe: 75€ (lunch), 180€ (dinner),
260€ (dinner, wine included).
A la carte: 160–190€.
Air cond. Terrace. Valet parking.

First, there is the grandiloquent setting dreamt up by César Ritz more than a century ago, with its gilding, stucco, wall hangings and painted ceiling. Then there is the repertoire of a virtuoso chef. Trained at the Ritz, where he has served loyally for more than twenty years (a two-year escapade at Lasserre aside), Michel Roth, holder of the Meilleur Ouvrier de France award and first winner of the Bocuse d'Or prize, is now running the kitchens of this luxury Paris hotel. His cuisine is both traditional and inventive, paying tribute to the culinary conventions that Auguste Escoffier made his trademark. The spider crab with avocado and citrus fruit couldn't be fresher. The asparagus, served with foie gras, comté and sauce Périgueux (a rich sauce flavored with Madeira and truffles) have never tasted so good. The Dover sole, braised in shellfish broth and served with zucchini aïoli, is a marvel of refinement, and the Pauliac lamb with foie gras, truffles and salsify reveals a myriad of flavors. Every last note of the delightful sweetbreads with baby artichokes and citrus polenta is calculated. Turning to the desserts, close your eyes and savor the iced chocolate dessert with milk bonbons or the Ritz's signature millefeuille. Some great vintages feature among the thousand wines the cellar has to offer, all harmonizing with these delicately crafted dishes.

● Goumard   ⓒ LUX

9, rue Duphot
Métro: Madeleine
Tel. 01 42 60 36 07. Fax 01 42 60 04 54
goumard.philippe@wanadoo.fr
www.goumard.fr
Open daily until 10:30 PM.
Prix fixe: 46€, 30€ (children).
A la carte: 135€.
Air cond. Private dining room. Valet parking.

Philippe Dubois, our Restaurateur of the Year 2006, is still riding high. First, his elegant establishment is a visual delight. We never tire of the woodwork, chandeliers and inlays by Lalique, or the engraved glass facade. The food is also a constant source of pleasure, thanks to the skills of Olivier Guyon. Having trained at Vernet and Daniel in New York, he is a master in the preparation of fish of every kind, using select produce to concoct brilliantly simple dishes. Charm does its work in the sautéed crayfish with green asparagus and peanuts, the roasted line-caught sea bass with sweet peas, baby artichokes and heirloom radishes and the sautéed wild squid served with a ricotta and savory ravioli, finished with lobster broth. The culinary display concludes with croustillant filled with wild strawberries, citrus mousse, fresh mango and sorbet of red fruits. Add attentive service and wines to match the exceptional nature of the dishes, and you have a recipe for maritime delight in the course(s) of a dinner or lunch to remember.

● Le Grand Véfour   ⓒ 🍴 LUX

17, rue de Beaujolais
Métro: Palais-Royal, Pyramides, Bourse
Tel. 01 42 96 56 27. Fax 01 42 86 80 71
grand.vefour@wanadoo.fr
Closed Friday evening, Saturday, Sunday, August. Open until 9:30 PM.
Prix fixe: 78€ (lunch). A la carte: 200€.
Air cond. Private dining room. Valet parking.

Guy Martin has been conducting his orchestra in the kitchens of the Véfour for nearly fifteen years. This native of Savoie (formerly of the Château de Coudrée, then the Château de Divonne overlooking Lake Geneva) is very much at home in this restaurant made fashionable by Raymond Oliver. The historic setting, with its red velvet seats, view of the Palais Royal, and plaques dedicated to eminent figures such as Balzac, Colette, Hugo, Cocteau, Berl, Malraux and Napoléon has the elegance of a Directoire shrine. Turning to the cuisine, Guy Martin reconciles tradition and modernity, exotic flavors and provincial produce. The golden frog's legs with a delicate sorrel sauce and the foie gras terrine with mango confit and ras el-hanout (an exotic blend of Moroccan spices) set the tone. Follow with the monkfish encrusted with mild spices and a light smoked cucumber emulsion, roasted Breton lobster with fennel, tomato and shiso (an aromatic Japanese green), filet of lamb with wasabi, baby fava beans and hearts of baby romaine lettuce or oxtail parmentier with truffles and potatoes. The melon fondant with sorbet and wild strawberries forms a dainty conclusion, while the hazelnut and milk chocolate lollypop with salted caramel ice cream offers a moment of delight. The 750 items on the wine list allow some highly appropriate matches, with Patrick Tamisier providing astute advice.

● Le Meurice   ⓒ V.LUX

Hotel Meurice, 228, rue de Rivoli
Métro: Concorde, Tuileries
Tel. 01 44 58 10 55. Fax 01 44 58 10 76
restauration@meuricehotel.com
www.meuricehotel.com
Closed Saturday, Sunday, February, beginning–end of August. Open until 10 PM.
Prix fixe: 75€ (lunch), 190€.
A la carte: 205€.
Air cond. Private dining room. Valet parking.

The decor in the dining room is inspired by the Salon de la Paix at Versailles Palace, and Yannick Alleno's cuisine mirrors it perfectly: grandiose, but not pompous. The master of ceremonies takes his duties as a maestro of flavors to heart. With a squad of 70 sous chefs under his command, this discreet native of the Lozère district wages battle without compromise, producing a spectacular cuisine that leaves nothing to chance, from the choice of raw materials to the methods of preparation and subtlety of cooking and seasoning to the presentation of the dish. This is great art, refined, delicately crafted and never found wanting. The smoked salmon and scallop coulibiac, the heart of "celtuce"—a delicious but little-known vegetable in the asparagus family—with caviar, the cod glazed with seaweed, the tender wild Adour river salmon served rare with Choron sauce (hollandaise with a touch of tomato purée), the Bresse hen with truffles and foie gras served with a celeriac and horseradish ravioli, the roasted suckling pig with blood sausage and creamed corn or the spit-roasted rack of milk-fed Pyrénées lamb provide a splendid feast. There is a bit of Carême, Escoffier and Vatel [considered to be the fathers of French cuisine] in Alleno. He unearths forgotten tastes, tracks the finest flavors to their lairs and gives pleasure without trying to impress. The millefeuille "as you like it" (vanilla, coffee or chocolate, made to order, as it should be) is a high point, and the paper-thin ravioli, iced with red fruit, topped with a champagne and basil infused whipped cream and gavotte fourrée (a crisp, thin, rolled-up pancake) are more sophisticated but equally irresistible. Turning to the cellar, you can choose from some 700 wines, with Nicolas Rebut to help you select the appropriate nectar. This is clearly one of the very greatest establishments in Paris today.

GOOD RESTAURANTS & OTHERS

● L'Absinthe   SIM

24, pl du Marché-Saint-Honoré
Métro: Pyramides, Tuileries
Tel. 01 49 26 90 04. Fax 01 49 26 08 64
www.michelrostang.com
Closed Saturday lunch, Sunday.
Open until 10:30 PM.
Prix fixe: 29€, 36€.
Air cond. Terrace. Private dining room.

Caroline Rostang, who was our 2006 Hostess of the Year, is still running her excellent eatery with boundless energy. The great Michel's daughter has turned this New York loft-style bistro into an elegant but relaxed establishment, carefully constructed

around a large glass wall with a combination of rough materials (concrete, wood, aged metal) and antique tables, Thonet chairs and industrial glass. As for the food, the tastes of the South of France add a ray of sunshine to Laurent Montgillard's roguish cooking. We cheerfully savor Roman ravioli with fresh tomato and verbena, the seared tuna with spices served with wheat risotto, a roasted veal steak with slow-roasted shallot confit, remembering to end on chocolate and coffee fondant. The wine list covers all of France and ventures well beyond its borders, to Italy, New Zealand and Chile.

● L'Ardoise   SIM

28, rue du Mont-Thabor
Métro: Tuileries, Concorde
Tel. 01 42 96 28 18
lardoise1@yahoo.fr
Closed Sunday lunch, Monday, beginning–end of August. Open until 11:30 PM.
Prix fixe: 31€. A la carte: 45€.
Air cond. Private dining room.

At Pierre Jay's Ardoise, you will find classics of good home cooking, sometimes reinterpreted, but always perfectly prepared. This veteran of La Tour d'Argent has no shortage of confidence or ideas (if not diffidence), as is shown by the dishes he concocts with ease. The yellow and ochre walls have a soothing effect, and when the food arrives, you will scarcely be disappointed by the langoustine ravioli, the foie gras terrine, the grilled scallops with sautéed shiitake mushrooms, the veal loin sautéed with morels and cream or the feuillantine of Gariguette strawberries. A fine selection of wines by the glass.

● L'Argenteuil   COM

9, rue d'Argenteuil
Métro: Pyramides, Palais-Royal
Tel. 01 42 60 56 22
Closed Saturday, Sunday.
Open until 10:30 PM.
Prix fixe: 16€ (lunch), 29,50€.
Air cond. Terrace.

The Viennes have taken over from the Schaeffers at this small, local restaurant with its boudoir chic. In the kitchen, Sylvain produces daring, lively, sometimes unexpected compositions, and Laetitia, his charming wife, welcomes guests with a smile. The crisp duck foie gras with Banyuls caramel and shallot confit, grilled sea bass with eggplant cannelloni, braised sweetbreads and chanterelle mushrooms or raspberry macaron with pistachio cream have an easy charm, like the short but shrewd wine list with an astute selection of wines by the glass, so you can enjoy yourself without breaking the bank.

● L'Arpent   € SIM

12, rue Jean-Jacques-Rousseau
Métro: Louvre-Rivoli, Palais-Royal
Tel. 01 42 36 52 90
Closed Sunday lunch, Monday lunch,
Tuesday lunch. Open until 11 PM.
Prix fixe: 14€ (weekday lunch).
A la carte: 25–30€.
Private dining room.

This wine bar takes great care of its food, too. A Bacchic frieze, exposed stonework and a small room with parquet flooring upstairs set the tone on the decor side. The atmosphere is friendly and the flavors authentic: Chicken liver terrine and foie gras *de maison*, cod brandade, steak tartare, pan-roasted small new potatoes or Lauragais cassoulet fulfill their promise. The lemon tart and pistachio crème brûlée are childhood treats.

● L'Atelier Berger   COM

49, rue Berger
Métro: Louvre-Rivoli, Châtelet, Les Halles
Tel. 01 40 28 00 00. Fax 01 40 28 10 65
atelierberger@wanadoo.fr
www.restaurant-atelierberger.com
Closed Saturday lunch, Sunday, Christmas.
Open until 11 PM.
Prix fixe: 14€ (lunch), 36€, 58€.
A la carte: 41€.
Terrace. Private dining room.

The French-Norwegian Jean Christiansen has made the most of his dual roots, as well as his experience with Rostang, Cagna and Vié. Here in his atelier he invites us to taste the end result. We are convinced by the tuna tartare, the smoked eel with marjoram sorbet, the lobster, parmesan, and penne gratin, the roasted veal kidneys, the pig's feet with slowly simmered vegetables and rosemary and the caramelized bananas, tapioca with passion fruit, and bitter chocolate ganache.

● L'Autobus Impérial   SIM

14, rue Mondétour
Métro: Les Halles, Etienne-Marcel
Tel. 01 42 36 00 18. Fax 01 42 36 00 31
www.autobus-imperial.fr
Closed Sunday, one week in mid-August.
Open until 10:30 PM.
Prix fixe: 15,50€ (lunch), 17,50€ (lunch),
24€ (dinner), 30€ (dinner). A la carte: 35€.
Air cond. Terrace. Private dining room.

The Guimard-style Métro decor has not changed. Arnaud Hiernard, who has taken over the establishment, has kept on Michel Vico, formerly at Chez Constant, in the kitchen. The Gascon crackling terrine with a foie gras center, the salt-roasted scallops with porcini mushrooms, the grilled calamari with squid-ink risotto, and the shepherd's pie with ham confit, sautéed wild mushrooms and game bird jus meet with no complaints. Well-chosen wines by the glass.

● Le Bar Anglais   N V.COM

Hotel Régina, 2, pl des Pyramides
Métro: Tuileries, Palais-Royal, Pyramides
Tel. 01 42 60 90 34. Fax 01 40 15 95 16
banqueting@regina-hotel.com
www.regina-hotel.com
Open daily until 10 PM.
Prix fixe: 24€. A la carte: 55€.
Air cond. Terrace. Private dining room.
Valet parking.

With its new English lounge look, the Régina's restaurant is cozier than ever. Hervé Riebbels' straightforward dishes are served in a British bar atmosphere. The chilled tomato and coriander soup and the arugula salad with artichokes and goat cheese are cool fare for warm days. The grilled tuna with wok-seared vegetables reflect current trends, the tender hand-chopped steak tartare slips down easily and the crème caramel *de grandmère* is unpretentious.

● Le Béarn   ● SIM

2, pl Sainte-Opportune
Métro: Châtelet
Tel. 01 42 36 93 35. Fax 01 45 08 59 12
le-béarn@noos.fr
www.lebearncafé.com
Closed Sunday, 2 weeks in August.
Noon–9 PM. Cont. service.
A la carte: 20€.
Terrace.

All that remains of the Béarn region is the béarnaise sauce. Yet this very pleasant Forties-style bistro does offer honest country cooking. The hard-boiled eggs with mayonnaise, the smoked herring marinated in oil, the perch with beurre blanc sauce, the strip steak with béarnaise sauce, the veal kidneys with mushrooms and Madeira wine and crème caramel give complete satisfaction. An attractive wine list with prices to match.

● Le Beau Vin   SIM

7, rue des Prouvaires
Métro: Châtelet, Les Halles, Louvre-Rivoli
Tel. 01 45 08 04 10
Open daily until 11:30 PM.
Prix fixe: 17€. A la carte: 38€.
Terrace.

Le Beau Vin has a selection of fine bottles displayed on the yellow and purple walls of this bistro run with gusto by Didier Gaillard. The classic dishes prepared by Claude Agnier meet with general approval. There are no complaints with the onion soup, bone marrow with toast, fresh fish from the market, beef filet with porcini mushrooms, the beautiful 12-ounce rib-eye steak or the warm chocolate cake, especially since these reasonably priced dishes are served promptly and with a smile.

● Gérard Besson   ○ LUX

5, rue Coq-Héron
Métro: Louvre-Rivoli, Palais-Royal
Tel. 01 42 33 14 74. Fax 01 42 33 85 71
gerard.besson4@libertysurf.fr
www.gerardbesson.com
Closed Saturday lunch, Sunday,
Monday lunch, 3 weeks in August.
Open until 9:30 PM.
Prix fixe: 105€. A la carte: 130€.
Air cond. Valet parking.

Classical and timeless: Gérard Besson has prospered for nearly thirty years in this unobtrusive street near the former wholesale food market. Tremendously experienced and a holder of the prestigious Meilleur Ouvrier de France award, he has successfully combined tradition with faultless technique in a cuisine that cares nothing for fashion. His restaurant is luxurious with its widely spaced tables and cozy nooks. Guests come to enjoy mushrooms, truffles and game in season. The fresh green asparagus from Pertuis with morel mushrooms and just a touch of cream, the filet of sole with morels served with pasta stuffed with wild mushroom duxelles, the sautéed blue lobster "Georges Garin" with truffle butter and savory fennel flan and the scallops of sweetbreads lightly sautéed in butter served with asparagus tips and a purée of sweet peas and savory are demanding, polished dishes. The unusual caramelized fennel served with Tahitian vanilla bean ice cream served as a dessert, and the mini baba au rhum with fresh pineapple and almond milk ice cream is memorable. We are left in no doubt: Besson is still Besson.

● Au Bistro   ● SIM

8, rue du Marché-Saint-Honoré
Métro: Tuileries, Pyramides
Tel. 01 42 61 02 45
Closed for dinner, Sundays.
Open until 3:30 PM.
A la carte: 35€.

Evelyne and Thierry Endringer have turned this corner bistro into a timeless spot. The checked tablecloths, wooden counter and relaxed atmosphere set the tone, along with such timeless, popular dishes as the bone marrow on toasted bread, omelet with truffles, andouillette AAAAA and tarte Tatin. Every day, a fresh dish touts its charms on the slate: paella, stuffed nicoise vegetables or cassoulet. Pleasant and tasty, washed down with cheerful wines.

● Le Bistrot Saint-Honoré   SIM

10, rue Gomboust
Métro: Pyramides, Tuileries
Tel. 01 42 61 77 78
Closed Saturday, Sunday,
Christmas–New Year's, August.
Open until 10:30 PM.
Prix fixe: 28€. A la carte: 60€.
Terrace.

Formerly a bartender at the Ritz, George V and Ledoyen, François-Joseph Christian is now his own boss, occupying the place of honor behind his counter with superb style. His two specialties are Burgundy and regional dishes. The oeufs en meurette (eggs poached in red wine with bacon and onion), the large escargots, the roasted wild turbot with beurre blanc and the perfectly prepared veal kidneys with Dijon mustard sauce will bring tears of emotion to your eyes. Add crème brûlée with Echiré cream and a selection of fine wines that are quick to inflate the check.

● Bistrot Victoires   SIM

6, rue La Vrillière
Métro: Bourse, Palais-Royal
Tel.-Fax 01 42 61 43 78
Open daily until 11:30 PM.
Sunday until 11 PM.
A la carte: 45€.
Terrace. Private dining room.

This genuine Parisian bistro adjacent to the place des Victoires owes a lot to François Saumet. This veteran of L'Ambroisie has breathed new energy into the former Souletin with continuously changing dishes based on market produce. The salads—landaise (green beans and foie gras) or Neapolitan-style—the salmon tartare served both raw and pan seared, the sautéed duck with creamy lime risotto and the warm chocolate cake

with a melted chocolate center served with homemade vanilla ice cream are the epitome of freshness.

● Aux Bons Crus   🏠 SIM

7, rue des Petits-Champs
Métro: Bourse, Palais-Royal
Tel. 01 42 60 06 45.
Closed Sunday, Monday evening,
2 weeks in August. Open until 10:30 PM.
A la carte: 30–35€.
Air cond.

A new team has taken over this circa 1900 bistro, which still makes an excellent impression with its freight elevator and zinc bar. At the stove, Stéphane Porte adds a Mediterranean touch to the appetizing house fare. The paper-thin beggar's purse filled with goat cheese, tomatoes and tapenade, the swordfish with beurre blanc, the rib-eye steak with morels, the lamb brochette with thyme and the pistachio crème brûlée raise the tone.

● Brasserie du Louvre   COM

Pl. du Palais-Royal
Métro: Palais-Royal
Tel. 01 42 96 27 98. Fax 01 44 58 38 01
restauration-louvre@concorde-hotels.com
brasseriedulouvre@concorde-hotels.com
www.hoteldulouvre.com
Daily noon–11 PM. Cont. service.
Prix fixe: 35€, 12€ (children).
A la carte: 60€.
Air cond. Terrace.

A brasserie in an ideal spot, with a terrace looking out on place du Palais Royal at the foot of the Louvre and the Comédie Française. Many tourists stop by, enchanted by such Gallic specialties as the chicken liver pâté with Espelette chili peppers, the sole (pan-fried in butter or grilled), the potatoes mashed with salted butter, calf's head with vinaigrette and baba au rhum with whipped cream and aged rum. Of course, all that does come at a price.

● Café Marly 🛉 COM

93, rue de Rivoli, in the Louvre
Métro: Palais-Royal
Tel. 01 49 26 06 60. Fax 01 49 26 07 06
s.a.marly@wanadoo.fr
www.marly.fr
Open daily until 12:30 AM.
A la carte: 60€.
Air cond. Terrace. Private dining room.

With its unobstructed view of the Louvre pyramid, this Costes brasserie has two great arguments in its favor: the Second Empire decor and the elegant cuisine—as long as price is no obstacle. The mache salad with endive and truffles, the sea bass with a balsamic reduction sauce and parmesan, the grilled lamb tenderloin chops with haricots verts and the petits macarons all deserve attention. However, the service falls short of perfection.

● Café Ruc SIM

159, rue Saint-Honoré
Métro: Palais-Royal
Tel. 01 42 60 97 54. Fax 01 42 61 36 33
Open daily until 12:30 AM.
A la carte: 55€.
Air cond. Terrace. Valet parking.

With its red velvet chairs, this Costes café opposite the Comédie Française suggests a diminutive theater itself. The food is improving and the perfectly choreographed service leaves nothing to chance. The baby artichokes, the grilled sesame-crusted tuna steak, the filet of beef with béarnaise sauce and the raspberry macarons deserve a touch of applause.

● Café Véry ☕ SIM

Jardin des Tuileries
Métro: Concorde, Tuileries
Tel.-Fax 01 47 03 94 84
contact@app-dt.com
Closed Christmas.
Noon–10:30 PM in summer; 7 PM in winter. Cont. service.
A la carte: 30€.
Air cond. Terrace.

Right in the middle of the Tuileries Gardens, a wooden cabin embellished with bay windows where you can enjoy tuna cakes, beef carpaccio, grilled salmon, chicken with morels and a tarte Tatin with apple and red currants. A relaxing break far from the bustle of the city.

● Carré Blanc 🆕 SIM

62, rue Jean-Jacques-Rousseau
Métro: Les Halles, Louvre-Rivoli
Tel. 01 40 28 99 04. Fax 01 40 28 09 62
www.lecarréblanc.resto.free.fr
Closed Saturday lunch, Sunday, Monday, 2 weeks in August. Open until 10 PM.
Prix fixe: 18€ (lunch), 15€ (lunch), 11€ (lunch). A la carte: 27€.
Terrace. Private dining room.

Exit Jules. Here, Christian Elizabé plays the modish, modest café card. The crumble of goat cheese with spinach, red tuna with sesame, spare ribs with honey and ginger and warm chestnut cake slip down effortlessly. All is served with a smile and, in the evening, in small porcelain clogs, lending the delicate dishes a cheerful tapas air.

● Les Cartes Postales SIM

7, rue Gomboust
Métro: Pyramides, Opéra
Tel. 01 42 61 02 93 / 01 42 61 23 40. Fax 01 42 61 02 93
lescartespostales@wanadoo.fr
Closed Saturday lunch, Sunday, Monday evening, December 24th–January 3rd, July 14th–July 31st. Open until 10 PM.
Prix fixe: 25€, 70€. A la carte: 60€.
Air cond.

Formerly with Dutournier at Aux Trou Gascon, Yoshimasa Watanabe has long been his own boss. He combines Japanese precision with French imagination in his delicately prepared concoctions. The crab cakes with grapefruit vinaigrette, the sautéed langoustines and scallops with wild mushrooms, a brochette of veal sweetbreads with truffles and his flaky almond pastries are very successful.

A SPECIAL FAVORITE

● A Casa Luna 🏠 🍴 COM

4-6, rue de Beaujolais
Métro: Palais-Royal
Tel. 01 42 60 05 11. Fax 01 42 96 16 24
acasaluna@noos.fr
www.acasaluna.com
Open daily until 11 PM.
Prix fixe: 15€ (lunch on weekdays), 20€.
A la carte: 35€.
Air cond.

Fond of Corsica? Well, here it is in Paris, just opposite the Palais Royal. Its charm is not restricted to the backdrop of old stone vaults, tables spread with crimson cloths, and attractive drapes, posters and photos but also lies in the cuisine, with its particularly Corsican accent, and the welcoming smile of Christine Sanna-Lefranc. Christine, who ran L'Alivi in the Marais quarter, has created a gastronomic showcase here for her native island. The savory tart infused with marjoram, the sardines marinated in fennel and olive oil, the cannelloni stuffed with brocciu (a Corsican goat cheese) and the lamb shank served in its own juices with butter beans are remarkable, even though young chef Laurent Benoit does tend to add pointless sprigs of dill and awkward pink berries to all his dishes. The food is accompanied by wines produced in vineyards from Sartène (exquisite red Fiumicicoli) to Patrimonio, along with Orezza water and finally a complimentary myrtle liquour that lends the world a rosy glow. Don't miss the shortbread with a lime pastry cream; what is actually a fine tarte sablée au citron frais makes a stunning, sweet (but not excessively so) dessert. It will have you melting on the spot!

● Le Caveau du Palais SIM

17-19, pl Dauphine
Métro: Pont-Neuf
Tel. 01 43 26 04 28. Fax 01 43 26 81 84
caveaudupalais@wanadoo.fr
Closed end of December–May 1st.
Open until 10:30 PM.
A la carte: 45€.
Terrace.

The building dates from the 16th century, the interior is rustic from its furniture to its exposed beams and stone, and the food is prepared in the domestic tradition with Southern French leanings. There is not a single false note in tomato tart with pesto, the filet of turbot with risotto, the chicken breast with morels, the veal kidneys and sweetbreads with honey and the delicate thin apple tart with vanilla ice cream and caramel sauce. Bordeaux takes pride of place on the wine list.

● Le Chalet de Diane €SIM

Allée de Diane, Jardin des Tuileries
Métro: Concorde, Tuileries
Tel.-Fax 01 42 96 81 12
Closed Christmas.
7:30 AM–10 PM (winter
8:30 PM). Cont. service.
A la carte: 30€.
Terrace.

Instead of mountain peaks, this chalet offers an unobstructed view of the Tuileries, its jewel case. The food is simpler than at Café Véry opposite but still very satisfactory. You only have to try the mozzarella and tomato salad, salmon with basil, traditional veal stew and fruit salad to be convinced.

● Au Chien qui Fume 🔔 SIM

33, rue du Pont-Neuf
Métro: Châtelet, Les Halles
Tel. 01 42 36 07 42. Fax 01 42 36 36 85
auchienquifume@club-internet.fr
www.au-chien-qui-fume.com
Closed Christmas. Open until 1 AM
(Friday, Saturday 2 AM).
Prix fixe: 23€, 29€, 30€, 36€.
A la carte: 50€.
Air cond. Terrace. Private dining room.

Founded in 1740, Au Chien qui Fume is an outstanding monument of the old Les Halles quarter. You can bring your canine friends and order the house standards until late: the escargots with wild mushrooms and garlic, medallions of monkfish with a wild mushroom sauce, kidneys braised in Chablis and fresh fruit gratin with Grand Marnier sabayon.

● Chez Clovis   🏠 SIM

33, rue Berger
Métro: Châtelet, Les Halles
Tel.-Fax 01 42 33 97 07
Closed Sunday, 10 days from
Christmas–New Year's, 1 week in August.
Open until 11:30 PM.
Prix fixe: 19,50€, 25,50€. A la carte: 40€.
Terrace. Private dining room.

This Thirties' bistro with its patinated decor is something of an institution in the Les Halles quarter. Its devotees have made it their dining room and, over the years, tirelessly continued to revel in the trio of terrines, fish of the day, slowly stewed calf's head, strip steak of Salers beef in red wine and shallots and chocolate profiteroles.

● Hôtel Costes   COM

239, rue Saint-Honoré
Métro: Tuileries, Concorde
Tel. 01 42 44 50 25. Fax 01 42 44 50 01
Daily noon–4 AM. Cont. service.
A la carte: 60–80€.
Air cond. Terrace. Private dining room.
Valet parking.

The Costes brothers have turned this discreet hotel and restaurant into one of the most "in" places in the capital. The Café Florian ambience, Venice fashion, with Napoleon III alcoves and patio have a certain chic. Well-heeled aficionados go straight for the lobster salad or haricots verts salad, spicy penne, line-caught sea bass, "tigre qui pleure" ("crying tiger" beef), generous veal rib chop and warm chocolate cake. And remember: The house serves until late.

● Le Dauphin   🏠 SIM

167, rue Saint-Honoré
Métro: Palais-Royal, Pyramides
Tel. 01 42 60 40 11. Fax 01 42 60 01 18
Closed Christmas. Open until 10:30 PM.
Prix fixe: 25€ (lunch Monday–Saturday),
37€. A la carte: 55€.
Terrace. Private Dining Room. Valet parking.

Didier Oudill and Edgar Duhr have been together for a long time. The two companions studied with Guérard at Eugénie, then went into partnership at the Café de Paris in Biarritz, before taking over this bistro institution: Le Dauphin. The menu has the singsong accents of Provence and the Southwest, and the generous dishes overflow with sun-drenched flavors as the succession of the Provençal-style escargot, a salmon in crispy phyllo pastry with asparagus, duck brandade with thick Morteau smoked sausage, a tangy sauce and chanterelle mushrooms and beggar's purse with honey ice cream and raspberry sorbet unfolds. Sheer joy!

● Les Dessous de la Robe   SIM

4, rue Bertin-Poirée
Métro: Pont-Neuf, Châtelet
Tel. 01 40 26 68 18.
contact@lesdessousdelarobe.com
Closed Saturday lunch, Sunday, Monday,
3 weeks in August. Open until 11 PM.
Prix fixe: 16€ (lunch), 21€ (lunch).
A la carte: 40€.
Terrace.

This 17th-century abode shelters a convivial offshoot of La Robe et le Palais (see page 17). Olivier Schvirtz provides a very businesslike welcome as Bruno Pohier concocts the delicious chow *du jour*. The sun-dried tomato and goat cheese gâteau, foie gras *maison*, cod with olives and mashed potatoes, rib-eye steak with Camargue salt, lamb shank braised with thyme and the fresh fruit sabayon are a delight to be savored under the solid beams.

● 234 Rivoli   V.COM

Hotel Intercontinental, 234, rue de Rivoli
Métro: Concorde, Tuileries
Tel. 01 44 77 10 40. Fax 01 44 77 10 24
réservation.01729@starwoodhotels.com
www.westin.com/paris
Open daily until 10 PM.
Prix fixe: 35€, 18€ (children).
A la carte: 50€.
Air cond. Terrace. Private dining room.
Valet parking.

The Westin chain has taken over this hotel, but it hardly provides a proper showcase for Patrick Juhel's food. The ersatz brasserie decor lacks soul and the service fails to match expectations. Yet the menu has plenty to offer: The artichoke purée with porcini mushrooms and poached egg, baked pike-perch covered with thin slices of black sausage, veal roast baked in a pastry crust with mozzarella cheese and mustard and a classic crème brûlée are highly successful.

● **L'Epi d'Or**   SIM

25, rue Jean-Jacques-Rousseau
Métro: Louvre-Rivoli, Palais-Royal
Tel. 01 42 36 38 12. Fax 01 42 36 46 25
www.epi-dor.fr
Closed Saturday lunch, Sunday, August.
Open until 11 PM.
Prix fixe: 18€, 22€. A la carte: 40€.

This timeless, *bouchon*-style restaurant, which would be quite at home in Lyon's rue du Garet, offers a staunchly classical experience in the hands of Pascaline and Larbi Diebli. The engraved glass panes have character, the welcome is friendly and the baked eggs with oyster mushrooms, Dover sole sautéed in butter, seven-hour leg of lamb and beggar's purse of caramelized pears are aptly pleasing in a solidly traditional style.

● **La Fermette du Sud-Ouest**   SIM

31, rue Coquillière
Métro: Palais-Royal, Les Halles,
Louvre-Rivoli
Tel. 01 42 36 73 55.
fso@noos.fr
Closed Sunday, 1 week in August.
Open until 10:30 PM.
A la carte: 40€.
Terrace.

Jacky Mayer continues to present dishes and wines from Southwest France in his Parisian "farmhouse." In surroundings of stone and exposed beams, guests enjoy Madiran, Gaillac, Cahors and Jurançon wines with fois gras, escargot stew, cassoulet, duck breast with porcini mushrooms and tarte Tatin prepared by the book and served with a smile.

● **Chez Flottes**   Ⓢ COM

2, rue Cambon
Métro: Concorde, Madeleine
Tel. 01 42 60 80 89. Fax 01 42 60 13 85
flottes@wanadoo.fr
www.flottes.fr
Daily noon–12:30 AM. Cont. service.
Prix fixe: 22€, 27€, 11€ (children).
A la carte: 38-50€.
Air cond. Terrace. Private dining room.
Valet parking.

No luck this year in the neo-1900 brasserie with its Mucha stained glass and frieze-ornamented bar. The pasta and chicken oyster salad fail to convince: a glutinous mound of undercooked pasta topped with laughably small morsels of dried-out chicken. The duck confit is nothing to write home about, while the Auvergne sausage was desperately overcooked and served with cold garlic-mashed potatoes. The sympathetic service is as considerate as ever and the wine list deserves study, but Chez Flottes is visibly struggling.

● **Les Fontaines Saint-Honoré**   SIM

196-200, rue Saint-Honoré
Métro: Palais-Royal
Tel. 01 42 61 46 65. Fax 01 42 60 49 74
groupes@restosparis.net
www.restosparis.net
Closed Tuesday.
Noon–11 PM. Cont. service.
Prix fixe: 13,98€, 16,55€, 22,85€.
A la carte: 30–40€.
Air cond. Terrace. Private dining room.

Here, everything smacks delightfully of Provence, from the decor to the food. The service is friendly and we eagerly dive into the lobster terrine with a subtle whiskey sauce, pike-perch filet, a potato stuffed with bacon served with spinach salad, lamb wrapped in bacon with bleu cheese and fresh tagliatelle, not forgetting the chocolate soup with gingerbread croutons.

Good Restaurants & Others

● Chez Gabriel `COM`

123, rue Saint-Honoré
Métro: Louvre-Rivoli
Tel.-Fax 01 42 33 02 99
www.restosparis@club-internet.fr
Closed Saturday lunch, Sunday, Christmas,
beginning–end August. Open until 10 PM.
Prix fixe: 32€, 40€. A la carte: 60€.
Air cond. Private dining room.

The decor has been refurbished, with leather benches, maritime pictures and cream paint lending a certain air of freshness to Serge Boullard's establishment. This freshness runs to the food, too, and the service has lost none of its energy. We indulge ourselves with the millefeuille of foie gras and crispy haricots verts in a truffle vinaigrette, roasted cod with lemon, grilled filet mignon with béarnaise sauce and seasonal fruit gratin with sabayon.

● Le Garde Robe `N` `●` `SIM`

41, rue de l'Arbre-Sec
Métro: Louvre-Rivoli, Châtelet, Les Halles
Tel. 01 49 26 90 60
Closed Sunday evening. Open until 10 PM.
A la carte: 22€.
Terrace.

The team at La Robe et le Palais and Les Dessous de la Robe have made this cellar grocery their third address. Perfect for a dinner with friends without breaking the bank as there are plenty of choices among the Bigorre ham, taramasalata on toasted baguette, grilled bread with tapenade, assorted charcuterie and marinated anchovies. The wines are chosen with impressive skill. Brunch on Sunday at noon.

● Le Grand Louvre `COM`

Louvre Museum
Métro: Palais-Royal
Tel. 01 40 20 53 41. Fax 01 42 86 04 63
marie-gabrielle.cave@elior.com
www.eliance.fr
Closed Tuesday, dinner reservations for groups except Monday and Wednesday.
Open until 10 PM.
Prix fixe: 29€, 37€. A la carte: 50€.
Air cond. Private dining room.

Just under the Louvre pyramid, with contemporary styling by Wilmotte, this restaurant does not simply rely on its dream location but also takes good care of its customers under the auspices of Yves Pinard, who busies himself in the wings preparing fine dishes. The crayfish salad with lentils and eel, cod simmered in coconut milk served with vegetable cannelloni, pan-roasted veal kidneys and Amarena cherry cake with chocolate hit the spot.

● Hamaïka `●` `SIM`

11, rue Jean-Jacques-Rousseau
Métro: Louvre-Rivoli
Tel. 01 40 28 91 15
Closed Sunday, Monday.
Tuesday–Saturday noon–3 PM; 7:30–11 PM.
Open until 2 AM.
A la carte: 25€.
Air cond. Private dining room.

Not a Japanese restaurant, but a tapas bar, offering authentic Basque produce. The attractions here are wines from Spanish Navarre and Irouléguy accompanying the Serrano ham, grilled squid, veal simmered with Espelette peppers and a Basque-style crème brûlée.

● Hôtel de Vendôme `N` `V.COM`

1, place Vendôme
Métro: Tuileries, Opéra, Concorde
Tel. 01 55 04 55 00. Fax 01 49 27 97 89
reservations@hoteldevendome.com
Open daily until 10 PM.
Prix fixe: 35€, 40€.
Air cond. Valet parking.

On the second floor of this charming hotel with its prestigious address, the dining room offers a change of scenery in the British manner. Chef Frédéric Fallope presents a golden opportunity with the set menu: delicious puff pastry "cigars" of duck confit, chilled crab appetizer, perfectly cooked swordfish steamed in banana leaves, roasted scallops and desserts that could have been better—overly sweet chestnut meringue and ordinary sorbets. The service could be more conscientious.

● **Juvéniles**   € SIM

47, rue de Richelieu
Métro: Palais-Royal, Bourse, Pyramides
Tel. 01 42 97 46 49. Fax 01 42 60 31 52
tim.grapes@wanadoo.fr
Closed Sunday, Monday lunch.
Open until 11 PM.
Prix fixe: 14,50€ (lunch, wine included),
18€ (dinner), 26€ (dinner). A la carte: 28€.

A Scottish devotee of wine worldwide, Tim
Johnston is the kind of Parisian we love. His
exquisite bottles accompany simple dishes
and excellent produce. Customers squeeze
into the dining room, cluttered with
wooden chests and precious vintages, to
savor the plate of Basque charcuterie,
sautéed calamari, Duval sausages served
with mashed potatoes and chutney or
apple crumble a la mode. (Also see Shops.)

● **Kai**   Ⓝ SIM

18, rue du Louvre
Métro: Louvre-Rivoli
Tel. 01 40 15 01 99
Closed Sunday lunch, Monday.
Open until 10 PM.
Prix fixe: 38€ (lunch), 58€, 90€ (dinner).
A la carte: 50–80€.

Tonkatsu-don, ohitashi, sakamushi,
chawanmushi, hoba miso, kani daikon:
fluent Japanese in the original. There is
nothing forced about the friendly welcome here. Although the prices won't
spoil you, you will not be disappointed by
the freshness of the produce, the authenticity of preparation and the rigorously
precise dishes: the seared tuna with avocado, pinenuts and wasabi, breaded pork
with red miso sauce, chicken grilled in
magnolia leaves, scrambled eggs with
steamed foie gras. Taste and marvel.

● **Lescure**   € SIM

7, rue de Mondovi
Métro: Concorde
Tel. 01 42 60 18 91. Fax 01 40 15 91 27
Closed Saturday, Sunday,
Christmas–New Year's, 3 weeks in August.
Prix fixe: 22,50€. A la carte: 30€.
Air cond. Terrace.

The Lascauds have been carrying on a
family tradition for nearly a century. With
unfailing reliability, they compose a
menu based on classics of the domestic
repertoire. There are no unpleasant surprises with the pâté cooked in a pastry
crust served on a bed of mixed greens,
genuine English-style poached haddock,
beef bourguignon with steamed potatoes
and carrots and triple chocolate fondant
with crème anglaise. The wine list is in
much the same vein.

● **Le Louchebem**   SIM

31, rue Berger / 10, rue des Prouvaires
Métro: Les Halles, Châtelet
Tel. 01 42 33 12 99. Fax 01 40 28 45 50
le-louchebem@wanadoo.fr
www.le-louchebem.fr
Closed Sunday. Open until 11:30 PM.
Prix fixe: 13,90€. A la carte: 40€.
Air cond. Terrace.

Butcher's son Etienne Jojot has taken over
this antique brasserie decorated by Slavik.
The meat is especially good, coming as it
does straight from the neighboring butcher
shop run by his cousin. In short, this is a
family business where Michel Maillard continues to apply his skills as a master of carnivorous arts. Sit down and choose a dish:
charcuterie, roast beef, leg of lamb, roasted
ham or prime rib of beef. Finish up with
profiteroles or homemade crème brûlée.

● **Macéo**   🔪 V.COM

15, rue des Petits-Champs
Métro: Palais-Royal, Bourse, Pyramides
Tel. 01 42 97 53 85. Fax 01 47 03 36 93
info@maceorestaurant.com
www.maceorestaurant.com
Closed Saturday lunch, Sunday,
3 weeks in August. Open until 10:30 PM.
Prix fixe: 30€, 36€. A la carte: 60€.
Private dining room.

Just a step away from the Palais-Royal, the
late Mercure Galant is enjoying a second
youth, thanks to Mark Williamson, who
has selected 250 wines from areas as far
flung as the Rhône Valley, Burgundy, Spain
and the United States. His choices perfectly complement the appealing dishes

prepared by Thierry Bourdonnais. Who could resist the tuna tartare with asparagus tips, foie gras with apples and figs in sangria caramel, duck prepared in two ways with mixed vegetables, pineapple and mascarpone macarons, especially when they are served with good humor and promptness? The setting (in a listed 18th-century building) plays on contrasting bright shades and contemporary paintings, offering a note of cheer.

● Le Noailles   Ⓝ COM

Hotel Saint-James & Albany,
202, rue de Rivoli
Métro: Concorde, Tuileries
Tel. 01 44 58 43 40
Closed Saturday lunch, Sunday, Monday.
Prix fixe: 19€ (lunch). A la carte: 70–85€.

The "vestibule" dining room lacks charm, but the bar provides a pleasant setting for a quick lunch, and the drab paved courtyard is pleasant on a sunny day. David Desplanques (who has taken over the kitchen after working with Patrice Tricali at Montparnasse 25, Robuchon and Ducasse) has devised a short menu based on fresh market produce. The red tuna with lime and coriander, sea bream with potatoes and julienned zucchini and filet of duck glazed with sweet spices accompanied by crispy zucchini and pear tagine show strong skills with an added dash of imagination, but the best is yet to come with the desserts, particularly the pina colada dessert with crisp candy caramel, mango and vanilla. The wine list needs to be entirely revised. The young dining room staff is very amiable. A place to watch.

● L'Ostréa   SIM

4, rue Sauval
Métro: Louvre-Rivoli
Tel. 01 40 26 08 07. Fax 01 40 26 04 93
Closed Saturday lunch, Sunday, 1 week for Easter, 3 weeks in August. Open until 11 PM.
A la carte: 40€.

It's not surprising that Jean-Pierre Devaux understands presentation: Before becoming a chef, he was a florist. Attractive dishes

then, consisting of seafood only. All the food is extremely fresh, since the menu is based on catches and tides. It includes, for example, Baltic herring, mussels in tomato sauce, sea bass flambé, tuna tartare and pan-seared jumbo shrimp. A refreshing meal that ends with a chocolate mousse or tarte Tatin.

● Paul   🍴 SIM

15, pl Dauphine / 52, quai des Orfèvres
Métro: Châtelet, St-Michel, Pont-Neuf
Tel. 01 43 54 21 48. Fax 01 56 24 94 09
restaurantpaul@wanadoo.fr
Closed Monday, mid August–end of August.
Open until 10:30 PM.
A la carte: 50€.
Terrace. Valet parking.

Chantal and Thierry Dieuleveut, owners of the neighboring Caveau du Palais, have made absolutely no changes to the decor of this timeless bistro or its trademark domestic repertoire, which is reliable and modest. The stewed escargots, skate in caper sauce, smoked haddock with beurre blanc, honey-glazed duck medallions, sautéed calf's liver with a vinegar sauce, warm chocolate cake and baba au rhum with whipped cream and Bing cherries are cheerfully dependable.

● Chez Pauline   ○ 🍴 COM

5, rue Villedo
Métro: Pyramides, Palais-Royal
Tel. 01 42 96 20 70. Fax 01 49 27 99 89
chez.pauline@wanadoo.fr
www.chezpauline.com
Closed Saturday lunch, Sunday.
Open until 10:30 PM.
Prix fixe: 27€ (lunch), 45€ (lunch),
55€ (dinner). A la carte: 70€.
Terrace. Private dining room.

A step away from the Palais Royal, André Génin's picturesque circa 1880 bistro is hidden behind an appealing paneled facade. The man's choice of friends suggests a true love of gourmet cooking: Lacombe in Lyon, Chabran in Pont-de-l'Isère and Rostang in Paris. He offers a warm welcome in this little treasure chest of stucco, mirrors, red benches and other jewels of bygone times.

His cuisine has character to spare, and the skillfully chosen produce is prepared with unfailing care. The terrine of parsleyed ham, lobster sautéed with new potatoes and shallots, sweetbreads baked in puff pastry "father Génin"–style and an enormous helping of cognac baba with mixed nuts, dried fruit and a touch of whipped cream are exemplary. Ideally, the wine list should be a little more substantial.

● **Pavillon Baltard**   Ⓝ SIM
9, rue Coquillière
Métro: Les Halles
Tel. 01 42 36 22 00
Daily, 24 hours. Cont. service.
A la carte: 35–45€.
Air cond. Valet parking.

No closing, prompt, amiable service and a fairly humdrum bistro-brasserie decor opposite the "tunnel" of the former Les Halles wholesale market. Stéphane Collaro has gently revived this institution of yesteryear, which also serves as a smoking room (you can smell the cigars!) and piano bar. In any case, we cannot fault the quality of the meat (rib-eye, flank steak and steak tartare) and the eggs mayonnaise, warm sausage, roasted cod, calf's liver fried in butter and delicious potato purée take pride in their traditional appeal.

● **Le Pavillon C**   SIM
14, rue Coquillière
Métro: Les Halles, Louvre
Tel. 01 42 36 51 60. Fax 01 42 36 53 93
pavillonc@wanadoo.com
Closed Monday evening, 2 weeks in early August. Open until 11 PM.
Prix fixe: 15€ (lunch), 16€ (lunch), 19€ (lunch). A la carte: 35–40€.
Air cond. Terrace.

Le Pavillon C has had no trouble in gaining acceptance after replacing the mediocre Bistrot Coquillière. We can only congratulate Jean-Marie Cauvet on his gastronomic initiatives, such as the pan-seared foie gras with apples, salmon steak with chives and cream, walnut cake, Salers beef and a tiramisu-style exotic fruit dessert.

● **Le Petit Mâchon**   SIM
158, rue Saint-Honoré
Métro: Palais-Royal
Tel.-Fax 01 42 60 08 06
Closed Monday, August. Open until 11 PM.
Prix fixe: 16,50€. A la carte: 38€.
Terrace. Valet parking.

This contemporary bistro redesigned in the traditional manner welcomes customers with a light, modern cuisine. The foie gras crème brûlée, crayfish salad, roasted pike-perch with extra virgin olive oil, monkfish ragout in a light pastry shell, sweetbreads with truffle juice and fried pastries with red currants and fresh mint are accompanied by Côtes du Rhône and Beaujolais.

● **Au Petit Théâtre**   COM
15, pl du Marché-Saint-Honoré
Métro: Pyramides, Opéra, Tuileries
Tel. 01 42 61 00 93. Fax 01 47 03 31 64
Closed Sunday, Monday, 3 weeks in August. Open until 10 PM.
Prix fixe: 18€ (lunch), 22,50€ (lunch), 28€ (dinner). A la carte: 50€.
Air cond. Terrace. Private dining room.

As we all know, "there's good eating to be had in every bit of a pig." Au Petit Théâtre has devoted a museum to the creature, featuring statuettes, posters, piggy banks and papier mâché sculptures. The food here, prepared by David Baroche, pork butcher by training and cook by vocation, also owes everything to the animal. The pork cheek and leek terrine, chicory salad with truffle oil vinaigrette, roasted scallops with smoked bacon, pork medallions with morels, and the apple shortbread tart with salted-butter caramel and vanilla ice cream meet with general approval.

● **Pharamond**   🏠 SIM
24, rue de la Grande-Truanderie
Métro: Etienne-Marcel, Les Halles
Tel. 01 40 28 45 18. Fax 01 40 28 45 87
jmc.corver@wanadoo.fr
www.le-pharamond.com
Closed Sunday, August. Open until 10:30 PM.
Prix fixe: 20,50€, 30€. A la carte: 45€.

This 1880 institution is changing hands. For now, it is too early to tell whether the Auvergne will still go hand in hand with Normandy, with the foie gras terrine, scallops with cider or Caen-style tripe remaining its staples. You can learn what to expect in next year's edition.

● Au Pied de Cochon   🔺 COM

6, rue Coquillière
Métro: Châtelet-Les Halles
Tel. 01 40 13 77 00. Fax 01 40 13 77 09
de.pied-de-cochon@blanc.net
www.piedecochon.com
Daily, 24 hours. Cont. service.
Prix fixe: 24€. A la carte: 50€.
Air cond. Terrace. Private dining room.
Valet parking.

This monument of the former Les Halles wholesale market has been successfully exploring the theme of pig's feet for more than fifty years. At any hour of the day or night, its two persistently packed floors welcome tipsy Parisians and tourists. The onion soup makes an excellent start to the proceedings, which continue with sole meunière or the famous "temptation of Saint Antoine" (pig's tail, ears, snout, and feet), baba au rhum and the ritual crêpes flambéed with Grand Marnier.

● Pierre au Palais-Royal   COM

10, rue de Richelieu
Métro: Palais-Royal, Musée du Louvre
Tel. 01 42 96 09 17. Fax 01 42 96 26 40
pierreaupalaisroyal@wanadoo.fr
www.pierre-paris.com
Closed Saturday lunch, Sunday,
3 weeks in August. Open until 11 PM.
Prix fixe: 34€ (on weekdays),
41€ (on weekdays). A la carte: 60€.
Air cond. Private dining room.

The set menus are still tempting, although the a la carte prices tend to soar a little. It must be said that David Frémondière does put quality first, both in his choice of products and in the way he puts them together. The results are persuasive, taking the form of seared foie gras with gingerbread, pear confit and reduced spiced red wine, the skate with brown butter, parmesan and cream, the sautéed fingerling potatoes with white asparagus and parsley, the roasted Quercy lamb with sweet garlic, watercress jus, eggplant caviar, sautéed cherry tomatoes, zucchini and Swiss chard, not to forget the traditional Bourbon vanilla millefeuille. The welcome could be a little friendlier.

● Pinxo   ◎ COM

Plaza Paris Vendôme, 9, rue d'Alger
Métro: Tuileries
Tel. 01 40 20 20 00. Fax 01 40 20 72 02
www.pinxo.fr
Closed August. Open until 11 PM.
A la carte: 45€.
Air cond. Valet parking.

Lunches for shopping enthusiasts from the chic Colette boutique or a business clientele: Pinxo's patrons vary, but the service invariably runs smoothly. Obviously, we would expect nothing less of Alain Dutournier, who has made a great success of this adjunct to the Carré des Feuillants—a chic refectory version—in the heart of the Plaza Vendôme hotel. Surrounded by its minimalist decor (Japanese-inspired tendencies all in black and white by Alberto Bali), we relax as we study the mouthwatering menu devised by Fabrice Dubos, formerly of the Café Faubourg. In no particular order, it offers sautéed small squid with garlic chips, rare sesame-glazed tuna, Aquitaine sirloin steak served both raw and seared and smoked pear with a dark chocolate cake and green tea sorbet. The wines are from all over the world. Apart from being well chosen, they are presented in a novel manner, according to price range, another way of looking at the question.

● **Point Bar** `SIM`

Hotel Régina, 40, pl du Marché-Saint-Honoré
Métro: Pyramides, Tuileries
Tel. 01 42 61 76 28. Fax 01 42 96 46 90
www.reservthebest.com
Closed Sunday, Monday, Bank Holidays,
Christmas–New Year's. Open until 11 PM.
Prix fixe: 16€ (lunch, wine included),
21€ (lunch, wine included), 26€ (lunch,
wine included), 20€ (dinner), 29€ (dinner),
38€ (dinner). A la carte: 50€.
Air cond. Terrace. Private dining room.

Like her mother, Sophie, from Tours, Alice Bardet brings a touch of exuberance to her modern little bistro. The contemporary decor, bright colors and Alain Kassis's cuisine go well together. Carpaccio, mini grilled ham and cheese sandwiches with arugula, foie gras with dried fruit chutney, seared tuna satay, veal in a parmesan crust, vanilla panna cotta and warm strawberry crumble with balsamic vinegar reflect current trends.

● **La Poule au Pot** `SIM`

9, rue de Vauvilliers
Métro: Louvre-Rivoli, Les Halles
Tel. 01 42 36 32 96
www.lapouleaupot.fr
Closed lunch, Monday.
7 PM–5 AM. Cont. service.
Prix fixe: 30€. A la carte: 55€.
Air cond. Terrace. Private dining room.

They serve until late in this traditional-style bistro, boldly boasting a cuisine no longer in vogue. Night owls come here to sup on eggs with foie gras, the house chicken salad, salmon with champagne sauce, duck confit and chocolate profiteroles.

● **Le Ragueneau** `SIM`

202, rue Saint-Honoré
Métro: Palais-Royal
Tel. 01 42 60 29 20. Fax 01 42 60 29 70
vincerp75@hotmail.com
www.ragueneau.fr
Closed Christmas, New Year's Day, May 1st.
Open until 10 PM.
Prix fixe: 9,60€ (lunch), 18,50€ (lunch),
23€ (lunch). A la carte: 35€.
Air cond. Terrace. Private dining room.

Vincent Sitz, who trained at Taillevent and with the Pourcels, has taken over this historic institution revamped in modern fashion, now a tearoom and stylish restaurant. On the first floor, customers perched on aluminum stools snack on savory tarts, salads and sweets; on the second, on bottle-green grained leather seats set against attractive red drapes, they enjoy cod brandade, braised beef with spices, millefeuille or divine almond tart.

● **Le Restaurant du Palais-Royal** `COM`

43, rue de Valois / 110, galerie de Valois
Métro: Bourse, Palais-Royal
Tel. 01 40 20 00 27. Fax 01 40 20 00 82
palaisrest@aol.com
www.restaurantdupalaisroyal.com
Closed Sunday, December 20th–mid January.
Open until 10:30 PM.
A la carte: 70€.
Terrace.

Immediately by the gardens of the Palais Royal, the terrace is one of the prettiest in Paris. The decor is elegant with its cheerful hues, while the food served up by Bruno Hees, formerly of the Récamier, is subtle, carefully prepared and made from fine ingredients, its only fault being its high price. In any case, we have no complaints about the sea bass tartare, eggplant caviar with Ibérico ham, grilled sea bass with olive oil or sautéed calf's liver with a spiced crumble.

● **La Robe et le Palais** `SIM`

13, rue des Lavandières-Sainte-Opportune
Métro: Châtelet
Tel.-Fax 01 45 08 07 41
contact@larobeetlepalais.com
www.robe-et-palais.com
Closed Sunday. Open until 11 PM.
Prix fixe: 15€ (lunch), 18€ (lunch).
A la carte: 40€.
Air cond. Terrace.

The cellar here boasts more than 300 wines, and taste buds are exercised on every side, by both the dishes and the drink. The cuisine has Southwestern French leanings. Food lovers will happily make short work of the Bigorre black ham terrine, squid risotto, chicken breasts marinated in ginger with spiced yogurt cream and a platter of farmer's cheeses served with bundles of dried fruit, figs and almonds.

● Le Rubis ● 🏠 SIM

10, rue du Marché-Saint-Honoré
Métro: Tuileries
Tel. 01 42 61 03 34.
Closed Saturday evening, Sunday,
school vacations, Christmas–New Year's,
2 weeks in August.
Open until 10 PM.
A la carte: 25€.
Air cond. Terrace.

Beaujolais, Bordeaux, Loire wines and Côtes du Rhône: These are the pearls in the cellar stocked by Albert Prat, who provides a family welcome in his Fifties'-era bistro with its original zinc counter lit by neon. In great simplicity, among the barrels and Formica tables, patrons relish the pig snout salad, homemade rillettes, pork knuckle with lentils, calf's head with mayonnaise, capers, herbs and hard-boiled egg and rice gâteau. There is also a very nice selection of charcuterie. (Also see Rendezvous.)

● Le Soufflé COM

36, rue du Mont-Thabor
Métro: Concorde
Tel. 01 42 60 27 19. Fax 01 42 60 54 98
crigaud@club-internet.fr
Closed Sunday.
Open until 10 PM.
Prix fixe: 29€, 33€. A la carte: 50€.
Air cond. Private dining room.

As the name suggests, everything here is a tribute to the shape and lightness of the soufflé, a style that apparently appeals to women. Claude Rigaud has made it his specialty (although he has no qualms about straying aptly into other areas). In any case, it is difficult to resist the asparagus soufflé, salmon and sorrel soufflé, calf's head with truffle vinaigrette or coconut soufflé.

● Le Stado SIM

150, rue Saint-Honoré
Métro: Louvre-Rivoli
Tel. 01 42 60 29 75.
www.lestado.com
Open daily until 11:30 PM.
Prix fixe: 12€ (lunch on weekdays),
15€ (lunch on weekends), 17€ (dinner).
A la carte: 30€.
Air cond.

Lovers of the Southwest and rugby football, this place is for you. The Tarbes club that gave its name to the restaurant would approve of the generous portions here, enough to revive any rugby player after a long night spent celebrating a victory. The landaise salad (foie gras and green beans), plate of foie gras, pike-perch filet with a shellfish sauce, the cassoulet, the duck confit and traditional Basque cake will satisfy even the most demanding.

● Table d'Hôte du Palais-Royal COM

8, rue du Beaujolais
Métro: Pyramides, Tuileries, Palais-Royal
Tel.-Fax 01 42 61 25 30 & 01 42 60 99 59
www.tablepalaisroyal-sinclair.com
Open daily until 11 PM.
Prix fixe: 15€, 19€, 28€, 39€.
A la carte: 45€.
Air cond. Private dining room.

Following its complete renovation last January, Caroll Sinclair's restaurant is more convivial than ever. We are fond of the black marble floor, the flowery facade with its pots of aromatic plants, and the wrought iron chairs and mosaic tables. On the food side, this self-taught purveyor of moveable feasts (formerly of boulevard Beaumarchais, then rue d'Argenteuil) makes fresh market produce her mainstay. According to season, patrons can savor the artichoke hearts with asparagus tips, foie gras baked en papillote, Provençal-style bass, beef cheeks in red wine, rump-steak filet with foie gras and morels and to finish, warm chocolate cake or apple crumble.

● **La Taverne de l'Arbre Sec**   ⊜ SIM
109, rue Saint-Honoré
Métro: Louvre-Rivoli
Tel. 01 40 41 10 36
Closed Sunday.
Open until 11:30 PM.
Prix fixe: 13,50€ (lunch). A la carte: 25€.
Terrace. Private dining room.

No showiness in Sylvain Lemarchand's tavern, just very solid dishes, reflecting the heavy beams and stones of the walls, and well-behaved prices, from the tomato and mozzarella millefeuille to rump steak to seared Provençal scallops, without forgetting the simple pleasure of the warm chocolate cake.

● **Aux Tonneaux des Halles**   ⊜ 🍴 SIM
28, rue Montorgueil
Métro: Les Halles
Tel. 01 42 33 36 19
Closed Sunday.
Open until 10:30 PM.
A la carte: 30€.
Air cond. Terrace.

Patrick Fabre has turned his traditional bistro into a refuge for those with solid appetites, nostalgic for the old Les Halles market. Patrons sit beneath vine branches and savor the pleasures of bygone days. Dried country sausage, Mediterranean scorpion fish sautéed with leeks, calf's head with a thick, tart vinaigrette and steamed potatoes and tarte Tatin all slip down easily. A good ambience fueled by quality Beaujolais. (Also see Rendezvous.)

● **La Tourelle**   ⊜ SIM
43, rue Croix-des-Petits-Champs
Métro: Bourse, Palais-Royal, Les Halles
Tel.-Fax 01 42 61 35 41
latourelle7501@yahoo.fr
Closed for dinner (except by reservation),
Saturday, Sunday, one week in August.
Prix Fixe: 9€ (lunch). A la carte: 20–25€.
Terrace. Private dining room.

A fine, stone-walled restaurant, a generous wine list with good, thirst-quenching vintages and deftly prepared home cooking: These are the strong points of Fabrice

Louvel's bistro, which regales the public with assorted charcuterie, sardine rillettes, roasted cod filet, grilled skirt steak, andouillette AAAAA and fromage blanc mousse.

● **La Tour Montlhéry**   🍴 SIM
5, rue des Prouvaires
Métro: Louvre-Rivoli, Les Halles
Tel. 01 42 36 21 82. Fax 01 45 08 81 99
Closed Saturday, Sunday, mid-July–
mid-August. Open until 6 AM.
A la carte: 55€.
Air cond.

An institution in the old Les Halles quarter, the Tour Montlhéry has seen many great figures pass through its portals. Still today, many journalists, politicians and other personalities continue to seat themselves around its tables under the gaze of General de Gaulle and Jeff Kessel, sketched by the late, much lamented artist Moretti, to savor the homemade fois gras, the chef's terrine, braised salmon with mustard sauce, prime rib roast, sautéed calf's liver, millefeuille and baba au rhum. The cellar is well stocked and the service prompt.

● **Chez la Vieille**   SIM
1, rue Bailleul, at the corner
of rue de l'Arbre-Sec
Métro: Louvre-Rivoli
Tel. 01 42 60 15 78. Fax 01 42 33 85 71
Closed Saturday, Sunday, Monday,
Tuesday evening, Wednesday evening, August.
Open until 9:30 PM.
Prix fixe: 27€ (lunch). A la carte: 55€.

Marie-José Cervoni has left her own mark on this legendary establishment in the Belly of Paris while remaining faithful to the memory of the "Vieille" (old woman), Adrienne Biasin. The photo-lined dining room never empties. Patrons crowd around the starter trolley to make their selection before enjoying an appetizing potau-feu or calf's liver sautéed with vinegar. Then back to the trolley, but the sweet trolley this time, where every dessert offers a whiff of childhood.

● Villa Lys `COM`

30, rue de Montpensier
Métro: Pyramides, Palais-Royal
Tel.-Fax 01 42 61 85 99
Closed Sunday evening. Open until 11 PM.
A la carte: 35€.
Air cond. Terrace. Private dining room.

With its terrace by the Palais Royal, this establishment has a cheerful appearance in red, fuchsia, black and white. Patrick Le Clec'h, who plies his trade in both dining room and kitchen, produces a fusion cuisine of vegetable spring rolls, shrimp and coconut milk soup, scallop and mushroom tagine or duck with dried fruits. The desserts, warm chocolate cake or lavender honey crème brûlée, are more typically French.

● Vin et Marée `COM`

165, rue Saint-Honoré
Métro: Palais-Royal, Pyramides
Tel. 01 42 86 06 96. Fax 01 42 86 06 97
vin.maree@wanadoo.fr
Open daily until midnight.
A la carte: 50€.
Air cond. Valet parking.

Here, opposite the Comédie Française, the tide offers up its catch of fresh fish, and informed aficionados savor a meal brimming with flavors of the sea. The menu often has a South of France feel, as does the cellar, largely devoted to the Rhône Valley. Langoustines roasted in hazelnut oil, sole with citrus butter, grilled sea bass with thyme and Zanzibar baba au rhum are all very well prepared.

● Willi's Wine Bar `SIM`

13, rue des Petits-Champs
Métro: Bourse, Pyramides
Tel. 01 42 61 05 09. Fax 01 47 03 36 93
info@williswinebar.com
www.williswinebar.com
Closed Sunday, 2 weeks in August.
Open until 11 PM.
Prix fixe: 25€ (lunch), 34€ (dinner), 19,50€ (lunch). A la carte: 40€.

Mark Williamson's wine bar is astonishingly good. Cultivating his passion for the divine nectar, this quiet Englishman has gradually built up an impressive cellar that reflects a weakness for the Rhône Valley but is not limited to France alone. By taking on a chef of François Yon's stature, he has also invested in quality cuisine. The result is convincing, with tuna tartare, the antipasti plate, sea bass filet, roasted cod with green vegetable risotto, pan-seared veal chops with sage and chocolate terrine.

● Wine and Bubbles `SIM`

3, rue Française
Métro: Etienne-Marcel
Tel. 01 44 76 99 84. Fax 01 44 76 04 89
nicolas@wineandbubbles.com
www.wineandbubbles.com
Closed lunch, Sunday, Bank Holidays.
Open until 11 PM.
A la carte: 30€.
Air cond. Terrace.

A wine bar in tune with today's trends that only serves food in the evening (useful when the neighboring theaters empty) as an adjunct to its carefully stocked cellar made up of wines from all over France and abroad (more than 500 labels). On the terrace, or more cozily on the mezzanine, with its many poufs and sofas, customers revel in fine cheese or charcuterie plates with Corsican sausage, aged comté and foie gras. (Also see Shops.)

● Zimmer `COM`

1, pl du Châtelet
Métro: Châtelet
Tel. 01 42 36 74 03. Fax 01 42 36 74 04
lezimmer@wanadoo.fr
www.lezimmer.com
Daily 8 AM–12:30 AM. Cont. service.
Prix fixe: 19,90€. A la carte: 40€.
Air cond. Terrace.

Entirely made over by Jacques Garcia, this discreet Châtelet brasserie has also acquired a new chef, Stéphane Graf, responsible for a welcome change in the menu, which was beginning to run out of steam. Now, we are very happy with the cream of carrot and spring pea soup, cod baked in a spice crust with passion fruit, Venetian steak tartare with parmesan, basil and olive oil and sautéed pears with gingerbread and vanilla ice cream.

INTERNATIONAL RESTAURANTS

● Il Cortile   🅿 ◎ V.COM

Hotel Castille, 37, rue Cambon
Métro: Concorde, Madeleine
Tel. 01 44 58 45 67. Fax 01 44 58 45 69
ilcortile@castille.com
www.castille.com
Closed Saturday, Sunday, 1 week from
Christmas—New Year's, August.
Open until 10:30 PM.
Prix fixe: 38€ (lunch), 48€ (lunch),
95€ (dinner). A la carte: 95€.
Air cond. Terrace. Private dining room.
Valet parking.

This was *the* Alain Ducasse Italian restaurant. Now, after a period of uncertainty, it is carrying on without him . . . and looks the picture of health! The tables on the patio—in the open air when the weather is fine—the young, assiduous waiters, the vast range of Italian wines at every price and the chef from Modena, Vittorio Beltramelli, who not only knows the score but performs it with an inspiration that mirrors the changing of the seasons: All is a recipe for success. Cream of celery root with littleneck clams or chilled spaghetti with Mediterranean bottarga served as an appetizer, calf's tongue with sweet and sour vegetables, pumpkin risotto with diced crisp prosciutto or mint, scallops with white truffle oil are right on target. The desserts, ranging from the classical (a giant creamy tiramisu) to the modern (a chilled soufflé with ginger and a pina colada sauce) also hit the mark. We drink selected wines by the glass, such as a Conte della Vipera white from Antinori and Ladoucette in Umbria and a Morgante Nero d'Avola from Sicily, delighted to be enjoying this fine restaurant again.

● Chez Vong   ◎ V.COM

10, rue de la Grande-Truanderie
Métro: Les Halles, Etienne-Marcel
Tel. 01 40 26 09 36 / 01 40 39 99 89.
Fax 01 42 33 38 15
chez-vong@wanadoo.fr
www.chez-vong.com
Closed Sunday. Open until 11:30 PM.
Prix fixe: 23,50€ (lunch). A la carte: 85€.
Air cond. Terrace. Private dining room.
Valet parking.

After twenty-five years of loyal service, Vong Kai Kuan seems as lively as ever, and his restaurant, certainly one of the best purveyors of Chinese cuisine in Paris, has in no way lowered its standards; quite the contrary. The dishes presented on the menu reflect the culinary traditions of Canton and Vietnam, competing in subtlety and range of flavor. The service is not fast, but remarkably unobtrusive and polite. The produce is carefully selected and nothing is left to chance. You can savor the steamed ravioli, line-caught sea bass salad, live young turbot (steamed to order) Szechwan beef filet, Peking duck or, ordered in advance, the famous Bresse chicken (also Peking style), sorbets, beignets and steamed cakes. Our host has not neglected the wine list, which promises some shrewd pairings. If the evening goes on long enough, he will even come and chat for a while at your table, taking his duties seriously enough to see you to the door, all with a delightful smile.

▼ SHOPS

KITCHENWARE & TABLETOP

▼ La Bovida

36, rue Montmartre
Métro: Les Halles, Etienne-Marcel
Tel. 01 42 36 09 99. Fax 01 42 33 05 72
9 AM—6:30 PM (Saturday 10 AM—7 PM,
Monday 10 AM—6:30 PM). Closed Sunday.
This Ali Baba's cave for cooking enthusiasts is not only a magnet for pros. Here, you will find stainless steel dishes, food processors and disposable plates, as well as spices, canned foods and preserves.

Shops

▼ La Chaise Longue

30, rue Croix-des-Petits-Champs
Métro: Palais-Royal, Louvre-Rivoli
Tel. 01 42 96 32 14. Fax 01 42 96 08 81
www.lachaiselongue.com
11AM–7PM (December 10 AM–8 PM).
Closed Sunday.

Gift ideas for every pocket can be found in this charming store, with glass candlesticks, ice buckets and toasters.

▼ Dehillerin

18 and 20, rue Coquillière
Métro: Louvre-Rivoli, Les Halles
Tel. 01 42 36 53 13. Fax 01 42 36 54 80
9 AM–6 PM (Monday 9 AM–12:30 PM,
2–6 PM). Closed Sunday, Bank Holidays.

Since 1820 this quality store has been offering cutlery, frying pans, cooking pots, plates and cake pans, as well as copper, tin, stainless steel and porcelain items prized by cooking buffs.

▼ Mora

13-15, rue Montmartre
Métro: Les Halles
Tel. 01 45 08 19 24. Fax 01 45 08 49 05
www.mora.fr
9 AM–6:15 PM (Saturday 8:30 AM–1 PM,
2–5 PM). Closed Sunday, Bank Holidays.

Established in 1814, this institution supplies both the trade and discerning households with a fine choice of porcelain plates and dishes, saucepans, ice buckets, spatulas, salad spinners, pastry molds and knives to be found here and here alone.

BREAD & BAKED GOODS

▼ Philippe Gosselin

125, rue Saint-Honoré
Métro: Louvre-Rivoli
Tel. 01 45 08 03 59. Fax 01 45 08 90 10
7 AM–8 PM. Closed Saturday,
3 weeks in July and August.

Philippe Gosselin, prince of sourdough, sesame and whole-grain breads, makes an award-winning baguette with a soft inside and crispy crust. His macarons, flaky brioches, and cakes—such as the Deauville or Royal, with berry mousse— are remarkable.

▼ Julien

75, rue Saint-Honoré
Métro: Louvre-Rivoli
Tel. 01 42 36 24 83. Fax 01 42 36 24 62
6:30 AM–8 PM. Closed Sunday,
3 weeks in July and August, May 1st.

Jean-Noël Julien is the local star. His baguette, two-time award winner, is one of the most famous in the capital. His crusty country-style loaf or wheat bread with apricots and hazelnuts are just as tasty. His chicken curry and poppy seed and salmon sandwiches are remarkable.

▼ Rault

4, rue des Lavandières-Sainte-Opportune
Métro: Châtelet
Tel. 01 42 33 82 68
7 AM–8 PM.
Closed Sunday, Monday, August.

The Raults have their eyes fixed firmly on excellence: The savory croissants and cakes, Auvergne "Volcan" bread and rolls with dried fruit, cheese and rye are delicious, as is the multigrain baguette, whose reputation has spread as far afield as Japan.

WINE

▼ Juvéniles

47, rue de Richelieu
Métro: Pyramides
Tel. 01 42 97 46 49
Noon–midnight. Closed Sunday,
Monday lunch, Christmas, May 1st.

Half cellar, half wine bar (see Restaurants): In Tim Johnston's lair, you can taste the merchandise before you buy. Wax lyrical over a Cairanne, Australian Shiraz, noble sherry or New Zealand Sauvignon.

▼ Lavinia

3-5, bd de la Madeleine
Métro: Madeleine
Tel. 01 42 97 20 20. Fax 01 42 97 54 50
www.lavinia.fr
10 AM–8 PM (Saturday 9 AM–8 PM).
Closed Sunday.

Thierry Servant takes us on a journey in the company of 2,000 foreign wines, 3,000 French wines and 1,000 spirits. He offers fine Bordeaux in their wooden boxes at reasonable prices, and more common vintages from promising French winegrowers. You can taste his best wines in his restaurant on the second floor.

▼ Wine and Bubbles

3, rue Française
Métro: Etienne-Marcel, Les Halles
Tel. 01 44 76 99 84 / 08 21 02 10 01. Fax 01 44 76 99 94
www.wineandbubbles.com
Bar 6 PM–2 AM, boutique 11 AM–9 PM (Monday 4–9 PM).
Closed Sunday, Bank Holidays.

Wines from all over the world, produced using new natural, biodynamic vinification processes, along with professional advice and free delivery in Paris, have built the reputation of these wine lovers (Also see Restaurants.)

CHOCOLATE

▼ Jean-Paul Hévin

231, rue Saint-Honoré
Métro: Tuileries
Tel. 01 55 35 35 96. Fax 01 55 35 35 95
jphevin.com
10 AM–7:30 PM. Closed Sunday, Bank Holidays, 10 days in August.

The honorable Jean-Paul Hévin. Customers flock to his establishment, drawn by the reliability and quality of chocolates, macarons, chocolate eclairs, ice creams and sorbets, which can be tasted on the second floor or taken out. Everything here contributes to the legend of this extraordinary confectioner.

▼ Michel Cluizel

201, rue Saint-Honoré
Métro: Tuileries, Pyramides
Tel. 01 42 44 11 66. Fax 01 42 44 11 70
www.chocolatmichelcluizel.com
10 AM–7 PM. Closed Sunday, August.

In Catherine Cluizel's window, a fountain pours out real chocolate. In the store, patrons taste chocolate bars made with 33% to 99% cocoa, chocolate rounds, and spiced or sesame pralinés. All the chocolate is produced to the highest standards by Michel Cluizel in Dampsmesnil, Eure.

CUTLERY

▼ Laguiole Galerie

1, pl Sainte-Opportune
Métro: Châtelet
Tel. 01 40 28 09 42. Fax 01 40 39 03 89
www.forge-de-laguiole.com
10:30 AM–1:15 PM, 2–7 PM.
Closed Sunday, Monday.

Laguiole cutlery, Nontron knives with pyrographed boxwood handles and waiter's corkscrews: This designer store has them all. Over the last two years the range has expanded, with Courrèges, Plexiglas, paper, children's, cigar smokers' and pipe smokers' knives.

▼ Saillard-Faugé Le Page

8, rue de Richelieu
Métro: Palais-Royal, Pyramides
Tel. 01 42 96 07 78. Fax 01 42 96 12 05
10 AM–7 PM. Closed Sunday.

On the first floor of this superb fin de siècle building you will find the finest blades from Corsica, Sweden, the Aveyron and Canada. However, the service is a little tight-lipped.

FRUITS & VEGETABLES

▼ Aux Beaux Fruits de France

304, rue Saint-Honoré
Métro: Concorde
Tel. 01 42 60 45 26
7 AM–8:30 PM.
Closed Sunday afternoon, Monday.

The fine fruits of France are to be found here, along with juicy Tunisian oranges and succulent Latin American dates, and, depending on the season, several potato varieties, mushrooms and wild strawberries.

▼ Opéra Primeurs

21, rue Danielle-Casanova
Métro: Pyramides, Opéra
Tel. 01 42 28 60 05
8 AM–7 PM. Closed Sunday.

Apart from the friendly service, you will find appetizing exotic fruits and all types of potatoes and garden-fresh vegetables here. The crisp lettuces, wild arugula and delicious strawberries are carefully selected.

COFFEE

▼ Starbucks Coffee Company

26, av de l'Opéra
Métro: Pyramides, Opéra
Tel. 01 40 20 08 37. Fax 01 40 20 07 75
Open daily (Monday–Thursday 7:30 AM–
9 PM, Friday 7:30 AM–10:30 PM, Saturday
8 AM–10:30 PM, Sunday 8 AM–9:30 PM).
America is enshrined in the decor of this
café, where you will find the famous
House Blend, Shade Grown . . . The finest
selections from Mexico, Kenya, Sumatra,
Guatemala, Antigua and Colombia feature on the menu, as well as the fullest flavored coffee beans.

▼ Verlet

256, rue Saint-Honoré
Métro: Palais-Royal, Pyramides
Tel. 01 42 60 67 39. Fax 01 42 60 05 55
9:30 AM–7 PM. Closed Sunday, August.
Since 1880, this institution supplying good
coffee has broadened its range with teas
and coffees from the Caribbean, South
America and Africa. Superb candied fruit,
generous salads and savory tarts have
place of honor in this establishment intelligently managed by Eric Duchossoy.

◆ RENDEZVOUS

BARS

◆ Bars du Ritz

Hotel Ritz
15, pl Vendôme
Métro: Madeleine, Pyramides
Tel. 01 43 16 30 30. Fax 01 43 16 33 75
Open daily 11 AM–1 AM.
Air cond. Terrace.
Hemingway celebrated the Liberation in
this cozy bar in 1944. Enjoy well-made
dishes or savor the renowned "Ritz Cider"
cocktail based on apple juice and champagne, as you wish. The clientele is international, elegant and discreet. In the
basement, the Ritz Club is as exclusive as
ever.

Rendezvous

◆ Le Normandy

7, rue de l'Echelle
Métro: Palais-Royal
Tel. 01 42 60 30 21. Fax 01 42 60 45 81
Open daily 11 AM–midnight
(Saturday, Sunday 6 PM–midnight).
This remnant of the Fifties was spared
when the hotel was renovated, and it is
still the headquarters of French satirical
publication *Le Canard Enchaîné*. With its
woodwork, period seats and Scottish carpet, it has a very British charm.

◆ Water Bar Chez Colette

213, rue Saint-Honoré
Métro: Pyramides, Tuileries
Tel. 01 55 35 33 90. Fax 01 55 35 33 99
11 AM–7 PM. Closed Sunday.
Air cond.
With its white designer decor, bay windows and glass tables, this stylish haunt
is a rendezvous for fashion victims. Customers are attracted by the selection of
200 waters and light small plates (carpaccio, chicken breasts and strawberry tarts)
and make a point of popping upstairs to
take a look at the latest gadget in vogue.

PUBS

◆ Café Oz

18, rue Saint-Denis
Métro: Châtelet
Tel. 01 40 39 00 18
5 PM–3 AM
(Thursday, Friday, Saturday 5 PM–4 AM).
Closed Christmas.
You can wash down a savory chicken tart
with a foaming beer in this Crocodile
Dundee–style Australian pub, with two
giant screens showing games broadcast
live from Australia.

◆ Carr's

1, rue du Mont-Thabor
Métro: Tuileries
Tel. 01 42 60 60 26. Fax 01 42 60 33 32
conall.carr@wanadoo.fr
www.carrsparis.com
Open daily noon–1:30 AM.

This pub with its Irish ambience has a convivial restaurant in its tavern area. It is well worth a visit for its nooks, stained glass and foaming Guinness, to be enjoyed while admiring the paneled decor.

◆ Le Sous-Bock

49, rue Saint-Honoré
Métro: Louvre-Rivoli
Tel. 01 40 26 46 61. Fax 01 40 26 59 36
Open daily 10 AM–5 AM.
Air cond. Terrace.

In this haunt and headquarters of the Sporting Union Agen rugby club, the 400 beers and 180 whiskeys are a great hit. Czech Pilsen, Chinese Tsingtao and Belgian Leffe co-exist harmoniously, fueling the crazy ambience of this sports bar.

◆ La Taverne des Halles

12, rue de la Cossonnerie
Métro: Les Halles
Tel. 01 42 36 26 44. Fax 01 40 41 92 25
8 AM–1 AM. Closed Sunday.
Terrace.

In this paneled setting brightened by the red faux-leather wall covering, you can try fifteen or so house draft beers: Guinness, Grimbergen and Adelscott star in relaxed surroundings.

◆ Au Trappiste

4, rue Saint-Denis
Métro: Châtelet
Tel. 01 42 33 08 50. Fax 01 40 13 92 25
Open daily 11 AM–2 AM
(Friday, Saturday 11 AM–4 AM).
Terrace.

This bar's success derives from its youthful ambience and kitsch decor. Twenty beer taps, steamed mussels, French fries, sauerkraut and sausage provide the atmosphere in this tavern managed by Philippe Dehan and Patrick Reagal.

WINE BARS

◆ Le Bar de l'Entracte

47, rue Montpensier
Métro: Pyramides, Palais-Royal, Bourse
Tel. 01 42 97 57 76
Open daily 10 AM–2 AM
(Saturday, Sunday noon–midnight).
Terrace.

This retro bistro opposite the Palais Royal has a communicative passion for pastas, assorted charcuterie, and fine vintages (Marionnet Gamay and Druet Bourgueil), all served in a good-natured atmosphere.

◆ Au Cabanon   Ⓝ

42, rue Croix-des-Petits-Champs
Métro: Louvre-Rivoli, Palais-Royal
Tel. 01 42 61 49 98
8:30 AM–8 PM (Saturday 8 AM–3 PM).
Closed Saturday afternoon, 2 weeks in August.
Terrace.

The former Tourne Bouchon has been refurbished in the colors of Southern France by Laurent Blancpain. Tartiflette (potatoes, bacon, and reblochon cheese casserole), sauerkraut, leg of lamb or rack of pork, as well as serious grilled open-faced sandwiches are washed down with reliably selected Cheverny, Gamay and Côtes du Rhône wines.

◆ La Cloche des Halles

28, rue Coquillière
Métro: Louvre-Rivoli, Les Halles
Tel. 01 42 36 93 89
8 AM–9 PM (Saturday 10 AM–4 PM).
Closed Saturday evening, Sunday,
3 weeks in August.
Terrace.

This atmospheric café ruled with an iron hand by Franck Lesage serves quiches, pissaladière (pizza-like onion tart with black olives and anchovies), aged cheeses and fruit clafoutis, washed down with polished Beaujolais.

Rendezvous

◆ Nicolas

17, av de l'Opéra
Métro: Opéra, Pyramides
Tel. 01 42 96 05 84
www.nicolas.fr
Noon–4 PM (Thursday, Friday noon–7 PM).
Closed Sunday.
Air cond. Terrace.

The paneled decor and warm colors are appealing. Smoked salmon and a trio of tartares are washed down with engaging wines served by the glass.

◆ Le Rubis 🍴

10, rue du Marché-Saint-Honoré
Métro: Tuileries
Tel. 01 42 61 03 34
7 AM–10 PM (Saturday 9 AM–3:30 PM).
Closed Saturday evening, Sunday,
1 week for Christmas, 3 weeks in August.
Air cond.

The Fifties' setting with its neon lighting, zinc counter and Formica tables is pretty as a picture. Rillettes, cheeses and assorted charcuterie and pâtés accompany its cheerful Beaujolais. The barrels set up on the terrace make for a convivial atmosphere. (Also see Restaurants.)

◆ Taverne Henri IV

13, pl du Pont-Neuf
Métro: Pont-Neuf
Tel. 01 43 54 27 90
11:30 AM–9:30 PM (Saturday noon–5 PM).
Closed Sunday.

This tavern is now run by the Virmouxs, who are struggling to take up the torch of what was Robert Cointepas' gourmet temple. The selection of Loire and Beaujolais wines has suffered, and the food is moderately damaged. But the assorted charcuterie, pâtés, and cheeses still have their fans in the Palais de Justice neighborhood.

◆ Aux Tonneaux des Halles 🍴

28, rue Montorgueil
Métro: Les Halles, Etienne-Marcel, Sentier
Tel. 01 42 33 36 19
8 AM–midnight. Closed Sunday.

Patrick Fabre carries on as if the Les Halles wholesale market were still there. We like this antique bistro setting with its zinc counter and vine branches, top-notch Beaujolais and excellent open sandwiches. (Also see Restaurants.)

◆ Vino's Ⓝ

29, rue d'Argenteuil
Métro: Pyramides
Tel. 01 42 97 52 43
7:30 PM–2 AM. Closed Sunday.

Under Japanese management, this discreet bar offers well-chosen wine in a lounge decor. Dark gray tones and soft chairs go well together. Combier Crozes accompanies the quality food.

CAFES

◆ Le Café de l'Epoque

2, rue du Bouloi
Métro: Palais-Royal
Tel. 01 42 33 40 70. Fax 01 40 26 68 98
Open daily 6:30 AM–midnight
(Sunday 6:30 AM–11 PM).
Terrace.

This fin de siècle café offers pleasant dishes of the day and honest wines to be enjoyed standing at the bar. Laurent Binvignat also shares his passion for staunchly regional cuisine.

◆ Le Cochon à l'Oreille 🍴

15, rue Montmartre
Métro: Les Halles, Etienne-Marcel
Tel. 01 42 36 07 56
Noon–3 PM, 6 PM–1 AM.
Closed Sunday, August.
Terrace.

This marvelous blue-collar café is equipped with Métro train seats, ceramics and frescos reminiscent of the atmosphere of the Les Halles wholesale market of yesteryear. When the weather is fine, the terrace is a joy.

◆ L'Imprimerie 🍴

29, rue Coquillière
Métro: Louvre-Rivoli, Les Halles
Tel. 01 45 08 07 08. Fax 0145 08 87 08
8 AM–2 AM. Closed Sunday.
Terrace.

The 19th-century frescos are enchanting, the dishes appealing (a delicate tart with tomato and basil, risotto with asparagus and arugula, a homemade soft chocolate cake), and you can enjoy an informal drink at the wood and ceramic bar.

◆ Le Nemours

2, galerie de Nemours / pl Colette
Métro: Palais-Royal
Tel. 01 42 61 34 14
Open daily 7 AM–1:30 AM
(Sunday 9:30 AM–9:30 PM).
Terrace.

This café, whose theatrical decor is reminiscent of the Comédie Française national theater, offers excellent sandwiches on Poilâne bread and wines by the glass. The terrace is next to the entrance to the Palais Royal.

TEA SALONS

◆ Angelina   🏠

226, rue de Rivoli
Métro: Tuileries
Tel. 01 42 60 82 00. Fax 01 42 86 98 97
www.angelina.fr
Open daily 9 AM–6:45 PM.
Air cond.

The star attraction of this circa 1900 café redolent of Vienna (it was the Rumpelmayer establishment) is its hot chocolate, creamy and sweet to a fault. You will need to be patient, though: There is always a wait. A Mont-blanc topped with whipped cream and chestnuts, the dark chocolate tart, the salads and the special of the day slip down effortlessly.

◆ Le Fumoir

6, rue de l'Amiral-de-Coligny
Métro: Louvre-Rivoli
Tel. 01 42 92 00 24. Fax 01 42 92 05 05
www.lefumoir.com
11 AM–11:30 PM (bar until 2 AM).
Closed Christmas, New Year's,
2 weeks in August.
Air cond. Terrace.

After visiting the Louvre museum, patrons soon fill this pretty tearoom with its library feel and adjoining lounges. Exquisite pastries, a good choice of teas, astute little dishes and a quiet atmosphere.

◆ Le Pain Quotidien

18, pl du Marché-Saint-Honoré
Métro: Pyramides, Tuileries
Tel. 01 42 96 31 70. Fax 01 42 96 31 72
7 AM–7 PM (May 1st–October 1st
7 AM–11 PM). Closed Christmas.

This timelessly charming rustic tearoom wins over visitors with plates of smoked salmon, carpaccio, and aged cheeses. The brunch is exquisite, with pots of honey and jam, served on solid pine communal tables.

◆ Chez Paul

70, rue de Rivoli
Métro: Châtelet
Tel. 01 42 71 54 59
8 AM–8 PM. Closed Sunday.

This chain establishment, a little temple of sweetness, is in good health. Savor its tarts, cakes and brioches in peace, upstairs with a view.

◆ Toraya

10, rue Saint-Florentin
Métro: Concorde, Madeleine
Tel. 01 42 60 13 00. Fax 01 42 61 59 53
www.torayagroup.co.jp/paris/
10:30 AM–7 PM. Closed Sunday,
Bank Holidays, 2 weeks in August.
Air cond.

A guaranteed touch of the exotic in this embassy of the Rising Sun, with its ceiling in the form of an inverted hull. We hesitate between choux puffs filled with sesame cream, an azuki bean–paste bar studded with apples and cakes with seasonal fruit. The elegant service is provided by waitresses in traditional costume.

○	Very good restaurant
⊙	Excellent restaurant
⊙⊙	One of the best restaurants in Paris
⊘	Disappointing restaurant
🏆	Good value for money
€	Meals for less than 30 euros
SIM	Simple
COM	Comfortable
V.COM	Very comfortable
LUX	Luxurious
V.LUX	Very luxurious

Red indicates a particularly charming establishment

🎫	Historical significance
🅿	Promotion *(higher rating than last year)*
🆕	New to the guide

●	Restaurant
▼	Shop
◆	Rendezvous

2ND ARRONDISSEMENT
HAUSSMANNESQUE
AND CHARMING

Rue de la Paix and place des Victoires are located in this district, a sign of its elegance, style and popularity. The district is romantic and captivating as well as historic. Pretty and multifaceted, this is the Haussmann arrondissement par excellence, although it is no stranger to urban renewal. The Bourse, the AFP press agency and typical brasseries and bistros (Gallopin, Vaudeville, Chez Georges, Le Grand Colbert) mingle with the latest places in vogue (Le Café Moderne, Liza, Sur un Arbre Perché) and lively Japanese restaurants (Bizan, Koetsu, Issé). Primarily an engaging district, it is home to our International Restaurant of the Year (Mori Venice Bar), which might lead you to mistake the vicinity of the Palais Brongniart for Venice's Grand Canal. Here all is monumental, predestined for inclusion in the register of listed buildings. The arcades are reliably chic. Poet and novelist Louis Aragon mapped out his *Paris Peasant* tour in the area. Passersby dine after the show, let their hair down around the Opéra, repeat the address of Harry's Bar with the traditional American accent ("Sank roo doe noo!") and finish the evening as errant funambulists. With its squares and arcades, the second gives the nod to Fargue or Fallet, playful pedestrians whose pleasure it was to confuse the secret alleys around the Palais Brongniart with the Grands Boulevards nearby. A thoroughly Parisian district in the heart of the City of Light.

● RESTAURANTS

GOOD RESTAURANTS & OTHERS

● Les Alchimistes `SIM`

16, rue Favart
Métro: Richelieu-Drouot
Tel. 01 42 96 69 86. Fax 01 40 20 92 95
lesalchimistes@wanadoo.fr
www.les-alchimistes.fr
Closed Saturday lunch, Sunday, August.
Open until 10 PM.
A la carte: 38€.
Air cond. Private dining room.

This restaurant's alchemy certainly seems to work. Apart from the decor—a combination of patina and contemporary furniture—there are the added attractions of Yvon and Jonathan Bismuth's welcome and Denis Dujour's colorful dishes. The menu changes with the seasons, offering a host of alternatives, such as cream of Jerusalem artichoke soup, red mullet served on a bed of bulgur with pumpkin and preserved lemon, duck parmentier and tropical fruit salad with lemongrass. Each day there is a new special, and the prices are inoffensive.

● Angl'Opéra `COM`

Hotel Edouard VII, 39, av de l'Opéra
Métro: Opéra
Tel. 01 42 61 86 25. Fax 01 42 61 47 73
info@angiopera.com
www.anglopera.com
Closed Saturday, Sunday, Bank Holidays,
3 weeks in August. Open until 11 PM.
A la carte: 45€.
Air cond. Terrace.

Gilles Choukroun, who has left his Café des Délices and advises the Sofitel Mogador in Essaouira, has made this chic, modern eatery on avenue de l'Opéra his Paris showcase. You may or may not like his new style. You can begin with the surprising cream of mint soup with crabmeat and popcorn, then carry on with asparagus, pomelo and licorice in a shaker. The sea bream served with stewed black olives, oranges and tomatoes and, in conclusion, watermelon milkshake with Espelette chili pepper and strawberry-flavored candy provide a pleasant interlude that remains agreeable . . . even when the check arrives.

● Bistrot Vivienne `SIM`

4, rue des Petits-Champs
Métro: Palais-Royal, Bourse
Tel. 01 49 27 00 50. Fax 01 49 27 00 40
Closed Sunday, Christmas, New Year's,
1 week in August. Open until 11 PM.
A la carte: 40€.
Terrace. Private dining room.

This traditional bistro, where red and wood are the main components of the decor, is a discreet neighbor to the handsome place des Victoires. The dishes have style, especially the millefeuille of goat cheese, slow-baked tomato and zucchini, the seared tuna steak with cold ratatouille or the lamb tenderloin with tarragon. And who can resist the tiramisu of red fruits?

● Bistro Volney `N` `T` `SIM`

8, rue Volney
Métro: Opéra
Tel. 01 42 61 06 65
Closed Saturday, Sunday,
dinner (Monday–Wednesday), August.
Open until 10 PM.
Prix fixe: 24€, 32€, 40€.
A la carte: 35–50€.
Terrace.

Aurélien Laffon and François Roger have restored vitality and youth to this old-style bistro reliant on its charm, with its large bar, wine racks and attractive, blue-tinted lights. Guests come for the atmosphere, simple cuisine and choice of shrewd vintages from an extravagant list. The salad with poached egg and mushrooms (that could use a bit more seasoning), the bouquet of shrimp, the guinea fowl (a bit dry) or well-prepared kidney served with soft French fries nicely accompany the Domaine Gauby Côtes du Roussillon or the Caronne Sainte Gemme Haut Médoc.

● Le Bougainville   € SIM

5, rue de la Banque
Métro: Bourse
Tel. 01 42 60 05 19
Closed dinner, Sunday, Bank Holidays,
February vacation, August. Open until 3 PM.
A la carte: 25–30€.
Terrace.

Unshakable good humor at Raymonde Maurel's Lyon *bouchon*-style restaurant. She never fails to welcome her guests with a smile. The classics on the menu are just the thing for journalists from the neighboring *Le Figaro* newspaper or AFP press agency, who come to enjoy the Aveyronnaise pork terrine, broiled sea bass, grilled rib-eye steak and seasonal fruit tarts.

● La Bourse ou la Vie   SIM

12, rue Vivienne
Métro: Bourse
Tel.-Fax 01 42 60 08 83
Closed weekends,
one week Christmas–New Year's
A la carte: 35€.

The boss is bigmouthed and the setting offbeat, but even so, you soon begin to enjoy yourself in this pocket restaurant, as long as you accept its eccentricities: lack of ceremony, tirades and "recommended" wines. The food is a delight, with a terrine of beef and cured ham, pan-roasted codfish steak, salmon in a pepper crust, whole veal kidney and apple tart. The prices are not extravagant.

● Le Café Moderne   SIM

40, rue Notre-Dame-des-Victoires
Métro: Bourse
Tel. 01 53 40 84 10. Fax 01 53 40 84 11
cafemoderne@wanadoo.fr
Closed Saturday lunch, Sunday,
Bank Holidays, Christmas, 2 weeks in
August. Open until 10:30 (weekends: 11 PM).
Pix fixe : 28€, 32€. A la carte: 51€.
Air cond.

One of them from the Vigny, the other from the rue Balzac, Frédéric Hubig and David Lanher are the soul of this modern-looking bistro, solidly established in its

neighborhood. At the stove, newcomer Benoît Hérault plays with today's flavors. The cream of cauliflower soup with herbed mushroom fricassée, seared tuna steak with sweet potato purée and ginger sauce, roasted veal with tomato and olive risotto and a crumble of apples and prunes flambéed with Calvados, served with a fromage blanc sorbet, work their charm. A fine wine list.

● Le Céladon   ○ LUX

Hotel Westminster, 15, rue Daunou
Métro: Opéra
Tel. 01 47 03 40 42. Fax 01 42 61 33 78
infos@leceladon.com
www.leceladon.com
Closed weekends, August.
Open until 9:30 PM.
Prix fixe: 55€ (lunch, wine included),
71€ (dinner), 110€ (dinner).
A la carte: 100€.
Air cond. Private dining room. Valet parking.

In a French Regency style by designer Pierre-Yves Rochon, decorated with Oriental touches, celadon walls and Chinese porcelain, Christophe Moisand gives free reign to his gastronomic inclinations. This conscientious chef, a graduate of Le Coq Saint-Honoré, deploys the full range of his skills. Meticulousness, subtlety and creativity are the watchwords of his expert repertoire. King crab with spring vegetables open the dance, followed by Breton langoustines, squid, farm-raised veal and Poitou rabbit. The desserts stay the course with wild strawberries, a tapioca pudding with ginger ice cream and a lemon sorbet and vodka float. On weekends, Le Céladon changes its decor to become Le Petit Céladon. The atmosphere is intentionally more relaxed, the tablecloths vanish from the tables and families come to eat after a tour of the Louvre or a stroll in the Tuileries. An astute set menu at 55€, including wine and coffee, and a well-devised children's menu help guests keep the cost down.

● Chorus Café `COM`

23, rue Saint-Marc
Métro: Bourse, Richelieu-Drouot
Tel. 01 42 96 81 00. Fax 01 40 20 07 06
chorus.cafe@wanadoo.fr
Closed Sunday, Monday, July, August.
Open until midnight.
Prix fixe: 40€ (dinner), 52€ (dinner),
68€ (dinner). A la carte: 55–60€.
Air cond.

After trying his hand at singing and winning the Eurovision Song Contest in 1965 with "*N'avoue jamais*" ("Never Admit"), Guy Mardel quietly turned to running a restaurant. He brings his guests together around a selection of timeless gastronomic standards: Foie gras *maison*, Provençal-style red mullet, grilled duck confit and nougat glacé are perfectly executed.

● Clémentine `SIM`

5, rue Saint-Marc
Métro: Bourse, Richelieu-Drouot,
Grands-Boulevards
Tel. 01 40 41 05 65
reservation@restaurantclementine.com
www.restaurantclementine.com
Closed weekends. Open until 10:15 PM.
Prix fixe: 27,50€. A la carte: 35€.
Air cond. Private dining room.

Franck Langrenne provides a warm welcome in this 1906 bistro on two floors, where he serves honest, generous dishes. We treat ourselves to sautéed duck hearts with garlic and parsley, sauerkraut with smoked haddock, cassoulet made with Tarbais beans and strawberry vacherin. A fine selection of wines from small vineyards. Each year in May, the restaurant flies the Corsican flag, adding wines from the Isle of Beauty to its list for the occasion.

● Les Coulisses du Théâtre `SIM`

19, pass. des Panoramas
Métro: Grands-Boulevards, Bourse
Tel. 01 44 82 09 52. Fax 01 44 82 06 52
les.coulisses@wanadoo.fr
www.restaurantlescoulisses.com
Closed Sunday, Bank Holidays.
Open until 10:30 PM.
Prix fixe: 29€ (dinner), 26€ (lunch), 22€.
A la carte: 35€.
Air cond.

The *coulisses* the name refers to are the theater wings of the Théâtre des Variétés. Stéphane Jeanty's restaurant stands opposite it, in the heart of the Passage des Panoramas arcade. After the show, everyone gathers for a convivial session over escargot pie, filet of red mullet in raw tomato and olive oil sauce, steak tartare made to order and homemade chocolate profiteroles. Note that the hours depend on what time the play ends.

● Aux Crus de Bourgogne `SIM`

3, rue Bachaumont
Métro: Sentier, Les Halles
Tel. 01 42 33 48 24. Fax 01 40 26 66 41
Open daily until 11 PM.
Prix fixe: 27€ (dinner). A la carte: 52€.
Terrace. Private dining room.

Not far from rue Montorgueil and the former Les Halles wholesale market, this distinguished bistro with its listed historic facade has stuck to its traditions. The service is formal but relaxed, the menu time-honored and the clientele made up of journalists from *Le Figaro* newspaper or *Le Nouvel Observateur* magazine who are attached to their ways. Like them, we easily enjoy the terrine of parsleyed ham, sole meunière, beef tenderloin with morels and baba au rhum. As the bistro's name suggests, the wine list pays special tribute to the vintages of Burgundy.

A SPECIAL FAVORITE

● **Dalva** Ⓝ 🏠 SIM

48, rue d'Argout
Métro: Sentier
Tel. 01 42 36 02 11. Fax 01 42 36 02 27
Closed Saturday lunch, Sunday,
Monday evening. Open until 10:30 PM.
Prix fixe: 14€ (lunch), 18€ (lunch).
A la carte: 35€.
Air cond.

An eye-catching red facade, a clean and simple bistro entrance, a bay window with a terrace in the summer, then, on the second floor, an attractively decorated room with two dining areas and a Murano chandelier; you soon feel at home in François Lelièvre and Agnès Clément's restaurant. Bruno Schaeffer, previously at L'Argenteuil, organizes the menu with skill. Spinach and smoked haddock ravioli in Charroux mustard sauce, cream of shellfish soup with croutons, roast cod and olive oil fork-mashed potatoes, tender rib-eye steak with small roasted potatoes are splendid, as is crème brûlée flavored with bergamot. Quality of produce remains the priority. The somewhat spare cellar is young and reasonable, with finds such as the Domaine de la Negly La Clape. The ideal place to meet friends for a gourmet spread.

● **Domaine de Lintillac** Ⓔ SIM

10, rue Saint-Augustin
Métro: Quatre-Septembre
Tel. 01 40 20 96 27
lintillac@free.fr
www.domainedelintillac-paris.com
Closed Saturday lunch, Sunday lunch,
May 1st, 1 week in August. Open until
10:15 PM (Friday and Saturday 11 PM)
Prix fixe: 8,80€ (lunch). A la carte: 25€.
Air cond.

The Fifties' bistro setting and generous cuisine from Southwest France are reassuring. The produce used to make the house dishes comes from the Domaine de Lintillac in the Corrèze. Whole duck foie gras marinated in Sauternes wine, cassoulet made with duck confit, black duck

sausage in a crust of ground walnuts and the walnut cake, Brive-style, are splendid. Modest prices.

● **Drouant** ◎ 🏠 V.COM

18, pl Gaillon
Métro: Opéra, Quatre-Septembre, Pyramides
Tel. 01 42 65 15 16. Fax 01 49 24 02 15
www.drouant.com
Closed 3 weeks in August.
Open until midnight.
Prix fixe: 42€ (lunch). A la carte: 90€.
Air cond. Terrace. Private dining room.
Valet parking.

Drouant has become "Drouant by Antoine Westermann." The master of the Strasbourg Buerehiesel has turned the venerable establishment that hosts the Goncourt literary awards into a modish, Zen, gourmet brasserie offering a series of meticulously prepared hors d'oeuvre and dishes. The vegetables, fish or classical dishes served on small plates tapas-style, cold asparagus cream soup, foie gras pâté en croûte and Simmental rib-eye steak with slow-roasted shallots: All await you here among a thousand other delights that change from season to season in a gaily refurbished setting in shades of yellow, or on the teak terrace. The desserts, rhubarb croquante in vanilla syrup, millefeuille filled with light cream and baba au rhum, are one of the house's strong points, as are the wines. The service is more relaxed than it was, and the cellar is resourceful. In short, Drouant has been rejuvenated. If France's literary giants can adjust to that, why not you?

● **L'Ecaille de la Fontaine** SIM

15, rue Gaillon
Métro: Quatre-Septembre
Tel. 01 47 42 02 99
Closed weekends, 2 weeks in the beginning of August. Open until 11:30 PM.
A la carte: 30–45€.
Air cond. Valet parking.

Gérard Depardieu, owner of La Fontaine Gaillon, has opened this seafood restaurant just opposite. It is again Laurent Haudiot, formerly of Marius et Janette, who presides in the kitchen. On the first floor, the oyster stall offers oysters and shellfish (oysters: spéciales from Quiberon, claires from Marennes-Oléron; Venus clams from Pors-Even; shrimp from Saint-Gilles-Croix-de-Vie; langoustines from Loctudy), while on the second floor with its view of the 18th-century square and its fountain, guests feast on dishes from across the street. Mackerel rillettes, langoustine ravioli, cold-dressed crab in vinaigrette, hand-chopped rump steak tartare and hazelnut millefeuille favorably impress. On the cellar side, we indulge ourselves with a carafe of Côtes du Rhône or Mâcon white.

● L'Escargot Montorgueil   🍴 COM

38, rue Montorgueil
Métro: Les Halles, Etienne-Marcel
Tel. 01 42 36 83 51. Fax 01 42 36 35 05
escargot-montorgueil@wanadoo.fr
www.escargot-montorgueil.com
Closed 2 weeks in the beginning of January, 3 weeks in August. Open until 1 AM.
A la carte: 80€.
Terrace. Private dining room. Valet parking.

Already in the days of Henri IV, the Montorgueil quarter was renowned for its escargots, eaten in large quantities there. In 1832, L'Escargot d'Or opened at number 38 in the street of the same name. Now Laurent Couegnas has taken over this Second Empire pearl, a listed historical monument, restoring it to a pristine state. Its stucco, moldings and red velvet seats have a nice effect. The Provençal-style sautéed frog's legs with chopped garlic and parsley, Breton lobster flambé with whiskey, veal sweetbreads stewed with vinegar and fresh foie gras and crêpes Suzette are up to standard, even though the prices tend to soar.

● Etienne Marcel   SIM

34, rue Etienne-Marcel
Métro: Etienne-Marcel, Les Halles
Tel. 01 45 08 01 03. Fax 01 45 08 09 26
Open daily until 2 AM
A la carte: 40€.
Air cond. Terrace. Private dining room.

The change of team at this umpteenth Costes brothers restaurant has also meant a chance to bring a few changes to the decor (while preserving the neo-Sixties' style that makes it special, though) and of course to the menu, making it even more appealing. The tomato confit and creamy goat cheese gâteau, filet of sea bass with balsamic vinegar and parmesan, steak tartare served with toasted Poilâne bread and mini cheesecake with fromage blanc sorbet are good examples.

● La Fontaine Gaillon   ◎ 🍴 V.COM

1, pl Gaillon / 1, rue de la Michodière
Métro: Opéra, Quatre-Septembre
Tel. 01 42 65 87 04. Fax 01 47 42 82 84
www.la-fontaine-gaillon.com
Closed Saturday, Sunday,
1 week in February, 3 weeks in August.
Open until midnight.
Prix fixe: 38€ (lunch). A la carte: 65€.
Air cond. Terrace. Private dining room.
Valet parking.

Gérard Depardieu and Carole Bouquet have turned this townhouse built by Jules Hardouin-Mansart into their gourmet showcase. When the sun is out, opposite the fountain that gives the restaurant its name, the terrace enjoys the restful sound of lapping water. Inside, five private dining rooms are available for more personal repasts. Laurent Haudiot is a conscientious chef. His menu reveals a staunch traditionalism and changes with the seasons. The cold-dressed crab in vinaigrette sauce, langoustine ravioli, whole deep-fried whiting, pan-fried John Dory with mashed potatoes, rack of lamb served in its natural juices or milk-fed veal chop are handled with skill. The praliné millefeuille and gariguette strawberries with mint leaves provide a delightful conclusion. The cellar is well stocked, mainly with wines from small growers, but there are also Sicilian vintages among its shrewd selection at friendly prices.

● Gallopin ☕🍴COM
40, rue Notre-Dame-des-Victoires
Métro: Bourse, Grands-Boulevards
Tel. 01 42 36 45 38. Fax 01 42 36 10 32
administration@brasseriegallopin.com
www.brasseriegallopin.com
Daily noon–midnight. Cont. service.
Prix fixe: 19,50€, 33,50€.
A la carte: 40–50€.
Air cond. Terrace. Private dining room.
Valet parking.

This former stockbrokers' refectory has just celebrated its 130th birthday and has lost none of its splendor, with its woodwork, mahogany bar, superb historic glass veranda and original chandeliers. The uniformed waiters are extremely attentive and serve the subtly prepared brasserie dishes gracefully. The beef and vegetables terrine, tuna tartare with French fries and green salad, pork medallion au gratin with almonds and pistachios, spiced fresh fruit soup with red fruit sorbet are of the best. They can be washed down with a selected Bordeaux or a *gallopin* of beer: 20 centiliters instead of the usual 25 in a silver tankard, a house invention.

● Le Gavroche 💶SIM
19, rue Saint-Marc
Métro: Bourse, Richelieu-Drouot,
Grands-Boulevards
Tel. 01 42 96 89 70. Fax 01 40 20 92 20
Closed Sunday, Christmas, New Year's,
1 week in February, August.
Open until 1:30 AM.
A la carte: 30€.

This genuine, old-fashioned local bistro encourages you to take your time with the standards of a timeless cuisine: dried sausage, fresh anchovies, roast prime rib for two, steak with peppercorn sauce and baba au rhum and "*service aux petits oignons*" (i.e., delightfully helpful waiters) and a fine selection of wines by the glass, including selected Beaujolais.

● Chez Georges 🍴SIM
1, rue du Mail
Métro: Bourse, Sentier, Palais-Royal
Tel. 01 42 60 07 11
Closed weekends, Bank Holidays, August.
Open until 10:15 PM.
A la carte: 52€.
Air cond.

This typical Parisian bistro has managed to preserve its turn-of-the-century decor (as shown by the counter, seats, stucco and mirrors) and proprietor Arnaud Brouillet ensures that great recipes of yesteryear continue to delight. Regulars or tourists in search of authenticity sit down to such classics as smoked herring and potato salad, salmon steak in sorrel sauce, grilled veal kidney Henri IV–style and iced profiteroles with warm chocolate sauce, washed down with a carafe of Chinon that tastes like an elixir of youth.

● Le Grand Colbert 🍴COM
2, rue Vivienne
Métro: Bourse
Tel. 01 42 86 87 88. Fax 01 42 86 82 65
le.grand.colbert@wanadoo.fr
Daily noon–1 AM. Cont. service.
Prix fixe: 19€ (lunch), 28€ (lunch),
34€ (dinner). A la carte: 50€.
Air cond. Valet parking.

Opposite the National Library, this 19th-century brasserie featured in *Something's Gotta Give*, starring Keanu Reeves, Jack Nicholson and Diane Keaton, explaining the fondness of American tourists for this quiet establishment. It has lived up to their expectations, though, and there will be few complaints about the baked onion soup, sole meunière, pan-fried calf's liver with caramelized pearl onions and profiteroles with warm chocolate sauce.

● La Grille Montorgueil 🍴SIM
50, rue Montorgueil
Métro: Etienne-Marcel
Tel. 01 42 33 21 21. Fax 01 42 33 70 21
Open daily until midnight.
Prix fixe: 14€ (lunch). A la carte: 35€.
Air cond. Terrace.

The counter that French film star Jean Gabin leaned on in the 1937 movie *Gueule d'Amour* (*Lady Killer*) is still intact, proof of its robustness. The same is true of the chalkboard, presenting classics of domestic cuisine. We make short work of the whole duck foie gras, grilled sea bass, hand-chopped steak tartare and poached pear with chocolate sauce. First-rate service.

● Un Jour à Peyrassol `SIM`

13, rue Vivienne
Métro: Bourse
Tel. 01 42 60 12 92. Fax 01 42 60 00 85
contact@peyrassol.com
www.peyrassol.com
Closed weekends. Open until 10 PM.
Prix fixe: 18€ (lunch on weekdays).
A la carte: 50€.
Private dining room.

The Commanderie de Peyrassol, which produces striking Côtes de Provence wines in three colors, has turned this Parisian restaurant devoted to truffles and Provençal specialties into its embassy. In a contemporary setting of exposed stone walls and pickled wood tables, we delight in the mache, goat cheese and truffle salad, large prawns with fork-mashed potatoes, scrambled eggs with winter truffles and chocolate cake. Just a step away from the restaurant, you can shop in the store.

● Aux Lyonnais ○ `SIM`

32, rue Saint-Marc
Métro: Bourse, Richelieu-Drouot
Tel. 01 42 96 65 04. Fax 01 42 97 42 95
auxlyonnais@online.fr
Closed Saturday lunch, Sunday, Monday, Christmas–New Year's, August.
Open until 11 PM.
Prix fixe: 28€. A la carte: 60€.
Private dining room. Valet parking.

Eric Mercier provides the unshakable "Ducasse" smile in this circa 1900 bistro where not a single element is missing: mirrors, woodwork, moldings, counter and lighting. Here we are happily reunited with the classics of Lyonnaise cuisine, Alain Ducasse–style, which apt pupil Sébastien Guénard prepares by the book. Taste buds

are in for a treat with the pike quenelles with crayfish, calf's liver with chopped garlic and parsley, quick-sautéed beef Lyonnaise style and the Grand Marnier soufflé, not to mention the hazelnut cream tart that will knock you off your feet. The cervelle de canut (fresh cheese seasoned with herbs and shallots) is *the* cheese to taste. The Beaujolais, Burgundies and Côtes du Rhône selected by Mathieu Buffet make an excellent impression, even if they can send the check sky high.

● Le Mellifère 🛉`SIM`

8, rue Monsigny
Métro: Quatre-Septembre
Tel. 01 42 61 21 71. Fax 01 42 61 31 71
a.mellifere@libertysurf.fr
Closed Saturday lunch, Sunday, Monday lunch. Open until 11:30 PM.
Prix fixe: 30€ (lunch), 34€ (dinner).
Terrace. Private dining room.

Ideal for refueling after a show at the neighboring Théâtre des Bouffes Parisiens, Alain Atibard's friendly bistro provides a delicious market produce–based cuisine that draws much of its inspiration from Southwest France. Having trained with the greats (Dutournier, Senderens, Lorain and Cagna), our playful, modest chef gives a faultless performance with eggs baked in a ramekin with foie gras, cod brandade, Basque blood sausage with old-fashioned mashed potatoes and Basque cake, a jam-filled butter pastry. Note the free set menu for children under 10.

● Mémère Paulette 🛉`SIM`

3, rue Paul-Lelong
Métro: Bourse
Tel. 01 40 26 12 36
chezmemerepaulette@free.fr
Closed weekends (except for group reservations), Monday evening (except for group reservations), Bank Holidays, 2 weeks in August. Open until 10 PM.
Prix fixe: 14€ (lunch), 16€ (lunch), 19€ (dinner).
Air cond. Private dining room.

In a rustic setting redolent of the country-side with its old advertising and agricultural competition medals, this wine bar, taken over by the dynamic Laurent Savary, has 200 different vintages in its cellar. In terms of cuisine, it menders along the by-ways of Southwest France, with the duck parmentier braised with white wine and mushrooms, lamb shank braised in Cahors red wine with prunes and dark chocolate ganache flavored with Szechuan pepper.

● Le Mesturet   SIM

77, rue de Richelieu
Métro: Bourse, Quatre-Septembre
Tel.-Fax 01 42 97 40 68
lemesturet@wanadoo.fr
www.lemesturet.com
Closed Saturday lunch, Sunday,
Christmas, New Year's, May 1st,
end of July–middle of August.
Open until 10:30 PM.
Prix fixe: 19€, 25€. A la carte: 35€.
Air cond. Private dining room.

Alain Fontaine has turned this corner bistro into a joyously traditional rendezvous that still gives a nod to today's flavors. We like the thin sardine tart with shallots confit and bell peppers, seared tuna with aniseed oil and Mediterranean vegetables, pig's feet in crispy pastry with sage jus and creamy mashed potatoes and plum clafoutis flavored with aged plum brandy, which go wonderfully with the fine selection of wines by the glass. (Also see Rendezvous.)

● Les Noces de Jeannette   COM

9, rue d'Amboise (at the corner of rue Favart)
Métro: Richelieu-Drouot
Tel. 01 42 96 36 89. Fax 01 47 03 97 31
paris@lesnocesdejeannette.com
www.lesnocesdejeannette.com
Closed December 24. Open until 9:30 PM.
Prix fixe: 19€, 27€, 30€ (wine included).
Air cond. Private dining room.

With its hallmark early 20th-century decor featuring theater and opera posters, Patrick Fracheboud's restaurant tends toward a sterling traditionalism. The rillettes of fresh and smoked salmon, steamed codfish, grilled top rump steak with green peppercorn sauce and chocolate Opéra

cake with crème anglaise are perfectly done, but unsurprising. When will there be a change of menu?

● Le Petit Vendôme   ●SIM

8, rue des Capucines
Métro: Opéra
Tel. 01 42 61 05 88
Closed dinner, Saturday, Sunday,
Bank Holidays.
7 AM–9 PM. Cont. service.
A la carte: 30–35€.
Air cond. Terrace.

In the shade of one of the most stylish locations in the capital, this Parisian Auvergnat café is unashamed of its roots. Apart from the retro charm of its Sixties' setting with neon lights and Formica, there is the added pleasure of generous portions of successive courses of charcuterie, dried sausage, rib-eye steak with béarnaise sauce and strawberry tart.•Fish on Friday only, according to what the market has to offer.

● Chez Pierrot   ●SIM

18, rue Etienne-Marcel
Métro: Etienne-Marcel
Tel. 01 45 08 00 10. Fax 01 42 77 35 92
Closed Sunday, 1st week of January,
3 weeks in August. Open until 11 PM.
A la carte: 40€.
Air cond. Terrace.

This elegant, relaxed, antique bistro refurbished in contemporary style is now decked out in fine brown and plum shades that offer a certain warmth. We are pleasantly surprised by the roasted and marinated bell peppers with mozzarella, red mullet with beurre blanc sauce, Aubrac rib-eye steak served with genuine French fries, rare-cooked veal kidneys and homemade chocolate profiteroles. The Beaujolais and Rhône Valley wines encourage us to wholeheartedly raise our glass.

● Le Press Café ● SIM

89, rue Montmartre
Métro: Sentier, Bourse
Tel. 01 40 26 07 30
www.presscafe.net
Closed Sunday. Open until 10:30 PM.
Prix fixe: 12,50€ (lunch).
A la carte: 25–30€.
Terrace. Private dining room. Valet parking.

In the Bourse district, a cradle of the French press, the name of Frank Bonin's and Jérémy Claval's restaurant was an obvious choice. Food-loving journalists share a love of Royans ravioli, codfish with baby spinach salad, grilled duck confit with sautéed potatoes and chocolate mousse at friendly prices, served in a relaxingly simple setting. One remark: The partners, old acquaintances from the Boucoléon and Blacherne, seem to have lost some of their former ambition.

● Le Pur'Grill 🅿 Ⓞ V.COM

Park Hyatt Vendôme, 5, rue de la Paix
Métro: Opéra
Tel. 01 58 71 10 60. Fax 01 58 71 10 61
www.paris.vendome.hyatt.com
Open daily until 11 PM.
A la carte: 110€
Air cond. Terrace. Valet parking.

Elegant, expensive, glamorous, fashionable and super (in the model sense)—in short, very much at home in its location between Cartier and Boucheron—this exquisite, charming hotel, somber in grayish beige, has acquired a chef of great character. Jean-François Rouquette, an engaging beanpole from the Aveyron region, who formerly trained under Constant at Le Crillon before moving to the Bourdonnais and then to Les Muses at the Hôtel Scribe, has caused a stir in rue de la Paix by adding a stamp of approval to the house cuisine, both in the lobby patio (Les Orchidées) and the gourmet restaurant known as Le Pur'Grill. The place now seems less "fusional" and more regional (but with no awkwardness, just a certain mischief). We delight in light lobster bisque, langoustines slit down the middle and flavored with lemongrass, scallops with

porcini mushroom caramel and the splendid roasted veal rump with diced sautéed zucchini. The desserts, with their geometric composition (the apple theme is exquisite), avoid gimmickry, and licorice macarons will have you melting. In a word, this is an establishment that deserves proper recognition. Superb wines by the glass, including a La Lagune that will leave you speechless.

● Le Saint-Amour SIM

8, rue du Port-Mahon
Métro: Quatre-Septembre, Opéra
Tel.-Fax 01 47 42 63 82
hervbrun@hotmail.fr
Closed Saturday lunch, Sunday, Christmas, 2 weeks in August. Open until 10:30 PM.
Prix fixe: 23€, 26€, 32€.
Air cond. Private dining room.

Halfway between the Bourse and the Opéra, this historic establishment focuses on seafood. In a marine-inspired decor, we make short work of marinated salmon served in a glass, roseval potato salad, langoustines risotto, grilled Argentinian rib-eye steak, hand-cut French fries and the strawberry soup. The menu changes each week according to what the market has to offer.

● Sur un Arbre Perché SIM

1, rue du Quatre-Septembre
Métro: Bourse
Tel.-Fax 01 42 96 97 01
about@surunarbreperche.com
www.surunarbreperche.com
Closed Saturday lunch, Sunday, Christmas, New Year's, 3 weeks in August.
Open until 10:30 PM.
Prix fixe: 20€ (lunch). A la carte: 50€.
Air cond. Private dining room.

In this fashionable establishment, the refined decor, with its prevailing verdant green and white tones, suits the cuisine, which is a touch sophisticated. We are won over by jumbo shrimp in phyllo pastry with lemongrass, a fancy dish of lobster and langoustines flavored with truffle essence, basil lasagna, lamb feuillantine flavored with coffee and served with an eggplant flan and soft chocolate cake with caramelized pineapple and white chocolate ice cream.

● **Le Vaudeville** 🅃 COM

29, rue Vivienne
Métro: Bourse
Tel. 01 40 20 04 62
www.groupeflo.fr
Open daily until 1 AM.
Prix fixe: 22,90€, 29,90€.
A la carte: 45€.
Terrace.

This is the archetypal Parisian brasserie with its clamor, characteristic Thirties' art deco style, beige marble, efficient service and perennially fashionable menu and execution, which has improved significantly. Banks nearby and the neighboring AFP press agency supply a large part of its clientele, who find suitable sustenance there in the form of duck foie gras, grilled Dover sole, skate with capers, stewed calf's head, andouillette AAAAA and millefeuille, all delicious. The choice of wines is appropriate, without hiking up the check excessively.

● **Le Versance** Ⓝ 🅃 COM

16, rue Feydeau
Métro: Bourse, Grands-Boulevards
Tel. 01 45 08 00 08. Fax 01 45 08 47 99
contact@leversance.fr
www.leversance.fr
Closed Saturday lunch, Sunday, Monday, August. Open until 10:45 PM.
Prix fixe: 32€ (lunch, wine included),
38€ (lunch, wine included).
A la carte: 50€.
Air cond. Private dining room.

Exit Le Petit Coin de la Bourse of gastronomic memory. Some of 19th-century stucco remains, but the place has acquired a more contemporary look in the hands of the dynamic Samuel Cavagnis. Atmosphere, staff and menu have all been rejuvenated. In any case, we cannot find fault with the seared foie gras with artichoke crumble, filet of sea bream in aniseed broth with slow-roasted tomatoes and Navy beans, slow-roasted lamb

shank with dried apricots or tear-shaped chocolate and praliné pastry with mango sauce.

INTERNATIONAL RESTAURANTS

**INTERNATIONAL
RESTAURANT OF THE YEAR**

Mori Venice Bar Ⓝ ◯ COM

2, rue du Quatre-Septembre
Métro: Bourse
Tel. 01 44 55 51 55. Fax 01 44 55 00 77
mori@massimomori.fr
www.massimomori.fr
Closed Saturday lunch, Sunday, August.
Noon–11:30 PM. Cont. service.
A la carte: 40–100€.
Air cond. Terrace. Private dining room.
Valet parking.

He was the most elegant, amusing and engaging maître d' in Paris, speaking perfect French acquired in Lausanne, Switzerland. Yet he, the Mantovan of Armani Caffé, decided he wanted more than that. Now, Massimo Mori displays his skills as host in his own restaurant, playing the part of Arrigo Cipriani in this Venetian answer to Harry's Bar. With a wave of his magic wand, the beguiling ristoratore will convince you that the Grand Canal is to be found here in the heart of Paris. Where the Bon II once stood opposite the Bourse (the Paris stock exchange), the Mori Venice Bar offers an elegant, startling leather and wood decor designed by Philippe Starck in lounge mode, setting the tone for a sharp, pure, produce-based cuisine. Mustardy carpaccio, cured ham from the Euganean hills, a seafood soup with clams, monkfish, scorpion fish, squid and croutons, sweet-and-sour marinated langoustines "en escabeche" (in the manner of sardines "in saor "): All wield an irresistible charm. Then there are veal tripe in cream, cuttlefish-ink risotto, clam linguini: Reliable, subtle and vigorous, this cuisine is good for both heart and soul. Everything here is steeped in character and has the flavor of true refinement, like the wines by the glass (including a Pio di Lei Umbrian Chardonnay, unstoppably fruity with a fine finish, and a La Rovinera Speri

Valpolicella with a black cherry nose). The desserts are a delightful experience—a creamy red fruit panna cotta, cooked perfectly, a tasty tiramisu and splendid pastries of the day—and the staff quick to satisfy your every wish. Massimo provides explanations and tells stories as he turns from one table to the next. All Paris slips softly in. As you will have realized by now, this is the great Italian event in the French capital.

▼ SHOPS

KITCHENWARE & TABLETOP

▼ Christofle
24, rue de la Paix
Métro: Opéra
Tel. 01 42 65 62 43. Fax 01 47 42 28 51
10:30 AM–7 PM. Closed Sunday.
Everything for the elegant dinner table at Fabrice David's establishment: porcelain, crystal, silver plate, plain or patterned damask tablecloths, sterling silver, silverplated and steel cutlery, as well as vases and frames of no little grace.

▼ Simon
48 and 52, rue Montmartre
Métro: Etienne-Marcel
Tel. 01 42 33 71 65. Fax 01 42 33 68 25
9 AM–6:30 PM. Closed Sunday, Monday morning (all day in August).
Quality at the right price in this institution in business since 1884: porcelain services, food processors, sharp Japanese knives, silverplate, copper saucepans and baking pans of every shape for professional or amateur cooks. The quality of service has its ups and downs, though.

BREAD & BAKED GOODS

▼ Au Panetier
10, pl des Petits-Pères
Métro: Sentier
Tel. 01 42 60 90 23. Fax 01 40 15 04 72
8 AM–7:15 PM. Closed Saturday, Sunday, 1 month July–August.
The charming Fabrice Cléret and his bread: saint-fiacre, rustic loaves, rye, wal-

nut, dried fig and raisin breads, specialty baguettes. The pine-nut tart, the pancake with a cream and raspberry filling, and the white chocolate bread also make a visit to this fine store dating from 1900 worthwhile.

WINE

▼ Legrand Filles & Fils
1, rue de la Banque
Métro: Sentier, Bourse
Tel. 01 42 60 07 12. Fax 01 42 61 25 51
www.caves-legrand.com
10 AM–7:30 PM (Saturday 10 AM–7 PM, Monday 11AM–7 PM). Closed Sunday
The spirit of the Legrands lives on in this establishment, which continues to promote the best from all the world's vineyards under the aegis of Christian de Châteauvieux (a perfect name for a man of his calling), a store devoted to the arts of wine, with glasses, decanters and a huge book section. At lunchtime, the tasting area offers a vast selection of wines by the glass, accompanying cheeses, charcuterie and foie gras.

▼ Versein & Minvielle
50, rue Sainte-Anne
Métro: Quatre-Septembre
Tel. 01 42 61 99 88. Fax 01 42 86 88 06
versein.minvielle@wanadoo.fr
10:30 AM–7:30 PM
(Tuesday 5:30–7:30 PM). Closed Sunday, Bank Holidays, 2 weeks in August.
A fine selection of growers' wines and a wide choice of spirits from Alsace, Bas Armagnac, Cognac and Calvados, as well as many different accessories, are all to be found here. Deliveries in France and abroad.

CHOCOLATE

▼ Debauve & Gallais
33, rue Vivienne
Métro: Bourse
Tel. 01 40 39 05 50
9:30 AM–6:30 PM. Closed Sunday, Bank Holidays.
20 years ago, Paule Cuvelier turned this fin de siècle store into the Paris embassy for

his chocolates, made in the Eure. Stucco and gilding offer the ideal showcase for his chocolate bars studded with broken cocoa beans and arabica coffee beans and nougatine, dome-shaped chocolates, not to mention the celebrated Kings' chocolate squares and Marie-Antoinette's coin-shaped chocolate drops.

CANDY & SWEETS

▼ Tétrel

44, rue des Petits-Champs
Métro: Pyramides
Tel. 01 42 96 59 58
9 AM–8 PM. Closed Sunday, Bank Holidays.
Yvonne Tétrel has turned this old-fashioned store into a temple of regional delicacies: aniseed candy, chocolate and caramel candy, bergamot-flavored drops, barley sugar, almond pralinés, soft nougatine drops in a crunchy coating, sugar-coated almond and candied fruit lozenges and pyramid-shaped fruit drops.

CUTLERY

▼ Kindal

33, av de l'Opéra
Métro: Pyramides
Tel. 01 42 61 70 78. Fax 01 42 61 75 34
10 AM–6:30 PM (Saturday 11 AM–6:30 PM). Closed Sunday, Bank Holidays.
In this excellent store you will find fine, shiny and solid blades from the Auvergne, Corsica and Scandinavia. The razors, corkscrews, pepper and salt mills will enchant devotees of rare items.

GROCERIES

▼ Detou

58, rue Tiquetonne
Métro: Etienne-Marcel
Tel. 01 42 36 54 67. Fax 01 40 39 08 04
8:30 AM–6:30 PM. Closed Sunday,
Bank Holidays, 2 weeks in August.
There is a little of everything in this fine grocery store: spices, confectionery, tea and coffee. Foie gras, salmon, champagne, wines and spirits at reasonable prices.

PASTRIES

▼ Stohrer

51, rue Montorgueil
Métro: Etienne-Marcel, Sentier
Tel. 01 42 33 38 20. Fax 01 40 26 41 64
7:30 AM–8:30 PM.
Closed 2 weeks in the beginning of August.
François Duthu and Pierre Liénard run one of the finest patisseries in Paris, with its frescoes under glass designed in 1864 by Paul Baudry. Baba au rhum, cream puffs filled with coffee or chocolate pastry cream, lemon pound cake and festive compositions of filled and glazed choux pastry are models of their genre. Excellent delicatessen dishes—puff pastry with a creamy savory foie gras filling, white boudin flavored with foie gras and truffle—complete the house range.

◆ RENDEZVOUS

BARS

◆ Bar Edouard VII

39, av de l'Opéra
Métro: Opéra, Pyramides
Tel. 01 42 61 56 90. Fax 01 42 61 47 73
www.edouard7hotel.com
Open daily 10:30 AM–1 AM.
Air cond. Terrace.
In a cozy, paneled setting, this hotel bar offers mini baguette sandwiches, croque-monsieur and assorted charcuterie. Every evening from 6 to 8, enjoy its champagne happy hour (by the glass, at half price).

◆ The Duke's Bar

Hotel Westminster, 13, rue de la Paix
Métro: Opéra
Tel. 01 42 61 55 11
Open daily 7 AM–1 AM.
Air cond.
This English-style bar is ideal for an aperitif, light lunch or peaceful dinner. Patrons who come to taste the joys of its restful atmosphere are lulled by the female jazz singer who performs in the evening on weekends, smoke cigars and succumb to the temptations of bartender

Gérard Bouidghaghen as he expertly touts his alluring cocktails, including the Sazerac, the Duke's Martini and the Sixth Avenue.

◆ Harry's New York Bar 🛏

5, rue Daunou
Métro: Opéra
Tel. 01 42 61 71 14. Fax 01 42 61 58 99
10:30 AM–4 AM. Closed Christmas.
Air cond.

This Thirties' bar has preserved its "British institution" ambience, moldings and patinated ceiling. On weekends, you need to be patient to place your order, and finding a seat in the barroom is something of a labor of Hercules. But weekday evenings are quieter. A fine collection of single malts.

◆ Sherwood

3, rue Daunou
Métro: Opéra
Tel. 01 42 61 70 94. Fax 01 42 61 05 64
Open daily noon–4 AM.
Air cond.

The selection of beers and cocktails is respectable. Practical when the neighboring Harry's is full.

PUBS

◆ The Frog & Rosbif

116, rue Saint-Denis
Métro: Etienne-Marcel, Réaumur-Sébastopol
Tel. 01 42 36 34 73. Fax 01 42 36 48 02
www.frogpubs.com
Open daily noon–1:30 AM.
Air cond. Terrace.

The most packed place in the capital on Saturday night or when soccer or rugby games are shown. The beer flows freely and the poulet à l'indienne (Indian-style chicken stew), like the cheesecake, are eaten hungrily.

◆ Kitty O'Shea's

10, rue des Capucines
Métro: Opéra
Tel. 01 40 15 00 30 / 01 42 96 02 99. Fax 01 42 56 49 54
Open daily 11 AM–1:30 AM
(Friday, Saturday 2 AM).
Air cond. Terrace.

Rendezvous

You could easily think yourself in Ireland in this paneled tavern serving rivers of Guinness. The seafood cocktail, strip steak in whiskey sauce, and Irish stew are worthy of its Dublin namesake.

◆ Le Manneken-Pis

4, rue Daunou
Métro: Opéra
Tel. 01 47 42 85 03. Fax 01 44 51 93 79
Open daily 11:30 AM–6 AM.
Air cond.

This discreet-looking Belgian bar is prized for its 200 beers—Chimays, Leffes and Gueuzes—steamed mussels with French fries and Ardenne smoked ham. In the basement, the dance floor is decorated with photos of celebrities.

WINE BARS

◆ Le Mesturet

77, rue de Richelieu
Métro: Bourse, Quatre-Septembre
Tel.-Fax 01 42 97 40 68
7:30 AM–11 PM.
Closed Saturday lunch, Sunday.
Air cond.

Alain Fontaine has turned a commonplace corner café into *the* congenial rendezvous in the Bourse district. Small plates, selected wines and good atmosphere go hand in hand. A choice of quality wines and first-rate open sandwiches. (Also see Restaurants.)

CAFES

◆ Bistrot des Petits Carreaux 🛏

17, rue des Petits-Carreaux
Métro: Sentier
Tel. 01 42 33 37 32
8 AM–1 AM. Closed Sunday evening.
Terrace.

This renovated Fifties' café is as friendly as ever. Wines by the glass, lemonade, unfussy dishes and copious salads can be enjoyed freely at any hour.

◆ Café du Croissant 🏠

146, rue Montmartre
Métro: Bourse, Grands-Boulevards
Tel.-Fax 01 42 33 35 04
7 AM–1 AM. Closed Sunday.
Terrace.

This old-fashioned café upholds the memory of Jaurès, the socialist French president assassinated in 1914, and the early 20th-century press. Customers take time out to enjoy the fish of the day, veal blanquette or duck parmentier.

TEA SALONS

◆ A Priori Thé

35-37, Galerie Vivienne
Métro: Bourse
Tel. 01 42 97 48 75. Fax 01 42 97 46 31
Open daily 9 AM–6 PM (Saturday 9 AM–6:30 PM, Sunday noon–6:30 PM).
Terrace.

Under the glass roof of the galerie Vivienne, Margaret Hancock devotedly watches over the cosmopolitan dishes and exquisite pastries that patrons savor in the cozy lounge or on the terrace under the arcade's glass roof.

◆ L'Arbre à Cannelle 🏠

57, pass. des Panoramas
Métro: Richelieu-Drouot, Grands-Boulevards
Tel. 01 45 08 55 87
11:30 AM–6:30 PM. Closed Sunday (except in December), Bank Holidays, evening, 2 weeks in August.
Terrace.

In this Second Empire arcade, under the coffered ceiling, three women make savory and sweet tarts, large salads (Périgord salad with foie gras and cured duck breast, "supreme" salad, "exotic" salad). Assorted charcuterie and cheeses from the Savoie region and tiramisu are on offer. Sunday brunch in December.

◆ Lina's Sandwiches

50, rue Etienne-Marcel
Métro: Etienne-Marcel
Tel. 01 42 21 16 14. Fax 01 42 33 78 03
www.linascafe.fr
9:30 AM–6 PM (Saturday until 6:30 PM).
Closed Sunday.

Quick meals with generous sandwiches (pastrami or steak-and-mozzarella) are offered at this modern deli. Lemon tart, crème brûlée and cookies are not bad.

◆ Le Pain Quotidien

33, rue Vivienne
Métro: Bourse, Richelieu-Drouot, Grands-Boulevards
Tel. 01 42 36 76 02. Fax 01 42 36 76 03
7 AM–6:30 PM.
Closed Christmas, New Year's.
Air cond. Terrace.

A step away from the Bourse, this rustic lounge offers delights in the shape of beef carpaccio, smoked salmon, tarts or assorted cheeses. Excellent country bread and delicious artisanal jams and preserves.

◆ Ventilo

27 bis, rue du Louvre
Métro: Sentier
Tel. 01 44 76 82 97 / 01 44 76 83 02.
Fax 01 44 76 83 03
10 AM–6 PM (Saturday until 7 PM).
Closed Sunday.

On the third floor, the bay window looks out over rue du Louvre. Seat yourself comfortably in one of the rattan chairs in this very cozy lounge and enjoy the tarts and crumbles. A moment of pleasure.

○	Very good restaurant
◎	Excellent restaurant
◎◎	One of the best restaurants in Paris
⑤	Disappointing restaurant
■	Good value for money
€	Meals for less than 30 euros
SIM	Simple
COM	Comfortable
V.COM	Very comfortable
LUX	Luxurious
V.LUX	Very luxurious

Red indicates a particularly charming establishment

🏛	Historical significance
🏷	Promotion *(higher rating than last year)*
Ⓝ	New to the guide

●	Restaurant
▼	Shop
◆	Rendezvous

3RD ARRONDISSEMENT
REFLECTIONS OF
PROVINCIAL FRANCE

The regions are encamped in the Marais quarter, where the street names are Bretagne, Poitou, Beauce, Forez and Saintonge. Its *hôtels*—historic residences—and their grounds are now open to the public. The former home of Madame de Sévigné has become the city's history museum. The Hôtel Sale is devoted to Picasso and the Hôtel de Marle to Swedish culture, while the Hôtel de Sens houses the Fornay library. Then there are the Hôtel de Soubise, the French history museum; the Hôtel de Saint-Aignan, the museum of Judaism; the Hôtel de Rohan-Guéméné, dedicated to Victor Hugo; and the Hôtel de Guénégaud, devoted to hunting and nature. The third arrondissement is a mosaic of gardens, small squares, alleys and streets running beside enclosed parks. This is not the heart of Paris, rather a certain idea of a tranquil, provincial France in a Medieval or Renaissance vein. The cafés have a rustic chic. The bistros (such as our special favorite, the playful Café des Musées, which offers the freshest of fresh produce at the lowest of prices) are good natured. Place des Vosges, terraces and mazes of streets where the grass grows green beneath the cobblestones... Do you know place du Marché Sainte-Catherine or rue du Parc-Royal with its noble facades? Not far away is the Pompidou Center, already another world, extending into the future.

RESTAURANTS

GOOD RESTAURANTS & OTHERS

● **L'Ambassade d'Auvergne** 🔊 V.COM

22, rue du Grenier-Saint-Lazare
Métro: Rambuteau, Etienne-Marcel
Tel. 01 42 72 31 22. Fax 01 42 78 85 47
info@ambassade-auvergne.com
www.ambassade-auvergne.com
Open daily until 10:30 PM.
Prix fixe: 28€. A la carte: 40€.
Air cond. Private dining room.

In the center of Paris, Françoise Petrucci's establishment is a friendly country inn offering attentive service in rustic surroundings. Everything is present: the old-fashioned dining room with exposed beams, raspberry wall hangings, communal tables, comfortable chairs and fresh produce from the Auvergne region, deftly prepared by a new chef, Emmerich de Backer. The Salers beef and tender leek terrine and vegetable millefeuille with walnut oil are excellent starters. We follow them up with estofinado (Provençal codfish stew with tomatoes, garlic and spices) or roasted free-range guinea fowl with garlic and—the icing on the cake—fresh peas, then come in to land with a trio of custards with a subtle taste of the Auvergne or sweet shortbread cookies with strawberries. Françoise Petrucci also offers a private dining room and meeting room. In fact, she has thought of everything, and is even open on Sunday.

● **L'Ami Louis** 🔊 SIM

32, rue du Vertbois
Métro: Arts-et-Métiers
Tel. 01 48 87 77 48
Closed Monday, Tuesday,
mid-July–mid-August. Open until 11 PM.
A la carte: 135€.

Bill Clinton loves the place, as does Jacques Chirac. This genuine bistro, whose soul and appearance have survived intact, provides uniformed service and timeless classics with tremendous panache. Of course, guests at L'Ami Louis are not short of a dollar or two; the prices are catastrophic, but if you are not afraid to share the dishes, which are huge, the check can prove manageable. Foie gras, escargots from Burgundy, beautiful seasonal asparagus, milk-fed lamb with sautéed garlic potatoes, whole roasted chicken served with a mountain of French fries have style to spare. The extraordinary wines do nothing to lighten the tab. Finally, it is worth pointing out that the restaurant is open on Sunday.

● **L'Auberge Nicolas Flamel** 🔊 COM

51, rue de Montmorency
Métro: Etienne-Marcel, Rambuteau
Tel. 01 42 71 77 78
nicolas-flamel@tele2.fr
www.auberge-nicolas-flamel.fr
Closed Saturday lunch, Sunday,
3 weeks in August. Open until 10:30 PM.
Prix fixe: 30€ (lunch, wine included),
49€, 59€. A la carte: 60€.
Private dining room.

In a medieval atmosphere (the restaurant is one of the oldest in Paris, dating from 1407), the cuisine is inventive and of good quality. A private dining room for more intimate occasions or a meeting room for working parties—the choice is yours. Creamy octopus risotto with sautéed peas and morels or delicious Noirmoutier potatoes mashed with sea snails and periwinkle butter are two of new chef Frédéric Le Guen-Geffroy's successful offerings. To end, the chocolate hazelnut dessert is delightful. A fine cellar.

● **Au Fil des Saisons** 🔊 SIM

6, rue des Fontaines-du-Temple
Métro: Arts-et-Métiers
Tel. 01 42 74 16 60
Closed Saturday lunch, Sunday,
Bank Holidays, August. Open until 10 PM
(weekends: 10:30 PM).
Prix fixe: 14€ (lunch), 17€ (lunch),
27€ (dinner), 31€ (dinner).

This snug, rustic restaurant just around the corner from the Carreau du Temple provides a cheerful welcome, fresh dishes and modest prices. We enjoy Burgundy escargots in a Chablis beurre blanc, oyster mushrooms sautéed with onions and pork belly, seared foie gras medallions with thyme and millefeuille with rhubarb and bergamot-infused cream. All this is chalked up on the blackboard and accompanied by the delicious house bread. The lunchtime set menu is quite a find.

● Le Bar à Huîtres `COM`

33, bd Beaumarchais
Métro: Chemin-Vert, Bastille
Tel. 01 48 87 98 92. Fax 01 48 87 04 42
barahuitres.bastille@barahuitres.fr
www.lebarahuitres.com
Daily noon–1:30 AM. Cont. service.
Prix fixe: 20€, 24€, 38€, 16€ (children).
A la carte: 45€.
Air cond. Terrace. Private dining room.
Valet parking.

The establishment has changed hands. The decor, by Jacques Garcia, is very new and handsome. This oyster bar boasts air conditioning, a terrace, a private dining room and valet parking (which makes life easier here in the heart of Paris). The cuisine makes no waves. Tart of slow-roasted caramelized tomatos, monkfish baked in puff pastry with mustard, fresh cod with aïoli, sautéed seasonal fruit in salted butter caramel are all well prepared.

● Le Baromètre `SIM`

17, rue Charlot
Métro: St-Sébastien-Froissart,
Filles-du-Calvaire
Tel. 01 48 87 04 54
Closed Sunday. Open until 10:30 PM.
A la carte: 32€.

Alain Larché has taken over this pleasant bistro in the heart of the Marais district, which has been soberly repainted in off-white colors. The wines are Sancerres, Beaujolais and Chinons. If you feel like a bite, country pâté, andouillette gratin—a bistro classic—or 10-ounce roasted prime rib will be just the thing. Alain and his daughter handle the service.

● Au Bascou `SIM`

38, rue Réaumur
Métro: Arts-et-Métiers, Réaumur
Tel.-Fax 01 42 72 69 25
Closed Saturday, Sunday,
1 week Christmas–New Year's, August.
Open until 10:30 PM.
Prix fixe: 18€ (lunch). A la carte: 40€.
Air cond.

Although Jean-Guy Loustau has been replaced by Bertrand Guéneron, Senderens' former lieutenant at the Lucas-Carton, neither the atmosphere nor the cuisine has changed an iota. There can be no doubt: We are still in the temple of Euskadi, the Basque country, and the ochre walls, covered with drawings, photos (especially of the previous proprietor), relics and miscellaneous diplomas are still the same. The menu breathes a delightful scent of the Pyrénées and the Atlantic, as evinced by the inevitable piperade (sautéed sweet bell peppers with tomatoes, onions and garlic) and also the sautéed shrimp with fennel salad, the pan-seared squid with Espelette chili peppers, Bayonnaise (Basque guinea hen), as well as "*le béret Basque*" (a traditional Basque chocolate cake) for dessert. A fine selection of Irouléguy (such as Ohitza) and Spanish wines adds the final touch to this highly colorful restaurant.

A SPECIAL FAVORITE

● Café des Musées `SIM`

49, rue de Turenne
Métro: St-Sébastien-Froissart, Chemin-Vert
Tel. 01 42 72 96 17. Fax 01 44 59 38 68
Closed mid-August–beginning of September.
Open until 11 PM.
Prix fixe: 12,50€ (lunch), 19€ (dinner).
A la carte: 35€.
Air cond. Terrace. Private dining room.

In the heart of the Marais district, just a step away from the Picasso and Carnavalet museums, this unassuming looking corner café is soon packed, proof that word of mouth is highly effective in the center of Paris. The young François Chenel (who trained at Fouquet's, La Gentilhommière

Good Restaurants & Others

in Tremblay-sur-Mauldre and Le Dôme du Marais) has taken over the business with a keen young team and prepares simple but striking dishes at the open stove. His lunch option at 12.50€ is a steal, and the chalkboard offers an array of dishes that are dynamic, honest and fresh. We adore the creamy, warm quiche-like tart with bacon and onions, the delicate beef piccata, and dishes that change to reflect the produce available at the market. The watercress soup, the solid rib-eye steak with crispy French fries and béarnaise sauce, the slowly cooked chicken with morels and loin of black Bigorre pork are a genuine delight. Add good-natured desserts—from the chocolate brownie-like Lorrain cake and the light raspberry and almond meringue cake—and carafe wines with plenty of good, common sense (Marionnet Sauvignon white, Côtes de Blaye red), and you realize that this is an opportunity you cannot afford to miss in today's Paris.

● Les Chineurs   🅝 SIM

55, rue de Bretagne
Métro: Arts-et-Métiers, République, Temple
Tel. 01 42 78 64 50. Fax 01 75 51 44 08
contact@leschineurs.com
www.leschineurs.com
Closed Sunday, Monday,
Christmas–New Year's, 3 weeks in August.
Open until 11 PM.
Prix fixe: 22€ (lunch), 28€.
A la carte: 40–55€.
Terrace.

Xavier Belvaux and Laurent Peccavet have decorated their restaurant with mirrors, curiosities and fine tableware: The result is startling and original. The saddle of baby rabbit stuffed with morels, filet of sea bass with golden polenta "matchsticks" and tomato confit, purée of fresh green peas, suckling pig stuffed with buttery cooked cabbage and foie gras, are very well prepared. Indecisive epicures will opt for the selection of eight different desserts. Note the choice of game in season.

● Le Clos du Vert Bois   SIM

13, rue du Vertbois
Métro: Temple, Arts-et-Métiers
Tel. 01 42 77 14 85
Closed Saturday lunch, Sunday (except for reservations), Monday, Christmas, New Year's, 3 weeks in August.
Open until 10 PM.
Prix fixe: 23€, 27€,
34,90€ (wine included).

In this rustic establishment in shades of orange, everything has been entirely refurbished: decoration and paintwork. Proprietor Franck Pinard has taken over the kitchen. There are still no a la carte dishes, but depending on the season and what the market has to offer, the set menu presents six or seven dishes for lunch and dinner. The brioche of pan-fried foie gras with langoustines, pike-perch with asparagus or beef tenderloin with morels are assiduously prepared and generously served. A restaurant to cherish.

● Le Connétable   COM

55, rue des Archives / 2, rue des Haudriettes
Métro: Rambuteau, Hôtel-de-Ville
Tel. 01 42 77 41 40 / 01 42 71 69 21.
Fax 01 42 77 84 66
www.leconnetable.com
Closed Saturday lunch, Sunday lunch, August. Open until 11 PM.
Prix fixe: 15€ (lunch), 21€.
A la carte: 50€.

Nothing has changed at Françoise Wilcz's establishment: The historic stones and beams of this building, once the townhouse of the Cardinal de Retz, are as enduring as the Aubusson tapestries, the plate of raw fish, duck breast with mango and the chocolate "Marquise" mousse. Good news: The prices have not changed either. Note that the restaurant is open on Sunday evening.

● **A Deux Pas du Trois**　　COM

101, rue Vieille-du-Temple
Métro: St-Sébastien-Froissart,
Filles-du-Calvaire
Tel. 01 42 77 10 52. Fax 01 42 71 40 59
Closed Saturday lunch, Sunday, Monday.
Open until 11:30 PM.
Pix fixe: 15€ (lunch on weekdays),
25€ (weekdays). A la carte: 46€.
Air cond. Terrace.

Close to the Picasso museum, Olivier Cornet's establishment has a rustic charm and the additional attraction of a terrace. Chef Stéphane Moa prepares the food with the greatest care and changes his menu two or three times a year. The foie gras and seasonal fruit terrine, seared filet mignon with fork-mashed fingerling potatoes and shallot confit will leave no one indifferent. To conclude, petite tuiles with rhubarb marmalade and the creamy mascarpone crème with salted butter caramel are as delicious as you could hope for.

● **Les Don Juan**　　€ SIM

19, rue de Picardie
Métro: Arts-et-Métiers, Filles-du-Calvaire,
République
Tel. 01 42 71 31 71
www.lesdonjuan.com
Closed Saturday lunch, Sunday,
3 weeks in August. Open until 10:30 PM.
Prix fixe: 12,20€ (lunch), 14,80€,
31€ (dinner). A la carte: 30€.
Air cond.

The atmosphere and cuisine of this rustic establishment are Mediterranean. The setting is agreeable and there is no smoking at all on the first floor, where guests savor sun-drenched dishes such as the Crete-style pork shoulder with spring vegetables to begin, followed by risotto with artichoke hearts and parmesan. Panna cotta with roasted mangos and "le secret du Vatican" (a white chocolate and pistachio meringue cake) are sweetly sinful.

● **Au Duc de Montmorency**　　€ SIM

46, rue de Montmorency
Métro: Rambuteau, Arts-et-Métiers
Tel.-Fax 01 42 72 18 10
leduccuisiniertraiteur@tiscali.fr
www.avecousanssauce.com
Closed dinner, Sunday, beginning of
August–end of August. Open until 8:30 PM.
Prix fixe: 7,90€ (lunch), 8,50€ (lunch),
9€ (lunch).

A few barstools stand at the counter of this delicatessen. Laurent Delcros, formerly at Laurent and L'Auberge Nicolas Flamel, keeps everyone guessing. He welcomes customers among his jars, cans and bottles and improvises according to the season, the produce available at the market and his mood. There is no permanent menu: The choices change every day and are a complete surprise. Open-face toasted sandwiches, plates of charcuterie, Corsican cheese, fish baked in parchment paper with aromatic vegetables, freshly cooked vegetables and desserts (chocolate cake, fruit tarts and flans) are all lovingly crafted.

● **L'Estaminet d'Arômes**　　€ SIM
　et Cépages

Enfants Rouges market, 39, rue de Bretagne
Métro: Filles-du-Calvaire, Arts-et-Métiers
Tel. 01 42 72 34 85. Fax 01 42 72 28 12
aromes-et-cepages@mangoosta.fr
www.aromes-et-cepages.com
Closed dinner, Sunday evening, Monday.
A la carte: 25€.
Terrace.

In the charming open market, this bistro with its communal wooden tables provides a friendly welcome. Thierry Poincin presents dishes as fresh as the morning dew. Soft-boiled eggs with a chestnut and mushroom cake, foie gras terrine with peppered aspic, sea bass infused with chervil and served with a shellfish broth, duck tagine with spices and preserved lemon and seven-hour lamb are impressive. The honey waffles with warm chocolate sauce will rekindle memories of childhood. (Also see Rendezvous.)

● **La Guirlande de Julie** `COM`

25, pl des Vosges
Métro: St-Paul, Bastille
Tel. 01 48 87 94 07. Fax 01 48 87 01 22
info@guirlandedejulie.com
www.latourdargent.fr
Closed Monday. Open until 10:30 PM.
Prix fixe: 25€. A la carte: 45–60€.
Air cond. Terrace.

Under the arches of place des Vosges, this, the second of two neighboring establishments (along with Coconnas) belonging to André Terrail of La Tour d'Argent, has been entirely renovated in shades of pink. In the dining room, decorated with flowers and adjoining a leafy courtyard, we savor traditional dishes revised by Eric Jolibois, formerly at Taillevent and the George V. Who could resist the foie gras terrine with a pear and Port aspic, grilled turbot with baby leeks and olive oil sabayon, classic pot-au-feu, veal filet with morels and cream, or the unusual poppy-seed ice cream parfait?

● **Chez Janou** `SIM`

2, rue Roger-Verlomme
Métro: Chemin-Vert
Tel. 01 42 72 28 41. Fax 01 42 76 00 03
chezjanou@wanadoo.fr
Closed December 24th. Open until midnight.
Prix fixe: 13,50€ (lunch). A la carte: 38€.
Air cond. Terrace.

With its wooden furniture and faux-leather seats, this Fifties' bistro in shades of pastis (Jean-François Roux says he has 80 different types of this liquor in his cellars, alongside Rhône Valley and Provence wines) is a congenial place. New chef Rani Mousli concocts a sunny cuisine with pleasant dishes that include the crayfish, avocado and grapefruit salad, grilled sea bass with pesto and blanc-manger with lemon. A charming, shady terrace.

● **Chez Jenny** `🍴` `COM`

39, bd du Temple
Métro: République
Tel. 01 44 54 39 00. Fax 01 44 54 39 09
chezjenny@blanc.net
www.chez-jenny.com
Daily 11:30 AM–1 AM. Cont. service.
Prix fixe: 19€, 23,50€, 28€.
A la carte: 45€.
Air cond. Terrace. Private dining room.
Valet parking.

Its red facade, twinkling lights, sumptuous woodwork, collection of Spindler marquetry and carved wooden figure of an Alsatian lady at the door offer a change of scenery. The dishes and drinks incite us to travel. The Alsatian quiche, haricots verts salad with smoked duck, salmon with sorrel with Alsatian pasta, grilled rib-eye steak with béarnaise sauce and Alsatian apple tart served a la mode with gingerbread are effortlessly accompanied by a Tokay Pinot Gris, Pinot Noir or Riesling.

● **Le Murano** `V.COM`

13, bd du Temple
Métro: Filles-du-Calvaire
Tel. 01 42 71 20 00. Fax 01 42 71 21 01
paris@muranoresort.com
www.muranoresort.com
Open daily until midnight.
A la carte: 70€.
Air cond. Terrace. Private dining room.
Valet parking.

Jérôme Foucault and chef Julien Chicoisne, formerly of the Sketch in London and Les Fermes de Marie in Megève, run this chic hotel restaurant with brisk efficiency. The style is neo-Starck in shades of white and plum. A private dining room, terrace and valet parking are all available to its well-heeled customers, who appreciate the meticulously prepared dishes showcasing flavors from all over the world. White bean purée, Japanese-style langoustines, gilthead sea bream or grilled Kobe beef with a purée of "forgotten" vegetables (crosnes, Jerusalem artichokes, rutabagas) impress favorably. The Guanaja chocolate sabayon completes the banquet beautifully. There is brunch on Saturdays and Sundays, with an option at 55€ including champagne. The sommelier is a competent young woman named Julia Dussert.

● **Chez Nénesse** ☕🏠SIM

17, rue de Saintonge
Métro: République, Filles-du-Calvaire
Tel. 01 42 78 46 49. Fax 01 42 78 45 51
Closed Saturday, Sunday, Bank Holidays, Christmas–New Year's, August.
Open until 10:30 PM.
A la carte: 23€.

The Leplu family runs this charming, friendly, traditional bistro without affectation. Roger, who presides at the stove, is a veteran of Prunier, Le Grand Véfour and Pierre au Palais-Royal. His cuisine is classical, sober, meticulous and unfussy. The smoked herring and potatoes marinated in olive oil, veal chops pan-fried with butter, lemon and parsley and raspberry clafoutis are of excellent character. This discreet haunt for gourmets also has a number of appealing wines to offer.

● **Le Pamphlet** ○COM

38, rue Debelleyme
Métro: Filles-du-Calvaire, St-Sébastien-Froissart
Tel. 01 42 72 39 24
Closed Saturday lunch, Sunday, Monday lunch, first 2 weeks in January, 3 weeks in August. Open until 11 PM.
Prix fixe: 33€, 55€.
Air cond. Private dining room.

A native of Pau trained at the Crillon by Christian Constant, Alain Carrère has not rested on his laurels. This year, he has opened a good-natured adjunct, Le Petit Pamphlet, just a short step from home. This does not prevent him from tending as conscientiously as ever in the great Pyrenean tradition to the parent establishment with its yellow and red hues and attentive service. The cuisine comes directly from the region and displays great character. The thin potato tart with marinated wild salmon, sea bream with vegetable fritters and pimento jus, seared mixed grill of meats served with Swiss chard with green

peppercorns and roasted breast of Challans duckling win our ready approval. The pistachio crumble and the roasted pear with ice cream and chocolate sauce are childhood delights.

● **Le Petit Marché** ⓃSIM

9, rue de Béarn
Métro: St-Sébastien-Froissart
Tel. 01 42 72 06 67
Open daily until midnight.
Prix fixe: 14€ (lunch). A la carte: 40–45€.
Air cond. Terrace.

This rustic, convivial corner bistro just behind place des Vosges and a step away from rue de Turenne does not only supply a variety of beverages at any hour. It also provides a very fashionable, slightly "fusion," genuinely market-based cuisine, chalked up on the blackboard and served with a smile on wooden tables set simply with table mats and attractive plates. The raw sesame tuna, the gravlax-style salmon, the sea bream grilled skin-side down, rare veal kidneys, veal chop wrapped in bacon with potatoes gratin provide an accurate, light example of its deft style. Fresh ideas emerge, the staff are cheerful and the waitresses charming. The prices are reasonable, especially since the wines by the glass enable customers to avoid pushing up the tab too much. A pleasant terrace in the summer. (Also see Rendezvous.)

● **Le Petit Pamphlet** Ⓝ🏠SIM

15, rue Saint-Gilles
Métro: Chemin-Vert
Tel. 01 42 71 22 21
Closed Saturday lunch, Sunday, Monday lunch, Christmas, first week of January, 3 weeks in August. Open until 11 PM.
Prix fixe: 31€. A la carte: 38€.
Air cond.

His Pamphlet in rue Debelleyme was not enough for him. Now with Laurence Lesieur, Alain Carrère has opened a good-natured offshoot just a step away from the parent establishment and not far from place des Vosges. The menu adapts to what the market has to offer without losing itself in pointless twists and turns. The prices are

Shops

realistic and the setting urbane. In short, we have only words of praise for this modest, very neat and tidy, new wave–style bistro. The lump crab with tomato and avocado tartare, Piquillo peppers stuffed with brandade of smoked haddock with chorizo chips, parmesan risotto with grilled shrimp or breast of duckling with seasonal fruit remind us that Alain Carrère learned his trade at the Crillon under Christian Constant. An engaging spiced cherry chaud-froid with vanilla ice cream and shrewdly chosen wines from Southwest France and Spain.

● Robert et Louise 🏠 SIM

64, rue Vieille-du-Temple
Métro: St-Paul, Filles-du-Calvaire,
Hôtel-de-Ville
Tel. 01 42 78 55 89
Closed Sunday, Monday, beginning of
July–end of August. Open until 10:30 PM.
Prix fixe: 12€ (lunch). A la carte: 38€.

Pascale Georget has taken up the torch of her recently deceased father, Robert. With her mother, Louise, she lovingly tends to the fortunes of this inn, always a delight with its rustic atmosphere and food cooked at the fire with feeling: grilled boudin, escargots, roasted prime rib, grilled lamb, homemade chocolate cake and seasonal fruit tarts are remarkable.

● Si Restaurant SIM

14, rue Charlot
Métro: Filles-du-Calvaire,
St-Sébastien-Froissart
Tel. 01 42 78 02 31
sirestaurant@wanadoo.fr
www.sirestaurant.fr
Closed Saturday lunch, Sunday,
3 weeks in August. Open until 10:30 PM
(Friday, Saturday 11 PM).
Prix fixe: 13,50€ (lunch), 17,50€ (lunch),
24€ (dinner), 29€ (dinner).

Quite hip, rather Seventies, with its globe lighting and ochre, orange and beige tones, this establishment located very close to the Picasso museum offers dishes with hot, spicy notes. Concocted by Julien Toujan, pan-seared scallops with cumin-spiced

pumpkin purée, filet of cod with red pesto, duck parmentier with shallot confit and sautéed mushrooms and sabayon and red berry gratin are drenched in sun.

● Au Vieux Molière ⊜ SIM

12, passage Molière
Métro: Rambuteau
Tel. 01 42 78 37 87. Fax 01 42 77 81 87
contact@auvieuxmoliere.com
www.auvieuxmoliere.com
Closed Saturday lunch, Sunday,
1 week in August. Open until 10:30 PM.
Prix fixe: 9,50€ (lunch, wine included).
A la carte: 30€.
Terrace.

In this old-style family inn with its picture-covered walls, the dishes vary from season to season. Sven Verardo welcomes guests with a smile, while Eric Kabongo meticulously prepares eggs baked in a ramekin with foie gras, lamb chops with old-fashioned mashed potatoes and "Old Molière's Delight." Terrace, reasonable prices and parking nearby.

▼ SHOPS

KITCHENWARE & TABLETOP

▼ Dot 🏠

47, rue de Saintonge
Métro: Filles-du-Calvaire
Tel. 01 40 29 90 34. Fax 01 42 74 76 22
dot.bon@wanadoo.fr
9:30 AM–6 PM. Closed Saturday (except in December), Sunday.
This Forties' glassworks has some fine antiques at reasonable prices. Marie-Ange Bon offers marrow spoons, asparagus and escargot tongs, knife rests, leg of mutton holders and fine sets of tableware from the luxury hotels of yesteryear at reasonable prices.

▼ Philippe Olivier

65, rue de Thurenne
Métro: St-Sébastien-Froissart
Tel. 01 42 78 20 87
Open daily 10 AM–8:30 PM.

A talented florist, Philippe Olivier is also a brilliant antiques dealer. Tableware, pottery, champagne glasses, salad bowls, earthenware, vases, floral decorations and antique household linen are on display at sensible prices.

BREAD & BAKED GOODS

▼ Fernand Onfroy
34, rue de Saintonge
Métro: Filles-du-Calvaire
Tel. 01 42 77 56 46
7:50 AM–1 PM, 3–8 PM.
Closed Saturday afternoon, Sunday,
1 month July–August.

Customers come here for the quality of the bread. Corinne and Aurélie Onfroy sell large round loaves of white bread, country loaves, and rye, whole grain and organic breads. Don't overlook the exquisite Viennese pastries.

▼ Au Levain du Marais
32, rue de Turenne
Métro: Chemin-Vert
Tel. 01 42 78 07 31
7 AM–8 PM. Closed Monday.

Thierry Rabineau has spread his talent around in Paris (in the ninth and eleventh arrondissements). He guarantees that no additives are used in any of the foodstuffs he supplies in this fine store. Various breads—rye, organic country sourdough, organic whole wheat, focaccia with cheese or bacon and rye with walnuts or raisins—are deftly prepared.

WINE

▼ Le Jardin des Vignes
91, rue de Turenne
Métro: St-Sébastien-Froissart
Tel. 01 42 77 05 00. Fax 01 42 77 70 89
lejardindesvignes@lejardindesvignes.com
2:30–7:30 PM. Closed Saturday (in summer), Sunday, August.

Every day (except Monday and Friday), Jean Radford presents two-hour oenology classes for groups of five or six people. In his cellar and library, you will find the best wines of the Loire, Rhône and other regions.

▼ Le Nectar des Bourbons
37, rue de Turenne
Métro: Chemin-Vert
Tel.-Fax 01 40 27 99 12
10:30 AM–2 PM, 4–8:30 PM.
Closed Sunday, Monday, August.

Alain Dechy offers shrewd advice and, once a month, organizes a tasting of his greatest finds in this former art gallery, open all week. High quality Côtes du Rhône, Beaujolais and Burgundies.

▼ Aux Trésors de Bacchus
4, rue du Pas-de-la-Mule
Métro: Chemin-Vert, Bastille
Tel. 01 48 87 27 07. Fax 01 48 87 80 38
centrale.dist@wanadoo.fr
10 AM–8:30 PM. Closed Monday, Tuesday,
2 weeks in August.

Near place des Vosges, Chantal Berthault's fine emporium offers carafes, glasses and corkscrews, great Bordeaux, old Armagnacs, selected vodkas and mature cheeses.

CUTLERY

▼ Le Laguiole du Marais
6, rue du Pas-de-la-Mule
Métro: Chemin-Vert, Bastille
Tel. 01 48 87 46 88. Fax 01 48 87 66 66
10 AM–12:30 PM, 1:30–7 PM
(Sunday 2–7 PM).

Just by the place des Vosges, an attractive, enchanting store devoted to Aveyron knives. The repair, sharpening and sale of knives with horn or boxwood handles, Laguiole cutlery and children's knives will appeal to aficionados.

GROCERIES

▼ Goumanyat
3, rue Charles-François Dupuis
Métro: Temple, République
Tel. 01 44 78 96 74
www.goumanyat.com
2–7 PM (Saturday 11 AM–7 PM).
Closed Sunday, Monday, 3 weeks in August.

Pierre Thiercelin, alias Goumanyat, selects the best condiments, dried fruits and fine liqueurs, some of them almost unknown. Spices, dried flowers and dried mushrooms have places of honor in his model grocery store.

CHEESE

▼ Fromagers de France

39, rue de Bretagne
Métro: Filles-du-Calvaire, Arts-et-Métiers
Tel. 01 42 78 52 61
8 AM–1 PM, 4–8 PM.
Closed Sunday afternoon, Monday.

We delight in William Jouannault's fresh goat cheese, aged cantal, beaufort d'alpage, camembert with cider and Calvados, échurgnac ripened with William Jouannault walnut liqueur. He showcases the Rhône-Alpes, Auvergne, Normandy and Loire regions in all their variety.

BOOKS

▼ Food

58, rue Charlot
Métro: Filles-du-Calvaire
Tel. 01 42 72 68 97
11 AM–1 PM, 2–7 PM.
Closed Saturday morning,
Sunday, Monday, August.

Claude Deloffre supplies delicacies and reading matter in his fine bookshop. Contemporary items and photographs mingle eclectically with Tea Together chutney and marmalade, Halen Môn spiced coarse salt, Liège syrups and Oliviera oil from Nice.

PASTRIES

PASTRY CHEF OF THE YEAR

▼ Le Pain de Sucre

14, rue Rambuteau
Métro: Hôtel-de-Ville, Rambuteau
Tel.-Fax 01 45 74 68 92
paindesucre75003@aol.com
9 AM–8:30 PM. Closed Tuesday,
Wednesday, July.

Didier Mathray and Nathalie Robert both served as pastry chefs with Pierre Gagnaire before going into business themselves on a modest scale, taking over a narrow baker's store in this gastronomic street. They have painted it a chocolate shade and now present the cream of today's cakes and pastries. Their specialty? Taking a fresh look at the classics, lightening and revamping them. Taste their version of chocolate eclair "crumble" fashion, shortbread pastry with red fruit, lemon tart, their very fashionable mason jars (Zanzibar with pineapple purée, Mister Tom with green apple, apricot "Don Quichotte") and puddings and custards. The chocolate "shock" and Castanea chestnut dessert are worth purchasing and tasting.

FRUIT & VEGETABLES

▼ Jardin du Marais

29, rue de Bretagne
Métro: Filles-du-Calvaire, Arts-et-Métiers
Tel. 01 42 72 61 02. Fax 01 42 72 48 04
6 AM–1 PM, 4–8 PM.
Closed Sunday afternoon, Monday, August.

Crunchy carrots, mushrooms in season (porcini from Burgundy, gyromitres, bolets) as well as juicy grapefruits and perfectly ripe tropical fruits look very appealing in this smart store.

TEA

▼ Le Palais des Thés

64, rue Vieille-du-Temple
Métro: Hôtel-de-Ville
Tel. 01 48 87 80 60
www.lepalaisdesthes.com
Open daily 10 AM–8 PM.

A selection of 200 teas from the finest plantations, which can be accompanied by different types of spice loaf and confectionery. Enthusiasts can learn more at three daily sessions entitled *découvertes* (discoveries), *connaissances* (knowledge) and *évasion* (getting away), with guest experts.

COFFEE

▼ Lapeyronie

3, rue Brantôme
Métro: Rambuteau
Tel.-Fax 01 40 27 97 57
www.lapeyronie.fr
8:30 AM (Saturday 10 AM)–7:30 PM.
Closed Sunday, Bank Holidays,
first 2 weeks in August.
Terrace.

Stéphane Martin offers a competent, warm welcome in his paneled store, which boasts the finest coffees from Guatemala, Costa Rica and Yemen, Ethiopian moka and Salvadorian or Kenyan arabicas. Taste the house blends (Napoli, Hauts Plateaux, Balthazar blond), Chinese black tea and other brews and enjoy the terrace.

PREPARED FOODS

▼ A la Mexicaine

68, rue Quincampoix
Métro: Rambuteau, Les Halles
Tel.-Fax 01 48 87 99 34
alamexicaine@wanadoo.fr
Call for hours

Yuriria Iturriaga, anthropologist and diplomat, proudly champions Mexico's culinary traditions. This former restaurateur now offers take-out versions of her chalupas (filled with shredded beef, chicken or pork), monkfish with garlic and chili pepper, pork or lamb tacos, as well as a soft chocolate cake.

◆ RENDEZVOUS

BARS

◆ The Quiet Man

5, rue des Haudriettes
Métro: Rambuteau, Les Halles
Tel. 01 48 04 02 77
5 PM–2 AM. Closed Christmas.
This little Irish pub pours cool Guinness, Kilkenny and Murphy's in cozy surroundings. The second establishment in avenue Victoria is just as pleasant. Live Celtic music.

◆ La Taverne République

5, pl de la République
Métro: République
Tel. 01 42 78 50 86. Fax 01 48 87 88 51
www.tavernerepublique.com
Open daily 8 AM–2 AM
(Friday–Saturday 8 AM–4 AM).
Air cond. Terrace.

In this tavern filled with laughter and giant sculptures, or on its terrace, patrons can enjoy beers from all over the world, along with steamed mussels with French fries and Irish stew. They can also browse through the collection of comic books and join in the karaoke on Friday and Saturday nights. Tuesday and Thursday are devoted to world music and song.

WINE BARS

◆ Le Barricou

1, bd du Temple
Métro: Filles-du-Calvaire
Tel. 01 42 72 20 53
7:30 AM–8 :30 PM. Closed Sunday, August.
Sylvie and Michel Gineston serve assorted charcuterie, skate with caper sauce, and "Segala," red-label veal served with mashed potatoes with garlic and tomme cheese. Enjoy their homey desserts (chocolate mousse, Breton pudding cake with prunes), and be sure to taste the Loire wines, all in a traditional Paris-bistro atmosphere.

◆ Bistrot de la Gaîté

7, rue Papin
Métro: Réaumur-Sébastopol
Tel. 01 42 72 79 45
7:30 AM–8 PM. Closed Sunday,
3 weeks in August.
Terrace.

Slimane Benakli has taken over this old bistro, which stands in a quiet square between two boulevards. He serves Beaujolais and Loire vintages accompanied by well-prepared dishes—rolled stuffed veal wrapped in bacon, salmon, beef tenderloin.

◆ Le Bouledogue   Ⓝ
20, rue Rambuteau
Métro: Rambuteau
Tel. 01 40 27 90 90
9:30 AM–midnight.
Closed Sunday, August.
Terrace.

This bistro pays homage to the eponymous bulldog in its every guise, and is hospitable to a fault. The attractions here are the traditional (steak tartare with French fries, andouillette AAAAA) and selected Burgundy and Rhône Valley wines from the right sources.

◆ Les Enfants Rouges
90, rue des Archives
Métro: Filles-du-Calvaire
Tel. 01 48 87 80 61
7 AM–7:30 PM (Thursday, Friday 2 AM).
Closed Sunday, Monday.

Dany Bertin-Denis and daughter Emmanuelle run this amusing bistro, located in the heart of the Enfants Rouges market, with great good humor. Carefully selected Loire and Rhône wines accompany an assortment of pork pâtés and cured meats and well-judged specials of the day. Busy late night service on Thursday and Friday.

◆ L'Estaminet d'Arômes et Cépages
Enfants Rouges market
Métro: Filles-du-Calvaire
Tel. 01 42 72 34 85 / 01 42 72 28 12
www.arome-et-cepages.com
10 AM–8 PM.
Closed Sunday afternoon, Monday.
Terrace.

Thierry Poincin competes rustically with Dany Bertin-Denis in this good-natured café. Grilled bread with smoked haddock, served open-faced, blood pudding parmentier and mixed fruit crumble are accompanied by selected Chinons and Beaujolais. (Also see Restaurants.)

◆ Le Taxi Jaune   Ⓝ
13, rue Chapon
Métro: Arts-et-Métiers
Tel. 01 42 76 00 40
8:30 AM–1:30 AM. Closed Saturday, Sunday,
1 week Christmas–New Year's,
3 weeks in August.

Rendezvous

This fun bistro with its Fifties' schoolroom look provides pleasant snacks, good dishes at lunchtime—celery rémoulade, quiche lorraine, radish salad, sea bream with verbena, coq au vin and tremendously shrewd wines.

BRASSERIES

◆ Arts et Métiers   Ⓝ
51, rue de Turbigo
Métro: Arts-et-Métiers
Tel. 01 48 87 83 25
Open daily 7 AM–11 PM
(Saturday, Sunday 2 AM).

This designer café makes a charming contemporary brasserie. The food is unremarkable, but the location is strategic, not far from the Pompidou Centre, opposite the Arts et Métiers school.

CAFES

◆ Andy Whaloo
69, rue des Gravilliers
Métro: Arts-et-Métiers
Tel. 01 42 71 20 38
Open daily noon–2 AM.
Air cond. Terrace.

This bar serves North African tapas full of vigor. Salads, stuffed crisp pastry parcels and tasty pastries slip down smoothly in a smoky atmosphere. Guaranteed to get you away from it all with a hookah under the supervision of Mourad Mazouz, the man behind the North African eatery 404.

◆ Métalozinc
43, rue Beaubourg
Métro: Rambuteau
Tel. 01 48 87 14 73
www.metalozinc.com
7 AM–2 AM. Closed Sunday.

This designer location in red and black hues with dimmer lighting enchants effortlessly. The snacks are pleasant enough—giant salads, grilled ham and cheese sandwiches, club sandwiches—and the sensible prices do not rock the boat.

◆ Le Petit Marché

9, rue de Béarn
Métro: Chemin-Vert
Tel. 01 42 72 06 67
8 AM–midnight.
Closed Christmas Eve, New Year's Eve.
Terrace.

This pleasant, convivial bistro offers sundry drinks, cold and hot soups, crisp phyllo pastry with jumbo shrimp, calf's liver with balsamic vinegar and rib-eye steak to hip locals. Sunday brunch on the terrace.

◆ Royal Bar

19, rue du Parc-Royal
Métro: Chemin-Vert
Tel. 01 42 72 33 03
10 AM–10 PM. Closed August.

The opening times of this picturesque café next to the Picasso museum depend on the proprietor's mood. Bohemian atmosphere and varied drinks.

TEA SALONS

◆ Les Bonnes Sœurs　　🄽

8, rue du Pas-de-la-Mule
Métro: Chemin-Vert, Bastille
Tel.-Fax 01 42 74 55 80
Open daily noon–11 PM.

Cécile and Alexandra Baconnet have enthusiastically taken over this cozy tearoom. Savory food (red tuna with crisp fennel, poached egg and slowly roasted caramelized tomatoes, charcuterie) competes with sweet (panna cotta, chocolate cake, oranges with fresh mint). Brunch on weekends and public holidays.

◆ Bouak　　🄽

47, rue de Turenne
Tel. 01 44 78 09 84
10 AM–11 PM. Closed Saturday, Sunday, 2 weeks in August.

In the new wave Marais, this kosher deli is considered a hip eatery. Pastrami sandwiches, poppy seed cake and strudel are inspected by the Beth Din, but can also be enjoyed by goyim.

◆ Brocco　　🄷

180, rue du Temple
Métro: Temple, République
Tel. 01 42 72 19 81. Fax 01 42 72 05 68
6:30 AM–7:30 PM. Closed Sunday.

This tearoom, which has been refurbished snack-bar style, still has its historic ceiling showing the goddess of the harvest. The crisp layered pastry with pralinés and bitter chocolate, negresco cake, Brazilian cake and baba au rhum are worth a visit and taste.

◆ Camille

24, rue des Francs-Bourgeois
Métro: St-Paul
Tel. 01 42 72 20 50
Open daily 8 AM–midnight.
Terrace.

Half tearoom, half bistro, this establishment has plenty of charm with its exposed stone walls and terrace. Sorbet, tarte Tatin and small plates are served with zest in a lively atmosphere.

○	Very good restaurant
○○	Excellent restaurant
○○○	One of the best restaurants in Paris
○	Disappointing restaurant
♟	Good value for money
€	Meals for less than 30 euros
SIM	Simple
COM	Comfortable
V.COM	Very comfortable
LUX	Luxurious
V.LUX	Very luxurious

Red indicates a particularly charming establishment

🏛	Historical significance
℗	Promotion *(higher rating than last year)*
Ⓝ	New to the guide

●	Restaurant
▼	Shop
◆	Rendezvous

4TH ARRONDISSEMENT
FROM ISLAND TO ISLAND

The fourth arrondissement of Paris encroaches on the Marais, surrounds rue des Rosiers, then dons the mantle of a gay citadel in rue Vieille-du-Temple before casting its gaze down toward the river. There, it crosses from island to island, the Ile de la Cité and Ile Saint-Louis its havens. But despite this insular aspect, it remains open, hospitable and good natured. Its bridges span "the Seine: neither blue, nor gray, boiling" (as Yves Martin sang), giving you the feeling you are traveling from one island to another. On Quai de Bourbon or Quai de Béthune by the river, on the Pont Louis-Philippe or in rue Saint-Louis-en-l'Ile, you are still in Paris. But step across to the far bank and you will discover what seems to be some sort of modern medieval world in rue des Barres or rue François-Miron. The bistros and brasseries of the fourth arrondissement have character (Bofinger, Benoît, Les Fous d'en Face, Mon Vieil Ami, Le Vieux Bistro) and one of its fashionable establishments (Georges) looks out breathtakingly over Paris from the Pompidou Center. Its charming restaurants (L'Orangerie, taken over by del Burgo, and Chez Julien) and rare great gastronomic institutions (L'Ambroisie) are like clubs. The local artisans (Gardil, Izraël, Calixte) are united in their love of quality. This corner of Paris favors hearty appetites, solid dishes and wines to pass the time, flowing like the Seine as it accompanies the runaway gourmet.

RESTAURANTS

GRAND RESTAURANTS

● L'Ambroisie ⓟ ⓒⓞ LUX

9, pl des Vosges
Métro: Bastille, St-Paul
Tel. 01 42 78 51 45
Closed Sunday, Monday, Christmas vacation,
February, end of July–end of August.
Open until 10 PM.
A la carte: 245–300€.
Air cond. Valet parking.

A true classicist, refusing to skimp on produce or quality, reassuring us in these days
of designer food, unwilling to "decon-
struct" dishes but able to deftly span the
gap between yesterday's and tomorrow's
cuisines: This is Bernard Pacaud, the discreet artisan of L'Ambroisie. The lobster
gazpacho, with a very Robuchon air about
it, herb and escargot cannelloni in a
creamy star anise–flavored broth, soft-
boiled eggs and asparagus with a watercress and caviar sabayon sauce, roasted
foie gras glazed with onion caramel,
served with caramelized turnips and
turnip greens, Bresse chicken breast with
crayfish and creamed morel mushrooms
are enchantingly correct, verging on a
serene perfection. There is a kind of timelessness in this beautiful setting, an 18th-
century residence restyled by François
Joseph Graf, with parquet flooring, tapestries and velvet chairs. The wines, described with shrewd precision by Pierre le
Mouliac (unbeatable on the Rhône Valley,
brilliant on Burgundy), Daniel Pacaud's
serene welcome, Pascal Vetoux's distinguished but unstilted dining room management and the meticulously crafted
desserts such as delicate chocolate shortbread tart, vanilla ice cream, thin caramelized puff pastry cookies served with
fromage blanc, oven-dried lemon and
rhubarb crisps: Here we recognize the discretion that once moved us at Alain
Chapel's establishment in Mionnay. A
craftsman of French cuisine, never faulted,
the overly discreet Bernard has more than

earned the three plates we readily return
to him after too long an interlude.

GOOD RESTAURANTS & OTHERS

● L'Alivi ⓔ SIM

27, rue du Roi-de-Sicile
Métro: St-Paul, Hôtel-de-Ville
Tel. 01 48 87 90 20
alivi@noos.fr
www.restaurant-alivi.com
Open daily until 11 PM.
Prix fixe: 22€. A la carte: 45€.
Air cond. Terrace.

Corsica is at home here in the heart of the
Marais, under the supervision of Alain
Cacciari. His rustic lair elongated by a
small terrace incites us to enjoy a pleasant
break over the authentic dishes. The fresh
sardines marinated with fennel, thin red
mullet tart with ratatouille, roasted young
goat stuffed with brocciu cheese and
cream puffs filled with chestnut mousse
celebrate the Island of Beauty without a
single false note.

● Auberge de Jarente SIM

7, rue de Jarente
Métro: St-Paul, Bastille
Tel.-Fax 01 42 77 49 35
Closed Sunday evening.
Prix fixe: 13€ (weekday lunch), 19€,
21€ (wine included), 30€. A la carte: 35€.
Air cond. Terrace. Private dining room.

This traditional inn has changed, but no
one has noticed. Regional produce from
the Basque country and Béarn is still very
much the thing for Christophe and Franck
Inderbitzin, presiding over the dining
room and kitchen, respectively. In the
vaulted cellar with its fine woodwork,
squid and chorizo casserole, marmitako de
thon (a Basque tuna stew), duck breast
with honey and red wine sauce and crème
caramel are accompanied by delightful
wines from the Pyrénées and the Atlantic
coast.

● **Baracane** SIM

38, rue des Tournelles
Métro: Bastille, Chemin-Vert
Tel. 01 42 71 43 33
info@l-oulette.com
www.l-oulette.com
Closed Saturday lunch, Sunday, Christmas,
New Year's, May 1st. Open until midnight.
Prix fixe: 16€ (lunch, wine included), 28€,
38€ (wine included). A la carte: 40€.

In this modest adjunct to their Oulette in the twelfth arrondissement, Marcel and Marie-Noëlle Baudis serve up the Lot region on a platter. The Quercy produce is prepared without fuss and the dishes presented informally. We need little urging to try beef marrow on toast with red wine sauce, roasted pike-perch with preserved lemon and celery root purée, pan-seared top rump steak with shallots and apple pie with a crisp puff pastry topping, especially since the prices have remained manageable.

● **Benoît** ○ 🛉 COM

20, rue Saint-Martin
Métro: Châtelet, Hôtel-de-Ville
Tel. 01 42 72 25 76. Fax 01 42 72 45 68
restaurant.benoit@wanadoo.fr
Closed Christmas, New Year's,
beginning–end of August. Open until 10 PM.
Prix fixe: 38€ (lunch). A la carte: 70–90€.
Air cond. Private dining room.

Alain Ducasse, gentleman globetrotter, and Thierry de la Brosse from L'Ami Louis previously worked together on the aggiornamento of Aux Lyonnais in rue Saint-Marc. Now they have taken over this bistro revered by Americans, just a step away from the Hôtel de Ville. Keeping their promise to the Petit family, they have retained both the spirit of the place and its postcard-bistro decor, with counter, brass coat pegs and banquettes perfectly intact. To replace the great Michel, they have brought in an efficient dining room maestro who trained at La Bastide de Moustiers, Daniel Finot. The cuisine favored by David Rathgeber, an Auvergnat (but of Alsatian extraction) who was formerly at Aux Lyonnais, has not changed an iota (apart from

the—temporary?—disappearance of excellent iced desserts like the coffee parfait with prunes or the Grand Marnier soufflé, which should make a comeback). Langue Lucullus (smoked ox tongue stuffed with foie gras), frog's legs with chopped garlic and parsley, herring-style smoked salmon marinated in oil, cod brandade, oven-roasted shoulder of Pauillac lamb, and signature tête de veau—a masterpiece of the genre—are simply superb. Good news: Visa cards, once refused, are at last welcome! And the wine list now stretches to noble Burgundies at every price.

● **Le Bistrot de la Place** SIM

2, pl du Marché-Sainte-Catherine
Métro: St-Paul
Tel. 01 42 78 21 32. Fax 01 42 78 32 36
http://www.haltya.com/html/bp_us_index.htm
Open daily until 11 PM.
Prix fixe: 13,50€ (lunch). A la carte: 35€.
Air cond. Terrace.

Although the decor echoes the Big Apple, Dominique Péladeau has remained faithful to the refined home cooking of his native Provence. Sitting on the tree-planted terrace looking out over a dream square, you can almost hear the song of the cicadas as you savor the lavish platter of assorted salads, fish of the day, salmon in golden crispy pastry with leek fondue and saffron sauce, Provençal-style beef-cheek stew and tiramisu: classic, but delicate, sun-drenched dishes. You should try to be a little more prudent than the grasshopper in the fable though, and remember to make a reservation.

● **Bofinger** 🛉 COM

5-7, rue de la Bastille
Métro: Bastille
Tel. 01 42 72 87 82. Fax 01 42 72 97 68
eberne@groupeflo.fr
www.bofingerparis.com
Open daily until 1 AM.
Prix fixe: 29,90€, 13,50€ (children).
A la carte: 40–66€.
Air cond. Private dining room. Valet parking.

In pure Belle Epoque surroundings—a glass roof dating from 1880, Panzani inlays and Hansi paintings—this monument of the brasserie world attracts all kinds of customers, including those who leave the chore of parking to a valet. Atmosphere, atmosphere . . . this is Paris indeed. In front of you is Jean-Luc Blanlot in his role as dining room manager, directing a flawlessly choreographed ballet, and a blamelessly fresh assorted shellfish platter or the timeless preparations of chef Georges Belondrade: foie gras, sole meunière, seafood choucroute, roasted lamb saddle in its own jus and individual baba au rhum. Attractive, appetizing and professional.

● **Au Bourguignon du Marais**   SIM
52, rue François-Miron
Métro: St-Paul, Pont-Marie
Tel. 01 48 87 15 40. Fax 01 48 87 17 49
Closed Sunday. Open until 11 PM.
A la carte: 40€.
Air cond. Terrace. Private dining room.

This gracious embassy in the heart of the Saint Paul quarter has changed hands. Its new head, Philippe Lalot, has been careful to maintain the spirit of the place while casting an eye on its dishes. The Côte d'Or, Côte Chalonnaise and Beaune wines recommended by former boss Jacques Bavard still hit the mark. Jean-Yves Boutin remains a fixture in the kitchen, a guarantee of authenticity for the œufs en meurette (poached eggs in a red wine and bacon sauce), Duval andouillette cooked in Aligoté wine and assorted Burgundian cheeses enjoyed on the terrace or in the hushed, tasteful setting inside.

● **Brasserie de**   SIM
l'Ile Saint-Louis
55, quai de Bourbon
Métro: Pont-Marie
Tel. 01 43 54 02 59. Fax 01 46 33 18 47
Closed Wednesday, Christmas,
New Year's, August.
Noon–11:30 PM. Cont. service.
A la carte: 35–47€.
Terrace.

Choucroute and draft beer are on the menu in this Alsatian brasserie more than a hundred years old, along with smoked Baltic herring in rémoulade sauce with warm potato salad, skate in brown butter sauce, parsleyed calf's liver fried in butter, homemade chocolate mousse and ice creams and sorbets from nearby Berthillon. You only pay for the part of the bottle of wine you drink as you while away the time delightfully, watching the Seine flow by.

● **Coconnas**   COM
2 bis, pl des Vosges
Métro: Bastille, St-Paul
Tel. 01 42 78 58 16. Fax 01 42 78 16 28
info@marcannibaldecoconnas.com
www.latourdargent.com
Closed Monday. Open until 10:15 PM.
Prix fixe: 25€ (lunch), 32€,
15€ (children). A la carte: 45–65€.
Air cond. Terrace.

There have been changes in this Terrail bistro under the place des Vosges arcades. A young team has arrived, bringing a more vital approach and a return to tradition. At a polished wooden table, we savor deliciously prepared dishes that have a strong sense of identity. Frédéric Salaün, formerly at La Tour d'Argent, orchestrates the service enthusiastically in the dining room, while Aymeric Kräml, a young Breton veteran of Ducasse, Savoy and Crillon, presides over the kitchen with flair. The results? Tasteful, roguish, rustic dishes. The porcini mushroom tart, grilled calf's head with beets and coffee tiramisu are marvels included in the set menu at 32€. A la carte, the poule au pot (stewed stuffed chicken with vegetables and cream sauce) served in two stages is very much an institution, while sole meunière fried in foamy bacon butter, roasted cod brandade, a juicy slow-roasted veal chop with salsify or brioche pain perdu, served with quince compote and fromage blanc sorbet, are enchanting. To accompany all this, the Guigal Côtes du Rhône and Héritage de Chasse-Spleen roll over the tongue like velvet.

● Le Coude Fou   SIM

12, rue du Bourg-Tibourg
Métro: Hôtel-de-Ville, St-Paul
Tel. 01 42 77 15 16. Fax 01 48 04 08 98
www.lecoudefou.com
Open daily until midnight.
Prix fixe: 16,50€ (lunch, wine included),
19,50€ (lunch, wine included), 25€
(weekday dinner). A la carte: 35€.
Air cond.

This wine bar, one of the first in the capital, is as beguiling as ever for lovers of fine vintages and minor revelations, but they would be wrong to stop there: The food also warrants attention. The lemon-marinated sea bream tartare, fried sea bass fingers, sliced sesame duck breast and Catalan-style crème brûlée are a delight.

● Dame Tartine   ● SIM

2, rue Brisemiche
Métro: Hôtel-de-Ville
Tel.-Fax 01 42 77 32 22
contact@app-dt.com
Daily 9 AM–11:30 PM. Cont. service.
Prix fixe: 9,90€ (weekday lunch),
9,90€ (children). A la carte: 25€.
Terrace.

For a quick snack after an exhibition at the Pompidou Center, this is the place to go, opposite the Niki de Saint-Phalle fountain. They serve open sandwiches but also more substantial dishes: duo of taramasalata and eggplant caviar, salmon in coconut sauce, lamb gâteau with slow-roasted vegetables, crêpe with vanilla cream filling and caramel sauce. Pleasant, light and cheaper than its (many) neighbors.

● Le Dôme Bastille   COM

2, rue de la Bastille
Métro: Bastille
Tel. 01 48 04 88 44. Fax 01 48 04 00 59
Closed 3 weeks in August.
Open until 11 PM approximately (in
accordance with the Opéra).
A la carte: 40–55€.
Air cond.

The blackboard displayed in front of the restaurant offers the freshest shellfish and fish, with varieties depending on the catch. So cozy, hushed, decorated in yellow and burgundy, all they need is a good chef. Frédéric Steffany's lively, precisely cooked dishes—grilled squid, jumbo shrimp and parmesan salad, roasted John Dory, Limousin rib-eye steak, warm apple tart, made to order—easily secure our approval. Pascal Debasseux's service achieves the same high standards in Slavik's surroundings.

● Le Dôme du Marais   🍴 COM

53 bis, rue des Francs-Bourgeois
Métro: Rambuteau, Hôtel-de-Ville, St-Paul
Tel. 01 42 74 54 17. Fax 01 42 77 78 17
domedumarais@hotmail.com
Closed Sunday, Monday, first week in
January, mid-August–beginning of
September. Open until 11 PM.
Prix fixe: 17€ (lunch), 23€ (lunch)
A la carte: 32€, 45€.
Terrace.

We are awed by the sense of history here under the dome of this former Mont de Piété auction gallery, now run by Brittany's Pierre Lecoutre (formerly at L'Atlantide in Nantes), assisted by Denis Groison in the kitchen. The appealing covered terrace and blaze of white and gold in the round hall have plenty of style. The realistically priced set menus offer langoustine spring rolls, John Dory with foamy shellfish and coriander oil sauce, roasted loin of Bigorre black pig with Sicilian lemon and warm Chartreuse soufflé.

● Don Juan II   COM

In front of 10 bis du quai Henri-IV
Métro: Quai-de-la-Rapée, Sully-Morland
Tel. 01 44 54 14 70. Fax 01 44 54 14 75
contacts@yachtsdeparis.fr
www.yachtsdeparis.fr
Open daily.
Prix fixe: 165€ (dinner).
Air cond. Terrace. Private dining room.

The excellent chef Jean-Pierre Vigato, manager Marc Bungener and cupbearer Jean-Luc Paris, welcome us on board this white wood yacht with its brass and mahogany decor, air conditioning, terrace and private dining room. Following renovation, the new drapes, lampshades and floral decorations provide an added charm. The carrot flan with foamy lobster sauce, spiced roasted sea bass and cannelloni filled with Provençal vegetables, duck breast with parsleyed porcini mushrooms, assorted cheeses and chocolate desserts make up tempting set menus

● **Le Dos de la Baleine**   SIM

40, rue des Blancs-Manteaux
Métro: Rambuteau, Hôtel-de-Ville
Tel. 01 42 72 38 98. Fax 01 43 45 43 34
Closed Saturday lunch, Sunday, Monday, 3 weeks in August. Open until 11 PM.
Prix fixe: 14,60€ (lunch), 29€ (dinner), 34€ (dinner).
Air cond.

There is no one chef in this Marais institution: Jean-David Temin has decided that the whole team should lend a hand. In a decor of old stone and bright red shades, we delight in the solid domestic dishes, including rabbit and foie gras terrine with prunes, poached cod filet with oyster mushroom sauce, beef shoulder braised in red wine served with freshly mashed potatoes and prune tart made to order. To our further delight, the prices have been scaled down.

● **L'Escale**   ●SIM

1, rue des Deux-Ponts
Métro: Pont-Marie, Cardinal-Lemoine
Tel.-Fax 01 43 54 94 23
isabelle.pierre@noos.fr
Closed Sunday, 3 weeks in August.
A la carte: 25€.

This amiable café-bistro has a number of arguments in its favor: Patricia Deltel's warm welcome, the supremely fresh seasonal produce, the pleasant wines by the glass and the gentle prices. Between noon and two in a rustic bistro setting, we make short work of the avocado in cocktail sauce, perch filet in beurre blanc, sausage-stuffed veal steak with assorted vegetables and pear tart.

● **Le Felteu**   ●SIM

15, rue Pecquay
Métro: Rambuteau, Hôtel-de-Ville
Tel. 01 42 72 14 51
le-felteu.jerry@wanadoo.fr
Closed Saturday lunch, Sunday,
Bank Holidays, August. Open until 10:30 PM.
A la carte: 30€.

This old, Fifties' bistro serves up well-mannered classics, such as savory tart *du jour*, sea bass grilled with fennel, sautéed veal kidneys, blood pudding with apples and potatoes and crème brûlée.

● **Le Fin Gourmet**   ⓃSIM

42, rue Saint-Louis-en-l'Ile
Métro: Pont-Marie
Tel. 01 43 26 79 27. Fax 01 43 26 96 08
magniezd@hotmail.com
www.lefingourmet.fr
Closed Monday, Tuesday lunch, first 10 days of January. Open until 10:30 PM.
Prix fixe: 25€ (lunch, wine included), 27€ (dinner, wine included), 35€ (dinner, wine included). A la carte: 50–55€.
Air cond. Private dining room.

Although the former Gourmet de l'Isle has been subtly renamed and the jovial Jean-Michel Mestivier has passed on the torch, the same spirit lives on under its 17th-century vaults in the form of traditional gourmet feasts concocted by Yohann Gerbout to reflect the changing seasons. In a neo-contemporary setting in warm hues, vanilla-marinated Scottish salmon with crisp fennel, herb-crusted John Dory with stewed leeks, roasted lamb rack with tangy jus and black truffle potato purée and homemade tarte Tatin warm the hearts of both tourists and locals.

● Les Fous d'en Face　　SIM

3, rue du Bourg-Tibourg
Métro: Hôtel-de-Ville, St-Paul
Tel. 01 48 87 03 75. Fax 01 42 78 38 03
Closed Sunday evening, Christmas,
New Year's, first 2 weeks in August.
Open until 11:30 PM.
Prix fixe: 14,90€ (lunch, except Sunday),
18,90€ (lunch, except Sunday), 24,90€
(dinner, wine included). A la carte: 40–50€.
Air cond. Terrace.

Despite the name, which means "the crazy people opposite," this City Hall refectory run by Philippe Llorca turns out to be not so crazy after all, with its air conditioning, two terraces, patinated tables, rustic wine bar charm (with bottles priced from 19€ to 1,600€—no, don't leave) and Pascal Guyader's appealing home dishes. Pan-seared duck foie gras with balsamic vinegar, seared tuna with olive oil and lemon, beef tenderloin with caramelized shallots, vanilla vacherin with red fruit sauce slip down effortlessly, accompanied by an organic wine, an astute winegrower's vintage . . . or why not a Château Pétrus, if City Hall is picking up the tab?

● Georges　　COM

Centre G.-Pompidou, espl Beaubourg
Métro: Châtelet, Rambuteau, Hôtel-de-Ville
Tel. 01 44 78 47 99. Fax 01 44 78 48 93
georges-costes@wanadoo.fr
Closed Tuesday.
11 AM–2 AM. Cont. service.
A la carte: 70€.
Air cond. Terrace. Private dining room.
Valet parking.

From the tables by the bay window, the four modern, colored dining areas or the vast terrace, why not take the city in your arms? Perched at the summit, master of all you survey, savoring some engaging, half-traditional, half-fusional concoction whipped up by Jean-Philippe Lebœuf with a light Oriental touch to boot? Conscientiously served by Messrs. Mharouk or Peret, or some charming vestal, here are crab-meat and mushroom millefeuille, tigre qui pleure ("crying tiger" beef salad), tom ka gai (chicken stewed in coconut milk) or a

club sandwich. Huge and modern with its refined decor in shades of gray, the Costes brothers' dining room on the top floor of the Pompidou Center offers a stunning, panoramic view of Paris.

● Au Grain de Sel　　N SIM

13, rue Jean-Beausire
Métro: Bastille
Tel.-Fax 01 44 59 82 82
info@augraindesel.com
www.augraindesel.com
Closed Sunday, Monday, 1 week for Easter,
1 week in August. Open until 10:30 PM.
Prix fixe: 16€ (lunch), 26€ (lunch), 35€.
A la carte: 52–76€.
Air cond. Terrace.

A season and a half ago, Nathalie Ben Samoun, former top maître d' of Le Train Bleu, opened this bright establishment with its comfortable furniture and art exhibited on light walls. She has entrusted the pots and pans to young chef Laurent Dupas, who tinkers with French tradition, adapting it to his own tastes. The snow pea, pink lentil and roasted-artichoke salad with a ginger truffle vinaigrette begins the dance, followed by ginger-bread-crusted sea bass with caramelized tomato and stewed fennel and veal tenderloin, sweetbreads and kidneys served with stewed spring vegetables. The set menu at 35€ provides a very satisfactory overview. There are also a market-based set menu and suggestions featured on the blackboard.

● Grizzli Café　　🏠 SIM

7, rue Saint-Martin
Métro: Châtelet
Tel. 01 48 87 77 56. Fax 01 48 87 34 12
grizzlicafe@wanadoo.fr
Daily 9 AM–11 PM. Cont. service.
A la carte: 40€.
Air cond. Terrace.

With all his usual taste, Didier Kerveno has brought an agreeable, modern, unsnobbish touch—with wooden chairs, brown banquettes and dumbwaiters—to this friendly, early-20th-century bistro, where the lime hues of the first floor blend with the browns and beiges of the attractively re-decorated second, reached by a spiral stair-case. Eric Law Kwang has adopted a tasteful, lively approach in his spiced crab and avo-cado appetizer, prawn risotto with red curry sauce, duck breast with five spices and caramelized banana in crisp phyllo pastry. A combination of regional produce and fusion, it slips down effortlessly.

● **L'Impasse** ● SIM

4, impasse Guémenée
Métro: Bastille
Tel. 01 42 72 08 45. Fax 01 42 77 43 79
www.limpasse.com
Closed Saturday lunch, Sunday,
Monday lunch, 1 week in winter, August.
Open until 11 PM.
Prix fixe: 10€ (lunch), 25€, 28€.
Terrace.

In her cul-de-sac near place des Vosges, Françoise Manguy-Sueur serves up the country on a platter. Perusing the sensible set menus in her peaceful restaurant graced with exposed beams and appealing 1930s' lighting, we succumb to the allure of the well-crafted domestic dishes. The duck foie gras terrine, roasted scallops in raw tomato and olive oil sauce, rack of lamb and tarte Tatin are a pure joy.

● **Chez Julien** 🏠 COM

1, rue du Pont-Louis-Philippe
Métro: Pont-Marie, St-Paul, Hôtel-de-Ville
Tel. 01 42 78 31 64. Fax 01 42 74 39 30
Closed Saturday lunch, Sunday,
Monday lunch, Christmas, 3 weeks in August.
Open until 11 PM.
Prix fixe: 25€ (lunch), 29€.
A la carte: 55€.
Terrace.

Outside and in, from the enchanting 1900s' bakery facade to the discreet, ro-mantic interior here on the edge of the Marais quarter, on the river bank opposite the Ile Saint-Louis, this idyllic setting is perfect for lovers who have not yet plucked up the courage to confess their feelings. The candlelit meal is served on a prettily dressed table in surroundings of antique woodwork and warm hues: foie gras ter-rine with champagne, sautéed scallops with basil, five-spiced beef tenderloin and strawberries Romanoff accompanied by carafes of Bordeaux or Burgundy. Those who have still not declared their passion after that must be very hung up indeed!

● **Mon Vieil Ami** ○ SIM

69, rue Saint-Louis-en-l'Ile
Métro: Pont-Marie
Tel. 01 40 46 01 35. Fax 01 40 46 01 36
mon.vieil.ami@wanadoo.fr
www.mon-vieil-ami.com
Closed Monday, Tuesday, first 2 weeks
of January, first 2 weeks of August.
Open until 11 PM.
Prix fixe: 39€.

Three dynamic, vigilant musketeers run this fine restaurant with its sober black and white decor and soothing materials and tones and a touch of Alsace in the bargain. Here, Antoine Westermann founded his first Parisian annex before Drouant, Adrien Boulouque welcomes guests and waits table in the dining room and Frédéric Cro-chet composes his opuses at the stove. What can you expect? Warm vegetable stew with raisins and almonds, seasonal mushrooms on toast—how carefully the vegetables are prepared!— Provençal stew of artichokes and fennel bulbs, roasted pollack, duck breast—cooked with the ut-most precision!— rhubarb compote, pis-tachio cake and red fruit sorbet all accompanied by engaging wines, particu-larly from Alsace. The place is lively, subtle, meticulous, generous, reliable and wel-coming, even on Sunday. "Mon Vieil Ami" is just the kind of old friend you want to have around.

● **L'Orangerie** COM

28, rue Saint-Louis-en-l'Ile
Métro: Pont-Marie
Tel. 01 46 33 93 98
Closed Sunday, Monday. Open until 11 PM.
Prix fixe: 55€, 95€. A la carte: 90–100€.
Air cond. Valet parking.

This discreet establishment in the middle of the Ile Saint-Louis long belonged to French actor Jean-Claude Brialy but has now changed hands. As we write, Michel del Burgo, formerly of Taillevent, Negresco and La Bastide de Gordes, used to a certain mobility, is about to take over and add his stamp to the place. So we had best put our evaluation on hold and simply say that great things may come of this elegant 17th-century establishment devoted so far to chic little suppers.

● Les Parisiennes   ⊜ SIM

10, rue Brisemiche
Métro: Rambuteau
Tel. 01 42 78 44 11
Daily 11 AM–11PM. Cont. service.
Prix fixe: 14€. A la carte: 25€.
Terrace.

The main attraction of Frédéric Robichon's establishment is the meat. Everything is made in-house under the watchful eye of the discreet Didier Quellier. Sitting on the terrace opposite the fountain, with its sculptures by Niki de Saint-Phalle and Jean Tinguely, we fully appreciate the tomato croustillant, rump steak with sautéed potatoes and Auvergne blue cheese and the homemade heart-shaped chocolate pudding.

● Le Petit Bofinger   🛈 SIM

6, rue de la Bastille
Métro: Bastille
Tel. 01 42 72 05 23. Fax 01 42 72 04 94
Open daily until midnight.
Prix fixe: 19,90€, 28,50€.
A la carte: 32–35€.
Air cond. Terrace.

There is the big Bofinger and then there is this little one opposite, run by Jean-Luc Delouche. It boasts a very personal retro charm, bistro decor, Parisian fresco, moderate prices, conscientious service and restrained, feminine dishes. We are grateful to Stéphanie Leblanc not only for the traditional starters (oysters and tuna rillettes), but also for the careful preparation of seafood sauerkraut (with salmon, cod, smoked haddock, mussels and scallops), pan-fried calf's liver and warm soft chocolate cake.

● Le Rouge-Gorge   ⊜ SIM

8, rue Saint-Paul
Métro: Sully-Morland, St-Paul
Tel. 01 48 04 75 89. Fax 01 45 43 38 31
Closed Sunday, first 2 weeks in August.
Open until 11 PM.
A la carte: 35€.

Aside from his Salon des Vins d'Auteurs (Creators' Wine Fair) in June, François Briclot champions his noble vintages and minor revelations throughout the year, with a selection revised every two weeks. This astute oenologist also has a very hearty appetite. The rabbit terrine with mango chutney, red mullet with julienned vegetables, duck sausage served with stewed quince and fiadone (Corsican cheesecake) impress us favorably, but the service is not always up to the same standard. This year, a friend was received there in a manner that would be better suited to a local café-tabac.

● Le Temps des Cerises   ⊜ SIM

31, rue de la Cerisaie
Métro: Sully-Morland, Bastille
Tel.-Fax 01 42 72 08 63
mboukobza@hotmail.com
Closed dinner, Saturday, Sunday evening,
1 week in February, August.
Prix fixe: 13,50€ (lunch). A la carte: 25€.

This vintage bistro has lost none of its soul. Michèle and Yves Boukobza have made sure of that. The facade decorated with crimson red mosaics, the old photos and the caricatures of guests immediately work their charm. Then the cuisine takes over with duck rillettes, sea bass in a raw tomato and olive oil sauce, Aveyron lamb tripe sausage stew and orange tart. N.B.: There is traditional music on Sunday afternoons, and concerts are held on the first and third Fridays of the month.

● La Tête Ailleurs   `SIM`

20, rue Beautreillis
Métro: Sully-Morland, St-Paul
Tel. 01 42 72 47 80. Fax 01 42 74 66 85
www.lateteailleurs-restaurant-paris.com
Closed Saturday lunch, Sunday, Christmas,
2 weeks in August. Open until 10:30 PM
(weekends 11:30 PM).
Prix fixe: 14,50€ (lunch).
A la carte: 35–40€.
Air cond.

You feel you are vacationing on the Mediter-ranean coast in this sober establishment run by Hugues Courage, with its orange-toned walls, colored cushions and large, scintillating chandeliers. It provides a guaranteed change of atmosphere with its Provençal and Italian flavors: pan-fried squid a la Provençal, fricassée of jumbo shrimp, squid and penne, rump steak and truffle-flavored potatoes and panna cotta, all delightfully fresh.

● Le Trumilou   `SIM`

84, quai de l'Hôtel-de-Ville
Métro: Hôtel-de-Ville
Tel. 01 42 77 63 98. Fax 01 48 04 91 89
Closed one week Christmas–New Year's,
2 weeks the beginning of August.
Open until 11 PM.
Prix fixe: 15,50€ (lunch), 18,50€ (lunch).
A la carte: 35€.
Air cond. Terrace. Private dining room.

Unpretentious but tasteful with its bour-geois decor, the Charvin's domestic estab-lishment is just the place for a pleasant family outing. Guests come to enjoy the well-prepared home-style dishes: instar du pounti (a warm spinach, prune and bacon savory pudding), warm goat cheese salad, sautéed scallops with garlic and parsley, braised veal sweetbreads and crème brûlée.

● Le Vieux Bistro   `SIM`

14, rue du Cloître-Notre-Dame
Métro: Cité, St-Michel
Tel. 01 43 54 18 95. Fax 01 44 07 35 63
levieuxbistro@free.fr
Closed Christmas. Open until 10:30 PM.
Prix fixe: 26€ (weekday lunch).
A la carte: 50€.
Air cond. Terrace.

Former Marée proprietor Eric Trompier has sold Le Vieux Bistro to Vincent Sitz, who runs Le Ragueneau in the first arrondissement and has preserved the soul of this Paris café. Equipped with the traditional zinc bar, it opens even just for drinks. In the kitchen, Michel Benaziz, formerly at Les Papilles in the fifth, has added his touch of innovation to the house style but avoided any unruliness or excessive audacity. The genuine head cheese, soft and creamy pike quenelles, coriander veal kidney served with bulgur and raisins and a tarte Tatin "94" are washed down with cheerful bottles of Sancerre or Beaujolais. Literary figures Robert Sabatier and Bernard Frank, Sun-day night regulars, still love the place.

● Vins des Pyrénées   `♠ SIM`

25, rue Beautreillis
Métro: Sully-Morland, Bastille, St-Paul
Tel. 01 42 72 64 94. Fax 01 42 71 19 62
Closed Saturday lunch, 2 weeks in August.
Open until 11:30 PM.
Prix fixe: 12,50€ (lunch, wine).
A la carte: 38€.

Old postcards, wooden wall seats and grandmotherly drapes feature in this for-mer wine cellar, whose dishes now offer excellent value for the price. The intriguing platter of starters, the herbed salmon roll with stewed fennel, roasted beef prime rib and roasted pineapple brochette are all gratifying, as is the wine list.

INTERNATIONAL RESTAURANTS

● Napoli Food 🏠SIM

6, rue Castex
Métro: Bastille
Tel. 01 44 54 06 61. Fax 01 44 54 00 33
delizieitaliane@wanadoo.fr
Closed Sunday, Monday lunch,
1 week between Christmas and New Year's,
Easter, 3 weeks in August.
Open until 10:30 PM (weekends 11 PM).
Prix fixe: 15€ (lunch). A la carte: 35€.
Air cond.

The success of Fabio Grossi's authentic trattoria continues virtually unabated. The stylish dishes prepared by Neapolitan Antonio Pacchiano change to reflect market produce. Cheerful colors have given the dining room a much younger feel. Béatrice enthusiastically serves mixed homemade vegetable antipasti with buffalo mozzarella, sea bass or lobster simmered with Vesuvian tomatoes, exquisite penne all'amatriciana for two served in a skillet and ricotta cake with pears or figs, tasteful and tasty to the last. With this fare, we drink a Campania Aglianico or a Nero d'Avola, wines of the South, fiery as volcanoes.

▼ SHOPS

KITCHENWARE & TABLETOP

▼ Cuisinophilie 🏠

28, rue du Bourg-Tibourg
Métro: Hôtel-de-Ville
Tel. 01 40 29 07 32. Fax 01 40 29 99 21
2–7 PM.
Closed Saturday, Sunday, Monday, August.
This small, unobtrusive loft presents rigorously chosen objects. Colanders, metal coffee pots, scales, jelly jars, aluminum milk jugs and other antique utensils delight cooking enthusiasts.

▼ Sentou

18 and 24, rue du Pont-Louis-Philippe /
29, rue François-Miron
Métro: St-Paul
Tel. 01 42 77 44 79 / 01 42 71 00 01 /
01 42 78 50 60. Fax 01 48 87 67 14
10 AM–7 PM. Closed Sunday, Monday,
2 weeks in August.
This gallery offers a vast selection of poetic and fun items for little and "not so little" children: volcano-shaped cake molds, jointed candlesticks, "hungry" plates, "thirsty" glasses and other zany designs from Tsé Tsé, tablecloths by Robert le Héros and black glass bowls by Sugahara.

BREAD & BAKED GOODS

▼ Malineau

18, rue Vieille-du-Temple
Métro: Hôtel-de-Ville
Tel. 01 42 76 94 54
7:30 AM–9 PM. Closed Tuesday.
Hervé Malineau produces a quality traditional baguette as well as individual rye, raisin and walnut loaves, a Saint-Paul specialty loaf, sourdough bread, and bacon focaccia, baked with care.

▼ Philippe Martin

40, rue Saint-Louis-en-l'Ile
Métro: Pont-Marie
Tel. 01 43 54 69 48. Fax 01 43 25 50 78
7 AM–1:30 PM, 3:30–8 PM. Closed Sunday,
Monday, 1 week in winter, August.
Philippe Martin has taken over his father's historic bakery. A disciple of Poujauran, he produces an organic wheat baguette, olive focaccia, Correzian rye, delicious flaky brioches and crispy croissants made with Charente butter.

▼ Du Pain et des Idées 🔃

24, rue St-Martin
Métro: Châtelet, Hôtel-de-Ville
Tel. 01 48 87 46 17
7 AM–8 PM. Closed Saturday, Sunday.
This new store in the traditional style has a certain charm. Already established in the tenth arrondissement, Christophe Vasseur presents his crispy baguette, country-style round loaf, large crisscrossed flat loaf, mini country breads and quality pastries.

WINE

▼ Caves du Marais

62-64, rue François-Miron
Métro: St-Paul
Tel.-Fax 01 42 78 54 64
10:30 AM–1 PM. 4–8 PM.
Closed Sunday, Monday, August.

The dynamic Jean-Jacques Bailly recommends and supplies the best that French vineyards have to offer. Guigal Côte Rôtie, Henri Gouges Nuits Saint Georges, a wonderful Côtes du Roussillon and organic Beaujolais are some of the delights in store.

▼ Cavestève

10, rue de la Cerisaie
Métro: Bastille, Sully-Morland
Tel.-Fax 01 42 72 33 05
www.cavesteve.com
10 AM–8PM (Monday 4–8 PM).
Closed Sunday, 3 weeks in August.

Under the direction of Antoine Borgey and the Nabuchodonosor company, the Club Amical du Vin founded by J.-C. Estève has grown into a refined, rational designer store, finding room for both great classics and new discoveries from all wine-growing regions, French and foreign. Tastings are linked to new deliveries, and meetings are organized with some of the top names of the moment. In short, a cellar to watch.

▼ Nicolas

64, rue Saint-Louis-en-l'Ile
Métro: Pont-Marie
Tel.-Fax 01 43 54 40 70
Open daily 10 AM–8:30 PM
(Sunday 10 AM–6 PM,
Monday 4:30–8:30 PM).

This charming Nicolas store with its attractive facade is well worth a visit because of its astute selections: old Médocs, great vintages of every kind and first-rate champagnes and single malt whiskeys. Excellent gift boxes.

GROCERIES

▼ Izraël

30, rue François-Miron
Métro: St-Paul, Hôtel-de-Ville
Tel. 01 42 72 66 23. Fax 01 42 72 86 32
9:30 AM–1 PM, 2:30–7 PM
(Saturday 9 AM–7 PM).
Closed Sunday, Monday, August.

This charming grocery store stocks the rarest of products: spices, dried fruit and nuts, Tarbais beans for cassoulet, green Lucques olives, candied ginger chunks and dried rosebuds. Preserved monkfish liver, Venezuelan rum, and artisan-produced almond syrup are house favorites.

▼ A l'Olivier

23, rue de Rivoli
Métro: St-Paul, Hôtel-de-Ville
Tel.-Fax 01 48 04 86 59
paris@olivier-on-line.com
www.olivier-on-line.com
9:30 AM–7 PM (Monday 2–7 PM). Closed
Sunday, Monday morning, 1 week in August.

This temple of top-quality oil specializes in Mediterranean products. A nice range of balsamic vinegars and olive, argan or rapeseed oils.

▼ Sources Vives de Jérusalem

10, rue des Barres
Métro: Pont-Marie, St-Paul
Tel. 01 48 04 39 05
www.jerusalem.cef.sr
10 AM–Noon, 2:30–4:30 PM.
Closed Sunday afternoon, Monday, August.

From thirty or so French abbeys, crunchy biscuits, artisanal jams and preserves, organic fruit syrups, exquisite honeys and jellied fruit served by the monks of the Communion of Jerusalem.

CHEESE

▼ Ferme Saint-Aubin

76, rue Saint-Louis-en-l'Ile
Métro: Pont-Marie
Tel. 01 43 54 74 54. Fax 01 47 97 03 99
8 AM–7:30 PM. Closed Monday

Impeccable quality from Christian Le Lann, butcher in the nineteenth arrondissement but cheesemonger on the Ile Saint Louis, who lightly matures cheeses in his cellar. Walnut brie, cantal, camembert cured with a fortified apple cider, tomme de Ranrupt, pélardon, and brebis de Carayac are all highly commendable.

▼ Fromages . . . ou desserts ✪

13, rue de Rambuteau
Tel. 01 42 72 73 56
10 AM–1 PM, 4–8
PM (Saturday 9 AM–1 PM, 4–8 PM).
Closed Sunday afternoon, Monday,
3 weeks in August.

There are more cheeses than desserts here, with splendid mountain cheeses, fine farm-produced goat cheeses, Basque brebis and jams or jellied fruit to accompany them.

▼ Trotté

97, rue Saint-Antoine
Métro: St-Paul, Bastille
Tel. 01 48 87 55 37
8 AM–1 PM, 4–7:45 PM. Closed Sunday afternoon, Monday, 3 weeks in August.

Sold with a smile in this tiny store, Jean-Philippe's and Pascal Trotté's cheeses are refined to perfection in the fine stone cellar. Roqueforts, stiltons, cheddars, delicious mimolette, fruity comtés, as well as an endless variety of farmhouse goat cheeses, make a favorable impression.

ICE CREAM

▼ Berthillon

31, rue Saint-Louis-en-l'Ile
Métro: Pont-Marie
Tel. 01 43 54 31 61
www.berthillon.fr
10 AM–8 PM. Closed Monday, Tuesday, vacations (except Christmas),
mid-July–beginning of September

The store has been enlarged and the parlor moved next door, but they still have the nerve to close for the summer! Of course, the Chauvins care nothing for fashion. Their ice creams and sorbets (caramel, pear, wild strawberry, mirabelle plum, mandarin orange, gianduja, praliné, peach and marron glacé) are still models of the genre.

PASTRIES

▼ Calixte

64, rue Saint-Louis-en-l'Ile
Métro: Pont-Marie
Tel. 01 43 26 42 28
8 AM–2 PM, 4–8 PM.
Closed Tuesday, August.

Bernard-Calixte Gonon keeps the tradition of light confections alive. We like his puddings, irresistible tarts, caramelized mille-feuille and famous truffle chocolate cake. The Bing cherry soufflé, almond meringue cake, and orange and almond pound cake are delicacies that will instantly melt your resolve.

▼ Dalloyau

5, bd Beaumarchais
Métro: Bastille
Tel. 01 48 87 89 88. Fax 01 48 87 73 70
www.dalloyau.fr
Open daily 9 AM–9 PM.

A gourmet establishment since 1802, this great caterer guarantees excellence of quality. You can come here to shop or enjoy macarons, chocolate Opéra cakes, mille-feuilles and fruit tarts, every one a delicacy, in the room upstairs.

REGIONAL PRODUCTS

▼ A la Ville de Rodez

22, rue Vieille-du-Temple
Métro: Hôtel-de-Ville, St-Paul
Tel. 01 48 87 79 36
www.aveyron.com
8:30 AM–1 PM, 3–7:30 PM.
Closed Sunday (except holidays),
Monday, Bank Holidays, August.

This charming store offers fine products from the Aveyron and surrounding region. Its Laguiole knives, Salers aperitif, Marcillac wine, prune-filled pastries, lamb tripe sausage stew, foie gras and goose cracklings are exquisite products for special occasions.

TEA

▼ Mariage Frères
30, rue du Bourg-Tibourg
Métro: Hôtel-de-Ville
Tel. 01 42 72 28 11. Fax 01 42 74 51 68
www.mariagefreres.com
Open daily 10:30 AM–7:30 PM.

Established in 1854, this tea store offers 500 varieties, each with its own refined flavor. There is a choice of shortbreads, jellies, tea cream-filled chocolates, as well as cast-iron, silverware, or ceramic teapots. Try the exclusive, quality Thé des Maharajas. (Also see Rendezvous.)

◆ **RENDEZVOUS**

BARS

◆ La Bodeguita del Medio
10, rue des Lombards
Métro: Châtelet
Tel. 01 44 59 66 90. Fax 01 44 59 66 91
Open daily noon–2 AM.

Dedicated to the famous Bodeguita in Havana, where Hemingway drank his mojitos, this Cuban bar has a salsa ambience. Add a wide range of colorful dishes and Havana Club rums, not to mention a selection of reasonable cocktails (Daiquiri or Havana Sunrise), plus a large choice of cigars, and you will realize the appeal of the place.

WINE BARS

◆ La Chaise au Plafond
10, rue du Trésor
Métro: St-Paul, Hôtel-de-Ville
Tel. 01 42 76 03 22. Fax 01 42 72 48 34
www.cafein.com
Open daily 9 AM–1:30 AM.
Air cond. Terrace.

Xavier Denamur, who runs this agreeable, modern café with gusto, serves pleasant aperitifs, cocktails and simple dishes—savory tarts and lamb stew for a mainly—but not exclusively—male clientele.

◆ Au Gamin de Paris
51, rue Vieille-du-Temple
Métro: Hôtel-de-Ville
Tel. 01 42 78 97 24
Open daily 8 AM–2 AM.
Air cond.

At the foot of an old building in the Marais, Claude Viars offers quality domestic dishes such as beef tenderloin in honey sauce or goat cheese with figs and assorted drinks. You can come at any time to quench your thirst and discuss the issues of the moment.

◆ Ma Bourgogne
19, pl des Vosges
Métro: St-Paul, Bastille
Tel. 01 42 78 44 64
Open daily 8 AM–1:30 AM.
Terrace.

Under the place des Vosges arcades, this bistro plays to packed houses. Daily specials and luscious open sandwiches and salads are washed down with every kind of Beaujolais.

◆ La Tartine
24, rue de Rivoli
Métro: St-Paul, Hôtel-de-Ville
Tel. 01 42 72 76 85
Open daily 8 AM–2 AM
(Sunday, Monday 10 AM–11 PM).
Terrace.

A genuine zinc bar, patinated walls and molded ceilings set the tone in this renovated, old-style bistro. You can enjoy Loire wines, Chinon or Bourgueil as a worthy accompaniment to honest Poilâne bread open sandwiches and assorted charcuterie or cheese plates.

CAFES

◆ Le Bistrot des Vosges
31, bd Beaumarchais
Métro: Chemin-Vert, Bastille
Tel. 01 42 72 94 85
Open daily 7:30 AM–11 PM.

In this traditional bistro you can enjoy a drink at the bar, laze on the terrace or succumb to the charms of authentic Auvergnat dishes—stuffed cabbage, spinach, prune and bacon pudding, lamb sausage stew—accompanied by engaging wines served by the glass.

◆ Brasserie Louis-Philippe 🛏

66, quai de l'Hôtel-de-Ville
Métro: Pont-Marie, Hôtel-de-Ville
Tel. 01 42 72 29 42
Open daily 10:30 AM–11 PM.
Terrace.

This old café on the banks of the Seine with its zinc counter and acid-etched glass has a timeless charm. Coffee and snacks are served at the tables inside and, in the summer, on the shady terrace.

◆ Café Beaubourg 🛏

100, rue Saint-Martin
Métro: Rambuteau, Les Halles
Tel. 01 48 87 63 96. Fax 01 48 87 81 25
Open daily 8 AM–1 AM (Thursday, Friday, Saturday 2 AM).
Terrace.

This stylish café opposite the Pompidou Center is considered a monument of the era, with its gray concrete decor and shelves of books. On the first floor and mezzanine, strong coffee, fresh plates or a popular brunch are served with gusto.

◆ Café Hugo

22, pl des Vosges
Métro: St-Paul, Bastille, Chemin-Vert
Tel. 01 42 72 64 04
Open daily 7 AM–2 AM.
Terrace.

Under the place des Vosges arcades, the terrace extends from a tastefully designed interior. Market-based cuisine and fashionable drinks. Jazz concerts on Thursday nights.

◆ Café Martini

11, rue du Pas-de-la-Mule
Métro: Chemin-Vert, Bastille, St-Paul
Tel. 01 42 77 05 04
Open 11 AM–2 AM.
Closed 3 weeks in August.
Air cond.

There is an international atmosphere in this chic, Italian-style café. Fresh sandwiches and strong coffee just off place des Vosges.

◆ Les Deux Palais 🛏

3, bd du Palais
Métro: Cité, Châtelet, St-Michel
Tel. 01 43 54 20 86. Fax 01 43 25 93 95
Open daily 6:30 AM–9:30 PM.
Terrace.

Opposite the Palais de Justice, this huge brasserie with its moldings, frescos, mirrors and terrace never empties. People come for a bite (smoked salmon, homemade duck confit) and a chat at the bar or tables.

◆ Le Flore en l'Ile

42, quai d'Orléan
Métro: Pont-Marie, Sully-Morland, Cité
Tel. 01 43 29 88 27. Fax 01 43 29 73 54
Open daily 8 AM–2 AM.
Terrace.

Standing like a sentinel on the Ile Saint Louis, this café is favored by patrons who drop in at any time to enjoy fresh salads, exquisite cakes and pastries, selected teas and strong coffee.

◆ Le Petit Fer à Cheval 🛏

30, rue Vieille-du-Temple
Métro: Hôtel-de-Ville, St-Paul
Tel. 01 42 72 47 47
www.cafeine.com
Open daily 9 AM–2 AM.
Terrace.

This circa 1900 bistro with its horseshoe-shaped bar is largely frequented by the local gay community. It offers reasonable libations, as well as snacks like well-garnished Poilâne bread open sandwiches.

◆ Le Petit Marcel ℕ

65, rue Rambuteau
Métro: Rambuteau
Tel. 01 48 87 10 20
Open daily 8 AM–1 AM.

This true Parisian bistro with ceramics, stucco and counter is worth a visit for its atmosphere and pleasant snacks at any hour. Likable wines by the glass and steak at meal times, served with hand-cut French fries.

TEA SALONS

◆ Les Fous de l'Ile

33, rue des Deux-Ponts
Métro: Pont-Marie
Tel.-Fax 01 43 25 76 67
Noon–11 PM. Closed Sunday, Monday,
Tuesday evening, end of June–beginning of
July, end of December–beginning of January.

This very cheerful tearoom serves family-style cooking: Provençal-style veal stew, a choice of pastries such as Belphégor chocolate cake or cheesecake, Mariage Frères teas and ice cream by Berthillon.

◆ Le Loir dans la Théière

3, rue des Rosiers
Métro: St-Paul
Tel. 01 42 72 90 61
Open daily 11:30 AM–7 PM
(Saturday, Sunday 10 AM–7 PM).

This pleasant little spot with its antique shop air is a cozy place indeed: Its patrons enjoy meeting here to relax in the old, battered armchairs, sip mint tea and savor the house tart. The name (meaning "the Dormouse in the Teapot") and atmosphere are drawn straight from Lewis Carroll. Brunch on Sunday.

◆ Mariage Frères

30, rue du Bourg-Tibourg
Métro: Hôtel-de-Ville
Tel. 01 42 72 28 11. Fax 01 42 74 51 68
www.mariagesfrères.com
Noon–7 PM. Closed May 1st.
Air cond.

Tea buffs love this timeless establishment. They enjoy the duck breast flavored with Earl Grey tea, delicate pastries, fresh salads and smoked salmon or foie gras sandwiches. (Also see Shops.)

◆ Chez Marianne

2, rue des Hospitalières-Saint-Gervais
Métro: St-Paul, Hôtel-de-Ville
Tel. 01 42 72 18 86. Fax 01 42 78 75 26
Open daily 12:30 PM–midnight.

The strategic location close to rue des Rosiers and the close-set tables attract lovers of pickelfleisch, pastrami, strudel and vatrouchka (Russian cheesecake). You can while away the time reading the philosophical inscriptions on the walls in this picturesque delicatessen located in the Marais quarter.

5TH ARRONDISSEMENT
FROM THE LATIN QUARTER
TO THE WORLD AT LARGE

Once, Latin was the lingua franca around the Sorbonne. Now, on place Maubert and in the surrounding streets, Greek, Chinese, Thai, Turkish and Arabic are spoken and the area is high in ethnicity (and indeed flavor). Its great culinary institutions have grown rare, while other restaurants have appeared (the latest Christophe is worth its weight in gold) or returned to favor (Atelier Maître Albert). The river is there, like a beacon, but the fifth arrondissement also holds rue Mouffetard, the church of Saint Médard, the best Greek (Mavrommatis) and Spanish (Fogon) restaurants in Paris, a graceful Moroccan (L'Atlas), a secret Vietnamese (Tao), a quality Argentinian (El Palenque), an authentic Turk (La Voie Lactée) and an interesting Peruvian (Machu-Picchu). It is convivial, tame and simple, with its amiable wine bars (Les Pipos, Chardonnay, Café de la Nouvelle Marie and X), *bouchon*-style restaurants as in Lyon and worthy Parisian cafes. Chez René is still there on the boulevard Saint-Germain. Au Moulin à Vent, La Rôtisserie du Beaujolais and Moissonnier are the district's landmarks, along with Le Pré-Verre and L'AOC. The ice creams are still looking good at Damman's, as is the earthenware at La Tuile à Loup. All excellent reasons to brush up on your Latin.

Grand Restaurants

RESTAURANTS

GRAND RESTAURANTS

● **La Tour d'Argent** CO fl V.LUX
15–17, quai de la Tournelle
Métro: Maubert-Mutualité, Cardinal-Lemoine
Tel. 01 43 54 23 31 / 01 40 46 71 11.
Fax 01 44 07 12 04
www.latourdargent.com
Closed Monday, Tuesday lunch.
Open until 10 PM.
Prix fixe: 70€ (lunch), 200€, 230€.
A la carte: 200€.
Air cond. Private dining room. Valet parking.

From his vantage point, Claude Terrail must be proud to see that while the world moves on, it is business as usual for La Tour. He has finally left us, leaving his son André to run his institution. Lovers of Paris should not worry, though: Come hell or high water, the Tour remains. We paid our visit just after Michelin took away one of the restaurant's stars in a very well-publicized move as chef Jean-François Sicallac was handing over the reins to his lieutenant, Stéphane Haissant, a veteran of Guérard, Loiseau and Senderens, before going to run the Coquille in Concarneau. We felt that the house cuisine had never been more effective. Admittedly, no one visits the Terrails' establishment (which was already in vogue in the 16th century) in search of trendy dishes that will be out of date as soon as the latest fad has peaked, but rather for a master class in a great, ambitious, classical tradition. In fact, the little appetizers, with mustard beignets, and vigorous starters, such as medallions of foie gras with a sea urchin cream sauce, silky pike quenelles with mushroom duxelles, duck with orange sauce served with crisp, twice-fried potato puffs and spinach gratin, whole veal kidneys cooked rare, garnished with crayfish and a Jura wine sauce and passion fruit and guava parfait were actually at the height of their powers. We might add that these marvels were a part of the lunchtime set menu, priced at a levelheaded 70€. The service in wing collar

and tails, and the panoramic setting overlooking the Seine, the Ile Saint Louis and the roofs of Paris still hold all their ineffable charm. The wine list, supervised by the expert David Ridgway, is still one of the most splendid in the world (a 1988 Château la Dominique was the choice accompaniment for our feast). Finally, pears poached in a vanilla cream and poire William with candied caramel, remains one of the most irresistible confections of all time. Marvelous Tour!

GOOD RESTAURANTS & OTHERS

● **L'AOC** SIM
14, rue des Fossés-Saint-Bernard
Métro: Jussieu, Cardinal-Lemoine
Tel. 01 43 54 22 52
aocrestaurant@wanadoo.fr
www.restoaoc.com
Closed Sunday, Monday, 3 weeks in August.
Open until 11 PM.
A la carte: 55€.
Air cond. Terrace. Private dining room.

As the name suggests, this agreeable bistro prettily decorated with antique objects only uses certified French regional products that must abide by strict production methods. Bull from Camargue, Bigorre black pig, Corrèze veal: Jean-Philippe Lattron, originally from the Sologne, delights us with roasted bone marrow with hand-harvested sea salt, crisply cooked pig's foot, French red tuna steak with smoked potato purée and suckling pig roasted on a spit. To cap it all, a well-stocked cellar and a warm welcome from Sophie Lattron. The prices are up there.

● **Atelier Maître Albert** COM
1, rue Maître-Albert
Métro: Maubert-Mutualité
Tel. 01 56 81 30 01. Fax 01 53 10 83 23
ateliermaitrealbert@guysavoy.com
www.guysavoy.com
Closed Saturday lunch, Sunday lunch,
Christmas–New Year's, 2 weeks in beginning
of August. Open until 11:30 PM
(Thursday–Saturday 1 AM).
A la carte: 50–65€.
Air cond. Private dining room. Valet parking.

The exposed beams and fine fireplace date from the Middle Ages, reminding us that this is the historic heart of Paris. Yet the gray and orange decor by Wilmotte is contemporary, elegant and chic. We are in the hands of Guy Savoy, and nothing is left to chance, not the "vinothèque" devoted to wines and tastings; the rotisserie at the end of the dining room, where chickens, hams and rib-eye steaks are masterfully spit-roasted; nor indeed Emmanuel Moncelier in the kitchen "*aux piano.*"* Seasonal salads and chicken livers, cured tuna croquettes with poached eggs, (roasted John Dory fish with spring pea and asparagus risotto, spit-roasted strip steak with potatoes au gratin, and a grapefruit terrine with tea sauce bewitch the palate. Watch out for the seasoning and overcooking, though! We were there on a Sunday evening when the mashed potatoes were too salty, the escargots were rubbery, the penne overcooked and the coffee tart, which tasted more like cream than coffee, also needed work.

* *In French you will often here the word* "piano," *referring to a stove in a restaurant, meaning "who is running the kitchen."*

● **Balzar**　　　　🏛 SIM

49, rue des Ecoles
Métro: Cluny-La Sorbonne, Maubert-Mutualité
Tel. 01 43 54 13 67. Fax 01 44 07 14 91
www.brasseriebalzar.com
Daily noon–11:45 PM. Cont. service.
Prix fixe: 19,90€ (dinner).
A la carte: 40–50€.
Air cond. Terrace.

Woodwork, mirrors, faux leather seats, clocks and ceramic vases: Today, this brasserie, so typical of the Left Bank of Paris, is in the hands of the Flo group, but it has not changed a jot. Nor has the chef, Christian René, who is sensibly modest enough to remain in the background, behind a timeless cuisine that we enjoy so much each time: pig snout salad, smoked Baltic herring with cream, skate pan-fried in butter, the house cassoulet,

and baba au rhum. The Sorbonne crowd delights in these dishes. There are no complaints.

● **Le Bar à Huîtres**　　SIM

33, rue Saint-Jacques
Métro: Cluny-La Sorbonne
Tel. 01 44 07 27 37. Fax 01 43 26 71 62
www.lebarahuitres.com
Daily noon–midnight. Cont. service.
Prix fixe: 24€, 43€.
Air cond. Terrace. Valet parking.

The Triadous have stepped down. Jean-Pierre Chedal has taken over this seafood chain restaurant, leaving the decor intact but refining the dishes. The ceiling covered with shells is spectacular and the sautéed squid with Espelette chili peppers, sea bass carpaccio with vanilla oil, codfish with aïoli and mustard-crusted monkfish are quite attractive. The appealing berry shortbread tart and iced profiteroles with hot chocolate sauce will bring back childhood memories.

● **Le Bistro des Cigales**　　♨ SIM

12, rue Thouin
Métro: Place-Monge, Cardinal-Lemoine
Tel.-Fax 01 40 46 03 76
lebistrodescigales@laposte.net
Closed Saturday lunch, Sunday,
2 weeks in August. Open until 11 PM.
Prix fixe: 11,90€ (lunch), 18,90€, 22,90€.
A la carte: 30€.
Terrace. Private dining room.

This inexpensive, amiable, sunny local bistro brings vacations to mind. Everything here suggests Provence, from the walls in pastel tones to the wines and dishes with their definite South of France leanings. Red mullet with colorful diced vegetables and lemongrass, jumbo shrimp brochette, lamb tagine with prunes and eggplant, baba au rhum with ginger-infused fruit all display character.

● Les Bouchons du 5e 🔆 COM

12, rue de l'Hôtel-Colbert
Métro: Maubert-Mutualité, St-Michel
Tel. 01 43 54 15 34. Fax 01 46 34 68 07
www.lesbouchonsdu5.fr
Closed Saturday lunch, Sunday,
Monday lunch. Open until 11 PM.
Prix fixe: 20€ (lunch, wine included),
26€ (lunch, wine included), 30€, 65€.
A la carte: 55–75€.
Air cond. Private dining room.

The former name of this restaurant, now run by Denis Blin, has begun to fade from memory. The young Savoy and Gagnaire veteran has discreetly become his own master. Like the restaurant's soberly modernized historic decor, the cuisine has grown more exuberant, astute and cheerful. Between the exposed stone walls of the vaulted 12th-century cellar or in the 17th-century first floor dining room, we happily savor goose foie gras prepared three ways, turbot and potatoes roasted in salt, spit-roasted pigeon with truffle risotto, and certainly the individual babas with dark rum, roasted pineapple and coconut. If it were not for the prices . . . .

● Le Brasier 🟢 SIM

88-90, rue Mouffetard
Métro: Censier-Daubenton, Place-Monge
Tel. 01 47 07 62 18. Fax 01 43 37 59 14
Open daily until 11:30 PM.
Prix fixe: 12€, 32€. A la carte: 32€.
Air cond.

The idea behind this diminutive temple for devotees of raclette and fondue has spread to other locations in Paris, but this was the first of its kind, born here in "La Mouffe." It showcases (but not exclusively) classics of chalet cuisine in winter or summer, with a brand new air-conditioning system. Escargots de Bourgogne, raclette, braserade (tableside grilling of thinly sliced meats) and floating island provide a delightful feast for parties of friends.

A SPECIAL FAVORITE

● Au Buisson Ardent 🔆🏠 SIM

25, rue Jussieu
Métro: Jussieu
Tel. 01 43 54 93 02. Fax 01 46 33 34 77
info@lebuissonardent.fr
www.lebuissonardent.fr
Closed Saturday lunch, Sunday,
Bank Holidays, New Year's, August.
Open until 10 PM.
Prix fixe: 13€ (lunch), 16€ (lunch),
29€ (dinner). A la carte: 38€.
Air cond. Terrace. Private dining room.

Two childhood friends have breathed new life into this bistro of character. Chef Stéphane Mauduit (who trained with Michel Rostang) and Jean Thomas Lopez (devotee of wines and music and a graduate of a major business school) were eager to take on this establishment, which still has its 1925 frescos. Market produce, inspired home cooking, a friendly welcome, prompt but not rushed service and reasonable prices are a winning combination. We enjoy croustillant with asparagus, mozzarella cheese and citrus and the veal and pork sausage with sage, served with a Swiss chard fondue. Among the desserts, chocolate and pistachio ganache with Amarena cherries provides a delightful conclusion. To this, add selected wines and the superb house bread.

● Chantairelle 🔆 SIM

17, rue Laplace
Métro: Maubert-Mutualité
Tel. 01 46 33 18 59
info@chantairelle.com
www.chantairelle.com
Closed Saturday lunch, Sunday,
1 week in August. Open until 10 PM.
Prix fixe: 16€ (lunch), 21€ (lunch), 30€.
A la carte: 40€.
Terrace.

Do not be put off by its modern exterior: Frédéric Bethe's little Livradois cabin has plenty of character. Welcomed by the sound of bells and cicada or birdsong, we plunge into the timelessness of the Auvergne, savoring the poached eggs with fourme d'ambert blue cheese, salmon trout with green Puy lentils or old-fashioned stuffed cabbage, without leaving out the blueberry cake, accompanied by wines (Chanturgue, Châteaugay) and mineral waters from the region. In summer, these pearls can be savored in the open air, in the attractive inner courtyard.

A SPECIAL FAVORITE

● **Christophe** Ⓝ 🏠 SIM
8, rue Descartes
Métro: Cardinal-Lemoine
Tel. 01 43 26 72 49.
Open daily until 11:30 PM.
Prix fixe: 16€ (lunch), 19€ (lunch).
A la carte: 32–42€.
Air cond. Terrace. Private dining room.

Opposite the Ecole Polytechnique engineering school, this small, innocent, but friendly bistro could well revolutionize the gourmet scene of the Montagne Sainte Geneviève quarter. Christophe Philippe, 26, has an impressive record. He was a pupil under Eric Briffard in the days of the Plaza and the Vernet, then joined Anne-Sophie Pic before moving to the Grill de Monaco. He treats us to Basque suckling pig, bacon and blood sausage spring rolls, quartet of langoustines in puff pastry with basil, seared filet of sea bream, lamb shoulder slowly roasted with sweet spices, white beans simmered with vanilla and chorizo sausage, sweetbreads pan-fried in butter with a light, delicious golden crust, paired with creamy whipped Pompadour potatoes. We also delight in the molten caraïbes chocolate cake and Valrhona chocolate mousse. The caramelized pineapple with cinnamon makes for a fine conclusion. When all the delicious desserts are priced at 6€, why not spoil yourself? This young chef's cuisine is definitely a Special Favorite. Tasting his dishes, there is no doubt as to the source of his inspiration and passion for good, well-made things.

● **Cosi** SIM
9, rue Cujas
Métro: Cluny-La Sorbonne, Cardinal-Lemoine
Tel. 01 43 29 20 20. Fax 01 43 29 26 40
www.le-cosi.com
Closed Sunday, 2 weeks in August.
Open until 11 PM.
Prix fixe: 15,50€ (lunch), 20€ (lunch).
A la carte: 40–50€.

Mischievous Corsicans have turned this Parisian bistro into a gourmet haunt devoted to their Island of Beauty. Aficionados of artisanal charcuterie will be delighted. Of course, there are other delicacies from this sunny isle: tomato tart with slowly cooked onions, John Dory with herbed quenelles and aïoli, slow-roasted lamb shoulder with sweet spices, sublime fiadone (Corsican cheesecake) and chestnut soufflé are all enchanting. The wines are from further afield. A welcome to remember from Olivier Andreani, whose mother runs an inn in Cateri.

● **Le Coupe-Chou** 🏠 COM
11, rue Lanneau
Métro: Maubert-Mutualité
Tel. 01 46 33 68 69. Fax 01 43 25 94 15
lecc@lecoupechou.com
www.lecoupechou.com
Open daily until 12:30 AM.
Prix fixe: 22€, 25€, 32€.
A la carte: 45€.
Air cond. Terrace. Private dining room.

Neither cutthroat nor cut-rate, Le Coupe-Chou (meaning "cabbage cutter") was named after the barber who had his shop here. In this discreet street in the Montagne Sainte Geneviève quarter, Christian Azzopardi has turned his restaurant, spanning three 14th, 16th, and 17th century buildings into a haven of charm. Enjoy the country duck pâté with cassis-infused onion jam, monkfish with olive oil, tomatoes and garlic, rack of lamb with fresh mint and strawberry gratin with sabayon by candlelight in one of the adjoining rooms connected by a maze of passages and stairs, or outside on the flower-filled terrace.

● L'Ecureuil, l'Oie et le Canard 🏠 SIM

3, rue Linné
Métro: Jussieu
Tel.-Fax 01 43 31 61 18
Closed Christmas, New Year's.
Open until 10:30 PM.
Prix fixe: 17€ (lunch), 20€ (lunch),
18€, 21€. A la carte: 40€.
Terrace.

Be warned: This is a den of rugby fans! This luxurious bistro, an ode to Southwest France, capably caters to their heroic appetites after the game (even when it is just on TV). Generous house foie gras marinated in muscat wine, Salers beef tenderloin and flaky puff pastry filled with apples doused with Armagnac. A real treat. Proprietor Jean-Claude Favre's usually jovial welcome may have its moods.

● L'Equitable 🏠 COM

47 bis, rue Poliveau
Métro: St-Marcel
Tel. 01 43 31 69 20. Fax 01 43 37 85 52
Closed Monday lunch, Tuesday lunch, August.
Open until 10:30 PM.
Prix fixe: 22€ (lunch), 30,50€.
A la carte: 41€.
Air cond. Private dining room.

Very close to the Jardin des Plantes botanical garden, this inn—which deserves its name—has a loyal clientele who appreciate its excellent value for money. Yves Mutin, formerly at Le Jules Verne and L'Ambassade d'Auvergne, has a personal, inventive way of preparing regional produce and choreographing his set menus. The crab salad with julienned vegetables and tomato sorbet, seared pike-perch with crispy skin and a celery root and potato parmentier, duck breast encrusted with coriander, raspberries in a warm strawberry jus with fromage blanc sorbet) are pure delights.

● L'Estrapade 🏠 SIM

15, rue de l'Estrapade
Métro: Place-Monge
Tel. 01 43 25 72 58
Closed Saturday, Sunday, 1 week at Christmas, August. Open until 10 PM.
Prix fixe: 28€. A la carte: 35€.

This 2006 Special Favorite still enchants us with its low ceiling, red banquettes, zinc counter and mirrors. Ariane and Frédéric Chalette continue to regale us with farmhouse dishes, often—although not exclusively—from their native Lorraine. We delight in the parsleyed suckling pig terrine, salmon and baby leek timbale, grilled red tuna with pesto jus, free-range pork with sauerkraut and bacon, dark chocolate pot de crème, as well as the fine growers' wines, smiling welcome and very gentle prices. An address to treasure!

● Les Fontaines SIM

9, rue Soufflot
Métro: Cluny-La Sorbonne, Luxembourg, Maubert-Mutualité
Tel. 01 43 26 42 80. Fax 01 43 54 44 57
Open daily until 11:30 PM.
Prix fixe: 15€ (lunch, wine included).
A la carte: 31€.
Terrace.

New oak furniture provides the first clue. Everything has changed at Les Fontaines, including the management, with the dynamic Jean-Luc Martin now at the helm. Chef Laurent Guillard concocts amiable combinations, such as the artichokes with foie gras, codfish served with a side of squid ink risotto and veal chop with morels and a wild nettle cake. The raspberry millefeuille, with fresh cream and a crisp tuile, is stunning.

● Au Jardin SIM

15, rue Gît-le-Cœur
Métro: St-Michel, Odéon
Tel. 01 43 26 29 44
pgomes@netcourrier.com
Closed Sunday, Monday, 3 weeks in August.
Open until 10:30 PM.
Prix fixe: 18€ (lunch), 23€ (lunch),
29,50€ (dinner). A la carte: 40€.
Air cond.

This urban *jardin* is rather bucolic, with its stone wall, wooden furniture, bottle-green and ivory hues, soft light and trompe-l'oeil windows. In this four-centuries-old house in the Latin Quarter, Philippe Gomes concocts polished dishes: pan-seared foie gras with peaches, warm goat cheese salad with melon marmalade, scallops with pesto, duck breast with mango, orange crème brûlée.

● **Le Jardin des Pâtes** ⊜ SIM

4, rue Lacépède
Métro: Place-Monge, Jussieu
Tel. 01 43 31 50 71
Open daily until 11 PM.
A la carte: 22€.
Terrace.

Taste the excellent homemade, organic fresh pasta at this small restaurant with its white walls and exposed stone. Students of the University of Paris know it well, and come to stoke up on barley pasta with salmon, rye pasta with ham, chestnut pasta with duck, accompanied by a plate of mixed raw vegetables or a plate of fresh goat cheese, organic apple juice or wine. A postprandial stroll in the nearby Jardin des Plantes is highly recommended.

● **Lagrange** ⊛ SIM

17, rue Lagrange
Métro: Maubert-Mutualité
Tel. 01 43 54 14 65. Fax 01 45 77 20 44
pierrerieutord@wanadoo.fr
Closed Sunday evening, Monday.
Open until 11 PM.
A la carte: 25–35€.
Terrace.

Pierre Rieutord has scarcely taken over this gourmet café and it has already been made over completely. In a dining room brightened by mauve, red and yellow shades, we dine on very simple bistro dishes without (excessive) damage to our pocket: Hard-boiled eggs with homemade mayonnaise, hanger steak, and homemade warm chocolate cake are generously served with a smile by Johanne Rieutord.

● **Le Languedoc** SIM

64, bd de Port-Royal
Métro: Censier-Daubenton, Port-Royal, Glacière
Tel. 01 47 07 24 47
Closed Tuesday, Wednesday,
10 days Christmas–New Year's, end of July–end of August. Open until 10 PM.
Prix fixe: 20€ (wine included).
A la carte: 22-35€.
Air cond. Terrace.

Languedoc? In a manner of speaking. Michel Dubois's cuisine plays from the classical score of Parisian bistros, simply and at a low price. Artichoke hearts with vinaigrette dressing, beef tenderloin with peppercorn sauce, homemade vacherin with seasonal fruits make unfussy meals, matching the perennial red gingham drapes.

● **Léna et Mimile** SIM

32, rue Tournefort
Métro: Place-Monge
Tel. 01 47 07 72 47
www.chezlenaetmimile.com
Closed Sunday, Monday, March.
Open until 11 PM.
Prix fixe: 15€, 39€, 43€.
Terrace. Private dining room.

Just off rue Mouffetard, this bucolic abode with its steps and sunny terrace is irresistible. Inside, the decor is rather Thirties with wood paneling. The glass verandas have been extended and a private dining room fitted out. In the hands of newcomer Christèle Gendre, the cuisine improvises easily on classical and modern themes. You can enjoy a slow-roasted vegetable terrine, scorpion fish salad with anchovy butter, roasted pork caramelized with ginger, panna cotta with red fruit or chilled chocolate mousse, or, if you are feeling more daring, try the "molecular gastronomy" menu put together with the help of physicist and chemist Hervé This. However, Léna and Mimile are not Adrià (Ferrán) and Juli (Soler).

● Le Louis Vins   ❸ SIM

9, rue de la Montagne-Sainte-Geneviève
Métro: Maubert-Mutualité
Tel. 01 43 29 12 12
www.fifi.fr
Open daily until 10:30 PM.
Prix fixe: 15€ (lunch), 23€, 26€ (dinner).
Air cond.

Jovial joker Philippe Bourgeois has taken over this establishment, which boasts a well-stocked cellar. The Loire and Rhône Valley wines, the great Bordeaux and finds from the vineyards of Languedoc are set off by tasty regional dishes. homemade foie gras with mixed greens, boneless breaded grilled pig's feet, grilled tuna medallions with a sweet and sour sauce, hanger steak with a camembert sauce and raspberries with Campari are meticulously prepared and generously served. The evening set menu at 26€ is quite a find.

● La Maison   COM

1, rue de la Bûcherie
Métro: Maubert-Mutualité, St-Michel
Tel. 01 43 29 73 57
Closed Monday, Tuesday lunch, 1 week
Christmas–New Year's. Open until 11 PM.
Prix fixe: 32€, 42€.
Terrace.

The proximity of Notre Dame is an asset and the restaurant is as charming as newcomer Helena Theresani's cooking. In this cozy red and white setting, the homemade foie gras, "seven hour" roasted lamb shoulder, and citrus fruit terrine with a mango coulis make an excellent impression. The regulars are still in attendance and tourists like the place.

● La Marée Verte   ❸ SIM

9, rue de Pontoise
Métro: Maubert-Mutualité
Tel. 01 43 25 89 41
www.maree-verte.com
Closed Sunday, Monday. Open until 11 PM.
Prix fixe: 34€. A la carte: 35€.
Air cond.

On the walls, posters of ocean liners; on the plates, fresh seafood and other dishes.

In this blue and beige restaurant, Sébastien Raiser meticulously prepares marinated anchovies and slow-roasted peppers, monkfish with citrus fruit, duck with Bing cherries and pear beignets with rosemary caramel. Just what you need before tackling a few laps in the fine 1950s' swimming pool close by.

● Marty   🛏 COM

20, av des Gobelins
Métro: Les Gobelins
Tel. 01 43 31 39 51. Fax 01 43 37 63 70
restaurant.marty@wanadoo.fr
www.marty-restaurant.com
Noon–11 PM. Cont. service.
Prix fixe: 30€ (lunch), 33€ (dinner).
A la carte: 40–55€.
Air cond. Terrace. Private dining room.
Valet parking.

This former coaching inn turned Parisian brasserie, established in 1913 by the grandparents of current proprietor Geneviève Péricouche, has style to spare with its Thirties' decor and comfortable terrace (covered in winter). Seafood platters are the specialty, but new chef Emilien Cilia takes a novel approach to tradition with the cured salmon with chive cream, codfish filet with fava beans and young peas, old-fashioned calf's head and melted equatorial chocolate cake with nougat chips.

● Moissonnier   🛏 SIM

28, rue des Fossés-Saint-Bernard
Métro: Jussieu, Cardinal-Lemoine
Tel.-Fax 01 43 29 87 65
Closed Sunday, Monday, August.
Open until 10 PM.
Prix fixe: 24€. A la carte: 30–40€.

Opposite the Institut du Monde Arabe, this Fifties' decor, *bouchon*-style restaurant inspired by Lyonnais and Franche Comté culture in equal measures serves a perennially fashionable traditional menu. Philippe and Valérie Mayet should pay more attention to the Lyonnaise salad bar, fourteen starters of varying quality. The sautéed tripe is too vinegary, but the beef tenderloin with morel mushroom cream sauce is enjoyable, and the generous portion of salt pork and the lentils and smoked Montbéliard sausage is respectable. Apart from this, there is a substantial selection of cheeses and desserts like grandmother used to make. The food as a whole is more generous than subtle. The wines served in carafes—like the 2004 Chiroubles at 12€— do not rock the boat.

● Au Moulin à Vent   🔒 SIM

20, rue des Fossés-Saint-Bernard
Métro: Jussieu, Cardinal-Lemoine
Tel. 01 43 54 99 37. Fax 01 40 46 92 23
alexandra.damas@aumoulinavent.fr
www.au-moulinavent.com
Closed Saturday lunch, Sunday, Monday,
1 week Christmas–New Year's, 3 weeks
in August. Open until 11 PM.
Prix fixe: 35€ (lunch). A la carte: 60€.
Terrace. Valet parking.

A step away from the Institut du Monde Arabe, we are firmly back in Paris with this typical old-style bistro run by the dynamic Alexandra Damas. The counter is zinc, the ceiling low, the banquettes in faux leather, the furniture wood and the menu prudently classical. We have no complaints about the Lyonnaise salad with chicory, poached egg and bacon, the eggplant and crayfish terrine, frog's legs with tomatoes, garlic and herbs, the thick filet of beef tenderloin with peppercorn sauce and baba au rhum. As for the wine, you can trust the proprietor. She is a sommelier and will guide you well (and not necessarily to the most expensive bottles).

● Les Papilles   🏠 SIM

30, rue Gay-Lussac
Métro: Luxembourg, Cluny-La Sorbonne
Tel. 01 43 25 20 79. Fax 01 43 25 24 35
Closed Sunday, 3 weeks in August.
Open until 10 PM.
Prix fixe: 28,50€. A la carte: 38€.
Air cond. Terrace. Private dining room.

This highly commendable bistro and gourmet shop run by Bertrand Bluy, formerly a pastry chef with Troisgros, Veyrat and Taillevent, is flourishing. Its friendly welcome, atmosphere and quality all go hand in hand. The single prix fixe menu of

fresh market produce at 28.50€ changes every day. It is copious and irreproachable. A young L'Ami Jean veteran accurately interprets the fresh, subtle menu. The plate of assorted cured meats and pâtés, codfish roasted skin-side down, roasted lamb shoulder, citrus salad and chocolate cappuccino make this a delightful spread. Since we are not the only ones who know about this place, it is a good idea to make a reservation.

● Perraudin   🔒 SIM

157, rue Saint-Jacques
Métro: Cluny-La Sorbonne
Tel. 01 46 33 15 75. Fax 01 46 33 52 75
restaurant-perraudin@wanadoo.fr
www.restaurant-perraudin.com
Open daily until 10:30 PM.
Prix fixe: 18€ (lunch), 28€.
Terrace.

The dynamic Monsieur Correy has taken over this institution, frequented since time immemorial by Sorbonne university students, without changing its style. Chef Philippe Dubois gently modernizes bistro classics. The pot-au-feu terrine, profiteroles with warm goat cheese, salmon filet with sorrel sauce, sole meunière, bœuf bourguignon and roasted leg of lamb slip down easily. The grandmotherly desserts—apple tart a la mode and homemade profiteroles—are remarkable.

● Le Petit Châtelet   SIM

39, rue de la Bûcherie
Métro: St-Michel-Notre-Dame,
Maubert-Mutualité
Tel. 01 46 33 53 40. Fax 01 46 33 16 53
Closed Sunday evening, Monday (in summer
closed Monday lunch). Open until 11 PM.
Prix fixe: 14,50€ (weekday lunch, wine
included), 24,50€. A la carte: 30–50€.
Terrace. Private dining room.

The warm, sun-colored decor of the dining room sets the tone in this establishment run by the Silly family for more than half a century. The unpretentious menu of *cuisine bourgeoise*—good plain French home cooking—offers delicate tart with warm goat cheese and pesto, roasted rack of lamb with fresh thyme and strawberries in red wine. Neat, impeccable and served with a smile.

● Le Petit Pontoise   SIM

9, rue de Pontoise
Métro: Maubert-Mutualité
Tel. 01 43 29 25 20
Open daily until 10:30 PM.
A la carte: 45–50€.
Air cond. Terrace.

The place has been smartened up, but the welcome is still as warm as ever. In his Fifties' dining room–style bistro with its close-set wooden tables, Philippe Tondetta presents his exclusively a la carte dishes. Artichoke and parmesan tart, sea bream roasted in salt, roasted quail with raisins, crème brûlée with caramelized almonds are all appetizing, but not cheap.

● Le Petit Prince de Paris   € SIM

12, rue de Lanneau
Métro: Maubert-Mutualité
Tel. 01 43 54 77 26
Closed lunch, 1 week Christmas–New Year's.
Open until 11:30 PM.
Prix fixe: 18€ (dinner), 24€ (dinner).
Air cond.

In its side street, this "little prince" is modest indeed. Admirers praise its welcome and the friendliness of the staff as well as the quality of the dishes they serve. Benoît Gadreau lovingly concocts zucchini flan with scallops and spiced toasts, crisp layered pastry with salmon tartare and fresh dill, suckling pig roasted with honey and red wine, baba au rhum with lime and salted caramel ice cream.

● Les Pipos   € SIM

2, rue de l'Ecole-Polytechnique
Métro: Maubert-Mutualité
Tel. 01 43 54 11 40. Fax 01 43 54 12 78
www.les-pipos.com
Closed Sunday.
11:30 AM–11 PM. Cont. service.
A la carte: 30€.
Terrace. Private dining room.

Whether you are a "Pipo" (a student at the nearby Polytechnique engineering school)

or not, you will enjoy this honest restaurant's pleasant, bistro-style menu—salad with slow-roasted gizzards and smoked duck breast, Duval andouillette, crème brûlée—and a well-stocked cellar, all at friendly prices.

● Le Port du Salut   SIM

163 bis, rue Saint-Jacques
Métro: Cluny-La Sorbonne
Tel. 01 46 33 63 21. Fax 01 46 33 08 69
oggynat@club-internet.fr
Closed Sunday, Monday. Open until 11 PM.
Prix fixe: 15,60€, 22€, 27€.
A la carte: 35€.
Air cond. Terrace. Private dining room.

Is it Nathalie Godeau or the market-based cuisine that keeps the customers coming back? In the mainly Burgundy-colored dining rooms, the Andalusian gazpacho, bourguignon and clafoutis take center stage. A good choice of French wines.

● Le Pré-Verre   SIM

8, rue Thénard
Métro: Maubert-Mutualité
Tel.-Fax 01 43 54 59 47
Closed Sunday, Monday, 1 week
Christmas–New Year's, 2 weeks in August.
Open until 10:30 PM.
Prix fixe: 12,50€ (lunch, wine included),
25,50€.
Air cond. Terrace.

Philippe and Marc Delacourcelle's restaurant could spark off another Battle of Hernani. Some are delighted by the cuisine, while others complain about the background noise and close-set tables. In any case, this bottle-lined bistro with its red tables, baroque clock and jazz posters is a success. Philippe, who trained with Loiseau, was a great hit at Le Clos des Morillons, before setting up more modestly here, with an eye to low prices. The set menu is pleasant and the dishes appealing. Raw marinated sardines with eggplant, Mediterranean scorpion fish with a smoked potato purée, tender suckling pig with crispy cabbage and the chocolate truffade are among his best tricks.

● **Le Refuge du Passé**   SIM

32, rue du Fer-à-Moulin
Métro: Censier-Daubenton
Tel.-Fax 01 47 07 29 91
Open daily until 11 PM.
Prix fixe: 18€ (lunch), 26€, 32€.
Air cond.

The management has changed and so has the chef, but the cheerful thrift shop decor with its theater posters and old vinyl records has remained. The set menus are now free of a certain Auvergnat influence, as shown by the crayfish salad with grapefruit and Provençal-style red mullet, but some of the old dishes remain, such as sautéed chicken with honey. The tarte Tatin supplies a happy ending.

● **Chez René**   🏠 SIM

14, bd Saint-Germain
Métro: Maubert-Mutualité
Tel. 01 43 54 30 23
Closed Sunday, Monday, 10 days
Christmas–New Year's, August.
Open until 10:30 PM.
Prix fixe: 32€ (lunch, wine included),
43€ (dinner). A la carte: 42–60€.
Terrace.

Specialties from Lyon and Beaujolais top the bill in this bistro from a bygone era, with its white tables, simple decor and attentive service. The concept of "staff turnover" is alien to Chez René. Jean-Claude Cinquin, who has a healthy pair of lungs, is the founder's son, while Jean-Yves Monnerie has been officiating in the kitchen for more than a quarter of a century. Assorted charcuterie and pâtés, fish of the day, rib-eye steak or beef bourguignon and the dessert or charlotte of the day are perfectly prepared and will delight enthusiasts.

● **Ribouldingue**   🅽 🕭 SIM

10, rue Saint-Julien-le-Pauvre
Métro: St-Michel
Tel. 01 46 33 98 80
Closed Sunday, Monday, Christmas,
New Year's, 2 weeks in August.
Open until 11 PM.
A la carte: 35€.
Air cond.

Young, mischievous and full of energy, they have taken the plunge in the hazardous area of variety meats with the blessing of Yves Camdeborde: Nadège Varigny in the dining room and Claver Dousseh in the kitchen perform an original, amusing score in this successor to the former Fogon. Catching on quickly, lovers of tripe, lamb's brain fried in butter, crispy cow's udder salad, calf's head carpaccio with mayonnaise, capers and herbs, roasted veal kidneys with potatoes au gratin and pig's snouts have set up their headquarters in this elongated restaurant with its close-set tables. The fresh produce and precise cooking and seasoning work wonders. The cheese board is alluring and for dessert, the rice pudding *grand-mère* or Guanaja dark-chocolate mousse are attractive propositions indeed.

● **La Rôtisserie du Beaujolais**   🕭 SIM

19, quai de la Tournelle
Métro: Maubert-Mutualité, Pont-Marie
Tel. 01 43 54 17 47. Fax 01 56 24 43 71
Open daily until 10:30 PM.
A la carte: 40€.
Air cond.

Claude Terrail turned this chic *bouchon*-style restaurant in a prime riverside location into a rendezvous for friends, rather than an adjunct of La Tour d'Argent. It is still there, offering quality produce, attentive service and tempting food. The kitchen with its grill and spits is open to the dining room. As the Challans chickens and beefsteaks sizzle, we begin with crayfish marinated in Macon white wine, œufs en meurette (poached eggs with wine, bacon and onions), or the leeks vinaigrette, then face a choice. Why not a perfectly grilled sea bass with fennel au gratin or an equally good Salers rib-eye steak with a béarnaise sauce? A praliné millefeuille concludes the feast beautifully. A major bonus: The place is open on Sunday.

● Au Sud de Nulle Part Ⓝ SIM

16, bd Saint-Germain
Métro: Maubert-Mutualité
Tel. 01 43 54 59 10. Fax 01 43 29 02 08
Closed Saturday lunch, Sunday, 1 week in
mid-August. Open until 10:30 PM.
Prix fixe: 10,50€ (lunch), 16€ (lunch), 24€
(lunch, wine included). A la carte: 40–50€.
Air cond. Terrace.

Exit the Bistrot Côté Mer. David Pagnard,
the new boss, has refurbished the facade
of what was once Raffatin et Honorine,
stripping the woodwork to restore its natural warmth and freshening the whole
place up. In the kitchen, Alain Hemery has
his sights set on the Mediterranean with
his golden brown lasagna with roasted
eggplant and langoustines, pike-perch
baked in parchment with ratatouille and a
white wine butter sauce, calf's liver glazed
with Modena balsamic vinegar and vanilla
custard with berries.

● La Table Corse SIM

8, rue Tournefort
Métro: Place-Monge
Tel. 01 43 31 15 00. Fax 01 43 31 12 51
Closed Sunday, Christmas–beginning of
January, August. Open until 11 PM.
A la carte: 40–50€

This eatery dedicated to Corsica, Island
of Beauty, is looking good. New chef
Philippe Gauthier, a veteran of Le Relais
du Parc in Robuchon's day, as well as Passard and Meneau, presents his subtle
take on Corsican cuisine: millefeuille with
eggplant and cured Corsican ham, John
Dory fish prepared with fresh Corsican
mint, braised black ham with chestnuts,
shiitake and porcini mushrooms or the
pain perdu with slow-roasted caramelized clementines and brocciu (fresh Corsican ewe's cheese). We might add that
Monsieur Garsi offers a meticulous,
friendly welcome.

● La Table de Fabrice Ⓝ SIM

13, quai de la Tournelle
Métro: Maubert-Mutualité, Pont-Marie
Tel. 01 44 07 17 57. Fax 01 53 62 13 39
Closed Saturday lunch, Sunday, 2 weeks in
August. Open until 11 PM.
Prix fixe: 40€. A la carte: 70–80€.
Air cond. Terrace.

Fabrice Deverly, who trained with Robuchon and Senderens, and at L'Arpège, has
taken over this cozy riverside restaurant
on two floors (formerly La Table de Michel)
next door to the La Tour d'Argent and runs
it with great energy. We quietly savor the
charms of its lively, shrewd, well-executed
dishes in a traditional spirit. Truffle
risotto is a high point. Millefeuille of crab
beautifully decorated with vegetables,
sea bass baked in parchment paper with
aromatic vegetables, seared tuna with an
herb crust or citrus-braised sweetbreads
are not bad, without unnecessary com-
plications. The service is friendly and the
raspberry tiramisu gratifying.

● La Truffière V.COM

4, rue Blainville
Métro: Place-Monge, Cardinal-Lemoine,
Luxembourg
Tel. 01 46 33 29 82. Fax 01 46 33 64 74
restaurant.latruffiere@wanadoo.fr
www.latruffiere.com
Closed Sunday, Monday, Christmas, August.
Open until 10:30 PM.
Prix fixe: 20€ (lunch). A la carte: 90€.
Air cond. Private dining room.

In the intimate, rustic setting of this 17th-
century establishment with its two
vaulted rooms, fireplace, cigars and aged
spirits, we are ready to try one of the 2,400
wines from its stunning cellar. Sommelier
Vincent Martin can point you to the right
vintages to properly accompany Jean-
Christophe Rizet's sophisticated dishes:
Crayfish with asparagus and leeks, bread
with olive oil, tomato and garlic topped
with a fried egg yolk and cream infused
with squid ink, tuna and foie gras croustillant served with caramel marinated carrots or pigeon, its roasted breast and legs
stuffed with creamy barley, all make a fine

impression. The astute wine and food pairings lead to discoveries. To finish, warm berries with fresh mint and coconut milk served with cassis sorbet is pleasantly refreshing. Supervised by Christian Sainsard, the service is faultless. Lunchtime menu aside, the check tends to rise rapidly.

● Les Vignes du Panthéon 🏠 SIM

4, rue des Fossés-Saint-Jacques
Métro: Place-Monge, Cardinal-Lemoine
Tel.-Fax 01 43 54 80 81
www.lesvignesdupantheon.fr
Closed Saturday lunch, Sunday, 2 weeks in beginning of August. Open until 10:15 PM.
A la carte: 48€.
Air cond. Private dining room.

Under the historic ceiling, near the patinated zinc counter, Lionel Malière gives lovers of good food and drink occasions to remember. The slow-roasted pressed duck and foie gras terrine, pan-seared veal kidneys and iced macaron glacé with pistachios go famously with wines chosen from all the right places.

● Watt ⓔ SIM

3, rue de Cluny
Métro: Cluny-La Sorbonne
Tel. 01 43 54 99 85. Fax 01 43 54 20 78
Closed Sunday evening, 1 week Christmas–New Year's, 3 weeks in August.
Open until 10:45 PM (weekends 11:30 PM).
Prix fixe: 13€ (weekday lunch), 14€ (weekday lunch). A la carte: 25€.
Air cond. Terrace. Private dining room.

A rather sharp, fashionable spot, where you can make up your prix fixe menu yourself from a fairly wide choice of quite small portions. The setting is amiable—a large, bright loft that has just been repainted—with a mezzanine library. You can also drop in for a coffee or a drink with friends. Tartine with saint-marcellin cheese and fig jam, filet of sole with coconut-basil sauce, kangaroo filet with slow-cooked onions and figs, chocolate mousse with oranges and Nestlé Crunch go down pleasantly enough. Brunch (American, Scandinavian or English) on Sunday.

INTERNATIONAL RESTAURANTS

● Les Délices d'Aphrodite 🍴 SIM

4, rue de Candolle
Métro: Censier-Daubenton
Tel. 01 43 31 40 39. Fax 01 43 36 13 08
infos@mavrommatis.fr
www.mavrommatis.fr
Open daily until 11 PM
Prix fixe: 18€ (lunch). A la carte: 38€.
Air cond. Terrace.

In this blue and white tavern, it's easy to imagine yourself in the Greek Isles. The Mavrommatis brothers maintain the illusion with their succulent cuisine. Pikilia micri (an assortment of appetizers, a Greek Cypriot speciality), pan-seared octopus with olive oil and parsley, jumbo shrimp with garlic and chopped tomato, grilled lamb stuffed with shallot confit and flavored with aged vinegar and cinnamon, feta cheese with olive oil and oregano, orange-infused cream and toasted pistachios delight us with their sun-drenched flavors. When the weather is bad, we can still enjoy the covered, heated terrace.

● Mavrommatis ◯ COM

42, rue Daubenton
Métro: Censier-Daubenton
Tel. 01 43 31 17 17. Fax 01 43 36 13 08
info@mavrommatis.fr
www.mavrommatis.fr
Closesd Sunday, Monday, 3 weeks in August.
Open until 10:30 PM.
Prix fixe: 22€ (weekday lunch), 34€.
A la carte: 60€.
Air cond. Terrace. Private dining room.

Precise, simple flavors, the taste of fresh local produce from sunny Greece. The Mavrommatis brothers invite us on a gourmet pilgrimage in their fine establishment, where you could imagine yourself to be in Limassol or the Cyclades. On a pleasant little square by the Mouffetard market, their restaurant stands opposite a terrace surrounded by imposing olive trees. The interior breathes 19th-century Athens: mainly pale-yellow shades, wooden furniture and black-and-white photos. We begin with tzatziki (cucumber yogurt sauce), taramasalata (a creamy mixture of carp roe, olive oil, lemon and breadcrumbs), dolmadès (stuffed grape leaves) or sardines marinated in spicy oil and marinated "giant" beans, then set about a delicious grilled red mullet filet, a splendid roasted lamb with an eggplant and feta casserole or delicately roasted quail wrapped in grape leaves with honey and thyme. Then we have just enough room left for a date parfait or rice pudding with dried fruit and spiced caramelized pears. Excellent wines from the Peloponnese and the islands accompany this sun-kissed meal.

● **Tao**   🔊COM

248, rue Saint-Jacques
Métro: Cluny-La Sorbonne
Tel. 01 43 26 75 92. Fax 01 43 25 68 69
Closed Sunday, end of July to end of August.
Open until 10:30 PM.
A la carte: 35€.
Terrace.

We feel at ease in the refined, very Zen surroundings of the Truong's long, narrow establishment, soberly decorated with photos of Vietnam. Aficionados can choose between different sizes of dish, depending on how hungry they are. We are tempted by the XL version of steamed dumplings, tender pork simmered in coconut milk and herbed jelly for dessert. Subtle, fresh, tasty, authentic and all made on the premises by chef Kim Nguyen.

▼ | **SHOPS**

KITCHENWARE & TABLETOP

▼ **La Tuile à Loup**

35, rue Daubenton
Métro: Censier-Daubenton
Tel. 01 47 07 28 90. Fax 01 43 36 40 95
www.latuilealoup.com
10:30 AM–7 PM. Closed Sunday,
Monday morning (all day Monday,
July–August), weekend of July 14th,
weekend of August 15th.

This embassy of regional crafts offers unique items: bread baskets, knives, glasses, tablecloths, placemats and glazed pottery. Each object is a tribute to a trade and reminds us of the history of a beautiful area of France.

BREAD & BAKED GOODS

▼ **Beauvallet**

6, rue de Poissy
Métro: Maubert-Mutualité
Tel. 01 43 26 94 24
7 AM–8 PM. Closed Wednesday,
mid-August–end of August.

This traditional bakery often wins awards in the contest for the best Parisian baguette. We enjoy a perfect golden crust on each loaf. Mohamed Ousbih makes sure his bread is fresh, baking two batches a day.

▼ **Boulange d'Antan**

6, rue Linné
Métro: Jussieu
Tel. 01 47 07 10 94
7:30 AM–8 PM.
Closed Saturday, Sunday, August.

Béatrice and Denis Hecht supply Parisians with sweet delicacies from Alsace: Kugelhopf, plum tart, streudel, cheesecake and beautiful Viennese pastries are all to be found in their delightful store.

▼ Le Boulanger de Monge

Dominique Saibron
123, rue Monge
Métro: Censier-Daubenton
Tel. 01 43 37 54 20
7 AM–8:30 PM. Closed Monday

Self-taught, gifted Dominique Saibron leaves us in no doubt with her light-textured baguette, organic sourdough, various grain breads and Viennese pastries, and rolls with bacon and cheese. Croissants, sticky buns, pistachio and lemon crumbles and fresh fruit tarts complete the quality selection.

▼ Le Fournil de Mouffetard

123-125, rue Mouffetard
Métro: Censier-Daubenton
Tel. 01 47 07 35 96
7:30 AM–8 PM (Saturday 7 AM–8 PM).
Closed Sunday afternoon, Monday.

The Moranges have taken over from Stéphane Delaunay's store. The country sourdough, rye, wheat with hazelnuts and raisins, whole-grain breads and artisanal thin baguettes are still remarkable, but the welcome needs work.

▼ Kayser

8 and 14, rue Monge
Métro: Maubert-Mutualité,
Cardinal-Lemoine
Tel. 01 44 07 01 42 / 01 44 07 17 81
6:45 AM–8:30 PM.
Closed Tuesday.

Eric Kayser is acquiring stores and tearooms, sometimes in partnership ("Be") in the eighth arrondissement with Ducasse). His slow-rising baguette is still as good as it gets. His speciality breads made with wheat, buckwheat, walnuts, spelt, bacon or cheese cannot be faulted. You can find his seasonal breads in the sixth, eighth and fifteenth arrondissements.

WINE

▼ Caves du Panthéon

174, rue Saint-Jacques
Métro: Luxembourg, Cardinal-Lemoine, Place-Monge
Tel. 01 46 33 90 35. Fax 01 43 26 76 49
9:30 AM–8:30 PM (Monday 2–8:30 PM).
Closed Sunday, Monday morning.

In this early 20th-century establishment, Michel Schuch cossets a range of wines from every region: Elian Daros Côtes du Marmandais, selected Côtes Rôties and new wave Languedoc vintages. Tastings organized every Saturday.

▼ De Vinis Illustribus

48, rue la Montagne-Sainte-Geneviève
Métro: Censier-Daubenton
Tel. 01 43 36 12 12. Fax 01 43 36 20 30
www.devinis.fr
11 AM–8 PM.
Closed Sunday, Monday.

Specializing in old vintages, this cellar has a rare choice of old wines from the 1900s on. Château Margaux 1929 and Hermitage la Chapelle 1947 are there, along with old cognacs, memorable champagnes and first-rate ports.

GROCERIES

▼ Les Comptoirs de la Tour d'Argent

2, rue du Cardinal-Lemoine
Métro: Maubert-Mutualité
Tel. 01 46 33 45 58. Fax 01 43 26 39 23
10 AM (Sunday noon)–midnight.
Closed Monday.

Opposite the Tour, this fine store offers a collection of colored china ducks, Saint Louis and Baccarat crystal carafes and tableware bearing the Tour d'Argent name. It also sells preserves, teas, coffees, champagnes, spirits and Trois Empereurs foie gras.

CHEESE

▼ La Ferme des Arènes

60, rue Monge
Métro: Place-Monge
Tel. 01 43 36 07 08
8:30 AM–12:30 PM, 3:30–7:30 PM.
Closed Sunday afternoon, Monday

Christian Le Lann, butcher in the twentieth arrondissement and cheesemonger both here and on Ile Saint-Louis, selects carefully matured, quality cheeses. Comté, beaufort, saint-marcellin, munster and goat cheese matured in wood ash are presented at the peak of their form and according to season.

▼ Foucher

118, rue Mouffetard
Métro: Censier-Daubenton
Tel.-Fax 01 45 35 13 19
8:30 AM–1 PM, 4–7:45 PM
(Friday 8:30 AM–1 PM, 3:15–8 PM;
Saturday 8:30 AM–7:45 PM).
Closed Sunday afternoon, Monday,
1 week in August.

The talented Marie and Alain Quatrehomme champion the cause of raw milk cheese. As in the parent establishment in the seventh arrondissement, here they present goat cheese from the Loire Valley, creamy saint-marcellin, beaufort d'alpage, reblochon, époisses, chevrotin from Savoie or hand-crafted roquefort matured with endless care.

ICE CREAM

▼ Damman's

1, rue des Grands-Degrés
Métro: Maubert-Mutualité, St-Michel
Tel. 01 43 29 15 10
11:30 AM–7 PM (in summer 11:30 PM).
Closed Monday,
beginning of November–mid-December,
beginning of January–mid-March.

Thomas Damman offers ice cream in natural flavors. His tiramisu, chocolate with hazelnuts and dried fruit, salted butter caramel, vanilla with chocolate shavings, passion fruit and mango are very successful. You can take home Bulgarian yogurt ice cream with raspberry sauce and grated white chocolate or enjoy it in the parlor opposite Notre Dame.

Shops

▼ Octave

138, rue Mouffetard
Métro: Censier-Daubenton
Tel. 01 45 35 20 56. Fax 01 45 35 03 07
10 AM–7:30 PM (in summer 11:30 PM;
Sunday, Monday, Tuesday 9 PM; Wednesday,
Thursday 11 PM). Closed Monday morning,
Monday and Tuesday in winter, 2 weeks in
January.

From Toulouse, Mathieu Mendegris sends his ice creams dedicated to friends, including "Seins de glacé" (Breasts of Ice Cream) for cartoonist Wolinski or "C'est une Garonne" in memory of singer Claude Nougaro. "Légende d'hiver" or Winter Legend (caramel orange truffle) and "Soleil noir" or Black Sun (Valrhona Gianduja dark chocolate with hazelnuts) are worth the visit.

BOOKS

▼ Librairie Gourmande

4, rue Dante
Métro: St-Michel
Tel. 01 43 54 37 27. Fax 01 43 54 31 16
www.librairie-gourmande.fr
10 AM–7 PM. Closed Sunday

This bookshop has more than 12,000 catalogued volumes and lives up to its name. Cookbooks and volumes on table arts, wines and cocktails are all in stock here, from the 17th century to today.

PASTRIES

▼ Bon

159, rue Saint-Jacques
Métro: Luxembourg, St-Michel,
Cluny-La Sorbonne
Tel.-Fax 01 43 54 26 44
www.bon-chocolat.fr
6:45 AM–8 PM. Closed Sunday afternoon,
Monday, 1 week in February, August.

Lemon tarts, mambo (coffee macaron with chocolate chips), brésilien au café (coffee-infused chocolate truffle cake) or meringues with Kirsch are some of the delights concocted by confection expert Serge Bousseronde.

REGIONAL PRODUCTS

▼ Au Cochon d'Auvergne
48, rue Monge
Métro: Place-Monge, Cardinal-Lemoine
Tel.-Fax 01 43 26 36 21
9:30 AM–1:15 PM, 4–8 PM. Closed Sunday afternoon, Monday, mid-July–end of August.
His heart set firmly in regional France, Bertrand Morizur supplies artisanal produce from the Auvergne, but not exclusively. Sauerkraut, baked ham on the bone, head cheese, sausages and boudin with chestnuts breathe new life into the genre.

▼ Pierre Champion
110, rue Mouffetard
Métro: Censier-Daubenton
Tel.-Fax 01 55 43 92 59
10 AM–1 PM, 3–7:30 PM (Saturday 10 AM–7:30 PM, Sunday 10 AM–1:30 PM). Closed Sunday afternoon, Monday (July–August), Christmas, New Year's.
In this contemporary temple to Southwest France, Pierre Champion personalizes gift boxes with fresh duck or goose foie gras sold partially cooked, in lobes, as a terrine or in glass jars. Customers also shop for duck confit, cured duck breast, duck rillettes and stuffed duck and goose necks, as well as Bordeaux and Cahors wines.

TEA

▼ La Maison des Trois Thés
1, rue Saint-Médard
Métro: Place-Monge
Tel. 01 43 36 93 84
11 AM–7:30 PM (tastings 1–6:30 PM). Closed Sunday, Monday, beginning of August–beginning of September
This famous tea cellar offers different families of tea with an eye to detail: red (Dian Hong Gong Fu), blue (Gao Shan Cha, Oolong), green (Xian Xia Lan Cui), white (Bai Hao Yin Zhen) and yellow. Yu Hui Tseng, a tea expert, travels in Asia for six months of the year in search of the best harvests.

COFFEE

▼ La Brûlerie des Gobelins
2, av des Gobelins
Métro: Censier-Daubenton, Les Gobelins
Tel. 01 43 31 90 13. Fax 01 45 35 83 00
10 AM–7 PM (Saturday 10 AM–1 PM, 2:30 PM–7 PM). Closed Sunday, Monday, Bank Holidays, afternoons.
Jean-Paul Logereau's paneled den presents around thirty varieties of freshly roasted coffee, such as Ethiopian Moka, Guatemalan maragogype and the San Remo blend, as well as a range of jams from Savoie and Anjou honeys.

PREPARED FOOD

▼ Guillemard
241, rue Saint-Jacques
Métro: Luxembourg, Cardinal-Lemoine, Place-Monge
Tel. 01 43 26 97 17. Fax 01 40 51 80 70
8:30 AM–4 PM. Closed Sunday, Bank Holidays, August.
Founded in 1926, Christophe Brun's establishment supplies hors d'œuvres, assorted grilled meats, ready-to-serve dishes and decorative pyramids of small pastries and handles the complete organization of all receptions. The quality of his services is impeccable.

◆ RENDEZVOUS

PUBS

◆ L'Académie de la Bière
88 bis, bd de Port-Royal
Métro: Les Gobelins
Tel. 01 43 54 66 65. Fax 01 46 33 85 23
www.acade-biere.com
10 AM–2 AM (Friday, Saturday 3 AM). Closed Christmas, New Year's.
Air cond. Terrace.
There could be nothing less academic than this bar, which serves draft beers, some of which cannot be found elsewhere, to accompany mussels in a cream sauce or sauerkraut. The terrace is packed with students taking a breather.

◆ Connolly's Corner

12, rue de Mirbel
Métro: Censier-Daubenton
Tel. 01 43 36 55 40 & 01 43 36 55 70
Open daily 4 PM (in summer 6 PM)–2 AM.

A little patch of Ireland recently renovated, where Guinness and Kilkenny flow like water. Every Sunday night Liam Connolly puts on concerts of Irish music.

◆ Finnegan's Wake

9, rue des Boulangers
Métro: Jussieu, Cardinal-Lemoine
Tel. 01 46 34 23 65
11 AM (Saturday 6 PM)–2 AM.
Closed Saturday morning, Sunday, August.

This authentic Irish pub named after Joyce's masterpiece also takes an interest in culture, offering Gaelic lessons on Wednesday and poetry on Sunday. Each weekend patrons enjoy Guinness and Kilkenny at a jazz concert in the vaulted cellar.

◆ La Gueuze

19, rue Soufflot
Métro: Luxembourg, Odéon
Tel. 01 43 54 63 00
Open daily 11 AM–2 AM (Saturday, Sunday 3 AM).
Terrace.

Much appreciated by students from the Sorbonne. Guy Aguilet offers them more than 150 beers, as well as welcome snacks: steamed mussels with French fries or andouillette AAAAA.

WINE BARS

◆ Café de la Nouvelle Mairie

19-21, rue des Fossés-Saint-Jacques
Métro: Luxembourg, Cardinal-Lemoine
Tel. 01 44 07 04 41
9 AM–9 PM (Tuesday, Thursday midnight).
Closed Saturday, Sunday, August.

Near a rustic square hidden by the Panthéon, Nicolas Carmarans offers wines selected from the finest sources in the Loire region. Cheerful snacks, good daily specials and a striking chocolate cake. As soon as the sun comes out, the terrace is packed.

Rendezvous

◆ Le Vin Sobre

25, rue des Feuillantines
Métro: Port-Royal, Censier-Daubenton
Tel. 01 43 29 00 23. Fax 01 43 29 09 43
8 AM–10:30 PM.
Closed May 1st, 1 week in August.
Terrace.

Bertrand Guillemain has turned this corner wine bar into a lively haunt with a terrace on rue Saint-Jacques. A wide choice of organic wines is accompanied by an assortment of charcuterie, pâtés and regional dishes.

CAFES

◆ Au Pain Quotidien

136, rue Mouffetard
Métro: Censier-Daubenton
Tel. 01 55 43 91 99
Open daily 8:30 AM–7 PM.
Terrace.

The communal table, country atmosphere, unupholstered wood furniture and weekend brunch set the tone. Fine round loaves of white bread, artisanal jams, teas and hot chocolates encourage visitors to take their time.

TEA SALONS

◆ Café de la Mosquée

39, rue Geoffroy-Saint-Hilaire
Métro: Censier-Daubenton, Jussieu
Tel. 01 43 31 18 14
Open daily 9 AM–11:30 PM.

This 1926 vintage Moorish café takes us back to the colonial era. The reliably prepared food—tagines, couscous, crisp filled phyllo, Moroccan savory pie, and Middle Eastern pastries—are commendable. Fine rooms are furnished with comfortable chairs; large trays serve as tables.

◆ La Fourmi Ailée

8, rue du Fouarre
Métro: Maubert-Mutualité
Tel. 01 43 29 40 99. Fax 01 43 25 09 22
jaev@wanadoo.fr
www.parisresto.com
Noon–midnight. Closed New Year's.
Terrace. Private dining room.

Near Notre Dame, this gourmet bookshop also offers tasty cakes and pastries plus home-style cooking prepared by a meticulous chef. Cécile Moresmo regales her guests with vegetarian dishes, lemon and prune tarts and soft chocolate cake.

◆ The Tea Caddy

14, rue Saint-Julien-le-Pauvre
Métro: Maubert-Mutualité, St-Michel
Tel. 01 43 54 15 56. Fax 01 49 59 01 75
postmaster@the-tea-caddy
www.the-tea-caddy.com
Noon–7 PM. Closed Tuesday, August.

Behind the church of Saint-Julien-le-Pauvre, Sophie Fort watches over this cozy, British-style tearoom. The light dishes, such as savory salmon pie, zucchini and eggplant au gratin, and the cakes and pastries, such as apple pie, muffins and crumble, are striking.

◆ Thé des Brumes

340, rue Saint-Jacques
Métro: Port-Royal, St-Jacques,
Censier-Daubenton
Tel. 01 43 26 35 07
11 AM–2:30 PM. Closed dinner, Saturday, Sunday, Bank Holidays, August.

Didier Parguel has changed tack and is now in the light lunch business. Salads and dishes of the day, as well as raspberry macarons, have us longing for the teatimes of yesteryear.

○	Very good restaurant
ⓒ○	Excellent restaurant
ⓒⓒ○	One of the best restaurants in Paris
⑤	Disappointing restaurant
🍴	Good value for money
⊜	Meals for less than 30 euros
SIM	Simple
COM	Comfortable
V.COM	Very comfortable
LUX	Luxurious
V.LUX	Very luxurious

Red indicates a particularly charming establishment

🏛	Historical significance
🅟	Promotion *(higher rating than last year)*
Ⓝ	New to the guide
●	Restaurant
▼	Shop
◆	Rendezvous

6TH ARRONDISSEMENT
SAINT-GERMAIN-DES-GOURMETS IS HERE

Once, Saint-Germain-des-Près was not a good place to eat, but now there is a wide choice of excellent restaurants, beginning with the quarters of our "Chef of the Year," the great Hélène Darroze in rue d'Assas, and including new or robust haunts, such as Ze Kitchen Galerie, Ferrandaise, 21, Comptoir du Relais, Méditerranée, Bastide Odéon and Racines. It is as if the Théâtre de l'Odéon were the center of a gourmet world, its influence radiating outward (but Cagna and Le Relais Louis XIII are just next door). There are fashionable exotic eateries too (the Indian Yugaraj, the Italian Casa Bini and the Japanese Yen and Azabu). Admittedly, we continue to casually frequent the terraces of Le Flore and Les Deux Magots, the ground floor of Brasserie Lipp or the stalls of rue de Buci, but with Armani Caffè, Le Paris and the establishments mentioned above, Saint-Germain-des-Gourmets seems to have arrived. Trattorias such as Alfredo Positano, Les Trois Canettes, Bartolo and Via Palissy form local islets of charm. There are also many highly skilled artisans: pastry and chocolate makers Constant, Hermé, Mulot and Hévin, butchers such as Bajon, bakers to rival the late lamented Poilâne and charcutiers Charles, Coesnon and Vérot, among others. The Saint-Germain quarter has become a matchless market.

RESTAURANTS

GRAND RESTAURANTS

CHEF OF THE YEAR

● **Hélène Darroze** 🅿 ⓒⓞ Ⓥ.COM
4, rue d'Assas
Métro: Sèvres-Babylone
Tel. 01 42 22 00 11. Fax 01 42 22 25 40
reservation@helenedarroze.com
www.helenedarroze.com
Closed Sunday, Monday.
Open until 10:30 PM.
Prix fixe: 68€ (lunch), 168€.
A la carte: 130–200€.
Air cond. Private dining room. Valet parking.

Yes, the day has come: Little Hélène has come of age. A onetime rookie from the provinces, her naïveté the butt of insidious jokes, a former tosser of salads in Monaco for Cousin Ducasse from Castelsarrasin, having spent years at Supdeco business school, Hélène is now her own mistress, rallying Paris society to her banner. She has published a large, successful book of sentimental recipes entitled *Personne ne me volera ce que j'ai dansé* (*No One Can Take What I Danced from Me*) and continued her ascent, earning the title "little princess of the Landes in Paris." Today, the empty weekday dining rooms that she and her father Francis once faced in Villeneuve-de-Marsan are no more. Now she choreographs the cuisine of her day, era, roots and personality in this elegant contemporary setting in red and gold, with shades of carrot, tomato and eggplant. Cry it from the rooftops: Southwest France has acquired another grand culinary temple to stand alongside Alain Dutournier's Carré des Feuillants. An embassy built on charm? There is something of that, but make no mistake: Hélène Darroze is inspired. Like a great conductor, she brilliantly leads her young, dynamic, keen kitchen and dining room staff. Anything we may taste in her restaurant is undeniably equal to the finest dishes produced by her peers. So Three

Plates for her simply poached white asparagus, served with frog's legs, the pan-fried milk-fed lamb sweetbreads with tandoori spices, the aerial and sublime citrus and ginger mousse, magnificent wild river salmon grilled on one side, served with fingerling potatoes and a smoked herring and wild sorrel foam, Landais foie gras grilled on a wood fire, and the artichoke ravioli served with a light Provençal-style jus with a touch of fermented anchovy paste. Then there are the Basque lamb saddle stuffed with chorizo and roasted with bay leaves, classic desserts such as rice pudding with muscovado sugar, tropical fruit cocktail, litchi jelly, coconut sorbet and Madong chocolate cake with lemon cream and roasted hazelnut sauce. You may have thought you had already tasted this produce unearthed in the freshest of French regions, the heart of the great Southwest, and these tried and trusted recipes elsewhere, but Hélène coaxes entirely new harmonies from them, her music touching us like a great sonata. Add the most seductive of wines presented by competent, articulate sommelier Gilles Mouligneau, a mine of information on the greater South of France and eternal Bordeaux, combined with tempting prix fixe menus and Armagnacs—aged in Hélène's father's cellar and pleading to be uncorked—and a great house is born to us. We were the first to gauge Hélène's true worth when she came to the capital. Now she looms over the Parisian culinary stage alongside all those she formerly admired. It is time to applaud her.

● **Le Relais Louis XIII** ⓒⓞ 🍴 Ⓥ.COM
8, rue des Grands-Augustins
Métro: Odéon
Tel. 01 43 26 75 96. Fax 01 44 07 07 80
contact@relaislouis13.com
www.relaislouis13.com
Closed Sunday, Monday, August.
Open until 10:30 PM.
Prix fixe: 45€ (lunch), 68€ (dinner), 89€.
A la carte: 130–150€.
Air cond. Private dining room. Valet parking.

This former post house's rich, historical decor, Louis XIII furniture, colors (predominantly red and purple) and medieval cellars impress, but it is Manuel Martinez's cuisine that holds our attention. Holder of the Meilleur Ouvrier de France award, trained at Ledoyen, the Bristol and the Crillon and chef at La Tour d'Argent, this maestro of the range proficiently interprets a reliable, flawless classical repertoire but is also at home with lighter dishes. The Breton lobster and foie gras ravioli with a porcini cream sauce, Breton langoustines in puff pastry with green asparagus and truffle juice, line-caught Dover sole with spider crab and herbed potato gnocchi, roasted Challans duck with strong spices and caramelized turnip purée or twice-cooked veal chop in red wine sauce with diced vegetables are his touchstones: academic, but far from dull. Add fine desserts, such as millefeuille filled with light vanilla cream and seasonal fruit clafoutis with ice cream, and you will realize that this is the perfect place to celebrate a birthday or other happy event in appropriate style. A great cellar of 1,500 wines tended to by the competent Emilie Cousin.

GOOD RESTAURANTS & OTHERS

● **L'Alcazar**　　　　　　　　　COM

62, rue Mazarine
Métro: Odéon
Tel. 01 53 10 19 99. Fax 01 53 10 23 23
contact@alcazar.fr
www.alcazar.fr
Open daily until 12:30 PM.
Prix fixe: 19€ (lunch, wine included), 22€ (dinner, wine included), 25€ (lunch, wine included), 29€ (lunch, wine included), 39€ (dinner). A la carte: 55€.
Air cond. Private dining room.

Attractive, good, inexpensive (if you stick to the reasonable prix fixe menus) and relaxed (if you come for Sunday brunch), Sir Terence Conran's Parisian connection, managed by Michel Besmond, is in good shape. We love the modern setting with its mezzanine, its glass ceiling and open kitchen. At the range, Guillaume Lutard still focuses on freshness: a millefeuille of tuna, avocado and mango, langoustines sautéed with coriander and the lamb

shoulder, slow-roasted with thyme, are polished preparations. The desserts—baba au rhum, a licorice and raspberry iced meringue sundae—are of a high standard and the range of wines is full of pleasant surprises, including choices from beyond the borders of France.

● **Allard**　　　　　　　　　　🏠 SIM

1, rue de l'Eperon
Métro: St-Michel, Odéon
Tel. 01 43 26 48 23. Fax 01 46 33 04 02
Closed Sunday, 3 weeks in August.
Open until 11 PM.
Prix fixe: 24€ (lunch), 32€.
A la carte: 65€.
Air cond. Private dining room.

Things have improved at the Layracs': They have taken over the neighboring Roger la Grenouille, along with this establishment. No blunders, no strokes of genius, just good, classic fare from chef Didier Remay, who remembers the distant days of Fernande Allard. Escargots in parsley butter, homemade duck foie gras, Challans duck with olives and a veal chop sautéed with wild mushrooms are honest dishes. For dessert, baba au rhum and paris-brest continue to appeal. The cellar still has its points of interest.

● **L'Arbuci**　　　　　　　　　Ⓢ SIM

25, rue de Buci
Métro: Mabillon
Tel. 01 44 32 16 00. Fax 01 44 32 16 09
arbuci@blanc.net
www.arbuci.com
Daily noon–1 AM. Cont. service.
Prix fixe: 15,50€ (lunch), 20€ (lunch), 30€ (dinner). A la carte: 35–45€.
Air cond. Terrace. Private dining room.

Not very good, to be honest. This modern local brasserie turned jazz club serves up some pretty dull chow. The banal mozzarella tagliatelle with fresh tomato, the tasteless warm goat cheese tart, jumbo shrimp with basmati rice and the (dried-out) roasted farm-raised chicken scarcely satisfy. The steak tartare is not bad, but the French fries are dry. On the other hand, the profiteroles and warm chocolate cake seem like unforgettable masterpieces in comparison.

● **Bastide Odéon** ○ COM

7, rue Corneille
Métro: Odéon
Tel. 01 43 26 03 65. Fax 01 44 07 28 93
bastide.odeon@wanadoo.fr
www.bastide-odeon.com
Closed Sunday, Monday, 3 weeks in August.
Open until 10:30 PM.
Prix fixe: 26€, 38€. A la carte: 40–50€.
Air cond. Private dining room. Valet parking.

Cheerful, friendly and flavorsome, Gilles Ajuelos's lair has an appealingly Provençal feel. This Rostang and Maximin veteran adds his own deft touch to familiar classics, teasing fresh notes from them. Since these sound dishes form part of an unpretentious set menu, they rapidly win us to their way of thinking. Macaroni with escargots and chestnut soup, Riviera-style eggplant millefeuille, roasted turbot with a creamy olive oil potato purée, gilthead sea bream served with crisp cabbage, roasted quail with risotto, a nice two-pound roasted prime rib for two are gratifying. Add to this traditional but striking desserts, such as creamy vanilla millefeuille or soft warm chocolate cake served with vanilla ice cream and first-rate Provençal wines, and you will start to think that this somber eatery with its off-white decor has a lot going for it.

● **Le Bélier** COM

Hôtel, 13, rue des Beaux-Arts
Métro: St-Germain-des-Prés
Tel. 01 44 41 99 01. Fax 01 43 25 64 81
eat@ll-hotel.com
www.l-hotel.com
Closed Sunday, Monday, 1 week Christmas–New Year's, August. Open until 10:30 PM.
Prix fixe: 50€. A la carte: 70€.
Air cond. Terrace.

A bombshell at Le Bélier: a change of management and a new chef. Regulars should not worry, though: The fine, spirited, produce-based cuisine is still very much on the agenda in this hotel redesigned by Jacques Garcia. Seated comfortably opposite the Claude-Nicolas Ledoux fountain, we delight in the crabmeat with argan oil and guacamole, roasted sea bass filet with mushrooms and almonds, rib-eye steak and macaroni gratin flavored with summer truffle and delicious spiced chocolate croustillant.

● **Le Bistrot d'Henri** SIM

16, rue Princesse
Métro: Mabillon
Tel. 01 46 33 51 12
Closed Christmas. Open until 11:30 PM.
A la carte: 32–36€.
Air cond.

David and Julien Poulat, worthy successors to their father Henri, conscientiously run this excellent *bouchon*-style restaurant. Chef Gérard Fleuri maintains the domestic tradition, but with definite Southern French leanings. The octopus salad, fresh goat cheese dressed with olive oil and tapenade, spiced red mullet with basmati rice, sea bass in a raw tomato and olive oil sauce, pepper-crusted beef tenderloin or hangar steak with shallots are down to earth. For dessert, crème brûlée or cherry clafoutis hit the mark every time.

● **Bistrot d'Opio** € SIM

9, rue Guisarde
Métro: Mabillon, St-Germain-des-Prés
Tel. 01 43 29 01 84. Fax 01 58 16 43 79
www.bistrot-opio.com
Open daily until 10:30 PM
(Saturday, Sunday to midnight).
Prix fixe: 9,90€ (lunch), 16,90€ (lunch), 21,70€ (dinner), 25,50€ (dinner).
A la carte: 37€.
Air cond.

Exquisite flavors of Provence . . . but why the succession of chefs? Alfred Fuabi has replaced Mathieu Toucas in the kitchen, producing dishes that unfailingly hit the right note. An eggplant gratin with mozzarella and pesto, sea bass filet with shredded mild chorizo, lime-flavored lamb "crumble" with slow-roasted tomato and banana mascarpone cream drench us with sun and fill us with delight.

● Au Bon Saint-Pourçain　SIM

10 bis, rue Servandoni
Métro: St-Sulpice, Mabillon
Tel. 01 43 54 93 63
Closed Sunday. Open until 10:30 PM.
Prix fixe: 25€ (lunch, wine included).
A la carte: 40€.
Terrace.

Far from the tumult of eateries in vogue, Au Bon Saint-Pourçain has its sights set on quality. Under the attentive eye of François Bonduel, Franck Pasquet continues to meticulously prepare a flood of French classics. In the dining room of this Fifties' bistro, regulars do homage to the jellied rabbit pâté, sole meunière, tarragon chicken and crème brûlée.

● Boucherie Roulière　Ⓝ SIM

24, rue des Canettes
Métro: Mabillon, St-Germain-des-Prés
Tel. 01 43 26 25 70
Closed Monday, August.
Open until 11:30 PM.
A la carte: 35–40€.
Air cond.

Not a butcher's store despite its name, but a contemporary bistro in a neat, sober setting: This is what you can expect from Jean-Luc Roulière, who owns Brasserie Fernand in rue Christine. Guests enjoy the friendly atmosphere, wooden tables and appealing new approaches to traditional dishes such as a pig's head terrine and grilled tuna steak with slow-roasted vegetables, not to mention the fine choice of meat, including a superb one-pound rib-eye steak! There are desserts to match, such as the hazelnut and caramel chocolate marquise. Cheerful service. Delicious, fresh wines.

● Bouillon des Colonies　COM

3, rue Racine
Métro: Odéon, Cluny-La Sorbonne
Tel. 01 44 32 15 64. Fax 01 44 32 15 61
Closed Christmas. Open until 11 PM.
Prix fixe: 22€. A la carte: 35€.
Air cond. Valet parking.

The decor is dedicated to Africa, with photos, fabrics and so on. Doubly supervised by proprietor Luc Morand and chef Alexandre Beltoise, the cuisine explores flavors from around the world with a degree of imagination. The Tahitian-style marinated raw tuna, with bell peppers and tomatoes slow-cooked in mild spices, seared tuna "tataki" with wild rice, lemongrass sautéed shrimp, slow-roasted cumin lamb served in a halved eggplant and Moroccan-style chicken tagine with preserved lemon are not bad. The orange and date salad with cinnamon is lightness itself.

● Bouillon Racine　🏠 COM

3, rue Racine
Métro: Odéon, Cluny-La Sorbonne
Tel. 01 44 32 15 60. Fax 01 44 32 15 61
bouillon.racine@wanadoo.fr
www.bouillonracine.com
Closed Christmas, August 15th.
Open until 11 PM.
Prix fixe: 15,50€ (lunch), 26€.
Air cond. Valet parking.

Bouillon Racine, which has acquired a little brother next door (see Bouillon des Colonies, above), has retained the art nouveau style that forms the basis of its charm, but dropped the Belgian cuisine. Luc Morand, who looks after both establishments, has entrusted the kitchen to young Alexandre Beltoise, who wields his utensils with great proficiency. We delight in the tarbais bean and smoked bacon soup, scallop carpaccio with truffle oil, pike-perch and spinach baked in phyllo pastry and stuffed suckling pig roasted on a spit served with mashed potatoes. The soft chocolate cake and velvety chestnut mousse flavored with Jack Daniels are not bad.

● Les Bouquinistes　SIM

53, quai des Grands-Augustins
Métro: St-Michel
Tel. 01 43 25 45 94. Fax 01 43 25 23 07
bouquinistes@guysavoy.com
www.lesbouquinistes.com
Closed Saturday lunch, Sunday, Christmas–New Year's. Open until 11:30 PM.
Prix fixe: 25€ (lunch), 28€ (lunch).
A la carte: 65€.
Air cond. Valet parking.

William Caussimon, an apt pupil of the master Guy Savoy, watches diligently over the dishes served in this fine riverside establishment. The green asparagus and soft-boiled egg, the crab and langoustine ravioli, turbot meunière, tuna prepared three ways, pan-seared foie gras with pink praliné crisp and finally the mango cappuccino all demonstrate the house's pleasing ability to suitably broaden its repertoire. A fine wine list and an expert welcome.

● **La Boussole**　　　　　　　 ⊜ SIM

12, rue Guisarde
Métro: Mabillon, St-Germain-des-Prés
Tel. 01 56 24 82 20. Fax 01 58 16 43 79
www.la-boussole.com
Open daily until midnight.
Prix fixe: 16,90€ (lunch), 20,30€
(Saturday, Sunday lunch), 25,40€ (dinner).
Air cond. Private dining room.

Pascal Teyssier offers a warm welcome in this local establishment devoted to the South(s). Its exposed stone and vaults are very appealing, and so is the food, which takes the form of pleasantly shrewd set menus. The eggplant turnover, vegetable spring rolls, roasted salmon with Cajun spices, fish tagine with artichokes, duck with honey and thick grilled steak in licorice sauce are brightly exotic in their conception. Those with a sweet tooth will enjoy the soft chocolate cake and the mango, litchi and kiwi tagine with coconut sorbet.

● **La Brasserie du Lutétia**　　　 COM

23, rue de Sèvres
Métro: Sèvres-Babylone
Tel. 01 49 54 46 76. Fax 01 49 54 46 00
lutetia-paris@lutetia-paris.com
www.lutetia-paris.com
Daily noon–11 PM. Cont. service.
Prix fixe: 34€, 39€, 41€. A la carte: 60€.
Air cond. Terrace.

This Saint-Germain institution is still as popular as ever. In a black-and-white decor designed by Slavik, tourists and regulars savor Philippe Renard's skilled

work as they watch the crowds pass. The black figs and goat cheese from the Loire Valley, Canadian lobster, seafood platters, beef tartare and berry-basil granita are exemplary.

● **La Cabane d'Auvergne**　　　 SIM

44, rue Grégoire-de-Tours
Métro: Odéon
Tel. 01 43 25 14 75
www.lacabane.fr
Closed Saturday lunch, Sunday, August.
Open until 11 PM.
A la carte: 35€.

Gérard Corminier's welcoming rustic cabin champions every aspect of the Auvergne. Chanturgues and Châteaugays go down pleasantly with the the ploughman's plate (a selection of assorted cured meats and pâtés), country cured ham, salmon in sorrel sauce, trout fried in butter with almonds, Auvergnat rib-eye steak, stuffed cabbage and blueberry tart.

● **Jacques Cagna**　　　　　　 ◑ V.COM

14, rue des Grands-Augustins
Métro: St-Michel, Odéon
Tel. 01 43 26 49 39. Fax 01 43 54 54 48
jacquescagna@hotmail.com
www.jacques-cagna.com
Closed Saturday lunch, Sunday, Monday lunch, Christmas, 3 weeks in August.
Open until 10:15 PM.
Prix fixe: 42€ (lunch), 95€.
A la carte: 110–130€.
Air cond. Private dining room. Valet parking.

The historic elegance, the dining room with its Flemish paintings, beams and 16th-century woodwork, Anny Logereau's welcome and a wine list rich in fine vintages: All these are the trump cards of Maison Cagna. Not to mention the lunchtime set menu at 42€, which featured omelet Curnonsky (with diced lobster and lobster bisque sauce) the other day: tremendous! In short, Jacques Cagna, who owns L'Espadon and Rôtisserie, is still hale and hearty in his Old Paris establishment. Here, tradition goes hand in hand with contemporary tastes. The pan-seared duck foie gras with caramelized fruit, roasted turbot with puréed Granny Smith apples, salt-and-rosemary-crusted veal sweetbreads, Vendée pigeon cooked with green Chartreuse (the breast meat roasted, the leg meat ground and baked in phyllo pastry with spices), and paris-brest "of my childhood" are fine work indeed.

● Caméléon ⓝ SIM

6, rue de Chevreuse
Métro: Vavin, Raspail
Tel. 01 43 27 43 27
Closed Sunday. Open until 11 PM.
A la carte: 50€.
Valet parking.

Jean-Paul Arabian, maestro of the dining room (a veteran of Restaurant in Lille, then Ledoyen and Pierre in Paris) has just acquired, renovated and relaunched this good-natured bistro, famous back in the day of Faucher senior. His ambition is simple: to turn it into a lively local haunt, dynamically combining the talents of grocery store, neighborhood bar and epicurean eatery. It is still too early to describe the changing menu. As we write these lines, the paint is still drying on the walls. Find out more in our next edition. (Also see Rendezvous.)

● Aux Charpentiers 🔒 SIM

10, rue Mabillon
Métro: Mabillon, St-Germain-des-Prés, Odéon
Tel. 01 43 26 30 05. Fax 01 46 33 07 98
auxcharpentiers@wanadoo.fr
Open daily until 11:30 PM.
Prix fixe: 19€ (lunch, wine included),
26€ (dinner). A la carte: 40–50€.
Air cond. Terrace. Private dining room.

Genial host Pierre Bardèche has turned his bistro, open seven days a week, into an oasis of conviviality. No frills, no glitter, just good, plain, simple fare. The homemade duck foie gras, eggplant caviar with fresh goat cheese, sole meunière, veal blanquette and cherry clafoutis are enchantingly straightforward.

● Le Christine SIM

1, rue Christine
Métro: Odéon
Tel. 01 40 51 71 64. Fax 01 43 26 15 63
www.restaurantlechristine.com
Closed at lunch. Open until midnight.
Prix fixe: 38€ (dinner). A la carte: 60€.
Air cond. Private dining room.

This honest, local canteen has its enthusiasts. Jovial Boris Bazan and Emilie Benoît welcome you to their convivial dining room with a smile, while Julien Trucret concocts his delights: foie gras terrine, Breton-style lobster in a tomato and brandy sauce, thyme-scented rack of lamb and red berry soufflé.

● La Closerie des Lilas 🔒 V.COM

171, bd du Montparnasse
Métro: Port-Royal, Vavin
Tel. 01 40 51 34 50. Fax 01 43 29 99 94
closerie@club-internet.fr
www.closeriedeslilas.fr
Open daily until 1 AM.
Prix fixe: 45€ (lunch, wine included).
A la carte: 60–90€.
Terrace. Private dining room. Valet parking.

Literary and artistic Parisian society continues to frequent this iconic locale, along with tourists and the curious. To music from a jazz pianist, the elegant crowd soaks up the atmosphere in the three areas that open before it: the bar, the lively brasserie and the restaurant, with its shady terrace sheltered from the street. The mosaic floor, scarlet seats and polished tables form a splendid setting. In the kitchen, Jean-Pierre Cassagne, long at Edgar, prepares his classic dishes with skill. The salmon with Belgian endive and horseradish cream, pike quenelles, beef tenderloin in marrow sauce, sautéed artichoke with smoke-scented jus, and the "supreme" orange and lime-scented chocolate mousse with saffron coulis are equal to the house's reputation. Jean-Jacques Caimant, former Robuchon maître d', watches over the dining room, and Evo Iacobozzi, our glasses.

● Le Comptoir du Relais   ○ 🛏 SIM

9, carrefour de l'Odéon
Métro: Odéon
Tel. 01 44 27 07 97. Fax 01 46 33 45 30
hotelrsg@wanadoo.fr
www.hotel-paris-relais-saint-germain.com
Open daily until 10:30 PM.
Prix fixe: 42€ (dinner weekdays).
Terrace.

An unusual restaurant? Absolutely. Yves Camdeborde's bistro, our last year's "event," can scarcely be compared with any other eatery. What you will find there by night is a chic bistro (seating 22 diners) with an impressive prix fixe menu, and at noon, a gourmet café with dazzling dishes and no reservations. At either time, you will need to wait your turn patiently to taste the "pressed" foie gras and porcini mushroom terrine served with artichoke purée, the heavenly cod brandade, a superb boned and breaded pig's foot with its wonderful potato purée, chilled wild strawberry and watermelon soup served with ewe's-milk ice cream and nougatine chunks. Fine wines from selected growers are an added bonus.

● Côté Bergamote   SIM

8, rue de Montfaucon
Métro: Mabillon
Tel. 01 43 26 50 56. Fax 01 58 16 43 79
www.bergamote.org
Open daily until 11:30 PM.
Prix fixe: 10,50€ (lunch), 14,70€ (dinner), 25,30€ (dinner).
Terrace.

The South of France in all its guises is Pascal Tayssier's thing. This is his third address. The crunchy goat cheese and cumin appetizer, artichoke heart in a tomato and olive marinade, baked sea bass with tea and aniseed, salmon with poppy seeds and the veal stew with preserved lemon are not bad. We finish with a strawberry dessert soup with basil and, of course, make short work of the Provençal wines. Good prix fixe menus at angelic prices.

● Les Editeurs   Ⓢ COM

4, carrefour de l'Odéon
Métro: Odéon
Tel. 01 43 26 67 76. Fax 01 46 34 58 30
info@lesediteurs.fr
www.lesediteurs.fr
Daily 8 AM–2 AM. Cont. service.
A la carte: 45€.
Air cond. Terrace. Private dining room.

Despite the mediocre quality of its food, this brasserie on the Odéon crossroads still attracts the busy people of Saint-Germain. Although its cozy setting is stylish in a book-filled library sort of way, sadly, the dishes do not live up to the setting. The eggplant caviar tart (tasteless), steamed salmon and vegetables (boring), homemade hamburger—(just acceptable) and a cool strawberry soup flavored with strong wine lack clarity. A pity.

● L'Epi Dupin   🍴 ⊜ SIM

11, rue Dupin
Métro: Sèvres-Babylone
Tel. 01 42 22 64 56. Fax 01 42 22 30 42
lepidupin@wanadoo.fr
Closed Saturday, Sunday, Monday lunch, August. Open until 10:30 PM.
Prix fixe: 22€ (lunch), 31€.
Terrace.

The place is noisy, packed—teeming even—but François Pasteau's cuisine doesn't disappoint. In his set menus, this François Clerc veteran (who learned his manners from the greats but has ultimately chosen modesty) continues to focus on quality, creating "modern domestic" dishes that have no shortage of ideas or taste. His caramelized endive and goat cheese tarte Tatin, langoustines with pineapple and ginger chutney, cod steak with spinach and smoked sausage, grilled skate with hazelnuts and dried fruit and tender cumin-scented pork belly with carrots and spring onions are enchanting. The warm pistachio and chocolate cake with a molten center and apples and prunes baked in phyllo pastry and served with black pepper ice cream are things of joy.

● L'Espadon Bleu   COM

25, rue des Grands-Augustins
Métro: Odéon, St-Michel
Tel. 01 46 33 00 85. Fax 01 43 54 54 48
jacquescagna@hotmail.com
www.jacquescagna.com
Closed Saturday lunch, Sunday,
Monday lunch, August.
Open until 10 PM
(Saturday, Sunday 10:30 PM).
Prix fixe: 25€, 32€. A la carte: 60€.
Air cond. Valet parking.

The blue of the sea and the two swordfish hanging from the ceiling set the tone for Jacques Cagna's marine adjunct. His nephew Julien Logereau provides a friendly welcome and watches over the service and food, while disciple Stéphane Courtin deftly prepares dishes as light and fresh as sea spray. The tuna tartare with ginger, langoustine spring rolls with soy sauce, whiting with fingerling potatoes and Dover sole meunière are a success. There is a Salers beef prime rib for inveterate carnivores and an iced caramel and walnut meringue sundae for those with a sweet tooth, including us.

● Fernand   SIM

9, rue Christine
Métro: Odéon
Tel. 01 43 25 18 55
Closed Christmas, New Year's, August.
Open until 11 PM.
A la carte: 35€.
Air cond.

Jean-Luc Roulière, who owns the butcher's shop and brasserie of the same name in rue des Canettes, runs this relaxed eatery with great verve. Guests come for the atmosphere and decor (beams, stone and garnet shades), but Guillaume Godon's cooking is not bad either. The eggplant and mozzarella casserole, truffle ravioli, grilled salmon and sautéed zucchini with basil, Provençal-style squid stew and pan-fried veal kidney in mustard sauce are very honest. The warm soufflé-like chocolate cake and creamy honey millefeuille slip down effortlessly.

A SPECIAL FAVORITE

● La Ferrandaise   ● Ⓝ SIM

8, rue de Vaugirard
Métro: Odéon, Luxembourg, Cluny-La Sorbonne
Tel. 01 43 26 36 36. Fax 01 43 26 90 91
laferrandaise@wanadoo.fr
www.laferrandaise.com
Closed Sunday, Christmas, May 1st, August.
Open until 10:30 PM
(Friday, Saturday 11:30 PM).
Prix fixe: 30€. A la carte: 35€.
Air cond. Private dining room.

This area is becoming extraordinarily gastronomic. It is home to Les Racines, Le Comptoir du Relais, La Bastide Odéon, La Méditerranée . . . and now La Ferrandaise. Local publishers (Jean-Claude Gawsewitch the first among them) and chic literati have noted the address. The quiet one of the group, Gilles Lamiot (who owns La Taverne de Nesle), has brought in a young team trained by his celebrated neighbor Manuel Martinez at Le Relais Louis XIII. A dynamic young waiter and chef Nicolas Duquénoy lend a touch of youth to this rather medieval haunt, with its beams from wall to ceiling and exposed stone. The 30€ prix fixe menu is quite a find. The egg and mushrooms baked in a ramekin, layered terrine of beef shin and foie gras, shellfish cream soup, Breton cod and mashed potatoes with andouille, roasted veal with mashed old-fashioned vegetables, farm-raised pork chop in a mustard and gherkin sauce are lively, flavorsome and full of oomph. The charming, thirst-quenching wines do not hike up the tab. The desserts—rum-flavored pineapple gratin, almond cream with dried fruit and nuts—hit the right note.

● Fish la Boissonnerie   SIM

69, rue de Seine
Métro: Mabillon, Odéon
Tel. 01 43 54 34 69. Fax 01 43 54 33 47
laboissonnerie@wanadoo.fr
Closed Monday, 1 week at Christmas,
1 week in August. Open until 10:45 PM.
Prix fixe: 10,50€ (lunch), 21,50€ (lunch),
28,50€, 32,50€.
Air cond.

With its large bay window in the form of an archway surrounded by green ceramic tiles, this former fishmonger's turned into a "drinkmonger's" by two Anglo-Saxon pranksters is so attractive it makes you want to hurry inside at once. You will be pleased you did. The wine list is spectacular and extremely well composed, especially with whites, rosés and reds of excellent character from Southeast France. As for the food, the inventive, talented Mathew Ong whips up little Mediterranean dishes that delight the regulars, preparing fish and pasta as expertly as he handles the fragrances of Provence. The menu changes every month, and to top it all, the prices are as friendly as the staff.

● Le Foyer "chez Castel"   SIM

15, rue Princesse
Métro: Mabillon
Tel. 01 40 51 52 80. Fax 01 40 51 72 74
castel.club@wanadoo.fr
Closed at lunch, Monday, August.
Open until 1 AM.
A la carte: 45–55€.
Air cond. Private dining room. Valet parking.

As in the days of Jean Castel, Xavier Legrand welcomes the personalities who have made this select club their refectory. On the agenda are the uncomplicated dishes that Claude Morin has been preparing for more than thirty years. You will need to pass inspection to gain entry and taste the mushrooms in vinaigrette, roasted salmon, sea bass roasted skin side down, house hamburger, grilled hanger steak with shallots, chocolate mousse and fruit tart. Not so snobbish after all.

● Au Gourmand   SIM

22, rue de Vaugirard
Métro: Odéon
Tel.-Fax 01 43 26 26 45
augourmand@wanadoo.fr
Closed Sunday, 1 week in mid-August.
Open until 11 PM.
Prix fixe: 16€ (lunch, wine included),
22€ (lunch), 28€ (dinner), 34€ (dinner).
Air cond.

Norbert Grissault, who runs Le Pétula in rue des Ciseaux, has taken over this contemporary restaurant with its red and yellow decor, which is still as warm and intimate as ever, but more relaxed. The food is quite deft, although the same style has been adopted and improvised on elsewhere. At least the duo of foie gras with onion chutney, seared tuna with basmati rice, sea bass with Mediterranean vegetable casserole, rosemary-seasoned lamb parmentier and grilled strip steak served with thick-cut homemade fries, avoid unnecessary complexity. Extra charges of 2€ or 3€ pad out the check a little, depending on the set menu. The raspberry macaron served with warm fudge sauce meets with general acclaim.

● La Grille Saint-Germain   SIM

14, rue Mabillon
Métro: St-Germain-des-Prés, Mabillon, Odéon
Tel. 01 43 54 16 87. Fax 01 43 54 52 88
Closed Christmas.
Noon–12:30 AM. Cont. service.
Prix fixe: 18€ (weekday lunch, wine
included). A la carte: 33–45€.
Air cond. Terrace. Valet parking.

Pleasant, authentic and traditional, but by no means set in its ways, this Saint-Germain-des-Prés bistro makes no attempt to impress. Customers come for the atmosphere, the Harcourt studio photos and the well-maintained Fifties' flavor, which applies to the food as well. Faithful chef Jean-Claude Poulnais watches over the Mère Brazier's terrine*, seafood blanquette, grilled prime rib of beef with béarnaise sauce or calf's head, a house specialty. The bistro is open every day, closes late and purveys its

Good Restaurants & Others 6TH ARR

pleasures at an honest price. We have no complaints about the traditional desserts: caramel pain perdu with fromage blanc ice cream and fresh fruit fondue in warm chocolate sauce. So . . .

* La mère Brazier, from Lyon, was a famous post-war female chef.

● **Joséphine** 🏠 SIM
117, rue du Cherche-Midi
Métro: Duroc, Falguière
Tel. 01 45 48 52 40. Fax 01 42 84 06 83
Closed Saturday, Sunday.
Open until 10:30 PM.
A la carte: 50–75€.
Terrace.

Frequented by the press, with *Le Point* magazine's epicurean journalists in the forefront, this bistro (which once had its moment of glory) still boasts the same 1880s' *bouchon*-style brasserie decor with a patina of age. Not content to simply manage his legacy, Jean-Christophe Dumonet has changed the approach that his father Jean once made fashionable. Fresh duck foie gras, crisp jumbo shrimp cakes with bisque vinaigrette, marinated salmon with potato purée, pigeon millefeuille with slow-roasted legs are not bad. A classic homemade millefeuille for two is light and airy, and the selection of great Bordeaux wines will turn your head.

● **Lapérouse** 🏠 LUX
51, quai des Grands-Augustins
Métro: St-Michel
Tel. 01 43 26 68 04. Fax 01 43 26 99 39
restaurantlaperouse@wanadoo.fr
Closed Saturday lunch, Sunday, August.
Open until 10:30 PM.
Prix fixe: 30€ (lunch, wine included),
45€ (lunch, wine included), 95€ (dinner),
120€ (dinner). A la carte: 110–140€.
Air cond. Terrace. Private dining room.
Valet parking.

To believe in Lapérouse or not, that is the question. This riverside establishment has been welcoming guests since 1766. The new management team, Dominique Romano and Judith Cohen, seem to have their eye on the future, and chef Alain Hac-

quard has a sure touch. The roasted langoustines with watercress and sea-urchin sauce, the sea bass, slow-roasted skin side down served with shellfish jus and leeks stewed with bacon as well as the smoked beef tenderloin served with a truffle and Madeira sauce, served with hand-beaten potato and old-fashioned vegetable purée, are his tours de force. The desserts—lime soufflé, thyme ice cream, and creamy warm chocolate pudding with chicory ice cream—are of good character and the cellar still shows flashes of its former glory.

● **Brasserie Lipp** 🏠 SIM
151, bd Saint-Germain
Métro: St-Germain-des-Prés
Tel. 01 45 48 53 91. Fax 01 45 44 33 20
lipp@magic.fr
www.brasserie-lipp.fr
Closed Christmas.
Noon–1 AM. Cont. service.
A la carte: 55–60€.
Air cond. Terrace.

Of course, this is no longer the great Cazès's brasserie, but dinner can still be an enjoyable experience opposite the Fargue ceramics, on faux leather seats, rubbing shoulders with personalities such as actors Anouck Aimée, Pierre Arditi and Philippe Noiret, writer Jean Dutourd or the Count of Paris (all seated in the same small area—though not at the same table—on the evening we were there, a Sunday). The enduring house classics live up to our expectations. We never tire of the cold sliced sausage in creamy vinaigrette sauce, Bismarck herring, sole meunière, stuffed pig's feet, baba au rhum and iced coffee parfait.

● **Le Mâchon d'Henri** ● SIM
8, rue Guisarde
Métro: Mabillon
Tel. 01 43 29 08 70
Open daily until 11:30 PM.
A la carte: 30€.

At both Le Bistrot and Le Mâchon, the Poulat dynasty, formerly of a Lyonnaise persuasion, is turning South. The goat cheese in olive oil, arugula and mushroom salad, smoked haddock brandade with green salad, 7-hour lamb tagine with prunes and calf's liver with onion compote are the picture of health. The grandmother-style fruit compote summons up childhood memories.

● **La Maison du Jardin**   SIM
27, rue de Vaugirard
Métro: Rennes, St-Placide
Tel.-Fax 01 45 48 22 31
Closed Saturday lunch, Sunday,
Christmas–New Year's, 3 weeks in August.
Open until 10 PM.
Prix fixe: 22,50€ (wine included),
24€, 29€.
Air cond. Private dining room.

Sadly, despite the name, the fine dining room entirely refurbished in ochre and orange shades boasts no garden, only the Jardin du Luxembourg nearby. In any case, the goat cheese ravioli in pesto sauce, the monkfish baked with bacon, the lamb pastilla (ground and baked in phyllo pastry) with lemon thyme and the iced strawberry macaron, reliably prepared by Philippe Marquis, provide easy comfort.

● **La Maison de la Lozère**   SIM
4, rue Hautefeuille
Métro: St-Michel
Tel. 01 43 54 26 64. Fax 01 43 54 55 66
contact@lozere-a-paris.com
www.lozere-a-paris.com
Closed Sunday, Monday, 1 week Christmas–
New Year's, mid-July–mid-August.
Open until 10 PM.
Prix fixe: 15€ (lunch, wine included), 21€.
A la carte: 35€.
Air cond.

Not gastronomic, the Lozère region, you say? Well just drop into this paneled bistro a step away from place Saint-Michel. There, Patrick Bioulac whips up delicious small plates based on products imported from the mountains of Aubrac and Causses. The charcuterie platter, juniper-scented pâté from the Causses region, salmon trout in chive sauce and rack of lamb from the Gévaudan region, roasted with whole garlic cloves, are generosity it-

self. Then you will need a Languedoc wine to accompany them, without forgetting the essential apples caramelized in chestnut honey, baked in phyllo pastry and served with sheep's milk ricotta.

● **Chez Maître Paul**   COM
12, rue Monsieur-le-Prince
Métro: Odéon
Tel. 01 43 54 74 59. Fax 01 43 54 43 74
chezmaitrepaul@aol.com
www.chezmaitrepaul.com
Closed Sunday, Monday (July–August).
Open until 10:30 PM.
Prix fixe: 22€ (lunch), 29€,
35€ (wine included). A la carte: 50–65€.
Air cond. Private dining room.

Jean-François Debert vigorously champions the gastronomic traditions of Franche Comté, as practiced by chef Alain Floriot. In a cozy setting, enjoy warm smoked Monbéliard sausage and potato salad, slices of smoked dried beef on lentil salad, chicken braised in yellow wine with morel mushrooms and pan-fried calf's liver deglazed with sweet wine. To conclude, remember the walnut cake and the crunchy caramelized apple dessert served with cinnamon ice cream. The wine list pays special tribute to Arbois, Pupillin and Château-Chalon.

● **Chez Marcel**   SIM
7, rue Stanislas
Métro: Notre-Dame-des-Champs
Tel. 01 45 48 29 94
Closed Saturday, Sunday, Bank Holidays,
August. Open until 10 PM.
Prix fixe: 16€ (lunch). A la carte: 35–40€.
Terrace. Private dining room.

A true bistro in the Parisian or Lyonnaise style, with its Fifties' decor, timeless atmosphere and delightfully dated cuisine, Jean-Bernard Daumail's eatery is the picture of health. Forgetting their calorie count, guests savor the sliced Lyon sausage with warm potato salad, crackling pig's ear, pike quenelle in crayfish sauce, skate in roquefort cheese sauce, coq au vin (a rare dish) and Lyonnaise-style andouillette. Not necessarily the lightest of food but generous to a fault. To add the final touch, the homemade chocolate tart will bring a tear of devotion to your eye.

● La Marlotte `SIM`

55, rue du Cherche-Midi
Métro: Rennes, St-Placide, Sèvres-Babylone
Tel. 01 45 48 86 79. Fax 01 45 44 34 80
info@lamarlotte.com
www.lamarlotte.com
Closed Sunday, Bank Holidays, 3 weeks in August. Open until 10:45 PM.
Prix fixe: 21,50€ (lunch, wine included).
A la carte: 36–45€.
Air cond. Terrace. Private dining room.

Country style, Eric Roset's rustic restaurant is appealing in its straightforwardness, old-style dishes and wines that go down delightfully. Admittedly, it is not a particularly trendy establishment, but the regulars could not care less as they set about the lentil salad with shallots, duck foie gras terrine, roasted codfish steak with pesto, pan-fried calf's liver with honey, boudin with applesauce, floating island and chocolate tart.

● La Méditerranée `○` `🎫` `V.COM`

2, pl de l'Odéon
Métro: Odéon
Tel. 01 43 26 02 30. Fax 01 43 26 18 44
la.mediterranee@wanadoo.fr
www.la-mediterranee.com
Closed Christmas–New Year's.
Open until 11 PM.
Prix fixe: 27€, 32€. A la carte: 70–80€.
Air cond. Terrace. Private dining room.
Valet parking.

Things have changed in this fine seafood restaurant opposite the Théâtre de l'Odéon since Geneviève Jabouille turned the kitchen over to Denis Rippa. This veteran of Le Divellec, L'Ambroisie and Taillevent delicately crafts quality produce and adds a very down to earth, personal touch to his dishes, with such success that the food in this Fifties' setting with its Cocteau carpet and drawings by Bérard and Vertès has never been so refined. Red tuna tartare with olive oil, sea bass carpaccio with wholegrain mustard, Mediter-

ranean bouillabaisse, gilthead sea bream glazed with ginger and served with polenta are of excellent quality, although carnivores may prefer the Lozerian lamb chop served with fennel or pan-roasted beef tenderloin served with olive-oil French fries. Turning to the desserts, the shortbread pecan pie served with passion fruit sorbet or, finally, a tangy apple marmalade with Bourbon vanilla crème brûlée make a first-rate impression.

● Le Midi-Vins `SIM`

83, rue du Cherche-Midi
Métro: St-Placide, Vaneau
Tel. 01 45 48 33 71.
Closed Sunday, Monday.
Open until 10:30 PM.
Prix fixe: 13€ (lunch), 18€ (lunch), 21€.
A la carte: 35€.
Terrace.

Christelle Marie presides over the dining room and kitchen in this flowery bistro where you choose your dishes from the blackboard. Fine wines accompany the generous but light domestic cuisine. The fish and bell pepper terrine, crayfish salad dressed in chive cream, grilled perch filet with slow-roasted shallots, sea bass in beurre blanc sauce, grilled andouillette in mustard sauce and grilled lamb steak with garlic confit make no waves. In conclusion, you will find the pear flan or the strawberry and raspberry duo, served with berry coulis, irresistible.

● Le Parc aux Cerfs `🎫` `SIM`

50, rue Vavin
Métro: Vavin
Tel. 01 43 54 87 83. Fax 01 43 26 42 86
Closed August. Open until 11:15 PM.
Prix fixe: 23,50€ (lunch), 29€ (lunch),
30€ (dinner), 35€ (dinner). A la carte: 38€.
Air cond. Terrace.

The lighthearted Paul Hayat runs this genuine Thirties' bistro, whose warm, cozy nature is still intact. Chef Eddy Grillon's cuisine plays lucidly on the flavors of the South of France. We have no complaints about the cabbage and shrimp salad, Serrano ham with green lentils and poached egg, sea bass roasted in olive oil or tuna with capers and arugula. The walnut-crusted veal is not bad and the cool mango and raspberry dessert provides a very digestible finale.

● Le Paris ⊙ V.COM

45, bd Raspail
Métro: Sèvres-Babylone
Tel. 01 49 54 46 90. Fax 01 49 54 46 00
lutetia-paris@lutetia-paris.com
www.lutetia-paris. com
Closed Saturday, Sunday, Bank Holidays, August. Open until 10 PM.
Prix fixe: 50€ (lunch, wine included), 70€, 130€. A la carte: 100–150€.
Air cond. Valet parking.

The decor by Slavik, which echoes one of the dining rooms of ocean liner *Normandie*, is still impressive. The service is elegant and the prix fixe menus tempting. Philippe Renard (who also looks after the house brasserie) has been here for more than a decade, but cannot be accused of resting on his laurels. The proof is in the eating: the morel mushrooms and white asparagus dressed in chervil and hazelnut vinaigrette, the duck foie gras with baby leeks and a mango, lemon and red onion salsa, mark a change in the house style. The line-caught sea bass with barberries, snow peas and seaweed, and roasted "blonde d'Aquitaine" veal chop served with chanterelle mushrooms, apricots and chervil have a charming peasant appeal. The Basque Axuria lamb is a fine cut of meat and, for dessert, the whole roasted Victoria pineapple served with a white rum and tropical fruit granita is a paragon of its genre. The wine list is very Bordeaux oriented and its prices rather forbidding.

● Pères & Filles SIM

81, rue de Seine
Métro: Odéon
Tel. 01 43 25 00 28. Fax 01 43 25 00 67
Closed Christmas Eve, Christmas, New Year's Eve, New Year's. Open until 11 PM.
Prix fixe: 14€ (lunch). A la carte: 50€.
Terrace.

Virtually new, but designed traditionally, as in the old days, this amusing bistro dreamt up by the team from the Plage Parisienne is generally acclaimed. The Royans ravioli, codfish in coconut milk, veal blanquette à l'orange and pineapple crumble are just the thing. The neo-1900 eatery decor, including zinc counter, sideboard and library nooks, has its charm.

● La Petite Cour COM

8, rue Mabillon
Métro: Mabillon
Tel. 01 43 26 52 26. Fax 01 44 07 11 53
la.petite.cour@wanadoo.fr
www.la-petitecour.com
Closed Saturday lunch. Open until 11 PM.
Prix fixe: 26€ (lunch), 37€ (dinner).
A la carte: 60€.
Air cond. Terrace. Private dining room.

Jean-François Larpin is firmly on course in this rustic, gourmet courtyard adjoining a Napoleon III dining room refurbished in yellow and red. On fine days, patrons enjoy subtle, well-orchestrated dishes in its shade. Emmanuel Gomez cooks skillfully with an eye to current trends: the foie gras beignet with Port wine caramel and half-cooked tuna slices with sesame seeds, truffle-flavored monkfish medallions with paprika and pan-fried calf's liver with green vegetables are mannered, but not excessively so. In conclusion, do not miss the exquisite, subtle caramelized pineapple in phyllo pastry with mascarpone, which is lightness itself.

● Le Petit Lutétia 🛉 SIM

107, rue de Sèvres
Métro: Vaneau
Tel. 01 45 48 33 53. Fax 01 45 48 74 59
Closed Christmas. Open until 11 PM.
Prix fixe: 30€. A la carte: 40–50€.
Terrace.

This pleasant 1900s' *bouillon*-style brasserie still has all the charm of its era, with frescos, moldings, mirrors and brass fittings. Raymond Poignant's cuisine is in much the same vein, prepared with seasonal produce that adds a fresh touch to the restaurant's natural classicism. The broiled stuffed mussels, homemade foie gras, roasted sea bream, steak tartare and duck confit are unpretentious. The crème brûlée is cleverly crafted and rice pudding with orange zest and raisins a neatly done, grandmotherly dessert.

● Le Petit Saint-Benoît   ◉ 🏠 SIM

4, rue Saint-Benoît
Métro: St-Germain-des-Prés
Tel. 01 42 60 27 92
Closed Sunday, August. Open until 10:30 PM.
A la carte: 25€.
Terrace.

Despite the constant succession of chefs, this traditional, vintage 1901 bistro is still a model of the genre. After Alain Doviller, it is now Michel Voisin's turn to present his take on its rustic, generous domestic cuisine, in the form of boiled leeks in vinaigrette, fish baked in parchment paper, grilled hanger steak and dark chocolate fondant. To cap it all, the prices remain manageable.

● Le Petit Verdot   SIM

75, rue du Cherche-Midi
Métro: St-Placide, Sèvres-Babylone
Tel.-Fax 01 42 22 38 27
idee@lepetitverdot.com
www.le-petit-verdot.com
Closed Sunday, Monday, 2 weeks in February,
2 weeks in August. Open until 11 PM.
Prix fixe: 20€ (lunch), 30€ (dinner).
A la carte: 60€.
Private dining room.

Hide Ishizuka, late of Hiramatsu, has turned this charming bistro with its beams and zinc counter into a gourmet haunt. The head cheese, pan-seared foie gras with caramel, pan-fried langoustine tails served with cauliflower cream would not disgrace the most opulent of establishments. Although the a la carte prices tend to soar, the prix fixe menus are to be applauded. Monkfish steak in tomato and brandy sauce, oxtail sausage braised in wine and Challans chicken with morel mushrooms are duly flavorsome. To conclude the meal, we enjoy the soft chocolate cake and fruit tiramisu. The wine list

reflects Hide's background: He was the expert sommelier at Château Cordeillan Bages.

● Le Petit Zinc   COM

11, rue Saint-Benoît
Métro: St-Germain-des-Prés
Tel. 01 42 86 61 00. Fax 01 42 86 61 09
www.petitzinc.com
Open daily until midnight.
Prix fixe: 23,50€ (lunch), 29€ (lunch),
35€ (dinner). A la carte: 45€.
Air cond. Terrace.

This umpteenth Blanc brothers offshoot is in perfect health. The art nouveau decor by Jean Bouquin has as many admirers as ever. In the kitchen, Nicolas Pedriset has replaced Jérôme Léoty, but the spirit of the place remains unchanged. The Norwegian salmon carpaccio, sea bass baked in a salt crust, calf's liver fried in butter and warm Grand Marnier soufflé are gentle reworkings of domestic standards.

● Polidor   ◉ 🏠 SIM

41, rue Monsieur-le-Prince
Métro: Odéon
Tel. 01 43 26 95 34. Fax 01 43 26 22 79
mailletpolidor.com@wanadoo.fr
Open daily until 12:30 AM.
Prix fixe: 12€ (lunch), 20€.
A la carte: 25–30€.
Air cond.

No revolution at Polidor, which has been serving domestic classics near the Luxembourg gardens since 1845 (veal blanquette, beef bourguignon, tarte Tatin). Writer and critic Paul Léautaud was fond of this place, which still has its old fashioned flavor. Cream of lentil soup with foie gras, guineafowl stewed with cabbage and chocolate mousse are among the essential dishes of this Lyon *bouchon*–style restaurant prized by students.

● Le Procope ⓈⓃ COM

13, rue de l'Ancienne-Comédie
Métro: Odéon
Tel. 01 40 46 79 00. Fax 01 40 46 79 09
procope@blanc.net
www.procope.com
Open daily until midnight
(1 AM Thursday, Friday, Saturday).
Prix fixe: 19€, 24€, 30€. A la carte: 55€.
Air cond. Private dining room.

Historic, but nothing to write home about, this eatery once frequented by Voltaire mistakenly imagines itself to be a gastronomic haven. An oil-soaked Sicilian vegetable caponata, a refrigerator-cold duck foie gras with toasted panettone and dried-out salmon steak in beurre blanc sauce are hardly the stuff that dreams are made of. However, the pepper-crusted beef tenderloin and brown sugar crème brûlée are edible.

● Les Racines SIM

22, rue Monsieur-le-Prince (at rue Racine)
Métro: Odéon, Luxembourg
Tel. 01 43 26 03 86. Fax 01 46 34 58 33
Closed Sunday. Open until 10 PM.
A la carte: 35€.

This corner café converted into a traditional-style bistro by Jean-François Debert of Maître Paul is a delightful spot with enduring appeal. We like its easygoing ambience, checked tablecloths, prewar café atmosphere and perfectly maintained taste for home cooking. Among the dishes featured on the blackboard, the slow-roasted rabbit terrine, tuna steak with fork-mashed potatoes, authentic calf's head in gribiche sauce and veal hanger steak in blue cheese sauce hit the mark. The chocolate marquise is memorable and prunes stewed in red wine, served with Berthillon vanilla ice cream, delicious. The Loire wines provide a natural accompaniment without hiking up the tab.

● Roger la Grenouille Ⓝ SIM

26, rue des Grands-Augustins
Métro: Odéon
Tel. 01 56 24 24 34
Closed Sunday. Open until 11 PM.
Prix fixe: 24€ (lunch), 32€ (lunch).
A la carte: 65€.

The Layracs, father and son, already manage Allard just a step away. Demonstrating their love of Saint-Germain institutions, they have recently taken over this charming old bistro with its many memories. The ghost of good old Roger, who as a child was a ward of the State and used to feed the local poor with his nourishing leftovers, lingers in the two dining rooms: the first, simpler and more relaxed in front by the street; the other, hung with red velvet and more suitable for dining tête-à-tête. Here, the Layracs serve uncomplicated classics: Provençal-style frog's legs with garlic and parsley, beautiful seasonal asparagus, slow-roasted lamb shoulder, grilled rib-eye steak with béarnaise sauce, tarte Tatin and profiteroles. The check makes no concessions, but there are some fine wines (such as the Château Patache d'Aux) that are quite reasonably priced.

● La Rôtisserie d'en Face SIM

2, rue Christine
Métro: Odéon, St-Michel
Tel. 01 43 26 40 98. Fax 01 43 54 22 71
rotisface@aol.com
www.jacques-cagna.com
Closed Saturday lunch, Sunday.
Open until 11 PM.
Prix fixe: 25€ (lunch), 28€ (lunch),
42€ (dinner). A la carte: 50€.
Air cond. Private dining room. Valet parking.

A Jacques Cagna offshoot close to its parent establishment, this grillroom, with its Provençal bistro air, appeals to us. The charming welcome, conscientious service and relaxed atmosphere will put you at your ease. As for the food, the house-smoked salmon, grilled squid brochette, spit-roasted farm-raised chicken and the iced walnut and caramel vacherin are accompanied by pleasant wines, all at a reasonable price.

● **La Rotonde Montparnasse** `COM`

105, bd du Montparnasse
Métro: Vavin
Tel. 01 43 26 68 84 / 01 43 26 48 26. Fax
01 46 34 52 40
www.rotondemontparnasse.com
Daily noon–1 AM. Cont. service.
Prix fixe: 15€ (weekdays, wine included),
35€, 43€ (wine included). A la carte: 55€.
Air cond. Terrace. Private dining room.

This monumental brasserie at the corner of
Raspail and Montparnasse has been rejuvenated under the aegis of the young
Tafanel brothers. The paneled decor in
black, red and gold, the all-day service and
the very reasonable set menu all argue in its
favor. We were there on May 1st with literati
Robert Sabatier and Bernard Frank and enjoyed some very fine oysters, nicely aged
Salers beef rib-eye steak, Auvergne cheeses,
including a marvellous cantal, and a genuine baba au rhum. Add a Cadet de Lar-
mande and Roques plum brandy from
Souillac and it will dawn on you that there
is a splendid time to be had at La Rotonde.

● **Claude Saintlouis** `SIM`

27, rue du Dragon
Métro: St-Sulpice, St-Germain-des-Prés
Tel.-Fax 01 45 48 29 68
Closed Sunday, Monday, Christmas–New
Year's, August. Open until midnight.
Prix fixe: 18,50€ (lunch, wine included),
29€. A la carte: 40–50€.
Air cond.

Pleasant, discreet and timeless, this Saint-
Germain bistro just keeps going, its soul
living on thanks to Daniel Vermot, who
has left the founder's name over the door.
Forty years already! The homemade pork
terrine, a tartare of tomato, sea bream or
salmon, a grilled top rump steak, a beautiful roasted prime rib for two and
authentic traditional millefeuille all do
you a world of good.

● **Le Salon** `SIM`

4, rue d'Assas
Métro: Sèvres-Babylone
Tel. 01 42 22 00 11. Fax 01 42 22 25 40
reservation@helenedarroze.com
www.relaischateaux.com
www.helenedarroze.com
Closed Sunday, Monday, August.
Open until 10:30 PM.
Prix fixe: 31,50€ (lunch), 41,50€ (lunch,
wine included), 83€ (dinner).
A la carte: 45–65€.
Air cond. Private dining room. Valet parking.

Hélène Darroze has turned her first floor
into a gourmet society salon, a splendid
place for those who love elegant, boudoir-
style tapas. The foie gras crème brûlée
with a green apple sorbet and peanut
cappuccino, caramelized foie gras tidbits,
grilled tuna belly, langoustines roasted
with tandoori spices, Axuria lamb organ
meat grilled on skewers and grilled baby
chops from the same variety of lamb
served with puréed artichoke are all extremely well prepared. The baba soaked
in Mr. Darroze's Armagnac is in the same
vein as on the second floor. Fine wines
from the South of France are available by
the glass . . . but watch out for the prices!

● **Aux Saveurs de Claude** `SIM`

12, rue Stanislas
Métro: Notre-Dame-des-Champs, Vavin
Tel. 01 45 44 41 74. Fax 01 45 44 41 95
claudelamin@hotmail.com
www.ausaveurdeclaude.fr
Closed Sunday, Monday, 1 week at Easter,
2 weeks in August. Open until 11:30 PM.
Prix fixe: 30€. A la carte: 40–50€.
Terrace. Private dining room.

Having trained with Guy Savoy at Cap Vernet and Bistrot de l'Etoile, Claude Lamin
has found himself a good, contemporary-
style family bistro, with fine produce, precise cooking, clear-cut ideas and not too
much fuss. The set menu is striking and the
crayfish and leeks in puff pastry (made to
order), asparagus, quail eggs and arugula
salad, pan-fried scorpion fish with shredded cucumber and blackened spice-
crusted tuna steak served with cauliflower

fricassée are honest work. A fine Norman beef rib-eye steak with mashed potatoes and strawberry-balsamic vinegar clafoutis, served with olive oil ice cream provide a superb conclusion.

● Sensing   N COM

19, rue Bréa
Métro: Vavin
Tel. 01 43 27 08 80. Fax 01 43 27 03 76.
Closed Sunday. Open until 11 PM.
A la carte: 65€.
Air cond. Private dining room.

One of the events of fall 2006 was Guy Martin's acquisition of Dominique, once a historic Russian restaurant, now an eatery devoted to the five senses. Designed with elegance, skill and a rather glamorous chic by Jérôme Fayans-Dumas, it has plenty of verve. A former Lasserre lieutenant who worked with Guy Martin at the Véfour, Rémy Van Péthegem has devised a menu full of surprises. The mackerel and fennel tart, herb-crusted veal and mushroom-stuffed pasta, lemon zest shortbread topped with grapefruit segments and grapefruit sorbet are promising, but as we go to press, it is still too soon to say more.

● Sud-Ouest et Compagnie   SIM

39, bd du Montparnasse
Métro: Montparnasse-Bienvenüe
Tel. 01 42 84 35 35. Fax 01 42 84 26 27
www.sudouestetcie.fr
Open daily until 11 PM.
Prix fixe: 34€.
Air cond. Terrace.

No unwelcome surprises at Gérard Constiaux's restaurant: The name says all you need to know about his fare. Duck foie gras, roasted salmon, cassoulet, duck confit and apple pie made with phyllo provide a worthy celebration of Southwest France.

● La Table du Périgord   COM

13, rue de Mézières
Métro: St-Sulpice
Tel. 01 45 48 30 38. Fax 01 45 44 36 23
Closed Sunday, Monday, August.
Open until 10 PM.
Prix fixe: 13€ (lunch), 21€ (lunch), 24€ (lunch), 23€ (dinner), 28€ (children, dinner), 45€ (dinner). A la carte: 50€.
Terrace.

Jean-François Le Guillou's Périgord is not only reflected in the stones and beams of the decor. The cuisine is in the same vein, redolent of the region and its traditions. The assortment of three foie gras, roasted sea bass, cassoulet with duck confit, veal sweetbreads with morel mushrooms, prunes stewed with aged plum brandy served with vanilla ice cream and pear croustade are washed down with the Cahors, Bergerac and Madiran wines that form the basics here.

● Le Timbre   SIM

3, rue Sainte-Beuve
Métro: Notre-Dame-des-Champs, Vavin
Tel. 01 45 49 10 40. Fax 01 45 78 20 35
Closed Sunday, Monday lunch, 3 weeks in August. Open until 10:30 PM.
Prix fixe: 22€ (lunch), 26€ (lunch).
A la carte: 36€.

Twenty-four places and no more in this highly appealing "postage stamp" near the Luxembourg Gardens. British he may be, but boss Chris Wright (formerly at Le Bouchon de la Grille) whips up dishes in a wholly French domestic tradition. Smoked duck breast salad with citrus vinaigrette, trout filet with fresh fava beans and country ham, sage-breaded lamb kidneys served with snow peas and millefeuille are all faultless. Try the British cheeseboard accompanied by a glass of Port: a neat, unobtrusive tribute to the land of Shakespeare.

● La Tourelle ⓔ SIM

5, rue Hautefeuille
Métro: St-Michel, Odéon
Tel. 01 46 33 12 47
Closed Saturday lunch, Sunday, Christmas–
New Year's, August. Open until 10:30 PM.
Prix fixe: 11€ (lunch, wine included),
18€ (dinner). A la carte: 30€.
Air cond.

Inexpensive, congenial and authentic, Robert Collard's first-rate fare served in his traditional establishment offers excellent value. Without breaking the bank, you can enjoy Basque fish pudding, chicken liver pâté, skate in caper sauce, smoked haddock fried in butter, duck stew, Oriental style lamb brochette, pear clafoutis and the chocolate "sublime" that very nearly is.

● Vagenende 🛉 COM

142, bd Saint-Germain
Métro: Odéon
Tel. 01 43 26 68 18. Fax 01 40 51 73 38
www.vagenende.fr
Closed 3 weeks in August. Open until 1 AM.
Prix fixe: 19€ (lunch), 23€. A la carte: 55€.
Air cond. Terrace.

The setting has the edge on the food. The authentic 1900s' decor, all woodwork and mirrors, really does make the visit worthwhile. Still, there are very few grounds for complaint with the onion soup au gratin, chicken liver pâté with Armagnac, roasted pike-perch on shredded endive, a thick veal chop in its own juice served with macaroni casserole and a traditional grandmother-style rice pudding. Decent prix fixe menus.

● Le 21 Ⓝ ○ SIM

21, rue Mazarine
Métro: Odéon
Tel. 01 46 33 76 90
Closed Sunday, Monday, August.
Open until 11:30 PM.
A la carte: 55€.
Air cond.

Loved or hated, Paul Minchelli springs from his ashes like the phoenix. One virtue cannot be denied him: He certainly knows his fish. Under his guidance, handkerchief-

sized restaurant La Cafetière has become a "club" for a select few. Here, this highly talented "non chef," who achieved great success at the Duc and wrote a cult volume on the subject with his brother Jean (his rule is to cook food as little as possible), serves up a simple seafood cuisine of exceptional quality: marinated mackerel with capers, red mullet poached in olive oil, grilled sardines with sweet potatoes, steamed sea bass with zucchini and chopped fresh tomatoes all have an easy charm. Add a very good baba au rhum, an excellent Floria coffee from Richard and a Prieur-Brunet Meursault red (37€), lending a celebratory air to this marine banquet. An obstacle to be ignored, if not forgotten, is the slow service, which favors friends of the clan only. The second floor will soon be opening as a smoking area, even more private than the first.

● Wadja 🚪 🛉 SIM

10, rue de la Grande-Chaumière
Métro: Vavin
Tel.-Fax 01 46 33 02 02
Closed Sunday, week of August 15th.
Open until 11 PM.
Prix fixe: 11€ (lunch), 14€ (dinner).
A la carte: 40–50€.

Thierry Coué, a chef with Senderens in the days of his former restaurant L'Archestrate (Alain Passard, Dominique Le Stanc and Michel Husser worked under him), has been brought in to bolster Denise Leguay's kitchen staff in this genuine, old-style bistro. The cuisine is contemporary and you can enjoy its appealing, proficient, well-made dishes without breaking the bank. The tart of marinated fresh sardines, lamb brain beignets, codfish with zucchini, tuna belly with tarbais white beans and bell peppers, pan-fried calf's liver with onion purée and roasted pig's head served with lentils in vinaigrette dressing offer a reminder of the days when Thierry was still demonstrating his talents to the staff of Les Amognes in the twelfth arrondissement. The crêpe filled with cardamom eggplant compote and chocolate charlotte in coffee sauce are choice delicacies.

● Ze Kitchen Galerie 🏠 ○ SIM

4, rue des Grands-Augustins
Métro: St-Michel
Tel. 01 44 32 00 32. Fax 01 44 32 00 33
zekitchen.galerie@wanadoo.fr
www.zekitchengalerie.fr
Closed Saturday lunch, Sunday, Christmas,
New Year's, May 1st, July 14th.
Open until 11 PM.
Prix fixe: 23€ (lunch, wine included), 34€
(lunch, wine included). A la carte: 60–70€.

This gourmet loft with its designer furniture, Cuzzini glass lamps, art by Daniel Humair and Starck metal tables and cutlery easily complements the cuisine prepared by William Ledeuil, a Guy Savoy veteran who formerly ran the neighboring Les Bouquinistes. His dishes are modern, inventive and flavorsome to boot. We begin with beet gazpacho with candied ginger, cucumber and shrimp with fresh Thai herbs, green asparagus and Burratta mozzarella fritters, cream of white asparagus with lemongrass and arugula and marinated tuna with coleslaw, green mango and asparagus. Next we turn to shrimp with softshell crab and grilled frog's legs, and grilled chicken and veal sweetbreads with carrot-mustard-ginger jus and milk-fed lamb (slow-cooked, then grilled) with lemongrass-kumquat jus and begin to realize that something fine and flavorsome has come to the rue des Grands-Augustins. Nice strawberry, pistachio and lemongrass cappuccino, wasabi emulsion with chocolate cream and caramelized coconut, roasted banana with coconut ice cream and wines from France and further afield that are well worth a glance . . . an assiduous tasting.

INTERNATIONAL RESTAURANTS

A SPECIAL FAVORITE

● Evi Evane 🅝 🍴 SIM

10, rue Guisarde
Métro: Mabillon
Tel. 01 43 54 97 86
Closed Sunday, 3 weeks in August.
Open until 11 PM.
Prix fixe: 14,90€ (lunch), 19,90€.
A la carte: 30–35€.

"Evi Evane" was the cry of the followers of Dionysus at their divine banquets. In the heart of Saint-Sulpice, this tavern with its exposed stone walls plays on the same delights. Maria Nikolaou's smile brightens the dining room, while sister Dina prepares her delicate dishes. The turnovers with two cheeses served on a bed of greens, mezze composed of very fresh white taramasalata, stuffed grape leaves, eggplant salad and tzatziki. The grilled beef meatballs with aromatic herbs, the lamb chops with sesame seeds and grilled sea bream are of excellent quality. The strawberry jelly, yogurt with honey, sesame halva and lavender ice cream make a splendid impression. The cellar is small but suitably represents the efforts of modern Greece. The friendly prices mean that this exploration of all things Hellenic does little harm to our pocket.

● Armani Caffè ○ SIM

149, bd Saint-Germain
Métro: St-Germain-des-Prés
Tel. 01 45 48 62 15. Fax 01 45 48 53 17
mori@emporioarmanicaffe.fr
www.emporioarmani.it
Closed Sunday.
Noon–midnight. Cont. service.
A la carte: 75–80€.
Air cond.

He manages to divide his time between the Bourse district, where he has his Mori Venice Bar, and this highly fashionable eatery. Mantoua's Massimo Mori copes with success, chatting with the beautiful people as they battle for a table in this packed setting in shades of mouse gray. Everything chef Ivan Schenatti has to offer bears the stamp of quality: light antipasti, Zibello cured ham, steamed then pan-roasted sea bass with mixed grilled vegetables, red tuna seared on a cast-iron grill, boned lamb chop roasted in caul with artichokes, small veal and Swiss chard ravioli with walnuts. Every pasta dish is worth tasting and the risottos are sublime. Then there are the delicious desserts: red fruit and pomegranate panna cotta, strawberry or Sorrento lemon ice cream, made to order, and vanilla ice cream doused with espresso, as well as some very stylish wines. In other words, there is never a dull moment at Armani Caffè!

● Fogon ○ COM
45, quai des Grands-Augustins
Métro: St-Michel
Tel. 01 43 54 31 33. Fax 01 43 54 07 00
Closed weekday lunch, Monday, December, 2 weeks in August. Open until midnight.
Prix fixe: 35€, 40€.
Air cond. Valet parking.

Alberto Herraiz, who formerly prospered near Saint-Julien-le-Pauvre, has now set himself up in a suitable contemporary setting by the Seine with an open kitchen and baroque banquettes straight out of Almodóvar. This grandson of restaurateurs from La Mancha, who came here from Valencia, has become the darling of Parisian diners. Bomba rice, cooked with rabbit, ham, snails, market vegetables, cuttlefish ink, squid, langoustines or shrimp, fish fumet but without fish ("a banda without a banda," he quips) acquires the aura of a noble dish. The tapas, both savory (garlic soup, mashed cod with potato, fried fresh anchovies) and sweet (rice pudding, crème catalane, turron ice cream with vine-ripened peaches) are equally appealing, while the Rioja, Mancha and Penedes wines will knock you off your feet. Arriba Herraiz!

● Yugaraj ○ COM
14, rue Dauphine
Métro: Pont-Neuf, Odéon
Tel. 01 43 26 44 91. Fax 01 46 33 50 77
Closed Monday, Tuesday lunch, August.
Open until 10:30 PM.
Prix fixe: 19€ (weekday lunch), 34€ (dinner).
Air cond. Private dining room.

Kulendran Meyappen, a terribly "British" Sri Lankan gentleman, runs the best Indian establishment in Paris with genuine warmth. The cuisine he serves up is in his image: generous and refined. Entrusted to the safe hands of chef Joseph Yhangérajha, it leaves little room for improvisation and

exerts an easy charm with its authentic dishes and highly elegant wines. The names: salade pattera, fish tikka, chingri bahar and matchli massala, ghost korma and ghost rada, not to mention thene ou chahat nam for dessert, will take on a whole new meaning after this memorable experience. The decor is a little limited, but the gilded wall bases and grayish beige wall coverings are full of character.

▼ | SHOPS

KITCHENWARE & TABLETOP

▼ La Cornue
18, rue Mabillon
Métro: Mabillon
Tel. 01 46 33 84 74. Fax 01 40 46 93 85
10:30 AM–6:30 PM.
Closed Sunday, 2 weeks in August.
Excellent stoves in wrought iron, sheet metal, enamel, brass and bronze, rustic casseroles, whetstones, carafes and glasses: a paradise for enthusiasts!

▼ Maison de Famille
29, rue Saint-Sulpice (at rue Garancière)
Métro: St-Sulpice
Tel. 01 40 46 97 47. Fax 01 46 33 99 91
10:30 AM–7 PM. Closed Sunday.
This contemporary store on two floors offers practical utensils, open work partitions, table and bath linen, lighting and furniture of all kinds.

▼ La Maison Ivre
38, rue Jacob
Métro: St-Germain-des-Prés
Tel. 01 42 60 01 85
10:30 AM–7 PM. Closed Sunday.
Traditional glazed ceramics from the greatest contemporary potters, plates, jugs, cups, salad bowls, dishes and condiment sets, as well as tablecloths, dishtowels and napkins with floral patterns, are carefully selected by Sylvine Nobecourt.

▼ Xanadou

10, rue Saint-Sulpice
Métro: Odéon
Tel. 01 43 26 73 43. Fax 01 40 51 03 30
11 AM–1 PM, 2–7 PM. Closed Sunday,
Monday, 2 weeks in August.

This small store is devoted to designer table arts: sets of pans, utensils, chopping boards, plates, cutlery and glasses by Starck, Ron Arad and Enzo.

BREAD & BAKED GOODS

▼ Boulangerie Madame

Francis Rault
48, rue Madame
Métro: St-Sulpice, St-Placide
Tel.-Fax 01 42 22 14 57
7 AM–2 PM, 3–8 PM (Sunday and
Bank Holidays: 7 PM).
Closed Wednesday, August.

Francis Rault's croissant made with Charentes butter will have you melting. His crusty baguette is striking, like his volcan (a wholemeal loaf with toasted almonds, hazelnuts, honey and crème fraîche), his flaky brioche and lemon tart.

▼ Poilâne

8, rue du Cherche-Midi
Métro: St-Sulpice, Sèvres-Babylone
Tel. 01 45 48 42 59. Fax 01 45 44 99 80
7:15 AM–8:15 PM. Closed Sunday.
Patron: Apollonia Poilâne

We loved Lionel dearly and his achievements live on in our hearts. Apollonia continues his work with great style. Sourdough baton, whole wheat with walnuts, rye bread, apple tart, sugar cookies and butter shortbread are still masterpieces of the baker's art.

WINE

▼ Caves Miard   🇳

9, rue Quatre-Vents
Métro: Odéon
Tel.-Fax 01 43 54 99 30
10 AM–10 PM.
Closed Sunday, Monday, August.

Pierre Jancou has turned this 1880 former crémerie (dairy store) into a temple of selected vintages. Burgundies and great bottles from the Rhône rub shoulders with finds from Tricastin and Corbières.

▼ La Dernière Goutte

6, rue Bourbon-le-Château
Métro: St-Germain-des-Prés, Odéon,
Mabillon
Tel. 01 43 29 11 62. Fax 01 46 34 63 41
Tuesday–Friday 10 AM–1:30 PM, 3 PM–
(Monday 4 PM)–8:30 PM, Saturday
10 AM–8:30 PM, Sunday 11 AM–7 PM.
Closed Monday morning, Christmas,
New Year's.

This refined store works its charm. Juan Sanchez favors winegrowers from Provence, Burgundy, Languedoc and the Rhône who champion natural methods. On Saturday, he organizes tastings of his favorite wines.

▼ Le Savour-Club

125 bis, bd du Montparnasse (pedestrians)
and 120-139, bd du Montparnasse (cars)
Métro: Vavin
Tel. 01 43 27 12 06. Fax 01 43 27 25 87
10 AM–8 PM. Closed Sunday afternoon,
Monday.

The place to find bargains, with crates everywhere, selected special offers from all wine growing areas, good advice and tasting sessions.

CHARCUTERIE

▼ Charles

10, rue Dauphine
Métro: St-Michel, Odéon
Tel. 01 43 54 25 19
8 AM–2 PM, 4–8 PM.
Closed Saturday, Sunday, 3 weeks in August.

White or black boudin, goose or duck foie gras, head cheese, York-style or Paris-style boiled ham and parsleyed ham terrine, and spiced pork pie are meticulously prepared by father and son Claude and Philippe Charles. Cured ham on the bone and andouillette are first rate.

▼ Coesnon

30, rue Dauphine
Métro: St-Michel, Odéon
Tel. 01 43 54 35 80. Fax 01 43 26 56 39
9 AM–7:30 PM. Closed Sunday (except in
December), August.

Master artisan *charcutier* Bernard Marchaudon produces fresh foie gras, Lyon-style sausage, cured ham, ham on the bone, terrines and eighteen different black or white boudin, all of high quality. The prepared delicatessen dishes are equally commendable.

▼ Gilles Vérot

3, rue Notre-Dame-des-Champs
Métro: St-Placide
Tel. 01 45 48 83 32. Fax 01 45 49 37 33
8:30 AM–8 PM. Closed Sunday, Monday,
2 weeks in August.

Gilles Vérot, specialist in foie gras pâté, slow-roasted pork chunks, and truffle-studded cooking sausage, as well as white or black boudin, Troyes-style or Norman-style andouillette, chicken liver terrine and pike quenelle. His head cheese will make your mouth water.

CHOCOLATE

▼ Jean-Paul Hévin

3, rue Vavin
Métro: Vavin
Tel.-Fax 01 43 54 09 85
10 AM–7 PM. Closed Sunday,
1 week in August.

In this modern store near the Luxembourg gardens, Jean-Paul Hévin invites you to taste his chocolate creations. His spiced ganaches, millefeuilles, soft macarons, as well as his bitter cocoa sorbet are mouth-watering delicacies.

▼ Pierre Marcolini

89, rue de Seine
Métro: Mabillon, Odéon
Tel. 01 44 07 39 07
10:30 AM–7 PM (Monday 2–6 PM). Closed Sunday, Monday morning, 3 weeks in August.
Famous in place des Sablons, Brussels, Pierre Marcolini has turned this modern little store into his Paris embassy. His praliné chocolates, thin-filled chocolates, 75% pure cocoa chocolates and allspice, crunchy-vanilla or cinnamon-filled chocolates are works of art.

CANDY & SWEETS

▼ Les Bonbons

6, rue Bréa
Métro: Vavin, Notre-Dame-des-Champs
Tel. 01 43 26 21 15
10:30 AM–7:30 PM.
Closed Sunday, Monday, August.

Provençal candied fruit, Montélimar nougat, sugar-coated almond and candied-fruit candies, Berck barley sugar, soft nougatine drops in a crunchy coating, chocolate and caramel candy, Tours barley sugar, Dijon gingerbread and bergamot-flavored drops from Nancy are enthusiastically presented in this tiny store.

GROCERIES

▼ Da Rosa

62, rue de Seine
Métro: Odéon
Tel. 01 40 51 00 09
10 AM–10 PM. Open daily.

José Da Rosa astutely runs this grocery store decorated by Garcia. It offers a panorama of world flavors. The pasta, smoked salmon and Iberian hams make you want to buy the entire inventory. Tastings are held at the store.

CHEESE

▼ Rouge Crème

46, rue Madame
Métro: St-Sulpice, St-Placide
Tel. 01 45 44 11 00
9:30 AM–1 PM, 4–8:30 PM. Closed Sunday afternoon, 1 week in August.

Thierry Rochas, wine buff, and Manuel Cadoso, cheese maturer and -monger, have turned this into an excellent setting for tastings. Basque brebis, Loire chèvre, mimolette (Northern Dutch-style cheese) go well with the nice wines such as a cru bourgeois Puy-Castera. The homemade specialties—cumin-coated goat cheese, camembert cured with apple brandy—will have you melting on the spot.

Shops

PASTRY

▼ Christian Constant

37, rue d'Assas
Métro: St-Placide, Rennes
Tel. 01 53 63 15 15. Fax 01 53 63 15 16
8:30 AM–9 PM (Saturday 8 AM–8:30 PM,
Sunday 8 AM–8 PM). Open daily.

Christian Constant, a true artist in the chocolate medium, works his magic with cinnamon or coffee ganaches, cocoa sorbets, and chocolate and walnut tart. His cakes and pastries are the epitome of refinement. Coffee and walnut meringue cake, eclairs (chocolate or coffee), fruit tart, vanilla millefeuille, Siclan (a flaky praliné pastry topped with light pistachio cream) are mouthwatering. Excellent catering service.

▼ Gérard Mulot

76, rue de Seine
Métro: Mabillon, Odéon
Tel. 01 43 26 85 77. Fax 01 40 46 99 34
7 AM–8 PM. Closed Wednesday,
1 week at Easter, 4 weeks in July–August.

Gérard Mulot is an institution, surfing easily over the waves of fashion. His flan, macarons, tutti frutti tart, fruitcakes and butter kugelhopf, the best in Paris, are works of art. His Amaryllis, an almond macaron filled with light vanilla cream and fresh raspberries, deserves praise.

▼ Pierre Hermé

72, rue Bonaparte
Métro: St-Sulpice
Tel. 01 43 54 47 77. Fax 01 43 54 94 90
10 AM–7 PM (Saturday 7:30 PM).
Closed Monday, 4 weeks in July–August.

An innovator (one of the few genuine artists in his field) and teacher of proper manners, Pierre Hermé is better known in Japan than in France. His store near the place Saint-Sulpice is small, but his talent huge. Double millefeuilles, Viennese pastries, Aztec, Azur (filled chocolate), Torsade or PH3 (white chocolate balls with varying degrees of sweetness and sourness) are gourmet tours de force. But his macarons are masterpieces: Coffee, americano-grapefruit, "Mosaic" (pistachio-Bing cherry), or "Plénitude" (uniting chocolate, caramel and fleur de sel), they have us melting with pleasure. (Also see the fifteenth arrondissement.)

REGIONAL PRODUCTS

▼ Huilerie Jean Leblanc

6, rue Jacob
Métro: St-Germain-des-Prés, Mabillon
Tel.-Fax 01 46 34 61 55
Monday 2–7 PM, Tuesday–Friday noon–7 PM,
Saturday 10 AM–7 PM. Closed Sunday,
Monday morning, 2 weeks in August.

Anne and Jean Leblanc supply oils with delicate aromas: hazelnut, walnut, rapeseed, peanut, almond, pistachio, pinenut, olive, truffle, toasted sesame, argan and pecan, not to mention vinegars: wine, champagne, cider, sherry, truffled, tarragon and raspberry, chosen with care.

TEA

▼ Mariage Frères

13, rue des Grands-Augustins
Métro: St-Michel
Tel. 01 40 51 82 50. Fax 01 44 07 07 52
10:30 AM–7:30 PM. Closed Christmas–New
Year's, May 1st.

In this small, yellow parlor on the second floor, you will find tea-flavored jellies, tea-flavored chocolates, shortbreads, bonbons, and 500 tea caddies, along with assorted tea chests and beautiful teapots. Enthusiasts will be equally fascinated by the tea museum.

COFFEE

▼ Comptoirs Richard

48, rue du Cherche-Midi
Métro: Sèvres-Babylone
Tel. 01 42 22 45 93
10:30 AM–2 PM, 3:15–7:30 PM.
Closed Sunday, Monday, 3 weeks in August.

Coffees from Colombia, Costa Rica, Papua and Jamaica, peppermint tea, chocolate as food or drink and a wide choice of spices are presented with admirable care. You can also savor apple sugar, cookies and licorice drops in the tearoom area, decorated with splendid sets of porcelain and coffee grinders.

◆ | RENDEZVOUS

BARS

◆ Bar du Lutétia

45, bd Raspail
Métro: Sèvres-Babylone
Tel. 01 49 54 46 09
Open daily 9 AM–1 AM.
Air cond.

This attractive, very "society" hotel bar is private and cozy. With its red velvet lounge decorated with photos of great cigar smokers, it is just the place for those who wish to see and be seen. From 3 to 6:30 PM, the afternoon tea is excellent. From Wednesday to Saturday, jazz in the evenings from 10:15 on.

◆ Le Sélect

99, bd du Montparnasse
Métro: Vavin
Tel. 01 45 48 38 24. Fax 01 45 44 56 45
Open daily 7 AM–4 AM.
Air cond. Terrace.

Stucco, moldings, wooden tables and banquettes: this 1920s' Montparnasse institution still boasts all its antique elegance. The fifty whiskeys and assorted cocktails alone are worth the visit.

PUBS

◆ The Frog & the Princess

9, rue Princesse
Métro: Mabillon, St-Germain-des-Prés
Tel. 01 40 51 77 38. Fax 01 43 29 12 14
www.frogpubs.com
5:30 PM (Saturday, Sunday noon)–2 AM.
Closed Christmas.

Beer fans come to quench their thirst in this neo-London bar with its British staff, offering pleasant snacks and expertly poured light, amber and dark beers. The decor is rustic, with the coats-of-arms of beer brands displayed on the walls.

◆ La Taverne de Nesle

32, rue Dauphine
Métro: St-Michel, Odéon
Tel.-Fax 01 43 26 38 36
tavernedenesle@chez.com
6 PM–4 AM (Saturday, Sunday 6 AM).
Closed 2 weeks in August.

This rendezvous for sports fans shows soccer, rugby and handball games late at night. In its setting of stone and beams, we succumb to the pleasures of fine beers chosen by Gilles Lamiot, who also owns La Ferrandaise. The meals are supervised by neighbor Manuel Martinez of the Louis XIII.

WINE BARS

◆ Le Nemrod

51, rue du Cherche-Midi
Métro: St-Placide, Sèvres-Babylone
Tel. 01 45 48 17 05
6:30 AM–2 AM. Closed 1 week in August.
Terrace.

Francis Tafanel has taken over this corner café, which still has a cheerful ambience along with assorted plates of cheeses and charcuterie and Auvergne dishes like pounti (a spinach, prune and bacon pudding), dried sausage and potato-and-ham gratin on offer. The terrace is in great demand.

CAFES

◆ Café Doucet

41, rue de Vaugirard
Métro: Rennes, St-Placide
Tel. 01 45 48 49 50
7:30 AM–9 PM. Closed Sunday,
1 week in August.

Opposite the library of the same name, we settle down comfortably on the banquettes of this corner bistro with its neo-Fifties' lighting. Served all day, open-face sandwiches, pepper-crusted steak and Troyes andouillette braised Lyonnaise-style, provide a gourmet break.

◆ Café de la Mairie

8, pl Saint-Sulpice
Métro: St-Sulpice
Tel. 01 43 26 67 82
Open daily 7 AM–2 AM
(Sunday 9 AM–9 PM).

This café immortalized by Georges Pérec remains a favorite rendezvous for the publishing world and its discreet talks and heated discussions. Assorted cheese and charcuterie plates, omelets and pastries on either floor or on the terrace.

◆ Caméléon   Ⓝ

6, rue de Chevreuse
Métro: Vavin, Raspail
Tel. 01 43 27 43 27
8 AM–midnight. Closed Sunday.

Jean-Paul Arabian, former assistant at Maxim's and manager of Ledoyen, is now a luxury café owner, welcoming friends to his fine local establishment. He serves breakfast at the counter, and as patrons enjoy the exquisite baguettes and fine butter, they can browse through the daily paper provided or watch the news on a plasma-screen TV opposite the bar. Customers come to eat, drink and chew the fat.. (Also see Restaurants.)

◆ Cuisine de Bar

8, rue du Cherche-Midi
Métro: Sèvres-Babylone, St-Sulpice
Tel. 01 45 48 45 69. Fax 01 45 48 25 53
8:30 AM–7 PM. Closed Sunday, Monday,
3 weeks in August.

Cédric Diot is now the host at this modern café founded by Lionel Poilâne. Crayfish on toast, a Landaise open-faced sandwich with duck liver pâté, various salads and apple tart are served in the small, lively dining room.

◆ Les Deux Magots   🛖

6, pl Saint-Germain
Métro: St-Germain-des-Prés
Tel. 01 45 48 55 25. Fax 01 45 49 31 29
7:30 AM–1: 30 AM.
Closed last 4 days of January.
Terrace.

A historic heritage site with its two sculpted Chinese magi standing on pillars, this elegant, literary, tourist café provides impeccable service. Visitors take time out to enjoy a hot chocolate or cocktail on the terrace or the legendary first floor.

◆ Le Flore   🛖

172, bd Saint-Germain
Métro: St-Germain-des-Prés
Tel. 01 45 48 55 26. Fax 01 45 44 33 39
Open daily 7:30 AM–1: 30 AM.
Terrace.

In an elegant, art deco style, this quality establishment with its mirrored room, red faux-leather banquettes and terrace has become a prestigious tourist attraction. Enjoy Météor beer on tap or Pouilly Fumé by the glass, surrounded by the most literary clientele in Paris.

◆ Le Luxembourg

58, bd Saint-Michel
Métro: Cluny-La Sorbonne, Luxembourg
Tel. 01 43 54 53 24. Fax 01 43 26 17 35
Open daily 8 AM–2 AM.
Air cond. Terrace.

This neo-1900s' brasserie with its view of the Luxembourg gardens is a meeting place for academics and students from the nearby Sorbonne. They come to sample carefully prepared dishes of the day and fine cakes and pastries. Philosophical debates are held on Sunday morning.

◆ La Palette   🛖

43, rue de Seine
Métro: St-Germain-des-Prés
Tel. 01 43 26 68 15
8 AM–2 AM. Closed Sunday.
Terrace.

Gallery owners, artists and devotees have turned this fine 1900s' café into their headquarters. In the summer, it takes a while to find a table on the terrace. Modest wines, nice cured ham and open-faced toasted sandwiches.

TEA SALONS

◆ L'Artisan de Saveurs
72, rue du Cherche-Midi
Métro: St-Placide, Sèvres-Babylone
Tel. 01 42 22 46 64
www.lartisandesaveurs.com
Noon–6:30 PM. Closed Wednesday,
Christmas–New Year's,
last week in July, August.
Terrace.

This snugly comfortable tearoom offers sustenance in the form of Patrick Loustalot-Barbé's sound dishes (breaded sea bream, rabbit stewed in cider) and delicious confections (iced espresso cream cake). Brunch on the weekend.

◆ Bagels & Brownies
12, rue Notre-Dame-des-Champs.
Métro: St-Placide, Notre-Dame-des-Champs
Tel. 01 42 22 44 15
9 AM–6 PM.
Closed Sunday, 3 weeks in August.
Air cond.

In this New York–style deli, we find fine small plates, bagels, cream cheese (the salmon-flavored one is superb) and pastrami sandwiches. We could almost believe we were in you know who's *Broadway Danny Rose*.

◆ Forêt Noire
9, rue de l'Eperon
Métro: Odéon, St-Michel
Tel. 01 44 41 00 09
Noon–6:30 PM. Closed Monday,
May 1, 2 weeks in August.

At lunchtime, Denise Siégel's tearoom provides polished light meals and savory delicacies. The Chinese and Indian teas, linzertorte, apple streudel and Black Forest cake are splendid.

◆ L'Heure Gourmande
22, passage Dauphine
Métro: Mabillon, Odéon
Tel. 01 46 34 00 40
Noon–7 PM. Closed May 1st.

A cozy tearoom where hot chocolate (one of the best in Paris, with melted bars and sweetened chilled whipped cream), selected teas, gourmet plates and Viennese pastries, as well as fruit tarts and crumbles, are a great success.

◆ Ladurée-Bonaparte
21, rue Bonaparte
Métro: St-Germain-des-Prés
Tel. 01 44 07 64 87
Open daily 8:30 AM–7:30 PM
(Sunday 10 AM–7:30 PM).

Around twenty kinds of macarons are on offer in this very "Louis-the-Something" boudoir tearoom, located in the heart of Saint-Germain-des-Prés. The gingerbread macarons, passion fruit and raspberry tart, lemon tea bread, selected teas and Viennese pastries are a hit.

◆ La Maison de la Chine
76, rue Bonaparte
Métro: St-Sulpice
Tel. 01 40 51 95 16. Fax 01 45 35 34 13
www.lamaisondelachine.fr
10:30 AM–7:30 PM.
Closed Sunday, 1 week in August.

The number one Chinese tour operator has opened the kind of teahouse formerly to be found in Beijing or Shanghai, with varnished wood furniture and refined table items. The yellow-orange, blue-green, black and smoked teas go wonderfully with the right cakes.

◆ Pâtisserie Viennoise
8, rue de l'Ecole-de-Médecine
Métro: Odéon, St-Michel
Tel. 01 43 26 60 48
9 AM–7 PM. Closed Saturday, Sunday,
Bank Holidays, mid-July–end of August.

Jean-Luc Guillot specializes in Viennese pastries such as strudels, praliné wafers, poppy seed cake, flanni, beigli (Hungarian Christmas cake), Bing cherry "Danube" cake. Also hot dishes, salads and fine Mitteleuropa products.

○	Very good restaurant
○○	Excellent restaurant
○○○	One of the best restaurants in Paris
⑤	Disappointing restaurant
⬤	Good value for money
ⓔ	Meals for less than 30 euros
SIM	Simple
COM	Comfortable
V.COM	Very comfortable
LUX	Luxurious
V.LUX	Very luxurious

Red indicates a particularly charming establishment

🏛	Historical significance
🏠	Promotion *(higher rating than last year)*
🆕	New to the guide

●	Restaurant
▼	Shop
◆	Rendezvous

7TH ARRONDISSEMENT
DISCREET AND GASTRONOMIC

"Where we live, the avenues are deep and peaceful, like the paths in a cemetery," wrote Blondin, who lived near Ecole Militaire during the period he describes in *Les Enfants du Bon Dieu* (*The Children of God*). The district has lost none of its legendary discretion, but locals continue to drop into the Le Sancerre or Au Sauvignon for drinks. Today, gastronomy has become an elitist art in the seventh, though, with Passard at L'Arpège and his pupils Heerah and Bodereau at Le Chamarré; Le Divellec, king of fish, welcoming guests under his own name, and Alain Reix at Le Jules Verne. We should also mention Christian Constant, who is building a small culinary empire in rue Saint-Dominique (Le Violon d'Ingres, Café Constant, Les Fables de la Fontaine). The district also boasts famous bakers (Secco and Malo), star cheesemongers (Marie-Anne Cantin, Quatrehomme, Barthélémy) and select chocolatiers (Hévin and Chaudun). Bistros of breeding (Le P'tit Troquet, Au Pied de Fouet, Au Babylone or La Fontaine de Mars) and strategic restaurants (the excessively snobbish Lei, Le Récamier—taken over by Idoux of La Cigale—Au Bon Accueil—which has restored Les Anges' soul—and Vin sur Vin) live on, while others offering good value (L'Ami Jean, L'Affriolé, Le Maupertu, Nabuchodonosor, Le Clos des Gourmets) assert their identity. The elegantly unostentatious seventh has a motto: Happiness means being well filled . . . but keeping quiet about it.

RESTAURANTS

GRAND RESTAURANTS

● **L'Arpège** ⓒⓞ V.COM

84, rue de Varenne
Métro: Varenne
Tel. 01 45 51 47 33. Fax 01 44 18 98 39
arpege.passard@wanadoo.fr
www.alain-passard.com
Closed Saturday, Sunday.
Open until 10:30 PM.
Prix fixe: 130€ (lunch), 340€ (dinner).
A la carte: 250€.
Air cond. Private dining room.

Oblivious to fashion and its diktats, Alain Passard remains true to form, loyal to the produce-based cuisine that is close to his heart. It has been a long time since critics questioned the lack of red meat on his menu. This grandmaster of the vegetable has won them all over with his skills. Creativity, originality, sensitivity and rigor are the everyday watchwords of this Breton trained by Kéréver, Boyer, then Senderens, as he prepares dishes of breathtaking freshness and vivacity. The lemon-infused sweet onion gratin, the thousand-and-one-flavors of the vegetable from the morning's harvest, the Chausey island lobster served thinly sliced and perfumed with Côtes-du-Jura wine and the Breton monkfish with Orléans mustard are odes to nature's gifts from the Mayenne, Finistère, Côtes d'Armor and Ile-et-Vilaine regions. Then, for the launch of the 1998 vintage Perrier Jouët Belle Epoque: raw scallops in a saffron velouté of zucchini blossoms, beechwood-smoked potato with white Côtes-du-Jura wine. The names are simple, the pleasures vast. If any doubts remain, sugar-coated young pigeon with honey wine and the sweetbreads with licorice root provide dazzling proof. Finally, what can we say about the desserts, except that they too attain summits of refinement? The caramelized tomato stuffed "with twelve flavors" refreshed with an orange sauce or the classic millefeuille offer moments of delight in this trove of elegance and serenity opposite the Rodin museum.

● **L'Atelier de Joël Robuchon** 🏠 ⓒⓞ SIM

5-7, rue Montalembert
Métro: Rue-du-Bac
Tel. 01 42 22 56 56. Fax 01 42 22 97 91
Open daily until 12 AM.
Prix fixe: 98€ (tasting menu).
A la carte: 70–100€.
Air cond. Valet parking.

Black granite, red lacquer and Indian rosewood, a direct view of the kitchen from the bar and valet parking: Joël Robuchon's snack bar strays on the side of chic. Needless to say, we are in the presence of *grande cuisine*, inspired by Joël the First and implemented by his four assistants, Eric Lecerf, Philippe Braun, Eric Bouchenoire and Antoine Hernandez, who alternately tend to the Table de Joël Robuchon in the sixteenth arrondissement. A virtuoso display! Sautéed squid with artichokes open the proceedings, followed by a mackerel tart, deep-fried whiting, tuna belly, eggs with caviar, milk-fed lamb from the Pyrénées, all executed with tremendous proficiency. If you still have a little room left, the warm chartreuse soufflé with pistachio ice cream (a house classic) will fill it neatly. An impressive cellar of French, Italian, Spanish, Californian and Australian wines, a produce-oriented tasting menu and a choice of small or standard portions a la carte ingeniously complete the range of this great restaurant's options. Two Plates this year.

● **Le Chamarré** ⓒⓞ COM

13, bd de la Tour-Maubourg
Métro: La Tour-Maubourg, Invalides
Tel. 01 47 05 50 18. Fax 01 47 05 91 21
Closed Saturday lunch, Sunday, Monday.
Open until 10:30 PM.
Prix fixe: 28€ (lunch on weekdays),
40€ (lunch on weekdays), 60€, 80€.
A la carte: 80€.
Air cond. Terrace.

In the quiet Invalides quarter, this French Mauritian restaurant will excite the most torpid of taste buds. In partnership with Chantal Dias, Antoine Heerah and Jérôme Bodereau concoct an ambitious fusion cuisine. Pupils of Alain Passard, they learned to select produce, prepare it appropriately (but creatively) and cook it to just the right degree under his supervision. As a result, the dishes we savor in this contemporary, sober dining room, with its red vases, origami-style lamps, chocolate-colored leather chairs and golden brown banquettes are rare and possibly even unique. The slow-roasted Atlantic octopus in Mauritius-style vindaloo curry sauce, crispy shrimp with carrot broth, seared tuna with two types of sesame and red mullet and squid seared in olive oil dart deliciously between sea and sun. The Sarthois suckling pig with a spiced chutney and the roasted pigeon wrapped in crisp phyllo dough with licorice play consummately on a sweet and savory theme. For dessert, roasted Victoria pineapple with vanilla and a baba au rhum leave the palate deliciously sated.

● **Le Divellec**   ⓒⓞ LUX

107, rue de l'Université
Métro: Invalides
Tel. 01 45 51 91 96. Fax 01 45 51 31 75
ledivellec@noos.fr
Closed Saturday, Sunday, Christmas–New Year's, 1 week at the end of July, 3 weeks in August. Open until 10 PM.
Prix fixe: 55€ (lunch), 70€ (lunch).
A la carte: 160€.
Air cond. Valet parking.

Jacques Le Divellec's marine restaurant is still on course for freshness. The politicians and celebrities aboard are happy as clams in its elegant nautical setting, with assurance to spare in the galley. Over decades, the place has built up a solid reputation for fish and shellfish at the peak of their form, reliable preparation and precise cooking. Proof comes in the form of the cassoulet of langoustines with truffles, the clam, cuttlefish and sea snail salad with a shellfish broth, the turbot carpaccio with lemon confit, not to mention the thinly sliced raw tuna with seared foie gras. The

ocean is there on our plates, vital and magnificent. For dessert, the warm raspberry soufflé with strawberries and the warm chocolate cake, with its melted chocolate center infused with verbena and served with sesame ice cream, are adept takes on current classics. The service comes with a smile and the list of great wines is thorough.

● **Le Jules Verne**   ⓒⓞ LUX

Eiffel Tower, south pillar, Champ-de-Mars
Métro: Bir-Hakeim,
Champ-de-Mars–Tour-Eiffel
Tel. 01 45 55 61 44. Fax 01 47 05 29 41
Open daily until 9:30 PM.
Prix fixe: 57€ (lunch on weekdays),
128€ (dinner). A la carte: 130–170€.
Air cond. Valet parking.

The visual impact was only to be expected. But the gustatory impact . . . now, that is a surprise! You could easily dismiss this place as a tourist trap. Far from it. For this is where the great (though discreet) *Périgourdin extraordinaire* Alain Reix has built his nest. His soufflé rolls, lobster brioche rolls, langoustines and crab with a shrimp broth, his turbot filet with mango and finely diced vegetable "risotto" and romaine lettuce consommé, the milk-fed veal with spring vegetables and the roasted calf's head are as thrilling as they are exquisite. The cellar attains the same high standards. A little more and we would simply step over the balustrade and take to the air! However, we control our emotions and come softly and sweetly back to earth with the warm passion fruit soufflé with a coconut milk emulsion and a large wild strawberry macaron with litchi cream. Sheer velvet! We grow a little drowsy until the check appears: a tidy sum, but that is only to be expected. The weekday lunchtime set menu is very honest, though. At the weekend, the price more than doubles, not to mention the evening! Still, it is worth a sacrifice or two to glide among the stars, high above the City of Light.

GOOD RESTAURANTS & OTHERS

● L'Actuel `SIM`

29, rue Surcouf
Métro: La Tour-Maubourg, Invalides
Tel. 01 45 50 36 20. Fax 01 45 50 36 75
Closed Saturday lunch, Sunday.
Open until 11 PM.
Prix fixe: 17€ (lunch), 29€ (dinner).
A la carte: 40€.
Terrace. Private dining room.

Actuel means modern, and this eatery lives up to its name. Everything here is extremely "today": the decor, tending toward shades of ecru and brown, and the menu, revolving around a very modish cuisine carefully prepared by Nicolas Curtil, who takes the opportunity to express his creativity in such dishes as a salad with rooster comb, celery root and Spanish pepper aspic, striped catfish medallions with yellow rice pilaf, veal filet, hand-cut tartare and tomato tarte Tatin with caramelized raspberry vinegar and green tea marshmallows. The other good news is that the prices are as disciplined as ever. Philippe Pola and Patrice Rodriguez's acquisition of this restaurant has worked out very well.

● L'Affriolé `SIM`

17, rue Malar
Métro: Invalides, Pont-de-l'Alma
Tel. 01 44 18 31 33. Fax 01 44 18 91 12
Closed Sunday, Monday, Bank Holidays
(long weekends), Christmas–New Year's,
3 weeks in August. Open until 10:30 PM.
Prix fixe: 19€ (lunch), 23€ (lunch),
29€ (lunch), 33€.
Air cond.

At first, in its small street and with its simple decor, this restaurant is really not that impressive, but it gradually grows on you. Served as an appetizer, the slices of Lyonaise sausage with olive butter are followed by a choice of "dish-based" set menus that change every month. On the day we visited, there was cream of tarbais bean with foie gras and pig's feet croquettes, followed by roasted monkfish tail with bacon or quail pâté with foie gras. The Guanaja chocolate soufflé, cocoa sorbet or little fried cakes with a soft citrus jelly closed the proceedings. A disciple of Senderens and Duquesnoy, Thierry Verola knows his trade. In the dining room, Maria Verola looks after her guests in three languages. We enjoy the quality of this discreet, creative restaurant. There is another friendly gesture at the end of the meal: The check comes with a small, lightly textured pot of vanilla cream.

● Altitude 95 `COM`

Eiffel Tower, 1st floor
Métro: Bir-Hakeim,
Champ-de-Mars–Tour-Eiffel
Tel. 01 45 55 20 04. Fax 01 47 05 94 40
altitude-95.rv@elior.com
www.toureiffel.fr
Open daily until 9:30 PM.
Prix fixe: 22,50€ (lunch on weekdays),
28,70€ (lunch on weekdays), 52€ (dinner).
A la carte: 65€.
Air cond.

The main thing is the view over the Seine from this tasteful brasserie designed by Slavik on the first level of the Eiffel Tower. In the kitchen, Fabrice Brossard pays homage to bistro classics. The duck foie gras seasoned with pepper and champagne, salmon steak, tenderloin with béarnaise sauce and molten chocolate caramel cake offer the delights of Paris on your plate as well as before your eyes. A tempting proposition for tourists of comfortable means.

● L'Ami Jean `SIM`

27, rue Malar
Métro: La Tour-Maubourg
Tel. 01 47 05 86 89. Fax 01 45 50 34 79
ami_jean@hotmail.fr
Closed Sunday, Monday,
1 week Christmas–New Year's, August.
Open until midnight.
Prix fixe: 30€.
Air cond.

Photos of Basque country *pelota* games on the walls, green and red colors, rustic furniture and packed tables: Stéphane Jego nails his flag to the mast. Anyone looking for a quiet meal should either move on or make the best of it: People are here to have fun and there is no room for pickiness. The menu, which changes every day, is as hot as the atmosphere. Formerly at La Régalade, Jego is full of verve and undeniably talented. His quick-seared squid with Spanish beans is irresistible. Fish plays an important role. Grilled sea bream with lemon and olive oil and l'axoa (a dish of ground veal, onions and Espelette chilis), brebis cheese and black cherry confiture have a special (and deserved) place in the cuisine and heart of our amiable Stéphane, who has a gift for transmuting very simple domestic recipes, as shown by the delicious rice pudding he offers as a dessert. A good choice of wines from Southwest France, especially from the Basque country, on both sides of the Pyrénées.

● **Chez les Anges**　　　⌂ ◎ V.COM

54, bd de La Tour-Maubourg
Métro: Invalides, La Tour-Maubourg
Tel. 01 47 05 89 86. Fax 01 47 05 45 56
Closed Saturday, Sunday, 3 weeks in August.
Open until 10:30 PM.
Prix fixe: 28€. A la carte: 65€.
Air cond. Terrace. Private dining room.

First, it was Armand Monassier's Les Anges. Then it became Jean Minchelli's seafood eatery. Now Jacques Lacipière from Au Bon Accueil has restored the original name, and brought an identity and style to the place. The setting in white tones is chic and modern, although slightly neutral, but the restaurant as a whole has refinement in plenty, with its long counter, attractively set tables and banquettes. In the kitchen, there is no cheating over the quality of produce or its preparation at the peak of freshness. Cream of pumpkin soup with smoked bacon, sea urchin with an emulsion of sea water and hazelnut oil, winter vegetables in a spicy marinade and pigeon terrine with dried fruits all featured on the menu the other day, and were served in small ramekins, tapas style. Then there is gray sea bream with tarbais beans and milk-fed veal roast with salsify and a spicy jus. Passion fruit cream or chestnut ice cream with dark chocolate mousse and coffee-hazelnut financier provide a delightful conclusion. The wines by the glass (from Languedoc or the Rhône Valley) have plenty of nose, and character is much in evidence, with the focus on quality.

● **L'Auberge Bressane**　　　COM

16, av de La Motte-Picquet
Métro: La Tour-Maubourg
Tel. 01 47 05 98 37. Fax 01 47 05 92 21
www.auberge-bressane.fr /
www.auberge-bressane.com
Closed Saturday lunch, 2 weeks in August.
Open until 10:30 PM.
Prix fixe: 20€ (lunch), 24€ (lunch),
29€ (lunch, wine included).
Air cond. Terrace. Valet parking.

Stéphane Dumant now runs this bourgeois establishment with Jérôme. Fifties'-style decor, woodwork, a terrace on a quiet street and valet parking: The scene is set. The welcome is warm and the classical cuisine has genuine merit. Eschewing trends, Alexis Blanchard carries the torch of tradition. Quality is his main concern. Those who simply dream of a cheese soufflé or œufs en meurette (poached eggs in a Burgundian wine sauce), pike fish quenelles, classic coq au vin or veal sweetbreads simmered with morel mushrooms will find them here, and very well prepared, too. Crêpes Suzette and Baked Alaska refuse to be outdone by the rest of the fare. The check is reasonable, the cellar very well stocked and we emerge at peace with the world.

● **Auguste**　　　◎ COM

54, rue de Bourgogne
Métro: Varenne, Assemblée-Nationale
Tel. 01 45 51 61 09. Fax 01 45 51 27 34
Web site under construction
Closed Saturday, Sunday, 3 weeks in August.
Open until 10:30 PM.
Prix fixe: 35€ (lunch). A la carte: 45–60€.
Air cond. Private dining room.

He arrived unobtrusively, direct from the Hotel Meurice, took over Les Glénans (formerly devoted to fish) and gave it a whole new meaning. Suddenly, Gaël Orieux, erstwhile assistant to Yannick Alleno, has become the new celebrity artisan of the culinary seventh. In an elegant, modern setting, this unassuming lad (whose handsome head is full of ideas) regales his informed aficionados with fine dishes to match the contingencies of the market. We love the sea snails in aspic and crisp fried oyster fritters, the soft-baked fingerling potatoes with chilled chicken oysters, the wild pigeon roasted with mild spices and Jerusalem artichokes and the whole veal kidneys cooked in wine with salsify. His lunchtime set menu at 35€ is impressive.

● **L'Auvergne Gourmande**   ●Ⓔ SIM

127, rue Saint-Dominique
Métro: Ecole-Militaire, Pont-de-l'Alma
Tel. 01 47 05 60 79
Closed Sunday, 1 week Christmas–New Year's, 1 week in February, 3 weeks in August. Open until 11 PM.
A la carte: 25–30€.
Terrace.

The Boudons have turned this former butcher's store into a lively, communal restaurant. You sit down casually at the counter, get to know your neighbor and give your order. If you have a healthy appetite, this is the place for you. Everything comes from the Auvergne, from the tomato tartare with fresh tomme cheese to the sausage served with a regional potato purée with cheese and garlic, Auvergne beef simmered in red wine with cheese from the region and red fruit. No fish—except in a brandade (classic salt cod and garlic purée)—and no set menu, but very moderate prices a la carte, and French (but no Burgundy) and Spanish wines in profusion. You can also eat on the terrace, but there are only two tables.

● **Au Babylone**   ●Ⓔ 🏠 SIM

13, rue de Babylone
Métro: Sèvres-Babylone
Tel. 01 45 48 72 13
Closed dinner on weekdays, Sunday, August.
Open until 2:30 PM.
Prix fixe: 19,50€ (lunch, wine included).
A la carte: 25€.

Liliane Garavana has knocked down a wall and repainted her old bistro, which has a very Parisian charm with its exposed stone and checked tablecloths. She watches over her customers as attentively as ever, and the very simple dishes come at truly moderate prices: a bargain in this district! Duck foie gras terrine, pike fish quenelle and Dover sole pan-fried in butter and seasoned with parsley and lemon, leg of lamb and farm-raised chicken, daily seasonal fruit tart and chocolate cake: good, old-fashioned French home cooking. In fact, those are Liliane's children waiting the tables.

● **Le Bamboche**   COM

15, rue de Babylone
Métro: Sèvres-Babylone
Tel. 01 45 49 14 40. Fax 01 45 49 14 44
lebamboche@aol.com
www.lebamboche.com
Closed Sunday lunch, 1 week in beginning of August. Open until 11 PM.
Prix fixe: 28€, 35€. A la carte: 75€.
Air cond. Private dining room.

The bijou decor, whitewashed walls, dark wooden furniture covered with red cloths and sober atmosphere in this tiny establishment are the same as ever. The waiters are just as staid, but the partnership of Serge Arce and Philippe Fabert (who have spent time knocking around in Paris, London and Rio de Janeiro) works well. The sunny, refined cuisine has a Southern French tang: caviar sorbet with smoked swordfish and young spinach to whet the appetite, followed by scallops, langoustines and vegetables in a light fava bean emulsion, a sole roulade with licorice coulis and marbled with fingerling and violet potatoes, or veal served with rice, nuts, flax seeds, sunflower seeds, morel mushrooms and wild mushrooms. . . . The desserts are in the same vein, for instance, caramelized apples with balsamic vinegar, cinnamon, Calvados and orange. A reliable address.

● **Le Basilic**   🍴COM

2, rue Casimir-Périer
Métro: Solférino, Varenne, Invalides
Tel. 01 44 18 94 64. Fax 01 44 18 33 97
www.lebasilic.fr
Closed Saturday lunch. Open until 11 PM.
A la carte: 35€.
Air cond. Terrace.

This art deco brasserie has changed hands. Fortunately, its new proprietors, Fabrice Naacke and Boris Dumeau, have left the decor intact, changing only the lighting. Marc Gramfort, a refugee from the Taillevent school, is still at home on the range. His bone marrow seasoned with Guérlande salt and the garlic and hot pepper–seasoned sea bream are done to a turn and a simmered regional veal dish with Basque peppers is cooked to perfection. A marbled millefeuille rounds off the meal beautifully. Organic and natural wines, and a covered terrace.

● **BistroB**   SIM

81, av Bosquet
Métro: Ecole-Militaire
Tel. 01 47 05 36 15. Fax 01 47 53 88 13
Open daily until 11 PM.
Prix fixe: 23€ (dinner).
Private dining room.

Comfort and epicureanism in this spacious neo-1930s'–style brasserie with mahogany and maple woodwork, a pewter bar and a private dining room that can hold up to thirty people. The facade is open and the sunlight pours in. The regional cooking is understated, but irreproachable. Sea bass pan-fried in white wine, shallots and parsley, a boneless ribeye steak with house fries and mousse au chocolat in an earthenware pot are washed down with selected wines.

● **Le Bistrot de Breteuil**   SIM

3, pl de Breteuil
Métro: Sèvres-Lecourbe, Ségur, Duroc
Tel. 01 45 67 07 27. Fax 01 42 73 11 08
bistrotbis@wanadoo.fr
www.bistot-et-cie.fr
Open daily until 11 PM.
Prix fixe: 33€ (wine included).
Air cond. Terrace.

With its 80-seat terrace adapted to all seasons and its meeting room, this luxurious brasserie in beige and red is an ideal, welcoming rendezvous in the heart of the government district. Marc Nouveau concocts traditional dishes. The avocado tartare with crayfish tails, asparagus in puff pastry, sea bass filet, beefsteak and rack of lamb, as well as the soft chocolate cake and strawberry gratin are all splendid. Considerate service.

● **Le Bistrot de Paris**   COM

33, rue de Lille
Métro: Rue-du-Bac, Solférino, Musée-d'Orsay
Tel. 01 42 61 15 84 / 01 42 61 16 83. Fax 01 49 27 06 09
Closed Saturday lunch, Sunday, Monday evening, Christmas–New Year's, August.
Open until midnight.
Prix fixe: 13,50€ (lunch on weekdays).
A la carte: 55€.
Private dining room. Valet parking.

This genuine faux-1900s' bistro designed by Slavik is still a favorite for the elegant inhabitants of the seventh, who like its red and gold decor and cuisine consisting of appealingly presented popular classics. The warm smoked herring and potatoes with oil, skate wing, calf's liver and baba au rhum are accompanied by one of the 100 French wines from its impressive cellar, by the glass or bottle.

● **Au Bon Accueil**   ◎SIM

14, rue de Monttessuy
Métro: Alma-Marceau
Tel. 01 47 05 46 11. Fax 01 45 56 15 80
Closed Saturday, Sunday.
Open until 10:30 PM.
Prix fixe: 27€ (lunch), 31€ (dinner).
A la carte: 60€.
Air cond. Terrace.

In the shadow of the Eiffel Tower, Jacques Lapicière's restaurant is true to its name: the "good welcome." Customers are always cordially received, to say the least, even when the proprietor is absent (he divides his time between this establishment and Chez les Anges in avenue de la Tour-Maubourg). The service is prompt and friendly, the decor has been refurbished in the best possible taste (mahogany and beige walls, tablecloths of freshly ironed gray linen) and the menu offers an inspired, market-based gourmet cuisine. The produce is fresh, the quality faultless and the dishes seasonal. We are beguiled by the creamy frog's leg risotto, the oven-crisped sea bass filet, green asparagus seasoned with truffle oil, Bresse chicken breast in a white cream sauce and with crayfish tails served with the roasted drumstick and oven-crisp polenta, as well as the raspberry millefeuille with vanilla cream. Fine wines chosen from every region with flair.

● Bruno Deligne ○ COM
"Les Olivades"

41, av de Ségur
Métro: Ségur, St-François-Xavier, Ecole-Militaire
Tel. 01 47 83 70 09. Fax 01 42 73 04 75
www.deligne-lesolivades.fr
Closed Saturday lunch, Sunday, Monday lunch, 1 week Christmas–New Year's, August. Open until 10:30 PM.
Prix fixe: 12€ (lunch on weekdays), 60€ (tasting menu). A la carte: 70€.
Air cond. Terrace. Private dining room.

Bruno Deligne's extended resume (Fauchon, Copenhague, Maximin, Girardet, Pic, Ritz, Taillevent) would make him the ideal candidate to run a great establishment. But no, here he is, perfectly at ease in his restaurant of Southern French inspiration with its warm, simple decor. His sun-drenched cuisine is in the same vein: sincere, authentic and pleasant. The roasted black tiger shrimp with finely minced papaya, pepper, and sweet onions, the seared grilled sea bass with gnocchi seasoned with truffle vinaigrette, the rack

of lamb and asparagus fricassée seasoned with thyme and lemon and the Grand Marnier soufflé with candied citrus zests warm our heart, as do the Italian and New World wines.

● Le Café de l'Alma COM

5, av Rapp
Métro: Alma-Marceau, Pont-de-l'Alma
Tel. 01 45 51 56 74. Fax 01 45 51 10 08
cafedelalma@wanadoo.fr
Open daily noon–midnight. Cont. service.
A la carte: 50–75€.
Air cond. Terrace. Private dining room.
Valet parking.

This being Alma, people of breeding come to enjoy the large terrace and the contemporary but elegant setting of this chic café. They like its deliberately restrained colors (red, green and lavender), discreet nooks and gentrified popular cuisine. The jumbo shrimp tempura with endive, the salmon medallions with roasted sesame, the farm-raised chicken with dried fruits and nuts served with mashed potatoes and the vanilla crème brûlée gratify Paris society. Which explains the size of the check.

● Café Constant ● ● SIM

139, rue Saint-Dominique
Métro: Ecole-Militaire, Pont-de-l'Alma
Tel. 01 47 53 73 34. Fax 01 45 55 00 91
Closed Sunday, Monday.
Open until 10:30 PM.
A la carte: 30€.
Terrace. Private dining room.

Two buildings away from his Violon d'Ingres, Christian Constant has opened this simpler Fifties' bistro. Here, the former Crillon chef presents a successful new take on domestic standards. So successful, in fact, that customers have to wait in line (no reservations, unfortunately), giving them time to examine the dishes on the blackboard, which change with the season. Try the "kako terrine" (a Basque pork filet with lentils and vinaigrette), cod served with a fennel and herb vinaigrette, house Toulouse sausages or Aquitane beefsteak with house potato purée. Strawberries Melba offer a neat conclusion, and you need have no worries about the tab. The upstairs room can be used as a private dining room.

● Café de l'Esplanade [COM]

52, rue Fabert
Métro: La Tour-Maubourg
Tel. 01 47 05 38 80. Fax 01 47 05 23 75
Open daily 8 AM–2 AM. Cont. service.
A la carte: 65€.
Air cond. Terrace. Private dining room.
Valet parking.

The Costes brothers have brought their full salvo of winning formulas to bear in their Invalides restaurant. Napoleon III decor by Garcia, beautiful waitresses, a long terrace and stylish, well-prepared dishes: Thai chicken and basil spring rolls, scallops with lemon butter, quick-seared steak seasoned with herbs and raspberry macarons. The check will leave you shell shocked.

● Café Max [SIM]

7, av de la Motte-Picquet
Métro: La Tour-Maubourg, Ecole-Militaire
Tel. 01 47 05 57 66
Closed Saturday, Sunday, 1 week at Easter, 3 weeks in August. Open until 11 PM.
A la carte: 40€.
Terrace. Valet parking.

A rather fashionable *bouchon*-style restaurant—red on black decor, gilded mirrors, tablecloths and candles—run by a Venetian: All this smacks of adventure! You will need to choose between crisp layered pastry with minced pig's ear over a bed of lentils and Italian meat bundles served on a frisee salad with polenta, between the Alsatian-style lemon-seasoned haddock and the fish carpaccio and all its accompaniments. The beef cut of the day, prepared with shallots, and the rabbit saddle with rosemary and red wine sauce and eggplant ravioli are quintessentially French. The wines are very affordable, as are the profiteroles. Open facade and old-fashioned bay windows.

● La Calèche [COM]

8, rue de Lille
Métro: Rue-du-Bac, Musée-d'Orsay
Tel. 01 42 60 24 76
Closed Sunday, 2 weeks in August.
Open until 10:30 PM.
Prix fixe: 25€. A la carte: 48€.
Air cond. Terrace.

This pretty 18th-century *calèche* (or carriage) with its white plaster and exposed beams travels some very Gallic roads. On the way, we stop for a vegetable basket, foie gras, grilled sea bass or sea bream, beef tenderloin steak or veal cutlet cooked with cider, profiteroles and flambéed crêpes, and glasses of Bordeaux, Beaujolais and Burgundy. This honest, traditional trip involves no detours and can be taken on the terrace: virtually a *déjeuner sur l'herbe*!

● Le Calmont [SIM]

35, av Duquesne
Métro: St-François-Xavier, Ecole-Militaire
Tel. 01 47 05 67 10. Fax 01 45 51 43 67
Closed Saturday, Sunday, Christmas–New Year's, Easter, August. Open until 9:30 PM.
A la carte: 40–55€.
Air cond. Terrace.

The hushed ambience of this restaurant in mauve tones is enlivened by good, honest regional cuisine. From the Aveyron, the Battut family—husband at the helm, wife serving and son at the stove—has its fair share of skills. Alexandre especially is adept at suiting his cuisine to the season and keeping it interesting. His smoked fish duo and his Savoie trout are as fresh as his region's rivers. The wood-fire roasted ham, like the cherry clafoutis, has the indefinable flavor of childhood. The 60 items on the wine list provide suitable accompaniments for these moments of pleasure.

● La Cigale Récamier [COM]

4, rue Récamier
Métro: Sèvres-Babylone
Tel. 01 45 48 86 58
Closed Sunday. Open until 11 PM.
A la carte: 45€.
Air cond. Terrace. Private dining room.

Opposite the Bon Marché department store, this former haunt of Parisian political and literary society, with its terrace in the trees at the end of the Impasse Récamier, has become a paradise for soufflé lovers. After some camembert soufflé, surely you'll try a little morel soufflé? Naturally followed by a salted caramel soufflé? Still, the beef tenderloin grilled with basil has not been whipped up to a feathery consistency and the classic beef tartare is well seasoned—after all, there is more to life than just soufflés. And the only thing rising in the vicinity of the well-stocked cellar is our sense of well being.

● Le Clos des Gourmets   🍴COM

16, av Rapp
Métro: Ecole-Militaire, Pont-de-l'Alma
Tel. 01 45 51 75 61. Fax 01 47 05 74 20
www.closdesgourmets.com
Closed Sunday, Monday. Open until 11 PM.
Prix fixe: 25€ (lunch), 29€ (lunch),
33€ (dinner).
Terrace.

Do not imagine for one minute that this quiet district is devoid of inventive eateries. Just take this restaurant with its Louis XVI–style furniture and sunny yellow colors. Its chef, Arnaud Pitrois, who trained with Guy Savoy and Christian Constant, serves precise, mischievous dishes at (French) republican prices: a sardine tempura with house pepper-dipping sauce, sea bass and shellfish cooked in a small casserole with star anise infusion, rotisserie chicken with a chanterelle mushroom fricassée and roasted pineapple seasoned with green anise seeds and cream whipped with dill, among others. Add polished service and, like us, you will be pleased you paid a visit to this little temple of gastronomy.

● Le Club "La Maison   COM des Polytechniciens"

Maison des Polytechniciens,
12, rue de Poitiers
Métro: Solférino, Musée-d'Orsay
Tel. 01 49 54 74 54. Fax 01 49 54 74 84
info@maisondesx.com
www.maisondesx.com
Closed Saturday, Sunday, Christmas–New Year's, August. Open until 9:30 PM.
Prix fixe: 36€ (for Polytechnic students).
A la carte: 75€.
Private dining room.

In the former Hôtel de Poulpry, dating from the 18th century, this restaurant with its yellow walls, engravings of *Polytechniciens* (graduates of France's great engineering school), wooden chairs and silver cutlery also serves lay customers, who enjoy its lively, precise, produce-based cuisine. A Provençal stew of violet artichokes, langoustines with an herb vinaigrette, John Dory fish with scallops served with a pesto-seasoned vegetable fricassée and lamb filet in spice bread crust served with eggplant gâteau with nuts gently add a touch of sophistication to sun-drenched classics. The fresh fruit suspended in coconut milk jelly with ginger offer a hint of sweet exotica. The wine list drawn up by Taillevent cannot be faulted. If only the same could be said of the check. . . .

● La Cuisine   COM

14, bd de la Tour-Maubourg
Métro: La Tour-Maubourg, Invalides
Tel. 01 44 18 36 32. Fax 01 44 18 30 42
christine.duboscq@wanadoo.fr
www.lacuisine.lesrestos.com
Closed Saturday lunch, Christmas, New Year's, 2 weeks in beginning of August.
Open until 10 PM.
Prix fixe: 24€ (lunch), 31€ (lunch),
34€, 42€. A la carte: 56€.
Air cond. Terrace. Private dining room.

Sobriety and quality are the hallmarks of this establishment, which boasts a terrace decorated with flowers and parasols during the summer. Christine Duboscq and her husband welcome guests and serve the food and beverages themselves, while

Sébastien Blettery prepares traditional dishes, adding his own personal touch. Potato cake with escargots and creamed garlic, roasted rack of lamb with garlic, two kinds of vegetable purée in stuffed tomatoes and tarte Tatin with salted butter caramel and Calvados-flavored whipped cream have what it takes to tease the taste buds. The boss provides good oenological advice and has every type of wine but Alsatian. Note that the house is now open on Sunday.

● **D'Chez Eux**   COM

2, av de Lowendal
Métro: Ecole-Militaire
Tel. 01 47 05 52 55. Fax 01 45 55 60 74
courtjp@wanadoo.fr
www.chezeux.com
Closed Sunday, Bank Holidays,
Christmas–New Year's, 3 weeks in August.
Open until 10:30 PM.
Prix fixe: 34€ (lunch), 40€ (lunch).
A la carte: 65–80€.
Air cond. Terrace. Private dining room.

Good humor is ubiquitous here: in the air, over the red and yellow walls, on the smiling faces, the heaped plates, the trolley holding "all" the hors d'oeuvre and the other holding "all" the desserts, and in the cassoulet pot . . . François Casteleyn, a fixture for thirty years, serves up standards such as Burgundian snails roasted in garlic and parsley butter, calf's liver cooked with shallots and fish of the day. . . . Among other famous gourmets, Jean-Pierre Court's clients include President of the Republic Jacques Chirac and veteran politician Philippe Séguin. Since all this warrants a celebratory drink, we now have the task of choosing from the 100 wines in the cellar. A terrace, private dining room and Darroze Armagnacs to crown it all.

● **Delicabar**   SIM

Bon Marché Rive Gauche,
26-38, rue de Sèvres
Métro: Sèvres-Babylone
Tel. 01 42 22 10 12. Fax 01 42 22 08 60
office@delicabar.fr
www.delicabar.fr
Closed Sunday.
Open until 7 PM (Saturday 8 PM).
A la carte: 23–38€.
Air cond. Terrace. Valet parking.

Although you might expect the worst of the restaurant in the very preppy Bon Marché department store, you will be pleasantly surprised! Colucci's designer setting with its globe lighting, red, orange and pink seats and immense snack bar is friendly and chic. Above all, Sébastien Gaudard, former pastry chef at Fauchon, works wonders with his sweet and savory combinations: savory crumble with celery root, carrot, and Serrano ham, a layered pastry with slow-cooked vegetables and eggplant caviar, a small leek, hazelnut and smoked mozzarella tart, and unusual colorful salads with olive oil and balsamic vinegar, all washed down with a glass of Bordeaux, Burgundy or tea—your choice. In summer, the tree-lined terrace is a haven of coolness.

● **Domaine de Lintillac**   ● SIM

20, rue Rousselet
Métro: Duroc, Vaneau
Tel. 01 45 66 88 23. Fax 01 45 66 88 28
michelcomby@wanadoo.fr
Closed Sunday, Monday, 3 weeks in August.
Open until 10:30 PM.
A la carte: 20–25€.

Here in this domain, confit and the customer are king. At unbeatable prices, Michel Comby serves up duck foie gras terrine with Montbazillac aspic, duck gizzards confit with mixed greens, gourmet cassoulet with duck confit, Mulard duck confit and potatoes sautéed in duck fat and garlic. . . . But why are we even mentioning this place? We should be keeping it a secret. Not a word will pass our lips about the small crème brûlée nor the regional walnut cake. Or the wines from Southwest

France at 2€ a glass, or the checked table-cloths. . . .

● Les Fables de la Fontaine 🦪SIM

131, rue Saint-Dominique
Métro: Ecole-Militaire, Pont-de-l'Alma
Tel. 01 44 18 37 55
Closed Sunday, Monday.
Open until 10:30 PM.
A la carte: 40€.
Terrace.

These fables are enchanting tales of the sea told by Christian Constant, former maestro of Le Crillon. Owner of Le Violon d'Ingres and Le Café Constant on the same street, he has decided to offer up a taste of sea spray in this former oyster bar, with a terrace next to the charming Fountain of Mars. We savor fish from the day's catch, as well as gourmet preparations presented as suggestions of the day. These include cold vegetable soup with boneless chicken filets, braised galinette (a fish of the mullet family), olive and parmesan polenta and an excellent Basque cake. The place is generally packed, so it is best to reserve.

● La Ferme Saint-Simon COM

6, rue de Saint-Simon
Métro: Rue-du-Bac
Tel. 01 45 48 35 74. Fax 01 40 49 07 31
fermestsimon@wanadoo.fr
www.fermestsimon.com
Closed Saturday lunch, Sunday, Bank Holidays, Christmas, 3 weeks in August.
Open until 10 PM.
Prix fixe: 31,50€ (lunch), 35€ (dinner).
A la carte: 60–70€.
Air cond. Private dining room.

This cozy "farm" has a rather British feel to it, with its yellow and burgundy fabrics. However, the cuisine is resolutely French, under the aegis of Francis Vandenhende, a pupil of Bocuse and Lenôtre, and joint master of the house with his wife Denise Fabre, the former French TV presenter. Among other dishes, it includes a salad of spaghettini with pan-fried jumbo shrimp, red mullet and pan-seared squid, a crisp phyllo with lamb, stuffed Mediterranean vegetables seasoned with wild thyme, and,

for dessert, variations on a strawberry theme millefeuille (pan seared and in a salad). The lavish wine list boasts 200 different libations.

● La Ferronnerie SIM

18, rue de la Chaise
Métro: Sèvres-Babylone
Tel. 01 45 49 22 43
Closed Saturday, Sunday,
1 week in February, 3 weeks in August.
Open until 10:15 PM.
A la carte: 40€.
Air cond.

A step away from Sciences Po, the Paris school of political science, Patrick Lejeune still has things well in hand with his clientele of rather intellectual regulars. There have been no upheavals in the kitchen, where Jean-Pierre Gloaguen still puts the finishing touches to the house specialties: poultry liver terrine and roasted rack of lamb. Then there are his dishes of the day to be reckoned with, especially the daily market fish, calf's liver with onion compote and his classic home-style fruit compote, all washed down with a few mouthfuls of Bordeaux, the perfect lubricant to keep the conversation going. If the discussion should grow heated though, the dining room has air conditioning.

● Le Florimond SIM

19, av de la Motte-Picquet
Métro: Ecole-Militaire, La Tour-Maubourg
Tel.-Fax 01 45 55 40 38
Closed Saturday lunch, Sunday,
Christmas–New Year's, 1 week in May,
3 weeks in August. Open until 10:15 PM.
Prix fixe: 19,50€ (lunch on weekdays),
34,50€. A la carte: 50–55€.
Terrace.

We still have a weakness for this cheerful, bright restaurant with its small terrace, competitive prices and fresh cuisine. Pascal Guillaumin lovingly concocts an escargot risotto with parsley and slow-cooked tomatoes, a lobster, langoustine and wild mushroom fricassée, veal sweetbreads pan-seared in Calvados-flavored butter with spinach and many other surprises. We conclude on a sweeter note with a vanilla-Bourbon millefeuille or champagne sorbet with wild strawberries and hibiscus syrup. Note the "no smoking" policy.

● La Fontaine de Mars 🏠SIM
129, rue Saint-Dominique
Métro: Ecole-Militaire, Pont-de-l'Alma
Tel. 01 47 05 46 44. Fax 01 47 05 11 13
cafedelalma@wanadoo.fr
Closed Christmas–New Year's.
Open until 11 PM.
Prix fixe: 23€ (lunch). A la carte: 50€.
Air cond. Terrace. Private dining room.

The art deco setting, cloth-covered tables, patinated walls and terrace are stylish. The cuisine seems to have improved a little (boudin noir sausage with apples and porcini mushroom pâté). Then there are cod with aïoli, cassoulet with duck confit and chicken with morel mushrooms washed down with a lively Cahors. Jacques and Christiane Boudon, who run the neighboring Café de l'Alma and Auvergne Gourmande, seem to have taken our advice. A delicious floating island.

● Chez Françoise COM
Aérogare des Invalides
Métro: Invalides
Tel. 01 47 05 49 03. Fax 01 45 51 96 20
info@chezfrancoise.com
www.chezfrancoise.com
Open daily until midnight.
Prix fixe: 29€, 25€ (lunch), 19€ (Saturday, Sunday dinner), 32€ (Sunday lunch, wine included), 9€ (children).
A la carte: 45–60€.
Terrace. Private dining room. Valet parking.

You cannot play fast and loose with the cream of the Assemblée Nationale, and this is their refectory. Comfort, contemporary design, impeccable service, a modern wooden bar, terrace, private dining room for 50 people, meeting room, valet parking and 100 wines in the cellar are all that is needed to settle even the most intractable disputes. Of course, Philippe Léglise, with his porcini mushroom fricassée with garlic, onions and parsley, his farm-raised pork filet glazed with spices and served with an

artichoke and endive compote and prunes soaked in Armagnac, has plenty of arguments too. On Sunday, the change in ambience is startling when a nice lady arrives at lunchtime to make children up with face paint. Astounding!

● Gaya Rive Gauche ○COM
par Pierre Gagnaire
44, rue du Bac
Métro: Rue-du-Bac
Tel.-Fax 01 45 44 73 73
Closed Saturday lunch, Sunday, August.
Open until 10:30 PM.
A la carte: 80€.
Air cond. Terrace.

To each chef his adjunct, and Pierre Gagnaire is no exception. Here he is, jointly managing this fully redesigned marine establishment. On two floors, Christian Ghion has dreamed up a bright, bluish, chic, contemporary, seaside cabin decor. On the food front, the chef from the rue Balzac excels himself. The produce is at its peak, the inventive preparations quite unambiguous, the cooking impeccable and the presentation polished. Results include pressed crab cake with salted turnips and a cauliflower mayonnaise sauce, Gagnaire's take on the classic croque-monsieur sandwich with gray shrimp, Dover sole served grilled, simply pan seared, or pan fried in butter and seasoned with parsley and lemon and braised red mullet with Jerusalem artichokes and Spanish chorizo. Equally refined are the desserts, including iced chocolate dessert seasoned with olive oil and served with a thick orange sauce and a rum-soaked baba with lightly whipped cream. The service is exemplary and the menu a pure joy. Paris Left Bank society is eager for more of the same.

● Chez Germaine ●SIM
30, rue Pierre-Leroux
Métro: Duroc, Vaneau
Tel. 01 42 73 28 34
Closed Saturday evening, Sunday, August.
Open until 10 PM.
Prix fixe: 12€ (lunch), 14€ (dinner).
A la carte: 30€.
Terrace.

Good Restaurants & Others

Laurent Joly has taken over this little domestic establishment and left its style more or less intact. Guests still enjoy the tasty home cooking priced at blue-collar levels. Roman-style ravioli, tomme cheese and fig salad, sea bass with olives, duck breast seasoned with honey served with scalloped potatoes and a soft chocolate cake, not to mention a classic Marie Brizard frozen soufflé, go down without a grimace.

A SPECIAL FAVORITE

● **Le Gorille Blanc** Ⓝ 🍴 SIM

11 bis, rue Chomel
Métro: Sèvres-Babylone
Tel.-Fax 01 45 49 04 54
Closed Saturday, Sunday, Christmas, New Year's, 3 weeks in August. Open until 11 PM.
Prix fixe: 19€ (lunch). A la carte: 35–40€.

We love this local bistro located near the Bon Marché department store, with its counter, wooden tables, ceramic floor (it was formerly La Cigale) and compact summer terrace. Bernard Arény, formerly at L'Ambassade d'Auvergne, has turned his energy to running the place and renamed it the "White Gorilla," confirming his fondness for animal metaphors (he previously owned Le Grizzli in the fourth). A native of the Pyrénées, he has lost none of his Ariège accent or enthusiasm. To officiate in the kitchen, he has brought in the talented Jérôme Catillat, formerly at Bistrot du Théâtre in Toulouse. This young man, who trained with Dutournier and at Le Crillon, knows his stuff. He concocts cunning, fresh, flavorsome dishes that follow today's trends, reflect timeless tradition and willingly adopt the accents of Southwest France. The lentil salad with pig's feet and foie gras, chestnut soup with a frothy porcini mushroom emulsion, small squid with squid ink risotto and partridge wrapped in cabbage (served in the hunting season), work wonders, while the simple rabbit fricassée with onions and Corinth raisins is a domestic delight. The desserts—thin dark chocolate tart and hazelnut

crème brûlée—slip down readily. Sensibly priced, thirst-quenching wines, such as Chermette "Cœur de Vendanges" Beaujolais, scarcely boost the check. A treasure trove not to be missed.

● **La Gourmandine** COM

29, rue Surcouf
Métro: La Tour-Maubourg, Invalides
Tel. 01 45 51 61 49. Fax 01 47 05 36 40
sabinesabine@msn.com
Closed Saturday lunch, Sunday, Christmas, 3 weeks in August. Open until 10:30 PM.
Prix fixe: 17€ (lunch, wine included), 30€.
A la carte: 45€.
Air cond. Terrace.

The dynamic Sabine Dreyfus-Weill has taken over Evelyne Gélin's bistro and left the cozy, hushed ambience and decor in red and sienna tones intact. There, we enjoy the eggplant caviar cannelloni with parmesean, fresh goat cheese terrine with black radishes, seared scorpion fish filet with Swiss chard gratin, monkfish with basil-roasted tomatoes and pan-seared lamb with sautéed peppers meticulously prepared by chef Fabien Edru and inoffensively priced. The desserts—milk chocolate "contrast" and pear tartare with fermented honey—are good.

● **Léo le Lion** SIM

23, rue Duvivier
Métro: Ecole-Militaire, La Tour-Maubourg
Tel.-Fax 01 45 51 41 77
Closed Sunday, Monday, Christmas–New Year's, August. Open until 10:30 PM.
A la carte: 45€.

In this restaurant run by Didier Méry, formerly with Le Divellec, there is no lion on the menu, just fish as fresh as the morning dew, game and other succulent meats to be savored on the newly restored oak tables of this bistro in Thirties'-style burgundy hues. The snails braised in champagne, thinly sliced John Dory fish with a seafood broth or farm-raised chicken and langoustines, like the pineapple carpaccio with kirsch and sorbet, are a pleasure to eat.

● **Maison de l'Amérique Latine** V.COM
217, bd Saint-Germain
Métro: Rue-du-Bac, Solférino
Tel. 01 49 54 75 00. Fax 01 40 49 03 94
commercial@mal217.org
www.mal217.org
Closed Saturday, Sunday, Bank Holidays,
Christmas–New Year's, 10 days in July,
3 weeks in August. Open until 10 PM.
Prix fixe: 40€ (lunch), 55€ (dinner).
Terrace. Private dining room.

The facade of this 18th-century residence
conceals one of the finest terraces in Paris.
In summer, among the trees and shrubs,
the butterflies of the Left Bank admire Pascal Jouan's skills. This veteran of Le
Toupary dreams up set menus that delicately balance tradition and modernity.
The scrambled eggs with truffles and crisp
toast, the thyme-seasoned pan-seared cod
with spring onion mashed potatoes, the
veal chop with sweet garlic and mascarpone polenta and the hot mango soufflé
and lime sorbet make up light, fresh meals.

● **Le Maupertu**   ☎ COM
94, bd de la Tour-Maubourg
Métro: La Tour-Maubourg, Ecole-Militaire
Tel. 01 45 51 37 96. Fax 01 53 59 94 83
info@restaurant-maupertu-paris.com
www.restaurant-maupertu-paris.com
Closed Sunday, 1 week in February,
3 weeks in August. Open until 10 PM.
Prix fixe: 22€ (lunch), 29€ (dinner).
A la carte: 45€.
Terrace.

There are not many good restaurants at
reasonable prices in this part of Invalides.
Fortunately, Sophie and Alain Deguest are
still here, ready to welcome us in their
bright establishment with its sought-after
terrace. In the kitchen, Mikael Loiseau
concocts sterling dishes of the South of
France. The brochette of jumbo shrimp
enrobed in smoked bacon with mixed
greens, sea bass filet with vegetable purée
and anise-seasoned cream and breast of
farm-raised chicken with cream sauce and
a fourme d'ambert cheese crust, served
with mashed potatoes with Port sauce, will
bring roses to your cheeks, as will the kiwi

carpaccio, served with red fruit sauce and
Bulgarian yogurt ice cream.

● **Les Ministères**   COM
30, rue du Bac
Métro: Rue-du-Bac
Tel. 01 42 61 22 37. Fax 01 42 86 87 33
ckubiak@easynet.fr
www.lesministeres.com
Closed Christmas, New Year's, August 15th.
Open until 10:30 PM.
Prix fixe: 16,80€ (lunch, weekdays),
33€ (wine included). A la carte: 36€.
Air cond. Terrace. Private dining room.

The facade has just been completely refurbished and chef Hervé Gueguen has a
spanking new kitchen. All the rest is still
there: the terrace, private dining room,
wooden alcoves and banquettes, the eggplant millefeuille with crushed tomatoes.
If you prefer, the saffroned poultry risotto
with jumbo shrimp and the duck breast
with blueberry sauce served with potatoes
and shallots sautéed in duck fat look good,
while fruit with a Grand Marnier sabayon
competes honorably with orange and
strawberries with meringue. The set menu
at 33€ includes an aperitif and wine.

● **Le Montalembert**   COM
Hotel Montalembert, 3, rue Montalembert
Métro: Rue-du-Bac
Tel. 01 45 49 68 03. Fax 01 45 49 69 49
restaurant@montalembert.com
www.montalembert.com
Open daily noon–10:30 PM. Cont. service.
A la carte: 50–65€.
Air cond. Terrace. Private dining room.
Valet parking.

Neighbor to publishers Gallimard, the
great bar and restaurant of the Hotel
Montalembert has named one of its small
lounges (which can be closed off for a private meal) after the firm. Everything is in
the same tone: the library fireplace corner
with its couch and armchairs, the large
bar, the elegance and sense of light, and
especially the flexibility: You can have a
drink or order a dish at any time from
noon to 10:30 p.m. in the bar or dining
room or on a couch. The modern menu is

divided into four chapters—vegetable, sea, land, sun—and each dish into two sizes—"*dégustation*" (tasting) or "*gourmet*." Sautéed baby artichoke hearts with wild mushrooms, sea bass tagine with vegetables, Iberian ham and Spanish goat cheese are pleasant. A good choice of vintages from every region.

● Nabuchodonosor   `COM`
6, av Bosquet
Métro: La Tour-Maubourg, Ecole-Militaire, Pont-de-l'Alma
Tel. 01 45 56 97 26. Fax 01 45 56 98 44
www.nabuchodonosor.net
Closed Saturday lunch, Sunday,
3 weeks in August. Open until 11 PM.
Prix fixe: 21€ (lunch), 31€ (dinner).
A la carte: 50–60€.
Air cond.

The atmosphere is as warm and comfortable as ever in this restaurant named after Nebuchadnezzar, King of Babylon, with its blond woodwork, sienna hues and Venetian blinds. Chef Thierry Garnier, formerly with Guy Savoy, summons you to royal repasts of slow-cooked shrimp and sea snail stew, fondue of leeks with seafood sauce, seared scallops with balsamic vinegar, spinach sautéed in butter, beef potau-feu seasoned with Szechuan pepper, pan-seared foie gras and other pearls. A brioche pain perdu dusted with browned almonds and apricot jam and a caramel and white chocolate cream millefeuille provide an excellent conclusion.

● La Note de Frais   `SIM`
47, rue de Bourgogne
Métro: Varenne, Invalides
Tel. 01 45 55 15 35
bovisage@yahoo.com
Closed Saturday, Sunday, 3 weeks in August.
Open until 10:30 PM.
A la carte: 40€.

A new chef, but the same familiar ambience and cuisine in this fashionable bistro in warm colors. Jean-Baptiste Beauvisage welcomes guests, while in the kitchen, Stéphane Moulières whips up pleasant, unpretentious dishes. Ravioli prepared in

the Savoie style, a tomato and anchovy tart, tuna carpaccio, sea bream sashimi, soy-infused pork filet as well as cake soaked in orange liqueur and soft chocolate cake make for a quiet meal with friends.

● L'Œillade   `COM`
10, rue de Saint-Simon
Métro: Rue-du-Bac
Tel. 01 42 22 01 60
restaurantloeillade@hotmail.fr
Closed dinner, Saturday, Sunday,
Bank Holidays, Christmas, New Year's,
2 weeks in August. Open until 2 PM.
A la carte: 26–40€.
Air cond. Private dining room.

Jean-Louis Huclin is back at the range in this shrewd restaurant after a long absence. We like the rustic setting with its ochre, beige and orange tones, and especially the very French cuisine based on invariably fresh produce, prepared by this veteran of Jacques Manière from the days of the Pactole and the Dodin Bouffant. No complaints about the all-you-can-eat house terrine, sea bass seared with Pastis, lamb shank with eggplant purée, nor the exquisite rhubarb tart. The menu changes each day. Wines from every region wash down these pleasant, competently conducted feasts.

● Les Ombres   `N` `V.COM`
Musée du Quai Branly, 27, quai Branly
Métro: Pont-de-l'Alma (RER C)
Tel. 01 47 53 68 00
Open daily until 10:30 PM
(Friday, Saturday 11 PM).
Prix fixe: 32€ (lunch). A la carte: 80€.

The all-glass architecture by Nouvel, the view of Paris, the unmistakably designer decor and the appeal of innovation: This museum restaurant entrusted to the Elior group has a lot going for it. The young Arno Busquet, former assistant at Chez Laurent, veteran of the Robuchon school, strives to get it right in reduced circumstances. Dodine de lapin Rex du Poitou en anchoïade (a rabbit and anchovy paste dish), shellfish risotto with frothy lemon reduction sauce, seared tuna belly with sesame and onion rings, duck seasoned with rosemary served with a lime-seasoned confit duck leg and regional shortbread cookies with cherry and pistachio, served with whipped creamy mousse and almond milk sorbet, are tempting and very ambitious. Let us give him time to sort out the teething problems. The place is new and the service is still finding its feet. An event to watch.

● **Les Ormes**   ◎ COM

22, rue Surcouf
Métro: La Tour-Maubourg, Invalides
Tel. 01 45 51 46 93. Fax 01 45 50 30 11
Closed Sunday, Monday, 1 week in January,
3 weeks in August. Open until 10 PM.
Prix fixe: 32€ (lunch), 38€ (lunch), 44€
(dinner), 79€ (dinner). A la carte: 70€.
Air cond.

Stéphane Molé, a Robuchon disciple who was formerly with Jamin in rue de Longchamp, produces works of art in his stylish establishment. He is everywhere at once, honing masterpieces worthy of a great chef. We begin dramatically with his mackerel tart with fennel or his pan-seared foie gras over soft caramelized rhubarb and turnips. To follow, who could resist the symphony of flavors offered by brill with sorrel sauce and marinated vegetables or braised beef tenderloin with soft cooked potatoes and foie gras sauce? After these flights of excellence, strawberries marinated with mint on a Breton shortbread with olive oil offers a soft landing, especially in such good company. Attentive service and a wine list featuring 100 items.

● **Pasco**   COM

74, bd de la Tour-Maubourg
Métro: La Tour-Maubourg
Tel. 01 44 18 33 26. Fax 01 44 18 34 06
restaurant.pasco@wanadoo.fr
www.restaurantpasco.com
Closed Monday, 4 days for Christmas.
Open until 10:30 PM.
Prix fixe: 19€, 24€. A la carte: 40€.
Air cond. Terrace. Private dining room.
Valet parking.

By Les Invalides, this amiable Mediterranean restaurant in warm, brick colors with a corner terrace offers a menu of fusional leanings, different every day and changing with the seasons. Benoît Dargere, who has taken over from Fabrice Amar, puts together smoked haddock rémoulade with Chinese cabbage, green apples and endives, seared and sliced red tuna seasoned with coriander, beef tenderloin served with a black pepper infusion and reggiano cheese, as well as praliné and hazelnut cookies and blood orange sorbet.

● **A la Petite Chaise**   COM

36, rue de Grenelle
Métro: Sèvres-Babylone, Rue-du-Bac
Tel. 01 42 22 13 35. Fax 01 42 22 33 84
lapetitechaise@yahoo.com
www.alapetitechaise.fr
Closed Christmas. Open until 11 PM.
Prix fixe: 29,50€. A la carte: 38€.
Air cond. Terrace. Private dining room.

The series of three small rooms (yellow, red and gold, respectively) is one of this historic establishment's great charms. With its 17th-century walls and 18th-century beams, it is the oldest restaurant in Paris. Laurent Bargeau carries off a neat balancing act in terms of value for money, and Christophe Capron's cuisine is fresh and unpretentious. His homemade foie gras with potatoes, fish fumet and julienned vegetables and grilled veal roast with camembert cream are very well mannered. For dessert diehards who are feeling full, white chocolate mousse with dark chocolate sauce will do deliciously. You can eat freely a la carte: The prices are quite reasonable.

● **Le Petit Niçois**   SIM

10, rue Amélie
Métro: La Tour-Maubourg
Tel. 01 45 51 83 65. Fax 01 47 05 77 46
www.lepetitnicois.com
Closed end of July–end of August.
Open until 10:30 PM.
Prix fixe: 18€, 30€. A la carte: 45–70€.
Private dining room.

Those who find they have a sudden craving for a bouillabaisse or aïoli after a visit to Napoleon's tomb can satisfy their appetites at Robert Belgiral's, where Jo Velia and Vincent Butet magically produce these wonders from hats in the form of cooking pots. Otherwise, they can choose pan-seared porcini and chanterelle mushrooms Provençal, or half of a roasted free-range duck with olives. And after a hot apple tart with vanilla ice cream, they can raise a toast to the apt Petit Niçois, which also has a private dining room for 12 people.

● Au Petit Sud-Ouest   `SIM`

46, av de la Bourdonnais
Métro: Ecole-Militaire
Tel. 01 45 55 59 59
Closed Sunday, Monday, August.
Open until 11 PM.
A la carte: 45€.
Air cond. Terrace.

Christian and Chantal André have renamed their former Ambassade du Sud-Ouest and refurbished it in a cozy, natural style mainly in stone and wood. In the kitchen, nothing has changed: The focus is still on Southwest France. We feel quite at home with foie gras salad or a plate of foie gras and duck breast, duck breast with sautéed potatoes and porcini mushrooms or duck seasoned with cherry fondant cooked to perfection, and, for dessert, a regional pastry dish from the Southwest with apples and Armagnac. The same spirit fills the place . . . and the glasses too, with wines from Bordeaux or further afield, but all from the Southwest, of course. You can also eat on the terrace. The region's cherished palmiped also has a place of honor in the store, where you can make your purchases as you leave.

● Au Petit Tonneau   `SIM`

20, rue Surcouf
Métro: La Tour-Maubourg, Invalides
Tel. 01 47 05 09 01. Fax 01 47 53 05 59
Closed August. Open until 11 PM.
Prix fixe: 20€ (lunch on weekdays).
A la carte: 36–50€.
Terrace.

The great fictional detective Maigret (and there is a plaque to prove it) was a regular of this Fifties' bistro with its colored tiling and oak counter. We can easily believe it. Ginette Boyer brilliantly supervises the smooth running of her establishment and concocts deliciously traditional dishes: lentils served with crayfish tails, classic blanquette, sirloin steak with roquefort cheese, crème caramel and tarte Tatin offer a delightful reminder of our childhood. Every day, the catch of the day and the main courses are served with scalloped potatoes or fresh vegetables.

● Petrossian   `V.COM`

18, bd de La Tour-Maubourg
Métro: La Tour-Maubourg, Invalides
Tel. 01 44 11 32 32. Fax 01 44 11 32 35
www.petrossian.fr
Closed Sunday, Monday, August.
Open until 10:30 PM.
Prix fixe: 35€ (lunch), 45€ (dinner).
A la carte: 75€.
Air cond. Private dining room. Valet parking.

The year's good news comes from this Parisian institution, which Sébastien Faré has handed over to his former assistant. So the task of rejuvenating Armen Petrossian's establishment has fallen to Rougui Dia, an attractive Fulani. The decor has been modernized with gray tones in the dining rooms and livelier colors around the windows, the prices adjusted downward and the cuisine invigorated with spices and fashionable preparation. So it is with a light heart that we head up to the second floor above the grocery store to taste sea bream tartare with olive oil and dill, sea scallops with julienned vegetables and herbed vodka sauce or slow-cooked lamb tagine (her finest achievement!) served with tagine-roasted fruit. For dessert, a Russian strawberry dessert with basil jelly and lime sorbet dispels any remaining doubts: Petrossian has a jewel here, one to watch.

Good Restaurants & Others

● Au Pied de Fouet ● 🍴 SIM

45, rue de Babylone
Métro: St-François-Xavier
Tel. 01 47 05 12 27
Closed Thursday evening, 1 week in August.
Open until 11 PM.
A la carte: 20–25€.

Today, this former coachmen's haunt enjoys a solid reputation among the capital's gourmet bistros. Perusing a menu that changes each day, you are sure to find something to suit your tastes among, for example, a lentil salad, slow-cooked duck gizzards in salad, sautéed poultry livers, homemade duck confit, crème caramel and soft chocolate cake, all for a truly minimal price. Ideally, you should drink your coffee at the bar to free a table for those still waiting impatiently.

● La Poule au Pot 🍴 SIM

121, rue de l'Université
Métro: Invalides
Tel. 01 47 05 16 36. Fax 01 47 05 74 56
Closed Saturday lunch, Sunday, 10 days Christmas–New Year's, 3 weeks in August. Open until 10:30 PM.
Prix fixe: 18,50€, 24,50€.
A la carte: 47€.
Terrace.

This bistro with its typical Thirties' decor instantly works its charm. The setting, the food, the welcome—everything appeals. The tasty, timeless dishes that Jacques Dumond concocts have a tang of authenticity. Crawfish tail salad, salmon tartare, poule au pot farcie d'Henri IV (classic poached stuffed hen) and Armagnac-soaked prunes with accompanying tea cakes will bring color to your cheeks and a smile to your face.

● Le P'tit Troquet 🔔 SIM

28, rue de l'Exposition
Métro: Ecole-Militaire
Tel.-Fax 01 47 05 80 39
Closed Saturday lunch, Sunday, Monday lunch, August. Open until 10:30 PM.
Prix fixe: 30€ (dinner), 19,50€ (lunch), 27€ (lunch). A la carte: 42€.
Private dining room.

Everything is a collector's item in Patrick Vessière's Twenties' bistro in beige and green hues: marble tables, coffee pots and enameled advertisements on the walls. The proprietor and chef takes a fresh approach to regional cuisine with caramelized endive, apple chutney, and tangy goat cheese tart, wild drum fish seasoned with soy sauce and black olive-braised rabbit with fork-mashed potatoes. The strawberry, meringue and lemon ice cream "igloo" provides a suitable conclusion for the feast. The portions are generous, and no smoking is allowed in the restaurant.

● Chez Ribe COM

15, av de Suffren
Métro: Bir-Hakeim,
Champ-de-Mars–Tour-Eiffel
Tel.-Fax 01 45 66 53 79
Open daily noon–11 PM. Cont. service.
Prix fixe: 16,90€, 21,90€.
A la carte: 37€.
Terrace. Private dining room.

The style is a tad colonial with an "Out of Africa" feel to it in this neo-1900s' bistro in cream and brown, with a terrace, private dining room and mezzanine (occasionally turned into another private dining room for 25 people). The talented Ismaël Garreau offers no flights of fancy, but serves up an eggplant gâteau with tomato sauce, cod with aïoli, grilled beef tenderloin and lavender crème brûlée with disarming simplicity. No lengthy, technical names on the set menu, just well-prepared, appetizing dishes on the table. Only the starters change on the menu, the rest stays put.

● Le Rouge Vif SIM

48, rue de Verneuil
Métro: Rue-du-Bac, Solférino
Tel. 01 42 86 81 87
www.lerougevif.com
Closed Saturday, Sunday, Christmas–New Year's. Open until 10 PM.
Prix fixe: 18,50€ (lunch). A la carte: 40€.
Air cond.

The exposed stone and savannah shades of this restaurant set in the former stables of a town house contrast with its contemporary style and dominant red. Patrick Rousseau hosts exhibitions of photos and paintings on the walls and has a gift for creating a convivial atmosphere. The meal lavished on us by Cyrill Tran begins with bone marrow on toast (rare enough in our bistros to be worth noting), continues with a brochette of four different fish served with a celery root mousse and concluded soberly with a slice of pain perdu or pear clafoutis with raspberry sorbet. Pure pleasure.

● **Le Soleil**   Ⓝ COM
153, rue de Grenelle
Métro: La Tour-Maubourg
Tel. 01 45 51 54 12
Closed Sunday. Open until 11:30 PM.
Prix fixe: 38€ (lunch). A la carte: 65€.
Air cond.

Taken over by Louis-Jacques Vanucci, who runs the eponymous establishment opposite the Saint Ouen flea market, the former Gildo is enjoying a second youth. The decor draws on the colors of the South of France. The floor is an *opus insertium* of large gray-green schist stones, the walls are a light terracotta shade and the lighting is of a Diego Giacometti–style sconce design. The cuisine? A stroll along the Mediterranean coast, from Capri to Andalusia, via Cap d'Antibes. In others words, sun-kissed dishes, such as the spirited pan-seared squid with basil, marinated anchovies with slow-cooked peppers, tagliarini with parmesan and cream and a beautiful pan-seared Corsican red mullet. Then there are great wines from every region served by the glass, elegant Burgundies and the ambient murmur of delighted diners. The prices reflect all this.

● **Tante Marguerite**   ◯ COM
5, rue de Bourgogne
Métro: Assemblée-Nationale
Tel. 01 45 51 79 42. Fax 01 47 53 79 56
tante.maguerite@bernard-loiseau.com
www.bernard-loiseau.com
Closed Saturday, Sunday, August.
Open until 10:30 PM.
Prix fixe: 34€, 65€. A la carte: 60€.
Air cond. Private dining room.

Nostalgic gourmets need not worry: The spirit of Bernard Loiseau continues to permeate this rustic, bourgeois adjunct with its solid, classical dishes. The menu still features a snail and herb ragout, roasted brill with red wine sauce, roasted veal sweetbreads with shallot mashed potatoes and molten Guanaja chocolate cake and coffee ice cream. As ever, the team and service are remarkable in every way and the Burgundies introduced by Gabriel Guibert provide a very apt accompaniment for the cuisine.

● **Le Télégraphe**   Ⓝ 🍴 V.COM
41, rue de Lille
Métro: Rue du Bac, St-Germain-des-Prés
Tel. 01 42 92 03 04. Fax 01 42 92 02 77
Closed Friday evening, Saturday lunch,
2 weeks in August. Open until 10:30 PM.
Prix fixe: 50€. A la carte: 70€.

Expensive and kosher, but also good and even surprising, this Beth Din-approved restaurant presents the creative cuisine of a young Ducasse veteran in a former residence for ladies in the employ of the Post Office. Cream of porcini with hazelnut oil, tomato confit tart with balsamic vinegar, foie gras served three ways (terrine, poached and crème brûlée), pan-seared tuna with pear and ginger compote, roasted lamb tenderloin with eggplant spread are very well judged. The pure, gleaming art nouveau decor with its ceramics and chandeliers, and the art deco furniture, have a genuine retro charm, modernized in attractive colors.

● **La Terrasse**   COM
2, pl de l'Ecole-Militaire
Métro: Ecole-Militaire
Tel. 01 45 55 00 02. Fax 01 45 55 94 67
terrasse7@wanadoo.fr
www.laterrasse7.com
Open daily 7:30 AM–2 AM. Cont. service.
A la carte: 32–45€.
Air cond. Terrace. Private dining room.

Going the extra mile to welcome the brasserie's smart clientele, David Bramoul, Rémi Baubla and Christophe Abadit provide a sophisticated reception worthy of the place's red, gray and black distinction. With a private dining room for 90 people, La Terrasse is a colossus, wavering between the modern and contemporary styles of its chic dishes. Artichoke and peppers slow cooked with coriander seasoning, jumbo shrimp grilled on skewers and lemon-seasoned chicken with basmati rice are direct, unpretentious and tasteful. As a sweet conclusion, espresso with three mini desserts: crème brûlée, strawberries on a skewer and a soft cake.

● Thoumieux 🏠 COM
79, rue Saint-Dominique
Métro: La Tour-Maubourg
Tel. 01 47 05 49 75. Fax 01 47 05 36 96
bthoumieux@aol.com /
thoumieux@thoumieux.com
www.thoumieux.com
Open daily until midnight.
Prix fixe: 20€ (lunch on weekdays), 35€.
A la carte: 50€.
Air cond. Private dining room.

Paris society has been flocking to the Bassalert family's Corrèze brasserie since 1923. Free from the dictates of fashion, guests gather under its antique beams every day with friends or family to enjoy its reliable, solid bistro cuisine. Duck foie gras terrine, Dover sole filet pan-fried in butter and seasoned with parsley and lemon, grilled sardines, cassoulet, a half-pound steak and brown sugar crème brûlée are first rate.

● Titi Parisien SIM
96, bd de La Tour-Maubourg
Métro: La Tour-Maubourg
Tel. 01 44 18 36 37. Fax 01 44 18 39 40
Closed 1 week from Christmas–New Year's, 3 weeks in August. Open until 11:30 PM (Friday, Saturday midnight).
A la carte: 50€.
Terrace.

Opposite the dome of Les Invalides, this invigorating "meat bistro" with its quiet terrace, red brick walls, wine racks, old-fashioned zinc counter and amiable cuisine makes an excellent impression.

Patrons come for bone marrow, small black boudin sausage grilled with potatoes or apples, the half-pound boneless rib steak, the two-pound prime rib for two and the violet, rose and green tea crème brûlée, which do them a world of good. A fine selection of wines where you only need pay for the part of the bottle you drink.

● Vin et Marée COM
71, av de Suffren
Métro: La Motte-Picquet–Grenelle
Tel. 01 47 83 27 12. Fax 01 43 06 62 35
vin.maree@wanadoo.fr
Open daily until 10:30 PM.
A la carte: 48€.
Air cond. Terrace.

The first Vin et Marée (Wine and Tide) opened here a little more than ten years ago. A recent fire provided an opportunity to refurbish it completely. The prevailing color of the contemporary, wood-trimmed decor is of course blue. On the food front, the fish is always fresh, coming as it does directly from the ports of Normandy. Wine also plays an important part. Dubœuf Mâcon, Foreau Vouvray and Colombo Crozes go perfectly with crisp-layered pastry with jumbo shrimp, grilled sardines, Dieppe-style grilled fish, Honfleur-style grilled turbot, thick-cut tenderloin and baba au rhum.

● Le Vin de Soif ● SIM
24, rue Pierre-Leroux
Métro: Vaneau, Duroc
Tel. 01 43 06 79 85
Closed Saturday lunch, Sunday, 3 weeks in August. Open until 10:30 PM.
Prix fixe: 13€ (lunch), 25€ (dinner), 21€ (dinner). A la carte: 30€.
Air cond. Terrace.

Formerly at the Mauzac, Stéphane Pelouard has drawn up a wine list that reflects the quality of his cellar. It offers few Bordeaux wines, but some great finds, all at very reasonable prices. Creamed white beans glazed with cumin mousse, pan-seared Argentinean thick-cut boneless rib steak with mashed potatoes or certified

Troyes andouillette AAAAA roasted and served with mustard and slow-cooked fennel are a marvel, accompanied by a Grameron Côtes du Rhône or Château Yvonne Saumur. For dessert, we vote unanimously for rice pudding with salted peanuts and Corinth raisins and whipped cream quenelle.

● Vin Sur Vin ○ COM

20, rue de Montttessuy
Métro: Pont-de-l'Alma
Tel. 01 47 05 14 20
Closed Saturday lunch, Sunday, Monday lunch (except from April-September), school vacation, Christmas–New Year's, August. Open until 9:30 PM.
A la carte: 80€.
Air cond.

Knowledgeable connoisseur Patrice Vidal has more than 600 wines from all over France on his list. Pascal Toulza, who once worked at L'Arpège, provides ambitious dishes to match. Inspired by the French regions, his preparations offer the best of land and sea from Brittany to Drôme. The cream of oxtail soup, foie gras pot-au-feu, pan-seared red mullet, roasted farm-raised pigeon, aged beef tenderloin and millefeuille seasoned with orange blossom are all capably matched with the right libation. The setting suggests the dining room of a bourgeois home, the tables are meticulously set and, above all, the cellar unfailingly provides the perfect, unsung wine to add zest to your meal. A rare little establishment.

● Le Violon d'Ingres ○ COM

135, rue Saint-Dominique
Métro: Ecole-Militaire, Pont-de-l'Alma
Tel. 01 45 55 15 05. Fax 01 45 55 48 42
violondingres@wanadoo.fr
www.leviolondingres.com
Closed Sunday, Monday. Open until 10:30 PM.
Prix fixe: 50€ (lunch), 100€ (dinner).
A la carte: 45€.
Air cond.

A radical new departure for Christian Constant: The former maestro of Le Crillon, who taught proper manners to Eric Fré-

chon, Thierry Breton and Yves Camdeborde, has founded a relaxed, gourmet empire a stone's throw from the Eiffel Tower. First came Café Constant and Les Fables de la Fontaine, so popular they were turning customers away. Now, his great Violon d'Ingres has become a cheerful, lively, amusing gourmet brasserie, with rotisserie dishes and other modish creations. The prices have been halved and the public has poured in, keen to witness this phenomenon of triumphant modesty, following the example of Alain Senderens at Le Lucas last year. With Constant, there is no trickery, nothing but the real McCoy. Juggling with fresh market produce, he still concocts a changing, appropriate, personal menu. A superb foie gras terrine, sea bass fried in an almond crust, caramelized pig's foot pie with fingerling potatoes, rotisserie-cooked chicken and grilled prime rib with parsley jus offer a chance to indulge without breaking the bank. The desserts focus on seasonal fruits and the cellar has opened its doors to new, natural wines and affordable prices. In short, this is an event. A new career is beginning (again) for Constant, a native of Montauban, in Ingres country.

● Le Voltaire ✓ COM

27, quai Voltaire
Métro: Rue-du-Bac, Musée-d'Orsay
Tel. 01 42 61 17 49
Closed Sunday, Monday, 1 week at All Saint's Day, 1 week Christmas–New Year's, 1 week in February, 3 weeks in August.
Open until 10:15 PM.
A la carte: 55–75€.
Air cond. Terrace.

NEXT DOOR LA PETIT VOL

Le Voltaire has been around for more than 60 years, showing just how well it understands its eminent customers' preferences. A venerable institution dedicated to traditional domestic cooking, it also has other attractions: a luxurious ambience and surroundings full of old-fashioned charm, with wall lamps, thick, dark carpeting, woodwork and soft light playing a crucial role. Like French literati Jean d'Ormesson and Angelo Rinaldi, regular visitors from the Académie Française, we waver between fresh crab salad, the house rendition of classic hard-boiled eggs and mayonnaise, grilled red mullet with shallots and anchovies, Dover sole filet pan-fried in butter, parsley and lemon, beef tenderloin with pepper, tender young chicken roasted with tarragon and chocolate mousse. The wines are from Bordeaux or Burgundy, with labels to be taken seriously indeed, although without sending the check sky high.

INTERNATIONAL RESTAURANTS

INTERNATIONAL RESTAURANT OF THE YEAR

● Aïda   Ⓝ○ SIM

1, rue Pierre-Leroux
Métro: Vaneau, Duroc
Tel.-Fax 01 43 06 14 18
Closed Saturday lunch, Sunday lunch, Monday, 1 week in February, 2 weeks in August.
Prix fixe: 38€ (lunch), 45€ (lunch), 68€ (dinner), 90€ (dinner).
Air cond. Private dining room.

His name is Koji Aida. This young, subtle, discreet native of Tokyo has studied oenology in Burgundy and prepares a remarkably elegant "knife cuisine" in his tiny cubbyhole in the heart of the 7th arrondissement. His sushi and sashimi are splendid (and the mackerel superb). The grilled main dishes, cooked teppanyaki style, are the height of perfection. The spinach salad with mushrooms, the radish broth with foie gras, the miso soup, and the tender Limousin beef filet (the meat comes from Hugo Desnoyer in the fourteenth arrondissement, who supplies Pierre Gagnaire and L'Ambroisie) are devilishly tempting. Looking around, we see a few tables, a bar where we can admire the master sculptor, a small Japanese style dining room with tatamis, and an area to stretch out our legs. In short, an exquisite, exotic establishment whose little lunchtime set menus are tickets to Tokyo or Kyoto at angelic prices.

● Tan Dinh   ○ COM

60, rue de Verneuil
Métro: Rue-du-Bac, Solférino
Tel. 01 45 44 04 84. Fax 01 45 44 36 93
Closed Sunday, Bank Holidays, August.
Open until 11 PM.
A la carte: 54€.
Air cond. Private dining room.

Here, we discover all the wealth and refinement of that great, insufficiently known art that is Vietnamese cuisine. In a simple, freshly renovated Oriental decor in cream and red, the Vifian brothers bring us high fashion. Using fresh, quality produce, they concoct asparagus velouté with crab ravioli, mango and coconut salad, jumbo shrimp beignets, sautéed lamb with Thai ginger and soursop sorbet. Since good things never come singly, these deliciously subtle dishes are set off by an excellent cellar, where Bordeaux, Burgundies and first rate Australian, Italian and American wines lie side by side. The welcome and service are on a par with the rest.

● La Taverna   ⓐ COM

22, rue du Champ-de-Mars
Métro: Ecole-Militaire
Tel. 01 45 51 64 59. Fax 01 53 59 92 60
Closed August. Open until 11 PM.
Prix fixe: 18€ (lunch), 22€ (lunch), 33€.
Air cond.

Our last year's Special Favorite has stuck to its guns. Gustavo Andreoli titillates our taste buds deliciously with his delicate taleggio, arugula and Parma ham tart and his eggplant millefeuille with smoked cheese, dried tomatoes and basil. Depending on our appetite, to follow, there is red mullet with lemon and oregano cooked to perfection, just like flambéed tagliatelle with parmesan and fusilli with young broad beans and calamari. The pineapple tiramisu provides a commendable conclusion. There is sunshine in the dishes, an excellent Montepulciano in our glass and a smile on every face.

▼ SHOPS

TABLETOP & KITCHENWARE

▼ Le Chambrelain
11, av de la Motte-Picquet
Métro: La Tour-Maubourg
Tel. 01 45 55 03 45
9:30 AM–5 PM (Friday 9:30 AM–2 PM).
Closed Saturday, Sunday,
mid-July–mid-August.
Philippe Carenton gives lessons in painting porcelain and presents fine tableware, coffee sets and teapots in this pleasant store near Les Invalides.

BREAD & BAKED GOODS

▼ Malo
54, rue de Sèvres
Métro: Duroc, Vaneau
Tel. 01 47 83 30 40
7 AM–8 PM. Closed Sunday.
Jean-Loïc Negaret bakes a superb country loaf, multigrain breads, almond biscuits, breakfast pastries, brioche and a signature slow-rising baguette.

▼ Pain d'Epis
63, av Bosquet
Métro: Ecole-Militaire
Tel. 01 45 51 75 01
7:30 AM–8 PM. Closed Saturday, August.
Thierry Dubois wins unanimous approval with the house baguette, stone ground whole wheat loaf, country bread, and round rye loaf. The almond croissants and prune pastries are irresistible.

▼ Pâtisserie Secco
20, rue Jean-Nicot
Métro: Invalides, La Tour-Maubourg
Tel. 01 43 17 35 20. Fax 01 45 55 00 96
8 AM–8:30 PM.
Closed Sunday, Monday, August.
In the former Poujauran bakery store, which still has its antique facade and ceramic floor, Stéphane Secco has his eye firmly on quality: slow-rising yeast baguette, flute, round country bread, hazelnut raisin bread, lemon, chocolate, and apple tarts, vanilla cheesecake with lime and vanilla cake baked in fluted molds are exemplary.

WINE

▼ Les Grandes Caves
70, rue Saint-Dominique
Métro: La Tour-Maubourg
Tel. 01 47 05 69 28. Fax 01 47 53 09 92
10:30 AM–8 PM. Closed Sunday,
Monday morning, 3 weeks in August.
Sébastien Mourier has taken over this dynamic cellar offering exquisite bottles of Alsace (Deiss and Kientzler), Burgundy (Jayer-Gilles, Comtes Lafon) and Rhône Valley (Domaine le Sang des Cailloux). He also presents superb Bordeaux at reasonable prices.

▼ Ryst-Dupeyron   ⋔
79, rue du Bac
Métro: Rue-du-Bac
Tel. 01 45 48 80 93
10:30 AM–7:30 PM (Monday 12:30 PM–7:30 PM). Closed Sunday, Monday morning, 10 days in August.
This Condom (Gers) establishment specializing in great Bordeaux and vintage Armagnacs also offers W.J. Hart Port, rare whiskeys, 1845 Madeira, hundred-year-old Calvados, great Médocs and honorable Saint Emilions in a fine retro decor.

CHARCUTERIE

▼ Charles
135, rue Saint-Dominique
Métro: Ecole-Militaire, Pont-de-l'Alma
Tel.-Fax 01 47 05 53 66
8 AM–8 PM. Closed Sunday.
The Charles family, father and son, tend to walk off with all the awards: 2004 champions of France with a superb andouillette, award-winning ham, veal sausages and award-winning boudin. The light sauerkraut, terrines, rillettes, goose and duck foie gras, and head cheese terrine are works of art.

CHOCOLATE

▼ Michel Chaudun

149, rue de l'Université
Métro: Invalides
Tel.-Fax 01 47 53 74 40
9:15 AM–7 PM (Monday 10 AM–6 PM).
Closed Sunday.

The irrepressibly innovative Michel Chaudun charms us with dark- or milk-chocolate eggs, "postage stamps" and "sausages" made of chocolate. Just taste the truffle pastes: Merida (orange blossom), Esmerelda (dark chocolate and crushed cocoa beans) and discover his coffee, pepper, lemon, basil, praliné and pistachio ganaches in his chocolate colored store.

▼ Debauve & Gallais 🏠

30, rue des Saints-Pères
Métro: Rue-du-Bac, St-Germain-des-Prés
Tel. 01 45 48 54 67. Fax 01 45 48 21 78
9 AM–7 PM. Closed Sunday.

This store has a Balzacian chic. Pralinés, Aubin-style boules, variously flavored ganache, almond cream puffs and chocolate-covered candied orange peels: resistance is futile.

▼ Jean-Paul Hévin

23 bis, av de la Motte-Picquet
Métro: Ecole-Militaire
Tel. 01 45 51 77 48. Fax 01 45 55 87 33
10 AM–7:30 PM.
Closed Sunday, Monday, August.

Jean-Paul Hévin's confectionery is pure "dynamite": ginger chocolates, cola nuts, chocolate bark, almond chocolate biscuits, crunchy praliné cookies, eclairs, dried fruit and nuts and spice-flavored chocolate bars. (Also see the first and sixth arrondissements.)

▼ Richart

258, bd Saint-Germain
Métro: Solférino
Tel. 01 45 55 66 00. Fax 01 47 53 72 72
www.richart.com
10 AM–7 PM. Closed Sunday (except holidays), Bank Holidays.

This designer store has many different varieties of chocolate on offer: balsamic ganache, grilled praliné, prune and pineapple, citrus zest, floral and spice. "Graine de Gourmet" (liquid orange zest, candied hazelnut, vanilla, cinnamon) and "Emotion Pure" (crushed roasted cocoa beans, vanilla, almond) are very well done.

CANDY & SWEETS

▼ Les Gourmandises de Nathalie

67, bd des Invalides
Métro: Duroc
Tel. 01 43 06 02 98
10 AM–7 PM (Monday, Saturday 10 AM–6:30 PM). Closed Sunday,
Bank Holidays, August.

In her store near Les Invalides, Nathalie Lagrange presents salted butter caramels from Quiberon, nougat from Montélemar, jellied fruit from Apt, calissons (almond lozenges) from Aix, bergamots from Nancy, negus from Nevers, and spice bread from Dijon in a gourmet Tour de France.

▼ Puyricard

27, av Rapp
Métro: Ecole-Militaire, Pont-de-l'Alma
Tel. 01 47 05 59 47. Fax 01 47 05 85 87
10 AM–7 PM.
Closed Monday in July, August.

Ninety-two varieties of chocolates, sugared almonds, dried fruit compotes, cognac, rum or cinnamon truffles, orange candy, almonds, fig and liqueur–flavored chocolates from Provence are all equally delectable.

FINE GROCERIES

▼ Epicerie Fine Rive Gauche

8, rue du Champ-de-Mars
Métro: Ecole-Militaire
Tel. 01 47 05 98 18. Fax 01 47 05 92 18
epiceriefine.rivegauche@wanadoo.fr
9 AM–1 PM, 3–7:30 PM. Closed Sunday afternoon, Monday, February, August.

Italian white and black truffled pastas, pepper from Penja and Jamaica, artisan-roasted coffee, olive oil from Aglandau, sardines from Mouettes d'Arvor, and balsamic vinegar from Cavalli are Pascal Mièvre's treasures.

▼ La Grande Epicerie de Paris

38, rue de Sèvres, at Bon Marché
Métro: Sèvres-Babylone
Tel. 01 44 39 81 00. Fax 01 44 39 81 17
www.la-grande-epicerie.fr
8:30 AM–9 PM. Closed Sunday.

This luxuriously modern grocery store offers the best of Italian, Japanese, English and French regional products. Selected wines, oils, condiments, pasta, fish and spices turn this store into a fabulous pantry.

CHEESE

▼ Barthélémy   🏠

51, rue de Grenelle
Métro: Rue-du-Bac
Tel. 01 45 48 56 75. Fax 01 45 49 25 16
8 AM–1 PM, 4–7:15 PM. Closed Sunday, Monday, 1 week in February, August.

Roland Barthélémy chooses, matures and pampers the finest farmhouse cheeses: earthy saint nectaire, creamy reblochon, camemberts from several regions, soft brie, green-streaked livarot, saint-marcellin. Not to mention fresh butte, unpasturized farm milk and famous Fontainebleau.

▼ Marie-Anne Cantin

12, rue du Champ-de-Mars
Métro: Ecole-Militaire
Tel. 01 45 50 43 94. Fax 01 44 18 09 56
8:30 AM–7:30 PM. Closed Sunday

Marie-Anne Cantin and Antoine Diaz are keen advocates of the finest aged cheeses. Mountain beaufort, artisanal roquefort, dried and fresh goat cheese, earthy saint-nectaire, coulommiers, creamy reblochon and truffled brie. The selection of wines is splendid.

▼ Quatrehomme

62, rue de Sèvres
Métro: Duroc, Vaneau
Tel. 01 47 34 33 45. Fax 01 43 06 06 96
8:45 AM–1 PM, 4–7:45 PM
(Friday, Saturday 8:45 AM–7:45 PM).
Closed Sunday, Monday.

Recipient of the Meilleur Ouvrier de France award for her cheeses, Marie Quatrehomme is a maestro of aged cheeses. The reblochon, brie from Melun, Combes

roquefort, four-year-old gouda and selles-sur-cher are marvels. The stilton, cheddar, manchego and parmigiano reggiano are delights that know no frontiers.

ICE CREAM

▼ Martine Lambert

192, rue de Grenelle
Métro: Ecole-Militaire, Pont-de-l'Alma
Tel. 01 45 51 25 30. Fax 01 45 51 25 39
10 AM–1 PM, 3–8 PM (Saturday,
Sunday 10 AM–8 PM; Sunday in winter
10 AM–1:30 PM). Open daily.

Deauville's queen of ice cream, Martine Lambert has brought her unique flavors to Paris. We surrender to the charms of the Quiberon (salted butter caramel) or the Martinique (vanilla with chocolate chips and slivers of candied orange). Her sorbet (raspberry from the Dordogne and tree-ripened peach) are true delicacies.

BOOKS

▼ Rémi Flachard

9, rue du Bac
Métro: Solférino
Tel.-Fax 01 42 86 86 87
10:30 AM–12:30 PM, 3–6:30 PM.
Closed Saturday, Sunday, Bank Holidays,
mid-July–end of August.

Specializing in both rare and culinary works, Rémi Flachard knows all there is to know about books from the 15th century to the present day. It is a pleasure to talk with him.

PASTRIES

▼ Millet

103, rue Saint-Dominique
Métro: La Tour-Maubourg
Tel. 01 45 51 49 80. Fax 01 44 18 07 58
9 AM–7 PM (Sunday 8 AM–1 PM). Closed
Sunday afternoon, August.

This master of cakes presides over the flowers of French pâtisserie: Saint-Honoré, millefeuille, eclairs, Saint-Marc, Sully (a Sauternes mousse with fruit) and baba au rhum are supreme examples of the genre.

▼ Rollet-Pradier

6, rue de Bourgogne
Métro: Solférino
Tel. 01 45 51 78 36. Fax 01 44 18 96 50
8 AM–8 PM (Sunday 8 AM–3 PM). Closed
Sunday afternoon, Bank Holidays, August.
An expert pastry cook who was formerly
head of Ladurée, Jean-Marie Desfontaines
watches over his eclairs, dacquoises, mille-
feuilles, macarons and chestnut bombe.
Also fine delicatessen dishes. (Also see
Rendezvous.)

COFFEE

▼ Comptoirs Richard

145, rue Saint-Dominique
Métro: Ecole-Militaire
Tel. 01 53 59 99 18. Fax 01 53 59 97 26
10 AM–7:30 PM. Closed Sunday, Monday,
Bank Holidays, end of July–end of August.
Coffee roasters since 1894, the Richards
supply coffees of certified origin in this
modern store. Attractive coffee pots, cups
and interesting blends of herbal tea, with
thyme or coriander.

◆ RENDEZVOUS

BARS

◆ Le Lenox

9, rue de l'Université
Métro: Rue-du-Bac, St-Germain-des-Prés
Tel. 01 42 96 10 95. Fax 01 42 61 52 83
www.lenoxsaintgermain.com
5 PM–1 AM (Saturday, Sunday 5:30 PM–
2 AM). Closed August.
Enjoy refined cocktails in this piano bar
with its Twenties' decor, leather club chairs
and hushed atmosphere, as you listen to
the jazz pianist who plays three nights a
week.

WINE BARS

◆ Le Sancerre

22, av Rapp
Métro: Pont-de-l'Alma
Tel. 01 45 51 75 91
8 AM–3 PM, 6:30–10:30 PM.
Closed Saturday evening, Sunday,
3 weeks in August.
This barrel-shaped, rustic bistro pays tribute to selected Sancerre wines. The
smoked ham, chicken liver terrine, charcuterie and aged cheeses as well as the parsley, chive, tarragon and chervil omelet are
excellent.

◆ Au Sauvignon

80, rue des Saints-Pères
Métro: Sèvres-Babylone
Tel. 01 45 48 49 02. Fax 01 45 49 41 00
8 AM–10 PM.
Closed end of July–end of August.
Terrace.
This corner café with its terrace on rue de
Sèvres has a healthy air. Marie-Françoise
Vergne serves pork cold cuts, various
cheeses, tartines on Poilâne bread, salmon
and foie gras, along with well-bred Chablis,
Sancerre and Beaujolais.

◆ Le Septième Vin

68, av Bosquet
Métro: Ecole-Militaire
Tel. 01 45 51 15 97
Noon–midnight. Open daily.
Terrace.
Exit, Le 20 sur Vins. This designer café
serves browned bone marrow, caramelized foie gras, duck breast seasoned with
orange and pan-seared calf's liver to provide some solid accompaniment for the
vintages selected by Frédéric Mennetier.

◆ Les Vieilles Vignes

149, rue de l'Université
Métro: Solférino, Pont-de-l'Alma (RER)
Tel. 01 45 51 03 71
7 AM–9 PM. Closed Saturday, Sunday.
Marc Fabre, formerly at La Côte in rue de
Richelieu, has taken over this little bar
near to the ministries and runs it with
gusto. Beaujolais, Bourgueil, Saumur and
Gaillac provide an excellent accompani-

ment for carefully prepared tartines and small plates.

BRASSERIES

◆ Le Tourville

43, av de la Motte-Picquet
Métro: Ecole-Militaire
Tel. 01 44 18 05 08
7 AM–2 AM. Open daily.
Terrace

At this large brasserie opposite the Ecole Militaire, you can enjoy fashionable dishes (ginger chicken spring rolls, tomato basil penne) or a snack if you are not so hungry, and have a drink at the counter or on the terrace.

CAFES

◆ Le Bizuth

202, bd Saint-Germain
Métro: Rue-du-Bac, St-Germain-des-Prés
Tel. 01 45 48 13 87
7 AM–9 PM. Open daily.

This Fifties' bistro refurbished with a more colorful, contemporary feel is frequented by Sciences Po (political science school) students, who come to review or maybe forget their lessons. A hushed ambience.

◆ Café Branly

Musée du Quai Branly, 27, quai Branly
Métro: Pont-de-l'Alma (RER C)
Tel. 01 47 53 68 00
9 AM–6:30 PM. Closed Monday.

Glazed and opening onto a terrace on the same level, this brand new café designed by Jean Nouvel on the first floor of the Musée du Quai Branly offers relaxation and choice snacks.

◆ Café Constant

139, rue Saint-Dominique
Métro: Ecole-Militaire, Pont-de-l'Alma
Tel. 01 47 53 73 34
8 AM–midnight. Closed Sunday, Monday.
A la carte: 30€.

This attractive, old-fashioned café, one of the most popular establishments in the district under the aegis of Christian Constant of Le Violon d'Ingres, is worth a visit for its timeless atmosphere, genuine zinc

counter and excellent breakfasts. Drinks all day outside meal times.

◆ Le Rouquet

188, bd Saint-Germain
Métro: St-Germain-des-Prés
Tel. 01 45 48 06 93
7 AM–9 PM. Closed Sunday.
Terrace.

The attractions of this Fifties' café at the corner of rue des Saint Pères are its zinc and Formica surroundings and literary ambience (publishers Fayard and Grasset are its neighbors). On the terrace, we snack on mackerel simmered in white wine, hamburgers or salads.

◆ Tabac de l'Université

151, rue de l'Université, at rue Malar
Métro: La Tour-Maubourg, Pont-de-l'Alma
Tel. 01 45 51 33 24
6 AM–8:30 PM (Saturday 8 PM).
Closed Sunday, 3 weeks in August.
Terrace.

This traditional café's chic lies in its tiled floor and large, old-style counter. A perfect rendezvous for friends and lovers to enjoy a drink or quick snack together.

TEA SALONS

◆ Les Deux Abeilles

189, rue de l'Université
Métro: Alma-Marceau, Pont-de-l'Alma
Tel.-Fax 01 45 55 64 04
9 AM–7 PM. Closed 2 weeks in August.

Located behind the Musée du Quai Branly, this charming little tearoom has attracted aficionados for 20 years with exquisite pastries, jams, lemonade with ginger and dishes for healthy appetites. The salmon and cucumber "parfait" and goat cheese quiche make an excellent impression.

◆ Les Nuits des Thés

22, rue de Beaune
Métro: Rue-du-Bac, Musée-d'Orsay
Tel. 01 47 03 92 07
11:30 AM–7 PM. Closed Sunday (except for private parties), August.

A neighbor of publishers Gallimard, Jacqueline Cédelle offers a friendly welcome and meticulously prepares poached eggs, composed salads, apple crumble and chocolate fondant. The choice of teas is impressive.

◆ Rollet-Pradier

6, rue de Bourgogne
Métro: Assemblée-Nationale, Solférino
Tel. 01 45 51 78 36
8 AM–8 PM (Sunday 8 AM–3 PM).
Closed 3 weeks in August.

This elegant tearoom near the Assemblée Nationale, France's House of Representatives, regales its food-loving politicians with fruit tarts, millefeuilles, raspberry macarons and chocolate eclairs. Catering service.. (Also see Shops.)

○	Very good restaurant
◎	Excellent restaurant
◎◎	One of the best restaurants in Paris
◎	Disappointing restaurant
◉	Good value for money
€	Meals for less than 30 euros
SIM	Simple
COM	Comfortable
V.COM	Very comfortable
LUX	Luxurious
V.LUX	Very luxurious

Red indicates a particularly charming establishment

🏛	Historical significance
🏠	Promotion *(higher rating than last year)*
Ⓝ	New to the guide

●	Restaurant
▼	Shop
◆	Rendezvous

8TH ARRONDISSEMENT
THE SUPREME DISTRICT

With 250 establishments listed here—brasseries, bars, luxury hotels, prestige restaurants and much loved institutions—the eighth arrondissement is, as Jacques Lacarrière said of Crete, not "an island, but a continent." It is not the largest arrondissement in Paris, but it is the most important . . . for gourmets, tourists and guides, obviously. Socialites, clubbers, businessmen, models and epicures: all will visit a restaurant in the eighth at one time or another. Every kind of establishment is here: innovative eateries that enchant or exasperate, timeless bistros, vintage bars, great names of tomorrow and famous facades. The eighth is home to Taillevent and Le Cinq, Laurent and Lasserre, the Bristol and Les Ambassadeurs, Pierre Gagnaire and Alain Ducasse at the Plaza (restaurant or brasserie), among others. It stands at the cutting edge of both culinary and social fashion (the new brasserie-style Senderens and the amusing Steak & Lobster). In short, nothing can sate its perpetual appetite. Fine foreign restaurants, seafood eateries and hotel brasseries all cluster together here. Under this monster's cold exterior bubbles a frenzy of activity. For good food and a good time, head for the eighth—chic or simple, whichever you prefer—where anyone can feel at home. If this supreme arrondissement is not to your taste, you might as well forget Paris!

RESTAURANTS

GRAND RESTAURANTS

● **Les Ambassadeurs** ⓒⓄ V.LUX

Hotel Crillon, 10, pl de la Concorde
Métro: Concorde
Tel. 01 44 71 16 16. Fax 01 44 71 16 03
ambassadeurs@crillon.com
www.crillon.com
Closed Sunday, Monday lunch, August.
Open until 10 PM.
Prix fixe: 70€ (lunch on weekdays).
A la carte: 200€.
Air cond. Private dining room. Valet parking.

This is very much like a trip to the theater. In the golden glow of the dining room, our first impression is of the table art. The contemporary style of the cutlery, plates and glasses contrasts with the historic surroundings. The scene is set by the dining room manager, Mathieu Foureau, and his young, dynamic and extremely professional team. The most eagerly awaited artist remains in the wings though. The Crillon has found the chef it deserves in the person of Jean-François Piège. Assisted by his loyal lieutenants Yann Meinsel and Christophe Saintagne, who are ready to step forward and play the lead at any moment, he works on the imagination. The appetizers are already a play on words, flirting with a TV dinner concept but diametrically opposed to the kind of experience that might suggest: common, quick and trite. Indeed, they are magnificent and eminently creative: the Lucien Tende–style gâteau, circa 2006, the croustillante with a slice of ham, the cromesquis of fresh peas and the lemonade (!) of tabouli convey their message intelligently. When the curtain rises, the first act, a nicoise salad, Parisian style, and spider crab served with an herbed reduction glows with freshness and truth. The second is an exercise in subtlety though. The line-caught sea bass minestrone and the golden caviar nage with langoustines turn out to be the exclusive stars of the play, their produce prepared in such a way as to underline all their natural qualities and distil their essences. Making their appearance in the third act, deboned pigeon and foie gras in olive oil reduction and the casse-croûte of blue lobster, red chanterelles and lemon confit bring an infinitely delicate twist to the plot. The intermission—in the company of some of France's finest cheeses matured to perfection—only sharpens the suspense, but finally the epilogue, a new take on cherry and verbena clafoutis or a kind of strawberry basil vacherin by pastry chef Jérôme Chaucesse, breathes its irresistible scents. Stage right, the additional little luxuries are the herbal teas (peppermint, balm, sage-pineapple), cut and prepared before you. Stage left, the wine list is endless and David Biraud, assisted by young sommeliers as competent as they are efficient, provides invaluable advice. A standing ovation for so much talent and cordiality combined.

● **Apicius** ⓒⓄ V.LUX

20, rue d'Artois
Métro: St-Philippe-du-Roule,
Franklin-D.-Roosevelt, George-V
Tel. 01 43 80 19 66. Fax 01 44 40 09 57
apicius@relaischateaux.com
Closed Saturday, Sunday, August.
Open until 10 PM.
Prix fixe: 140€. A la carte: 150–180€.
Air cond. Terrace. Private dining room.
Valet parking.

Jean-Pierre Vigato is a great champion. After a spectacular start, we might have expected him to settle down to a more leisurely pace. Not at all. In the slightly over-the-top decor of Apicius, he is keeping up a perfectly steady rhythm like a marathon runner. His cuisine delights his preppy clientele, for whom he produces ever more imaginative dishes. He plays ingeniously on the changing seasons, offers a very personal take on the hunting season when autumn comes, and prepares seafood with infinite constancy. His hand-chopped langoustine meat, lightly seared on the grill, is a festival of marine flavors that explode on the tongue. The large turbot with spices, for two, is a simple, yet exceptionally tasty dish. We adore the roasted Pyrénées leg of lamb seasoned with parsley, and if we yield to the temptation of dessert, our vote goes to dark chocolate soufflé with unsweetened whipped cream. The service is a joy. If the Hervé Millet discoveries we select from the wine list hike up the check to a slightly higher sum than is reasonable, we still have no regrets.

● **Le Bristol**   ⬤⬤⬤ V.LUX

Hotel Bristol,
112, rue du Faubourg-Saint-Honoré
Métro: Miromesnil
Tel. 01 53 43 43 00. Fax 01 53 43 43 01
rcourant@lebristolparis.com
www.lebristolparis.com
Open daily until 10:30 PM.
Prix fixe: 80€ (lunch), 175€.
A la carte: 200€.
Air cond. Terrace. Valet parking.

Eric Fréchon continues to amaze us. He has a thousand and one tricks up his sleeve and (when the time is right) a happy ability to distill all that is best about the season onto our plates. When unrestricted imagination is brought to bear in the kitchen, the secret of great dishes lies in superior produce and perfect execution. Both are very much in evidence here. The bouillon with cubes of duck foie gras is combined with langoustines cooked "al dente" with ginger, coriander and leeks, sole with a slightly creamed fishbone reduction with Jura wine, stuffed with chanterelle mushrooms. The Sargasses eel, cooked in butter and seasoned with parsley, joins exquisitely with mashed smoked fingerling potatoes with parsley jus, seasoned with garlic. The Bresse hen for two, enveloped in a pig's bladder and slow poached in Jura wine, is served with green asparagus, morel mushrooms and a reduction sauce. The dessert prix fixe is a delight. While we especially love the apricots and Caribbean vanilla–flavored risotto with nougat cream; we also have a weakness for the frozen parfait infused with fresh mint, served with whole raspberries and milk chocolate. The welcome here is exemplary and the service, under

the eye of Raphaël Courant, first rate. Sommelier Jérôme Moreau is discreet and provides excellent advice. The check is, of course, open ended: this is one of the most prominent luxury hotels in Paris and the restaurant is absolutely first class.

● **Le Cinq**   ⬤⬤⬤ V.LUX

Hotel Four Seasons George V,
31, av George-V
Métro: George-V
Tel. 01 49 52 71 54. Fax 01 49 52 71 81
par.lecinq@fourseasons.com
www.fourseasons.com
Open daily until 10:30 PM.
Prix fixe: 75€ (lunch), 120€, 210€
(dinner). A la carte: 180–200€.
Air cond. Private dining room. Valet parking.

One day they will raise a statue to the glory of Philippe Legendre. He will certainly find the very idea unwelcome, but he deserves such a mark of respect, simply because he turns dinner in his restaurant into a trip to paradise. Although you are overwhelmed by choices when you read the prix fixe, very fortunately, Eric Beaumard and his dining room team are there to point you in the right direction. The large green asparagus with parmesan and truffles with a slow-cooked black olive polenta whet the appetite with a spectrum of scents that excite the palate. The anthology continues with cod seasoned with roasted peppercorns, underlining the aromas of the truffle tart served simultaneously. Roasted pigeon with peppermint and Sauternes takes on a traditional air next to that brilliant creation, farm-raised veal sweetbreads, pan-fried with orzo pasta "paella" style. The desserts are in the same vein: innovative and high in color and light, such as a crisp layered pastry with simply roasted fresh pineapple frosted with lime and coconut, or soft Guanaja chocolate streussel cake with cocoa sorbet. The cellar is one of the capital's finest, and Enrico Bernardo, privy to all its secrets, has been voted World's Best Sommelier.

● Alain Ducasse ⓒⓞ V.LUX

Plaza Athénée, 25, av Montaigne
Métro: Alma-Marceau, Franklin-D.-Roosevelt
Tel. 01 53 67 65 00. Fax 01 53 67 65 12
adpa@alain-ducasse.com
www.alain-ducasse.com
Closed Saturday, Sunday, Monday lunch,
Tuesday lunch, Wednesday lunch, 1 week at
the end of December, mid-July–end of July,
3 weeks in August. Open until 10:15 PM.
Prix fixe: 200€, 300€. A la carte: 250€.
Air cond. Valet parking.

Obviously, the Master, Alain Ducasse, is not always present, but the kitchen team led by Christophe Moret and his lieutenant Josselin Herland is one of the most brilliant anywhere. Its members put all their heart into their work and their preparations are remarkable, both in the precision of their execution and for their originality. The products are selected with extreme care, when they are not supplied exclusively to the Plaza. The fresh pasta with cream, truffles and giblets is a magnificent starter. Seasons are observed to the letter here. The line-caught sea bass is accompanied by green asparagus and fresh peas in the spring, but comes with citrus fruits, leeks, and spring onions in the fall. The smoked tea-glazed pigeon reveals entirely new flavors that bring out the full taste of turnips in sweet and sour sauce. Dessert is always a high point, but for those who are happiest straying from the beaten path, there can only be one choice—soft fresh ewe's cheese, peppered caramel, and strawberry-tree honey. Supervised by Denis Courtiade, the service attains summits of excellence, and the cellar, governed by Laurent Roucayrol, is extraordinary. The check is, of course, just as striking, but the most contemporary works of art are priceless and "Monsieur Ducasse" is and remains an artist with an eye to everything, from the decor designed by his associate Patrick Jouin, to minor details with a major impact, such as the cutlery and plates, and the style of the glasses.

● Les Elysées du Vernet ⓒⓞ LUX

Hotel Vernet, 25, rue Vernet
Métro: George-V, Charles-de-Gaulle–Etoile
Tel. 01 44 31 98 98. Fax 01 44 31 85 69
reservations@hotelvernet.com
www.hotelvernet.com
Closed Saturday, Sunday, Monday noon,
end of July–end of August. Open until 10 PM.
Prix fixe: 59€ (lunch), 94€ (dinner),
130€ (dinner). A la carte: 135€.
Air cond. Private dining room. Valet parking.

The Vernet's restaurant is one of the most splendid in the Champs-Elysées area. The decor is extraordinary, with its glass roof designed by Gustave Eiffel. Eric Briffard, long Joël Robuchon's second in command in the Jamin days, cultivates discretion, but still displays incomparable skill and, more than just ideas, wit, when planning the prix fixe. He expertly selects the finest produce and develops its promise to the full. The crunchy honey spice cake, pear, and smoked eel lend a mischievous air to the Landes duck foie gras which has been steamed and seasoned with a touch of ginger, and those who enjoy exoticism within reason will then choose blue lobster, salt-cooked and perfumed with aromatics served with fennel, artichokes, and coriander lemon gnocchi for its precise cooking and perfectly sustained flavors. In comparison, young pigeon with five-spice glaze, tamarind reduction, turnips, dates and lemon confit seems more traditional. The splendid conclusion takes the form of Saint Domingues "grand cru" chocolate, raspberry soufflé tart, and green tea sorbet. As for the wine, you can depend on Patrick Vidaller's instinct (although he found it difficult to find us a bottle that tasted more of fruit than wood when we last visited). To avoid insolvency, go for the set prix fixes at lunch or dinner.

● Pierre Gagnaire ⓒⓒ LUX

6, rue Balzac
Métro: George-V
Tel. 01 58 36 12 50. Fax 01 58 36 12 51
p.gagnaire@wanadoo.fr
www.pierre-gagnaire.com
Closed Saturday, Sunday lunch, Wednesday
lunch, 2 weeks in beginning of August.
Open until 9:30 PM.
Prix fixe: 90€ (lunch), 235€ (lunch).
A la carte: 300€.
Air cond. Private dining room. Valet parking.

As on the opening night of Victor Hugo's play *Hernani*, there are champions and critics, cheers and boos, with some praising it to the skies and others shooting it down in flames. Yes, Pierre Gagnaire is controversial, which is no bad thing. This genius of flavors has always been a mine of ideas, constantly revising the thousand and one dishes he invents and his ways of presenting them. The aim here is innovation as well as originality. Thrill to the exhilarating millefeuille with arugula whipped cream seasoned with spring onion jus, the speck ham and peppered mint with cherry juice, the golden Bresse liver gâteau with glazed crayfish nage seasoned with Pouilly-Fuissé accompanied by Perthius asparagus tips, new onions, and Menton lemon paste. Gasp at the daring langoustines with a green mango tartare and crunchy sheet of nougatine and mustard currant syrup that are pan-fried with "Terre de Sienne" spices, served with a broth foam and a slice of black radish-chilled consommé dusted with carob powder. The performance is not over yet. We applaud as the curtain rises on rack of Lozere lamb, roasted and poached with oregano, served with crisped fresh herbs and swiss chard enrobed with pan juices, cloves of garlic, shallots, and eggplant and chili-seasoned Madagascar jumbo shrimp cooked with prune eau de vie, grilled medallions of lamb with rich lamb sauce, zuchinni flowers, and cold reduction sauce as a condiment. Barely a moment to recover and Pierre Gagnaire's grand finale is with us: nine desserts inspired by French pâtisserie, made with seasonal fruit, lightly sugared confections, and chocolates. The service is perfection itself, including the choice of wines, which can be left unreservedly to Raphaël Huet. However, such prodigies come at a price.

● Le Jardin ⓒⓒ LUX

Hotel Royal Monceau, 37, av Hoche
Métro: Charles-de-Gaulle–Etoile
Tel. 01 42 99 98 70. Fax 01 42 99 89 94
restauration@royalmonceau.com
www.royalmonceau.com
Closed Saturday, Sunday, Monday lunch,
3 weeks in August. Open until 10 PM.
Prix fixe: 59€ (lunch), 95€ (dinner), 125€
(dinner). A la carte: 130€.
Air cond. Terrace. Private dining room. Valet
parking.

Christophe Pelé formerly worked with Cirino, Del Burgo and Gagnaire. He learned from these masters that in culinary terms, nothing can compare with the light personal touch that is the hallmark of a great dish. That touch is often imperceptible: You have to taste the cherry chutney that is served with browned duck foie gras to be sure it is really there. The mousse of artichoke provides whole John Dory fish seasoned with wild fennel with an additional note that thrills the palate. Liquorice-stick reduction sauce and roasted veal kidneys served in a covered dish with Joel Thilbault's young carrots becomes a unique creation. The desserts are in the same vein, including the caramel tofu with pimpernel spice ice cream. Stéphane Lochon will skillfully point you toward the wines from the South of France or Italy that will best complement your chosen dishes. The welcome and service are first rate, and the check reasonable. When the weather is fine, what a joy it is to eat on the terrace!

● Lasserre ⓒ 🔒 V.LUX

17, av Franklin-D.-Roosevelt
Métro: Franklin-D.-Roosevelt,
Champs-Elysées–Clemenceau
Tel. 01 43 59 53 43 / 01 43 59 67 45.
Fax 01 45 63 72 23
lasserre@lasserre.fr
www.restaurant-lasserre.com
Closed lunch (except Thursday, Friday),
Sunday, August. Open until 10 PM.
Prix fixe: 75€ (lunch), 185€ (tasting Prix
fixe). A la carte: 180–200€.
Air cond. Private dining room. Valet parking.

Monsieur Lasserre is no longer with us, but his great establishment opposite the Palais de la Découverte science museum marches on, more splendid than ever. Jean-Louis Nomicos, a close associate of Alain Ducasse for years, presents a prix fixe that skillfully reconciles tradition and modernity. Priority is given to produce, and everything here is a question of balance, as evinced by truffle and foie gras macaroni. The Breton lobster in classic simmered stew seasoned with honey, chestnuts and rosemary is always a must, but turbot in a crust of black truffle, artichokes and green pea purée is today's true event. The pigeon served with seasonal fruits and vegetables is to cooking what a Rembrandt is to painting, but you may prefer the milk-fed veal chops with lemon and ginger cream sauce. The chocolate soufflé is splendid. The service is fully what you would expect from such a noble establishment, and the check reflects that magnificence. The sommelier's name is Antoine Petrus, which already gives food for thought. When the weather is fine, the roof of the elegant dining room opens to the sky. The effect is magical and never stales.

● Laurent ⓒ V.LUX

41, av Gabriel
Métro: Champs-Elysées–Clemenceau
Tel. 01 42 25 00 39. Fax 01 45 62 45 21
info@le-laurent.com
www.le-laurent.com
Closed Saturday lunch, Sunday,
Bank Holidays. Open until 10:30 PM.
Prix fixe: 75€, 150€. A la carte: 180€.
Air cond. Terrace. Private dining room.
Valet parking.

With Edmond Ehrlich gone, many had their doubts about Laurent's future. They had not reckoned with the determination of its team of great professionals and the arrival of a conscientious chef. In the dining room, the good-humored Philippe Bourguignon welcomes regulars and first-time visitors with equal courtesy. In the kitchen, Alain Pégouret, who has worked with Joël Robuchon and Christian Constant, is at the summit of his art, as shown by pan seared duck foie gras that opens the proceedings. Beneath a classical exterior, red mullet filet seasoned with saffron, bone marrow and caramelized shallot sauce is an exceptionally modern dish. The Corrèze veal flank steak, simply braised and presented with Swiss chard and a reduction sauce, is congenial and tasty, while hot soufflé perfumed with Anis de Ponrarlier is a highly successful confection. Patrick Lair always provides good advice when the time comes to choose a wine. The price of all this splendor is reasonable, and there is a terrace for when the sun shines.

● Ledoyen ⓒ 🔒 V.LUX

Carré des Champs-Elysées, 1, av Dutuit
Métro: Champs-Elysées–Clemenceau
Tel. 01 53 05 10 01. Fax 01 47 42 55 01
pavillon.ledoyen@ledoyen.com
Closed Saturday, Sunday, Monday lunch,
August. Open until 9:45 PM.
Prix fixe: 85€ (lunch on weekdays), 198€
(lunch on weekdays), 284€ (wine included on
weekdays). A la carte: 200€.
Air cond. Private dining room. Valet parking.

The Napoleon III style has been lovingly maintained, and guests here lunch or dine in one of the most elegant settings in the capital. Christian Le Squer's cuisine is in tune with these surroundings as he consummately champions the colors of "his" Brittany, enchanting his enthralled audience with oven-crisped langoustines served in a citrus olive oil emulsion sauce. Straying a little further from the beaten path, the concentré of assorted Belon and spéciales oysters makes a succulent marine starter. Sobriety does not rule out a touch of mischief, and the astute oven-crisped slices of filet of sole acquire a somewhat Jurassic flavor, prepared as they are with Jura wine. The ingenious sautéed spiced suckling pig with gnocchi and semi-dried tomatoes seems native to the land of Brittany and is toothsome to a fault. For dessert, thin crisp dark chocolate sheets with iced pistachio milk will have you swooning. The service is in the delicious style practiced in bourgeois homes. The check climbs rather higher than Brittany's unspectacular Arrée Mountains, but without giving undue offence.

● **Stella Maris**   ◎◎ COM

4, rue Arsène-Houssaye
Métro: Charles-de-Gaulle–Etoile
Tel. 01 42 89 16 22. Fax 01 42 89 16 01
stella.maris.paris@wanadoo.fr
www.tateruyoshino.com
/www.stellemarisparis.com
Closed Saturday lunch, Sunday,
1 week in mid-August. Open until 10 PM.
Prix fixe: 43€ (lunch), 53€ (lunch), 85€,
130€. A la carte: 110€.
Air cond.

Tateru Yoshino could have made his fortune in the Land of the Rising Sun, but instead chose to set up in the land of his masters: Troigros, Senderens and Robuchon. Le Stella Maris has never emptied since. Regular customers shower praise on his very French cuisine, mischievously revised in the Japanese manner. They appreciate its originality and lightness. The langoustine ravioli with fish and shellfish couscous, and the rabbit tourte with green pea purée are irresistibly charming. For dessert, Traou Mad (a Breton shortcake biscuit) with rhubarb compote, accompanied by a strawberry sauce and fromage-blanc ice cream, combines Celtic charm with more exotic Nipponese notes. Michiko Yoshino's welcome is simply delicious, and although the food cannot be described as cheap, there are no regrets, for this establishment has a pleasantly outlandish feel to it. The Michelin guide has finally listened to us and given it a star this year, so anything is possible, even a sudden burst of open mindedness on the part of Bibendum, the Michelin Man.

● **Taillevent**   ◎◎ V.LUX

15, rue Lamennais
Métro: George-V
Tel. 01 44 95 15 01. Fax 01 42 25 95 18
mail@taillevent.com
www.taillevent.com
Closed Saturday, Sunday, end of July–end of
August. Open until 10 PM.
Prix fixe: 70€ (lunch), 140€, 190€.
A la carte: 200€.
Air cond. Private dining room. Valet parking.

Alongside the "modernists" and their sometimes controversial concoctions, the "classicists" have their place, but must obviously still bring their cuisine into line with today's tastes. This is exactly what Jean-Claude Vrinat asks of the chefs at "his" Taillevent, a timeless (but not changeless) restaurant. Alain Solivérès, a creative craftsman who trained with Maximin, Ducasse and Cirino, has planned a prix fixe that seems traditional on first sight. Only when it is explained by the master of the house do you realize that nothing could be further from the truth. This is confirmed when Sault spelt wheat risotto with browned frog's legs or John Dory fish with olives arrive. The sun-filled cuisine reaches its zenith with lamb saddle in a reduction sauce seasoned with regional wild herbs. The desserts, such as the feuille à feuille, a layered dessert of three chocolates, or baba au rhum with liquor-soaked raisins seem a million years old but still topical. The wine list is endless and the setting—a Second Empire town house with contemporary art providing interior decoration—exceptional, as is the service. The check rapidly adds up, but this comes as no shock, since the restaurant is at the peak of its achievements.

GOOD RESTAURANTS & OTHERS

A SPECIAL FAVORITE

● **A L'Abordage**　Ⓝ ▪ SIM
2, pl Henri-Bergson
Métro: St-Augustin
Tel. 01 45 22 15 49
Closed dinner (except Wednesday), Saturday, Sunday, end of July–end of August.
Open until 11 PM.
A la carte: 35–40€.
Terrace.

It looks like just another corner café with roadwork going on by its terrace behind Saint Augustine's church. But there is an omen: just a step away is a plaque marking the house where Curnonsky, prince of gastronomes, lived and died. Inside, there are the bar, the groups of friends (often famous chefs, who come to play cards after work) and the blackboard displaying the day's dishes. Bernard Fontenille serves up impeccable chow made with fresh produce prepared at its best in a tasteful, "club" atmosphere. A good country-style pork terrine, fresh salmon tartare, superb boneless rib-eye steak, paris-brest (choux pastry ring filled with a praliné buttercream), crème brûlée or (splendid) baba au rhum washed down with Foillard Morgon. But hush! Let's keep this private haunt our secret!

● **A l'Affiche**　SIM
48, rue de Moscou
Métro: Europe, Rome
Tel. 01 45 22 02 20. Fax 01 42 93 38 78
Closed Saturday lunch, Sunday, 3 weeks in August. Open until 10:30 PM.
Prix fixe: 13,80€, 19,90€, 22,90€.
A la carte: 40€.
Terrace. Private dining room.

Bruno Depoulain has turned this discreet bistro between place de Clichy and the Saint Lazare rail station into a cheerful spot indeed. There are movie posters, a bar

that resounds to the clink of well-filled glasses and domestic cuisine meticulously prepared by the faithful Rémi Pommerai. Crab steamed in a pouch, eggplant galette, cod aïoli, braised lamb shank and roasted veal kidney are very pleasant, as are the frozen vacherin with strawberries and the baba au rhum.

● **L'Alsace**　COM
39, av des Champs-Elysées
Métro: Franklin-D.-Roosevelt
Tel. 01 53 93 97 00. Fax 01 53 93 97 09
de.alsace@blanc.net
www.restaurant-alsace.com
Open daily 24 hours.
Prix fixe: 18,50€ (lunch), 24€,
30€ (dinner). A la carte: 38–65€.
Air cond. Terrace.

The Blanc brothers' establishment offers the taste of tradition 24 hours a day. Enthusiasts enjoy duck foie gras with Gewurztraminer aspic, assorted fish on a bed of sauerkraut, honey-braised pork shank with slow-roasted vegetables and blueberry tart in a charged, very "brasserie" ambience.

● **Aux Amis du Beaujolais**　€ SIM
28, rue d'Artois
Métro: St-Philippe-du-Roule,
Franklin-D.-Roosevelt, George-V
Tel. 01 45 63 92 21 / 01 45 63 58 64.
Fax 01 45 62 70 01
restaurantauxamisdubeaujolais@wanadoo.fr
bernard.picolet@wanadoo.fr
www.auxamisdubeaujolais.com
Closed New Year's, 3 weeks in August.
Prix fixe: 20,90€ (dinner). A la carte: 30€.
Air cond.

The atmosphere is always sunny in Bernard Picolet's eatery, where he celebrates bistro cuisine in the purest tradition. The superb classic boiled eggs with mayonnaise, smoked haddock with butter, beefsteak and fries and classic crème brûlée delight his regulars. Beaujolais is available in its every form, and the tab is reasonable.

● **Chez André** 🏠 SIM

12, rue Marbeuf
Métro: Franklin-D.-Roosevelt
Tel. 01 47 20 59 57. Fax 01 47 20 18 82
restaurant@chez-andre.com
www.rest-gj.com
Open daily noon–1 AM. Cont. service.
Prix fixe: 32€, 9,50€ (children).
A la carte 50€.
Air cond. Terrace.

One of the most popular street corners in the neighborhood. In this bistro, whose faux Thirties' style delights Americans, René Ambanelli serves Burgundian snails served in the shell with garlic and herb butter, frog's legs sautéed with garlic and half a roasted chicken with tarragon reduction sauce, which all work their casual charm. We also enjoy dark chocolate quenelles with orange zest and the staff's smiles as they run and run. Keep an eye on the prices, which tend to climb rather too steeply.

● **L'Angle du Faubourg** ◎ COM

195, rue du Faubourg-Saint-Honoré
Métro: Charles-de-Gaulle–Etoile,
George-V, Ternes
Tel. 01 40 74 20 20. Fax 01 40 74 20 21
angledufaubourg@cavestaillevent.com
www.taillevent.com
Closed Saturday, Sunday, August.
Open until 10:30 PM.
Prix fixe: 35€, 70€ (dinner).
A la carte: 80€.
Air cond. Private dining room.

This second establishment run by Jean-Claude Vrinat (of Taillevent) is a success. Its contemporary setting is a little noisy—especially at lunchtime—but full of light, and it offers vigorous dishes by Laurent Poitevin, who learnt his trade with Michel Del Burgo. A sober technician with skills beyond his years, he enables seasonal produce to express itself to the full. Who could resist the onion ravioli with bluefin tuna conserve and creamy artichoke sauce, slow-cooked cod with romaine lettuce cream and Avruga caviar and pan-fried foie gras seasoned with Banyuls wine? Then the soft wild strawberry macaron will sweep you off your feet. Mari-

anne Delhomme, the charming sommelier, will help you choose the right wine for each dish. Finally, Fernando Rocha is the kind of dining room manager we should see more often.

● **L'Appart'** COM

9-11, rue du Colisée
Métro: Franklin-D.-Roosevelt
Tel. 01 53 75 42 00. Fax 01 53 75 42 09
lappart@blanc.net
www.lappart.com
Open daily until 11:30 PM.
Prix fixe: 18€ (lunch), 23€ (lunch),
30€ (dinner). A la carte: 38–55€.
Air cond. Private dining room.

Kitchen and appurtenances: This restaurant (part of the Blanc brothers' empire) really is organized like an apartment. Chef Samuel Letorriellec acts as the master of the house, concocting very topical dishes. What can we say about slow-cooked eggplant seasoned with rosemary tomatoes and olive oil pesto, grilled salmon filet with pepper-stuffed phyllo pastry, mild spiced roasted duck breast with sage polenta, or soft chocolate cake with orange saffron chutney, except that they are honestly prepared?

● **L'Astor** LUX

Hotel Astor, 11, rue d'Astorg
Métro: St-Augustin, Madeleine
Tel. 01 53 05 05 20. Fax 01 53 05 05 30
hotelastor@aol.com
www.hotel-astorsainthonore.fr
Closed Saturday, Sunday, August.
Open until 10 PM.
Prix fixe: 33€, 47€ (lunch), 49€ (dinner).
A la carte: 80€.
Air cond. Private dining room. Valet parking.

Fine, well-executed fare, where tradition has the edge, despite a few fairly successful modish escapades presented by Jean-Luc Lefrançois. The sea bream tartare, red mullet with a Thai spice stuffing and thin crunchy pastry with chorizo sausage, veal filet with a gingerbread crust, casserole of spring carrot and radishes and then, on the dessert front, variations on the lemon theme: lemon tart, thin sesame tuiles, and assorted lemon sorbets are meticulously prepared. The service is perfect. Although the prices come as a blow, the surroundings are relaxing and the welcome warm.

● L'Atelier des Compères   N SIM

6, rue Galilée
Métro: George-V
Tel. 01 47 20 75 56
Closed Saturday, Sunday.
Open until 10:30 PM.
Prix fixe: 33€, 40€.

Jacques Boudin has opened this unusual, convivial haunt in a private courtyard hidden off the Champs-Elysées. There he offers traditional but light cuisine accompanied by selected wines. The dishes chalked up on the slate change every day. The millefeuille of slow-cooked vegetables, scallop carpaccio, duck foie gras terrine, poultry with cider sauce, veal filet with morel mushrooms and fresh pasta, Grand Marnier soufflé and pear clafoutis will do.

● L'Atelier Renault   SIM

53, av des Champs-Elysées
Métro: Franklin-D.-Roosevelt
Tel. 01 49 53 70 70. Fax 01 49 53 70 71
reservation.atelier-renault@renault.com
www.atelier-renault.com
Open daily 11 AM–1:30 AM. Cont. service.
Prix fixe: 23€, 29€. A la carte: 30–45€.
Air cond. Terrace.

The former Pub Renault has been refurbished as a stylish designer gourmet restaurant with Marc Veyrat in a consulting role. Under his guidance, a young team whips up light dishes with a contemporary feel. The small sardines in oil, fresh vegetable tart, crunchy vegetable salad, penne with bacon and parmesan sauce, "21st century hamburger" with a choice of either beef or tuna and fries are entertaining, without seeking to impress. Served by the glass, unpretentious wines from South Africa, California and other regions slip down smoothly. Fine ice cream (cappuccino, coconut or yogurt) from Sorbets de Paris and a good cheesecake with red berry sauce and blackcurrant sorbet.

● L'Avenue   COM

41, av Montaigne
Métro: Alma-Marceau, Franklin-D.-Roosevelt
Tel. 01 40 70 14 91. Fax 01 40 70 91 97
Open daily until 1 AM.
A la carte: 70€.
Air cond. Terrace. Private dining room.
Valet parking.

This contemporary brasserie is expensive and snobbish, but still popular with a clientele that frequents the avenue's luxury stores or RTL and Europe 1 broadcasting. The crab millefeuille, the cod "hakkasan" (silver cod with champagne and roasted honey) and the mandarina crispy duck (a variation on Peking duck) set the tone. A plus mark for the six (really) small macarons to share. The service is excellent.

● Bar des Théâtres   SIM

6, av Montaigne
Métro: Alma-Marceau, Franklin-D.-Roosevelt
Tel. 01 47 23 34 63. Fax 01 45 62 04 93
Closed August. Open until 1 AM.
A la carte: 40€.
Air cond.

Featured in the Danièle Thompson movie *Fauteuils d'Orchestre* (*Orchestra Seats*), this bar, where people gather after the play or concert just opposite at the Théâtre des Champs-Elysées, has adopted an elegant and not too pricey bistro format. On the menu are Dover sole filet pan-fried in butter and seasoned with parsley and lemon, a classic beef tartare, calf's liver and a tarte Tatin prepared without frills. The latest news is that the place is said to be in danger of closing, despite the distinction lent it by the lovely Cécile de France in the role of an apprentice waitress, so remember to check before you go.

● Le Berkeley   Ⓢ COM

7, av Matignon
Métro: Franklin-D.-Roosevelt,
Champs-Elysées–Clemenceau
Tel. 01 42 25 72 25. Fax 01 45 63 30 06
www.leberkeley.com
Open daily 8 AM–midnight. Cont. service.
Prix fixe: 28€ (weekdays), 30€,
34€ (weekdays). A la carte: 50–65€.
Air cond. Terrace. Private dining room.
Valet parking.

The English decor redesigned by Jacques Garcia will delight aficionados, but the cuisine is not always up to the same standard. The house-smoked Scottish salmon with toast, grilled tuna and olive oil–seasoned mashed potatoes, quick-seared chicken breast seasoned with curry and chutney served with basmati rice and warm dark chocolate cake still have room for improvement, year after year. As does the service, in fact.

● Le Bistro de l'Olivier   COM

13, rue Quentin-Bauchart
Métro: George-V, Franklin-D.-Roosevelt
Tel. 01 47 20 78 63. Fax 01 47 20 74 58
Closed Saturday lunch, Sunday, 3 weeks in August. Open until 10:30 PM.
Prix fixe: 27€ (lunch), 33,50€.
A la carte: 65–70€.
Air cond.

The South of France is honored here. Young chef Aurélien Marion delicately prepares dishes with the appetizing smell of Provence: grilled vegetable puff pastry with puréed slow-cooked tomatoes, grilled sea bream with nicoise ratatouille and pesto, Mediterranean slow-roasted beef with fresh pasta and citrus-infused cream stand up to any criticism. A sun-drenched address to remember.

● Le Bistrot de Marius   SIM

6, av George-V
Métro: Alma-Marceau
Tel. 01 40 70 11 76. Fax 01 40 70 17 08
Open daily until 11:30 PM.
Prix fixe: 28€, 32€. A la carte: 50€.
Terrace. Valet parking.

The sole ambition of this small offshoot of the great Marius et Janette next door is to serve seafood prepared at its freshest and at rather friendlier prices. The fish soup, grilled sea bream in salt crust, steamed cod with olive oil–seasoned mashed potatoes are well devised. The small strawberry tart and soft chocolate cake provide very suitable conclusions.

● Bistrot du Sommelier   COM

97, bd Haussmann
Métro: St-Augustin
Tel. 01 42 65 24 85. Fax 01 53 75 23 23
bistrot-du-sommelier@noos.fr
www.bistrotdusommelier.com
Closed Saturday, Sunday, 1 week
Christmas–New Year's, August.
Open until 10:30 PM.
Prix fixe: 32–54€ (lunch, wine included),
60–100€ (dinner, wine included).
Air cond. Private dining room.

Philippe Faure-Brac, a former World's Best Sommelier, has turned his establishment into a chic bistro. Locals flock here at lunchtime to pay homage to the pressed duck breast and fois gras, a nage of scallops and shrimp with citrus fruits and risotto or parmesan-seasoned pork filet with a morel reduction sauce served up by Jean-André Lallican. The desserts are in good taste, particularly pear tart with almond cream with dulce de leche ice cream. Xavier Guillien offers sound advice to help us choose among the wines selected by the master of the house.

● Le Bœuf sur le Toit   COM

34, rue du Colisée
Métro: St-Philippe-du-Roule,
Franklin-D.-Roosevelt
Tel. 01 53 93 65 55. Fax 01 53 96 02 32
www.boeufsurletoit.com
Open daily until 1 AM (midnight in August).
Prix fixe: 22,90€, 29,90€,
14,50€ (children). A la carte: 50€.
Air cond. Private dining room. Valet parking.

This jewel in the crown of the Flo group still appeals with its Thirties' bistro look. The "chic brasserie spirit" cuisine is tasteful. Along with the classics, Ming Wang of–

fers caramelized endive, blue cheese and cured ham tart, skin-seared salmon filet with aromatic herbs and ratatouille, thyme-seasoned grilled lamb chops with fresh green beans, a beautiful prime rib (but unfortunately served with potatoes pigswill-style when we last visited) and, for dessert, warm chocolate cake with vanilla ice cream, all looking good. The welcome and service are very friendly, and the check moderate.

● Dominique Bouchet ○ COM

11, rue Treilhard
Métro: Miromesnil, Villiers
Tel. 01 45 61 09 46. Fax 01 42 89 11 14
www.dominique-bouchet.com
Closed Saturday, Sunday, Bank Holidays,
1 week in February, August.
Open until 9:30 PM.
A la carte: 70€.
Air cond. Private dining room.

This restaurant is small in size, but stands tall in terms of quality. Dominique Bouchet, who was an assiduous pupil of Joël Robuchon before leaving the nest to manage the kitchen of Les Ambassadeurs, has imagination to spare. The produce is fresh and carefully selected, the execution extraordinarily precise and each preparation is a miniature masterpiece. The petite crab charlotte with basil-seasoned tomatoes is exquisitely simple, pasta with lobster and mushroom purée and reduction sauce is worth the visit in itself and grilled brioche-breaded pig's feet cakes napped with truffle reduction sauce can safely be called a great dish. The eclair "Sao-Tomé" (chocolate ganache with black cherry and cocoa ice cream) is a giddying treat. The service is discreetly tasteful, and shrewd sommelier Michaël Cives presents wines by the glass, enabling us to keep the damage down to a manageable sum.

● Le Bouchon Gourmand SIM

25, rue du Colisée
Métro: Franklin-D.-Roosevelt,
St-Philippe-du-Roule
Tel. 01 43 59 25 29
www.cityvox.comrestaurantlebouchongourmand
Closed Saturday lunch, Sunday, August.
Open until 11 PM.
Prix fixe: 18€ (lunch), 22€ (dinner).
A la carte: 35–45€.
Air cond. Private dining room.

In the hands of happy owners Danièle and Dominique Hinsinger, this convivial neo-1900s' bistro lives up to its name. The cuisine here is virtually home cooking. Admirably accompanied by one of the little wines from the cellar, the French onion soup, pike-perch filet with paprika, duck confit with garlic-seasoned potatoes and white chocolate mousse satisfy even the healthiest appetites.

● Le Boucoléon SIM

10, rue de Constantinople
Métro: Europe, Villiers
Tel. 01 42 93 73 33. Fax 01 42 93 95 44
Closed Bank Holidays, Saturday lunch,
Sunday, 2 weeks in August.
Open until 10:15 PM.
A la carte: 45€.
Air cond. Terrace.

Richard Castellan is the one-man band at this embassy of the Basque country in Paris. The homemade foie gras terrine, roasted cod filet with chorizo, minced artichoke hearts and black olives, trio of lamb chops slow cooked with honey and mild spices and the melon and apple sorbet compote are a very pleasurable experience, especially when accompanied by pleasant wines from Southwest France. The master of the establishment has a second address, just as convivial and devoted to tapas, at No. 17 in the same street (Tel.: +33(0)1 44 70 00 72).

● Ma Bourgogne `SIM`

133, bd Haussmann
Métro: Miromesnil
Tel. 01 45 63 50 61. Fax 01 42 56 33 71
mabourgogne@neuf.fr
Closed Friday evening, Saturday, Sunday,
1 week Christmas–New Year's, 2 weeks
in August. Open until 10 PM.
Prix fixe: 29€ (lunch), 38,50€ (lunch).
A la carte: 50€.
Air cond. Terrace.

This Burgundian establishment on boulevard Haussmann has changed hands again: Marie Kaoudio has taken over in the kitchen, with Nicolas Pasqua in the managerial role. Otherwise, it is business as usual. The plate of thinly sliced Lyonnaise-style dried sausage, pan-fried swordfish with a spicy sauce, classic beef bourguignon and brioche pain perdu with ginger caramel stay the distance—accompanied by Burgundy wines, of course—and the check keeps its head.

● Brasserie Lorraine `V.COM`

2-4, pl des Ternes
Métro: Ternes
Tel. 01 56 21 22 00. Fax 01 56 21 22 09
lorraine@blanc.net
Open daily 7 AM–1 AM. Cont. service.
A la carte: 60€.
Air cond. Terrace. Private dining room.
Valet parking.

Open again after being completely restored, this traditional brasserie now run by Frederic Hoepffner welcomes both Parisian society and local customers. All appreciate the neo-Fifties' decor, the original mosaics and the Saint Louis crystal chandeliers. The shellfish buffet is impressive, but guests can also enjoy traditional fare, such as foie gras with Montbazilliac aspic, Dover sole filet pan-fried in butter and seasoned with parsley and lemon, served with steamed potatoes or grilled lamb chops with green beans, while the paris-brest meets with unanimous approval. The large terrace is an attraction when the sun shines.

● Café Faubourg `COM`

Faubourg Sofitel, 15, rue Boissy-d'Anglas
Métro: Concorde
Tel. 01 44 94 14 14. Fax 01 44 94 14 28
h1295@accor-hotels.com
www.sofitel.com
Closed Saturday lunch, Sunday lunch,
3 weeks in August. Open until 10 PM.
A la carte: 70€.
Air cond. Private dining room. Valet parking.

It is good for a hotel of this class to have a restaurant giving such a good image of contemporary French cuisine. Jérôme Videau has put together a prix fixe that changes with the seasons and often has the flavor of the South of France. The crab millefeuille, red mullet served with a vegetable medley with garlic and pesto sauce and beef strip loin with olive-seasoned mashed potatoes are fine concoctions. Then for dessert we enjoy a classic layered pastry from Gascony served with Armagnac-flavored ice cream, reminding us that the chef worked with Alain Dutournier. A very warm welcome and highly conscientious service.

● Café M `COM`

Hyatt Regency Paris-Madeleine,
24, bd Malesherbes
Métro: Madeleine, St-Augustin
Tel. 01 55 27 12 57. Fax 01 55 27 12 35
resto@hyattintel.com
www.paris.madeleine.hyatt.com
Closed Saturday, Sunday, Bank Holidays.
Open until 10:30 PM.
Prix fixe: 45€ (lunch), 50€ (lunch).
A la carte: 70€.
Air cond. Private dining room. Valet parking.

Franck Paget, who has worked at La Grande Cascade, Le Jules Verne and La Cantine des Gourmets, has enthusiastically taken over at the stoves of this contemporary hotel restaurant in shades of brown. The setting is elegant, the wines by the glass well chosen and the cuisine manages to remain stylish without growing fussy. The crab and avocado layered pastry seasoned with thai ginger, the asparagus and green pea risotto, the sea bass filet with lemon confit and the herb-encrusted roasted rack of lamb are undeniably impressive. With frozen meringue vacherin flavored with vanilla, hazelnuts and milk chocolate or warmed salted caramel millefeuille to conclude, we realize why this excellent establishment for businesspeople quietly fills up at lunchtime.

● Café Terminus   COM

Hotel Concorde Saint-Lazare,
108, rue Saint-Lazare
Métro: St-Lazare
Tel. 01 40 08 43 30. Fax 01 40 08 43 65
stlazare-cafe-terminus@concorde-hotels.com
www.concordestlazare-paris.com
Open daily until 10 PM.
Prix fixe: 41€, 50€ (wine included).
A la carte: 58€.
Air cond. Valet parking.

Both the Gustave Eiffel architecture and the interior decoration help create a rather retro 1900s' ambience here, but chef Guy Pommelet's cuisine is conjugated very much in the present tense. The seasonal fish tartare, red mullet, beef compote seasoned with red wine served with artichoke mousseline, a layered lamb and potato dish with white onion confit and salad greens and an Earl Grey flavored blancmanger with fresh fruit sauce provide delightful confirmation of this very modern approach to travelers from the nearby Saint-Lazare rail station.

● La Cantine du Faubourg   SIM

105, rue du Faubourg-Saint-Honoré
Métro: St-Philippe-du-Roule
Tel. 01 42 56 22 22. Fax 01 42 56 35 71
resa@lacantine.com
Open daily until 1 AM.
Prix fixe: 40€ (lunch, wine included).
A la carte: 60€.
Air cond. Private dining room. Valet parking.

There is some progress in this year's program. The smoked tuna carpaccio with asparagus and the roasted monkfish with green pea risotto and beet sauce are certainly more deserving than the simple but enjoyable (to be honest) farm-raised chicken breast. The tea-flavored tiramisu is not to be sniffed at. At the end of the day,

if we were paying ten euros less, we would be quite happy to eat here on a regular basis, since the service is flawless.

● Le Cap Vernet   COM

82, av Marceau
Métro: Charles-de-Gaulle–Etoile
Tel. 01 47 20 20 40. Fax 01 47 20 95 36
Closed Saturday lunch, Sunday, Christmas, May 1st. Open until 11 PM.
A la carte: 50–65€.
Air cond. Terrace. Private dining room.

Jean-Marc Lemmery is keeping this comfortable seafood restaurant on a steady course, insisting on freshness and precise preparation. The shallot and parsley seasoned jumbo shrimp with chopped tomatoes, grilled sole served with asparagus in layered pastry, as well as veal filet mignon sautéed and served with tea-seasoned glaze reduction and chocolate ganache rolled in crushed hazelnuts are not bad, although they are slightly spoiled by their complexity. Still, their creativity compensates for the service, where there is room for improvement, and the check, which errs on the side of gluttony.

● Le Carré   COM

12, pl Saint-Augustin
Métro: St-Augustin
Tel. 01 44 69 00 22. Fax 01 44 69 33 19
restaurantlecarre@wanadoo.fr
www.restaurantlecarre.com
Closed Sunday. Open until 11:30 PM.
A la carte: 60€.
Air cond. Terrace.

The contemporary decor in black leaves us with a faint sense of déjà vu, but we are in the presence of quality here. The concassé of avocado and crab, sea bream with ginger-peanut sauce, tagine roasted lamb shank and chocolate cake with fruits and nuts served with bittersweet cocoa sorbet are well done. The price is high; the terrace pleasant.

● La Casa del Fox   COM

41, rue du Colisée
Métro: Franklin-D.-Roosevelt
Tel.-Fax 01 45 62 35 75
contact@foxrestaurant.com
www.foxrestaurant.com
Closed Saturday, Sunday. Open until 5 AM.
Prix fixe: 16€ (lunch), 36€ (dinner).
A la carte: 50€.
Air cond. Private dining room.

On the first floor is a hushed, intimate restaurant; in the basement, a vaulted cellar dining room and a lively bar, often with entertainment in the evening. The establishment is, in any case, presided over by Jean-Marie Bourbon. He and Gérald Barthélémy have devised a respectable prix fixe, with foie gras with fig confiture, herb and butter fried tuna steak and beef tenderloin with oyster mushrooms, then a pain perdu made with coconut milk for dessert.

● Cat Corner   🄽 SIM

89, rue du Rocher (at rue Monceau)
Métro: Villiers
Tel. 01 44 70 01 61
Closed Saturday lunch, Sunday.
Open until 11:30 PM.
Prix fixe: 34€.

Philippe Thull, a pure native of Metz and former dining room stalwart at La Table des Guilloux in Luxembourg, has turned this pleasant café-lounge with its wooden bar, gold leaf walls and red seats into a relaxed, tasteful gastronomic haunt. The set prix fixe encourages thrift. There can be no objections to the green Puy lentils and salmon with orange, the crayfish, celery and beet salad, skate wing with capers, lemon and hazelnut butter, duck breast and scalloped potatoes, macaron tiramisu and classic tarte Tatin with cream. The unassuming Pays d'Oc Merlot practically drinks itself.

● Chez Catherine   ◎ V.COM

3, rue Berryer
Métro: St-Philippe-du-Roule, George-V
Tel. 01 40 76 01 40. Fax 01 40 76 03 96
Closed Saturday, Sunday, Bank Holidays,
New Year's, 1 week in beginning of May,
3 weeks in August. Open until 10:30 PM.
Prix fixe: 40€ (lunch), 45€ (lunch),
50€ (dinner), 65€ (dinner). A la carte: 75€.
Air cond. Private dining room.

Catherine Guerraz remains true to form. She seems to delight in coming up with new dishes that surprise the most loyal of her regulars with their explosive flavors. Her langoustine and tarragon ravioli with shellfish broth are prepared just so, her minced catfish with a savory/sweet sauce, citrus vinaigrette and mango spaghetti takes your breath away and the smoothness of veal sweetbreads and duck foie gras with asparagus and morel mushrooms leaves you rooted to the spot. The desserts, too, are audacious to a fault, as shown by soft chocolate bonbon and praliné ice cream with chocolate mint sauce. The check is on the heavy side, but not exaggeratedly so, thanks to the set prix fixe option and the wines by the glass selected by Frédéric and the young Cyril Denonfoux.

● Chez Cécile "La Ferme   SIM
des Mathurins"

17, rue Vignon
Métro: Madeleine, Havre-Caumartin
Tel. 01 42 66 46 39
cecile@lafermedesmathurins.com
www.chezcecile.com
Closed Saturday lunch, Sunday, end of
July–end of August. Open until 10:30 PM.
Prix fixe: 22–32€ (lunch), 30€ (dinner),
35€ (dinner). A la carte: 50–55€.

Cécile Desimpel has taken over the helm in what used to be a traditional bistro, and her chef, Stéphane Pitré, has radically revamped the prix fixe. The liver parfait with an acidic Campari sauce served with crisp layered pastry and dried fruits, wine poached jumbo shrimp on a bed of crushed artichoke hearts served in pots oiled with pistachio oil, lamb saddle seasoned with lemon, the chef's slow-cooked peppers with potatoes and the roasted cocoa bean panna cotta with dulce de leche all derive their modernity from a firm grasp of fusion cuisine.

● Les Champs `V.COM`

Marriott Champs-Elysées,
70, av des Champs-Elysées
Métro: Franklin-D.-Roosevelt, George-V
Tel. 01 53 93 55 44 / 01 53 93 55 00.
Fax 01 53 93 55 01
www.mariott.com
Closed Saturday, Sunday (except for breakfast: 7 AM–2 PM). Open until 10 PM.
Prix fixe: 35€. A la carte: 70€.
Air cond. Terrace. Private dining room.
Valet parking.

Olivier Chéron's classic prix fixe has a New York French bistro quality that fits perfectly into the American environment of this contemporary-style hotel, contrasting with the preppy setting of the restaurant. No need to worry: Marco Polo shrimp—an original creation—tuna steak with both oven-baked and pan-tossed mushrooms and calf's liver with mashed potatoes weave an effortless charm. The "Symphony of Sweetness"—soft chocolate cake, small pistachio cake and mini crème brûlée—provides a delightful conclusion for the reasonably priced meals here.

● Chiberta ○ `V.COM`

3, rue Arsène-Houssaye
Métro: Charles-de-Gaulle–Etoile
Tel. 01 53 53 42 00. Fax 01 45 62 85 08
chiberta@guysavoy.comcom
www.lechiberta.com
Closed Saturday lunch, Sunday, 1 week Christmas–New Year's, 3 weeks in August.
Open until 11 PM.
Prix fixe: 60€, 100€. A la carte: 80–90€.
Air cond. Private dining room. Valet parking.

One of the most attractive establishments in the capital. With its decor by Jean-Michel Wilmotte, this new Guy Savoy address has quickly reached cruising speed. Gilles Chesneau's cuisine is worthy of the master's, and Jean-Paul Montellier's dining room management is exemplary. We delight in the spicy crisp jumbo shrimp served with a spicy avocado salad and corn crisps, whole turbot pan-fried in butter and seasoned with parsley and lemon served with artichokes, grilled pigeon with chickpeas, young corn, and eggplant seasoned with sage. The desserts are in the same vein, the creamy pistachio and rhubarb gelatin served with vanilla ice cream, a must. The wine list is worth a close look, with some excellent bottles at affordable prices.

● Citrus Etoile ○ `COM`

6, rue Arsène-Houssaye
Métro: Charles-de-Gaulle–Etoile
Tel. 01 42 89 15 51. Fax 01 42 89 28 67
info@citrusetoile.fr
www.citrusetoile.fr
Closed Saturday lunch, Sunday,
Bank Holidays, 2 weeks in August.
Open until 11 PM.
A la carte: 60€.
Air cond.

Gilles Epié has made his Paris comeback just a step away from the Arc de Triomphe. Although the dining room is run by his sparkling Californian wife, Elizabeth, he often leaves the kitchen to liven things up a little, moving from table to table and explaining how he works. He has a fertile imagination and produces dishes that are hard to resist. The scallops served on the half shell, prime oysters with white Landais asparagus and grilled tuna with foie gras are works of precision. The rabbit leg is a heroic achievement and the coconut ice cream beignets are simply beguiling. Jean-François Marteil oversees the cellar and provides intelligent advice. The prices are in no way excessive, and if you really want to get a table here, a word of advice: Reserve.

● Clovis ○ V.COM

Sofitel Paris-Arc de Triomphe,
14, rue Beaujon
Métro: Charles-de-Gaulle–Etoile
Tel. 01 53 89 50 53. Fax 01 53 89 50 51
h1296@accor-hotels.com
Closed Saturday, Sunday, Bank Holidays,
Christmas–New Year's, August.
Open until 9:45 PM.
Prix fixe: 39€ (lunch), 85€ (dinner).
A la carte: 80–90€.
Air cond. Private dining room. Valet parking.

How boring this place would be if François Rodolphe were not here to give it color and taste. His prix fixe is classical, but he is always ready to add a personal touch to his preparations. Mango and sweet citrus marinade prettily grace the fried langoustines, pistou (the traditional Provençal garlic and vegetable soup) brightens steamed sole with herbs and a vegetable tagine, with dates and lemon confit with rosemary, charmingly "orientializes" lamb from Paulliac. The house baba au rhum and mango and pineapple marinated with lime and coconut milk provide a marvelous conclusion. Olivier Pellier's recommendations are welcome when choosing the wine. The lunchtime set prix fixe is a bonus.

● Le Coin ℕ ⓔ SIM

88, rue du Rocher
Métro: Villiers
Tel. 01 43 87 58 96
Closed Sunday. Open until 10:30 PM.
A la carte: 30€.

A slightly wayward touch in a chic neighborhood, likeable wines, quality produce, the prix fixe chalked up on the blackboard changing daily and reasonable prices into the bargain—this is what you can expect from this street corner bistro. Depending on the season, we enjoy terrines, scalloped potatoes with saint-nectaire cheese, rabbit in a cream and mustard sauce, andouillette AAAAA, beef stew with carrots, chocolate mousse, crème brûlée and selected wines. The terrace soon fills up whenever the sun shows its face. (Also see Rendez-vous.)

● Le Cou de la Girafe COM

7, rue Paul-Baudry
Métro: St-Philippe-du-Roule,
Franklin-D.-Roosevelt
Tel. 01 56 88 29 55
www.coudelagirafe.com
Closed Sunday, Monday, 2 weeks in August.
Open until 11 PM.
Prix fixe: 24€. A la carte: 32–46€.
Air cond. Terrace. Valet parking.

After a few months spent here, Grégory Coutanceau moved on, but Le Cou de la Girafe has remained. Frédéric Claudel (formerly with Alain Solivérès, then at La Poêle d'Or) has taken over very successfully. Pierre-Yves Rochon's luxurious but unostentatious decor, with its elegant materials and warm colors, has remained unchanged. The traditional prix fixe and bistro dishes are welcome. The rabbit rillettes served in a pot, crab in lettuce cream, beef cheeks, poultry fricassée served in a Dutch oven and the more sophisticated sea bream in bouillabaisse are enjoyable, copious and well prepared. A successful change of management with a significant lowering of prices is an unusual occurrence in this business district, where inflation is the usual theme.

● Les Coupoles SIM

55, rue des Mathurins
Métro: St-Augustin, St-Lazare
Tel. 01 42 65 31 58
Closed Saturday, Sunday, Bank Holidays,
1 week Christmas–New Year's,
1 week in May, August. Open until 9 PM.
A la carte: 28–35€.
Terrace.

Aficionados of genuine traditional bistros should note this address carefully. The cantal cheese tart, regional Auvergne sausage with an accompanying Auvergnat cheese and potato dish, seasonal fish and house chocolate mousse would not shame the great "mères Lyonnaises" of yesteryear. The prices are sensible too, which is no bad thing.

● **La Cour Jardin**   Ⓝ ◯ V.COM

Plaza Athénée, 25, av Montaigne
Métro: Alma-Marceau
Tel. 01 53 67 66 02
Closed mid-September–mid-May.
Open until 10:30 PM.
A la carte: 90€.

The secret Parisian treasure of the "Ducasse Group"? The patio at the Plaza, with its ivy covered walls, young, enthusiastic dining room staff and Cédric Bechade's marvelously lyrical cuisine. Paella-style risotto, slow-cooked monkfish in its sauce, sardines in tomato sauce and marinated assorted raw vegetables are delightful "in the style of . . ." dishes. Then poached egg in aspic with pepper sauté and onion jus and turbot with salsa verde are a nod to the Basque country, suggesting that the chef, who trained at the Biarritz Palais, has left his heart somewhere between Bayonne and Hendaye. The red mullet with gnocchi in cheese sauce and the admirable desserts (chocolate raspberries or cherries refreshed with almond milk granita and pain perdu) are refined confections indeed. We help all this along with a thoroughbred Fessy Brouilly or Grisard Mondeuse, thinking that life in avenue Montaigne may not be so dull after all.

● **Le Crétois**   ⊜ SIM

19, rue Treilhard
Métro: Miromesnil, Villiers
Tel. 01 45 63 34 17. Fax 01 45 61 48 97
Closed Bank Holidays, Saturday, Sunday,
dinner, 3 weeks in August.
Open until 9:30 PM.
A la carte: 30€.
Air cond. Terrace.

Aside from its unpretentious prices, simplicity and a sense of tradition have helped this simple wine bistro to flourish in a very elegant neighborhood. The name (The Cretan) is taken from a fresco there. Much of the wine list focuses on the Rhône Valley. The leeks with raspberry vinaigrette, flank steak with shallots and daily house pastries are commendable.

● **Daniel Lounge**   SIM

Hotel Daniel, 8, rue Frédéric-Bastiat
Métro: Franklin-D.-Roosevelt,
St-Philippe-du-Roule
Tel. 01 42 56 17 00. Fax 01 42 56 17 01
hoteldanielparis@wanadoo.fr
www.hoteldanielparis@hoteldanielparis.com
Closed Saturday, Sunday (except for hotel
clients), 10 days in July, 3 weeks in August.
Open until 10:30 PM.
A la carte: 60€.
Air cond. Valet parking.

Discretion is the rule in this stylish hotel. The simplicity of the market-based set prix fixe contrasts with the excessive sophistication of the dishes a la carte. Even so, the roquefort and pear soufflé, sea bass filet roasted with lobster butter, rack of lamb rib roast with honey and curry-roasted chickpeas and soft chocolate cake, grapefruit sauce and fresh fromage blanc sorbet are admirable. A charming welcome.

● **Devèz**   ⑤ COM

5, pl de l'Alma
Métro: Alma-Marceau
Tel. 01 53 67 97 53. Fax 01 47 23 09 48
contact@devezparis.com
www.devezparis.com
Open daily until 12:30 AM.
A la carte: 45–55€.
Terrace.

Christian Valette has left, taking with him his chef and, it seems, everything that made this establishment so charming and successful. The prix fixe has not changed, but the Aubrac tapas are not what they were. The boneless rib-eye steak, always first-rate, is no longer perfectly cooked. The house strawberry and mascarpone dessert with cotton-candy flavored gelatin dessert is a touch parsimonious. The prices have not come down though, and the service has its ups and downs.

● **Entrenous aux Ternes** €️ COM

89, bd de Courcelles
Métro: Ternes
Tel. 01 43 80 78 22. Fax 01 43 80 20 18
entrenous4@wanadoo.fr
Closed Saturday lunch, Sunday, Christmas,
New Year's, 3 weeks in August.
Open until 11 PM.
Prix fixe: 15€ (lunch). A la carte: 30€.
Terrace. Private dining room. Valet parking.

"Entrenous" means "between you and me", an apt name indeed, given the relaxed, friendly service offered by the "boss". Christophe Chaillouté, and his disciple Pierre Barret. The cuisine by Emmanuel Verbruggen is in excellent taste. The mille-feuille of celery and crab, pan-fried sea bass on a bed of slow-cooked eggplant and veal parmigiana stay the distance, as does tapioca with coconut milk and vanilla served with fine mango slices. A few good wines, a reasonable check, an address to remember.

● **L'Evasion** SIM

7, pl Saint-Augustin
Métro: St-Augustin
Tel. 01 45 22 66 20. Fax 01 40 75 04 32
famillebrenta@wanadoo.fr
Closed Saturday, Sunday.
Open until 10:30 PM.
Prix fixe: 40€ (dinner). A la carte: 55–70€.
Air cond. Terrace.

This little corner bistro has been turned into a rather select little club. Laurent and Catherine Brenta's cellar offers a wealth of choice, with fabulous bottles selected by neighbor Marc Sibard from the Cave Augé nearby. Christophe Cavallo's dishes are of excellent parentage: fresh duck foie gras, truffle omelet, pan-fried squid with ham, traditional veal blanquette, superb prime rib by master butcher Hugo Desnoyer followed by a professional paris-brest (choux pastry ring filled with a praliné butter-cream) and panna cotta with red fruits. Fortunately, the food is lighter than the tab.

● **Fermette Marbeuf 1900** COM

5, rue Marbeuf
Métro: Alma-Marceau, Franklin-D.-Roosevelt
Tel. 01 53 23 08 00. Fax 01 53 23 08 09
fermettemarbeuf@blancs.net
www.fermettemarbeuf.com
Open daily until 11:30 PM.
Prix fixe: 24,50€ (lunch), 19,50€ (lunch),
30€ (dinner). A la carte: 60€.
Air cond. Terrace. Private dining room.

Beneath the 1898 glass roof of this chic brasserie, everything is classical to a fault. Duck foie gras, salmon with vegetables, chicken braised and served in a small casserole and Grand Marnier soufflé are assiduously prepared by Gilbert Isaac. The welcome is cheerful, the service prompt and the prices a la carte a little high.

● **Au Fin Bec** 🍴 COM

7, rue Roy
Métro: St-Augustin, Miromesnil
Tel.-Fax 01 45 22 22 46
Closed Saturday, Sunday, 1 week
Christmas–New Year's, 3 weeks in August.
Open until 9:30 PM.
Prix fixe: 34€ (wine included).
A la carte: 55€.
Private dining room.

In this Twenties' Parisian bistro, Daniel Niveau continues to delight a clientele of regulars who are warmly welcomed by Marie-Claude Mousty. We simply savor the seasonal salad with crayfish tails and foie gras medallions, mixed sauté of sole, sea bass, scallops, and jumbo shrimp, veal cutlet with oyster mushrooms and, finally, tarte Tatin.

● **Le Fouquet's** 🍴 V.COM

99, av des Champs-Elysées
Métro: George-V
Tel. 01 47 23 50 00. Fax 01 47 23 60 02
evigoureux@lucienbarriere.com
www.lucienbarriere.com
Open daily until 12:30 AM.
Prix fixe: 78€. A la carte: 75€.
Air cond. Terrace. Private dining room.
Valet parking.

People come for breakfast or to sit out on the terrace. But now eating here is no longer the gamble it once was, thanks to Jean-Yves Leuranguer, winner of the Meilleur Ouvrier de France award. Avoiding facile solutions, this seasoned pro—a veteran of the Martinez—serves up classic dishes that are not necessarily devoid of a modern touch. There can be no objections to lobster ravioli, marbled foie gras terrine with spiced wine, crayfish tail in scented aspic and roasted veal chops to share. The light millefeuille goes down well, too. The prices are still very steep, but the service has improved considerably.

● Chez Francis COM

7, pl de l'Alma
Métro: Alma-Marceau
Tel. 01 47 20 86 83. Fax 01 47 20 43 26
Open daily until midnight (12:30 AM Friday, Saturday). Cont. service.
Prix fixe: 28€, 34€. A la carte: 55–70€.
Air cond. Terrace. Valet parking.

The new chef at this institution, Lionel Accolas, is marking time, but not blindly. He serves well-made traditional dishes such as a beautiful Dover sole pan-fried in butter and seasoned with parsley and lemon, grilled lamb saddle serve accompanied by a classic potato gratin but also a more exotic tandoori chicken served with basmati rice. The warm dark chocolate cake with vanilla ice cream and a rice pudding with red fruit coulis offers a pleasing conclusion. The prix fixe menus can help keep the check down to manageable proportions.

● Fromages & Affinités ⬤SIM

58, rue des Mathurins
Métro: Havre-Caumartin, St-Augustin
Tel.-Fax 01 40 06 96 18
celtys.contact@free.fr
Closed dinner, Saturday, Sunday,
Bank Holidays.
A la carte: 25€.
Air cond. Terrace

Pierre Lévy has turned this little cheese cellar into a remarkable delicatessen. Open only for lunch, we go there to taste all kinds of aged and fresh cheeses, a goat cheese sorbet, toasts garnished with comté (an alpine cheese) and honey, fresh goat cheeses and coppa ham, salads featuring ricotta, spinach, and drizzled with a savory tomato and basil syrup, soups and pasta. No full meat dishes, no fish, but some unique combinations of flavors found only on the farm.

● Garnier ◯V.COM

111, rue Saint-Lazare
Métro: St-Lazare
Tel. 01 43 87 50 40. Fax 01 40 08 06 93
Closed end of July–end of August.
Open until 11:30 PM.
Prix fixe: 30€. A la carte: 55–90€.
Air cond. Valet parking.

Seafood tops the bill in this fine restaurant, whose great attraction is the wood and mirror decor designed by Dominique Honnet. The impeccably fresh shellfish buffet is also an incentive, as are the whole lobster salad with balsamic vinegar and light spiced tomato sauce, cod filet with basil minestrone and Dover sole pan-fried in butter and seasoned with parsley and lemon accompanied simply by small potatoes, all prepared with precision and creativity by Ludovic Schwartz. This is not to say that the meats are in any way inferior, and the herb-crusted rack of lamb and tender lard-fried potatoes are anything but slapdash. The desserts, such as puff pastry with egg-based chocolate sauce, are in excellent taste. Sadly, the a la carte check is much less of a pleasure.

● Les Gourmets des Ternes ⯅SIM

87, bd de Courcelles
Métro: Ternes, Courcelles
Tel. 01 42 27 43 04
Closed Saturday, Sunday,
10 days Christmas–New Year's, August.
Open until 10:15 PM.
A la carte: 55€.
Terrace.

Jean-Francois Marie is keeping this fine Parisian bistro in the family. Supervised by the meticulous Dat Hunguyen, the cuisine is well made, traditional and quintessentially French. Artichoke hearts in vinaigrette, white asparagus with goose foie gras, Dover sole pan-fried in butter and seasoned with parsley and lemon, grilled beefsteak served with marrow and baba au rhum will entice you back here, even if the prices have risen slightly.

● Le Goût des Hôtes `SIM`

33, rue de Constantinople
Métro: Villiers
Tel. 01 45 22 15 02. Fax 01 45 22 35 03
www.legoutdeshotes.canalblog.com
Closed Saturday lunch, Sunday, Bank
Holidays, 1 week Christmas–New Year's,
3 weeks in August. Open until 10:30 PM.
A la carte: 35€.
Terrace.

A change of proprietor and chef in this rustic bistro located in the Europe neighborhood. Simplicity is still the watchword, with Said Elbahoty's smile in the dining room and Eric Lefebre's unfussy cuisine. Foie gras baked in a salt crust, soberly priced at 8€, a ramekin of eggs with smoked salmon, sea bream in salt crust, beef filet with peppercorn sauce, duck breast with honey, profiteroles and floating island are all comfortingly well mannered.

● Le Grenadin Gourmand `COM`

44-46, rue de Naples
Métro: Villiers
Tel. 01 45 63 28 92. Fax 01 45 61 24 76
Closed Saturday lunch, Sunday,
Monday evening, 2 weeks in August.
Open until 10:30 PM.
Prix fixe: 30€, 38€. A la carte: 70€.
Air cond. Private dining room.

Sandra Combrisson and Alain Stéphan have put the color back into Le Grenadin after a fraught start. The prix fixe is a little tortuous, but what you might think were genuinely bad ideas turn out to be well founded, such as soft-cooked oxtail with honey and foie gras, jumbo shrimp and parmesan risotto seasoned with porcini mushrooms and truffle oil or "7-hour" herb and garlic roasted lamb and their seasonal accompaniments. The millefeuille with vanilla and red fruits is not bad but does not

compare with the one served up by Patrick Cirotte, the restaurant's founder. The set prix fixes offer good value.

● Hédiard "La Table d'Hédiard" `COM`

21, pl de la Madeleine
Métro: Madeleine
Tel. 01 43 12 88 99. Fax 01 43 12 88 98
www.hediard.com
Closed Sunday, August. Open until 10 PM.
Prix fixe: 50€ (dinner), 60€ (dinner, wine included), 70€ (dinner, wine included).
A la carte: 60–68€.
Air cond. Private dining room. Valet parking.

This establishment is a rendezvous for local shopaholics who enjoy its colonial decor and restrained fusion cuisine. The shrimp and vegetable tempura seasoned with mint and coriander, grilled tuna steak accompanied by tomato and anchovy tart, roasted beef filet with black peppercorn sauce served with thick-cut house fries and vanilla millefeuille make up a tasteful meal. Watch out for the check, a little on the heavy side.

● Hôtel de Sers `N` `COM`

41, av Pierre-1er-de-Serbie
Métro: George-V,
Tel. 01 53 23 75 75
www.hoteldesers.com
Open daily until 11 PM.
A la carte: 60€.
Air cond. Terrace. Valet parking.

Contemporary but quite at home in its 19th-century setting, this elegant, modern, discreet designer hotel in the heart of the Paris Golden Triangle also has a good eatery, which doubles as a bar and lounge, and serves voguish light dishes and delicacies. Tuna tartare, scallop carpaccio, veal T-bone steak and tender slow-cooked lamb shank are very successful. Chef Rémy Delbart (who trained with Alain Dutournier) and Eric Briffard must be talented indeed to work effectively in such a small space. Visitors can also snack on a club sandwich or enjoy a cocktail, depending on the hour and their fancy.

● Le Jardin des Cygnes LUX

Prince de Galles, 33, av George-V
Métro: George-V
Tel. 01 53 23 78 50. Fax 01 53 23 78 78
hotelprincedegalles@luxericollection.com
www.luxericollection.com/princedegalles
Closed Sunday evening. Open until 10 PM.
Prix fixe: 51€, 95€ (dinner, wine included).
A la carte: 110€.
Air cond. Terrace. Private dining room. Valet parking.

Continuing to run the kitchens at his own pace, Benoît Rambaud has modernized this luxury hotel's prix fixe with successive touches. The foie gras terrine seasoned with garlic, skin-seared sea bass filet with coconut milk butter, slow-cooked venison served with gingerbread and wild blueberry game sauce, soft coconut and pinapple cake infused with verbena and served with fromage blanc ice cream are not bad at all. The wine list is classical to a fault, the service extremely elegant and the check easier on the pocket than one might expect, especially at lunchtime. Then there is the Thirties'-style patio, delightful when the sun shines.

● Café Lenôtre COM

Carré Marigny, 10, av des Champs-Elysées
Métro: Franklin-D.-Roosevelt,
Champs-Elysées–Clemenceau
Tel. 01 42 65 85 10. Fax 01 42 65 76 23
www.lenotre.fr
Closed Bank Holidays, 2 weeks in August.
From 9 AM–11 PM. Cont. service.
A la carte: 40–60€.
Air cond. Terrace. Private dining room. Valet parking.

The modern charm of this café's orange and mauve decor works instantly, and Robuchon veteran Alain Despinois's highly subtle cuisine does the rest. The creamed sea urchin with slow-cooked tomatoes, simmered vegetables and monkfish with classic bouillabaisse seasonings, duck breast roasted on skewers with shallot confit, apricots and creamy polenta are unaffectedly excellent as they lead up to one of the parent establishment's famous desserts. To accompany all this, Olivier

Poussier, World's Best Sommelier in 2000, presents a selection of wines at very reasonable prices.

● Libre Sens COM

33, rue Marbeuf
Métro: Franklin-D.-Roosevelt
Tel. 01 53 96 00 72. Fax 01 53 96 00 84
libresensgroupebertrand@hotmail.com
Open daily until 3 AM.
Prix fixe: 19,50€ (lunch). A la carte: 40€.
Air cond. Private dining room.

Do they actually mean anything, the chic decor of this stylish eatery, the prix fixe trying to find its way between fusion food and unspectacular classicism, and the annoyingly affected service? Fortunately, the food—crisp phyllo pastry with goat cheese, tomato and pesto, sea bass filet with parmesan risotto and truffled veal reduction and even beef tartare or soft chocolate cake—will reconcile you to this restaurant, where you could do worse for 40€ or so.

● Lloyd's Bar COM

23, rue Treilhard
Métro: Miromesnil, Monceau
Tel.-Fax 01 45 63 21 23
Closed Saturday, Sunday,
1 week Christmas–New Year's, August.
Open until 10:30 PM.
Prix fixe: 35€ (lunch), 40€ (lunch),
28€ (dinner), 33€ (dinner).
Air cond. Terrace.

This former American bar converted into an authentic English pub is prized for its peaceful ambience (especially in the evening), Luc Lasry's amiable welcome and Laurent Dewaeles's harmonious dishes. The millefeuille of tomato, goat cheese and tapenade, cod filet in a green vegetable fricassée, quail with classic provençal ratatouille and small pot of chocolate mousse, red berries, and warm madeleines are entirely enjoyable, but moderately priced.

**HOSTESS
OF THE YEAR**

● **La Luna** 🏠 ○ V.COM

69, rue du Rocher
Métro: Villiers
Tel. 01 42 93 77 61. Fax 01 40 08 02 44
Closed Sunday, Christmas,
3 weeks in August. Open until 10:45 PM.
A la carte: 85–100€.
Air cond. Valet parking.

We have criticized this famous seafood
restaurant for various reasons in the past.
Now though, it has opted for sobriety and
has reached the peak of its form. The gracious Catherine Delaunay, who runs her
dining room with charm and virtuosity,
has refurbished it with a certain discreet elegance in gray and burgundy. The place
has chic to spare with its banquettes and
nooks. The beautiful hostess sets the quietly convivial tone and now the cuisine reflects the ambience perfectly. The sea
bream, salmon and tuna tartare, galette of
langoustines with tender Zanzibar leeks,
sole cooked in butter and seasoned with
parsley and garlic with Noirmoutier potatoes, sea bream cooked in banana leaf,
simmered lobster and spring vegetable
casserole and a gigantic baba au rhum with
vanilla cream—a masterpiece of the genre,
easily enough for two or three—all have an
easy appeal. The prices take no prisoners,
but do reflect the quality. An establishment
that deserves proper recognition.

● **La Maison de l'Aubrac** SIM

37, rue Marbeuf
Métro: Franklin-D.-Roosevelt
Tel. 01 43 59 05 14. Fax 01 42 25 29 87
maison.aubrac@wanadoo.fr
www.maison-aubrac.fr
Open daily 24 hours.
A la carte: 37–60€.
Air cond. Terrace. Private dining room.

An Aubrac livestock farmer, Christian
Valette showcases his region's deservedly
famous meat in his Paris restaurant. The
country-style beef salad, prime rib of beef
for two, excellent local cheeses and pain
perdu prepared with brioche reflect the
simple, reliable beauty of the high plateaus
of the Massif Central range. The restaurant
is open 24 hours a day, the cellar has 1,100
wines to offer, the service is cheerfully
prompt and the check realistic. Happiness
is just around the corner.

● **La Maison Blanche** 🏠 ○ LUX

15, av Montaigne
Métro: Alma-Marceau
Tel. 01 47 23 55 99. Fax 01 47 20 09 56
info@maison-blanche.fr
www.maison-blanche.fr
Closed Saturday lunch, Sunday lunch.
Open until 10:45 PM.
Prix fixe: 40€ (lunch), 65€ (lunch, wine
included). A la carte: 120€.
Air cond. Terrace. Private dining room.
Valet parking.

Reliable staff in both dining room and
kitchen, the determination of the Pourcel
twins to achieve new heights of quality, a
decor in shades of white and a view of the
Eiffel Tower over the roofs of Paris are all to
be found here. Now there is scarcely any
reason not to award a Plate to Thierry
Vaissière for his subtle, delicate, slightly
Mediterranean fare with its new take on
classics. The zucchini and porcini mushroom lasagna with truffled reduction
broth, a coconut risotto with grilled jumbo
shrimp stuffed with crab, a baked sea bass
with a white bean and olive crust and the
minced beef with potato, ham, porcini
mushroom and egg yolk terrine with an
acidic reduction sauce are the picture of
health. The desserts are in the same vein—
coconut millefeuille and mojito sorbet,
regional shortbread from Brittany and
chocolate tart with tea-flavored sauce. The
wine list focuses on Languedoc and the
Mediterranean. The prices are no one's
idea of a joke, but you will still have to fight
for a table, especially in the evening.

● Mandalaray `COM`

34, rue Marbeuf
Métro: Franklin-D.-Roosevelt
Tel. 01 56 88 36 36. Fax 01 42 25 36 36
contact@mandalaray.fr
www.mandalaray.fr
Open daily until midnight.
A la carte: 60€.
Air cond. Private dining room. Valet parking.

The bubble has burst. The chef's departure has been quite a blow for this restaurant, which despite its vast size, is packed with customers eager to taste its "world" cuisine. We fare reasonably well with the sea bream tartare seasoned with coriander and sweet and sour tomato marmalade, the old-fashioned roasted free-range chicken served with small roasted potatoes and artichokes with truffle oil and the lightly caramelized custard perfumed with Bora Bora flowers. The welcome and service are very friendly and so they should be, at prices like these.

● Le Marcande `V.COM`

52, rue de Miromesnil
Métro: Miromesnil
Tel. 01 42 65 19 14. Fax 01 42 65 76 85
info@marcande.com
www.marcande.com
Closed Saturday lunch, Sunday,
Christmas–New Year's, 2 weeks in August.
Open until 10 PM.
Prix fixe: 34€, 91€ (wine included).
A la carte: 60–90€.
Air cond. Terrace. Private dining room.

At Emmanuel Cazaux's establishment, we realize it takes time to produce masterpieces. So we wait patiently to savor Stéphane Ruel's inventive, skillfully prepared cuisine. The lime-marinated sea bream carpaccio, roasted langoustine tails served with a thyme and lemon risotto, roasted saddle of lamb seasoned with thyme and the millefeuille with gingerbread and orange marmalade are faultless. Only the check singularly lacks that lightness of touch.

● Marius et Janette ○`COM`

4, av George-V
Métro: George-V, Alma-Marceau
Tel. 01 47 23 41 88. Fax 01 47 23 07 19
Open daily until 11 PM.
Prix fixe: 46€ (lunch, wine included), 48€.
Air cond. Terrace. Valet parking.

Bernard Pinaud is a master of seafood. He does not just cook it to perfection, he seems to change its very nature to serve it with all its freshness and authentic flavor intact. The crunchy fried langoustines, the splendid tuna carpaccio and the fried whiting with tartar sauce, as well as the simple grilled line-caught sea bass all offer confirmation of his skills. The vanilla millefeuille is a paradigm of sweetness (but not excessively so). The welcome on board this luxury yacht of a bistro is excellent and the service impeccable and urbane. The prices are high, but justifiably so. The wine list is short but has some interesting items.

● Market ○`COM`

15, av Matignon
Métro: Champs-Elysées–Clemenceau,
Franklin-D.-Roosevelt
Tel. 01 56 43 40 90. Fax 01 43 59 10 87
prmarketsa@aol.com
www.jean-georges.com
Open daily until 11:30 PM.
Prix fixe: 34€ (lunch). A la carte: 100€.
Air cond. Terrace. Private dining room.
Valet parking.

New York superstar Jean-George Vongerichten's Paris restaurant is one of the most entertaining anywhere. The beautiful people that flock there do not detract from the Christian Liaigre decor. The dining room staff, led by Eric Précigoux and Sylvain Bonnafé, is first rate and their comments on the prix fixe will make your mouth water. The "black plate"—shrimp brochette, crisp phyllo pastry with crab, tuna roll, lobster seasoned with daikon radish and spiced quail—is a must, but in the kitchen, Wim Van Gorp has more than one string to his bow. His paprika-seasoned codfish and potato ravioli, like the boneless rib-eye steak with exotic peppercorns, marinated cucumbers and green asparagus, are anything but commonplace. For dessert, playing the Sorcerer's Apprentice, he presents a coconut panna cotta and marinated fruit with litchi sorbet in the style of Ferran Adria. The weekend brunch is a high point in the life of Paris society. The selection of wines is shrewd. Sadly, all this comes at a price.

● La Mascotte   Ⓢ SIM

270, rue du Faubourg-Saint-Honoré
Métro: Ternes
Tel. 01 42 27 75 26. Fax 01 42 27 75 22
Closed Saturday evening, Sunday,
Christmas, New Year's, 10 days in August.
Open until 11 PM.
A la carte: 40–60€.
Air cond. Terrace. Private dining room.
Valet parking.

New owners the Turlans have changed the decor, putting on a show of comfortable modernity that rejuvenates this newly chic Aveyron café a tad, but chef Yves Moreau is still at the range. Regulars do not seem disconcerted by céleri rémoulade (banal), seasonal fish, Aubrac beef filet with classic blue cheese sauce (overcooked) served with fried potatoes seasoned with green peppercorns and the house recipe of chocolate fondant and vanilla custard sauce. The dining room staff, who forget the half bottles and charge a supplement for a strawberry tart (sodden) topped with a scoop of ice cream is clearly intent on getting customers to spend as much as possible.

● Maxan   COM

37, rue de Miromesnil
Métro: Miromesnil
Tel. 01 42 65 78 60. Fax 01 49 24 96 17
rest.maxan@wanadoo.fr
Closed Saturday lunch, Sunday, Monday
evening, 10 days in August. Open until 11 PM.
Prix fixe: 30€, 45€ (dinner).
A la carte: 45–55€.
Air cond. Private dining room.

An amusing contemporary setting, a wall streaked with vertical lines of color, chandelier and decorations made of white paper: The former Poêle d'Or's refurbishment is a success. Laurent Jazac, Gérard Vié's lieutenant at Les Trois Marches, has taken over, along with Serge Conquet, François Clerc's maître d'. The delicious duck foie gras terrine with tart roasted figs, saffron potatoes with aïoli, lump crabmeat and almond milk gazpacho and veal filet braised with a mushroom fricassée are delicious, as is the chocolate fondant and cocoa ice cream. A fine business restaurant that deserves another visit.

● Maxim's   🏛 V.LUX

3, rue Royale
Métro: Concorde
Tel. 01 42 65 27 94. Fax 01 42 65 30 26
maxims@wanadoo.fr
www.maxims-de-paris.com
Closed Saturday, Sunday, Monday.
Open until 10 PM.
A la carte: 250€.
Air cond. Private dining room. Valet parking

This prestige establishment has become a shrine visited by nostalgics from all over the world keen on its Fifties' surroundings and old-fashioned service. A la carte, the langoustine salad, Dover sole braised with vermouth, beef filet with morel mushroom sauce and, finally, the Grand Marnier soufflé delight customers in search of a culinary museum. The wine list has riches to spare. Before stepping inside, make sure you do, too.

● Le Merisier   COM

28, rue Jean-Mermoz
Métro: St-Philippe-du-Roule, Miromesnil
Tel. 01 42 25 36 06. Fax 01 40 75 05 01
Closed Saturday, Sunday, Bank Holidays,
10 days on Easter, May. Open until 9:30 PM.
Prix fixe: 38€. A la carte: 52€.
Air cond. Private dining room.

The all (cherry) wood decor is charming to a fault. Jean-Paul Boyrie, who likes to present good, fresh dishes, is not averse to adding an original touch to traditional fare, such as the melon seasoned with spices accompanied by a shallot soufflé, or to change his cuisine to reflect the market produce of the moment. The turbot served with vegetable noodles, oven-baked duck breast and raspberry custard tart beguile effortlessly, as does Françoise Boyrie's smile as she offers subtle guidance to those studying the inspired wine list.

● 1728 `COM`

8, rue d'Anjou
Métro: Concorde, Madeleine
Tel. 01 40 17 04 77. Fax 01 42 65 53 87
restaurant1728@wanadoo.fr
www.restaurant-1728.com
Closed Saturday lunch, Sunday,
1 week Christmas–New Year's, August.
Open until midnight.
A la carte: 70€.
Air cond. Private dining room. Valet parking.

This 18th-century town house has been converted into a charming restaurant by Yang Lining, a world class sitar player. There is no faulting the decor, woodwork, period furniture, tapestries or antique paintings, but the cuisine has its ups and downs, which, given the prices here, are a little hard to swallow. Be that as it may, Yannick Quéré does fairly well with the *Désir thaï* (Thai desire: sea bream, smoked haddock, oven-crisped squid), *Côte ouest/côte est* (West Coast/East Coast: plump grilled scallops in a curry sauce with a balsamic vinegar foam) and Chinese crystal (chicken cooked in banana leaves). There is also a wonderful cocoa cream and pralinés in layered pastry with hot pistachio sauce for dessert.

● Mollard `🏠 COM`

115, rue Saint-Lazare
Métro: St-Lazare
Tel. 01 43 87 50 22. Fax 01 43 87 84 17
espace.clients@mollard.fr
www.mollard.fr
Open daily until 1 AM.
Prix fixe: 39,50€ (wine included), 51€.
A la carte: 52–75€.
Air cond. Private dining room.

Edouard Niermans' art nouveau decor and the listed Sarreguemines ceramics and frescos are certainly impressive, but we have also come to enjoy Joël Prodhomme's first-rate French cuisine. The scallop

carpaccio with coriander vinaigrette, classic Mediterranean rockfish bouillabaisse, veal kidneys flambéed with cognac and the house dessert omelet flambéed with Grand Marnier are exquisitely timeless.

● Music-Hall `Ⓢ COM`

63, av Franklin-D.-Roosevelt
Métro: Franklin-D.-Roosevelt,
St-Philippe-du-Roule
Tel. 01 45 61 03 63. Fax 01 45 61 03 88
www.music-hallparis.com
Closed Saturday lunch, Sunday lunch.
Open until 12:30 AM (late night menu:
12:30 AM–6 AM).
A la carte: 55€.
Air cond. Terrace. Private dining room.
Valet parking.

There seems to be a curse on this house. It was here that we met Marshall from California, who left us with some unwelcome memories. The service does its best in a modern setting not overburdened with charm (although comfortable to a degree). The cuisine, though, determinedly shuns any hint of flavor. Our meal? A bland rendition of veal Milanese using veal and tuna; tartare goat and maroilles cheese salad—insipid, amazingly, despite the strong cheese; rubbery, tasteless scallops; overcooked sea bream with limp artichokes; uncrisp duck breast flanked by laughable chocolate noodles, all making us seriously consider going on the lam. Not to mention the salmon (unappetizing) with vegetables (almost nonexistent). The place is supposed to be stylish and musical, but there is no one at the piano. The management's explanation? "The pianist only comes on Tuesday."

● L'Obélisque `COM`

Hotel Crillon, 6, rue Boissy-d'Anglas
Métro: Concorde
Tel. 01 44 71 15 15. Fax 01 44 71 15 02
restaurants@crillon.com
www.hoteldecrillon.com
Closed 1 week in February, 3 weeks in July.
Open until 10 PM.
Prix fixe: 50€. A la carte: 65–75€.
Air cond. Terrace. Valet parking.

Le Crillon's other eatery enjoys the same attentions as Les Ambassadeurs. Jean-François Piège tends to its needs with shrimp ceviche marinated in lime, with avocado, the "k-bio" marinated in squid ink, pigeon with fresh peas in cream and a chocolate lemon hazelnut cake. Fine wines served by the glass and first-rate service enhance the quality of this adjunct, with its Murano chandeliers and woodwork.

● **Pershing Hall**　　　COM
49, rue Pierre-Charron
Métro: Franklin-D.-Roosevelt, George-V
Tel. 01 58 36 58 36. Fax 01 58 36 58 01
info@pershinghall.com
www.pershinghall.com
Open daily until midnight.
A la carte: 70€.
Air cond. Terrace. Valet parking.

We are a little lost. The team at this chic hotel designed by Andrée Putman has changed again and the cuisine has become simpler, in a Costes brasserie style. Form your own opinion of salmon tataki with miso sauce and herbed green salad, crab gratin with a creamy spicy sauce, Argentinean boneless rib-eye steak with fries and—a memory of childhood—cotton candy sorbet with Tagada strawberry sauce. Guests come for the ambience, the patio and Patrick Blanc's vertical garden.

● **Le Petit Chablisien**　　　SIM
44, rue de Londres
Métro: St-Lazare, Liège
Tel.-Fax 01 43 87 46 15
Closed Bank Holidays, Saturday, Sunday, Monday evening, Christmas, New Year's, last week in July–end of August. Open until 9 PM.
A la carte: 35–50€.
Air cond. Terrace.

Robert Chervy and Alain Binot's bistro has a delightful authenticity. Along with the Chablis, Irancy and Epineuil wines favored by the masters of the house (although not exclusively), you can enjoy the simple pleasures of the tomato, mozzarella and basil tart, scallops with vermouth sauce, boneless rib-eye Aubrac steak weighing in at about three quarters of a pound and

baba au rhum with English rum without breaking the bank.

● **Le Pichet de Paris**　　　COM
68, rue Pierre-Charron
Métro: Franklin-D.-Roosevelt
Tel. 01 43 59 50 34. Fax 01 42 89 68 91
Closed Saturday, Sunday, Christmas–New Year's, 1 week in May, August.
Open until 11 PM.
A la carte: 75€.
Air cond.

We always enjoy our visits to Gaël Devergies and his associate in the kitchen for the last 30 years, Alain Larsonneur, in this establishment favored by the late President Mitterrand and his people. It continues to be a refectory of choice for media society and politicians of the right or left. Its "chic brasserie" spirit encourages us to try the shellfish buffet, one of the best in Paris, and to follow it up with red tuna steak with spinach or veal chop with lemon sauce. We conclude with the traditional millefeuille. Attentive service, high prices.

● **La Place**　　　COM
Radisson SAS, 78, av Marceau
Métro: George-V, Charles-de-Gaulle–Etoile
Tel.-Fax 01 53 23 43 43
mickael.shanclous@radissonsas.com
www.radisson.com/paris
Closed Saturday, Sunday, Christmas–New Year's, 3 weeks in August. Open until 10 PM.
A la carte: 70€.
Air cond. Terrace. Private dining room. Valet parking.

The decor is inspired by North America, but the cuisine is refreshingly French. Didier Pioline is gifted and mischievous on occasion, and we enjoy the slow-cooked potato and lobster with smoked herring caviar cream, broiled langoustines with Savoie pasta with a cauliflower and curry sauce, saddle of lamb with North African spices served with dried fruit polenta and, for dessert, crispy gaufres flavored with wild strawberries and white chocolate ice cream. The service is impeccable and the patio a haven in summer.

● **Pomze** SIM

109, bd Haussmann
Métro: St-Augustin, Miromesnil
Tel. 01 42 65 65 83. Fax 01 42 65 30 03
contact@pomze.com
www.pomze.com
Closed Sunday (July–August), Monday
(July–August), Christmas, New Year's,
May 1st. Open until 11 PM.
Prix fixe: 14€ (wine included with lunch
on weekdays), 25€ (lunch), 32€.
A la carte: 48–56€.
Air cond. Terrace. Private dining room.

Everything here takes its cue from the
apple. The walls are decorated with photographs of apple trees and picture of growers, and the dishes all feature the Pride of
the Orchard. The creamed spring vegetables with escargots and apple butter, asparagus risotto with shrimp flambéed with
Calvados, slow-cooked rabbit with eggplant cream, apples and pinenuts and
cheesecake with caramelized apples illus-
trate the many flavors of this fruit. But although tribute is paid to cider and
Calvados, the wines of our fine regions are
also much in evidence.

● **Le P'tit Bouco** ⊜SIM

17, rue de Constantinople
Métro: Europe, Villiers
Tel. 01 44 70 00 72
Closed Saturday, Sunday, Monday evening,
Tuesday evening, 3 weeks in August.
Open until 10:30 PM.
A la carte: 25€.
Terrace.

The sole purpose of this pleasant, convivial, *bouchon*-style restaurant, an offshoot of Le Boucoléon across the street, is
to provide honest sustenance in the form
of fine platters. Richard Castellan's aim is
to turn it into a San Sebastian–style bar.
Tapas, gourmet sandwiches, fresh salads,
daily specials and fruit tarts are all very
pleasant, accompanied by reds and whites
from Spain and Southwest France, and still
kind to your pocketbook.

● **40 BC Black Calavados** ⊛SIM

40, av Pierre-Ier-de-Serbie
Métro: Franklin-D.-Roosevelt, George-V
Tel. 01 47 20 77 77. Fax 01 47 20 77 01
info@bc-paris.fr
www.bc-paris.fr
Closed lunch, Sunday, 2 weeks in August.
Open until 3:30 AM.
A la carte: 75€.
Air cond. Valet parking.

The former Calavados has become a
fashionable restaurant for night owls. The
food—jumbo shrimp salad, foie gras and
popcorn, Waygu beef cheeseburger, panna
cotta, chocolate mousse—is snobbish and
expensive, but not necessarily inept. The
waitresses are more charming than
resourceful. The obvious question is: Will it
last?

● **R Café** COM

6, rue Chauveau-Lagarde
Métro: Madeleine
Tel. 01 44 71 20 85. Fax 01 42 65 19 49
info@rcafeparis.com
www.new.new-hotel.com
Closed Saturday lunch, Sunday,
mid-July–mid-August.
Open until 10:30 PM.
Prix fixe: 19€ (lunch, wine included),
10€ (children). A la carte: 50–55€.
Private dining room.

This restaurant on the first floor of an unobtrusive hotel is certainly not one of the
best known in Paris, but it is the kind you
tell your friends about. We enjoy the peace
and quiet here and the dependability of the
dishes prepared by Benoît-Joseph Dulieu,
who changes his prix fixe each month. The
sardines marinated in aromatic herbs with
leek vinaigrette, grilled redfish with white
beans and fennel-stuffed tomatos, pan-
fried sweetbreads with pepper and
vanilla–flavored pain perdu have a delightfully sunny side and the brioche pain perdu
is beautifully decorated with rhubarb
sauce and licorice ice cream.

● **Relais-Plaza**   Ⓥ V.COM

Plaza Athénée, 21, av Montaigne
Métro: Alma-Marceau
Tel. 01 53 67 64 00. Fax 01 53 67 66 66
reservation@plaza-athenee-paris.com
www.plaza-athenee-paris.com
Open daily until 11:30 PM.
Prix fixe: 45€. A la carte: 80€.
Air cond. Private dining room.
Valet parking.

A chic eatery, stylish food and a historic setting. The Plaza Athénée's Forties' brasserie, with its dining room inspired by the ocean liner *Normandie*, and its manager, the elegant Werner Kuchler, featured this year (both the restaurant and Werner himself) in the credits of the Danièle Thompson movie *Fauteuils d'Orchestre* (*Orchestra Seats*). Alain Ducasse, who loves the place and does more than just run an eye over the prix fixe, has entrusted the kitchen to the reliable Philippe Marc, who presents classic, flawless, well-made dishes: crab with red curry sauce, roasted wild-netted jumbo shrimp, vegetable risotto, breaded and fried veal cutlet, iced vacherin and baba au rhum with Beaujolais wine, all washed down with a thoroughbred Fessy Brouilly. Service fit for a great establishment and a smart clientele.

● **Royal Madeleine** 🍴 SIM

11, rue du Chevalier-Saint-Georges
Métro: Madeleine, Concorde
Tel. 01 42 60 14 36
royal.madeleine@wanadoo.fr
www.royalmadeleine.com
Closed 1 week in January, August.
Open until 11 PM.
A la carte: 60€.
Air cond. Terrace.

An inconspicuous little street, an equally unobtrusive 1900s' style bistro and a classic, seasonal prix fixe: This is the package presented by Laurent Couegnas, who also owns L'Escargot Montorgueil. Foie gras, sole cooked to your taste, simmered sweetbread cassoulet with mild vinegar sauce and warm profiterole of the day with hot chocolate sauce are prepared by Valérie

Paget to the delight of Carole Colin's guests. Uncompromising prices.

● **Rue Balzac** Ⓥ V.COM

3-5 rue Balzac (at 8, rue Lord-Byron)
Métro: George-V, Charles-de-Gaulle–Etoile
Tel. 01 53 89 90 91. Fax 01 53 89 90 94
ruebalzac@wanadoo.fr
www.ruebalzac.com
Closed Saturday lunch, Sunday lunch,
3 weeks in August. Open until 11:30 PM.
A la carte: 75€.
Air cond. Private dining room. Valet parking.

This cult corner establishment cultivates the legend of Johnny Hallyday, France's perennial rock star. Hallyday, born Jean-Philippe Smet, and his pal Claude Bouillon own the place. Like one of the father of French rock's stadium shows, the cuisine is planned down to the last note. Oven-crisped langoustines, house-style boiled and coddled eggs, fine pasta seasoned with green olives and baba au rhum with lightly whipped cream and rum-raisin ice cream are all highly persuasive. The ambience is pleasant, Vavro's decor stimulating, and while you wait for a table, you can relax at the bar, now situated near the door. The prices are ferocious, but when you're a fan, who's counting?

● **Le Safran** Ⓝ COM

Hilton Arc de Triomphe,
51-57, rue de Courcelles
Métro: Courcelles
Tel. 01 58 36 67 00
edouard.galisson@hilton.com
www.hilton.com
Open daily until 11 PM.
A la carte: 40–80€.

This quiet hotel restaurant decked out in purple and styled by Jacques Garcia is looking healthy. Bernard Fiemeyer, formerly at Le Concorde in Metz, prepares a dynamic fusion cuisine skillfully and with a light touch. The crab and avocado with wasabi, swordfish with lime, hearts of lettuce with mustard vinaigrette, sweet and sour grilled jumbo shrimp and scallops are extremely well done. The lunchtime business customers enjoy the food. The service is dynamic, the wines by the glass quite well chosen and the desserts (crème brûlée, apple tart, mango sablé with almond cream) deftly classical.

● Le San Régis   V.COM

Hotel San Régis, 12, rue Jean-Goujon
Métro: Champs-Elysées–Clemenceau,
Franklin-D.-Roosevelt
Tel. 01 44 95 16 16. Fax 01 45 61 05 48
message@hotel-sanregis.fr
www.hotel-sanregis.fr
Closed Sunday, August.
Open until 10:30 PM.
Prix fixe: 35€ (lunch on weekdays).
A la carte: 65€.
Air cond. Private dining room. Valet parking.

This elegant, discreet restaurant is very popular with journalists and businesspeople in the area, who get together to talk shop over green asparagus risotto, bay shrimp with sweet and sour sauce or veal filet seasoned with pineapple and honey meticulously prepared by Christophe Le Ricolais. Those with a sweet tooth will be unable to resist soft caramel cake with walnut. Today, with corporations keeping a close watch on expense accounts, the lunchtime set menu is a hit.

● Le Sarladais   COM

2, rue de Vienne
Métro: St-Lazare, St-Augustin, Europe
Tel.-Fax 01 45 22 23 62
www.lesarladais.com
Closed Saturday, Sunday, Christmas–New
Year's, 1 week in May, August.
Open until 9:30 PM.
Prix fixe: 29€, 35€. A la carte: 75€.
Air cond. Private dining room. Valet parking.

The changeless prix fixe has a Southwestern French accent. What could be more natural than to succumb to the temptation of duck foie gras with Sauternes aspic, classic Southwestern cassoulet and an Armagnac-flavored layered pastry. Also fine seasonal dishes, such as crayfish-tail salad and scallops. A superb welcome from André Perriau and appealing prices.

● Les Saveurs de Flora   ○ V.COM

36, av George-V
Métro: George-V
Tel. 01 40 70 10 49. Fax 01 47 20 52 87
www.lessaveursdeflora.com
Closed Saturday lunch, Sunday,
1 week in February, 3 weeks in August.
Open until 11 PM.
Prix fixe: 28€ (lunch), 38€, 65€.
A la carte: 80€.
Air cond. Terrace. Private dining room.

Flora Mikula prepares well-bred, contemporary dishes in these elegant surroundings. She successfully avoids the pitfalls of excess, only presenting produce in its simplest expression. Having worked with Alain Passard for a number of years, she shares this philosophy and passion for authenticity with him. The flavors of the lobster spring roll with coriander are underlined by puréed mango and avocado sorbet, the sole stuffed with gray shrimp is accentuated by orange and coriander and served on angel-hair pasta, the veal chop seasoned with garlic and rosemary grows more tender and expressive still when accompanied by the spelt risotto seasoned with parmesan. The desserts are small miracles, like the strawberry spring rolls soaked in a mint strawberry sauce or roasted pears with salted butter caramel and Carambar taffy in its every form. The dream continues even when the check arrives.

● Saveurs et Salon   COM

3, rue de Castellane
Métro: Madeleine
Tel. 01 40 06 97 97. Fax 01 40 06 98 06
contact@saveursetsalon.com
www.saveursetsalon.com
Closed Sunday lunch, Sunday evening.
Open until 10:30 PM.
Prix fixe: 20€ (lunch, wine included), 38€.
A la carte: 55€.
Air cond. Private dining room.

Talented host Rémus Nica hedges his bets. The prix fixe affects a modern style, with the foie gras carpaccio with sea salt and balsamic vinegar, or tagine of lamb shoulder with lime and ginger, but chef Paul Bougygues is at his best when he turns to classic dishes: scallop brochette and jumbo shimp with slow-simmered tender leeks, beef tenderloin with garlic and rosemary new potatoes and even a series of different crèmes brûlées for dessert. A delicious welcome and (almost) reasonable prices.

● Savy
🍴 SIM

23, rue Bayard
Métro: Franklin-D.-Roosevelt
Tel. 01 47 23 46 98. Fax 01 47 23 32 05
Closed Saturday, Sunday, Bank Holidays, August.
Prix fixe: 23,50€ (lunch), 28,50€ (dinner).
A la carte: 40€.
Air cond. Terrace. Private dining room.

Located just opposite RTL broadcasting, this old-fashioned bistro has always been used as a stylish refectory by the journalists and advertising people who work nearby. Lionel Dégoulange regales his guests with green Puy lentils with vinaigrette and sautéed bacon, grilled rib-eye steak with marrow and seasonal fruit tarts. The saint-nectaire cheese is superb. The service is a little hasty at lunchtime, but the prices are not excessive.

● Seafood Bar Caviar House Prunier
🅝 COM

15, pl de la Madeleine
Métro: Madeleine
Tel. 01 47 42 98 98. Fax 01 47 42 98 99
www.prunier.fr
Closed Sunday, August. Open until midnight.
Prix fixe: 19€. A la carte: 35–200€.
Air cond. Valet parking.

Chic, expensive, glamorous, attractive and stylish, with something of the modern lounge-style seafood bar about it, this healthy looking little temple to Aquitane caviar offers absolutely first-rate produce. Smoked herring with crème fraiche and grated horseradish, salmon tartare, Gillardeau Atlantic coast oysters and then, for sure, the entire line of domestic caviars produced in the Southwest with their "just like the Baltic" flavor (the "Tradition Prunier" is simply sublime) offer special treats at every price in this new shrine to

gourmet luxury. The contemporary setting is very refined and the view of the Madeleine unobstructed.

● Senderens
🅝 ○ 🍴 V.COM

9, pl de la Madeleine
Métro: Madeleine
Tel. 01 42 65 22 90. Fax 01 42 65 06 23
restaurant@senderens.fr
www.senderens.fr
restaurant@senderens.fr
www.senderens.fr
Closed Saturday (July–August), Sunday (July–August), May 1st.
Open until 11:30 PM.
Prix fixe: 105€ (wine included), 115€ (wine included). A la carte: 90–120€.
Air cond. Private dining room. Valet parking.

"Senderens nouveau" is here! Sixty years old but in great shape, with an assistant brought in from L'Ambroisie, a rejuvenated team and modern decor with neat tables in a industrial material and shades of gray by Noé Duchaufour-Lawrence. We are fond of the great Alain, even though we are not absolutely certain he can still offer all the magic of the wizard we once knew, the magic of rue de l'Exposition or rue de Varenne in the days of L'Archestrate. The vegetable-stuffed open ravioli, lightly smoked Scottish salmon with ribbon-cut cucumbers, red mullet cooked with seaweed and fennel confit served with olive oil cubes and the veal and langoustine tartare are not bad, even if they are not works of genius. Add to that the ever-persuasive wine-dish pairings, a less alarming tab when compared to the ferocious prices at Lucas Carton, and desserts that are obviously the house's strong point (the fine dacquoise seasoned with Szechuan peppercorns and served with lemon marmalade and ginger ice cream) will have you swooning.

● Sens Ⓝ COM

23, rue de Ponthieu
Métro: Franklin-D.-Roosevelt
Tel. 01 42 25 95 00
www.lacompagniedescomptoirs.com
Closed Saturday lunch, Sunday,
3 weeks in August. Open until 11:30 PM.
Prix fixe: 18€ (lunch), 25€ (lunch).
A la carte: 50–70€.
Air cond. Valet parking.

Just how far will they go? The Pourcel brothers' empire already extends to Montpellier, Avignon, Shanghai, Bangkok, Singapore and London, and they are now offering further feasts for the Senses in Paris. After the Maison Blanche, they have moved into the former Tanjia, turning it into a fashionable, sexy, gourmet spot that offers a ballet of attractive waitresses, an upper floor and mezzanine—with a movie screen to watch—plus polished cuisine from young disciple Pierre Altobelli. The chestnut broth or white bean soup and the lox-style tuna with caper-seasoned aïoli provide a gentle introduction. The main courses are more spirited and very well chosen, among them the slow oven–cooked cod and squid with chard and parmesan stuffing and especially the fine piece of farmhouse pork (a pork cutlet with blood sausage ravioli and sweet onions). Then there are the superb desserts such as warm and frozen cappuccino and highly the appropriate wines from around the world (Cabernets, Shirazes and Mourvèdres from South Africa). In short, a place to watch.

● Senso COM

16, rue de La Tremoille
Métro: Alma-Marceau, Franklin-D.-Roosevelt
Tel. 01 56 52 14 14. Fax 01 56 52 14 13
senso@hotel-tremoille.com
www.hotel-tremoille.com
Closed Saturday lunch, Sunday.
Open until 11 PM.
Prix fixe: 32€ (lunch, wine included),
39€ (lunch, wine included).
A la carte: 70€.
Air cond. Terrace. Private dining room.
Valet parking.

This restaurant is a mystery. Depending on what you choose, you get a masterpiece or a mockery. Frédéric Duca is still searching for his individual style and sometimes gets lost. "Limp" grilled jumbo shrimp, but a John Dory fish served with superbly cooked green gnocchi; saddle of rabbit with chard that is not bad at all, but which comes with a sticky parmesan polenta. The licorice soufflé is a great achievement. Everything is in contrast here, even the prices, expensive a la carte when you can also lunch for about 30€.

● Les Signatures COM

8, rue Jean-Goujon
Métro: Franklin-D.-Roosevelt,
Champs-Elysées–Clemenceau
Tel. 01 40 74 64 94. Fax 01 40 74 79 29
h1184-fb@accor.com
www.pressclub.fr
Closed dinner, Saturday, Sunday,
Christmas–New Year's, 3 weeks in August.
Open until 11 PM.
Prix fixe: 34€, 38€, 47€. A la carte: 65€.
Air cond. Terrace. Private dining room.
Valet parking.

Members of the Press Club, TV stars and great columnists or just plain ordinary journalists are at home here, enjoying a prix fixe with a very international flavor. The seared tuna with finely sliced vegetables and Chinese spices, the cod filet roasted with slivered carrots and vitelotte potatoes with soy, sesame, and ginger, the grilled ostrich filet with an orange and green pepper infusion, the asparagus tips served with a herbed "minestrone" of exotic fruits and the floating island served with spiced custard sauce are fairly successful. Fortunately, the set menus provide a less expensive option. A fine terrace in the summer.

● **Spicy** SIM

8, av Franklin-D.-Roosevelt
Métro: St-Philippe-du-Roule,
Franklin-D.-Roosevelt
Tel. 01 56 59 62 59. Fax 01 56 59 62 50
www.spicyrestaurant.com
Closed May 1st. Open until midnight.
Prix fixe: 20€ (lunch), 28€ (dinner),
15€ (children). A la carte: 42–50€.
Air cond. Terrace. Valet parking.

The house's commitment to spices is
meant to be trendy, but ironically, the result is often bland. The stuffed vegetables
with olive oil, shark steak seasoned with
honey and tumeric served with Chinese
noodles and chives, rib-eye steak with sea
salt and tuile with cream and a note of dark
chocolate come close to culinary modernity without fully achieving it. Go for the
set prix fixes to keep the tab to manageable
proportions.

● **Spoon** COM

14, rue de Marignan
Métro: Franklin-D.-Roosevelt
Tel. 01 40 76 34 44. Fax 01 40 76 34 37
spoonfood@marignan-elysees.fr
www.spoon.tm.fr
Closed Saturday, Sunday, New Year's, end of
July–end of August. Open until 10:15 PM.
Prix fixe: 38€ (lunch), 45€ (lunch),
85€ (dinner). A la carte: 80€.
Air cond. Valet parking.

The Spoon is still the Spoon, but with all
the innovations on which Alain Ducasse's
reputation is based. Christian Laval is in
the kitchen refining his art, while Stéphane
Colé is in the dining room explaining and
describing the basics of fusion food. Things
start off gently with lime-marinated raw
shrimp with nut and mimosa garnish, then
we move on to grilled squid in mango
sauce served with Thai rice, unless we
prefer the Australian-raised Wagu beef
served with barbeque sauce and lettuce
hearts, from livestock massaged and fed
with beer and sake. We return to Earth with
cheesecake served with yogurt ice cream
and red fruit compote (a confection
Americans envy us). The wine list takes us
around the world, and the restaurant is

entirely nonsmoking. The prices are
ridiculously high.

● **Steak & Lobster** SIM

26, rue Jean-Mermoz
Métro: Franklin-D.-Roosevelt,
Champs-Elysées-Clemenceau
Tel. 01 53 53 98 00. Fax 01 45 63 27 09
Closed Saturday lunch, Sunday,
5 August–21 August. Open until 11:30 PM.
Prix fixe: 24€ (lunch, wine included),
15€ (children). A la carte: 45–60€.
Air cond. Valet parking.

Lobster in all its forms, in bisque, grilled or
in sauce, grilled filet of sole, excellent red
meats served with fries: This is the fare presented by the shrewd Henri Baché, who
ran a flourishing eatery of the same name
in La Baule. This ad man turned fashionable restaurateur mingles cheerfully with
his communicative clientele. An initial experience with overcooked lobster and undercooked fries left us doubtful. A second,
with a new chef and an excellent, well-
seared rib-eye steak, crunchy fries and a
splendid millefeuille, showed that the
house had taken a turn for the better. The
check is uncompromising.

● **La Table du Lancaster** ○ COM

Hotel Lancaster, 7, rue de Berri
Métro: George-V
Tel. 01 40 76 40 76. Fax 01 40 76 40 00
restaurant@hotel-lancaster.fr
www.hotel-lancaster.fr
Closed Saturday lunch, Sunday lunch,
Bank Holidays, August. Open until 9:45 PM.
Prix fixe: 60€ (lunch), 120€.
A la carte: 110€.
Air cond. Terrace. Private dining room.
Valet parking.

Michel Troisgros has made this hotel
restaurant into his Paris laboratory. The
Master of Roanne has turned his hand to
"slow food" with a 300% success rate. He
creates and directs, leaving the execution to
Fabrice Salvador. The goat cheese
cannelloni with olive oil, cod broth with
koshi-hikari rice and the glazed suckling
pig with green mango salad offer proof of
Troisgros's innovative spirit and Salvador's

skills. We end on a high note with the light cappuccino truffle, then burn our fingers on the check. The chic bijou decor has a great deal of charm. So much originality and quality are priceless. The service is perfect.

● **Tante Louise** ○ 🏠 COM

41, rue Boissy-d'Anglas
Métro: Madeleine, Concorde
Tel. 01 42 65 06 85. Fax 01 42 65 28 19
tantelouise@bernard-loiseau.com
www.bernard-loiseau.com
Closed Saturday, Sunday, Bank Holidays, August. Open until 10:30 PM.
Prix fixe: 34€ (lunch), 40€ (dinner).
A la carte: 65€.
Air cond. Private dining room.

Bernard Loiseau's first Parisian establishment, redecorated in summer 2006, deserves only praise. The pan-fried duck foie gras, seared sea bass, simply served, in season, with green asparagus and a tomato garlic herb sauce or oven-roasted saddle of lamb with rosemary are very much in the spirit of the house. The molten guanaja chocolate cake with amerena cherry sauce will bowl you over. The a la carte tab is not cheap, but you can get off more lightly with the prix fixe, especially if you choose wine by the glass.

● **Terre de Truffes** SIM

21, rue Vignon
Métro: Madeleine
Tel. 01 53 43 80 44. Fax 01 42 66 18 20
terredetruffes.paris@wanadoo.fr
www.terredetruffes.com
Closed Sunday, Bank Holidays.
Open until 10 PM.
Prix fixe: 65€ (lunch), 95€.
A la carte: 80–100€.
Air cond. Private dining room

Clément Bruno is the great name in truffles. Working out of Provence, he is building up an empire around the Prince of Fungi. His Paris address has acquired a second dining room this year, where black Périgord and white Alba truffles are showcased from starter to dessert. Roasted asparagus with veal sweetbreads

and fresh morel mushrooms, potatoes with truffle-seasoned cream, truffled brie de Meaux cheese and a sampling of three desserts incorporating truffles are luscious. Of course, when you are dealing with produce of this nature, the check is never going to be within everyone's grasp, and the prix fixe menu at 65€ looks like a bargain.

● **Toi** COM

27, rue du Colisée
Métro: St-Philippe-du-Roule, Franklin-D.-Roosevelt
Tel. 01 42 56 56 58. Fax 01 42 56 09 60
restaurant.toi@wanadoo.fr
www.restaurant-toi.com
Open daily noon–2 AM. Cont. service.
Prix fixe: 17€ (lunch, except Sunday), 22€, 12€ (children). A la carte: 60€.
Air cond. Terrace. Private dining room. Valet parking.

The welcome is friendly, the prix fixe mouthwatering and the preparations audacious to a fault. Even so, we think a little more simplicity is needed to make it convincing. The fig, goat cheese, arugula, and white bean terrine seasoned with parmesan, quick-seared tuna with flavored olive oil, wok-sautéed vegetables with slow-cooked lamb shoulder, crunchy vegetables seasoned with cumin and a dessert of red fruits stay the distance, but at what a price!

● **Trend** SIM

37, rue du Colisée
Métro: St-Philippe-du-Roule
Tel. 01 42 56 50 75. Fax 01 42 56 34 75
contact@letrend.fr
www.letrend.fr
Closed Sunday, Christmas, May 1st, August.
Open until 11 PM.
Prix fixe: 16€ (lunch), 22€ (lunch), 36€ (dinner), 43€ (dinner). A la carte: 36–50€.
Air cond. Private dining room. Valet parking.

Laurent Ameel is now in charge of the kitchen, adding a touch of modernity and a few Southern French notes to the prix fixe. The goat cheese and vegetable terrine with pepper-spiced tomato sauce, sea bream with tapenade and slow-cooked tomatoes, braised lamb shank with olive-seasoned reduction sauce served with scalloped potatoes and soft Nutella cake gratify, while remaining moderately priced.

● **Le 36**   Ⓝ SIM

36, rue du Colisée
Métro: St-Philippe-du-Roule,
Franklin-D.-Roosevelt
Tel. 01 45 62 94 00.
saveursetterroir@free.fr
Closed Saturday lunch, Sunday,
3 weeks in August. Open until 11 PM.
Prix fixe: 25€. A la carte: 35€.
Air cond.

The Lacombes are affable hosts. While the prix fixe is a tribute to the Quercy region, the choice is more eclectic a la carte. The crab flan with curry, cod with balsamic vinegar, roasted veal filet and soft chocolate cake simply slip down. Skillfully selected growers' wines and friendly prices.

● **Virgin Café**   Ⓔ SIM

52-60, av des Champs-Elysées
Métro: Franklin-D.-Roosevelt
Tel. 01 42 89 46 81. Fax 01 49 53 50 41
cafe.champs@virginstores.fr
Closed Christmas, New Year's, May 1st.
Open until 11:30 PM.
A la carte: 28€.
Air cond.

This chic snack bar on the top floor of the Virgin Megastore has impressed us favorably for many a year. Between two stints of cultural retail therapy, without wasting time or breaking the bank, you can refuel with a potato and smoked salmon "burger," citrus-seasoned roasted cod with spring cabbage, strip steak with green mustard sauce and crème brûlée made with two sugars. There are also vegetarian options.

● **W**   Ⓞ V.COM

Hotel Warwick, 5, rue de Berri
Métro: George-V
Tel. 01 45 61 82 08. Fax 01 45 63 75 81
www.warwickhotels.com
Closed Saturday, Sunday, Bank Holidays,
August. Open until 9:30 PM.
Prix fixe: 49€. A la carte: 75–85€.
Air cond. Private dining room. Valet parking.

This luxury hotel has a restaurant with a fully justified reputation. Orchestrated by Christophe Moisand (who also officiates at Le Céladon), the prix fixe set to music by disciple Frédéric Lesourd is full of attractions. It is original without straying into excess and meticulously executed. The red tuna seasoned with parmesan sauce and picholine olives, red mullet with stuffed vegetables served with grilled eggplant or pan-fried lamb with basil crust and garlic herb-seasoned reduction sauce make an excellent impression. The desserts are in the same vein, especially frozen crunchy guanaja chocolate with an accompaniment of sautéed rhubarb. Excellent service and a peaceful ambience, perfect for a business meal.

● **Zo**   COM

13, rue Montalivet
Métro: Miromesnil,
Champs-Elysées–Clemenceau, Madeleine
Tel. 01 42 65 18 18. Fax 01 42 65 10 91
info@restaurantzo.com
www.restaurantzo.com
Closed Saturday lunch, Sunday,
mid-August–end of August.
Prix fixe: 16€ (lunch on weekdays).
A la carte: 50€.
Air cond. Terrace. Private dining room.
Valet parking.

The prix fixe has grown more sober, the prices have been reduced (slightly) and we now feel free to enjoy a visit to Michaël Memmi and Olivier Haski's eatery. The buffalo mozzarella and Parma ham served with young spinach, the salmon tartare served with wok-sautéed vegetables, the pecorino, arugula and Parma ham risotto and, for dessert, the house chocolate mousse are not bad at all.

INTERNATIONAL RESTAURANTS

● Il Carpaccio ⊙ V.COM

Hotel Royal Monceau, 37, av Hoche
Métro: Charles-de-Gaulle–Etoile
Tel. 01 42 99 98 90. Fax 01 42 99 89 94
restauration@royalmonceau.com
www.royalmonceau.com
Closed August.
Open until 10:00 PM. Cont. service.
A la carte: 100€.
Air cond. Private dining room. Valet parking.

Orazio Ganci, formerly at Sadler's in Milan after training with Marchesi in Erbusco, has brilliantly succeeded his compatriot Angelo Agliano in this fine Transalpine restaurant cheerfully restyled by Garcia. The handpicked staff deftly serves a salad of raw artichokes, parmesan and arugula, a fritto misto of langoustines, shrimp and calamari, saffron risotto with chanterelle mushrooms and handmade Sardinian-style pasta with sardines and bottarga. We also enjoy the more sophisticated medallions of monkfish with eggplant, cuttlefish and zucchini. The vanilla ice cream with Seville orange is a model of conclusive freshness. The fine wine list covers the whole of Italy and notably includes Tuscan reds chosen by Bruno Malara. The sublime service and the check—(almost) reasonable for such a grand experience—are the trademarks of the French capital's finest Italian restaurant.

● Le Copenhague ⊙ V.COM

142, av des Champs-Elysées
Métro: Charles-de-Gaulle–Etoile, George-V
Tel. 01 44 13 86 26. Fax 01 44 13 89 44
floradanica@wanadoo.fr
www.restaurantfloradanica.com
Closed Saturday, Sunday, Bank Holidays,
3 weeks in August. Open until 10:30 PM.
Prix fixe: 51€ (lunch), 70€ (lunch),
110€ (dinner). A la carte: 100€.
Air cond. Terrace. Private dining room.
Valet parking.

As we know, consuls are not always nationals of the countries they represent, and the Ambassador of the Kingdom of Denmark should confer this honor on Georges Landriot, who has turned this eatery into an academy of authentic Danish cuisine. His Danish-style foie gras poached in beer would bring a smile to the lips of the little mermaid, and Andersen would have loved lightly salted cod with a clam foam and glazed cucumbers. Her Majesty Margrethe II herself would appreciate the refined execution of the reindeer medallions with a red wine sauce and Danish-style croustillant filled with speck. Then the crown princes, the future Frederik X and his brother Joachim, would readily share in aquavit-soaked baba, caramelized pineapple, and vanilla whipped cream. The check is princely too, but we have no regrets, especially when the weather is good enough for us to dine on the landscaped terrace.

● Kinugawa ⊙ COM

4, rue Saint-Philippe-du-Roule
Métro: St-Philippe-du-Roule, Champs-
Elysées–Clemenceau, Franklin-D.-Roosevelt
Tel. 01 45 63 08 07. Fax 01 42 60 57 36
Closed Saturday lunch, Sunday,
Christmas–New Year's. Open until 10 PM.
Prix fixe: 32€ (lunch), 75€.
A la carte: 75€.
Air cond.

This is one of the fashionable Japanese restaurants between the Champs-Elysées and Opéra. The decor is Zen, the dining room team a little less so and the customers not at all when they get the tab. At lunchtime, patrons vie to order their bento boxes as fast as possible. Things are quieter in the evening, when customers enjoy the sushi bar (on the first floor), the sashimi and the makis or sakamushis (fish filet or shellfish braised in sake), unless they are set on meat, in which case they can choose between the thinly sliced beef and vegetables cooked in broth and seared beef with teriyaki sauce.

● Le Stresa

7, rue Chambiges
Métro: Alma-Marceau
Tel. 01 47 23 51 62
Closed Saturday, Sunday, Christmas
vacation, August. Open until 10 PM.
A la carte: 100€.
Air cond. Terrace. Private dining room.

You do not get much for 100€ these days
. . . except here in the Faiola brothers'
Fifties' decor restaurant. Tony in the dining room and Marco at the stove trans-
port their clientele of socialite gourmet
connoisseurs away to deepest Italy. There,
they savor stuffed zuchini blossoms, thin-
flaky-crust pizza, divine spaghetti car-
bonara, white truffle risotto, in season
(that has them melting), Dover sole with
olive oil and lemon, César-style beef filet
or finally caramel, almond and hazelnut
cake. The finest Transalpine wines feature
on the list and the Antinori Peppoli slips
down smoothly.

▼ | SHOPS

KITCHENWARE & TABLETOP

▼ Baccarat

11, pl de la Madeleine
Métro: Madeleine
Tel. 01 42 65 36 26. Fax 01 42 65 06 64
10 AM–7 PM. Closed Sunday.
Founded in 1764 in the town of Baccarat,
this great establishment offers different
lines of Lorraine crystal: superb glasses,
carafes, vases, dishes and tumblers.

▼ Bernardaud

11, rue Royale
Métro: Madeleine
Tel. 01 47 42 82 66. Fax 01 41 12 52 17
10 AM–7 PM.
Closed Sunday, Bank Holidays.
Bernardaud, star of Limoges porcelain,
supplies haute cuisine establishments
from Paris to New York with contemporary
styles—especially black and white stripes
or splendid white plates—among the
genre's finest. Its workshops in Oradour-

sur-Glane carry on the tradition of hand-
made porcelain with a very modern chic.

▼ Christofle

9, rue Royale
Métro: Concorde
Tel. 01 55 27 99 00. Fax 01 55 27 99 22
10:30 AM–7 PM.
Closed Sunday, Bank Holidays.
This great firm works with the most eminent designers to offer fine selections of
silverware, porcelain, crystal and silver or
silver-plated cutlery.

▼ Cristallerie de Saint-Louis

13, rue Royale
Métro: Concorde, Madeleine
Tel. 01 40 17 01 74
10 AM–6:30 PM.
Closed Sunday, Bank Holidays.
Acquired by Hermès, this is the oldest es-
tablished crystal glassworks in the Pays de
Bitche. The firm continues to sway be-
tween tradition and creativity. The glasses
and carafes are works of beauty.

▼ Lalique

11, rue Royale
Métro: Concorde, Madeleine
Tel. 01 53 05 12 12. Fax 01 53 05 12 13
10 AM–6:30 PM (Saturday 7 PM)
(Thursday–Friday 9:30 AM–6:30 PM).
Closed Sunday, Bank Holidays.
Since 1884, the Lalique workshops of
Wingen-sur-Moder (Bas-Rhin) have been
manufacturing vases, buckets, ashtrays and
dishes in opalescent crystal. Then there are
plates from Coquet in Limoges, not to men-
tion jewelry, candlesticks and doorknobs.

▼ Puyforcat

2, av Matignon
Métro: Franklin-D.-Roosevelt, Champs-
Elysées–Clemenceau
Tel. 01 45 63 10 10. Fax 01 42 56 27 15
10:15 AM–6:30 PM.
Closed Sunday, Bank Holidays.
PATRON : Jean-Louis Duval
Since the Thirties, the trademark of this
company has been the three-pronged
fork. The silver champagne buckets and
silver-plated Christmas ornaments are
also famous.

▼ Territoire

30, rue Boissy-d'Anglas
Métro: Madeleine, Concorde
Tel. 01 42 66 22 13. Fax 01 40 07 05 27
10:30 AM–7 PM. Closed Sunday,
Bank Holidays, 1 week in August.

This delectable, old-fashioned little store presents a collection of fun or nature-related decorative objects. Fine books and Nontron and Laguiole knives complete its stock.

BREAD & BAKED GOODS

▼ René Saint-Ouen

111, bd Haussmann
Métro: Miromesnil
Tel. 01 42 65 06 25
8 AM–7:30 PM. Closed Sunday,
Bank Holidays, August.

René Saint-Ouen, king of bread sculpture, shapes his dough into amusing forms, as with presidential baguette, rye bread with raisins and walnuts, leavened bread and foccacia. The kugelhof is remarkable.

WINE

▼ Cave Dubœuf

9, rue Marbeuf
Métro: Alma-Marceau
Tel. 01 47 20 71 23
9 AM–1 PM, 3–7 PM.
Closed Sunday, Monday, August.

Georges Dubœuf, king of Beaujolais, offers a fine selection of Mâconnais, Haut Poitou and Ardèche vintages, as well as Parent Pommard, Tollot-Beau Savigny and a fine range of New World wines.

▼ Caves Augé 🏠

116, bd Haussmann
Métro: St-Augustin
Tel. 01 45 22 16 97. Fax 01 44 70 08 80
9 AM–7:30 PM. Closed Sunday,
Monday morning, Bank Holidays.

In this 1850s' cellar with its woodwork and antique freight elevator, Marc Sibard shares his favorite vintages. Here, you will find the finest prestige wines, discoveries and unusual libations. Gramenon Côtes du Rhône, Nuits Saint Georges from

Shops

Gouges or Meylet Saint Emilion go hand in hand with Drappier "Nature" Champagne. The store has many unpretentious, fruity young wines and offers a wide range of foreign vintages.

▼ Caves Taillevent

199, rue du Faubourg-Saint-Honoré
Métro: Charles-de-Gaulle–Etoile, Ternes
Tel. 01 45 61 14 09. Fax 01 45 61 19 68
9 AM–7:30 PM. Closed Sunday, Monday
morning, 2 weeks in August.

Valérie Vrinat runs the family cellar with style. Among the Côtes de Bourg, Côtes de Blaye, Languedoc, distinguished Burgundy and flavorsome Bordeaux vintages, you are bound to find the bottle your heart is set on. There are also carafes with the Taillevent name and magnificent gift boxes (macarons, champagnes or cigars).

▼ Maison du Whisky

20, rue d'Anjou
Métro: Madeleine
Tel. 01 42 65 03 16
9:15 AM (Monday 9:30 AM)–8 PM (Monday
7 PM, Saturday 7:30 PM).
Closed Sunday, Bank Holidays.

Established in 1956, this embassy specializes in selected quality whiskeys. It is hard to choose between classics and newer items—between Tullibardine, 32-year-old Springbank or 1947 Glendronach, all sensational. The house also presents vodka, gin and ports of all kinds.

▼ Nicolas

31, pl de la Madeleine
Métro: Madeleine
Tel. 01 42 68 00 16 / 01 49 24 08 52.
Fax 01 47 42 70 26
9:30 AM–8 PM.
Closed Sunday, Bank Holidays.

First to offer wine for sale by the bottle rather than by volume, Nicolas offers a wide range of great Bordeaux, Sauternes, Meursault and Chambertin vintages from exceptional years. Also wines from South Africa, Argentina, Chile, Australia, Greece and Hungary.

▼ Verger de la Madeleine

4, bd Malesherbes
Métro: Madeleine
Tel. 01 42 65 51 99. Fax 01 49 24 05 22
www.verger-madeleine.com
10 AM–8 PM.
Closed Sunday, Bank Holidays.

This store, established in 1937, offers a vast range of great wines, brandies and spirits: choice rums, cognacs, Armagnacs, Madeiras from 1902 to 1943, liqueurs, Calvados and vodkas. Gilles Monoy selects the fruits of the great wine-growing regions of France at their best.

CHARCUTERIE

▼ Vignon

14, rue Marbeuf
Métro: Franklin-D.-Roosevelt, Champs-Elysées–Clemenceau
Tel. 01 47 20 24 26. Fax 01 47 20 15 14
8:45 AM–8 PM.
Closed Sunday, Bank Holidays.

Philippe Vignon enthusiastically champions traditional charcuterie: cured meats and sausages, York ham, pig's feet, wild game terrine, foie gras and smoked salmon for connoisseurs.

CHOCOLATE

▼ Au Chat Bleu

85, bd Haussmann
Métro: St-Augustin
Tel.-Fax 01 42 65 33 18
9:15 AM–7 PM.
Closed Saturday, Sunday, August.

As in Le Touquet, the store presents pralinés with crisp nougatine. Confectionery such as bitter chocolate with prunes, spiced chocolate, Saintonge chocolate made with 70% cocoa or Brazilian coffee ganache are of artisanal quality.

▼ La Maison du Chocolat

225, rue du Faubourg-Saint-Honoré
Métro: Ternes
Tel. 01 42 27 39 44. Fax 01 47 64 03 75
10 AM–7:30 PM (beginning of November–April), 10 AM–7 PM (May–October).
Closed Sunday, Bank Holidays.
(Other addresses: 52, rue François-Ier, 8th arr.,
Tel. 01 47 23 38 25.
19, rue de Sèvres, 6th arr.,
Tel. 01 45 44 20 40.
8, bd de la Madeleine, 9th arr.,
Tel. 01 47 42 86 52.
89, rue Raymond-Poincaré, 16th arr.,
Tel. 01 40 67 77 73).

Robert Linxe, great-hearted wizard of ganache, cultivates his love of excellence. All his chocolates are meticulously prepared: chocolate slices with dried fruit, caramel truffles, apricot truffles, marrons glacés, fruit jellies. Then there are the blends that have built the firm's reputation, such as fennel, Andalusian lemon, sylvia au lait, rigoletto and habanera peach plum, all supremely delicate and refined.

▼ La Reine Astrid

33, rue de Washington
Tel. 01 45 63 60 39. Fax 01 45 62 86 10
Métro: George-V
10:15 AM–7 PM. Closed Sunday, August.

You are welcomed with a bright smile in this little store. Raspberry ganache, champagne chocolates, chocolate nougat cakes or candied ginger strips are delicacies to melt over.

CANDY & SWEETS

▼ Fouquet

22, rue François-Ier
Métro: Franklin-D.-Roosevelt
Tel. 01 47 23 30 36. Fax 01 47 23 30 56
10 AM–7:30 PM. Closed Sunday,
Bank Holidays.

This confectionery institution favors full and aromatic notes with no bitterness. We delight in the jams, honey, dried fruits filled with almond paste and Russian-style dried fruits, orange-scented chocolate fondants, candied ginger, candied fruit peel or chocolate truffles. Taste the salvador, a soft caramel with hard caramel coating.

▼ Aux Miels de France 🏠

71, rue du Rocher
Métro: Villiers
Tel. 01 45 22 23 13
9:30 AM–2 PM (Saturday 1 PM),
2:30 PM–7 PM. Closed Sunday,
Bank Holidays, Monday, August.

Honey in all its forms is king here. We love the house jams, especially the bitter orange, honey drops, chocolates or artisanal gingerbread of impeccable quality.

GROCERIES

▼ BE

73, bd de Courcelles
Métro: Courcelles, Ternes
Tel. 01 46 22 20 20. Fax 01 46 22 20 21
www.boulangerepicier.com
7 AM–8 PM.
Closed Sunday, end of July–end of August.

This bakery and grocery store opened by Alain Ducasse and Eric Kayser offers food to take away or eat on the spot. You will find Spanish chili peppers, hand-harvested sea salt, licorice and calissons (Provençal almond candy), and, on the bakery front, a choice of speciality breads with walnuts, figs, tomatoes, olives and/or whole grain. If you feel like a bite at lunchtime, Kayser salad (chicken and crayfish), mushroom soup, salmon glazed with balsamic vinegar, sesame tuna, pear tart or salted caramels are all well prepared.

▼ Granterroirs

30, rue de Miromesnil
Métro: Miromesnil
Tel. 01 47 42 18 18. Fax 01 47 42 18 00
9 AM–8 PM. Closed Saturday, Sunday,
Bank Holidays, 3 weeks in August.

Jean-François Gimenez has turned his fine store into a showcase for all kinds of regional produce. Delicious foie gras terrine, goat cheese, smoked duck and duck gizzard confit are available to take away or eat at communal tables at lunchtime. Sardines, Acquerello rice and fleur de sel de Guérande (hand-harvested sea salt) make wonderful gifts.

▼ Maille

6, pl de la Madeleine
Métro: Madeleine
Tel. 01 40 15 06 00. Fax 01 40 15 06 11
10 AM–7 PM.
Closed Sunday, Bank Holidays.

Marie-Hélène Greczka provides house mustards in pots or from the pump, quality oils and vinegars (truffle, champagne), aromatic mustards (with dried apricot, marc, violet, herbs, honey, cognac, Calvados, green peppercorn or caramelized orange). Discover the superb earthenware pots of honey.

▼ La Maison de la Truffe

19, pl de la Madeleine
Métro: Madeleine
Tel. 01 42 65 53 22. Fax 01 49 24 96 59
9:30 AM–9 PM. Closed Sunday (except for Christmas–New Year's), Bank Holidays.

Guy Monier flaunts the truffle in all its forms: in omelets, terrines or sauces. He also offers vintage spirits, such as Armagnac and cognac, and luxury products of every kind: smoked wild salmon, caviar, foie gras, goose confit, fruits steeped in Armagnac, candies, chocolate truffles. An impressive cellar.

▼ Albert Ménès

41, bd Malesherbes
Métro: St-Augustin
Tel. 01 42 66 95 63. Fax 01 40 06 00 61
10:30 AM–2 PM, 2:45 PM–7 PM. Closed Saturday, Sunday, mid-July–mid-August.

Almost a hundred years old, this store offers a wide range of confectionery, candies, jams, honeys, provincial almond cake, teas, coffees, chocolates, Breton butter cookies, canned fish and spices, all of immaculate quality.

PASTRIES

▼ Ladurée 🏠

16, rue Royale
Métro: Concorde, Madeleine
Tel. 01 42 60 21 79. Fax 01 49 27 01 95
8:30 AM (Sunday 10 AM)–7 PM.
Closed Sunday, July 15th–August 15th.

Louis-Ernest Ladurée founded this famous store, decorated with moldings, in 1862.

Today, customers still flock to his establishment (now run by the Holder family) to savor or take away caramel- or rose-infused cream puffs, famous macarons, licorice millefeuilles, small sandwiches and rhubarb or wild strawberry tarts.

TEA

▼ Betjeman et Barton

23, bd Malesherbes
Métro: Madeleine
Tel. 01 42 65 86 17. Fax 01 42 65 19 71
10 AM–7 PM. Closed Sunday,
2 weeks in beginning of August.

Since 1919, this store has been offering a range of strong, flowery and spicy teas. We adore the Beryl Blend (Chinese tea with the aromas of orange, pineapple and lilac petals), the Parlez-moi d'amour (raspberry, jasmine and orange), the Ylang-Ylang and Ballade Irlandaise (with the aroma of whiskey cream). Also fine iron, porcelain and ceramic teapots.

COFFEE

▼ Torréfaction Marbeuf

25, rue Marbeuf
Métro: Franklin-D.-Roosevelt
Tel.-Fax 01 47 23 95 75
9:30 AM–7 PM.
Closed Saturday, Sunday, August.

Marie-Paule Brunet meticulously roasts coffees from all over the world: Ethiopia, Kenya, Lebanon, Yemen, Guatamala, Antigua, Guadeloupe, Lekempti and Costa Rica. Subtle blends of organic honey and miscellaneous, bewitching teas.

PREPARED FOOD

▼ Dalloyau

101, rue du Faubourg-Saint-Honoré
Métro: St-Philippe-du-Roule
Tel. 01 42 99 90 00. Fax 01 45 63 82 92
8 AM–9 PM. Open daily.

This gourmet delicatessen established in 1802 is a center of excellence and creativity. The preserved fruits, macarons, exquisite homemade white bread, truffles and mendiants (mixture of figs, almonds, hazelnuts and raisins) are delightful achievements. Upstairs, customers enjoy savory chicken and foie gras tourte, cured sausage studded with pistachios in brioche and carrots with cumin. The cakes and pastries are superb.

▼ Fauchon

26, pl de la Madeleine
Métro: Madeleine
Tel. 01 70 39 38 00. Fax 01 70 39 38 20
9 AM–9 PM. Closed Sunday.

This great institution has been a touchstone since 1886. Each year, the product range is examined with the greatest care. In the grocery section: cookies, coffees, teas, jams, compotes, spices. In the cakes, pastries and bakery section: orange- or tea-flavored eclairs, chocolates, macarons, ice creams and jellied fruits. The cellar boasts more than 2,500 vintages.

▼ Hédiard

21, pl de la Madeleine
Métro: Madeleine
Tel. 01 43 12 88 88. Fax 01 42 66 31 97
9 AM–9 PM. Closed Sunday.

For 150 years, this great establishment has been offering more than 6,000 products from the regions of France and beyond. There are terrines, pâtés, soups, biscuits, coffees, teas, condiments, exotic fruits, and spices in a store with a colonial flavor and a gilded, red and black decor.

◆ RENDEZVOUS

BARS

◆ Bar du Crillon

Hotel du Crillon, 10, pl de la Concorde
Métro: Concorde
Tel. 01 44 71 15 39
www.crillon.com
11:30 AM–2 AM. Open daily.

This bar on place de la Concorde, designed by sculptor César and decorated by Rykiel, has a timeless charm. Enjoy a whiskey, tea or cocktail there to the soothing sounds of the house piano. A lunch option at noon.

◆ Bar du Plaza

Plaza Athénée, 25, av Montaigne
Métro: Alma-Marceau
Tel. 01 53 67 65 00
www.plaza-athenee-paris.com
6 PM–2 AM. Open daily.

Elegant and contemporary, a stylish bar with a translucent glass counter that lights up when touched and snacks by Ducasse. Taste the special cocktails: Flower Power (distilled flower elixir in a revitalizing oxygen-rich water), Rose Royale (champagne and raspberry cocktail), Fashion Ice (cocktails in the form of a popsicle), Jelly Shots (jellified cocktails). An excellent club sandwich, refined herbal teas and delectable cakes and pastries can be savored in the gallery passage.

◆ Bar 30

Sofitel Faubourg
15, rue Boissy d'Anglas
Métro: Concorde
Tel. 01 44 94 14 14
9 AM–2 AM (Sunday 1 AM). Open daily.

This neo-Thirties' bar by Rochon offers a very personal welcome until late. The Hermès crowd comes here for a light supper from the kitchens of the Café Faubourg or a carefully prepared cocktail.

◆ L'Envue

39, rue Boissy-d'Anglas
Métro: Concorde
Tel. 01 42 65 10 49. Fax 01 40 17 09 28
www.lenvue.com
8 AM–2 AM.
Closed Sunday, 1 week in August.
Air cond. Terrace.

This stylish, baroque bar offers a range of cocktails and sophisticated foods (langoustine ravioli, lamb chops with an herb crust). The toilets are worth seeing.

◆ Le Forum 🛏

4, bd Malesherbes
Métro: Madeleine
Tel. 01 42 65 37 86. Fax 01 42 68 11 87
www.bar-le-forum.com
Noon–2 AM (Saturday 5:30 PM–2 AM).
Closed Sunday, 1 week in August.

The attractions of this Forties' bar are its hushed atmosphere, leather armchairs,

collection of vodka, cachaça, pisco and malt whiskeys and its selection of 250 cocktails.

◆ Le Fouquet's 🛏

99, av des Champs-Elysées
Métro: George-V
Tel. 01 47 23 50 00. Fax 01 47 23 50 55
www.lucienbarierre.com
8 AM–2 AM. Open daily.

Looking out onto the world's most beautiful avenue since 1899, this paneled bar has remained perennially fashionable. Patrons savor well-prepared classics, such as the Americano, Porto Flip and Bloody Mary, as well as a fine selection of whiskeys and eaux de vie.

◆ Mathi's

3, rue de Ponthieu
Métro: George-V
Tel. 01 53 76 01 62
7:30 PM–2 AM. Closed Sunday.

Gérald Nanty is the living key to Paris nightlife. His hotel bar and restaurant is the headquarters of French TV presenter Thierry Ardisson and the crowd from the Paris Première channel. Patrons enjoy smoked salmon, sea bass with a tangy butter sauce, rotisserie chicken on one side of the establishment and a drink on the other, until late. A select haunt.

◆ The Polo Room

3, rue Lord-Byron
Métro: George-V,
RER A Charles-de-Gaulle–Etoile
Tel.-Fax 01 40 74 07 78 / 01 40 74 02 23
11 AM–2 AM.
Closed Saturday lunch, Sunday lunch.
Air cond. Terrace. Valet parking.

Behind the Lido, this jazz bar offers international cuisine and delicately prepared cocktails, notably 30 martinis. Old movies in black and white are shown on large screens.

◆ Prince de Galles

Hotel Prince de Galles, 33, av George-V
Métro: George-V
Tel. 01 53 23 77 77
11:30 AM–2 AM. Open daily.

A luxury hotel bar that has maintained its British style and timeless air. Champagne cocktails (Bellini with peach, Miami Beach with orange, apricot and gin) star here.

◆ Royal Bar au Royal Monceau

Hotel Royal Monceau, 37, av Hoche
Métro: Etoile, Ternes
Tel. 01 42 99 88 00
9 AM–1 AM. Open daily.

Jacques Garcia renovated this bar, giving it a new lease on life with soft lights, large couches and crimson velvet. You can enjoy a grappa, perfect americano or iced vodka, not to mention some exquisite dishes (tempura, carpaccio risotto) here. Singing and music in the evening.

PUBS

◆ The Cricketer Pub

41, rue des Mathurins
Métro: St-Augustin, Havre-Caumartin
Tel. 01 40 07 01 45
4:30 PM–2 AM (Saturday,
Sunday 1 PM–2 AM).
Closed 2 weeks in August.

The blue front and woodwork set the tone. The cuisine is international (tandoori chicken, Tex-Mex or chicken pie) and the beer flows like water when there is a game to be watched on the three TV screens.

WINE BARS

◆ Le Coin   ⓝ

88, rue du Rocher
Métro: Villiers
Tel. 01 43 87 58 96
6:30 AM–11 PM. Closed Sunday.

Good wines at the counter, a selection of cured pork sausages and pâtés and aged cheeses and dishes of the day chalked up on the blackboard: This is what you can expect from this simple corner café, which lends a touch of the blue collar to this exclusive area of Paris. (Also see Restaurants.)

◆ L'Ecluse

15, pl de la Madeleine / 64, rue François Ier
Métro: Madeleine, George-V
Tel. 01 42 65 34 69 (Madeleine) /
01 47 20 77 09 (François Ier)
www.leclusebaravin.com
11:30 AM–1 AM. Open daily.

Opposite the Madeleine, the veranda has a countryside feel to it. You can snack on cheeses, tartare, foie gras or a superb chocolate cake. Dominique Dhyser presents the finest Bordeaux served by the glass.

◆ Le Griffonnier

8, rue des Saussaies
Métro: Miromesnil,
Champs-Elysées–Clemenceau
Tel. 01 42 65 17 17
8 AM–9 PM (Thursday 11 PM).
Closed Saturday, Sunday, 3 weeks in August.
Air cond.

The dynamic Cédric Duthilleul has taken over this wine bar, which made Robert Savoye (gone to LeCaffé nearby) famous, and which is frequented by literary neighbor Bernard Frank. Treat yourself to the oxtail terrine sold by the slice, sausages from the Auvergne region, rib-eye steak with marrow or crème brûlée. The Beaujolais are always appealing.

◆ Savoye Caffé   ⓝ

13, bd de Courcelles
Métro: Courcelles
Tel. 01 42 89 20 99
7 AM–11 PM. Open daily

Robert Savoye, who made such a success of Le Griffonnier, has turned this large, modern café with its horseshoe-shaped bar into a cheerful rendezvous. He serves serious, solid food (toasted open-faced sandwiches with cold cuts from the Massif Central region) or aged cheeses, fine grilled red meats, ice creams produced by Octave, as well as André Dussourt's Alsace wines, Château de Belleverne Saint Amour and his name-mate Pierre Savoye's Morgon. Brunch on Sunday.

CAFES

◆ Joe's Café

277, rue Saint-Honorê
Métro: Madeleine, Concorde
Tel. 01 49 27 05 54. Fax 01 49 27 01 82
10 AM–6 PM. Closed Sunday.

This Zen café welcomes patrons for a snack in its basement with light, fresh world cuisine. The thin slices of swordfish marinated in Tuscan olive oil, pasta with tomato and basil and jumbo shrimp risotto are remarkable. In the afternoon, you can enjoy French toast with ice cream.

◆ Le Paris

93, av des Champs-Elysées
Métro: George-V
Tel. 01 47 23 54 37. Fax 01 47 23 61 96
8 AM–6 AM. Open daily.
Terrace

This brasserie standing right on the Champs-Elysées is the picture of health. Guest come to enjoy timeless dishes (tomatoes and mozzarella, parmesan and arugula), grilled tartare, roasted salmon and delicious cocktails in a very Costes atmosphere.

◆ Rival

1, rue Marbeuf / 20, av George-V
Métro: Alma-Marceau
Tel. 01 47 23 40 99.
7 AM–2 AM. Open daily.
Terrace.

This elegant brasserie has two entrances and two terraces, plus a cozy interior with leather sofas and a mahogany bar. Refuel with organic eggs with salmon, golden-roasted chicken breast and delicious carpaccio.

TEA SALONS

◆ Ladurée

75, av des Champs-Elysées
Métro: George-V, Franklin-D.-Roosevelt
Tel. 01 40 75 08 75. Fax 01 40 75 06 75
www.laduree.fr
7:30 AM–12:30 AM. Open daily.
Air cond.

The five rooms with their cozy atmosphere have a perennially modish charm. Under the Ladurée label, Philippe Andrieu makes subtle desserts, including the famous chocolate, vanilla, rose or pistachio macarons.

◆ Maison Kayser

"Au Comte de Malesherbes"
85, bd Malesherbes
Métro: St-Augustin, Monceau
Tel. 01 45 22 70 30
www.maisonkayser.com
7 AM–8 PM. Closed Sunday,
Bank Holidays (except for Epiphany),
Christmas, New Year's.
Air cond. Terrace.

Eric Kayser runs a modern store and elegant tearoom, enabling customers to enjoy his range of bread. The pasta (rye macaroni, spelt-wheat spaghetti), simply cooked fresh fish and pastries all look good.

◆ Mariage Frères

260, rue du Faubourg-Saint-Honoré
Métro: Ternes
Tel.-Fax 01 46 22 18 54
www.mariagefrères.com
10:30 AM–7:30 PM. Closed Christmas,
New Year's, May 1st.
Air cond. Terrace.

Passion, refinement and sophistication are the house watchwords. Pastries and tea cakes are accompanied by brews from the finest plantations.

◆ Au Rythme de l'Opéra ⓝ

3, rue Vignon
Métro: Madeleine
Tel. 01 40 06 07 05. Fax 01 40 06 00 22
11:30 AM–6 PM. Closed Sunday,
2 weeks in August.
Terrace.

Roselyne Paris has taken over this deli, which offers pastrami sandwiches, bagels, poppy seed cakes, strudels and cheesecake.

9TH ARRONDISSEMENT
AN ARTISTIC RETREAT

The Costes brothers, who understand the city, have turned their eyes to the ninth arrondissement, delighting Paris society with their young, fashionable Hôtel Amour, a sign that the district can create trends but stands hostage to none. Under the name of Nouvelle Athènes, it was a 19th-century retreat and residential development built to shelter artists. Delacroix, George Sand, Renan, Gustave Moreau, Horace Vernet, Jean-Jacques Henner and Viollet-le-Duc lived there. They have been replaced by the media (*Le Figaro* newspaper and *L'Express* magazine are based nearby) and bohemian middle class. On the culinary front, the ninth is a forum. Its fine restaurants (from La Casa Olympe to Velly and L'Art des Choix to Georgette) set the tone. Some are regional, international, entertaining (Romain, Dell'Orto, Lo Spuntino, Wally, Sizin, Yorgantz, La Petite Sirène de Copenhague, Les Diamantaires, Le Paprika, Fuxia). There are also plenty of good stores. Between rue des Martyrs and Notre-Dame-de-Lorette, Paris is still an open-air market. Superb bakers, exquisite confectioners (Seurre, Rabineau, Delmontel) and quality butchers abound. In addition, delicious foreign "embassies" (Massis Bleue, Heratchian, L'Epicerie) cheerfully rub shoulders. This is a friendly, companionable arrondissement, the kind of ode to the pedestrian we dream of: gourmet and Parisian.

● RESTAURANTS

GOOD RESTAURANTS & OTHERS

● L'Annexe SIM

15, rue Chaptal
Métro: N-D.-de-Lorette, Blanche
Tel. 01 48 74 65 52
www.annexe-restaurant.com
Closed Saturday, Sunday, 3 weeks in August.
Open until 10 PM.
A la carte: 35€.
Terrace.

Opposite the Musée de la Vie Romantique, this local bistro does business amiably. Masson Yoni has taken over the kitchen with little difficulty, and the two proprietors, Patrice Perodeaud and Maxime Delplanque, offer a friendly welcome. The baked egg with sorrel, warm goat cheese salad with pears poached in wine, cod with ginger sauce, haddock with lemon cream sauce, duck medallions with raspberry sauce, beef with roquefort and apples, rhubarb tart and homemade profiteroles play to a traditional, domestic little score that has its charm.

● L'Art des Choix 🚘 ⊜ SIM

36, rue Condorcet
Métro: Anvers, Cadet
Tel. 01 48 78 30 61. Fax 01 48 78 16 29
www.e-quartier.com
Closed Saturday lunch, Sunday, Monday evening, 1 week Christmas–New Year's, 3 weeks in August. Open until 10:30 PM.
Prix fixe: 16€, 21€, 23€, 29€.
Private dining room.

Last year, Patrice Gras's small establishment was one of our Special Favorites. This Alain Dutournier disciple, whose local bistro has been refurbished in a cheerful, contemporary style, offers a convincing, light cuisine that adapts to the market produce of the day. The amiability of the prices matches the meticulousness of the preparations. You will not be disappointed by the warm asparagus with soft-boiled eggs and toast strips for dipping, the avocado "cassoulet" with warm goat cheese, pan-seared turbot with Bayonne ham, scallops with slow-roasted endives or the pork shank fricassée with hazelnuts. The beef tenderloin roasted in red wine (reasonably priced at 16€) is a choice morsel indeed. An apple-pear gelatin dessert with salted-butter caramel ice cream and a crisp pastry with Guérande salted chestnuts are treats for well-mannered children. The house also plans to open a store selling regional products.

● Auberge du Clou Ⓢ SIM

30, av Trudaine
Métro: Pigalle, Anvers
Tel. 01 48 78 22 48. Fax 01 48 78 30 08
auberge-du-clou@free.fr
www.aubergeduclou.fr
Closed Christmas, January 1 and 2.
Open until 11 PM.
Prix fixe: 15€ (lunch, wine included), 32€.
A la carte: 55€.
Terrace.

Since the Meillons left, the Clou has lost a lot of its charm. Prices have risen significantly, including for wine, now chosen with less discernment. The chilled cream of asparagus (ice cube-like) with a hard tomato granita, the smoked salmon, herring-style with potatoes (undercooked), cod (overcooked, a bit dry) with an orange sauce (nondescript) served with a fennel purée and sautéed lamb (dry) with mint sauce (but served with nice steamed vegetables) are not very persuasive. However, the tiramisu with strawberries that resembles a soft panna cotta and a raspberry tart with pistachios (despite its sodden pastry) provide an acceptable conclusion to the meal.

● Les Bacchantes SIM

21, rue de Caumartin
Métro: Madeleine, Auber (RER), Havre-Caumartin
Tel. 01 42 65 25 35. Fax 01 47 42 65 87
Closed Sunday, Monday, Bank Holidays, Christmas, 1 week in mid-August.
Open until midnight.
A la carte: 35€.
Air cond.

Things are better this year in this restaurant that we hold dear. Michel Gautier has taken the service in hand and brought a smile to the dining room, breathing new life into what was our favorite bistro in the days of its founder, Raymond Pocous. The bone marrow with Guérande salt, the chef's terrine, jumbo shrimp cassoulet, fresh Atlantic cod, leg of lamb and slow-cooked beef cheeks are irreproachable. Guests come to taste the splendid wines by the glass, chew the fat and enjoy old-fashioned desserts (chocolate fondant with crème anglaise, flan served by the scoop with caramel). Just one criticism: The restaurant formerly welcomed diners after shows at the Olympia theater, but the service now ends earlier.

● **Barramundi** COM

3, rue Taitbout
Métro: Richelieu-Drouot
Tel. 01 47 70 21 21. Fax 01 47 70 21 20
contact@barramundi.fr
www.barramundi.fr
Closed Saturday lunch, Sunday, August 2nd.
Open until midnight.
Prix fixe: 23€ (lunch), 33€ (lunch).
A la carte: 45€.
Air cond. Private dining room.

This discreetly hip establishment with its basement dining room, all-wood decor and openwork partitions offers a relatively unpretentious world cuisine. The upside-down tomato tart, crispy green bean salad, sea bream with a light reduction sauce, and the chicken tempura are up to standard and hardly call for comment. The same goes for the dessert of three chocolates and the sabayon with two types of oranges. The atmosphere is pleasant, customers are welcome until late and the restaurant turns into a discotheque every Saturday night from midnight until 5 a.m.

● **Bistrot des Deux Théâtres** SIM

18, rue Blanche
Métro: Blanche, Trinité
Tel. 01 45 26 41 43. Fax 01 48 74 08 92
www.bistrot-et-compagnie.fr
Open daily until 12:30 AM.
Prix fixe: 33€.
Air cond.

Why change a winning format? Willy Dorr, the more modest J.-P. Bucher of the bistro world, attracts less attention than the founder of the Flo group. However, his various bistros with their "all included" prix fixe menus have proved an ongoing success. Opposite the Théâtre de Paris, this one pulls in the crowds. Its decor (including a fresco featuring celebrities), counter, tables and banquettes form a traditional setting. On the food side, we have no complaints about the potato cake with duck foie gras and morel mushroom reduction, puff pastry with asparagus, pan-seared fresh scallops, or lamb à la Provençal. The soft chocolate cake with salted-butter caramel is not bad at all, and the Duboeuf Côtes du Rhône goes down wonderfully with all this.

● **Le Bistrot Papillon** SIM

6, rue Papillon
Métro: Cadet, Poissonnière
Tel. 01 47 70 90 03. Fax 01 48 24 05 59
Closed Saturday lunch, Saturday evening
(May-September), Sunday, Christmas–New
Year's, 1 week in beginning of May,
3 weeks in August. Open until 10 PM.
Prix fixe: 27€. A la carte: 50€.
Air cond.

Amiable and so out of date that it may well come back into fashion one of these days, Jean-Yves Guion's inn is delightful. At the foot of square Montholon, in this old, slightly kitsch pink and green setting decorated with woodwork, we feel as if we are visiting small-town cousins. The set menu is still the best deal here, and the house dishes are in a classical (but not monotonous) vein. The foie gras terrine, filet of sole with orange sauce, rabbit saddle seasoned with rosemary served with mushroom polenta and veal kidneys with morel mushroom are unpretentious. The nougat flavored with Grand Marnier offers a moment of pleasure.

● **Café de la Paix** ⊙ 👔 V.COM

2, rue Scribe
Métro: Opéra
Tel. 01 40 07 36 36. Fax 01 40 07 36 13
legrand@ichotelsgroup.com
www.paris.intercontinental.com
Open daily until 11:30 PM.
Prix fixe: 45€ (lunch),
85€ (dinner on weekdays). A la carte: 65€.
Air cond. Terrace.

Neutral, standardized, factory-style chic in a tourist trap guise: It seems to us that this archetypal Paris brasserie, renovated a few seasons ago, has lost its soul. Admittedly, they have kept the stucco, moldings and Garnier frescos, but what can we say this year about the tasteless dry foie gras, probably taken from the refrigerator just before it was brought to the table, the yawningly commonplace and equally bland onion soup, the sole meunière apparently left on the stove three minutes too long (which is a lot!) and the tough rib-eye steak (not properly hung), followed by a dry and hardened millefeuille. In comparison, the well-seasoned steak tartare served with good crunchy fries looks like a masterpiece. The restaurant, which has reinvested large sums of money and hired an extra chef, Laurent Delabre, needs further attention and a painful reappraisal.

● **Café Guitry** 👔 COM

Théâtre Edouard VII, 10, pl Edouard-VII
Métro: Madeleine, Opéra, Auber (RER)
Tel. 01 40 07 00 77. Fax 01 47 42 77 68
www.theatreedouard7.com
Closed Sunday, Monday evening, 3 weeks in August. Open until 11 PM.
Prix fixe: 26€ (lunch), 32€.
A la carte: 45€.
Air cond. Terrace. Private dining room.

We like this theater restaurant and not only because of its Napoleon III surroundings, red walls, collection of black-and-white photos of actors and vintage

advertising. Its cuisine, refined by chef Philippe Le Guen with intelligent advice from Andrée Zanat-Murat, author of cookbooks and wife of the manager, Bernard Murat, wields a ready charm. The shrimp salad with mango, coriander and lime, the tuna steak baked in a pepper crust served with ratatouille, the roasted cod filet with zucchini and a veal tagine with dried apricots and almonds and served with fine semolina are well done dishes. The rhubarb compote served with whipped mascarpone and strawberries slips down smoothly.

A SPECIAL FAVORITE

● **Carte Blanche** Ⓝ 🍴 COM

6, rue Lamartine
Métro: Cadet
Tel. 01 48 78 12 20. Fax 01 48 78 12 21
Closed Saturday lunch, Sunday, Christmas, end of July–mid-August.
Open until 10:30 PM.
Prix fixe: 25€, 28€, 35€, 38€.
Air cond.

Jean-François Renard, chef at Beauvilliers in the days when Edouard Carlier welcomed Paris society to his Montmartre showcase, has joined forces with Claude Dupont, formerly maître d' with Gagnaire in Saint-Etienne and then Paris. In a renovated rustic setting of stone walls and wooden tables, they offer a courteous welcome. The place settings and the appearance of the dishes? Modish, but not excessively so. Unusual tins of tuna, salmon and sardine are as delicious as the presentation is innovative. Toast topped with foie gras and cured calf's foot is a delight. Peppers stuffed with Basque charcuterie, scallop carpaccio with green apples, the pepper, tomato, onion and tuna tart and the wild mallard duck breast, like the unusual sea bass cooked in a Portuguese tagine, are well executed. We love the plats *du jour* for two, such as the slow-roasted shoulder of milk-fed lamb with vegetables served in a "Staub" marmite. All these dishes are part of a set menu that is well balanced given the quality of produce served. The desserts are up to the same standard: praliné, chocolate and sour cherry croustillant or soft caramel ginger cake served with individual madeleines. A very short, well-selected wine list, with a Grange de Quatre Sous 2002 at 30.50€. Pay a visit before the fashionistas find out.

● Casa Olympe ○ SIM

48, rue Saint-Georges
Métro: St-Georges
Tel. 01 42 85 26 01. Fax 01 45 26 49 33
Closed Saturday, Sunday, 1 week
Christmas–New Year's, 1 week in May,
3 weeks in August. Open until 11 PM.
Prix fixe: 38€.
Air cond.

She is one of a kind: grouchy and marvelous, a cook with golden fingers and a brilliant reinventor of the traditional domestic dish. Dominique Versini, a.k.a. Olympe, is still as appealing as in the days when she was playing the Paris society luminary in Montparnasse. The intimate decor with its close-set tables, Provençal fabric, stucco-style walls and Murano chandeliers is an exercise in charm. The dishes are precise in tone, well handled, appetizing and sometimes roguish. We delight in the crisp layered pastry filled with blood sausage and served with mixed greens, the sardines marinated in sea salt served with beet rémoulade, tuna with bacon and onions, langoustine ravioli, lamb shoulder for two and beef tenderloin with peppercorn sauce. The desserts (pots of chocolate with red fruit sauce, parisbrest, coffee crème brûlée) are in the same vein. A clientele of dedicated aficionados (film director Claude Berri, Francis Ford Coppola when he is in Paris and TV presenter Emmanuel Chain, among others) help to make the place feel like a friendly club.

● Le Charlain 🔴 SIM

23, rue Clauzel
Métro: St-Georges
Tel. 01 48 78 74 40. Fax 01 48 78 20 96
charlain@noos.fr
www.lecharlain.fr
Closed Saturday lunch, Sunday,
August 13th–August 20th.
Open until midnight.
A la carte: 40€.
Air cond. Private dining room.

Exit Auberge & Compagnie, enter Charlain. Why Charlain? It is a combination of the first names of new proprietors Charlène and Alain Dollinger, who run the dining room and kitchen, respectively, of this timeless establishment with its soberly refurbished stone and wood decor in the unobtrusive rue Clauzel. The dishes are rigorously classical with soft-boiled quail egg with diced foie gras or cassolette d'escargots with chanterelle mushrooms, cod with spinach and garlic or a whole duck breast with shallot confit and blackberry liqueur and scalloped potatoes, not to mention a classic crème brûlée (100% cream!). Amiably done, with no pretension or genius, but that is really not the point. The prices have remained honest.

● Charlot Roi des Coquillages V.COM

12, pl de Clichy
Métro: Place-de-Clichy
Tel. 01 53 20 48 00. Fax 01 53 20 48 09
de.charlot@blanc.net
www.charlot-paris.com
Open daily until midnight.
Prix fixe: 19,50€ (lunch), 25€ (lunch, wine included). A la carte: 75€.
Air cond. Private dining room. Valet parking.

We would like a new decor, a nonsmoking dining room a little larger than a closet, a more exciting wine list and more attentive service. Yet with oysters, bouillabaisse and Grand Marnier soufflé served opposite the bay window looking out on place Clichy and the giant movie posters of the Wepler theater, we still enjoy eating in this seafood restaurant. This year, we have no complaints about the terrine of red mullet, monkfish carpaccio seasoned with ginger and lime, sea bream in salt crust or the filet of Dover sole meunière reliably prepared by chef Elvis Carcel.

● Chartier

7, rue du Faubourg-Montmartre
Métro: Grands-Boulevards
Tel. 01 47 70 86 29. Fax 01 48 24 14 68
bouillon.chartier@wanadoo.fr
www.bouillon-chartier.com
Open daily until 10 PM.
A la carte: 22€.
Air cond.

For more than a century, this *bouillon*-style restaurant (vintage 1896) has been offering salvation for the thrifty in search of uncomplicated sustenance. Neither the decor—revolving door, faux leather banquettes, mirrors and brass work—nor the ballet of black-and-white clad waiters has changed since our student days. Hearts of palm vinaigrette, beef muzzle salad, oven-baked sea bream, flambéed sea bass served with fennel, pot-au-feu, calf's head and the house pastries are all terribly good natured.

● Le Chêne Vert COM

Galeries Lafayette, 99, rue de Provence
Métro: Havre-Caumartin, Chaussée-d'Antin–La Fayette, Auber (RER)
Tel. 01 40 23 52 31. Fax 01 40 23 52 60
afresnil@galerieslafayette.com
Closed dinner, Sunday.
Prix fixe: 38€.
Air cond. Private dining room.

David van Laer, whom we met at Le Bamboche and then Le Maxence, has become the enlightened chef of this paneled restaurant in the heart of the Galeries Lafayette department store. Now, between stints of shopping, we can savor his delicious dishes and enjoy the very appealing wines selected by Fabien Moglia. Duo of pork confit and foie gras, lobster and green bean salad with a citrus and argan oil vinaigrette, sole stuffed with finely diced sautéed mushrooms served with lemon butter, Iberian cured ham served with Swiss chard in a reduction sauce and fried herb cakes and grilled sea bass with pesto-

grilled baby vegetables are the successive chapters of a well-chosen set menu. For dessert, the strawberries with Penja pepper and olive oil ice cream and the chocolate and coconut dessert show an unfailing professionalism.

● Ch'Ti Catalan SIM

4, rue de Navarin
Métro: N.-D.-de-Lorette, Pigalle, St-Georges
Tel. 01 44 63 04 33
Closed Saturday lunch, Sunday,
Bank Holidays. Open until 11 PM.
Prix fixe: 13,50€ (lunch). A la carte: 30€.
Terrace.

This innocuous local bistro wedged between the Costes brothers' Hôtel Amour and star baker and confectioner Delmontel brings together the traditions of northern France and Catalonia. We have no complaints about the dark surroundings in shades of red and gold or the changing, spirited dishes listed on the blackboard: Marouilles cheese tart, escalivade (Catalan roasted vegetables), morue à la catalane (Atlantic cod cooked in a garlic, pepper, onion and tomato sauce), mixed grilled fish with a garlic and parsley–seasoned sauce, crème brûlée seasoned with cinnamon and the ginger cookie mousse go down easily. A miniature terrace in the summer.

● A la Cloche d'Or COM

3, rue Mansart
Métro: Blanche
Tel. 01 48 74 48 88. Fax 01 40 16 40 99
Closed Saturday lunch, Sunday, August.
Open until 1 AM.
Prix fixe: 17€ (lunch), 25€ (lunch), 29€ (lunch), 27€ (dinner). A la carte: 45€.
Air cond. Private dining room.

This restaurant with its rustic Fifties' charm does not serve as late as before, but still until one in the morning. The service is lively, the welcome friendly, the prices reasonable and the dishes reliably traditional. The foie gras in pastry, baked camembert, salmon cooked skin side down with roasted pinenuts, as well as the prime rib, duck confit, rack of lamb and hand-chopped beef tartare are hard to fault, and both the profiteroles and the authentic tarte Tatin slip down effortlessly.

● Le Clos Bourguignon [SIM]

39, rue de Caumartin
Métro: Havre-Caumartin
Tel. 01 47 42 56 60
Open daily until 10:30 PM.
A la carte: 35€.

Louis Deconquand does it all himself: cooking, welcome, service and advice on wine, as well as chewing the fat. In other words, he sets the tone in this restaurant frequented by Olympia theatergoers before the show, along with artists and journalists such as our friend Jacques Pessis. The restrained cuisine, the homey atmosphere, the zinc counter and the faux leather banquettes immediately work their charm, as do the warm sausage and potatoes, the shrimp salad with avocado, Auvergne-style salt cod, beef tongue and veal sweetbreads and the pear and cherry clafoutis that would not hurt a fly.

● Les Comédiens [SIM]

1, rue de la Trinité
Métro: Trinité
Tel. 01 40 82 95 95. Fax 01 40 82 96 95
Closed Saturday lunch, Sunday.
Open until midnight.
A la carte: 40–55€.

Gilles Bellot is still enthusiastically running this restaurant, perfect for supper after the show. The loft decor with its large counter and exposed stone is terribly pleasant. The dishes served up by this competent pro (who traveled quite a bit before settling in this Nouvelle Athènes abode just behind the Trinité church) are skillfully prepared with selected produce. The gorgonzola ravioli, sea bass and salmon tartare, thick veal chop, thick-cut Salers beef tenderloin and the rotisserie chicken are well chosen, and the melted chocolate cake is a treat for good children.

● Côté 9e [SIM]

5, rue Henri-Monnier
Métro: St-Georges, Pigalle
Tel. 01 45 26 26 30
www.cote9.com
Closed Saturday lunch, Sunday, Saturday evening (July–August). Open until 10:45 PM.
A la carte: 35–40€.

Frédéric Ecollan has taken over this small restaurant with its regular clientele, which serves a market produce-based cuisine in a neat setting refurbished designer-style in brown and red shades. Chef Eric Lexuan, who has been here since the restaurant was called La Table de la Fontaine, regales his customers with good, simple dishes. The salad of fresh beans with pesto, tuna tartare with spinach shoots, cod with parmesan, veal kidneys with herbed mashed potatoes and "*grand-mère moderne*" desserts (chocolate cake with vanilla ice cream, crème brûlée seasoned with bergamot) are well prepared.

● Les Diables au Thym [SIM]

35, rue Bergère
Métro: Grands-Boulevards
Tel.-Fax 01 47 70 77 09
Closed Saturday lunch, Sunday, 1 week at Easter, 1 week at the end of July, 2 weeks in beginning of August. Open until 10:30 PM.
Prix fixe: 20,95€ (lunch), 26,20€.
A la carte: 40€.
Air cond.

Serge Uriot is the last of the Mohicans in this area of fast food joints off the Grands Boulevards. An excellent pro, he continues to serve up a tasteful, domestic, rural cuisine that is quite uninfluenced by fashion. Lobster ravioli with soft-cooked leeks, crawfish tails rémoulade served with finely diced vegetables, pike-perch in cabbage and butter sauce and medallions of rabbit with morel mushroom stuffing all look good. The beggar's purse with chocolate and pistachio sauces and the soft chocolate cake with salted-butter caramel ice cream slip down without any trouble.

● Domaine de Lintillac @ SIM

54, rue Blanche
Métro: Trinité, Blanche
Tel. 01 48 74 84 36
www.domainedelintillac-paris.com
Closed Saturday lunch, Sunday. Open until
10:15 PM (Friday, Saturday 11 PM).
Prix fixe: 8,80€ (lunch).
A la carte: 25–30€.
Air cond.

Young people adore this restaurant with its foie gras at bargain prices. It now belongs to a regional produce business in the Corrèze region that has opened establishments in Paris. The decor of the old Auberge de Ribeauvillé has not been touched. There are toasters on the tables along with foie gras prepared with Sauternes wine at 10.80€ and duck breast with potatoes and shallots sautéed in duck fat at 9.70€. The duck, goose and pork rillettes on warm toast and the duck confit, as well as the crème brûlée and the creamed chestnut with whipped cream and ice cream are unpretentious.

● En Haut de Là ℕ SIM

14, rue de Clichy
Métro: Trinité, Liège
Tel. 01 48 74 51 27
Closed Monday evening, 2 last weeks in
August. Open until 11:30 PM.
A la carte: 50€.

The attractive Emmanuelle Perret, who worked at the Hôtel Costes and Coco et sa Maison, has taken over this café-brasserie just a step away from the Casino de Paris. The setting is convivial and vintage posters set the tone. The cuisine is Costes style, well prepared with fresh produce. The crab and avocado, the tomato and mozzarella millefeuille, sea bass with spinach, beef tenderloin with béarnaise sauce, beef tartare and the vanilla panna cotta are familiar but tuneful melodies. The check is not insubstantial, but the Château des Tours Brouilly goes down easily, and the meal as a whole is very well mannered.

● Le Faux-Filet @ SIM

16, rue Joubert
Métro: Havre-Caumartin, Chaussée-d'Antin-
La Fayette
Tel.-Fax 01 40 16 81 81
faux-filet@voila.fr
Closed dinner, Saturday, Sunday, August.
Open until 2:30 PM.
Prix fixe: 16€ (lunch). A la carte: 25–30€.
Air cond.

Just behind the Galeries Lafayette department store, this neo-Thirties' bistro provides simple fare. The walnut salad, the smoked herring with potatoes and olive oil, salmon steak with béarnaise sauce, sirloin steak with fries and the waffle with vanilla ice cream and hot chocolate sauce make a lot of people happy.

● Fontaine Fiacre ℕ COM

8, rue Hippolyte-Lebas
Métro: N.-D.-de-Lorette, Cadet
Tel. 01 53 20 88 70. Fax 01 53 20 88 73
g.haillot@wanadoo.fr
www.fontainefiacre.com
Closed Saturday lunch, Sunday.
Open until 10:30 PM.
Prix fixe: 12,50€ (lunch), 21€, 27€.
A la carte: 40€.
Terrace. Private dining room.

An open kitchen, modern decor (part loft, part lounge), a young team and pleasant cuisine: That is the deal from this corner restaurant just by rue Milton and not far from rue des Martyrs. Alexandre Nicolas, who has worked with Westermann in Strasbourg, among others, applies his mischievously revised classical style. The onion, mozzarella and tomato tart, the marinated salmon served with celeri rémoulade, pan-seared tuna with tomato confit, parmentier de canard (a layered duck and mashed potato dish), beef cheeks simmered in red wine, a chocolate cream cake and the plums poached in red wine and spices, served over a cinnamon streudel, are well made and well chosen.

● Georgette   SIM

29, rue Saint-Georges
Métro: N.-D.-de-Lorette
Tel. 01 42 80 39 13
Closed Saturday, Sunday, 1 week in May,
1 week for Ascension, August.
Open until 11 PM.
A la carte: 40€.
Private dining room.

Georgette is Marie-Odile Chauvelot, proud
mother of her amiable Nouvelle Athènes
bistro. We love the amusing setting with its
beams and Formica tables and casual
atmosphere. We also enjoy the fare, which
is delicious and simple (although not *that*
simple). Depending on what the market
has to offer, Florys Barbier (who trained at
the neighboring Olympe) produces all
kinds of delicacies: a poached egg served
with mushrooms, grilled fennel and olive
oil, dill-marinated salmon and oven-
crisped veal served with sautéed potatoes.
The desserts (shortbread cookie with
cream and salted-butter caramel ice
cream or spiced roasted figs with chestnut
honey ice cream) conjure up childhood
memories.

● Grand Café Capucines   COM

4, bd des Capucines
Métro: Opéra
Tel. 01 43 12 19 00. Fax 01 43 12 19 09
www.legrandcafe.com
Open daily 24 hours.
Prix fixe: 24,50€ (lunch). A la carte: 55€.
Air cond. Terrace. Private dining room.

This Maxim's for limited budgets is one of
the nuggets of the Blanc empire. It does
not offer culinary genius but a professional
welcome and alert nonstop service at fairly
well-behaved prices. Shellfish bisque with
a golden crust, grilled langoustines seasoned with mild spices, grilled sea bass
flambéed with anise liquor and a pan-
seared veal kidney with foie gras sauce are
the house specialties. The crêpes flambéed
with Grand Marnier are worth the visit.

● A la Grange Batelière   SIM

16, rue de la Grange-Batelière
Métro: Richelieu-Drouot
Tel.-Fax 01 47 70 85 15
lagrangebateliere@wanadoo.fr
Closed dinner (except for the first and the
third Wednesday of each month), Saturday,
Sunday, 1 week Christmas–New Year's,
beginning of August–end of August.
Prix fixe: 30€ (lunch), 25€ (lunch).
A la carte: 70€.

Actress Mimie Mathy and her cook husband Benoist Gérard have taken over this
post Second Empire bistro successfully. It
has kept its counter and pigeonholes but
acquired wooden tables and a little space.
Dishes of the day are chalked up on the
blackboard and showbiz friends come and
enjoy the seafood millefeuille, the crayfish
and asparagus in puff pastry, pan-seared
scallops served with a mild brandade, as
well as the Mediterranean grilled red mullet tartine. We should also mention the
thick sautéed veal chop and the authentic
Salers chateaubriand served with roasted
new potatoes with shallots, mushrooms
and olive oil and offer a reminder that the
house opens mainly for lunch (but now
also for dinner two Wednesdays a month).
The desserts (vanilla, coffee and chocolate
creams in little pots) and a croquant of
sour red fruits are charming; the prices,
sadly, much less so.

● Hôtel Amour   SIM

8, rue Navarin
Métro: St-Georges, N.-D.-de-Lorette
Tel. 01 48 78 31 80. Fax 01 48 78 14 09
Open daily until 11:30 PM.
A la carte: 35€.

Fun, congenial and brought to us by the
Costes brothers—who have shrewdly
struck again, this time in the heart of Nouvelle Athènes—this amusing, offbeat,
modern allusion to Pigalle hotels of the
past is a success. Guests enjoy the bright
rooms, amusing surroundings and contemporary art on the corridor walls. However the restaurant is also well planned. Its
Fifties' decor, young wait staff and revised
classic dishes (roast chicken in a creamy

205

aspic with Piccadilly sauce, garnished ham served with a lettuce salad, macaroni gratin, grilled Atlantic cod with a salad of green peas, steak frites do the job gracefully. The fruit tarts come from neighboring Delmontel. The young and hip are legion. If this is not a major event, it certainly looks like one.

● Le Jardin des Muses   SIM

1, rue Scribe
Métro: Opéra
Tel. 01 44 71 24 19. Fax 01 44 71 24 64
Open daily until 10 PM.
Prix fixe: 26€ (lunch), 32€ (dinner).
Air cond. Private dining room. Valet parking.

Franck Charpentier, who runs Les Muses restaurant just above, has turned this eatery into a lively gourmet spot. Vanilla and bourbon marinated salmon served with asparagus purée, red tuna served with lemony black radishes and a shrimp-broth risotto served with grilled squid seasoned with lime. Add to that spare ribs roasted with spices served with rosemary-mashed potatoes and a delicious frozen Gariguette strawberry meringue and ice cream dessert and you realize this is a good place to have a pleasant meal at a reasonable price.

A SPECIAL FAVORITE

● Le Jardinier   🏠🍴 COM

5, rue Richer
Métro: Grands-Boulevards
Tel.-Fax 01 48 24 79 79
le.jardinier@wanadoo.fr
www.lejardinier.lesrestos.com
Closed Saturday lunch, Sunday, Monday evening, 1 week in July, 2 weeks in August.
Open until 10 PM.
Prix fixe: 30€. A la carte: 40€.

This is a good local restaurant in an unexpected location. An anonymous-looking hotel, a dining room boasting circa 1880 stucco and a rather dated look, but a good chef, Christophe Bouillault, a veteran of the Plaza and Bristol, and an alert proprietor, Patrice Dupenher, who brings a little

life to the place. In any case, the crab soup with chanterelle mushroom turnovers, squid-ink risotto, pig ears cooked with shallots and apple tart are splendid. A spot to watch.

● Jean   COM

8, rue Saint-Lazare
Métro: N.-D.-de-Lorette
Tel. 01 48 78 62 73. Fax 01 48 78 66 04
chezjean@wanadoo.fr
Closed Saturday, Sunday, 1 week at Easter, 1 week in July, 3 weeks in August.
Open until 10:30 PM.
Prix fixe: 36€, 56€ (dinner), 69€ (dinner), 78€ (dinner). A la carte: 65–80€.
Air cond. Private dining room.

Have we gone crazy? Here is a restaurant that secures a star from Michelin just as we remove the Plate we gave it long ago. You see, while we are as fond as ever of the modernized brasserie setting and Taillevent veteran Jean-Frédéric Guidoni's polished service, we find Benoît Bordier's cuisine overblown and impossibly complicated—on the verge of hitting the ceiling and succumbing to a nervous breakdown, to put it bluntly. Is the wind of fashion in any way responsible? At any rate, we find it very hard to enjoy the jumble of genres and unrelieved use of sweet and savory in dishes such as the frog's legs and spicy sausages served with guacamole with mint and pine seasoning or soft-cooked sardines served with a pickle aspic and a banana parsley "milkshake." Not to mention the cod and thiny sliced roasted veal, served with beets, peppers and chocolate wasabi sauce! The customers here have been turned into guinea pigs. The same goes for the langoustines, split peas and mussels with cinnamon and different condiments and the roasted lamb with kiwi, litchi and rosemary. To console ourselves, there remains the eight-hour roasted pork belly with carrots, apricots and roasted lemons seasoned with sage and a chocolate pineapple tart seasoned with cardamom, which has the look of a "real" dessert.

● J'Go   SIM

4, rue Drouot
Métro: Richelieu-Drouot
Tel. 01 40 22 09 09. Fax 01 40 22 07 15
Parisdrouot@lejgo.com
www.lejgo.com
Closed Sunday, Christmas.
Open until midnight.
Prix fixe: 16€ (lunch), 21€ (lunch),
11€ (children); A la carte: 40€.
Air cond.

Everything we love: excellent produce, a pleasant atmosphere, amiable people with the accent of the South of France and prices that are not too pretentious. As in Toulouse, opposite the Victor Hugo market, here is a gourmet embassy of Southwest France, next to the *mairie* of the ninth arrondissement. On either paneled floor (downstairs, there is also a bar), you can savor the Gascon black pig pâté, the slow-cooked foie gras terrine, whole lamb shoulder roasted on the bone and a classic French rice pudding, washed down with a spirited Côtes du Frontonnais.

● Les Muses   ⌂ ○ LUX

Hotel Scribe, 1, rue Scribe
Métro: Opéra, Madeleine
Tel. 01 44 71 24 26. Fax 01 44 71 24 64
h0663-re@accord.com
www.accorhotels.com
Closed Saturday, Sunday, Bank Holidays,
1 week Christmas–New Year's, August.
Open until 10 PM.
Prix fixe: 45€ (lunch), 75€, 95€.
A la carte: 70–85€.
Air cond. Private dining room. Valet parking.

Admittedly, the decor of this chic hotel restaurant—windowless and confined to the basement—is not the most charming imaginable. However, the tables are widely spaced and very well set, the service is impeccable and the sommelier a master of his art. Then the food prepared by Franck Charpentier from W, who enthusiastically took over the kitchen here when Jean-François Rouquette left for the Park-Hyatt, is subtle, precise and polished. His dishes are attractive, good, technically accomplished and shrewd, and exert an effortless

charm. We like the Tudy Island oysters with greens and lemon seawater foam, his parmentier fumé (smoked country-style bacon with mashed potatoes and truffles—in fact a smoked bacon and potato soup with black truffles and a fried egg—a great moment!), as well as pan-seared scallops with crisp beef and foie gras–filled pastry served with celery root ravioli. The meats (Vendée pigeon served with a small covered dish of simmered vegetables or pork belly with Colonnata lard, served with truffle and foie gras ravioli) are frankly inspiring. The desserts (spiced pumpkin waffle and a coffee cream infusion) are equally refined. This is obviously an excellent establishment to revisit.

● No Stress Café   ⊜ SIM

2, pl Gustave-Toudouze
Métro: St-Georges
Tel.-Fax 01 48 78 00 27
Closed Monday (except in summer),
Christmas, New Year's, 3 weeks in January.
Open until 11:30 PM.
Prix fixe: 15€ (lunch). A la carte: 25–30€.
Terrace.

This casual rendezvous with its large terrace on a Peynet-style square urges you to take your time. Swordfish steak with aïoli, scallops sautéed in a wok, glazed duck with sesame and rhubarb crumble follow a totally relaxed, exotic approach.

● L'Œnothèque   SIM

20, rue Saint-Lazare
Métro: N.-D.-de-Lorette
Tel. 01 48 78 08 76. Fax 01 40 16 10 27
loenotheque@hotmail.fr
Closed Saturday, Sunday, Bank Holidays,
3 weeks in August. Open until 10:30 PM.
Prix fixe: 24€. A la carte: 50€.
Air cond.

Daniel Hallée, who remembers his days as a sommelier at Jamin, has founded a club for connoisseurs in his restaurant-library-gallery in shades of red, where the pictures change monthly. Here he champions quality produce and presents vintages he especially appreciates. Crayfish tail salad, foie gras, tuna steak seasoned with olive oil, black mullet with ginger sauce, rotisserie-roasted spicy veal kidneys, baba au rhum, and crème brûlée are accompanied by his latest wine discoveries. Yveline Hallée welcomes guests and provides friendly advice, and the cigar box is always worth inspecting.

● Pakito ⊜ SIM

11, rue Rougemont
Métro: Grands-Boulevards, Bonne-Nouvelle
Tel. 01 47 70 78 93
contact@pakito.fr
www.pakito.fr
Closed Sunday, 1 week Christmas–New Year's, 3 weeks in August.
Open until 10:30 PM.
Prix fixe: 14€ (lunch, wine included), 14€ (dinner). A la carte: 20–30€.
Air cond. Terrace.

This Basque bar offers refreshment after the (rugby) game and half-time drinks at any time. In a noisy, good-humored ambience, guests come to enjoy assorted tapas while drinking sparkling Txakoli, Eki beer or Irouléguy. Squid in its own ink, gazpacho, chicken simmered with onions, peppers, garlic and Basque spices as well as axoa de veau (a Basque dish of simmered peppers and veal) and a Basque cake will sate your appetite pleasantly.

● Le Petit Canard ⊜ SIM

19, rue Henry-Monnier
Métro: St-Georges
Tel. 01 49 70 07 95
Closed lunch, Saturday, Sunday.
Open until 11 PM.
A la carte: 25–30€.

Duck to distraction: foie, gizzards, breast and confit . . . . In fact, duck in its every delicious dimension. This is the fare provided by a graphic artist who came here because he wanted to meet people and introduce them to fine products from his brother-in-law's farm. You can indulge yourself here without breaking the bank. The cakes baked by a confectioner friend supply a suitably effective sugar rush.

● Au Petit Riche 🏠 COM

25, rue Le Peletier
Métro: Richelieu-Drouot, Le Peletier
Tel. 01 47 70 68 68. Fax 01 48 24 10 79
aupetitriche@wanadoo.fr
www.aupetitriche.com
Closed Sunday. Open until midnight.
Prix fixe: 22,50€ (lunch), 25,50€, 29,50€, 11€ (children). A la carte: 55€.
Air cond. Private dining room.

Stucco ceilings, engraved glass, faux leather banquettes and lacquered walls: This circa 1880 institution still offers all the charm of Old Paris. The cuisine is in the same vein, playing on tradition and matching timeless dishes to Loire Valley wines. The pork belly confit served with lentils, the eggs baked in ramekins with foie gras, the pike-perch with beurre blanc, English-style poached haddock, a traditional roasted veal chop and calf's head served with a thick vinaigrette with shallots and herbs are all enjoyable. The vanilla millefeuille is exquisite and the paris-brest delicious.

● Le Pétrelle ◯ COM

34, rue Pétrelle
Métro: Anvers, Poissonnière
Tel. 01 42 82 11 02. Fax 01 40 23 05 69
Closed lunch, Sunday, Monday,
Christmas–New Year's, mid-July–mid-August.
Open until 10 PM.
Prix fixe: 27€ (dinner). A la carte: 60€.

This restaurant only opens in the evening, serves a cuisine dear to its heart and has dreamt up a decor all its own: a romantic library style with fine bouquets, shelves of books and choice linen. Jean-Luc André, an almost wholly self-taught native of the Ardèche who has opened Les Vivres, a bistro and grocery store open from noon to 7 p.m., just next door, is a charming loner. The menu is intelligent, the dishes are market produce-based, lively, fresh and light, and the cuisine is cheerfully kitchen garden, all added attractions. Dishes include the white asparagus and morel mushroom fricassée, marinated baby artichokes served with chevril root chips, scallops and truffles in season, line-caught sea bass roasted with sea salt and crispy herbs and leg of lamb with fava beans, seasoned with thyme and lemon. The desserts (slowly cooked rhubarb with wild strawberries and dark chocolate cake) are delightful.

● **Le Pré Cadet** 🖼 SIM

10, rue Saulnier
Métro: Cadet
Tel. 01 48 24 99 64. Fax 01 47 70 55 96
flomicadet@wanadoo.fr
Closed Saturday lunch, Sunday, New Year's,
May 1st, May 8th, 3 weeks in August.
Open until 10:30 PM.
Prix fixe: 30€. A la carte: 40€.
Air cond.

Discreet, rustic and welcoming, with its plaster walls and friendly atmosphere, Michel Le Boulch's "little club" is one of the secret haunts of the ninth arrondissement (Mayor Jacques Bravo is a regular and the "brothers" of the rue Cadet pay neighborly gastronomic calls). We enjoy the lively cuisine, prepared with what the market has to offer by the modest José Marquès. It never disappoints. The menu is splendid and the dishes change. Crisp pastry with a basil bouquet, escargots prepared with parsley and garlic butter, cod filet roasted with olive oil and served with olive oil–seasoned mashed potatoes, sole meunière, poached calf's head terrine, boneless rib-eye steak, the chocolate cake and the floating island are all first rate.

● **Le Relais Beaujolais** SIM

3, rue Milton
Métro: N.-D.-de-Lorette
Tel. 01 48 78 77 91
Closed Saturday, Sunday, Bank Holidays,
last week of July–the end of August.
Open until 10:15 PM.
Prix fixe: 29€. A la carte: 45€.

A true bistro, Alain Mazeau's place is perfect for a get together between friends. Guests enjoy themselves simply and to the full here, over selected Beaujolais and fine meats. A former butcher, Alain chooses his steaks skillfully, as he does his Morgon and Brouilly vintages. Patrons savor poached

eggs en meurette (with a red wine and bacon sauce), parsleyed ham terrine, crayfish gratin, veal kidneys with a mustard sauce and, certainly, a 10-ounce boneless rib-eye Salers steak with sea salt. The cream puffs and Grand Marnier soufflé crêpes end the party on a sweeter note.

● **Le Roi du Pot-au-Feu** ● 🏠 SIM

34, rue Vignon
Métro: Madeleine, Havre-Caumartin
Tel. 01 47 42 37 10
Closed Sunday, Bank Holidays.
Open noon–10:30 PM.
A la carte: 30€.
Terrace.

Nothing changes in this authentic bistro with its talkative proprietors, retro decor with neon lighting, brass, mirrors, counter and companionable welcome, serving a pot-au-feu with a bowl of bouillon and tender meat. The house terrine, the hachis parmentier (a ground meat and potato dish similar to shepherd's pie) and the chocolate mousse are equally commendable.

● **16 Haussmann** 🏠🖼 COM

Hotel L'Ambassador, 16, bd Haussmann
Métro: Richelieu-Drouot, Chaussée-d'Antin–
La Fayette
Tel. 01 48 00 06 38. Fax 01 44 83 40 57
16 haussmann@concorde-hotels.com
www.hotelambassador-paris.com
Closed Saturday lunch, Sunday,
3 weeks in August. Open until 10:30 PM.
Prix fixe: 28€, 32€.
Air cond. Terrace. Private dining room.
Valet parking.

All right then, we shall award Michel Hache his "Pot" for good value for money. This fine chef who used to work with Senderens has never disappointed us with his set menu, considerably kept down to 32€. The place is worth seeing with its modern decor, cheerful coloring in shades of blue, fine woodwork and Starckian chairs. The good Michel copes professionally with groups, while his cuisine, consistent, subtle and fresh, wins converts to its cause with its crab and crayfish with celeri rémoulade, a mushroom salad with purslane, the roasted sea bass with asparagus pan fried in butter with parsley and the sole cooked in salted butter with finely diced sautéed mushrooms, shallots and cream. The quick-seared leg of lamb rubbed with Provençal herbs and served with baked vegetables makes you want to drop everything and tour the Côte d'Azur, while the fraîcheur (a dessert of fresh strawberry, litchis and chocolate) fully deserves its name.

● La Table d'Anvers   🏠🚇COM

2, pl d'Anvers
Métro: Anvers
Tel. 01 48 78 35 21. Fax 01 45 26 66 67
phiphi.colin@wanadoo.fr
www.latabledanvers.fr
Closed Saturday lunch, Sunday, 1 week Christmas–New Year's, 2 weeks in beginning of August. Open until 11 PM.
Prix fixe: 15€ (lunch, wine included), 23€ (lunch), 29€, 35€ (dinner, wine included).
Air cond. Terrace. Private dining room.

Philippe Collin has the gift of ubiquity. This Girardet veteran who ran the refined Clos Juillet in Troyes manages to be present in both his Why Not in the seventeenth arrondissement and this, the former abode of the Conticinis, now more sedate in a modern bistro style. King of organ meats Philippe and his young team work their charm with roguish dishes offering both taste and accent. There is a veal and tuna tartare, pig's foot carpaccio served with a thick vinaigrette with shallots and herbs, the house rabbit terrine, a formidable calf's head with tongue served with mayonnaise, capers, herbs and hard-boiled egg, the classic andouillette de Troyes with champagne sauce, served with the house purée "Léa" (named after the chef's daughter). Those who are not fond of offal can console themselves with grilled sea bass with an olive vinaigrette or cod served with lobster sauce and basmati rice. The wines by the glass (Chablis or Languedoc) are well chosen. The young maîtresse d' is charming and the desserts (soft chocolate cake with carambar candy ice cream or Sarlat sour cherries and vanilla ice cream) take us back to our childhood.

● La Taverne Kronenbourg   COM

24, bd des Italiens
Métro: Richelieu-Drouot
Tel. 01 55 33 10 00. Fax 01 55 33 10 09
reservationtaverne@blanc.net
www.taverne.com
Open daily 11:30 AM–midnight. Cont. service.
Prix fixe: 18,50€ (lunch, wine included), 24€, 28€. A la carte: 35–50€.
Air cond. Terrace. Private dining room.

Not very refined, but highly enjoyable, this brasserie on the boulevard offers an unfussy welcome. The attractions are the traditional dishes: salmon tartare, quiche lorraine, poached smoked haddock, sole meunière, lamb shank, a nice choucroute and sorbet with marc. The check is easy on the pocket.

● Velly   🚇SIM

52, rue Lamartine
Métro: N.-D.-de-Lorette
Tel.-Fax 01 48 78 60 05
Closed Saturday, Sunday, Bank Holidays, 3 weeks in August. Open until 10:30 PM.
Prix fixe: 23€ (lunch), 31€.
Private dining room.

This small restaurant run by Alain Brigant, formerly at Le Bristol and Fauchon, is in good shape, even when the master of the house is absent. When we ate there, an assistant—a young Asian woman—prepared dishes from both menu and blackboard with great dexterity. The setting, with its low ceiling, art deco lighting and second floor with a few tables, has character. So does the cuisine, as witnessed by the baked goat cheese, avocado and grapefruit "crumble", pan-fried razor clams with spicy sausage, pan-fried curried monkfish served with a broccoli coulis, pollack filet with cabbage, the suckling pig served with fork-mashed potatoes and finally a veal hanger steak with peppercorn sauce that we savor with pleasure. The desserts (baba au rhum and a chocolate palet) are excellent. The service provided by Thierry Lerosey is dynamic.

● **Le Vin Vignon** SIM

20, rue Vignon
Métro: Madeleine, Havre-Caumartin
Tel. 01 40 06 02 64
alphadel@wanadoo.fr
Closed Saturday evening, Sunday,
Monday lunch, Christmas, New Year's.
Open until 10:30 PM.
Prix fixe: 23€, 27€ (dinner).
A la carte: 25–35€.
Air cond. Terrace.

Isabelle Delmotte has changed her chef (the new one is called Stéphane Belloir) without anyone noticing in this modern yellow and orange bistro, warmed by a little woodwork. The house foie gras, Basque bull with a ratatouille risotto, grilled leg of lamb with rosemary and saddle of rabbit with thyme are washed down with selected wines. An appealing red berry gratin with sabayon and an exquisite apple fondant with caramel.

● **Le Zinc des Cavistes** ●SIM

5, rue du Faubourg-Montmartre
Métro: Grands-Boulevards
Tel. 01 47 70 88 64. Fax 01 44 79 01 83
lezincdescavistes@wanadoo.fr
Closed Sunday, Christmas, 2 weeks in
beginning of August. Open until midnight.
Prix fixe: 15€ (lunch).
Air cond. Terrace.

Four great Parisian cellars—Les Grandes Caves (seventeenth), Caves du Panthéon (fifth), Coteaux du 9e (ninth) and Cave Saint-Clair (Boulogne-Billancourt)—have joined forces here to found a modern, simple, agreeable "wine restaurant". Three hundred different wines accompany shrewd dishes. At an ordinary or pedestal table, in a very chummy ambience, patrons savor an avocado served with creamy crab, tomato and goat cheese terrine topped with basil, sea bass with fennel served with a curry and star anise and lamb shank tagine. The trio of crèmes brûlée is not bad.

INTERNATIONAL RESTAURANTS

● **La Boule Rouge** ●SIM

1, rue de la Boule-Rouge
Métro: Grands-Boulevards, Cadet
Tel. 01 47 70 43 90 / 01 48 00 07 69.
Fax 01 42 46 99 57
Closed Sunday, August.
Open until 11:30 PM.
Prix fixe: 25€, 35€. A la carte: 40–45€.
Air cond. Private dining room.

Like singer Enrico Macias, who is more or less at home here, we are happy to spend time with Raymond Haddad. His affable establishment is warm and flavorsome. The setting is pleasant with its desert-themed fresco and the cuisine refuses to be outdone. The fish served whole—gilt head sea bream, cod just like you'd find in Goulette (the main port in Tunis), a beautiful Dover sole of 600 g, fried red mullet, or gray mullet served grilled or with "the works"—are impeccable. Then there are the Moroccan tapas, minina (chicken and egg soufflé), crisp phyllo pastry stuffed with tuna, merguez (spicy lamb or beef sausage), couscous made with beans, l'akoud (tripe in a cumin tomato sauce) and the couscous bkaïla (with spinach and beans) at lunchtime on Saturday (go for the ambience!), all delightful in this inexpensive kosher restaurant. The service is affable, the Listel rosé slides down effortlessly and, for dessert, watermelon, melon, Algerian pastries made with semolina dough or the pastries made with honey are delicious. Sheer enjoyment!

● **Fuji-Yaki** ●●SIM

20, rue Henri-Monnier
Métro: Pigalle, St-Georges
Tel.-Fax 01 42 81 54 25
Closed Sunday lunch, mid-August–beginning
of September. Open until 11 PM.
Prix fixe: 7,50€, 9€, 12€, 20€.
Air cond.

The management has changed at this reasonably priced Japanese restaurant, but we hardly notice. The sober snack bar setting is rather dull, but the delightfully warm welcome, polished dishes, gentle prices and purity are gratifying. Without fuss, we savor the miso soup, fried dumplings, langoustine tempura, seafood salad flavored with vinegar, spicy tuna maki, salmon and yellow tail tuna sashimi, meat brochettes yakitori and black or white sesame ice cream, which are just splendid. All this is also available to take away.

● La Petite Sirène de Copenhague   🍴 SIM

47, rue Notre-Dame-de-Lorette
Métro: St-Georges, N.-D.-de-Lorette
Tel. 01 45 26 66 66
Closed Saturday lunch, Sunday, Monday, Christmas, New Year's, 3 weeks in August.
Open until 11 PM.
Prix fixe: 28€ (lunch), 32€.
A la carte: 55€.

This sober, pleasant, chic, delicious Danish embassy is run by Peter Thulstrup. This expert technician (who trained at Le Crillon, the Kong Hans in Copenhagen and La Tour d'Argent) is a jack of all trades. He moves from kitchen to dining room, promoting the splendid lunchtime option with gusto, along with his aquavits and Cérès beer. He also provides knowledgeable explanations as he presents Danish-style herring, imperial smoked salmon, braised cod filet with red cabbage and a wonderful duck with caramelized potatoes for our approval. The remarkable desserts (nougat glacé, warm cherries with cardamom cream, rhubarb crumble) and relaxed atmosphere are an incitement to eat here on a regular basis.

● Romain   🅿 ◎ COM

40, rue Saint-Georges
Métro: St-Georges, N.-D.-de-Lorette
Tel. 01 48 24 58 94. Fax 01 42 47 09 75
Closed Sunday, Monday, 3 weeks in August.
Open until 10:30 PM.
Prix fixe: 24€ (lunch), 26€ (lunch), 32€.
A la carte: 60€.
Air cond.

Former chic classicists of the tenth, the Châteaubriant's Burcklis have brought their Lorjou and Carzou paintings and innate warmth from rue de Chabrol to this modern den in the Nouvelle Athènes quarter. Guy has lost none of his skill in the kitchen, as we discover when we taste his exceptional Milanese-style risotto made with saffron. Annick still brightens the dining room with her smile and natural charm. She is assisted there by her son Romain, who is in charge of the wines and has modernized the choice of house vintages from both sides of the Alps. The move has been successful: We have never eaten so well at their table. Eggplant lasagna and roasted sardines topped with mozzarella cheese, thin pizza made with a puff pastry crust, a duo of fried shrimp and calamari with tartar sauce, green and white angel hair pasta with a country tomato sauce with foie gras and the ham and squid ink risotto charm us with their generosity. We might criticize Guy for using more butter than olive oil in his dishes, but this native of Ticino has more in common with the Piedmontese or the Valdostans than with the Lombards. The tiramisu, like the raspberry panna cotta with raspberry coulis, are wonderful concoctions and the 32€ menu is a fabulous bargain. One plate this year.

A SPECIAL FAVORITE

● Sizin   🅿 🍴 ◎ SIM

47, rue Saint-Georges
Métro: St-Georges
Tel. 01 44 63 02 28
ekilic@free.fr
www.sizin-restaurant.com
Closed Sunday, last 3 weeks in August.
Open until 11 PM.
Prix fixe: 13,90€ (lunch). A la carte: 30€.
Air cond. Terrace.

Which is the best Turkish restaurant in Paris? This little corner establishment, presided over with sincere warmth by the young Erdal Kilic. The decor has been gently restyled in shades of white, with souvenirs of Anatolia and photos of Istanbul on the walls. The unfailingly charming cuisine consists of light, spicy, eloquent, faultless dishes. The extra fresh mezze, or Turkish tapas (vegetable fritters, pan fried shrimp with paprika, flaky pastry stuffed with cheese, light tara-masalata, hummus, stuffed eggplant), ex-quisite wood-grilled meats (marinated lamb and beef skewers) and ali nazik adana (chopped meat brochette with yo-gurt and eggplant) are all remarkable. Desserts (baklava and others) follow, the Yakut Kavaklidere slips down easily and the prices are amiable to a fault.

● Wally le Saharien ◎ COM
36, rue Rodier
Métro: Anvers, N.-D.-de-Lorette
Tel. 01 42 85 51 90. Fax 01 45 86 08 35
Closed Sunday, Monday.
Open until 10:30 PM.
Prix fixe: 40,40€ (dinner).
Air cond. Private dining room.

One of a kind, Wally, the former Foucauld company camel driver turned sedentary Parisian restaurateur, is a something of a storyteller and quite a cook. He has been pulling the wool over our eyes for three decades with a symphony of a menu. The flaky phyllo pastry stuffed with roasted pi-geon, stuffed sardines, harira (traditional bean soup with herbs), a flavorful roasted leg of lamb, and his famous couscous (its grains fine and light as snow) with peas are a quality experience. We also savor the tchatchouka (a north African ratatouille), chicken and prune tagine and the farm-raised chicken with slowly cooked cara-melized onions, all of equal excellence, just to experience new pleasures. The pastries with a glass of mint tea, the north African cake with seasonal fruit coulis and the Al-gerian wines, including Dahra red, are all part of the festivities.

▼ **SHOPS**

BREAD & BAKED GOODS

▼ Boulangerie Dupuy
13, rue Cadet
Métro: Cadet
Tel. 01 48 24 54 26. Fax 01 48 24 59 37
7 AM–8 PM. Closed Sunday afternoon, Tuesday, August.

Jérémy Dupuy, who has replaced his father Daniel here, supplies organic baguettes, sourdough, and also the famous almond and orange tuiles and classic pastries equally conscientiously.

▼ Jean-Paul Lamé
64, rue Notre-Dame-de-Lorette
Métro: St-Georges, Pigalle
Tel. 01 48 74 46 52
7 AM–8 PM (Sunday 7 AM–6 PM; Sunday in July and August 7 AM–2 PM).
Closed Monday.

Jean-Paul Lamé enchants us with his flûte Gana, his round country loaf, his whole-grain bread and exquisite house foccacia. We love the breakfast pastries and crois-sants and delicious brioches, almond turnovers, pound cake and fried treats with a jam center.

▼ Le Levain du Marais ⓝ
10, rue des Martyrs
Métro: N.-D.-de-Lorette
Tel. 01 48 78 20 17
6:45 AM–8 PM (Sunday 7:30PM).
Closed Tuesday.

Thierry Rabineau, also present in the eleventh (boulevard Beaumarchais and avenue Parmentier) and the third (rue de Turenne), has managed to find himself a niche in a street where bakers are legion . . . and king. His crispy baguette is to die for, his whole-grain bread, focaccia, big sour-dough country loaf and quality breakfast pastries are among the finest in Paris. An attractive corner store.

▼ Le Pain au Naturel
7, rue Bourdaloue
Métro: N.-D.-de-Lorette
Tel. 01 48 74 04 55
7 AM–8:30 PM. Closed Sunday.

Michel Moisan and his excellent tradi-tional breads have spread to this gourmet district, taking over the historic Bourdaloue establishment. The rustic bread, baguette and brioches are to be par-ticularly recommended.

PASTRIES

▼ Arnaud Delmontel
39, rue des Martyrs
Métro: N.-D.-de-Lorette
Tel.-Fax 01 48 78 29 33
www.arnaud-delmontel.com
7 AM–8:30 PM. Closed Tuesday,
2 weeks in beginning of August.

There is an almost permanent line of customers on the sidewalk outside this 19th-century building decorated with an attractive red sign. Arnaud Delmontel offers exquisite creations: the Renaissance baguette with hand-harvested Guérande salt, focaccia, round country loaf, cinnamon kugelhofp, fried treats with a jam center, meringue-layered almond cakes with dried passion fruits and nuts or lemon puff pastry. His rich almond croissant is a phenomenon.

WINE & SPIRITS

▼ La Cave des Martyrs   ⓝ
39, rue des Martyrs
Métro: N.-D.-de-Lorette
Tel. 01 40 16 80 27
10 AM–8 PM (Sunday 7 PM). Open daily.

This cellar offers the best of France's regions at competitive prices, with seasonal offers, eaux de vie, traditional aperitifs and quality champagnes.

▼ Champagne et Collections
6, rue Blanche
Métro: Trinité
Tel.-Fax 01 48 74 41 85
louis.hellin@wanadoo.fr
10 AM–7 PM. Closed Sunday, Monday.

The finest vintages of the sparkling wine par excellence are the stock in trade of this fine store, where unfamiliar names rub shoulders with the great classics. From Billecart-Salmon to Roederer, Bollinger to Gosset and Krug to Trouillard, Louis Hellin selects champagnes for every taste and pocket. He also has 300 different spirits and wines from every region.

Shops

▼ Le Dit Vin
68, rue Blanche
Métro: Blanche, Trinité
Tel. 01 45 26 27 37. Fax 01 45 26 28 38
10 AM–10 PM (noon–3 PM lunch by reservation). Closed Saturday, Sunday. Terrace.

This corner cellar, also a wine bar, has refurbished its storefront in youthful colors: denim blue and violet. On the street terrace, you can taste vintages from the Loire, Languedoc and other regions, then take them home. Small tasting plates served in the evening with the latest, must-try wines.

▼ Les Granges de Pigalle
32, rue Pigalle
Métro: Pigalle, Trinité
Tel.-Fax 01 49 70 69 46
lesgrangespigalle@wanadoo.fr
Monday 4 -8:30 PM.
Tuesday, Friday 10 AM–1 PM, 4 -8:30 PM.
Wednesday, Thursday 3:30–8:30 PM.
Saturday 11 AM–8:30 PM.
Closed Sunday, Monday morning, Wednesday morning, Thursday morning, August.

Jean-Luc Sengelé selects champagnes and vintages from Alsace, Languedoc, the Marmandais and the Rhône Valley. His regional products tend toward the South and Southwest of France: foie gras from the Landes region, sausages from Ardèche, duck confit and cassoulet. Tasting on Saturday.

CHARCUTERIE

▼ Charcuterie Lyonnaise
58, rue des Martyrs
Métro: Pigalle
Tel.-Fax 01 48 78 96 45
9 AM–1:30 PM, 4:30–7:30 PM.
Closed Sunday afternoon, Monday, August.

Jean-Jacques Chrétienne presents a sabodet as good as many in Lyon, along with truffled white sausages, pâté en croûte, pike fish quenelles, regional Lyonnaise dried sausage, parsleyed ham terrine, and pork shank terrine.

CANDY & SWEETS

▼ La Bonbonnière de La Trinité

4, pl d'Estienne-d'Orves
Métro: Trinité
Tel.-Fax 01 48 74 23 38
9:30 AM–7 PM. Closed Sunday, Monday
(July–August).

This store with its retro charm supplies great classics of confectionery: bergamote, spéculos, calissons, négus, violettes as well as homemade chocolates, bitter chocolate truffles, praliné and hazelnut bites, chocolate-covered orange or ginger, madrilènes and various artisanmade jams.

▼ A l'Etoile d'Or 🏠

30, rue Fontaine
Métro: Blanche, Pigalle
Tel. 01 48 74 59 55. Fax 01 45 96 01 71
11 AM–7:30 PM (Monday 3–7:30 PM).
Closed Sunday (except holidays), Monday morning, August.

This circa 1900 store has plenty of appeal. Boxes of every color delight the eye, and the confectionery thrills the palate. With great gusto, her hair in bunches, Denise Acabo boasts 33 kinds of chocolates, salted-butter caramels from Leroux in the Quiberon, mandarin, négus and papillotes, traditional wrapped Christmas chocolates from Lyon.

▼ Fouquet 🏠

36, rue Laffitte
Métro: Le Peletier, Richelieu-Drouot
Tel. 01 47 70 85 00. Fax 01 47 70 35 52
www.fouquet.fr
10 AM–6:30 PM. Closed Saturday, Sunday.

This venerable 19th-century establishment offers delicious acidulés, caramels, fruit gelées, honeys, jams, jellies, black or green tea, cookies and short breads, pure almond or hazelnut pralinés, raspberry and orange ganaches, flat chocolates and sour cherries in kirsch liquor.

▼ La Maison du Miel

24, rue Vignon
Métro: Madeleine, Havre-Caumartin
Tel.-Fax 01 47 42 26 70
9:15 AM–7 PM. Open daily.

This discreet store restored as new still presents 40 varieties of honey: Gâtinais, Larzac, heather, wild thyme, rosemary, lime, buckwheat, lemon tree, and acacia. As a bonus, royal jelly and honey candy.

▼ A la Mère de Famille 🏠

35, rue du Faubourg-Montmartre
Métro: Le Peletier
Tel. 01 47 70 83 69. Fax 01 47 70 51 37
www.lameredefamille.com
9 AM–8 PM
(Monday, Saturday 10 AM–8 PM).
Closed Sunday afternoon.

This is the oldest confectionery store in Paris, established in 1761. Etienne Dolfi has refurbished the place with a careful eye to tradition. Calissons (prune, orange or lemon), chocolate-covered pralinés, homemade ice creams, traditional candies (cotignacs, bêtises, bergamotes, négus, nougats, pâtes de fruits, marrons glacés and dragées) and jams (rhubarb, melon, peach cinnamon) work their wonders.

GROCERIES

▼ Les Vivres

28, rue Pétrelle
Métro: Anvers, Barbès-Rochechouart
Tel. 01 42 80 26 10
11 AM–9 PM. Closed Sunday, Monday,
1 week in Christmas, mid-July–mid-August.

Half bistro, half grocery store, under the supervision of poetic chef Jean-Luc André, this fine establishment offers convenience food at lunchtime, just like at home. You can take away snacks, preserves, condiments, artisinal products and select wines at reasonable prices. (Also see Restaurants.)

CHEESE

▼ Molard

48, rue des Martyrs
Métro: N.-D.-de-Lorette
Tel.-Fax 01 45 26 84 88
9:30 AM–1 PM, 4:30–8 PM
(Saturday 9:30 AM–1:30 PM, 3:30–8 PM;
Sunday 10 AM–1 PM).
Closed Sunday afternoon, Monday,
Tuesday morning, end of July–end of August.

Josiane Molard is a lover of artisan-made cheeses (banon in its chestnut leaf, lavort ewe's cheese, camembert with cider, mâchecoulais from cow's milk, creamy reblochons, saint-nectaire with its taste of the earth, fruity beaufort, pérail from the Averyron and bleu from Velay). She is to be found at the Breteuil market on Thursdays and Saturdays.

ICE CREAM

▼ Zagori

6, rue La Fayette
Métro: Chaussée-d'Antin-La Fayette
Tel. 01 47 70 81 37. Fax 01 49 24 03 41
7 AM–8 PM (Saturday 10 AM–8 PM).
Closed Sunday.

Ivan Zagori, who supplies many restaurants, also offers exotic fruit sorbets for the general public. Our favorites are coconut, mango and green apple. The pure-cream ice creams (chocolate, vanilla, licorice, tiramisu, coffee) are polished work indeed.

PASTRIES

▼ Rousseau et Seurre

22, rue des Martyrs
Métro: N.-D.-de-Lorette
Tel. 01 42 81 29 89. Fax 01 44 53 03 31
8:30 AM–1:30 PM, 4–7:30 PM.
Closed Sunday afternoon, Monday.

Gérard Seurre combines tradition and innovation, and that is what we like about him. When faced with his classics, such as the famous pistachio cake, profiterole-style tart, his crisp millefeuille or fresh lemon tart, resistance is useless. The framboisier (a raspberry cream Genoise cake), the pear charlotte, specialty cakes like the Truffélia, the Antigua and the dark chocolate Elodie, as well as the Ardechois (made with chestnut mousse), are a delight.

Shops

FRUIT & VEGETABLES

▼ Maxi Fraîcheur

17, rue Hippolyte-Lebas
Métro: N.-D.-de-Lorette
Tel. 01 40 23 02 55
7 AM–7:30 PM.
Closed Sunday afternoon, Monday.

This fine corner store supplies fruit and vegetables at the peak of their freshness, as the sign says. Green or white asparagus, baskets of raspberries: All the produce looks truly appealing. Reasonable prices.

REGIONAL PRODUCTS

▼ Henri Ceccaldi "Lu Spuntinu"

21, rue des Mathurins
Métro: Havre-Caumartin, St-Lazare
Tel. 01 47 42 66 52
8:30 AM–7:30 PM.
Closed Saturday, Sunday, August.

Henri Ceccaldi chooses the finest products of Corsica for his little store. The brocciu (Corsican cheese), lonzu (smoked pork filet), figatelli (liver sausages), fadone (Corsican cheesecake), oils and honeys, beignets made from brocciu, canistrelli (traditional Corsican anise cakes) and quality wines (Etienne Suzzoni Clos-Columbu, Domaine de Leccia and Domaine Torraccia) are all expertly selected.

▼ Aux Saveurs d'Auvergne

21, rue des Martyrs
Métro: N.-D.-de-Lorette
Tel. 01 48 78 30 19
8:30 AM–12:45 PM, 4:15–7:30 PM.
Closed Sunday afternoon, Monday, beginning of July–end of August.

Tasteful tripous (a sheep's feet dish), Salers gentiane liqueur, cantal and laguiole cheeses, fouace (a regional brioche-like cake), dried sausage and mountain ham have their home here.

COFFEE

▼ Méo

95, rue Saint-Lazare
(other address: 1, bd Denain, 10th arr.)
Métro: Havre-Caumartin
Tel. 01 48 74 36 77
contact@meo.fr
www.meo.fr
9 AM–7 PM.
Closed Sunday, Monday, August.

The Méo establishment has been roasting quality coffee since 1945. Blue Montain, Java Lintung, organic Méo Bio and Bugoma Noble coffee are all to be found here, along with selected teapots, cast iron and porcelain cups, and coffee pots (Chambord, Eileen, Kontessa), which make excellent gifts.

 # RENDEZVOUS

BARS

◆ Casa del Campo

22, rue de la Chaussée-d'Antin
Métro: Havre-Caumartin, Chaussée-d'Antin–La Fayette
Tel. 01 42 46 02 48. Fax 01 42 46 02 49
10:30 AM–midnight
(Saturday, Sunday 2 AM).

This Bilbao- or Seville-style beer and tapas bar offers an intelligent gourmet exoticism, based on Iberian wines and beers accompanied by ham, chorizo, chicken croquettes. A friendly welcome.

PUBS

◆ Le Général Lafayette

52, rue La Fayette
Métro: Le Peletier
Tel. 01 47 70 59 08. Fax 01 47 98 34 13
8 AM–4 AM. Open daily.
Terrasse.

This art nouveau brasserie with its brass beer taps has something of the Deux Magots café about it. The draft beers (including Lutterbach and Bitburger) accompany charcuterie from the Averyron, beef tartare with fries, Duval andouillette and

changing dishes of the day. Terrace on the street, service in back, open late.

◆ Saint-Georges Tavern's

46, rue du Faubourg-Montmartre
Métro: Le Peletier
Tel.-Fax 01 49 49 01 84
8:30 AM–1:30 AM. Closed Sunday.
Air cond.

This English-style pub, where you can watch the game on a large screen, serves darft and bottled beer at the bar. At any time, you can eat onion soup gratin, grilled andouillette and brownies accompanied by one of its range of beers, an aged whiskey or a delicious cocktail.

WINE BARS

◆ Le Beaujolais Drouot

7, rue Rossini
Métro: Richelieu-Drouot, Le Peletier
Tel. 01 42 46 09 20
6:30 AM–4 AM. Closed Sunday,
Bank Holidays.

This old-style café offers Xavier Benier Beaujolais Villages, Foillard Morgon Côte de Py and Domaine de Grand-Cour Fleurie, with charcuterie plates and aged cheeses. The dishes of the day (at lunchtime) follow a regional and seasonal approach.

◆ Le Bistrot des Artistes

10, rue Saulnier
Métro: Cadet
Tel. 01 47 70 50 88
Noon–2:30 PM, 7 PM–11:30 PM.
Closed Saturday lunch, Sunday, Monday evening, Bank Holidays, 10 days in July, 2 weeks in beginning of August, 3 days for Christmas.

This intimate bistro is dedicated to good Loire vintages. Vouvray, Anjou, Saumur, Gamay and Chinon wash down Salers prime rib, blood sausage with apples, calf's liver, warm sausages and andouillette.

Rendezvous

◆ La Cave Drouot

8, rue Drouot
Métro: Richelieu-Drouot
Tel. 01 47 70 83 38. Fax 01 45 23 56 66
7 AM–9 PM. Closed Sunday, August.
Terrace.

This corner café opposite the Hôtel Drouot welcomes workers from the auction gallery, who enjoy tasteful domestic dishes here. Terrines, poached skate, Basque blood sausage or leg of lamb are washed down with cold Chenas.

◆ Le Chenin

33, rue Le Peletier
Métro: Le Peletier
Tel. 01 47 70 12 01
9 AM–5 PM. Closed Saturday, Sunday, Christmas–New Year's, August.

Decorated with old bills, photos of artists and billiard cues, this bistro has character. Patrons enjoy traditional dishes (slow-cooked pork cheek dish with onions, veal blanquette, Salers beefsteak) and cheese from the splendid board, accompanied by Beaujolais or Sancerre.

◆ La Clairière

43, rue Saint-Lazare
Métro: Trinité
Tel. 01 48 74 32 94. Fax 01 42 03 46 28
7:30 AM–7 PM (Saturday 7:30 AM–3 PM).
Closed Sunday, last week in August.

Opposite the Taitbout post office, this Parisian *bouchon*–style restaurant offers domestic dishes and selected vintages. Its warm sausage, beef bourguignon, duck legs with oyster mushrooms and clafoutis are solid snacks.

◆ La Pause Terroir

8, rue Godot-de-Mauroy
Métro: Madeleine
Tel. 01 42 65 22 64
6:30 AM–6 PM. Cont. service.
Closed Sunday, 2 weeks at the end of January.

Croissants made with organic flour from Moisan, charcuterie and cheeses direct from a Basque farm, fresh foie gras, growers' wines (Chinon, Madiran, Pacherenc) and house desserts comprise the worthy fare of Laurence and Philippe Pocous's bistro. The dishes and produce from Southwest France are also available to take away.

CAFES

◆ Blabla   ℕ

66, rue Blanche (at rue Chaptal)
Métro: Blanche
Tel. 01 49 70 06 75
10:30 AM (Saturday 4 PM)–1 AM.
Closed Sunday.

This new, contemporary café in shades of gray, with its corner bar and double room with Fifties' and Sixties' furniture lends a modern touch to this chic area of Nouvelle Athènes. Amiable snacks (plates of assorted tapas, sushi, picnic items or Iberian ham, grilled rib-eye steaks, spare ribs, Argentinean barbeque) and a pleasant terrace on the street.

◆ Café Gallery

78, rue de Provence
Métro: Chaussée-d'Antin–La Fayette, Havre-Caumartin
Tel. 01 48 74 55 63
7 AM–9 PM. Closed Sunday.
Terrace.

This stylish café makes an excellent impression with its brown hues and attractive lighting. Guests come to take a break from shopping, grab an andouillette or an Auvergne-style salad and enjoy the exhibition of designer furniture.

◆ Café Mazarin

16, bd Montmartre
Métro: Grands-Boulevards, Richelieu-Drouot
Tel. 01 47 70 80 15
7 AM–2 AM. Closed Christmas.
Terrace.

Opposite the Théâtre des Variétés, this large, modern café offers salads, starters, and tiramisu. Tequila sunrise, piña colada and Berthillon ice cream are served at any time.

◆ Le Café des Roses ⓝ

1, rue Vintimille
Tel. 01 53 20 96 57
7:30 AM–midnight. Open daily.

An authentic Parisian café with zinc counter, pink walls and beige furniture, Le Café des Roses focuses on tradition and low prices with an old-fashioned air that will appeal to the genre's purists. Brunch on Sunday.

◆ Fuxia

25, rue des Martyrs
Métro: St-Georges
Tel. 01 48 78 93 25. Fax 01 48 78 99 04
10 AM–11 PM (Saturday, Sunday cont. service). Closed May 1st.
Air cond. Terrace.

For a coffee or Italian wine at any time, inside or out on the terrace, this trattoria acts as a café outside meal times.. (Also see Restaurants.)

◆ Hôtel Amour ⓝ

8, rue Navarin
Métro: N.-D.-de-Lorette, Pigalle, St-Georges
Tel. 01 48 78 31 80
8 AM–11:30 PM. Open daily.

The bohemian middle-class event in Nouvelle Athènes is this offbeat hotel with its shady little courtyard, school canteen–style dining room, Fifties' furniture and terrace. Visitors are welcome at any time for morning coffee or a mojito in the evening. All Paris society is going, has gone or will go there.. (Also see Restaurants.)

◆ Omnibus

13, pl Pigalle
Métro: Pigalle
Tel. 01 45 26 82 04
8:30 AM–2 AM (Friday, Saturday 8:30 AM–3 AM). Open daily.

This exotic restaurant and bar with pink armchairs attracts fans of electronic music. Honest brasserie fare (omelets, beef tartare, fromage blanc with honey) served with a smile.

◆ Sélect Café ⓝ

37, rue des Martyrs
Métro: N.-D.-de-Lorette, St-Georges
Tel. 01 53 20 00 67
7 AM–11:30 PM. Open daily.

A drink on the terrace in this rising street, a coffee at the counter or a generous lunchtime set menu (€16 all inclusive) are what you can expect from this pleasant, brisk establishment opposite star baker Delmontel.

TEA SALONS

◆ Les Cakes de Bertrand

7, rue Bourdaloue
Métro: N.-D.-de-Lorette
Tel. 01 40 16 16 28
www.lescakesdebertrand.com
April 15th–October 15th: Monday–Friday noon–3:30 PM, Saturday 9:30 AM–7 PM, Sunday noon–6 PM.
October 16th–April 14th: Monday noon–5 PM, Tuesday–Friday noon–7 PM, Saturday 9:30 AM–7 PM, Sunday noon–6 PM.
Closed Christmas–New Year's, August.

This attractive neo-19th-century tearoom with its chandeliers and pendants offers crumbles, fruit tarts and cakes for a gourmet clientele, while also managing Thé dans le Jardin (Tea in the Garden) at the Musée de la Vie Romantique.

◆ La Jolie Vie

56 bis, rue de Clichy
Métro: Place-de-Clichy
Tel. 01 53 20 04 04. Fax 01 53 20 00 10
www.lajolievie.com
10 AM–7 PM.
Closed Sunday, 3 weeks in August.

This tearoom with its colored walls presents assorted teas (green, jasmine, red fruits or Japanese), cinnamon-scented chocolate as well as terrines, soups, savory tarts and prune flan.

◆ Les Pipalottes Gourmandes

49, rue de Rochechouart
Métro: Cadet, Poissonnière
Tel. 01 44 53 04 53
10 AM–6 PM
(for take-out: open until 10 PM).
Closed mid-July–mid-August.

This attractive gourmet tearoom offers traditional cuisine, exotic snacks (moussaka or lasagna) and hot and cold gourmet dishes according to the season. A brunch option on Sundays and holidays.

◆ Rose Bakery

46, rue des Martyrs
Métro: N.-D.-de-Lorette
Tel. 01 42 82 12 80
9 AM–7 PM (Sunday 5 PM).
Closed Monday, 2 weeks in August.

Very fashionable and very organic, this chic cavern-style French-English tearoom serves prepared dishes, vegetable buffet, exquisite pastries (muffins, crumble), ice cream and fresh fruit juices. Service in summer on the terrace, with amusing iron chairs.

◆ Tea Follies

6, pl Gustave-Toudouze
Métro: St-Georges
Tel.-Fax 01 42 80 08 44
11 AM–9 PM (in summer 11 PM,
Saturday, Sunday, Monday 11 AM–7 PM).
Closed Christmas, New Year's.

This easygoing establishment on a bucolic square offers savory tarts, large composed salads, crumbles and fruit tarts. Exhibitions are organized in partnership with neighboring galleries.

10TH ARRONDISSEMENT
POETIC AND DEMOCRATIC

Léon-Paul Fargue saw this district as "the most poetic in the capital," with its "brasseries filled with women of easy virtue," Canal Saint Martin, two rail stations—Gare du Nord and Gare de l'Est—and noisy avenues leading to other destinations. The tenth arrondissement has managed to remain modest. Its delicious restaurants are less expensive than those of comparable quality elsewhere. It is no accident that the historic jewels in the crown of the Flo group, which specializes in gourmet establishments with a historic flavor (Brasserie Flo, Julien, Terminus Nord), are to be found here. The "in" crowd frequents the bistros close to the canal. The district's charm actually lies in its easy blend of modernism and nostalgia. Behind the church of Saint-Vincent-de-Paul, Thierry Breton has modernized two vintage establishments and, with a deft touch, made them accessible to all (Chez Michel and Casimir). The wine bars (Le Rallye and Le Réveil du Xe) are full of conviviality. Local restaurants are experiencing a renaissance here (Aux Zingots is the latest event, but Hôtel du Nord has also made a fresh start). Newcomers (Le Martel, Côté Canal, Le Pachyderme, Le Verre Volé) show that the parishioners of the tenth, once a workaday, blue-collar neighborhood, stand in the vanguard of fashion today.

RESTAURANTS

GOOD RESTAURANTS & OTHERS

● Aux Armes de Colmar `COM`
13, rue du 8-mai-1945
Métro: Gare-de-l'Est
Tel. 01 40 34 94 50. Fax 01 42 46 07 02
Open daily until 11 PM.
Prix fixe: 16,50€, 32€. A la carte: 35€.
Terrace.

When Alsatians (by birth or nature) passing by the Gare de l'Est are struck by a sudden craving for choucroute or creamy onion tart, they naturally turn to this recently renovated brasserie. Here, the region's great classics are prepared with an eye to tradition. Onion soup gratinée, monkfish steak in pepper sauce, old-style smoked haddock filet, thick rib-eye steak with a peppercorn sauce and apple streudel accompanied by Pinot Noir and Riesling. When it is in season, make sure you try the mirabelle plum tart!

● Balbuzard Cafe `SIM`
54, rue René-Boulanger
Métro: République
Tel. 01 42 08 60 20
Closed Sunday. Open until midnight.
Prix fixe: 10,50€ (lunch), 12€ (lunch, wine included), 19€ (dinner), 21€ (dinner).
A la carte: 25€.
Air cond. Private dining room.

Noël Romani's bistro has been enlarged, providing more space for its regular customers, all lovers of Corsica, the Island of Beauty, who know full well what culinary delights they can expect: wild boar terrine, grilled jumbo Corsican shrimp, figatelli (traditional Corsican sausage) with lentils and fiadone (Corsican cheesecake). Corsican wines only and a delicious chestnut liqueur to end the meal.

● Brasserie Flo `COM`
7, cour des Petites-Ecuries
Métro: Château-d'Eau, Strasbourg-St-Denis
Tel. 01 47 70 13 59. Fax 01 42 47 00 80
www.brasserieflo.com
Open daily until midnight.
Prix fixe: 19,90€ (lunch), 22,90€ (lunch).
A la carte: 45€.
Terrace. Valet parking.

The cour des Petites-Ecuries is a picturesque spot that warrants a visit, ending with a meal in this vintage-1880s brasserie. Carved woodwork, stained glass, frescos paying tribute to Alsace and the brewer's art, and comfortable leather banquettes are all here. The menu is tastefully classical and the preparation has improved. The duck foie gras, spéciales oysters from Gillardeau, French onion soup, salmon grilled on one side, Colmar-style sauerkraut, leg of lamb roasted with thyme and the authentic baba au rhum and chocolate profiteroles will do you a world of good.

● Cafe Panique `SIM`
12, rue des Messageries
Métro: Poissonnière
Tel. 01 47 70 06 84
www.cafepanique.com
Closed Saturday, Sunday, 3 weeks in August.
Open until 10 PM.
Prix fixe: 19€ (lunch, wine included), 30€.
A la carte: 40€.
Private dining room.

What makes this innocuous street special is the Cafe Panique with its contemporary loft chic. In the dining room, which is bathed in light, Odile Guyader serves up dishes reflecting current trends and adapting to the season and vagaries of the marketplace. The foie gras ravioli with spices in lemon verbena "cappuccino", monkfish tail with artichokes and an orange sauce, veal loaf cooked with white wine and a soft almond, honey and lemon cake are pleasantly surprising.

● Chez Casimir ⬤ SIM

6, rue du Belzunce
Métro: Gare-du-Nord
Tel. 01 48 78 28 80. Fax 01 44 53 61 31
Closed Saturday, Sunday, August.
Open until 11 PM.
A la carte: 35€.
Terrace.

This nearby offshoot of Chez Michel is closely supervised by maestro Thierry Breton, even though he spends more time there than in this bistro. We are pleased to find ourselves back here, enjoying the convivial atmosphere and chatting over a drink and generous dishes concocted by Cédric Lefevre. The country terrine, eggplant and goat cheese millefeuille, cod brandade served with mixed greens, Burgundy-style stewed beef cheeks and pear Belle-Hélène are gratifying and a bargain at the price. The dishes of the day on the blackboard reflect the season and adapt to what is on offer at the market.

● La Chandelle Verte ⬤ SIM

40, rue d'Enghien
Métro: Bonne-Nouvelle
Tel. 01 47 70 25 44.
Closed dinner, Saturday, Sunday, August.
Prix fixe: 15€, 21€.

We all remember the words of Ubu Roi, composed by Alfred Jarry's mischievous pen: "Yes, by my green candle, I'm starving!" So if you are famished, push open the door of Ursula and Michel Monnier's "Green Candle" bistro and try their market produce-based dishes. The pork terrine with green peppercorns, the marinated salmon with dill and the veal shoulder with mushrooms, like the airy dark chocolate and coffee mousse, go down smoothly. One-third of the wine list consists of organic wines that go perfectly with the vegetarian plate, 100% organic and ecological.

● Le Coin de Verre ⬤ SIM

38, rue Sambre-et-Meuse
Métro: Colonel-Fabien, Belleville
Tel. 01 42 45 31 82
Closed lunch, Sunday, 1 week Christmas–New Year's. Open until 11 PM.
A la carte: 25€.

On the heights of Sainte Marthe, hidden behind a red-draped door, this bistro for a few select connoisseurs regales guests with fine fare served by the hearth at reasonable prices. Hugues Calliger takes great care with his assorted charcuterie and cheese platters, family dishes like veal blanquette, andouillette, beef bourguignon, grandmother-style desserts and "natural" wines.

● Aux Deux Canards COM

8, rue du Faubourg-Poissonnière
Métro: Bonne-Nouvelle
Tel. 01 47 70 03 23. Fax 01 47 70 18 85
lesdeuxcanards@aliceadsl.fr
www.lesdeuxcanards.com
Closed Saturday lunch, Sunday,
Monday lunch, 1 week in beginning of January,
July 24th–August 24th.
Open until 10 PM.
Prix fixe: 17€ (lunch). A la carte: 40€.
Air cond.

Gérard Faesch's restaurant, formerly run by his mother Catherine, takes its name from the French slang for a newspaper: *canard* or duck, since most of its clientele once came from the offices of two dailies: *Combat* and *Le Matin*. In a retro decor, where school blackboards have replaced the traditional slates and jars of orange peel sit on red and white checked tablecloths, we delight in the basil and goat cheese flan, porcini mushrooms marinated in olive oil, signature duck bourguignon (stewed in red wine and orange blossom honey), a wonderful andouillette AAAAA in red butter and a luscious millefeuille of soufflé crêpes in warm chocolate sauce.

● La Grille   🏠 COM

80, rue du Faubourg-Poissonnière
Métro: Poissonnière
Tel. 01 47 70 89 73
Closed Saturday, Sunday, 3 weeks in August.
Open until 9:30 PM.
A la carte: 45€.
Air cond.

Once you have crossed the threshold, you feel you have been plunged into the past, surrounded as you are by the antique ornaments, hat stands and lace that make up the decor here. Geneviève Cullerre offers her guests a smiling welcome, while Yves, her husband, sets to work in the kitchen, concocting brilliant dishes. The homemade duck terrine with hazelnuts, the mackerel stewed in white wine, the celebrated turbot served with beurre blanc, pan-grilled tenderloin chateaubriand, old-style beef bourguignon and the custard flan and profiteroles à la royale have not dated at all. They even seem rejuvenated by a glass of Clément Menetou-Salon.

● Hôtel du Nord   🏠 COM

102, quai de Jemmapes
Métro: Jacques-Bonsergent
Tel. 01 40 40 78 78. Fax 01 40 40 99 20
Open daily until midnight.
Prix fixe: 13,50€ (lunch on weekdays).
A la carte: 40€.
Air cond. Private dining room.

Atmosphere is the key in this Hôtel du Nord, refurbished in an art deco brasserie style by Julien Labrousse. The place has become a fashionable haunt for young middle-class bohemians, attracted as much by the relaxed ambience as by the fine dishes cooked up by Pascal Chenaut, formerly with Janou in rue Verlomme. We make short work of the antipasti (including buffalo mozzarella), monkfish and grilled shrimp brochette, duck breast with a potato and Salers cheese galette, as well as the gingerbread tiramisu. There is a bonus: the terrace, which soon fills up whenever the sun shows its face.

● Le Jemmapes   Ⓢ SIM

82, quai de Jemmapes
Métro: République, Jacques-Bonsergent
Tel. 01 40 40 02 35
Closed Tuesday lunch. Open until midnight.
A la carte: 30€.
Terrace.

This retro canal street has been modernized by the local bohemian middle class. Sylvester Kolomi's bistro is reaping the benefits, especially since the ambience is amiable and the traditional cuisine unpretentious. The smoked herring and potato salad, strip steak in peppercorn sauce with potato gratin and the chocolate fondant delight both regulars and curious passers-by.

● Julien   🏠 COM

16, rue du Faubourg-Saint-Denis
Métro: Strasbourg-St-Denis
Tel. 01 47 70 12 06. Fax 01 42 47 00 65
p.henriques@groupeflo.fr
Open daily until 1 AM.
Prix fixe: 22,90€, 29,90€.
A la carte: 50€.
Air cond. Valet parking.

There is the facade, all in wood, then the dining room with its superb art nouveau decor and Majorelle bar, Trézel muses, glass roofs and floral patterns. Then come the culinary delights. The menu pays tribute to the fine tradition of brasserie dishes, regaling us with salmon rillettes, chicken liver terrine, stewed cod with vegetables, sea bass beurre blanc, grilled leg of lamb, rib-eye steak with béarnaise sauce and warm chocolate profiteroles. Turning to the cellar, Bordeaux wines predominate, with a few excellent bottles that are reasonably priced (the Haut Marbuzet is at trade price). Neither do we have any complaints about the professional, attentive service.

● **La Marine**   SIM

55 bis, quai de Valmy
Métro: République
Tel. 01 42 39 69 81
Closed Christmas, New Year's.
Open until midnight.
Prix fixe: 13€ (lunch). A la carte: 30€.
Terrace.

From the terrace of this flourishing quai de Valmy institution, you can watch the barges passing on the canal. Inside, we tread the century-old floor that must have borne the weight of many a bargeman before the new bohemian middle-class crowd moved into the neighborhood. The menu tends toward modified bistro classics, with an honest oxtail and foie gras terrine, fresh roasted codfish with natural sea salt, exquisite caramelized spareribs and a more banal charlotte with five flavors.

● **Chez Michel**   ○ COM

10, rue de Belzunce
Métro: Gare-du-Nord, Poissonnière
Tel. 01 44 53 06 20. Fax 01 44 53 61 31
Closed Saturday, Sunday, Monday lunch.
Open until midnight.
Prix fixe: 30€.
Terrace. Private dining room.

A step or two away from the Gare du Nord, just behind the church of Saint Vincent de Paul, the aptly named Thierry Breton, formerly at the Ritz and Crillon, brings together lovers of Brittany and other food enthusiasts over dishes based on regional produce and the ocean. The 1939 vintage dining room is decorated with a few paintings of the Breton coast between Morlaix and Carnac. Downstairs is a cellar vaulted with undressed wood and wrought iron. Whether you choose to eat there or upstairs, take your time; you are in for a memorable experience. Slow-cooked tuna with coriander and Breton-style tabouli, roasted John Dory with sweet potato purée, thick tuna steak with eggplant caviar, Breton pot-au-feu with buckwheat dumplings and roasted milk-fed veal with young turnips make a fine feast, which ends with the inevitable kouign-amann (Breton flaky butter and sugar pastry) or an

outstanding paris-brest (choux pastry ring filled with praliné cream). The wine list offers a wide range of vintages at reasonable prices. You can also try some excellent ciders from the Cornouaille district as well as Breton beers, especially oat and buckwheat brews. We strongly recommend you reserve.

● **Le Pachyderme**   SIM

2 bis, bd Saint-Martin
Métro: République
Tel. 01 42 06 32 56. Fax 01 42 06 36 52
www.pachyderme.fr
Closed Christmas. Open until 11 PM
(midnight: Thursday, Friday, Saturday).
Prix fixe: 13€ (weekday lunch, wine included). A la carte: 35€.
Air cond. Terrace.

Do not worry, the dishes are not as heavy as the name of the restaurant might suggest. Quite the opposite, in fact. The herbed fresh and smoked salmon terrine, red tuna and lime tartare, duck breast with Espelette chili pepper and the citrus terrine with vanilla essence are the epitome of freshness. The hip young musical ambience, very friendly welcome and terrace are all excellent reasons to pay a visit to this establishment just off place de la République.

● **Le Petit Cafe**   € SIM

14, bd de Strasbourg
Métro: Strasbourg-St-Denis, Château-d'Eau
Tel. 01 42 01 81 61
Closed Sunday, Monday, August.
Open until midnight.
Prix fixe: 11€ (lunch). A la carte: 30€.
Terrace.

The Théâtre Antoine's Petit Cafe never empties. Before or after the show, actors and audience share the same culinary pleasures, with Basque country specialties lovingly prepared by Jean-Louis Fontanieu. The salt cod-stuffed piquillo peppers, boned and breaded pig's feet served on a bed of peppers and tomatoes, Basque-style squid, Basque tuna stew, lamb neck slow-roasted in olive oil, Basque butter cake filled with cherry jam and prune pie topped with crisp phyllo are enjoyable. Basque wines from both France and Spain take place of honor.

● Le Phénix　●🛈SIM

4, rue du Faubourg-Poissonnière
Métro: Bonne-Nouvelle
Tel. 01 47 70 35 40
lephenixcafe@wanadoo.fr
www.lephenixparis.com
Closed Saturday lunch, Sunday,
Bank Holidays, 1 week Christmas–New
Year's, August. Open until 11:30 PM.
Prix fixe: 12€ (lunch). A la carte: 30€.
Air cond. Terrace.

This circa-1880 bistro is enjoying a second youth under the aegis of Fabien Gadeau. This young proprietor and sommelier has brought a new sparkle to its bar, stucco and oilcloths, with solid, boarding house cuisine to match. The Lyonnaise sausage, salmon carpaccio, duck confit and chocolate mousse gratify without breaking the bank.

● Ploum　SIM

20, rue Alibert
Métro: Goncourt
Tel. 01 42 00 11 90
www.ploum.fr
Closed Saturday lunch, Sunday lunch,
Monday, beginning of August–end of August.
Open until 11 PM.
Prix fixe: 15€ (lunch), 18€ (lunch).
A la carte: 30€.

Not far from the Saint Louis hospital, set back slightly from the fashionable part of the Canal Saint Martin, this French Japanese restaurant with its unusual decor, disconcerting to say the least (electric cables on the bare concrete walls), has plenty of arguments in its favor. Come and take a seat, enjoy the good-humored ambience and taste the spinach in sesame cream, gray mullet steak with olive oil and basil, quickly seared salmon tartare, cuttlefish with ginger flambéd with sake, the assorted sushi, bo bun–style beef salad and green-tea tiramisu. Surprises and discoveries abound, and you will soon find yourself under the spell of this subtle alliance of Japanese tradition and contemporary cuisine, all overflowing with inspiration.

● Restaurant de Bourgogne　●SIM

26, rue des Vinaigriers
Métro: Jacques-Bonsergent, Gare-de-l'Est
Tel. 01 46 07 07 91
Closed Saturday lunch, Sunday, 3 weeks
in August. Open until 11 PM.
Prix fixe: 8,50€ (lunch), 9,50€ (lunch),
12€ (lunch), 13,50€ (dinner).
A la carte: 20€.
Air cond. Terrace.

A rustic decor, red-and-white checked tablecloths, staunch bistro classics and a short but thorough wine list, mainly from Burgundy, as you might imagine. With minimal damage to our pocket, we enjoy marinated smoked herring, tuna steak, grilled top rump steak in peppercorn sauce, tartiflette (a baked casserole of potatoes and reblochon cheese) and chocolate mousse—enough to satisfy even the healthiest of appetites.

● Le Sainte-Marthe　ⓃSIM

32, rue Sainte-Marthe
Métro: Belleville
Tel. 01 44 84 36 96
Closed Monday lunch, Tuesday lunch,
December 24th. Open until 11:30 PM.
Prix fixe: 11€ (except on Sunday).
A la carte: 35€.
Terrace.

Looking out onto an appealing Parisian square, this old-style bistro steeped in tradition delights both locals and tourists. All enjoy the poached bone marrow on toast, roasted monkfish with sesame seeds, a huge Irish prime rib roasted with coarse sea salt and apple-raspberry crumble. The service is with a smile and the check has a sense of proportion.

● **Le Sporting** 🛉 SIM

3, rue des Récollets
Métro: Gare-de-l'Est
Tel. 01 46 07 02 00. Fax 01 46 07 02 64
www.lesporting.com
Closed Christmas–New Year's.
Open until 11:30 PM.
Prix fixe: 14€ (lunch on weekdays).
A la carte: 40€.
Terrace.

Strolling by the Canal Saint Martin, you come upon this Thirties' bistro, still with its wooden bar, unvarnished parquet flooring and lacquered walls. Its modish, gourmet clientele comes to savor a fresh market-based cuisine. The dishes are chalked up on the blackboard: homemade foie gras, grilled jumbo shrimp served with arugula salad, sea bass filet with fresh green beans, beef tartare with sautéed small new potatoes, strip steak from the Aubrac region, crème brûlée and, in season, a succulent strawberry tart. The wines from selected small growers are enjoyable.

■ **La Table du Pavillon** 🛉 V.COM

Holiday Inn Opéra, 38, rue de l'Echiquie
Métro: Bonne-Nouvelle
Tel. 01 42 46 98 84. Fax 01 42 47 03 97
thierry.viot@hi-parisopera.com
www.table-du-pavillon.com
Open daily until 10 PM.
Prix fixe: 16€ (lunch), 21€ (lunch), 37€ (wine included).
A la carte: 45€.
Air cond. Private dining room.

Originally a hunting lodge belonging to King Henri IV in 1593, then a brasserie in the 1920s, this historic abode now houses a traditional restaurant, whose art deco–style has remained intact, with mahogany woodwork, mosaics, mirrors and stained glass paneling. The place has style, and the menu lives up to its promise with a combination of tradition and modernity. The foie gras with rhubarb, shellfish ravioli, sea bass cooked with coarse sea salt, herb-marinated lamb, beefsteak in Chivas sauce and chocolate macaron with Bourbon vanilla ice cream are all pleasant sur-

prises, accompanied by an astute selection of wines at gentle prices.

● **Terminus Nord** 🛉 COM

23, rue de Dunkerque
Métro: Gare-du-Nord
Tel. 01 42 85 05 15. Fax 01 40 16 13 98
terminusnord@groupeflo.com
Open daily 11 AM–1 AM. Cont. service.
Prix fixe: 19,90€ (after 10:30 PM), 22,90€, 29,90€. A la carte: 35–60€.
Air cond. Terrace. Private dining room.

While you wait for your train to leave, or after getting off one, you can take refuge in this delightful, authentic Parisian brasserie opposite the Gare du Nord. The interior is richly decorated, fluently blending art deco and art nouveau (mosaic tiling, frescos, high ceilings). The menu tends toward a tasteful classicism and its execution has improved significantly. The smoked herring and potato salad, seafood platters, bouillabaisse, choucroute, pan-roasted farm-raised veal with morel mushroom sauce and fresh tagliatelle and chocolate profiteroles are enough to satisfy any appetite. A courteous welcome, attentive service and a wide choice of wines by the glass.

● **La Vigne Saint-Laurent** € SIM

2, rue Saint-Laurent
Métro: Gare-de-l'Est
Tel. 01 42 05 98 20
Closed Saturday, Sunday, 1 week Christmas–New Year's, August.
Open until 10:30 PM.
Prix fixe: 13,50€ (dinner, wine included).
A la carte: 30€.

Patrons visit this Lyon *bouchon*–style restaurant near the Gare de l'Est as much for the fruits of the vine, selected from the Beaujolais region and the Rhône Valley, as for the regional produce from the four corners of France. François Bidal's service is good humored and Gérard Cochet's cuisine delightful. We indulge ourselves with the charcuterie plate, scorpion fish filet with pesto, "Rhône bargemen"–style beef and raspberry clafoutis.

Shops

A SPECIAL FAVORITE

● **Aux Zingots** Ⓝ🅰SIM

12, rue de la Fidélité
Métro: Gare-de-l'Est, Strasbourg-St-Denis
Tel. 01 47 70 19 34
Closed Sunday, Monday lunch.
Open until 1 AM.
A la carte: 40€.

It was formerly Nicolas, KOH, then the Boca. Now the place—1880s' brasserie-style, with moldings, stucco and ornate staircase plus Fifties' style lighting and banquettes—has recovered its soul. The "in" crowd meet here, led by movie director Cédric Klapisch and actor Jean-Pierre Daroussin. At the helm, Gilles Bénard, from Chez Ramulaud in the eleventh arrondissement, and Denys Clément, former photographer with the sports daily *L'Equipe*, have restored the restaurant and entrusted the kitchen to Véronique Melloul, previously at the Cafe de l'Homme. We savor the langoustine tartare with pig's feet, blood pudding parmentier with chestnut chips, calf's liver with honey vinegar along with beet and foie gras carpaccio with coarse sea salt, marinated grilled beef tenderloin with freshly made fries and béarnaise sauce, codfish in a creamy sauce with braised lettuce and caramelized onions. All the dishes have character, and the desserts range from the traditional to the tastes of today, with brioche pain perdu with creamy caramel or authentic baba soaked with mandarin liquor. Among the 150 items on the wine list, you are bound to find the right bottle to go with your particular spread. The Tour des Gendres Bergerac white and the Breton Chinon are elixirs to cure all ills.

▼ SHOPS

KITCHENWARE & TABLETOP

▼ Limoges Unic

34, rue de Paradis
Métro: Gare-de-l'Est, Poissonnière
Tel. 01 47 70 61 49. Fax 01 45 23 18 56
limogesunicmadronet@wanadoo.fr
www.limoges-unic-madronet.com
10:30 AM–6:30 PM (Monday, Tuesday, Friday), 11 AM–6 PM (Wednesday, Thursday, Saturday). Closed Sunday, Bank Holidays, 3 weeks in August.

Jacques Madronet offers high-quality porcelain, crystal creations and silverware in this store established in 1932. Bernardaud, Haviland, Raynaud, Lalique, Daum, Saint-Louis, Baccarat and Christofle are all represented.

BREAD & BAKED GOODS

▼ Du Pain et des Idées Ⓝ

34, rue Yves-Toudic
Métro: Jacques-Bonsergent
Tel. 01 42 40 44 52
7 AM–8 PM. Closed Saturday, Sunday.

Christophe Vasseur, fashion salesman, waited until his forties to learn the baking trade. Now, in a historic store that is worth a visit in itself for its mirrors and paintings under glass, his wonderful breads, Parisian baguettes, country-style round loaves, pain Polka (a large, criss-crossed flat bread) and small sourdough loaves are works of art.

CANDY & SWEETS

▼ Furet Tanrade

63, rue de Chabrol
Métro: Poissonnière
Tel. 01 47 70 48 34. Fax 01 42 46 34 41
www.le-furet-tanrade.com
8 AM–7:30 PM (Sunday 9 AM–7 PM).
Open daily.

Alain Furet, king of fine preserves, weaves his spell with quality blends of fruit. Customers also come in search of his choice teas, fruit jellies, pastries, chocolates and savory eclairs: Lot (sausage, lentils, red wine sauce) or Dauphinois (potato gratin with bacon bits).

CHEESE SHOPS

▼ Laurent Bouvet

Marché Saint-Martin:
31-33, rue du Château-d'Eau
Métro: Château-d'Eau
Tel. 01 40 40 73 25
9 AM–1 PM, 4–8 PM. Closed Sunday afternoon, Monday, 1 week in mid-August.
Laurent Bouvet rallies the gourmets of the marketplace with his aged cheeses: two-year-old appenzeller cheese, creamy reblochon, high-altitude beaufort, artisanal roquefort, fruity comté or Basque brebis. A selection of wines to match and fig or sour cherry preserves to accompany these fine cheeses.

PASTRIES

▼ Pain et Fruit

12, rue du 8-Mai-1945
Métro: Gare-de-l'Est
Tel. 01 40 35 74 07
7 AM–8 PM (Sunday 7:30 AM–7:30 PM).
Closed Monday.
Gilles Louzon presents millefeuille, flan, chocolate and fruit tarts in his fine, traditional cake store.

▼ Tholoniat

47, rue du Château-d'Eau
Métro: Château-d'Eau
Tel. 01 42 39 93 12. Fax 01 47 70 05 21
tholonia@club-internet.fr
8 AM–7:30 PM (Sunday 8:30 AM–5 PM).
Closed Monday, 20th July–1st September.
Christian Tholoniat excels in the art of traditional-style cakes. Caramelized millefeuille, lemon tart, maple syrup "Bouchard" tart and crispy raspberry pastry make an admirable impression. Chocolates filled with raspberry, quince or red-currant jelly and whiskey-flavored chocolate truffles complete the house range.

REGIONAL PRODUCTS

▼ Schmid

76, bd de Strasbourg
Métro: Gare-de-l'Est
Tel. 01 46 07 99 02. Fax 01 46 07 83 92
schmid2@wanadoo.fr
www.schmid-traiteur.com
9 AM (Saturday 8:30 AM–8 PM).
Closed Sunday, 1st and 8th of May,
July 14th, August 15th.
This store close to Gare de l'Est has been paying tribute to the Alsace region since 1904. Sweet or savory kugelhopf, Tempé brand pork charcuterie, raw or cooked sauerkraut, Black Forest cake, apple strudel, pretzels, Gertwiller gingerbread, jams and preserves and famous "gendarmes" (thin smoked sausages), eaux de vie and Météor beer go well together.

◆ RENDEZVOUS

BARS

◆ Delaville Cafe

34, bd Bonne-Nouvelle
Métro: Bonne-Nouvelle
Tel. 01 48 24 48 09
Noon–midnight. Open daily.
Terrace.
Decorative glass, columns, iron staircase and 19th-century mosaics set the fin de siècle tone of this modish café. Bloody Mary, hamburger or foie gras risotto go down cheerfully. Brunch on Sunday.

WINE BARS

◆ L'Enchotte

11, rue de Chabrol
Métro: Gare-de-l'Est
Tel. 01 48 00 05 25
Noon–2:30 PM, 7:30 PM–10:30 PM.
Closed Saturday lunch, Sunday,
3 weeks in August.
Equipped with a freight elevator, this wine bar opposite the Saint Quentin market has atmosphere to spare. Patrons come at noon on the dot to enjoy the dishes of the day (calf's head, salad with duck breast),

drink thirst-quenching wines and shoot the breeze at the counter.

◆ Le Rallye

267, rue du Faubourg-Saint-Martin
Métro: Stalingrad
Tel. 01 46 07 22 83
6:30 AM–8:30 PM. Closed Sunday,
Christmas–New Year's, 1 week for Ascension,
3 weeks in August.
Terrace.

Parisian and Auvergnat, this café, enthusiastically run by Antoine Deconquand, provides good humor, tripe stew, Auvergnat pork and sausage pot-au-feu, country-style cherry clafoutis and apple meringue tart, accompanied by cheerful Beaujolais.

◆ Le Rallye du Nord

94, rue La Fayette
Métro: Poissonnière
Tel. 01 47 70 28 30. Fax 01 48 00 94 05
7 AM–10:30 PM. Open daily.
Terrace.

This café on a busy street is worth a visit for its simple ambience, vintages by the glass and dishes chalked up on the blackboard. Omelet, lamb tripe stew, toasted ham and cheese on Poilâne bread satisfy without making waves.

◆ Le Réveil du Xe

35, rue du Château-d'Eau
Métro: Jacques-Bonsergent, République
Tel.-Fax 01 42 41 77 59
7:30 AM– 9:30 PM.
Closed Saturday evening, Sunday,
Bank Holidays.

Pierre Cure and Aurélie Vidalenc represent the new generation in this Sixties' café. Patrons come to lunch here amid the noise and cheer of solid dishes: terrines, regional pâtés, pork, duck or goose confit, a savory prune, spinach and bacon pudding, grilled sausage with cheese-and-potato purée, potato and bacon gratin, potato pie and fruit tarts. The Beaujolais are superb.

◆ Le Tire-Bouchon

118, rue de La Fayette
Métro: Gare-du-Nord
Tel. 01 48 24 58 46
7 AM–11 PM. Closed Sunday

Jean-Philippe Bruel, whose heart is solidly anchored in the Cantal district, offers honest Auvergne cheeses: saint-nectaire, cantal, Salers, as well as stuffed cabbage, stuffed veal breast and grilled sausage with cheese-and-potato purée. To wash them down cheerfully, Beaujolais, Loire wines and Irancy.

◆ Le Verre Volé

67, rue de Lancry
Métro: Jacques-Bonsergent
Tel.-Fax 01 48 03 17 34
10:30 AM–2 AM.
Closed Christmas–New Year's,
1 week in August

This mini bistro is a grocery store, cellar and good-natured haunt. We taste Cyril Bordarier's selections and savor the andouillette, mini pork pâtés, country-style sausage and aged cheeses, which complement the Métras Fleurie, Gramenon "Côtes" and the Dard and Ribo Crozes.

CAFES

◆ Le Château d'Eau ♟

67, rue du Château-d'Eau
Métro: Château-d'Eau
Tel. 01 47 70 11 00
7 AM–2 AM. Open daily.

With its marble counter and green ceramic tiles, this old-style bistro rouses the love of Paris that slumbers in us. Coffee, sandwiches and grilled meats are there for the asking.

◆ Merci Charlie

42 bis, bd Bonne-Nouvelle
Métro: Bonne-Nouvelle
Tel. 01 45 23 01 77. Fax 01 45 23 06 55
8 AM–2 AM. Open daily.
Terrace.

This cocktail bar just next to the Rex movie theater offers a range of drinks and inspired dishes: smoked haddock carpaccio, duck breast in honey sauce, banana-chocolate tarte Tatin. On the first floor you can take time out to watch a big-screen film, then enjoy a dinner time DJ set that turns the air electric.

◆ Le Poisson Rouge

112, quai de Jemmapes
Métro: Château-Landon
Tel. 01 40 40 07 11
10:30 AM–2 AM.
Closed Christmas–New Year's.
Terrace.

This pleasant café in a registered building offers a youthful ambience and refined cuisine: sautéed veal, made to order, fish quenelle in chive sauce and pan-fried tangerines in lemon cream accompanied by well-chosen growers' wines. Terrace in summer.

◆ Chez Prune

71, quai Valmy
Métro: République
Tel. 01 42 41 30 47
8 AM–2 AM. Closed Christmas, New Year's
Terrace

This bohemian middle-class café with its stucco and bar made over in a young, colorful style, welcomes patrons inside or on the terrace. The place reflects the changes in these neighborhoods gripped by fashion (Agnès B. is not far away). Small assorted cold plates to snack on, better than hot food!

◆ Sur les Quais

37, quai de Valmy
Métro: République
Tel. 01 40 40 70 55
Noon–3 PM, 6 PM–2 AM. Closed Sunday.

This retro café makes you want to pause in your wanderings. It offers Auvergne blue-cheese pie, grilled meats, smoked duck breast and wines by the glass. Every month an exhibition provides a change of decor on the walls.

◆ Les Voisins

27, rue Yves-Toudic
Métro: République, Jacques-Bonsergent
Tel. 01 42 49 36 58
9 AM–2 AM.
Closed Sunday, Christmas, New Year's
Terrace

Between quai de Valmy and boulevard Magenta, this vintage café serves drinks all day and substantial dishes at lunch and dinner time. Patrons can snack on tapas while listening to the local gossip.

○	Very good restaurant
◐	Excellent restaurant
◖◗	One of the best restaurants in Paris
◍	Disappointing restaurant
■	Good value for money
€	Meals for less than 30 euros
SIM	Simple
COM	Comfortable
V.COM	Very comfortable
LUX	Luxurious
V.LUX	Very luxurious

Red indicates a particularly charming establishment

🏛	Historical significance
🅿	Promotion *(higher rating than last year)*
🅽	New to the guide
●	Restaurant
▼	Shop
◆	Rendezvous

11TH ARRONDISSEMENT
AN AREA IN A STATE OF FLUX

Formerly a working-class district, now middle-class bohemian and intellectual, the eleventh arrondissement has become the haunt of new Paris society. Already a decade ago, director Cédric Klapisch portrayed the district in a movie called *When the Cat's Away*. It has not aged in the slightest. The cafés are still just the same, and some have become excellent eateries. Ramulaud, frequented by actor Jean-Pierre Darroussin (*Red Lights* and *A Very Long Engagement*), Klapisch and others, Le Vieux Chêne, Chardenoux, Le Bistrot Paul Bert, Le Temps au Temps, Le Villaret and Astier are just some of the restaurants that have made their mark on the district (and on their era, in fact). There are also excellent international establishments, from Amici Mei to Mansouria, as well as La Bague de Kenza. In this district, everyone can shape their own world and plot their own frame of reference. The slightly neutral, slightly gray architecture, the places that shun luxury, the delightful terraces, the bistros whose only aim is to please (La Muse Vin, Les Bas-Fonds, Le Clown Bar)—all are effortlessly congenial. The latest trends parade from one brasserie to the next. In rue de Lappe, Madrilenian and Cuban tapas bars have replaced the Auvergnat cafés. Yet the people we see seem thick as thieves, which actually sums it up: Of all the arrondissements, the eleventh is definitely the only one that belongs to all Parisians—here, there and everywhere.

● RESTAURANTS

GOOD RESTAURANTS & OTHERS

● L'Aiguière `COM`

37 bis, rue de Montreuil
Métro: Faidherbe-Chaligny
Tel. 01 43 72 42 32. Fax 01 43 72 96 36
patrick.masbatin@wanadoo.fr
www.laiguiere.com
Closed Saturday lunch, Sunday.
Open until 10:30 PM.
Prix fixe: 29€, 55€, 65€. A la carte: 80€.
Air cond. Private dining room. Valet parking.

His training as a sommelier has left Patrick
Masbatin with a passion for wine in its
every guise. His cellar, tirelessly restocked
on the basis of 300 items covering every region, is the proof. There is also great attention to detail on the culinary front, with
chef Pascal Viallet, formerly at the Plaza, in
the kitchen. The restaurant was once an
inn frequented by King Louis XIII's musketeers. In its hushed ambience, we revel in
the sweetbreads with artichoke hearts and
langoustines, a goat cheese briquette with
acacia honey ice cream, red pandora fish
with a lemon jus and old-fashioned
braised sweetbread medallions before the
soft dark chocolate cake with sherry caramel and walnut-honey ice cream.

● A l'Ami Pierre `€` `SIM`

5, rue de la Main-d'Or
Métro: Ledru-Rollin
Tel. 01 47 00 17 35
Closed Sunday, Monday, August.
Open until midnight.
A la carte: 28€.

At the Ami Pierre, Marcel effortlessly regales us with the assorted charcuterie, cod
brandade, flank steak with shallots, veal
blanquette, crème brûlée and the chocolate cake. We savor these authentic, perennially fashionable bistro classics under the
attentive eye of Marie-Jo, always alert to
her guests' needs.

● Les Amognes `COM`

243, rue du Faubourg-Saint-Antoine
Métro: Faidherbe-Chaligny, Nation
Tel. 01 43 72 73 05
Closed Sunday. Open until 11 PM.
A la carte: 41€.
Terrace.

Exposed beams and dressed stone set the
scene in this Norman cottage–style
restaurant run by Jean-Louis Thuillier.
This veteran of Robuchon and Fauchon
conscientiously prepares scallop medallions with Espelette chilis, foie gras with
fig jam, monkfish served with risotto,
roasted lamb shank with honey and
croustillant of caramelized apples. You
can have a good time here without over-
stepping your budget.

● L'Armagnac `€` `SIM`

104, rue de Charonne
Métro: Charonne
Tel. 01 43 71 49 43
Open daily until 11:30 PM.
A la carte: 28€.

This old-style bistro with its stucco, zinc
counter, woodwork and engraved glass has
an antique charm. The gourmet menu and
inoffensive prices make it a favorite rendezvous for locals. Savor the goat cheese millefeuille, foie gras pâté with toast, steak
tartare, sirloin steak, orange-infused crème
brûlée and soft chocolate cake with crème
anglaise. Fish is also served, but only on Friday, as Catholic tradition dictates. A fine selection of wines by the glass.

● Astier `🍴` `€` `SIM`

44, rue Jean-Pierre-Timbaud
Métro: Parmentier, Goncourt
Tel. 01 43 57 16 35
www.restaurant-astier.com
Open daily until 11:30 PM.
Prix fixe: 18,50€ (lunch), 23,50€ (lunch),
28€ (dinner).
Air cond.

This sound local bistro, which offers value
for money, a relaxed atmosphere, selected
wines and refined dishes of the day, has
changed hands, but remains true to its call-

ing. Frédéric Hubig, who owns the Café Moderne behind the Paris stock exchange, has taken it over but has refrained from tampering with all those things that have made it a success: smoked herring with potatoes and olive oil, wonderful terrines, roasted monkfish with basmati rice, traditional veal blanquette and crème caramel like grandmother makes are all simple delights. New chef Benjamin Bajol was Yannick Alleno's lieutenant at the Meurice, and Robert Henry in the dining room is a Hotel Bristol veteran, but they have adapted easily to this more modest establishment.

● Auberge Pyrénées-Cévennes COM

106, rue de la Folie-Méricourt
Métro: République, Goncourt
Tel. 01 43 57 33 78
Closed Saturday lunch, Sunday,
Christmas—New Year's, 2 weeks in August.
Open until 10:30 PM.
Prix fixe: 27,50€. A la carte: 45€.
Air cond.

Although Françoise and Daniel Constantin's restaurant mainly pays tribute to Southwest France, they take us on a genuine gustatory tour of the French regions in their inn with its waxed beams. The salad with foie gras, the Puy caviar (French green lentils, that is), skate with capers, pike quenelles, andouillette, cassoulet, nougat glacé (frozen dessert with candied fruit and whipped cream) and chocolate profiteroles are quite enough to satisfy every appetite. The decor is refined and the welcome extremely warm.

● Bar-Bat SIM

23, rue de Lappe
Métro: Bastille
Tel. 01 43 14 26 06. Fax 01 48 06 89 05
www.barbat.fr
Closed lunch, Christmas—New Year's.
Open until 2 AM.
Prix fixe: 38€ (wine included), 40€ (wine included), 45€ (wine included).
A la carte: 34€.
Air cond.

Right in the heart of the Bastille district, in a welcoming, brightly colored decor,

reliable dishes inspired by Corsica are revised by the young, talented Frédéric Ottolenghi. We savor the thinly sliced cured Italian sausage with honeyed ewe's cheese and ginger, the pan-seared sea bream with parsley, garlic and olive oil, the caramelized spare ribs with rosemary, fennel and juniper berries, the roasted lamb with rosemary and garlic confit and a coffee and chestnut infused tiramisu. Corsican wines only. Catering services are also available.

● Le Bar à Soupes Ⓝ Ⓔ SIM

33, rue de Charonne
Métro: Ledru-Rollin, Bastille, Charonne
Tel.-Fax 01 43 57 53 79
info@lebarasoupes.com
www.lebarasoupes.com
Closed Sunday, Bank Holidays, last week of July—end of August. Open until 11 PM.
Prix fixe: 9,50€. A la carte: 10€.
Private dining room.

Behind Bastille on a bend in rue de Charonne, this bright yellow facade marks an eatery for monomaniacs, serving soup—almost exclusively soup. We join the young and hip, and families on a tight budget, to eagerly enjoy "oriental" cream of chickpea soup, Portuguese chorizo soup and salted butter chocolate cake. Practical, good and inexpensive.

● Les Bas-Fonds SIM

116, rue Amelot
Métro: Filles-du-Calvaire
Tel.-Fax 01 48 05 00 30
infos@lesbasfonds.com
www.lesbasfonds.com
Closed Sunday lunch, 2 weeks in August.
Open until midnight.
A la carte: 40€.
Air cond. Terrace. Private dining room.

Along with the contemporary decor, David Souma presents two distinct culinary themes in two separate areas. One is decisively modern and inventive, in tune with current trends, while the other, wine-based and focused on tradition, is served in the basement. Whichever style you choose, you will find plenty to enjoy in the haricots verts salad, brochette of Japanese-style breaded sardines, roasted scallops with a creamy coconut curry risotto, Creole-style braised chicken, rib-eye steak with ginger and the coconut milk panna cotta with raspberry coulis and pineapple juice.

A SPECIAL FAVORITE

● Le Bistrot Paul Bert ▪ SIM

18, rue Paul-Bert
Métro: Faidherbe-Chaligny, Charonne
Tel. 01 43 72 24 01. Fax 01 43 72 24 66
Closed Sunday, Monday, August.
Open until 11 PM.
Prix fixe: 16€ (lunch), 30€ (dinner).
Terrace.

Bertrand Auboyneau, who gave up law and the stock exchange because of his love of good food and fine wines, has made a success of his career change. He has turned this bistro into a warm, welcoming place, bringing in Thierry Laurent, who has a talent for fine, generous, flavorsome dishes, playing with produce and the seasons to express his art to the full. Enjoy the superb rib-eye steak on the bone with homemade French fries, the pan-seared veal sweetbreads or delicate apple tart with rhubarb ice cream. The wines are selected with genuine flair (a striking Dard et Ribo Saint-Joseph) and the set menus are a gift. This is a haven for astute food lovers.

● Le Brespail ▪ SIM

Passage Saint-Bernard,
159, rue du Faubourg-Saint-Antoine
Métro: Ledru-Rollin
Tel. 01 43 41 99 13
lebrespail@free.fr
Closed Sunday, Christmas. Open until 11 PM.
Terrace. Private dining room.
Prix fixe: 12€ (lunch), 14€ (lunch), 35€ (dinner). A la carte: 43€.

Southwestern French cuisine is generous, as the guests here know. Those on a diet will have to put it on hold, for one meal at least. It is impossible to resist the carpaccio of fresh foie gras, thick smoked duck breast with foie gras, lamb chops, soft chocolate cake and rhubarb and raspberry tart. Marie Levayer is well aware of this and serves up substantial portions.

● Le C'Amelot ▪ SIM

50, rue Amelot
Métro: Chemin-Vert
Tel. 01 43 55 54 04. Fax 01 43 14 77 03
Closed Saturday lunch, Sunday,
Monday lunch, August. Open until 10:30 PM.
Prix fixe: 17€ (lunch), 24€ (lunch),
32€ (dinner).

Formerly at the Crillon, Didier Varnier took over this little dive and turned it into one of the district's most prized restaurants. We like his slapdash decor (stainless-steel tables, straw-bottomed chairs, mismatched plates), good-natured ambience and excellent dishes with all the flavor of simplicity. We just cannot get enough of the green asparagus braised in chicken broth, roasted cod with aromatic vegetables, eggplant caviar, lamb shoulder cannelloni with Italian parsley and almond crème brûlée with cane sugar and cherry compote.

● Cartet ▪ SIM

62, rue de Malte
Métro: République, Oberkampf
Tel. 01 48 05 17 65
Closed Saturday, Sunday, August.
Open until 9:30 PM.
A la carte: 45–55€.

The Nouailles would like us to leave them in peace and just forget about their *bouchon*-style restaurant, reserved for a select few. However, their tenacious defense of traditional pleasures and retro ambience makes it hard for us to keep their little lair a secret. Assorted charcuteries and pâtés, organ meats and wayward dishes vie for our attention, including mutton feet with a thickened lemon, parsley and butter sauce, lentils with sausage, poached beef and bugnes (traditional Lyonnaise doughnuts). A gourmet hideout.

● **Chardenoux** 🔨 SIM

1, rue Jules-Vallès
Métro: Charonne, Faidherbe-Chaligny
Tel. 01 43 71 49 52. Fax 01 43 71 80 89
Open daily until 10:30 PM.
A la carte: 55€.
Terrace.

The Belle Epoque–style of this hundred-year-old bistro is still intact, with mirrors, ceiling painted with clouds and sky and rococo Fallières bar. After his time at Chez Francis, Philippe Roche took over and has breathed new life into this place. Recently promoted to the kitchen, Lydie Dupraz offers her take on a classic menu, including foie gras terrine with gingerbread, duck terrine with figs, codfish with aïoli, lamb stew with baby vegetables, raspberry millefeuille and jasmine crème brûlée. The cellar is well stocked and you will have no trouble finding the right wine to quench your thirst among its treasures.

A SPECIAL FAVORITE

● **Le Chateaubriand** 🏠🍴🔨 SIM

129, av Parmentier
Métro: Goncourt
Tel.-Fax 01 43 57 45 95
Closed Saturday lunch, Sunday, Monday.
Open until 11 PM.
Prix fixe: 13€ (lunch), 30€ (dinner),
36€ (dinner). A la carte: 40€.
Terrace.

We first came across him at La Famille in the eighteenth arrondissement and immediately made him a Special Favorite. Inaki Aizpitarte, the Bounding Basque, has been out in the suburbs, advising a modern art museum and its gourmet restaurant (Le Transversal) and still finding time to successfully take this 1900s'-style bistro in hand, together with his pal Frédéric Peneau, formerly at Café Burq. The two have changed the lights, kept the banquettes, slapped on a cheerful coat of yellow paint and above all brought a new spirit to the place, speeding up its transformation. So here it is, the new wave of gourmet bistro—very 21st century, with an eye to its roots.

The lunchtime option at 13€ for two courses hits the spot. Over the bar pass glasses of Gramenon (Poignée de Raisin), Foillard (Côtes de Py Morgon) and Dard et Ribo, a tribute to nature and the grape. The food is lively and fortifying, taking shrewd new approaches to traditional ideas. The first time we lunched here, the julienned cucumber with shredded smoked fish, the orange-infused veal stew, the banana compote with maple syrup and the chocolate mousse were resourceful indeed. Of course, there are also "luxury" items (wild Baltic salmon or the seared tuna with fork-mashed potatoes and salad), which can push up the tab (forgetting the rather dry Lomo pork loin). In the evening, prices soar and the food becomes showier, with mackerel ceviche with tabasco, seared tuna with asparagus and chorizo, sautéed veal medallions with Pompadour potatoes and pork belly with celery root and licorice. Watch your step: The set menu is at 36€ not including drinks, and the enticing bottles on the wine list can clean you out.

● **Cielo** ⒩ SIM

25, rue Oberkampf
Métro: Oberkampf
Tel.-Fax 01 48 06 28 23
Open daily until midnight.
Prix fixe: 14€ (lunch). A la carte: 32€.

Exit Le Vin de Zinc, replaced by the Cielo with its blackjack table and fusion cuisine from Guillaume Cara. New boss Guillaume Pierre is a keen host. A little refurbishment has given this cheerful haunt a whole new look, with ochre walls and contemporary art. The cheerfully modish menu offers surprises: Magali gazpacho, artichokes with mozzarella, Asian noodles with satay sauce, blue-cheese hamburger, rib-eye steak with parsley, garlic and butter and tiramisu with red berries.

● Le Clown Bar 🛖 SIM

114, rue Amelot
Métro: Filles-du-Calvaire
Tel. 01 43 55 87 35. Fax 01 43 55 38 20
www.clown-bar.fr
Closed Sunday lunch, 2 weeks in August.
Open until midnight.
Prix fixe: 13,50€ (lunch), 25€ (dinner).
A la carte: 35€.
Terrace.

A step away from the Cirque d'Hiver, Joël Vitte's (registered historic) bistro is appealing indeed with its clownish decor, a menu touting timeless classics and attentive service. We happily set off around the ring to savor œufs meurette (eggs poached in red wine, with bacon and onions), green salad with crispy phyllo-wrapped saint-marcellin cheese, cod brandade, spice-encrusted pork medallions and Valrhona Guanaja melted-chocolate cake. Loire, Alsace and Rhône Valley wines accompany this gentle spread.

● Les Crâneuses Ⓝ ⊜ SIM

72 bis, rue J.-P.-Timbaud
Métro: Parmentier
Tel. 01 47 00 37 59
Closed lunch, Sunday, Christmas, New Year's, 2 weeks in August. Open until 2 AM.
A la carte: 25€.

This amiable feminine bistro offers a smiling welcome, shrewd, mainly organic wines and impeccable Meurdesoif charcuterie, cheese from Le Lann and Olsen smoked fish. The two proprietresses, Corinne Blouch and Catherine Girardière, welcome guests and prepare the food.

● L'Ecailler du Bistrot 🚢 SIM

22, rue Paul-Bert
Métro: Faidherbe-Chaligny
Tel. 01 43 72 76 77. Fax 01 43 72 24 66
Closed Sunday, Monday, August.
Open until 11 PM.
Prix fixe: 16€ (lunch), 45€ (dinner).
A la carte: 49€.
Air cond.

Cadoret, a familiar name in the world of oyster farming, is the family name of Gwenaëlle, who runs this establishment, and her brother, who supplies her at the source in Riec-sur-Belon. The marennes, pleine mer and spéciales claires oysters provide a wide range of the best produce available. The catch comes from Guilvinec, and we find ourselves caught up in a veritable festival of marine flavors when the tuna tartare, duo of fresh crab with avocado, fresh shellfish platter and brill (a delicate fish similar to turbot) arrive. To finish, the delicious thinly sliced apples with salted butter caramel really hits the mark. The Loire wines follow naturally and the marine decor with its gleaming woodwork forms a suitable background for this oceanic repast.

● Les Fernandises COM

19, rue de la Fontaine-au-Roi
Métro: République, Goncourt
Tel. 01 48 06 16 96
Closed Saturday lunch, Sunday.
Open until midnight.
Prix fixe: 13€ (lunch), 15€ (lunch), 18€ (dinner). A la carte: 33€.

Sister and brother Anne and François Crespo, natives of Southwest France, have breathed new life into this cheerful local bistro. The walls have acquired a touch of color (sponge-painted ochre shades), as has the food, which works with sunny flavors and regional produce to provide some delightful culinary moments. We take pleasure in sautéed escargots, calamari with parsley, garlic and butter, Basque-style tuna, duck breast served with potatoes sautéed in duck fat, verbena-perfumed pork medallions with a tomato cake and crème brûlée with raspberries and thyme. We are also agreeably surprised by the skillfully chosen wines from small growers.

● La Galoche d'Aurillac 🛖 SIM

41, rue de Lappe
Métro: Bastille
Tel. 01 47 00 77 15
www.lagalochedaurillac.com
Closed Monday. Open until 11:30 PM.
Prix fixe: 25€, 35€ (wine included).

The Bonnets' Auvergnat inn contrasts with the fashionable bars of rue de Lappe. It is a genuine pleasure to sit down here under the hanging clogs, hams, traditional musical instruments and farming implements, and taste authentic produce, such as the Auvergnat salad, veal breast stuffed with bacon and vegetables, goose confit with Guérande salt, truffade (layered, fried potato pancake with bacon and Cantal cheese), aligot (mashed potatoes with tomme cheese and garlic) and pounti (pork loaf that typically includes Swiss chard or spinach and prunes), not to mention the sweet treats that form the delightful conclusion with old-fashioned Bing cherries or prunes stewed in wine. A reinvigorating rustic break.

● Les Jumeaux

73, rue Amelot
Métro: St-Sébastien-Froissart
Tel.-Fax 01 43 14 27 00
lesjumeaux@noos.fr
Closed Saturday lunch, Sunday, Monday,
1 week Christmas–New Year's, 2 weeks in
August. Open until 10:30 PM.
Prix fixe: 20€, 30€. A la carte: 42€.

Helena Kryztofiak has taken over the Vandevelde brothers' establishment. Renovation work has smartened up the decor of this contemporary restaurant, mainly in brown and orange tones. At the stove, Frédéric Gillaizeau works with fine produce, combining classics with today's flavors. We have no complaints about the millefeuille with escargot and pig's feet, scallop parmentier with lobster sauce, English-style calf's liver with bacon, a caramelized custard with balsmaic vinegar and brioche pain perdu with vanilla ice cream and a caramel "dome" with cinnamon. The jazz ambience is relaxing and the cellar correctly stocked.

● Le Marsangy

73, av Parmentier
Métro: Parmentier, St-Ambroise
Tel.-Fax 01 47 00 94 25
Closed Saturday lunch, Sunday, 2 weeks
Christmas–New Year's, 2 weeks Easter,
2 weeks in August. Open until 10:30 PM.
Prix fixe: 22€.
Air cond.

Francis Bonfillou, who formerly officiated at the Concorde Lafayette under Joël Robuchon, has turned this restaurant into a gourmet haunt. His produce is rigorously selected and deftly prepared. In the dining room, with its old-fashioned pink hues, slates and mirrors, we enjoy the duck confit terrine with foie gras, sea bass filet with white beans in cream, lamb filet with eggplant caviar and chocolate fondant with basil. The cellar, boasting at least a hundred items, pays tribute to Burgundy. The service is prompt and attentive, and the prices behave themselves.

● Mélac

42, rue Léon-Frot
Métro: Charonne
Tel. 01 40 09 93 37. Fax 01 43 70 73 10
melac@bistrot-melac.com
www.melac.fr
Closed Sunday, Monday, Christmas,
Easter, August. Open until 10:30 PM.
Prix fixe: 14,50€ (lunch on weekdays).
A la carte: 27€.
Air cond. Terrace.

Mélac senior, who left the Aveyron region for Paris, opened this cheerful bistro more than sixty years ago. Originally called Le Palais du Bon Vin, it was taken over in 1977 by his son Jacques, who decided to add solid fare to the liquid refreshments. Since then, patrons have delighted in its succulent food and delicious nectars. In the evening, Guillaume Brachet is happy to prepare us eggs baked in ramekins, savory sausage cakes, lamb chops with mashed potatoes with tomme cheese and garlic and mutton tripe. Jacques has been producing his own wine for three years now, a Corbières named Domaine des Trois Filles, which he presses from the fruit of the five acres he owns near Lézignan. There is no fuss or ceremony here: The atmosphere is good natured, diners move over to make room for newcomers and, with the help of the wine and ambience, you will soon find yourself chatting with your neighbor.

● La Muse Vin   SIM

101, rue de Charonne
Métro: Charonne
Tel.-Fax 01 40 09 93 05
lamusevin@free.fr
www.lamusevin.com
Closed Sunday. Open until 11 PM.
Prix fixe: 25€ (dinner), 30€ (dinner), 10€ (lunch, wine included), 14€ (lunch).
Terrace.

Guillaume Dubois and Guillaume Dupré both nurture a passion for wine. After their time at the Verre Volé and Chez Ramulaud, they founded this bistro dedicated to the fruit of the grape. The dining room has been recently enlarged and is now more comfortable for patrons enjoying the dishes prepared by Dubois and Nicolas Pailhes. Cooked and raw foie gras with seaweed, skate encrusted with hazelnuts, pork chops with watercress mousse and poached spiced-pear tart meet the same high standards as the 350 wines in the cellar, among them Dard et Ribo Crozes, Baux Clos Milan and a sparkling Corsican. We also appreciate Guillaume Dupré's highly attentive service and knowledgeable advice.

● Paris Main d'Or   SIM

133, rue du Faubourg-Saint-Antoine
Métro: Ledru-Rollin, Faidherbe-Chaligny
Tel.-Fax 01 44 68 04 68
Closed Sunday. Open until 11 PM.
Prix fixe: 12€ (lunch). A la carte: 31€.
Air cond. Terrace.

Jean-Jacques Raffiani has created a discreet Corsican haunt here, after Le Vivario in rue Cochin. The colors glow and the menu tends toward simplicity. We enjoy some truly epicurean moments with pastry turnover filled with meatballs and onions, stuffed sardines, Provençal lamb casserole and chestnut flour crêpes. The wines are from the Island of Beauty and we cannot resist a glass of Cap Corse Muscat or a Fiumicicoli red.

● Le Passage des   ●SIM
Carmagnoles

18, passage de la Bonne-Graine
Métro: Ledru-Rollin
Tel. 01 47 00 73 30. Fax 01 47 00 65 68
Closed Sunday evening. Open until 11:30 PM.
A la carte: 28€.
Air cond. Valet parking.

Antoine Toubia, an oenologist by training, has acquired this little local bistro where he can share his passion for wine with passing aficionados. Just visit the cellar and take a glance at the labels, and you will realize he does not do things by halves. To enhance our enjoyment of these precious elixirs, he also provides for other appetites. What could be more convincing than the escargot in puff pastry shell, fish with curry spices, thinly sliced beef with spices, andouillette AAAAA and chocolate fondant?

● Chez Paul   🔨SIM

13, rue de Charonne (at rue de Lappe)
Métro: Bastille, Ledru-Rollin
Tel. 01 47 00 34 57. Fax 01 48 07 02 00
chezpaul@noos.fr
Open daily until 12:30 AM.
A la carte: 31€.
Terrace. Private dining room.

The patina in this Twenties' bistro is genuine. With its old-fashioned charm, the setting is a popular one, and the sensibly priced classics cannot be faulted. The bone marrow with toast, stuffed hard-boiled eggs, salmon filet with sorrel, steak tartare with sautéed potatoes, crème caramel and chocolate charlotte are simple but excellent. A special mention for the service, which is charming and attentive despite the crowds of tourists that fill the place.

● La Plancha ⓃⒺ SIM

34, rue Keller
Métro: Ledru-Rollin, Bastille, Voltaire
Tel. 01 48 05 20 30
Closed Sunday, Monday, 1 week
Christmas–New Year's, 3 weeks in August.
Open until 1:30 AM.
A la carte: 30€.
Air cond.

From aperitif time to late at night, Hervé and Patrice's tiny establishment never empties. Aficionados of tapas and pinxos served up in a highly charged bodega ambience gather here in a decor dedicated to the Basque country, over the fried squid, stuffed peppers, grilled tuna, lamb steak cooked to order and cakes (Basque, of course).

● Les Portes SIM

15, rue de Charonne
Métro: Bastille, Ledru-Rollin
Tel. 01 40 21 70 61
lesportes@wanadoo.fr
www.lesportes.fr
Open daily until midnight.
Prix fixe: 12€ (lunch on weekdays),
27€, 35€. A la carte: 45€.
Terrace. Private dining room.

There has been a never-ending succession of proprietors and chefs in this establishment, but fortunately the cuisine is as conscientious as ever. On the first floor, refurbished in chocolate tones, or in the newly opened basement, the duck breast carpaccio with porcini mushroom oil, sea bass with a sorrel beurre blanc, pepper-encrusted filet of beef flambéed with cognac and roasted figs with red berries offer subtle new approaches to domestic classics.

● Le Pure Café SIM

14, rue Jean-Macé
Métro: Faidherbe-Chaligny, Charonne
Tel.-Fax 01 43 71 47 22.
Closed Christmas Eve, Christmas,
New Year's Eve. Open until 11:30 PM.
Prix fixe: 11€ (lunch). A la carte: 40€.
Terrace.

On tables bathed in light around a fine, horseshoe-shaped bar, this old corner bistro offers contemporary dishes featuring original, often winning combinations. The tuna roll with pesto and avocado ice cream, grilled sesame squid with rhubarb compote over spiced bulgur wheat, lamb shank with artichoke tartare and dark chocolate spring rolls are not bad. The service is alert and the prices not too pompous.

● Chez Ramulaud 🍴 SIM

269, rue du Faubourg-Saint-Antoine
Métro: Faidherbe-Chaligny, Nation
Tel. 01 43 72 23 29. Fax 01 43 72 57 03
Closed 1 week in December, 1 week in April.
Open until 11 PM.
Prix fixe: 16€ (lunch), 29€ (dinner).
A la carte: 40€.
Air cond. Terrace.

Market-based dishes, a vintage bistro setting, a personalized welcome and floods of bottles (the cellar numbers nearly 350 vintages) are the arguments in favor of this restaurant, run by the mischievous Gilles Bénard, who has a gift for putting people at their ease. Here we sometimes meet movie director Cédric Klapisch or actor Jean-Pierre Darroussin, who, like us, delight in the fricassée of baby artichokes and langoustines, filet of pageot (a type of sea bream) with hibiscus jus, eggplant compote, oxtail crumble, calf's feet with foie gras and sautéed cherries with black pepper and lemon mousse.

● La Ravigote Ⓔ SIM

41, rue de Montreuil
Métro: Faidherbe-Chaligny, Rue-des-Boulets
Tel.-Fax 01 43 72 96 22
Closed Saturday evening, Sunday, August.
Open until 10:30 PM.
Prix fixe: 13€ (lunch), 18€ (dinner).
Air cond.

The name heralds the house specialty: the sauce ravigote (thick vinaigrette sauce with white wine, shallots and herbs), which accompanies the calf's head. Pierre Fava prepares it to perfection and has other practiced tricks up his sleeve, which we enjoy discovering, such as the preserved pork liver terrine, head cheese, grilled sea bass with fennel, duck fricasée, paris-brest (crown-shaped choux pastry filled with praliné butter cream and topped with chopped almonds) and the chocolate cake. His wines from Southwest France are impressive. It is not hard to work out why this highly colorful establishment has been packing in patrons for more than 35 years.

● Le Réfectoire   SIM

80, bd Richard-Lenoir
Métro: Richard-Lenoir
Tel. 01 48 06 74 85. Fax 01 48 06 74 61
Closed 1 week in August. Open until 11 PM.
Prix fixe: 10€ (lunch), 14€ (lunch), 17€
(lunch). A la carte: 38€.
Air cond. Terrace.

After the success of La Famille in Montmartre, Patrick and Yannig Famot decided to open a sibling: this Réfectoire near Bastille. The ambience is just as electric, the clientele fashionable, the service unfussy and the cuisine modern. Add to that a shrewd selection of wines in the cellar and you can see why it deserves a visit. The cuttlefish with veal kidneys, stewed rabbit with dried fruit, crisp tuna with basil, free-range chicken breast with Campari contribute to the festival of flavors changing daily on the blackboard. The decor is from the Seventies, in red, white and black, seasoned with colorful frescos. Brunch on Sunday.

● Le Repaire de Cartouche   COM

8, bd des Filles-du-Calvaire
Métro: St-Sébastien–Froissart,
Filles-du-Calvaire
Tel. 01 47 00 25 86. Fax 01 43 38 85 91
Closed Sunday, Monday, 1 week in February,
1 week in May, August. Open until 11 PM.
Prix fixe: 16€ (lunch on weekdays), 25€
(lunch on weekdays). A la carte: 40€.

This timeless inn with its rustic surroundings and old-fashioned charm owes its name to the famous, hotheaded bandit Cartouche, who is said to have frequented the place. Is that why the restaurant has

two entrances? In any case, Rodolphe Paquin, the current master of the house, reserves a warm welcome and a tempting menu for his guests. This staunch Norman concocts generous dishes, including the cold purée of peas with country ham, steamed hake filet with tomatoes, lemon confit and olive oil, the veal sautéed until golden with fava beans, roasted pigeon with baby vegetables and soft chocolate cake with cream. The menu changes to reflect the produce on offer at the market, and the cellar is well stocked.

● Au Rond-Point   € SIM

65-67, bd de Ménilmontant
Métro: Père-Lachaise
Tel. 01 40 21 13 35. Fax 01 40 21 13 39
aurondpoint@aurondpoint.com
www.aurondpoint.com
Closed Christmas. Open 11 AM–10 PM.
Prix fixe: 12,90€, 23€ (wine included),
7,50€ (children, with beverage).
A la carte: 29€.
Air cond. Terrace. Private dining room.

Opposite Père Lachaise cemetery, this neo–art nouveau brasserie offers classic dishes all day long, with a special eye to the regions. The warm Lyonnaise sausage with pistachios, salmon steak braised in beer with Puy lentils, honey-roasted duck breast with rhubarb compote, Salers beef rib-eye steak with potatoes and cantal cheese and chocolate fondant are meticulously executed and sensibly priced.

● Les Sans-Culottes   SIM

27, rue de Lappe
Métro: Bastille
Tel. 01 48 05 42 92. Fax 01 48 05 08 56
hotel.lessansculottes@wanadoo.fr
www.lessansculottes.com
Closed Monday. Open until 11:30 PM.
Prix fixe: 23€. A la carte: 55€.
Terrace. Private dining room.

Despite its name, this traditional hotel is not in the least revolutionary. Its great, typically French standards are performed from a very familiar score with never a false note. The stuffed salmon timbale, beggar's purse of pike-perch with foie gras, sweetbreads with chanterelle mushrooms and pears poached in muscat wine with sabayon are reliability itself, but the prices are not for the downtrodden masses.

● Le Sofa SIM

21, rue Saint-Sabin
Métro: Bastille, Bréguet-Sabin
Tel. 01 43 14 07 46
contact@lesofa.com
www.lesofa.com
Closed lunch, Sunday, Monday.
Open until 11 PM.
Prix fixe: 19€ (dinner). A la carte: 31€.
Air cond.

With its patinated red walls, the azuleijos that decorate the bar and a menu tending toward foreign flavors, the Sofa is a voyage in itself. Cidalia Alvès, a young woman of Portuguese origin who used to live in the United States, regales her guests with a millefeuille with green apples and smoked haddock, salmon baked in pastry crust perfumed with spices, saddle of rabbit with black-olive paste and citrus fruit in a verbena-infused broth. French and Portuguese wines.

● Le Sot l'y Laisse SIM

70, rue Alexandre-Dumas
Métro: Alexandre-Dumas, Avron
Tel.-Fax 01 40 09 79 20
Closed Sunday, Monday, 1 week
Christmas–New Year's, August.
Open until 10 PM.
Prix fixe: 13€ (lunch), 17€ (lunch).
A la carte: 36€.

How could we pass up the chance to taste the herbed langoustine soup, filet of sea bream with braised endive, pigeon with sautéed mushrooms or stewed peaches? Cyril Esneault, a veteran of Clos Longchamp and Maison Blanche, excels in the preparation of these choice dishes. He is a very amiably modest man and you will have a pleasant time in his pastel yellow bistro.

● Suds SIM

55, rue de Charonne
Métro: Ledru-Rollin
Tel. 01 43 14 06 36. Fax 01 47 00 37 40
www.suds.fr
Closed Saturday, Sunday lunch, Monday.
Open until 11 PM.
Prix fixe: 9,90€ (lunch), 19€ (dinner).
A la carte: 35€.
Air cond. Terrace. Private dining room.

Jérôme Lagarde's restaurant sets the tone with its palm trees and red and orange hues: We are heading south and the ambience is "muy caliente," fired by the intermixed flavors of a fusion menu. The foie gras with sweet potatoes, shark filet with spicy tomato chutney, mahi-mahi cooked in banana leaves, sugar-rubbed duck breast, Argentinean rib-eye steak and banana mousse with two chocolates all favorably impress. The wines are from the Rhône Valley, Roussillon, Argentina, Chile and Australia. A cocktail full of vitality with energy to spare. Invigorating.

● La Table de Claire Ⓝ COM

30, rue Emile-Lepeu
Métro: Charonne
Tel.-Fax 01 43 70 59 84
latabledeclaire@wanadoo.fr
Closed Sunday, Monday, Tuesday, August.
Open until 10:30 PM.
Prix fixe: 13€ (lunch), 16€ (lunch).
A la carte: 45€.
Terrace.

Before reaching retirement age, Serge and Claire Haguenauer left the cutthroat world of advertising to open this establishment on a bend in a back street of the eleventh arrondissement. Their excellent initiative enables locals and visitors to enjoy the peaceful surroundings in this old-fashioned bistro, its selected wines and especially Claire's cuisine *bonne femme*. Unaccountably sure of touch, this self-taught cook shrewdly whips up parsleyed ham terrine, sautéed squid with peppers, calf's liver and blanc-manger with berry coulis.

● **Le Temps au Temps** 🎦 SIM
13, rue Paul-Bert
Métro: Faidherbe-Chaligny
Tel.-Fax 01 43 79 63 40
Closed Sunday, Monday, 10 days
Christmas–New Year's, August.
Open until 10:30 PM.
Prix fixe: 12€ (lunch), 14€ (lunch),
16€ (lunch), 28€ (dinner). A la carte: 36€.
Terrace.

Its facade brightened by red shutters, a visit to this pocket bistro definitely ought not to be rushed. Take your time savoring the dishes prepared by Lyon's Sylvain Sendra. The crisp calf's head with foie gras vinaigrette, Mediterranean red tuna with green asparagus and fresh peas, risotto with pig's feet and morel mushrooms and white chocolate ice cream "cappuccino" with a coffee emulsion all point to a perfect mastery of his art. Add fine bottles, such as the Foillard Côte de Py Morgon or bio-dynamically produced wines—the Quartz 2003 from Courtois, for instance—and you have the ideal recipe for a very special meal in a unique setting.

● **La Vache Acrobate** €⃝ SIM
77, rue Amelot
Métro: St-Sébastien-Froissart
Tel. 01 47 00 49 42. Fax 01 47 00 49 09
www.lavacheacrobate.com
Closed Saturday lunch, Sunday.
Open until 11 PM.
Prix fixe: 13,50€ (lunch on weekdays),
15,50€ (weekday lunch, wine included).
A la carte: 30€.
Terrace.

This acrobatic cow has landed on its feet. Its circus act has been polished to perfection by Laurent Helly and Frédéric Ramel, who run their restaurant with great energy. The service is good humored and the dishes overflow with sunshine, their glow inspired by Provence and the Southwest. The potato terrine, tuna steak with pesto, grilled salt and pepper steak or tiramisu are accompanied by fine wines by the glass. The decor is full of color and the ambience relaxed.

● **Au Vieux Chêne** 🎦 SIM
7, rue du Dahomey
Métro: Faidherbe-Chaligny
Tel. 01 43 71 67 69.
Closed Saturday lunch, Sunday,
Christmas–New Year's, 1 week at Easter,
end of July–mid-August.
Open until 10:30 PM.
Prix fixe: 13€ (lunch), 29€ (dinner).
A la carte: 45€.
Air cond. Terrace.

One of our better finds in the district. This old bistro with its patinated counter and whitewashed walls fills lovers of spirited, mischievous cuisine with delight. Concocted by Stéphane Chevassus, the Sot l'y Laisse veteran trained by Rostang, Cagna and Savoy, the oxtail medallion with potatoes and andouille sausage, monkfish with lentils and a shellfish cream sauce, quail filet and thigh with green asparagus and dried tomatoes and the strawberries and rhubarb with almond cream are washed down with highly impressive, shrewd little wines.

● **Le Villaret** ◯ SIM
13, rue Ternaux
Métro: Parmentier
Tel. 01 43 57 89 76
Closed Saturday lunch, Sunday,
Christmas–New Year's, August.
Open until midnight.
Prix fixe: 22€ (lunch), 27€ (lunch),
52€ (dinner). A la carte: 52€.
Air cond.

This ageless bistro has stood up well to the tests of time and fashion without losing its soul or allowing its style to grow stale. The rustic stone and wood are a foil to the precision of dishes appealingly orchestrated by Olivier Gaslain, who has an eye to both tradition and innovation. We are both reassured and pleasantly surprised by the cold cream of tarbais bean soup, langoustine tails with dried tomatoes and crushed avocado, Breton John Dory fish baked in the oven with wild asparagus and caramelized garlic, sweetbreads encrusted with gingerbread with baby artickoes and tender potatoes or pineapple and mango ice ice cream sundae with coconut cream and aged rum ice cream. The cellar has plenty of ideas and, in the dining room, Joël Homel is gratifyingly attentive and friendly to a fault.

● Vin et Marée `COM`

276, bd Voltaire
Métro: Nation, Rue-des-Boulets
Tel. 01 43 72 31 23. Fax 01 40 24 00 23
vin-et-maree@wanadoo.fr
www.vin-et-maree.com
Open daily until 10:30 PM.
Prix fixe: 18,50€, 24,50€.
A la carte: 50€.
Air cond. Terrace. Private dining room.
Valet parking.

With its four restaurants in Paris, the legendary Vin et Marée can pride itself on its continuing success. Its secret? A daily delivery of supremely fresh produce from Breton or Norman boats, simply prepared with all its taste intact. Naturally, the menu changes daily depending on the catch. The dishes include grilled sardines with Guérande salt, a croustillant of jumbo shrimp, grilled sole with citrus butter or codfish. Diehard meat eaters can tear into a chateaubriand and sweet-toothed gourmets will adore the celebrated Zanzibar baba au rhum.

INTERNATIONAL RESTAURANTS

● Mansouria ○`COM`

11, rue Faidherbe
Métro: Faidherbe-Chaligny
Tel. 01 43 71 00 16. Fax 01 40 24 21 97
Closed Sunday, Monday lunch, Tuesday lunch, 1 week in mid-August. Open until 11 PM.
Prix fixe: 30€, 46€. A la carte: 45€.
Air cond. Terrace. Private dining room.

A native of Oujda, former ethnologist Fatema Hal has always been keen to share her taste for "Cooking Connections", and that is exactly what she does at her restaurant, in her books and more recently with her own grocery brand. Newcomers or regulars, she welcomes her customers like old friends in the four dining rooms decorated in Moorish style. Whether we are there to

taste her cuisine for the first time or enjoy its familiar pleasures for the umpteenth, we never fail to wonder at its tremendous refinement and sweetness. Among the essential dishes here, we should mention the flaky phyllo pastry stuffed with roasted pigeon, the mourouzia (a slowly simmered lamb stew flavored with 27 different spices), the chicken tagine with walnut-stuffed figs, the puff pastry filled with custard and the sliced oranges with orange blossoms.

▼ SHOPS

KITCHENWARE & TABLETOP

▼ Le Fiacre

24, bd des Filles-du-Calvaire
Métro: Filles-du-Calvaire, St-Sébastien– Froissart
Tel. 01 43 57 15 50
www.lefiacreanglais.com
www.lefiacreanglais.com
10 AM–1 PM, 2–7 PM. Closed Sunday, Monday, 3 weeks in August.
Dishes for children, English porcelain (Beatrix Potter, Mason's, Burleigh, Wedgwood and Minton), attractive teapots and fragrances for the home coexist happily in this British shop.

BREAD & BAKED GOODS

▼ L'Autre Boulange

43, rue de Montreuil
Métro: Faidherbe-Chaligny
Tel.-Fax 01 43 72 86 04
7:30 AM–1:30 PM, 3:30–7:30 PM.
Closed Saturday afternoon, Sunday, Monday, August.
Michel Cousin uses a wood oven to cook various walnut and bacon breads, thin baguettes, organic and country-style breads. Regional pastries (tarte Tatin, Breton pudding-cake with figs, Alsatian tart) are attractive indeed.

▼ Au Levain du Marais 🏠

28, bd Beaumarchais / 142 av Parmentier
Métro: Bastille, Chemin-Vert, Goncourt
Tel.-Fax 01 48 05 17 14 / 01 43 57 36 91
7 AM–8 PM. Closed Tuesday, Wednesday,
Sunday, Monday (av. Parmentier),
Christmas, New Year's Day.

Thierry Rabineau, who has opened other stores across Paris, has turned these two fine establishments into attractive bastions indeed. Baguettes, country loaf, focaccia, Viennese pastries, vanilla cake baked in fluted molds are prepared with care. The pastries (royal, paris-brest, délice du Marais, millefeuille) are just delicious. (Also see the third and ninth arrondissements.)

WINE

▼ Caves de la Nation 🏠

55, av Philippe-Auguste
Métro: Nation, Rue-des-Boulets
Tel. 01 43 71 08 04. Fax 01 43 71 14 33
9:30 AM–1 PM, 3–8 PM.
Closed Sunday afternoon, Monday.

This magnificent 1920s' cellar brings together a fascinating selection of Languedoc, Burgundy, Champagne and Rhône Valley wines. Among other delights, Jean-Noël Lemière enthusiastically presents a collection of honorable whiskeys, Armagnacs, cognacs and selected eaux de vie.

CHARCUTIERIE

▼ Ronceret

138, rue de la Roquette
Métro: Voltaire
Tel.-Fax 01 43 79 71 19
8 AM–1:15 PM, 4–8 PM (Friday, Saturday
8 AM–8 PM). Closed Sunday afternoon,
Monday, 3 weeks in August.

Philippe Ronceret deftly prepares head cheese or country pâté, garlic sausage, black or white truffled boudin, cured ham shank, pink cooked ham, hand-made andouillette, all of high quality. The head cheese won a bronze medal in 2006.

GROCERIES

▼ Alicante

26, bd Beaumarchais
Métro: Bastille, Chemin-Vert
Tel.-Fax 01 43 55 13 02
10 AM–1 PM, 2–7 PM.
Closed Sunday, 2 weeks in June.

This cutesy store specializes in oils: winter squash seed, pistachio, argan, plum kernel oil. Also safflower oil, recommended to counter the ageing process.

▼ Andraud 🏠

12, rue de la Roquette
Métro: Bastille
Tel. 01 47 00 59 07
10:15 AM–6:45 PM. Closed Sunday,
Monday, 10 July–end of August.

A step away from the Bastille, this establishment (almost a hundred years old) presents excellent candies, nougats, honeys, jams, chocolates, cognacs, whiskeys and other assorted delights.

PASTRIES

▼ Pâtisserie Demoulin

6, bd Voltaire
Métro: République, Oberkampf
Tel. 01 47 00 58 20. Fax 01 47 00 72 33
www.chocolat-paris.com
8:30 AM–7:30 PM (Sunday :
8 AM–1:30 PM, 3–7 PM).
Closed Monday, end of July–end of August.

Philippe Demoulin, as fine a chocolate maker as he is an expert pastry cook, carefully prepared chocolate ganaches with Earl Grey, rum, licorice and passion fruit. The chocolate mousse made with Valrhona Guanduja chocolate, his Montélimar nougat, lemon madeleines, kirsch cream, macarons and mendiant (mixture of figs, almonds, hazelnuts, and raisins) or chocolate truffles will overcome your resolve on the spot.

REGIONAL PRODUCTS

▼ Aux Produits d'Auvergne

6, rue de Lappe
Métro: Bastille
Tel.-Fax 01 47 00 41 28
9:30 AM–1 PM, 4–8 PM. Closed Sunday,
Monday, August.

Since 1931, this store has provided pork rillettes, almond cookies, boudin, preserved
poultry and meats, as well as cantal, saint
nectaire and tomme cheeses, along with
wine and liqueurs made in the Auvergne.

◆ RENDEZVOUS

BARS

◆ Boca Chica

58, rue de Charonne
Métro: Ledru-Rollin
Tel. 01 43 57 93 13. Fax 01 43 57 04 08
labocachica@labocachica.com
10:30 AM–2 AM (Friday, Saturday 5 AM).
Closed Sunday.
Air cond. Terrace.

A step away from the Bastille, this bodega
is a public forum with a Latino ambience.
Tapas, chili con carne, grilled cod, paella
are washed down with mojitos and sangria
in a setting straight out of Almodovar.

◆ Havanita Café

11-15, rue de Lappe
Métro: Bastille
Tel. 01 43 55 96 42. Fax 01 43 55 96 19
5 PM (4 PM Saturday and Sunday)–2 AM.
Closed Christmas.
Air cond.

This cocktail bar is also a restaurant offering Cuban and South American specialties.
Patrons savor stuffed crab or veal simmered in coconut milk and sip mojitos and
daiquiris at any hour.

◆ Le Réservoir

16, rue de la Forge-Royale
Métro: Ledru-Rollin, Faidherbe-Chaligny
Tel. 01 43 56 39 60. Fax 01 43 56 31 73
lereservoir@free.fr
www.reservoirclub.com
8 PM–2 AM (Friday, Saturday 5 AM;
Sunday 11:30 AM & 2 PM: jazz brunch).
Closed 2 weeks in August.
Air cond.

This former textile warehouse is worth a
visit: The highly successful decor employs
an Italian Renaissance style. We enjoy the
electro-jazz on Sunday.

WINE BARS

◆ Le Café du Passage

12, rue de Charonne
Métro: Ledru-Rollin, Bastille
Tel. 01 49 29 97 64
lecafedupassage@aol.com
6 PM (Saturday noon)–2 AM.
Closed Bank Holidays.

This comfortable, cozy café offers more
than 200 different wines. Wash down the
risotto with porcini mushrooms, fresh
mozzarella with basil or fruit crumble with
a vintage by the glass.

◆ Le Macassar

112, bd Richard Lenoir
Métro: Oberkampf, Parmentier
Tel. 01 47 00 24 77
7 AM–midnight. Closed 3 weeks in August.

Selected quality wines to taste by the glass
on the premises and take away "if you enjoyed them": That is the program at this
fashionably renovated, old-style café, with
its cheerful ambience and love of good
things. Polished light dishes, prepared with
care, appear on the blackboard and
change daily.

◆ La Muse Vin

101, rue de Charonne
Métro: Charonne
Tel. 01 40 09 93 05
lamusevin@free.fr
www.lamusevin.com
11 AM–11 PM. Closed Sunday.

Guillaume Dubois and Guillaume Dupré
serve their favorite wines for tasting at the

bar: Jo Landron Muscadet, Lemaire-Fournier Vouvray, Anne Godin Cahors and Jean Foillard Côte de Py Morgon. Do not leave without trying the good charcuterie or a delicious house dish. (Also see Restaurants.)

◆ Le Nouveau Nez

112, rue Saint-Maur
Métro: Parmentier, Rue-St-Maur
Tel.-Fax 01 43 55 02 30
aunouveaunez@yahoo.fr
3–9 PM. Closed Sunday,
Bank Holidays, August.

Nadine Decailly's list includes around fifty "natural" wines. At her two tables or on her eight stools, customers can taste her special favorite of the moment, nibbling charcuterie and cheeses while enthusiastically discovering, savoring and discussing the vintage.

CAFES

◆ L'Armagnac 🛖

104, rue de Charonne
Métro: Charonne
Tel. 01 43 71 49 43. Fax 01 46 59 12 24
www.pariszoom.com
7:30 AM (Saturday, Sunday 10 AM)–2 AM.
Closed Christmas.

This corner café is well worth a visit with its stucco, engraved glass, woodwork and counter. Come and have a snack or drink and engage in topical discussion in a timeless setting.

◆ Le Bistrot du Peintre 🛖

116, av Ledru-Rollin
Métro: Ledru-Rollin
Tel. 01 47 00 34 39. Fax 01 46 36 13 09
7 AM–2 AM (Sunday 9 AM–1 AM).
Closed Christmas.

Every day, this genuine art nouveau bistro with mirrors, banquettes and frescos draws the crowds. Patrons drink selected wines as they savor beef bourguignon, roasted rabbit, Salers beef rib-eye steak or crème caramel.

◆ Café Charbon 🛖

109, rue Oberkampf
Métro: Parmentier, Rue-St-Maur
Tel. 01 43 57 55 13. Fax 01 43 57 57 41
Open daily 9 AM–2 AM (Thursday, Friday, Saturday 4 AM).
Closed daytimes for 15 days in August.

Pleasant and relaxed, this 19th-century workmen's café with its large mirrors, counter, banquettes and frescos has a popular Parisian chic. Customers enjoy osso buco or tarte Tatin and meet over brunch.

◆ Café de l'Industrie 🛖

15, 16 and 17, rue Saint-Sabin
Métro: Bréguet-Sabin
Tel. 01 47 00 13 53. Fax 01 47 00 92 33
10 AM–2 AM. Closed Christmas, July 14th.

Having spread to the other side of the street (No. 15), this large café is seeing double. The welcome is charming; the atmosphere warm and companionable. Patrons enjoy solid dishes (pâté, lamb shank) and sandwiches in a Fifties setting featuring a maze of rooms and a terrace in the summer.

◆ Le Paris 🄝

24, bd Richard-Lenoir
Métro: Bréguet-Sabin
Tel. 01 47 00 87 47
7 AM–midnight (Sunday 6 PM). Open daily.

Baroque, both old and new, this café on the boulevard attracts hip young people from new wave Bastille for pleasant suppers, simple snacks and drinks of every kind in a timeless atmosphere.

◆ Pause Café

41, rue de Charonne
Métro: Ledru-Rollin
Tel. 01 48 06 80 33. Fax 01 43 57 63 78
7:30 AM–2 AM (Sunday 9 AM–8 PM).
Closed Christmas.
Terrace.

Appreciated by the local bohemian middle classes, especially since the filming of the movie *When the Cat's Away*, an ode to the eleventh arrondissement, this café allows you to laze around on the terrace and, at meal times, enjoy a duck breast with honey and creamy rice pudding.

◆ Le Petit Baïona

90, rue de Charonne
Métro: Charonne
Tel. 01 43 48 98 82. Fax 01 43 48 13 00
www.petitbaiona.com
7 AM–2 AM. Closed Christmas.

This Basque café presents the same dishes
they serve in Bayonne (octopus salad, tiny
eels, traditional Basque cake, pan-fried
young eel) accompanied by Irouléguy red.
Dedicated to rugby and soccer fans, it
shows games on a giant screen.

◆ Le Rouge Limé

167, bd Voltaire
Métro: Charonne
Tel. 01 43 73 45 55. Fax 01 45 31 22 06
elenebruel@free.fr
7 AM–2 AM. Open daily.

"Founded since it was established" says
the mischievous sign of this "old-new"
café immediately opposite Charonne
Métro station. The wines by the glass are
shrewd and the grilled open sandwiches
honest.

○	Very good restaurant
◎	Excellent restaurant
◎◎	One of the best restaurants in Paris
◍	Disappointing restaurant
◒	Good value for money
€	Meals for less than 30 euros
SIM	Simple
COM	Comfortable
V.COM	Very comfortable
LUX	Luxurious
V.LUX	Very luxurious

Red indicates a particularly charming establishment

▌	Historical significance
▲	Promotion *(higher rating than last year)*
Ⓝ	New to the guide
●	Restaurant
▼	Shop
◆	Rendezvous

12TH ARRONDISSEMENT
THE BERCY REVIVAL

The new twelfth arrondissement has a Bercy appeal. The wine warehouses have turned into chic bistros, tempting terraces and souvenir stores. CinéCité, Sofitel and the Palais des Sports are now the district's latest landmarks, close to the Seine. A new bridge leads to the thirteenth, Austerlitz and its rail station. Daumesnil is admittedly quieter, with its elegant provincial flavor, but on the outskirts, along the old railway viaduct that has been made over into an ecological park (the *coulée verte* or green streak), a different identity asserts itself: part bucolic, part urban. Fashionable restaurants, modish brasseries and lazy terraces form a delicious garland. On the horizon stand the bell tower of the Gare de Lyon (like its sibling in Limoges) and the Bastille column. The modern opera house is near, yet nearly distant. The twelfth's star restaurants (Au Trou Gascon, Le Quincy and L'Oulette) are inns imbued with the accents of rural France, while its more fashionable gourmet eateries (O'Rebelle, Sardegna a Tavola, La Pibale/Club 308) flaunt their modish charms. The new Bercy is like a provincial town. Its new alleys and the church looking out over its flock from place Lachambaudie all seem to be enclosed by modern spaces. However, true provincial France begins with the Foire du Trône carnival, out at Porte de Reuilly.

RESTAURANTS

GOOD RESTAURANTS & OTHERS

A SPECIAL FAVORITE

● L'Alchimiste 🏠🚇€ SIM
181, rue de Charenton
Métro: Montgallet, Reuilly-Diderot
Tel. 01 43 47 10 38
Closed Sunday, Monday, 3 weeks in August.
Open until 10:30 PM.
Prix fixe: 14€ (lunch), 18€ (lunch),
20€ (dinner), 25€ (dinner).

Jean-Michel Garby runs this tasteful bistro enthusiastically. It is an affable establishment with its beige tones and stenciled frieze, and the set menu with its various options is well thought out. Chef Marc Ranger plays an elegant, neoclassical score that hits the mark with its fine produce. The pan-seared foie gras with gingerbread, sweet onions and cinnamon apples, the gratin of Royans ravioli with saffron, the tuna and shrimp brochette with mashed vitelotte purple potatoes, the codfish "baked at the oven door" with bell pepper cream and the chorizo and duck confit baked in phyllo pastry do their jobs beautifully. A dark chocolate fondant with coffee-pecan sauce slips down effortlessly.

■ L'Auberge Aveyronnaise COM
40, rue Gabriel-Lamé
Métro: Cour-St-Emilion
Tel. 01 43 40 12 24. Fax 01 43 40 12 15
lesaubergistes@hotmail.fr
Closed Christmas, 2 weeks in beginning of
August. Open until 11:30 PM.
Prix fixe: 17,80€ (lunch), 19,40€ (dinner),
23,10€ (lunch), 24,60€ (dinner).
A la carte: 45€.
Air cond. Terrace. Private dining room.

The theme is the Aveyron, topical and timeless, just a step away from cour Saint Emilion in this modern inn. Although no one could accuse the decor of excessive warmth, Fabien Gayraud's cuisine is more congenial, with its pan-seared foie gras on creamy chestnut purée, salad of quail confit, pan-fried sea trout with hazelnuts and balsamic vinegar, grilled sausage with cheese-and-potato purée or shoulder of milk-fed lamb. The traditional-style millefeuille and the Valrhona chocolate charlotte are marvelous treats.

● A La Biche au Bois 🚇 SIM
45, av Ledru-Rollin
Métro: Gare-de-Lyon, Quai-de-la-Rapée,
Bastille
Tel. 01 43 43 34 38
Closed Saturday, Sunday, 1 week Christmas–
New Year's, July 25th–August 25th.
Open until 11 PM.
Prix fixe: 23,20€. A la carte: 38€.
Terrace.

We are fond of this firmly rooted rural inn near the Gare de Lyon, with more than just one foot in provincial France. Eric Broutin takes his cuisine seriously and to heart, the prices are sensible and Céline and Bertrand Marchesseau's welcome is civility itself. The homemade duck foie gras, country terrine, salmon with wild mushrooms, game in season (from September to March) and whole grilled veal kidney do you a world of good. The Opéra Biche (homemade chocolate Opéra cake with custard sauce) and seasonal fruit tart are polished desserts.

● Les Bombis Ⓝ SIM
22, rue de Chaligny
Métro: Reuilly-Diderot
Tel. 01 43 45 36 32
Noon–3 PM, 8 PM–10:30 PM.
Closed Saturday afternoon,
Sunday, Bank Holidays.
Terrace.

A wooden bar, varnished tables, banquettes, yellow walls, pleasant wines and refined dishes: All this awaits you here, with a relaxed ambience in the bargain. Depending on what the market provides, we savor the eggplant, goat cheese and country ham roll, the roasted rack of lamb au jus and crème brûlée. However, the place is mainly worth a visit for its decor.

● Café Barge `COM`

5, port de la Rapée
Métro: Gare-de-Lyon
Tel. 01 40 02 09 09. Fax 01 40 02 02 95
mls@cafebarge.com
www.cafebarge.com
Open daily until 2 AM.
Prix fixe: 26€ (lunch), 31€ (dinner),
33€ (lunch), 38€ (dinner).
Terrace. Private dining room. Valet parking.

Roland Bijaoui, who has dropped PR but not showbiz, has turned this former oil barge near the Ministry of Finance into a friendly haunt. Guests come to feast (modestly) on the set menu, which offers a cuisine that amiably follows fashion (but yesterday's on occasion). The foie gras poached in Madeira wine, eggplant charlotte, lobster fricassée flambéed with whiskey, grilled tuna with olive oil potato purée and spiced lamb shank with raisin couscous slip down easily. A good chocolate mousse.

● Café Ké `COM`

Sofitel Bercy, 1, rue de Libourne
Métro: Cour-St-Emilion
Tel. 01 44 67 34 71. Fax 01 44 67 34 01
H2192@accor-hotels.com
www.accor.com
Closed Saturday, 3 weeks in August.
Open until 10:30 PM.
Prix fixe: 25€, 27€, 33€.
Air cond. Terrace. Private dining room.
Valet parking.

This modern, cozy, paneled café is a welcoming place. Eric Sanchez, who worked at the Madrid Sofitel and the Dodin-Bouffant, presents an elegantly classical cuisine all week. The duck foie gras with citrus chutney, tomato tarte Tatin made with tomato confit and balsamic vinegar caramel, cod with asparagus and fresh peas, Dover sole with fork-mashed rattes potatoes, pork prepared three different ways—roasted, slow-cooked or salt-cured—are well chosen and deftly prepared. Interesting wines by the glass. Brunch on Sunday.

● Chai 33 `COM`

Bercy Village, 33, cour Saint-Emilion
Métro: Cour-St-Emilion
Tel. 01 53 44 01 01. Fax 01 53 44 01 02
info@chai33.com
www.chai33.com
Open daily until 11:45 PM (Monday, Sunday 11 PM; Friday–Saturday 12:30 AM).
Prix fixe: 15€, 21€. A la carte: 45€.
Air cond. Terrace.

Located in one of the old wine storehouses that formed the backbone of Bercy Village, Grégory Boubert's restaurant and cellar puts forward some serious arguments on the wine front, with 350 different vintages in stock. On the food side, there is plenty to satisfy gourmets. The dishes prepared by Alain Préault include the crispy chicken salad, tomato-basil "smoothie", roasted cod, tasty grilled flank steak, warm chocolate cake and strawberry millefeuille.

● Le Chalet du Lac `SIM`

At the edge of the bois de Vincennes
Métro: St-Mandé-Tourelle
Tel. 01 43 28 09 89. Fax 01 43 98 92 58
contact@chaletdulac.fr
www.chaletdulac.fr
Closed Monday. Open until 10:30 PM.
Prix fixe: 20€ (lunch). A la carte: 25–45€.
Air cond. Terrace. Private dining room.
Valet parking.

Take a break in this rustic chalet without putting your finances into the red. Its neo-art nouveau setting reconstructed on the edge of the woods has plenty of character. Guests enjoy the smoked salmon, salad with thinly sliced foie gras, grilled salmon with raw tomato and olive oil sauce, beef prime rib grilled on a wood fire and dark chocolate fondant with no fuss or frills. Dancing with a band and DJ every night from Wednesday to Sunday.

● . . . Comme Cochons `SIM`

135, rue de Charenton
Métro: Reuilly-Diderot
Tel. 01 43 42 43 36. Fax 01 53 33 04 23
www.commecochons.com
Open daily until 10:30 PM.
Prix fixe: 12€ (lunch), 15€ (lunch, wine included), 21€ (dinner), 35€ (dinner, wine included). A la carte: 35€.
Terrace.

The name is based on a French expression: "pals like pigs." The convivial dinners provided by Arnaud and Jean-Philippe Bonny and chef Jean-Michel Bourgouin in their colorful bistro are inevitably a success. The three hosts offer a genial welcome and the tempting menu lives up to its promises. Accompanied by a well-chosen wine, the eggplant millefeuille, sea bass grilled with fennel, oven-roasted ham hock and crème brûlée delight the food-loving guests.

● La Connivence `SIM`

1, rue de Cotte
Métro: Ledru-Rollin
Tel. 01 46 28 46 17. Fax 01 46 28 49 01
Closed Sunday, Monday, 2 weeks in August.
Open until 11 PM.
Prix fixe: 14€ (lunch), 17€ (lunch), 17€ (dinner), 25€ (dinner).
Air cond. Terrace.

Pascal Kosmala, from Bar le Duc in the Meuse district, formerly at the Gastrolâtre in Nancy, the Maison Kammerzell in Strasbourg and Schillinger in Colmar, has settled in this corner of the East of Paris. His cuisine is classical, subtle, flavorful and sensibly priced, and patrons have no trouble finding something to their taste in the prix fixe menus. The brioche stuffed with Burgundy snails in garlic cream, pikeperch stewed with fava beans and bacon, grilled beef hanger steak with chopped olives served in a tart crust, duck prepared three ways, as well as the dessert of three chocolates and the dame blanche (vanilla ice cream with hot fudge sauce) are generous, carefully crafted preparations.

● Le Daktari Café `N` `COM`

4, pl Edouard-Renard
Métro: Porte-Dorée
Tel. 01 43 43 39 98. Fax 01 43 43 32 43
Open daily noon–midnight. Cont. service.
Prix fixe: 14,90€, 18,90€, 9,80€ (children). A la carte: 35€.
Terrace.

Exit the Potinière du Lac. Christian Delpuech has taken the place over, changing the name and adding other more fashionable concoctions to the Auvergnat dishes. The predominantly red decor on an animal theme (hence the restaurant's name) has a certain warmth. We casually enjoy the Cantal pâté, jumbo mussels roasted with garlic and parsley, grilled codfish and grilled country sausage with cheese-and-potato purée. Crème brûlée or gingerbread croque-monsieur slip down readily.

● Le Duc de Richelieu `SIM`

5, rue Parrot
Métro: Gare-de-Lyon
Tel. 01 43 43 05 64. Fax 01 40 19 08 70
Closed Sunday, August. Open until 1 AM.
Prix fixe: 14,50€ (lunch). A la carte: 35€.
Terrace. Private dining room.

Having left the Bourse district and his Gavroche in rue Saint-Marc, Stéphane Derre has nailed his flag to the mast near the Gare de Lyon. Like its host, this pleasant *bouchon*-style restaurant is sincere and frank. The endive salad, pike quenelle with beurre blanc, free-range chicken, grilled Charolais beefsteak, baba au rhum and millefeuille are cheerfully washed down with worthy Beaujolais vintages.

● L'Ebauchoir `SIM`

43-45, rue de Cîteaux
Métro: Faidherbe-Chaligny
Tel. 01 43 42 49 31
www.lebauchoir.com
Closed Sunday, Monday lunch.
Open until 11 PM.
Prix fixe: 13,50€ (lunch, wine included), 23€ (lunch). A la carte: 38€.
Air cond.

This mustard-yellow and red bistro with its Fifties' flavor is as cheerful as it is gastronomic. Its lunches are quick and inexpensive; its dinners more elaborate. Thomas Dufour, who has "done" Baumanière, Arpège and Laurent, has a gift for producing flavorsome, fresh dishes at affordable prices. The smoked herring and potato salad, tuna tartare with mashed avocado, whiting with pesto sauce, a surprising grilled tuna steak with white chocolate and black olives, thyme-roasted chicken, Irish rack of lamb with tapenade and turmeric, chocolate mousse and iced vacherin with mango sorbet are right on target. Thierry Bruneau handles the prompt service.

● L'Eglantine   Ⓝ ⊜ SIM

21, rue Fabre d'Eglantine
Métro: Nation
Tel. 01 44 67 73 40
Closed Sunday, 1 week in August.
Open until 11 PM.
Prix fixe: 15€ (lunch). A la carte: 30€.
Terrace.

Just off place de la Nation, Jean-François Sahnes, a dynamic young Aveyronnais, runs this genuine old-fashioned bistro with great energy. Everything is new, but in an antique vein, with red hexagonal floor tiles, a pewter counter by Nectoux, a terrace, and dishes chalked up on the blackboard and served on attractive wooden tables. The top quality meat carries local produce certification, including the sausage aligote and the charcuterie. Without too much damage to our bank balance, we treat ourselves to the salmon tartare, hard-boiled egg with mayonnaise, half-cooked foie gras, a nice 10-ounce ribeye steak, roasted prime rib with coarse sea salt, a hearty steak tartare and chocolate profiteroles. The service is lively and the thirst-quenching wines do not hike up the tab.

● L'Encrier   Ⓝ SIM

55, rue Traversière
Métro: Ledru-Rollin, Bastille, Gare-de-Lyon
Tel.-Fax 01 44 68 08 16
Closed Saturday lunch, Sunday, Christmas, New Year's, August. Open until 10:45 PM.
Prix fixe: 13€ (lunch), 18€ (dinner), 22€, 33€. A la carte: 33€.

Near the Gare de Lyon in a street perpendicular to the arches of the avenue Daumesnil viaduct, this local restaurant with its brick and wood decor offers set menus at amiable prices and is full at both lunch and dinner time. The dishes are well chosen. We feast on roquefort cheese and pears, homemade terrine, pan-fried salmon steak, duck confit, beef tenderloin with escargot sauce and an iced nougat with raspberry coulis. The portions are generous and Ahmed Azzoug's smile is part of the decor.

● Entre les Vignes   🛏 SIM

27 ter, bd Diderot
Métro: Gare-de-Lyon
Tel. 01 43 43 62 84
Closed Saturday, Sunday, Christmas–New Year's, 3 weeks in August.
Open until 10:30 PM.
Prix fixe: 19€, 23€. A la carte: 35€.
Terrace.

This genuine 1905 bistro in yellow and orange shades has lost none of its vintage character. We come for sustenance in the form of simple, refined market-based dishes. The Lyon-style poached sausage with potato salad, country terrine, roasted codfish with lime and ginger, mahi-mahi with rosemary, Salers beef flank steak with shallots and the gingerbread tiramisu slip down straightforwardly.

● **L'Européen** `COM`

21 bis, bd Diderot
Métro: Gare-de-Lyon
Tel. 01 43 43 99 70. Fax 01 43 07 26 51
euro@brasserie-leuropeen.fr
www.brasserie-leuropeen.fr
Open daily 11 AM–1 AM. Cont. service.
Prix fixe: 19€, 26€, 29€,
10,50€ (children). A la carte: 55€.
Air cond. Terrace. Private dining room.

The a la carte prices tend to soar, but the prix fixe menus are well chosen and the Seventies' style neo-art nouveau brasserie setting by Slavik has acquired a certain patina. There are no complaints about the veal and andouillette terrine, lentil and piquillo pepper salad, steak tartare with French fries—even though the green salad is charged as an extra—nor about the calf's liver deglazed with raspberry vinegar. The service lacks warmth, but it is prompt (especially when you have a train to catch). The nougat glacé is splendid and the Château de Corcelles Brouilly slips down smoothly.

● **A La Frégate** `COM`

30, av Ledru-Rollin
Métro: Gare-de-Lyon, Quai-de-la-Rapée
Tel.-Fax 01 43 43 90 32
Closed Saturday, Sunday, 3 weeks in August.
Open until 10 PM.
Prix fixe: 31€, 36€.
Air cond.

Gilles Goueffon provides a cheerful welcome. He has left the kitchen to David Périllaud, who has continued in the same fishy vein with a certain degree of sophistication. The thin tart of fresh sardines, ricotta and preserved lemon, the shrimp tempura with orange-mango gazpacho, the roasted cod with soy sauce, the pan-fried sea bass with pesto, and the chocolate "sphere" with crushed raspberries, rose-hip jam and vanilla ice cream would benefit from a little more simplicity. The blond wood and blue surroundings are pleasantly warm.

● **Jean-Pierre Frelet** `SIM`

25, rue Montgallet
Métro: Montgallet
Tel. 01 43 43 76 65
Closed Saturday lunch, Sunday, August.
Open until 10 PM.
Prix fixe: 18,50€ (lunch), 26,50€ (dinner).
Air cond.

His past training with Delaveyne in Bougival and Michel Oliver at the Bistrot de Paris has left Jean-Pierre Frelet with a good sense of produce and a feel for the right taste. In his old-fashioned bistro he provides a well-managed cuisine based on extensive experience. As the market produce changes, his inspiration goes to work again and you will scarcely be disappointed by the stuffed roasted suckling pig, escargots sautéed in anchovy butter, saffron risotto with squid and langoustines, fresh cod parmentier with young vegetables, calf's liver with carrots and onions, and the sautéed lamb with Provençal-style vegetables. To conclude, the dark chocolate fondant with Espelette chili pepper is explosive.

● **La Gazetta** `N` `SIM`

29, rue de Cotte
Métro: Ledru-Rollin
Tel. 01 43 47 47 05. Fax 01 43 47 47 17
team@lagazetta.fr
www.lagazetta.fr
Closed Sunday evening, Monday, Christmas,
New Year's, August. Open until 11 PM
(Friday, Saturday 11:30 PM).
Prix fixe: 14€ (lunch), 26€ (dinner).
A la carte: 37€.
Air cond.

A step away from the Aligre market, this "in" bistro created by the shrewd team from the China Club and Fumoir provides uninterrupted service in a decor of the South of France with red hexagonal tiles, pistachio-green walls and a bar in dark wood. The ambience is convivial and the dishes sun drenched. Patrons enjoy the tuna ceviche, Provençal-style shredded lamb, sautéed squid, tenderloin lamb chops with thyme jus and raspberry-pistachio shortbread. The wines from

Provence and the Rhône Valley are very appropriate.

● **Les Grandes Marches** `V.COM`

6, pl de la Bastille
Métro: Bastille
Tel. 01 43 42 90 32. Fax 01 43 44 80 02
Open daily until midnight.
Prix fixe: 22,90€, 29,90€,
13,50€ (children).
Air cond. Terrace. Private dining room.
Valet parking.

This establishment located at the foot of the Bastille Opera House is the hip offspring of the Flo group. Its refined, modern setting and topical cuisine go hand in hand. Chef Tony Rodrigue's dishes have a very contemporary flavor. The avocado and crayfish tartare with hearts of palm in vinaigrette sauce, curried shrimp in crisp phyllo pastry, sesame-crusted tuna steak and the thick-cut calf's liver with salted-butter potato purée are not bad. For dessert, the raspberry millefeuille filled with light vanilla cream brings you back to earth.

● **Inédit Café** `SIM`

4, rue Taine
Métro: Dugommier, Daumesnil
Tel. 01 43 43 21 80
Open daily until 11:30 PM.
A la carte: 26€.
Air cond. Terrace. Private dining room.

François Saumet has turned this gourmet café in light-brown and brick-red shades into a convivial haunt. Chef Maxime Cachard plays from a simple, unfussy score, preparing goat cheese salad, salmon tartare, grilled rib-eye steak with thyme, steak tartare, chocolate cake and banana pastry croustillant, all sensibly priced.

● **Jacquot de Bayonne** `SIM`

151, rue de Charenton
Métro: Reuilly-Diderot
Tel.-Fax 01 44 74 68 90
Closed Sunday, Monday, August.
Open until 9:45 PM.
Prix fixe: 27,20€, 28,20€.

We formerly met Jacques Lozada at the Royal Palm, Mauritius. Now he has opted for more modest surroundings in this local bistro with a Southwestern French flavor. At a reasonable price and in good company, patrons savor the mussels stuffed with almond butter, homemade charcuterie, squid stewed in their ink, roasted duck breast and sautéed veal tenderloin, not to mention an impeccable Landais apple pastry topped with crisp phyllo served with vanilla ice cream.

● **O'Rebelle** `SIM`

24, rue Traversière
Métro: Gare-de-Lyon
Tel. 01 43 40 88 98. Fax 01 43 40 88 99
www.o-rebelle.fr
Closed Saturday lunch, Sunday,
Bank Holidays, August. Open until 10:30 PM.
Prix fixe: 30€, 38€.

Mr. Trappe is more globetrotter than rebel. His establishment has a ready charm, with its modern setting in bright colors, exotic wood tables and pictures by Australian artists. The escargot galette served with polenta, balsamic vinegar sauce and ratatouille, the codfish millefeuille with Sarawak black pepper, date coulis and fork-mashed potatoes, the lamb prepared two ways served with eggplant tagine and mascarpone and the banana and Espelette chili pepper sabayon provide original combinations of flavors. The wine list spans the world.

● **L'Oulette** `V.COM`

15, pl Lachambeaudie
Métro: Cour-St-Emilion, Bercy
Tel. 01 40 02 02 12. Fax 01 40 02 04 77
info@l-oulette.com
www.l-oulette.com
Closed Saturday, Sunday, Bank Holidays.
Open until 10:15 PM.
Prix fixe: 32€ (lunch), 48€ (wine included),
70€, 82€ (wine included). A la carte: 70€.
Air cond. Terrace.

With its contemporary decor, terrace sheltered by thujas and a mouthwatering menu with Southwestern French accents, this restaurant belonging to Marcel

Baudis, native of Quercy and pupil of Alain Dutournier, encourages us to indulge ourselves, and that is exactly what we do with the baby artichokes with coriander, fresh mint and cured pork loin, the spice-crusted roasted codfish served with rice cooked in milk with onions, lemon and olive oil foam, the sautéed veal sweetbreads with foie gras flan and a Guanaja chocolate mousse served on a bed of pear granita. All are quite acceptable, although a little short of oomph here and there. The interesting wine list focuses on the Southwest, Bordeaux and Languedoc-Roussillon. Attentive service with a smile.

● **Pataquès**   SIM
40-42, bd de Bercy
Métro: Bercy
Tel. 01 43 07 37 75. Fax 01 43 07 36 64
pataquesbercy@aol.com
www.pataques.fr
Open daily until 10:30 PM.
Prix fixe: 15,50€ (lunch, wine included),
30€. A la carte: 35€.
Air cond. Terrace.

Despite the name, there is no "shambles" in this sunny bistro. Its yellow hues, fun-loving atmosphere and light dishes are all charming. The stuffed sardines, tuna millefeuille, cuttlefish cooked in its own ink, scorpion fish with creamed fresh fava beans, rabbit loin in Provençal herbs and beef brochette with rosemary carry you south to Cassis and Le Lavandou.

● **Le Petit Porcheron**   SIM
3, rue de Prague
Métro: Ledru-Rollin
Tel. 01 43 47 39 47
Closed Sunday. Open until 11 PM.
Prix fixe: 15€ (lunch, wine included).
A la carte: 30–35€.
Terrace.

This old-style bistro serves up sound, elaborate dishes. The warm chicken liver flan, baked camembert with almonds, scallop mousse with lobster sauce, roasted monkfish with cured ham, duck leg sautéed with olives and grilled top rump steak in peppercorn sauce are honestly prepared. The

semolina pudding with caramel and salted butter brings back childhood memories.

● **La Pibale / Club 308**   SIM
308, rue de Charenton
Métro: Porte-de-Charenton
Tel.-Fax 01 44 75 01 55
lapibale308@hotmail.fr
www.lapibale.com
Closed Saturday lunch, Sunday, Monday dinner, 1 week at Easter, 3 weeks in August. Open until 10 PM (Friday, Saturday 10:30 PM).
Prix fixe: 19€, 22€, 30€, 40€ (menu concert Friday and Saturday evenings).
A la carte: 45€.
Air cond.

Jean-Charles Diehl, once King of Paris at Jean-Charles et ses Amis, rue de La Trémoille, is now the Little Prince of his stretch of street (which is a very long one!). He still flies the flag of Southwest France, holds his jazz club on the weekend and cheerfully serves up tuna tartare, mackerel with sesame, squid cooked in its own ink, piquillo peppers, veal stew with tomatoes, peppers and Espelette chilies, pork loin baked with chorizo and Basque butter cake with lemon zest to his eager guests.

● **Le Quincy**   ○ COM
28, av Ledru-Rollin
Métro: Gare-de-Lyon
Tel.-Fax 01 46 28 46 76
Closed Saturday, Sunday, Monday, Christmas–New Year's, mid-August–mid-September Open until 9:30 PM.
A la carte: 50–70€.
Air cond. Terrace.

Michel Bosshard, a.k.a. Bobosse, has turned his old-fashioned inn into a compact gourmet theater. He offers a warm welcome and vigorously touts his traditional cuisine. The atmosphere soon grows companionable. With a keen appetite, we dine on the homemade foie gras, farm-style terrine with cabbage and garlic, codfish brandade, a copious stuffed cabbage, oxtail stew and rabbit stew with white wine and shallots, exemplary in their genre. The chocolate mousse has a silky texture; the vanilla ice cream is homemade. Credit cards are still off limits, but the house continues to present devotees with a plum flambé.

● Le Saint-Amarante `SIM`

4, rue Biscornet
Métro: Bastille
Tel. 01 43 43 00 08
Closed Saturday, Sunday, 1 week in August.
Open until 11 PM.
Prix fixe: 15€ (lunch). A la carte: 45€.
Terrace.

Thierry Maricot has taken over this gourmet bistro and lowered its prices, while maintaining its quality. The tone is classical and unsurprising, although very tasteful. Among the house's successful dishes, the chicken liver terrine with Port wine, poached eggs in red wine sauce with slow-roasted garlic, scorpion fish filets with saffron jus and fork-mashed potatoes with olives and the calf's head are splendid. As you savor the warm chocolate cake or the apple-rhubarb crumble it may well occur to you that this little eatery is quite a find.

● Le Square Trousseau `T` `SIM`

1, rue Antoine-Vollon
Métro: Ledru-Rollin
Tel. 01 43 43 06 00. Fax 01 43 43 00 66
Closed Sunday, Monday. Open until 11:30 PM.
Prix fixe: 20€, 25€.
Terrace. Private dining room.

Things have improved in this fine 1900s' bistro boasting stucco, mirrors and carved wooden bar, which has simply been the victim of its own success. Philippe Damas, a veteran of Le Crillon, deploys his culinary skills to cope with the influx of customers, close-set tables and noisy atmosphere. This year, we have no complaints about the tuna and cucumber tartare, nor the ravioli with basil, tomato and beaufort cheese. The seven-hour roasted lamb shanks hit the right note and the prune "bonbons" roasted with Armagnac are still excellent.

● La Table d'Aligre `€` `SIM`

11, pl d'Aligre
Métro: Ledru-Rollin, Gare-de-Lyon
Tel. 01 43 07 84 88. Fax 01 43 46 36 87
cyr75@wanadoo.fr
Closed Monday, Christmas,
2 weeks in August.
Open until 10:30 PM.
Prix fixe: 12,20€ (lunch), 14,50€ (lunch, wine included), 22,50€ (dinner), 27,50€ (dinner).
Terrace. Private dining room.

The conscientious Marc Baudry, who has worked with Senderens, Barrier and Guérard, continues to run this modest bistro, where Hervé Ruy seconds him in the dining room and kitchen. The place has been renovated in orange-brown shades, the prix fixe menus are tempting and the dishes flirt with current tastes, although not to excess. The marinated baby cuttlefish with fennel with orange, cold peach and Serrano ham soup, codfish gazpacho with stewed onions and tabbouleh, spring lamb and vegetable stew and roasted fresh figs with pistachio ice cream are enjoyable.

● La Table de Julie `N` `SIM`

234, rue du Faubourg-Saint-Antoine
Métro: Nation, Faidherbe-Chaligny
Tel.-Fax 01 43 70 83 22
Closed Sunday, Monday dinner.
Open until 10:30 PM.
Prix fixe: 18€ (lunch). A la carte: 27€.
Terrace.

The former Saint-Pourçain has become La Table de Julie, providing an opportunity for a makeover. The entirely revamped decor in attractive red and apricot tints is inspired by the South of France. The menu also counts on sunshine and good humor. Michel and Nelly Garanger (late of Antoine et Antoinette in the seventh arrondissement, then Le Moniage Guillaume, the renowned fish restaurant in the fourteenth) take a tastefully modest approach here, treating their small, local clientele to arugula salad with parmesan cheese, red tuna salad with spicy oil, roasted Charolais prime rib and a cream of red fruits prettily accompanied by wines from Southwest France or Languedoc.

● Le Temps des Cerises · SIM

216, rue du Faubourg-Saint-Antoine
Métro: Faidherbe-Chaligny
Tel. 01 43 67 52 08. Fax 01 43 67 60 91
Closed Monday (except Bank Holidays),
2 weeks in August. Open until 10:30 PM.
Prix fixe: 15€ (lunch on weekdays),
20€ (lunch on weekdays), 22€ (dinner,
except Sunday), 30€ (dinner, wine included).
A la carte: 55€.
Air cond. Terrace. Private dining room.

Lydie Corbin-Poulet has taken over this fine inn with her children. She welcomes guests and supervises the service, and has kept on the excellent chef, Bernard Bergounioux, a pupil of Alain Dutournier, who prepares a forthright, honest cuisine. The eggplant, goat cheese and basil mille-feuille, homemade foie gras, sea bream roasted in a potato crust, fish baked in parchment paper, and thyme-roasted lamb shank are well made. To conclude, the "Temps des Cerises" ("Cherry Season"), a dessert made from preserved cherries and fromage blanc, slips down smoothly.

● Le Train Bleu · V.COM

Gare de Lyon, pl Louis-Armand
Métro: Gare-de-Lyon
Tel. 01 43 43 09 06. Fax 01 43 43 97 96
reservation.trainbleu@ssp.fr
www.le-train-bleu.com
Open daily until 11 PM.
Prix fixe: 45€ (wine included), 48€,
15€ (children). A la carte: 70€.

Established in 1901, this restaurant with its sumptuous, rococo decor is still the finest rail station buffet in France. Visitors can admire frescos paying homage to the Paris-Lyon-Mediterranean railroad, as well as the gilding, stucco, moldings, wood-work and crystal chandeliers. Turning to the food, tradition is properly maintained once more with the homemade duck foie gras, sea bream in the style of the South of France, roasted leg of lamb with potato gratin and baba au rhum soaked with amber Saint James rum. A delicious way of

passing the time while waiting for a train. Nothing has been done about the prices, though.

● Le Traversière · SIM

40, rue Traversière
Métro: Gare-de-Lyon
Tel. 01 43 44 02 10. Fax 01 43 44 64 20
Closed Sunday evening, Monday, 3 weeks in August. Open until 10:30 PM.
Prix fixe: 23€ (lunch), 29€, 39,50€.
A la carte: 56€.
Terrace.

The contrast between the wood facade, decorated with old-fashioned glazed tiles in a provincial inn style, and the decisively modern dining room decor is surprising. Johnny Bénariac's menu, which depends on carefully selected regional produce, changes with the seasons. We treat ourselves to the lobster and chanterelle mushroom croustillant, the duck foie gras carpaccio, the saffron-roasted monkfish with endive tarte Tatin, sautéed veal kidneys and sweetbreads and the raspberries and strawberries served with a macaron, and enjoy the wide range of wines served by the glass. The prix fixe menus are welcome.

● Au Trou Gascon · COM

40, rue Taine
Métro: Daumesnil
Tel. 01 43 44 34 26. Fax 01 43 07 80 55
carre.des.feuillants@wanadoo.fr
www.autrougascon.fr
Closed Saturday, Sunday, Bank Holidays,
1 week Christmas–New Year's, August.
Open until 10 PM.
Prix fixe: 36€ (lunch), 50€ (dinner).
A la carte: 80€.
Air cond.

Alain Dutournier's first abode is still on the right track. The bistro setting made over by designer Alberto Bali takes a minimalist approach in gray tones. In the dining room, Claude Tessier and Nicole Dutournier's supervision is unfailingly attentive, while the kitchen carries on the traditions of Southwest France (but not exclusively) under the aegis of apt pupil

Jean-Charles Paquet. The pan-seared Landais duck foie gras steak with artichoke and asparagus salad, quick-grilled squid with tomato, eggplant and olive stew, hake steak with eggplant and wild mushrooms and red mullet filet with spelt in green curry sauce forge ahead. The cassoulet made with haricots maïs—a regional bean—is still the best in Paris and the sliced and grilled veal sweetbread or kidneys are polished works of craftsmanship. Finally, the warm and crispy tourtière with salted-butter caramel ice cream and the pistachio-filled dacquoise served with honey-roasted pineapple and pistachio ice cream are paradigms of confection. A great Bordeaux cellar and Armagnacs to die for.

● **Le Viaduc Café** SIM

43, av Daumesnil
Métro: Gare-de-Lyon
Tel. 01 44 74 70 70. Fax 01 44 74 70 71
www.viaduc-cafe.fr
Open daily until midnight.
Prix fixe: 17€ (lunch on weekdays).
Terrace. Private dining room.

Marc Le Boudec has taken over this modern brasserie with its terrace below the verdant viaduct that once carried trains to Bastille, and has left its style intact. Christophe Le Corre's cuisine tends toward fashionable dishes. The tuna tataki with black sesame seeds, tomato tart with basil sorbet, red mullet croustillant, pan-seared saddle of lamb with mozzarella and thyme and a crispy spiced chicken and caramelized apricot tart make no waves.

● **Le Vinea Café** Ⓢ SIM

Bercy Village, 26-28, cour Saint-Emilion
Métro: Cour-St-Emilion
Tel. 01 44 74 09 09. Fax 01 44 74 06 66
www.vinea-cafe.com
Open daily noon–1 AM (Friday,
Saturday 4 AM). Cont. service.
Prix fixe: 13,50€ (lunch on weekdays),
16,80€ (lunch on weekdays),
29,50€ (dinner), 9€ (children).
Air cond. Terrace. Private dining room.
Valet parking.

Among the appealing eateries of the cour Saint-Emilion is this modern brasserie in burgundy and orange shades. Served until late, its cuisine reflects current fashions but is intended to please everyone. Actually, this year, we felt a tasteless carpaccio, a badly seasoned Caesar salad and a tasteless Canadian lobster tagine with a dried-out piece of salmon, all poorly reheated in the microwave, were frankly dreary. The welcome could be more perceptible and the service, though pleasant, is amateurish. However, the codfish and zucchini croustillant is not bad and the crème brûlée is quite well done. In short, there is room for improvement.

● **Les Zygomates** ● 🏠 SIM

7, rue de Capri
Métro: Daumesnil, Michel-Bizot
Tel. 01 40 19 93 04. Fax 01 44 73 46 63
info@leszygomates.fr
www.leszygomates.fr
Closed Sunday, Monday, August.
Open until 10:30 PM.
Prix fixe: 14,50€ (lunch) 24€, 30€.
Air cond.

Pleasant, inexpensive and shrewd, Patrick Fray's establishment has become part of life in the twelfth arrondissement. In his hands, this 1900s' butcher's store has become a modish, gourmet haunt. There are no unpleasant surprises in store with the raw duck foie gras and pinenut salad, langoustine ravioli, roasted codfish with tapenade and the Moroccan-style pigeon pie. The wines are skillfully selected and not unreasonably priced, and the service is fast and friendly. Like the exquisite beggar's purse of apples and almonds in salted caramel sauce, the other desserts are right on target.

▼ | SHOPS

KITCHENWARE & TABLETOP

▼ Constance Maupin ▥

11, rue du Docteur-Goujon
Métro: Daumesnil
Tel. 01 43 07 01 28
10 AM–1 PM, 2:30 PM–7:30 PM.
Closed Sunday, Monday, Bank Holidays,
beginning of August–beginning of September.
Constance Maupin enthusiastically selects silver cutlery, crystal carafes, fine porcelain and earthenware, late 19th- and 20th-century glassware, embroidered tablecloths and linens, mirrors, vases and antique pictures.

BREAD & BAKED GOODS

▼ Jacques Bazin ▥

85 bis, rue de Charenton
Métro: Ledru-Rollin, Bastille
Tel.-Fax 01 43 07 75 21
7 AM–8 PM. Closed Wednesday, Thursday,
1 month July–August.
This vintage-1880 store offers organic baguettes, fig bread, bacon bread, bazinette (a house specialty), farm-style sourdough walnut bread, country bread and a tremendous sandwich loaf. Apple pastries, crumble and millefeuille are worth the visit.

▼ Yann Chantrelle

57, av du Docteur-Arnold-Netter
Métro: Porte-de-Vincennes
Tel. 01 43 43 91 73
7 AM–8 PM. Closed Wednesday, Thursday,
3 weeks in August.
In his renovated store, Yann Chantrelle charms customers with his sourdough breads and delicate cakes and pastries, soft almond cake, "Saudade" (a lemon cake filled with honey, nougatine and pistachio mousse) and spiced biscuits filled with vanilla cream, praliné mousse and Italian meringue.

▼ Chejy

83, av du Docteur-Arnold-Netter
Métro: Porte-de-Vincennes
Tel. 01 43 46 06 32
7 AM–8 PM.
Closed Sunday afternoon, Monday,
1 month July–August.
Hassan Chejy bakes his bread the traditional way in an old-fashioned wood oven. He produces organic breads, roquefort bread, and sourdough country breads. The palmiers, shortbreads, orange-peel cookies and gingerbread are splendid.

▼ Maître Pain

225, rue de Charenton
Métro: Dugommier
Tel. 01 43 43 52 48. Fax 01 75 51 40 31
7 AM–8:30 PM (Sunday 7:30 AM–2 PM).
Closed Thursday.
Emmanuel Merlhes, star of the street, impresses with his "Bagatelle" baguette (light and cream-colored inside), "Bercy" sourdough loaf, made from three different flours, and flawless Viennese pastries, flaky brioche and fouace (a regional sweet bread with orange flower water).

▼ Moisan "le Pain au Naturel"

5, pl d'Aligre
Métro: Ledru-Rollin
Tel. 01 43 45 46 60
7 AM–8 PM.
Closed Sunday afternoon, Monday
Michel Moisan, who has other stores around Paris, is still in residence here, supplying breads made from certified organic flour. His brioche and sweet breads, traditional-style country breads, organic cuminseed bread, wholemeal bread, baguettes, croissants made with traditionally churned butter and flûte sur poolish (a thin baguette made from twice-fermented dough) are a treat.

WINE

▼ Caves Michel Renaud 🏠

12, pl de la Nation
Métro: Nation
Tel. 01 43 07 98 93. Fax 01 40 02 06 16
9:30 AM–1 PM, 2:30 PM–8:30 PM.
Closed Sunday afternoon, Monday morning.
Owner of Le Clos Joliette in Jurançon and Le Domaine du Tauzia in Cazaubon, Bas Armagnac, Michel Renaud offers exquisite local wines in three colors and thoroughbred ports from Quinta do Castelinho, as well as great Burgundies, rare Malagas and fine Riedel carafes.

CHARCUTERIE

▼ Rigault

4, rue Marsoulan
Métro: Picpus
Tel. 01 43 43 89 57
8 AM–1 PM, 4–7:30 PM.
Closed Sunday afternoon, Wednesday,
beginning of August–end of August.
Gilles Rigault, cooked-meat maestro, prepares quality pork pies, head cheese, country terrines, quenelles, as well as Norwegian smoked salmon, sauerkraut, ham on the bone and dried sausage.

ICE CREAM

▼ Raimo

59-61, bd de Reuilly
Métro: Daumesnil
Tel. 01 43 43 70 17
9 AM–midnight. Closed Monday, February.
For three generations, the Raimos have carried on the tradition of Italian ice cream and offer more than 40 flavors of pure-cream ice creams and pure-fruit sorbets: honey, fresh cream, ginger, Vermont maple syrup, white chocolate, bitter chocolate, nougat, muscat grape, red currant, mandarin orange, banana, chestnut or spice.

PASTRIES

▼ Saffers

24, pl de la Nation
Métro: Nation
Tel. 01 43 43 77 36
8:30 AM–1:30 PM, 3–7:45 PM.
Closed Monday, Tuesday,
1 week in February, August.
Take time out to enjoy the scent of the giddying perfumes that waft from Philippe Saffers's delicious store. Cointreau "burnt" pudding, charlotte, mandarin, red currant, sweet-lemon omelet, millefeuille, coffee and meringue cake, wild strawberry tart and champagne pudding are delightful.

▼ Stéphane Vandermeersch

278, av Daumesnil
Métro: Porte-Dorée
Tel. 01 43 47 21 66
7 AM–8 PM. Closed Monday, Tuesday,
1 week in March, 1 month July–August.
Master of the baguette and specialty breads, Stéphane Vandermeersch also provides quality cakes and pastries. Individual fruit tarts, Mont-Blanc, pistachio-filled cream puffs, chocolate-pear Saint-Honoré pudding and millefeuille will make you melt. In season, the galette des rois (frangipane-filled puff pastry cake) is a work of art.

REGIONAL PRODUCTS

▼ Fine Bouche

3, rue du Rendez-Vous
Métro: Picpus
Tel.-Fax 01 46 28 43 63
www.finebouche-fromager.com
9 AM–1 PM, 4–7:30 PM.
Closed Sunday afternoon, Monday,
end of July–end of August.
This mouthwatering store promotes products from the Auvergne. Duck foie gras, boudin, stewed lamb tripe sausage, layered terrines, stuffed duck breast, sauerkraut, Auvergne cheeses, cabécou (small aged goat cheeses), jams and preserves are all available from Claude and Geneviève Soler.

▼ Sur les Quais

Beauvau covered market, pl d'Aligre
Métro: Ledru-Rollin
Tel. 01 43 43 21 09. Fax 01 43 43 03 16
surlesquais@club-internet.fr
9:30 AM–1 PM, 4:30–7:30 PM
(Saturday 9:30 AM–1:30 PM, 4–7:30 PM,
Sunday 9:30 AM–1:30 PM). Closed Sunday
afternoon, Monday, August.

This temple of olive oil holds more than 80
varieties, as well as kitchen accessories to
go with it. Also rare spices, grains of paradise, peppers, tonka bean, vadouvan (a
South Indian mix of spices and fried
onions), various vinegars, and green olives
from Lucques, Lyon or Les Baux

COFFEE

▼ Pascal Guiraud

21, bd de Reuilly
Métro: Dugommier, Daumesnil
Tel. 01 43 43 39 27. Fax 01 43 43 46 00
pascal.guiraud@919.fr
10 AM–8 PM (Tuesday 10 AM–7 PM).
Closed Sunday, Monday, Bank Holidays,
2 weeks in August.

Thirty or so quality coffees are meticulously
roasted by Pascal Guiraud: Moka Sidamo,
Maragogype and Mysore. A wide choice of
teas and, in the gourmet food department,
quality pastas, vinegars and mustards.

◆ RENDEZVOUS

BARS

◆ Barrio Latino

46-48, rue du Faubourg-Saint-Antoine
Métro: Bastille, Ledru-Rollin
Tel. 01 55 78 84 75. Fax 01 55 78 85 30
www.buddhabar.com
Noon–2 AM (Friday noon–2:30 AM,
Saturday noon–3:30 AM). Closed May 1st.
Air cond. Private dining room.

Near the Bastille Opera House, this fashionable bar covers three floors: a restaurant on the first, a Cuban bar on the second
and a VIP bar on the last. Patrons enjoy
tacos, Mexican tortilla dishes, Acapulco-
style tuna steak and "buena suerte" jumbo

Rendezvous

shrimp. Customers must wait in line and
get past the forbidding doormen!

◆ China Club

50, rue de Charenton
Métro: Ledru-Rollin, Bastille
Tel. 01 43 43 82 02. Fax 01 43 43 79 85
ww.chinaclub.cc
7 PM–2 AM. Closed New Year's, August.
Air cond.

The colonial decor, 45-foot bar and large
dining room set the tone. We like the Ping
Xiang platter, fried dumplings, iced lime tart.
Concerts on Friday and Saturday nights.

WINE BARS

◆ Le Baron Rouge

1, rue Théophile-Roussel
Métro: Ledru-Rollin
Tel. 01 43 43 14 32
10 AM–2 PM, 5–10 PM (Saturday
10 AM–10 PM, Sunday 10 AM–3 PM).
Closed Monday.
Air cond.

The ambience is pleasant, the wines amiable, the oysters from Cap-Ferret very fresh
and the assorted charcuterie plates and
goat cheeses unpretentious.

◆ Au Compteur

25, bd de Reuilly
Métro: Dugommier, Daumesnil
Tel. 01 43 41 77 27
9 AM–3 PM, 6:30 PM–midnight.
Closed Saturday lunch, Sunday, Monday
evening, 1 week Christmas–New Year's.

Dany and Patrice Bach serve selected
wines from the Rhône Valley and Roussillon to accompany duck breast, duck confit, Duval andouillette and smoked garlic
sausage. A tasteful ambience.

◆ Lolo et les Lauréats

68 bis, rue de Reuilly
Métro: Montgallet
Tel.-Fax 01 40 02 07 12
7:30 AM–8 PM. Closed Sunday.
Terrace.

We enjoy relaxing on the heated terrace and
in this lively bar, where domestic dishes
and unpretentious wines go hand in hand.

CAFES

◆ Gudule

58, bd de Picpus
Métro: Picpus
Tel. 01 43 40 08 28
8 AM–1:30 AM. Open daily.
Terrace.

Yann Bayet has taken over this relaxed bistro that offers pleasant drinks, tartines and snacks and nibbles. Regulars gather for Sunday brunch.

◆ La Mère Pouchet   🄽

168, bd Diderot
Métro: Nation, Reuilly-Diderot
Tel. 01 43 43 87 66
7 AM–2 AM. Open daily.

This young, new corner café, whose style is very Klapisch East Paris, is a lively place to meet, at the bar or on the terrace. It also provides satisfying sustenance in the form of fresh salads, traditional specials of the day such as blanquette or roast chicken and grandmother-style desserts.

◆ Pictural Café

40, bd de la Bastille
Métro: Bastille
Tel. 01 53 17 01 98
8 AM–2 AM.
Closed Sunday (except in summer).
Terrace.

Two strong points: the view of the Canal de l'Arsenal and the unusual decor. The food includes broiled camembert, porcini mushroom ravioli, duck parmentier. Latin and techno evenings are held every two weeks, as well as photo and painting exhibitions.

TEA SALONS

◆ Tarte Thé Tartine

129, bd Diderot
Métro: Nation, Reuilly-Diderot
Tel. 01 46 28 64 55
9 AM–10 PM. Closed 2 weeks in August.
Air cond. Terrace.

Anita Bessis is the queen of tarts, quiches and open sandwiches. The eggplant, zucchini and grilled tomato tart and the chocolate and banana tart are splendid.

◆ Tea Melodie

72, bd de Picpus
Métro: Picpus
Tel. 01 44 68 91 77
Saturday, Monday 9 AM–6:30 PM;
Tuesday–Friday 9 AM–11 PM.
Closed Sunday, Christmas–New Year's.
Terrace.

This little tearoom with its relaxed atmosphere wins over visitors with its milkshakes, iced coffee, gingerbread tarte Tatin, fruit crumbles, Mariage Frères teas and hot chocolate. Classical music and small exhibitions.

◆ Tesnime Pâtisserie   🄽

207, rue du Faubourg-Saint-Antoine
Métro: Faidherbe-Chaligny, Ledru-Rollin
Tel. 01 43 48 60 97. Fax 01 43 48 63 88
8 AM–9 PM. Closed Monday morning.
Air cond. Terrace.

This welcoming tearoom with its decor in warm tones and small library presents m'hadjeb (hand-kneaded semolina flatbread), baked almond-stuffed crescent-shaped pastries, pistachio pastries and samsa (fried almond-filled pastries in syrup) with mint tea.

○	Very good restaurant
◎	Excellent restaurant
◎◎	One of the best restaurants in Paris
⑤	Disappointing restaurant
🛎	Good value for money
⊜	Meals for less than 30 euros
SIM	Simple
COM	Comfortable
V.COM	Very comfortable
LUX	Luxurious
V.LUX	Very luxurious

Red indicates a particularly charming establishment

♜	Historical significance
🏠	Promotion *(higher rating than last year)*
🕸	New to the guide
●	Restaurant
▼	Shop
◆	Rendezvous

13TH ARRONDISSEMENT
A MULTICOLORED DISTRICT

Motley, colorful, modern and splintered, the thirteenth arrondissement has changed. The Grande Bibliothèque, France's new national library, dominates the bank of the Seine, marking out a new sector. Beyond the towers of avenue de Choisy, Chinatown already defines another neighborhood. The overhead Métro line cuts across the horizon like a frontier. The "free" commune of La Butte aux Cailles lives on, with its old alleyways and housing developments imitating English lanes or Alsatian villages. This is the arrondissement of hippy culture and quiet bistros. Deepest Asia seen from the Tang store, Chinese and Thai Sunday feasts, colorful stores and little cafés where spring rolls can be had for pennies . . . all this and more is of course to be found in the thirteenth. We can lose ourselves by the Seine at the crossroad of the Pont de Tolbiac, straight out of a Léo Malet novel, or catch a movie at the Marin Karmitz multiplex. We can eat fashionably at Jules et Jim or more traditionally at Le Terroir or Chez Paul, discover the L'Avant-Goût and L'Ourcine, stroll around the church of Jeanne d'Arc, up rue Véronèse or down rue des Cinq-Diamants (do you know the Cailloux?) and venture into the Gobelins quarter. In the end, despite the changes, the soul of Old Paris seems to have survived here, one way or another.

● RESTAURANTS

GOOD RESTAURANTS & OTHERS

● L'Anacréon 🎦 SIM
53, bd Saint-Marcel
Métro: Les Gobelins
Tel. 01 43 31 71 18. Fax 01 43 31 94 94
www.restaurant-anacreon.com
Closed Saturday lunch, Sunday, Monday,
1 week Christmas–New Year's,
1 week in May, 3 weeks in August.
Open until 10 PM.
Prix fixe: 20€ (lunch), 32€.
Air cond.

Christophe Accary, who has been running this excellent local establishment since last year, has rejuvenated its classics of bistro cuisine with a touch of modernity and a great deal of lightness. The vine-ripened tomato gazpacho with cucumber foam, the pan-seared scorpion fish with saffron potatoes and argan oil, the sweetbreads braised in Jura wine and the Plougastel strawberry melba are enhanced here and there with highly appealing hints of exotic flavor. The check is civilized.

● Assis, au Neuf SIM
166, bd Vincent-Auriol
Métro: Place-d'Italie, Nationale
Tel. 01 45 82 69 69. Fax 01 45 82 68 69
assisauneuf@wanadoo.fr
www.a609paris.com
Closed Christmas, New Year's.
Open until 11:30 PM.
Prix fixe: 13€ (lunch on weekdays).
A la carte: 37–50€.
Terrace.

When the weather is fine, we sit until late at a table on the terrace of Alexandre Fayad's restaurant. The goat cheese wrapped in phyllo with honey, scallops pan-seared in garlic butter, rack of lamb with thyme and the apple terrine with gingerbread, with their delicious accents of the South of France, are accompanied by a Southern wine from France, Spain, Portugal or Argentina. The moderate tab is another of the place's many charms.

● Auberge Etchegorry 🏠 SIM
41, rue de Croulebarbe
Métro: Corvisart, Les Gobelins
Tel. 01 44 08 83 51. Fax 01 44 08 83 69
Closed Sunday, Monday.
Open until 10:30 PM.
Prix fixe: 26€, 32,50€, 37,60€.
A la carte: 38–80€.
Air cond. Terrace. Private dining room.

Henri Laborde has brought the Basque country to stay in what was formerly a cabaret frequented by Victor Hugo and the entertainer Béranger. The facade remains, but the dining room is now very much of our century and the cuisine is engagingly generous. The seared foie gras medallions with grapes, small squid in its own ink, duck breast with potatoes sautéed in goose fat and traditional Basque cake have the sweet smell of the Pyrénéen Southwest. Appealing wines from France and Spain selected by the chef and master of the house add to the warm atmosphere.

● L'Avant-Goût 🎦 SIM
26, rue Bobillot
Métro: Place-d'Italie
Tel. 01 53 80 24 00. Fax 01 53 80 00 77
Closed Saturday, Sunday, Monday,
1 week in beginning of January, 1 week
in May, 2 weeks in beginning of August.
Open until 11 PM.
Prix fixe: 31€.
Air cond.

Christophe Beaufront, who trained under Guérard and Savoy, and ages ago already held our yearly Best Value for Money award, has forgotten none of his illustrious mentors' creative precision. His set menus change along with the seasons and according to his inclinations, and we relish his sharp, fresh dishes. We fondly remember the pairing of fresh goat cheese with tapenade, creamy pea soup with fresh mint, sesame-crusted codfish, spiced pork pot-au-feu served with its traditional bouillon and melon soup with anise and a tarragon ice, all faultless. Pascal Gesret provides shrewd advice on how best to complement them with a well-chosen wine.

● Le Bouche à Oreille   Ⓝ SIM

10, pl Paul-Verlaine
Métro: Place-d'Italie
Tel. 01 45 89 74 42. Fax 01 45 89 83 60
lebao@wanadoo.fr
Closed Sunday, Monday evening,
Tuesday evening, 3 weeks in August. Open
until 10:30 PM (Monday, Tuesday 9 PM).
Prix fixe: 8,50€ (lunch), 11€ (lunch),
13,50€ (lunch). A la carte: 35€.

Opposite the Butte aux Cailles swimming pool, this local bar with its Fifties' vintage bistro appearance is worth a visit. The proprietor's welcome may not always be first rate, but his fine selection of wines from all over France and his regional cuisine speak for him. Oeufs en meurette (eggs poached in red wine with bacon and onions), calf's liver with raspberry vinaigrette and the tarte Tatin are impeccable.

● Café Bibliothèque   SIM

MK2 Bibliothèque,
128-162, av de France
Métro: Bibliothèque-François-Mitterrand,
Quai-de-la-Gare
Tel. 01 56 61 44 00. Fax 01 56 61 44 12
sandrine.gay@mk2.com
www.mk2.com
Closed Christmas, New Year's. Open until
11 PM (Friday, Saturday midnight).
Prix fixe: 15,90€ (lunch), 20,90€.
A la carte: 30–40€.
Air cond. Terrace. Private dining room.

Before or after a movie, you can eat in the designer setting of this MK2 multiplex café. Tomato and mozzarella millefeuille drizzled with olive oil, a tuna steak with ginger, nutmeg, white pepper and cloves and crispy pan-fried vegetables, chicken breast with morel mushrooms served with a potato flan and zucchini sautéed with thyme and the berry crumble with vanilla ice cream provide a gourmet screenplay with nonstop action thanks to the fast service.

● Café Fusion   ● SIM

12, rue de la Butte-aux-Cailles
Métro: Place-d'Italie, Corvisart
Tel. 01 45 80 12 02
Closed Sunday evening.
Open 11:30 AM–11:30 PM. Cont. service.
Prix fixe: 16€, 23€. A la carte: 30€.
Terrace.

Not everyone appreciates the orange- and metal-based contemporary decor and Pierre Bonnefille's wall panels, but the cuisine, which (as the place's name suggests) draws inspiration from all over the world, is consensually modern. The croustillant with saint-nectaire cheese, salmon "fusion," coconut chicken crumble and sautéed peach soup with fresh mint win both enthusiasts and neophytes over to this culinary trend rooted in current fashion.

● Djoon   COM

22, bd Vincent-Auriol
Métro: Quai-de-la-Gare
Tel. 01 45 70 83 49. Fax 01 45 70 83 57
contact@djoon.fr
www.djoon.fr
Closed Saturday lunch, Sunday, Monday
evening, 2 weeks in August.
Open until 11:30 PM.
Prix fixe: 17,90€ (lunch), 35€ (dinner).
A la carte: 38–55€.
Air cond. Terrace.

Of Iranian origin ("djoon" means "life" in Persian), Afshin Assadian has chosen a baroque decor whose columns, couches and frescos are inspired by Eastern and Mediterranean styles. On the food front, the foie gras terrine with artichokes, jumbo shrimp (in spite of the useless pink peppercorns) with curry and basmati rice, honey-roasted rack of lamb with sesame, and strawberry soup with fresh mint carry us around the world. All this attracts a heterogeneous crowd, ranging from the staff of major corporations and government departments located nearby to the bohemian middle classes who have recently settled in this radically changing district.

● A la Douceur Angevine `SIM`

1, rue Xaintrailles
Métro: Bibliothèque-François-Mitterrand
Tel.-Fax 01 45 83 32 30
Closed dinner (except Thursday, Friday),
Saturday, Sunday, 1 week at the end of July,
3 weeks in August.
Open until 11:30 PM (2 AM for drinks).
A la carte: 30–40€.
Terrace.

Catherine Thébaud pays tribute to a region, her region: Anjou, which is well worth a culinary visit. The chicken liver gâteau, line-caught sea bass, cabbage with sausages and strawberry clafoutis have the fine flavor of tradition handed down on the banks of the Loire, and vintages from the region hold a place of honor on the wine list. The mistress of the house provides a friendly, attentive welcome that makes guests feel at home immediately.

● La Girondine `SIM`

48, bd Arago
Métro: Glacière, Les Gobelins
Tel. 01 43 31 64 17
Closed Sunday evening. Open until 11:30 PM.
Prix fixe: 15,90€ (lunch on weekdays),
18,90€, 30€ (wine included).
Terrace.

The team here changed at the start of the year, but this gourmet brasserie has stuck with the same successful strategy in renovated surroundings. The morel mushrooms in a pastry crust, scallops served over a bed of sweet potato purée, lamb shank braised with garlic and chocolate quiche display the charms of proficiently mastered tradition. The shady terrace is a marvelous find, and we are equally delighted with the moderate prices.

● Chez Jacky `COM`

109, rue du Dessous-des-Berges
Métro: Bibliothèque-François-Mitterrand
Tel. 01 45 83 71 55. Fax 01 45 86 57 73
Closed Saturday, Sunday, Bank Holidays,
1 week Christmas–New Year's, August.
Open until 10:30 PM.
Prix fixe: 43€ (wine included).
A la carte: 50–65€.
Air cond. Private dining room.

Jacky Minet was once a butcher, and when it comes to selecting meats, he is a strict connoisseur. In fact, he applies the same approach to all the produce conscientiously prepared by Joël Dubeau, his alter ego in the kitchen for the last thirty years. The homemade foie gras terrine, emperor red snapper filet with morels and fresh saffron pasta, "La Villette" calf's head with two sauces and a crisp layered pastry with warm cinnamon apples are accompanied by selected wines. An amusing, old-fashioned hostelry decor.

● La Nouvelle Gare `●` `SIM`

49, bd Vincent-Auriol
Métro: Chevaleret, Quai-de-la-Gare
Tel. 01 45 84 74 29
Closed Saturday, Sunday. Open until 4 AM.
Prix fixe: 12€ (lunch), 14€ (dinner), 21€.
A la carte: 20–27€.
Terrace. Private dining room.

In this establishment run by Rose-Angela Guénard (a.k.a. Poupa), the food is well prepared, appetizing and inexpensive. The chicken liver salad, salmon with sorrel, rabbit in mustard sauce and seasonal fruit tart delight staff from the nearby Ministry of Finance and, later on, night owls from the neighborhood or farther afield, since the house is open until the wee hours. Poupa's really is an excellent eatery. We will be returning there soon.

● L'Ourcine ● SIM

92, rue Broca
Métro: Les Gobelins, Glacière
Tel. 01 47 07 13 65. Fax 01 47 07 18 48
Closed Sunday, Monday, 1 week at the end of
July–mid-August. Open until 10:30 PM
(11 PM with reservations).
Prix fixe: 16€ (lunch), 28€.

After seconding Yves Camdeborde at the Régalade, then running the kitchens of the 70, Sylvain Danière now supervises his own restaurant. This old-style bistro looks good. It offers impressive value for money and displays plenty of creativity in the content of the set menu, changed every day. The farm-raised parsleyed pork terrine over mesclun salad greens, roasted pollack with olive oil and roasted and stuffed free-range Gers chicken with sautéed chinese cabbage are among its successful dishes. When it is time for dessert, do not miss miniature chocolate pralinés with Valrhona Guanaja chocolate ganache, a true delicacy. Both the welcome and Vassanthy Danière's service are delightful.

● Chez Paul SIM

22, rue de la Butte-aux-Cailles
Métro: Corvisart, Place-d'Italie
Tel. 01 45 89 22 11. Fax 01 45 80 26 53
Closed December 23rd–January 3rd.
Open until midnight.
A la carte: 40–50€.
Terrace.

Amiable and generous, Paul Desaivre's bistro regularly focuses on French quality. Oxtail terrine, homemade foie gras, monkfish with Espelette peppers, suckling pig with sage, baba au rhum and salted caramel brioche pain perdu are classics that never stale. Chiroubles wine follows naturally, accompanying this feast of friends.

● Pearl COM

53 bis, bd Arago
Métro: Les Gobelins, Glacière
Tel. 01 47 07 58 57
pearlparis@free.fr
www.pearlparis.com
Closed Saturday lunch, Sunday evening.
Open until 10:30 PM.
Prix fixe: 19€ (lunch on weekdays),
27€, 37€. A la carte: 55€.
Air cond. Terrace.

Attentive service, a pearl-gray and white decor with baroque and imitation Louis XV furniture and world cuisine prepared by Jean-Baptiste Legros, formerly of the Cap Est (Relais & Châteaux's star resort in Martinique): This is the gourmet journey that awaits you here. Vegetable casserole with morel sabayon, tomatoes prepared three ways (stuffed, carpaccio, gazpacho), Asian-style tuna tataki and pork medallions with Kerala black pepper butter are satisfyingly exotic. To conclude, the lime soufflé with dark chocolate sorbet is excellent.

● Le Percheron COM

12, rue Véronèse
Métro: Place-d'Italie
Tel.-Fax 01 43 36 65 45
coudray@restaurant-lepercheron.com
www.restaurant-lepercheron.com
Closed Saturday lunch, Sunday, Monday,
1 week Christmas–New Year's, mid-June–
mid-August. Open until 10 PM.
Prix fixe: 13,50€, 17,50€, 19€, 25€.
A la carte: 35–40€.

Gino and Danielle Coudray provide a friendly welcome and run the place, she in the kitchen, he in the dining room. They maintain a family atmosphere and manage the perfectly orchestrated rustic menu, regaling us with a duo of foie gras and smoked salmon, a filet of red mullet with tarragon, a generous cassoulet "au gratin" with goose confit and a homemade seasonal fruit tart.

Good Restaurants & Others

● **Le Petit Marguery** `COM`

9, bd de Port-Royal
Métro: Les Gobelins
Tel. 01 43 31 58 59. Fax 01 43 36 73 34
marguery@wanadoo.fr
www.petitmarguery.fr
Closed Sunday, Monday, Christmas, August.
Open until 10:15 PM.
Prix fixe: 23,20€ (lunch), 26,20€ (lunch),
30€, 35€.
Terrace. Private dining room.

Familiar to aficionados of game, this restaurant presents seasonal dishes prepared according to what the market has to offer and the quality of the year's produce. Head cheese with andouille, roasted scorpion fish with tapenade, rooster with foie gras and truffles (replaced by hare during the hunting season) and Grand Marnier soufflé enjoy the company of selected wines and after-dinner drinks and are attentively served. There are, of course, many regular customers.

● **Le Temps des Cerises** €`SIM`

18, rue de la Butte-aux-Cailles
Métro: Place-d'Italie, Corvisart
Tel. 01 45 89 69 48. Fax 01 45 88 18 53
alphag@club-internet.fr
Closed Saturday lunch, Sunday.
Open until 11:45 PM.
Prix fixe: 7,50€ (lunch), 14,50€, 22,50€.
A la carte: 30–35€.
Private dining room.

In the heart of the Butte aux Cailles quarter, Gérard Alpha's restaurant, run as a workers' cooperative, is a social and gourmet institution. Its name, meaning "The Cherry Season," is the title of a song associated with the Paris Commune. In any case, chef Hedris Londo conscientiously regales his guests with beef cheek confit salad, Antilles-style fish, rib-eye steak with roquefort sauce and chocolate cake, all flawlessly prepared. The prices are always restrained.

● **Le Terroir** `SIM`

11, bd Arago
Métro: Les Gobelins
Tel. 01 47 07 36 99
Closed Saturday, Sunday, Christmas–New Year's, August. Open until 10:15 PM.
A la carte: 55–65€.
Terrace.

Pleasant, solid and copious, the cuisine in this genuine old-style bistro justifies the trip over to boulevard Arago. The house pâté, grilled turbot, hanger steak "La Villette" and chocolate mousse prepared by Daniel Mangin are remarkably generous. The proprietor, Michel Chavanon, formerly at Chez Pierrot in rue Etienne Marcel, is an affable host who knows his wines. Only the prices will make you flinch.

● **Virgule** 🆕🍴`SIM`

9, rue Véronèse
Tel. 01 43 37 01 14
Closed Wednesday, 3 weeks in August.
Open until 11 PM.

French Cambodian Heng Dao smilingly serves us his "local gastronomy". which made him a "Special Favorite" of ours a few years ago. Schooled at Lenôtre and Jules Verne, his dependability never flags. We are, as ever, crazy about his subtle touches of spice and perfectly cooked dishes. Sautéed small scallops served with oyster sauce and celeri rémoulade, monkfish in a wine sauce, whole duck breast with Bing cherries, along with suckling pig with sweet spices and a generous portion of potato gratin, and the Baked Alaska make up cheerful meals at moderate prices.

● **La Zygothèque** €`SIM`

15 bis, rue de Tolbiac
Métro: Bibliothèque-François-Mitterrand
Tel. 01 45 83 07 48
www.lazygotheque.com
Closed Saturday lunch, Sunday, August.
Open until 10:30 PM.
Prix fixe: 14€ (lunch), 29€.
Private dining room.

The whiskey list is the strong point of Jean-Michel Noël's bistro, moored in the new district of the "Very Big Library." Ordering our aperitif, we are spoiled for choice with more than fifty possibilities. The grilled foie gras terrine, sea bass with langoustine coulis, veal piccata with asparagus and tiny wild mushrooms and the ginger cream with pineapple chutney are reliably meticulous.

INTERNATIONAL RESTAURANTS

A SPECIAL FAVORITE

● A Le Bambou ⓝ 🍴 ⓔ SIM
70, rue Baudricourt
Métro: Tolbiac
Tel. 01 45 70 91 75
Closed Monday. Open until 10:30 PM.
A la carte: 20€.

In a street besieged by Oriental restaurants of every kind, this one stands out. Patrons constantly beat a path to its door, ensuring its ongoing success. There is no mystery here: Madeleine Nguyen painstakingly presides over this small Viet embassy, where freshness is the demanding master. Large and small bowls of phô (sliced rare beef soup with meat balls and noodles) like those found in Saigon, papaya salad, omelet-style crêpes stuffed with shrimp, bò bun (spring rolls, grilled beef and julienned vegetables over rice noodles), steamed dumplings and fresh mango are simply delightful.

● L'Appennino 🍴 SIM
61, rue de l'Amiral-Mouchez
Métro: Cité-Universitaire
Tel.-Fax 01 45 89 08 15
lappennino@wanadoo.fr
Closed Saturday, Sunday, Bank Holidays, 1 week Christmas–New Year's, 2 weeks in August. Open until 10:30 PM.
A la carte: 35–40€.
Private dining room.

Vittorino Marzani fervently orchestrates the flavors of Emilia-Romagna in his trattoria done out in shades of pink. The dishes are generous and the vitello tonnato, tuna with lemon, homemade pasta

with Parma ham, like the sabayon, take us on a highly enjoyable journey. Including several organic vintages, the Italian wines presented by Marie-Christine Marzani underline the authentic fare with their sunny notes.

▼ SHOPS

BREAD & BAKED GOODS

▼ L'Artisan du Pain 🏠
104, rue Bobillot
Métro: Place-d'Italie, Tolbiac
Tel. 01 45 80 12 96. Fax 08 25 18 15 46
7 AM–8 PM.
Closed Sunday, Monday, August.
Christophe and Séverine Coët have eagerly adopted this 1920s' store with its historic tiled ceiling and walls. The traditional baguette, organic sourdough bread, financiers and macarons are first class.

▼ Aux Délices de la Butte
48, rue Bobillot
Métro: Place-d'Italie
Tel. 01 45 89 45 55
7 AM–8 PM. Closed Saturday, Sunday, 2 weeks in August.
This friendly store supplies Rétrodor bread. The pistachio and raspberry flans, the vanilla cakes baked in fluted molds, crumbles, the tourtières (Southwestern pastry tarts filled with apples and/or prunes with Armagnac) and craquelins de nougatine (Breton nougat-filled pastries) will have you melting with pleasure.

▼ Laurent Duchêne
2, rue Wurtz
Métro: Glacière
Tel. 01 45 65 00 77
7:30 AM–8 PM. Closed Sunday.
Holder of the 1993 Meilleur Ouvrier de France pastry cook award, having trained with Millet, Hellegouarch and Peltier, Laurent Duchêne is an expert in subtle, fresh cakes. His bakery store is first rate, with a dense traditional baguette with a light airy center, amazing sourdough, and top-quality rye, poppy and bacon breads.

But the Viennese pastries, sweet desserts and puddings, eclairs, millefeuille with rum-infused cream, chocolate cakes and fruit tarts are of the highest order.

▼ Soulabaille

112, av d'Italie
Métro: Maison-Blanche
Tel. 01 45 89 70 40. Fax 01 53 80 33 02
7:15 AM–8 PM. Closed Sunday afternoon, Monday, August.

Paul Soulabaille makes an excellent tourtière from Gascogny with apples or prunes, as well as a pure-butter kouing-aman, but it is his flûte Gana, focaccia and country loaf that win our highest approval.

▼ Stéphane Pouget

90, bd August–Blanqui
Métro: Glacière
Tel. 01 43 31 72 00
8 AM–7:30 PM. Closed Sunday afternoon, Monday, August.

Stéphane Pouget concocts exquisite breads with apricot, sunflower and puffed rice, as well as a splendid "sportif" bread stuffed with dried fruits and pistachios.

WINE

▼ Cave des Gobelins

56, av des Gobelins
Métro: Les Gobelins, Place-d'Italie
Tel.-Fax 01 43 31 66 79
ericmerlet@aol.com
9 AM–1 PM, 3–8 PM. Closed Sunday, Monday, August.

In this fine paneled cellar slumber rare vintage Armagnacs, old Calvados, sixty or so whiskeys, François I Pineau and Paul Bara champagnes. On Saturday afternoon, there is a tasting session hosted by Eric Merlet.

▼ Tous à la Cave   🏠

119, rue Léon-Maurice-Nordmann
Métro: Glacière
Tel. 01 45 35 39 34. Fax 01 45 35 40 55
tousalacave@wanadoo.fr
10:30 AM–1 PM, 4–8 PM. Closed Sunday afternoon, Monday, end of July–mid-August.

Moselle wines, Heiligenstein Klevener, Château Gueyrosse, Saint Emilion and Guillevic cider coexist harmoniously in this fine Thirties' cellar. Also excellent regional products.

CHARCUTERIE

▼ Meurdesoif

8, rue Albert-Bayet
Métro: Place-d'Italie
Tel. 01 42 16 81 83
8:30 AM–1:30 PM, 4–8 PM.
Closed Sunday, August.

Using traditional methods, Joël Meurdesoif produces our favorite cured meats, pâtés and pork products: boudin noir, head cheese, Troyes-style andouillette, ham with the bone in, pork cracklings, foie gras, terrines and caillettes (pork sausage with spinach, garlic, onions, parsley, bread and egg). His cooked dishes, such as beef tongue in a spicy sauce, veal blanquette and stuffed cabbage, are of equally high quality.

CANDY & SWEETS

▼ Les Abeilles

21, rue de la Butte-aux-Cailles
Métro: Place-d'Italie, Corvisart
Tel. 01 45 81 43 48. Fax 01 45 80 75 58
11 AM–7 PM.
Closed Sunday, Monday, August.

Jean-Jacques Schakmundes, who has a demonstration apiary for his customers, presents honey in its every form: acacia, rhododendron, holly, mint, lavender and raspberry bush. He also supplies gingerbread, prepared pastry dough, mendiants de Narbonne (a mixture of figs, almonds, hazelnuts and raisins) and honey mustard.

CHEESE

▼ Fil O' Fromage

12, rue Neuve-Tolbiac
Métro: Bibliothèque-François-Mitterrand
Tel. 01 53 79 13 35. Fax 01 53 79 12 85
10 AM–7:30 PM (Thursday, Friday 11 PM).
Closed Sunday, 1 week in August.

Sylvie and Chérif Boubrit introduce customers to cheese and jelly combinations. Upstairs, photos on the theme of cheese are exhibited. A tasting bar presents Gex blue cheese, Corsican brocciu, Vinage carré, brebis from the Pyrénées, poivre d'âne, Berthault époisses and munster flavored with eau de vie and cumin.

PASTRIES

▼ Mathon
10, pl d'Italie
Métro: Place-d'Italie
Tel. 01 43 31 33 93
7:30 AM–8 PM. Closed Sunday, Monday,
3 weeks in August.

Jean-Paul Mathon shares his passion for old-fashioned breads, petits fours and small sweet and savory pastries. "Le Grand Louvre" (a chocolate orange biscuit with dark and white chocolate mousse), eclairs, dacquoise, chocolate Royal and his "cake of kings" are masterpieces of sweetness.

▼ Les Pâtissiers de la Chapelle
5, bd Arago
Métro: Les Gobelins
Tel. 01 47 07 52 61. Fax 01 43 36 79 06
7 AM–8 PM. Closed Wednesday, 3 weeks in July–beginning of August.

Philippe Legendre wins us over with his valentin (cassis mousse with apple and shortbread pastry), sainte-aimée (apricot mousse, green apple and almond sponge cake), caramel mousse, macarons, millefeuilles and his exquisite ice creams.

REGIONAL PRODUCTS

▼ Genty Gastronomie
169, bd Vincent-Auriol
Métro: Nationale
Tel. 01 45 85 29 45. Fax 01 44 23 89 26
10 AM–1 PM, 3:30–7:45 PM.
Closed Sunday, Monday morning,
Wednesday morning.

The fine cheese store with its ageing cellar, the excellent charcuterie and cheese section featuring regional produce and the vast wine cellar fail to eclipse Jacky Genty's large delicatessen department.

◆ RENDEZVOUS

BARS

◆ Batofar
Facing 11, quai François-Mauriac,
port de la Gare
Métro: Bibliothèque-François-Mitterrand,
Quai-de-la-Gare
www.batofar.org
8 PM–4 AM.
Closed Sunday, Monday (in winter).

This imposing red iron shop topped with a lighthouse presents electronic music and a range of cocktails. Enjoy the happy hours on Tuesday and Thursday until 9:30 p.m.

◆ La Folie en Tête
33, rue de la Butte-aux-Cailles
Métro: Corvisart, Place-d'Italie
Tel. 01 45 80 65 99
6 PM–2 AM.
Closed Sunday, Christmas–New Year's.

This bar enthusiastically showcases percussion and African instruments. Patrons take time out to enjoy beers and cocktails.

WINE BARS

◆ Au Soleil d'Austerlitz
18, bd de l'Hôpital
Métro: Gare-d'Austerlitz
Tel. 01 43 31 22 38. Fax 01 43 31 73 55
7 AM–10 PM.
Closed Saturday evening, Sunday.
Terrace.

Cyril Dos Santos has taken over this café opposite the rail station with everyday, home-style cooking, Aveyron produce and selected Beaujolais. A convivial ambience.

CAFES

◆ Café Bibliothèque
MK2 Bibliothèque, 162, av de France
Métro: Bibliothèque-François-Mitterrand,
Quai-de-la-Gare
Tel. Fax 01 56 61 44 12
www.mk2.com
Noon–4 PM, 7 PM–midnight (Saturday Sunday noon–midnight). Closed Christmas.

This modern loft has chic to spare. We adore the enormous lengths of bamboo in the large dining room, with its screen-printed glass and bright red from floor to walls. The gourmet platters are substantial snacks indeed.

◆ Le Réveil-Matin

32, av des Gobelins
Métro: Les Gobelins
Tel. 01 43 31 11 84
8 AM–8 PM (groups must reserve in the evening). Closed Sunday, Bank Holidays, Christmas–New Year's, August.
Terrace.

This beige and white establishment covering three floors serves mixed grills and homemade French fries, andouillette, duck breast and assorted salads with zest.

CREPERIES

◆ Crêperie du Thimonier

11, bd Saint-Marcel
Métro: St-Marcel
Tel. 01 47 07 59 69
//creperieduthimonier.free.fr
11:45 AM–2 PM, 6:45–10 PM.
Closed Sunday, Monday evening, August.

Vinh Sach Nguyen offers amiable French Asian dishes of the day, along with traditional crêpes. Menu in Braille and large characters for the visually impaired.

TEA SALONS

◆ L'Art Home Café

44, bd Arago
Métro: Les Gobelins
Tel.-Fax 01 43 31 91 30
11AM–10:30 PM (Sunday 5 PM).
Closed Sunday, Monday, Easter, August.
Terrace.

All redecorated in white, mauve and black under the supervision of Massogbe Villard, this tearoom offers grilled open-face sandwiches, salads, daily specials (exotic, and some not so exotic), plates of Creole specialties in the afternoon and cocktails.

◆ L'Empire des Thés

101, av d'Ivry
Métro: Tolbiac
Tel. 01 45 85 66 33. Fax 01 45 84 62 15
edt@kawa.fr
11 AM–8 PM. Closed Monday.
Air cond.

In this orange-red tearoom, patrons savor a wide range of teas: Fujian Yin Zhen, Anhui green tea and Ti Kuan Yin Imperial blue green tea. These brews are accompanied by green tea or sesame eclairs, financiers with Sencha green tea, citrus cake or chocolate tart infused with Earl Grey.

◆ L'Oisive Thé

10, rue de la Butte-aux-Cailles
Métro: Place-d'Italie, Corvisart
Tel. 01 53 80 31 33
www.loisivethe.free.fr
Noon–7 PM (Friday–Sunday noon–8 PM).
Closed Monday, August.

This delicate tearoom that serves brunch in a neo-colonial setting has 50 or so selected teas to offer, accompanied by shortbread cookies, pound cake or rhubarb and plum tart.

◆ Pose T

126, rue Nationale
Métro: Nationale
Tel. 01 45 85 80 55
www.poset.canalblog.com
9:30 AM–7 PM. Closed Saturday, Sunday
Air cond.

We take a break and enjoy one of the 25 selected teas (Darjeeling, Sencha, etc.) and fine fruit tarts, a delicious crumble, chocolate from Catherine Custodio. Between mouthfuls, we can visit her husband's adjoining photo gallery and store.

14TH ARRONDISSEMENT
MONTPARNASSE GOURMETS

Montparnasse is only part of the fourteenth arrondissement, and the artists who once filled the boulevard's cafés are long gone. Yet the village of Montparnasse remains highly influential, with its tower dominating the horizon and its cemetery, where so many illustrious figures are buried, including Sartre, Fargue and Baudelaire. The city limits feel of rue du Château, rue de l'Ouest and rue Didot, and the suburban taste of avenue du Maine and rue d'Alésia are highly deceptive. Rue Daguerre has a friendly village air to it. The district's bistros and stores speak with the voice of wisdom. A few well-known restaurants here and there (L'Assiette, Le Duc, Le Dôme, Le Cagouille, Montparnasse 25, La Maison Courtine) suggest a modest glory, but the local inhabitants, who like to be left in peace, do not care. The fourteenth is also bucolic, with its secret gardens, cul-de-sacs and rustic villas between rue Boulard and the cemetery, and suits those with hearty appetites. It is home to many modest eateries. High chic is not the local style. Its spirited cheesemongers, inspiring cellar owners, reliable butchers (such as the star Hugo Desnoyer), gifted bakers (Pierre Thilloux, Basile Kamir, Bruno Thual) and tasteful confectioners (Gerstenmeyer) express a love of genuine fare. Fuss is the enemy here. We do not look down on Montparnasse, but from it, admiring Paris from its peaceful vantage point. It is a village once again.

● RESTAURANTS

GRAND RESTAURANTS

● Montparnasse 25 ◎◎ LUX

Hotel Méridien-Montparnasse,
19, rue du Cdt-René-Mouchotte
Métro: Montparnasse-Bienvenüe, Gaîté
Tel. 01 44 36 44 25. Fax 01 44 36 49 03
meridien.montparnasse@lemeridien.com
www.m25.fr
Closed Saturday, Sunday, Bank Holidays,
mid-July–end of August.
Open until 10:30 PM.
Prix fixe: 49€ (lunch), 108€ (dinner).
A la carte: 105–145€.
Air cond. Private dining room.

You may or may not like the neo-Thirties, slightly colonial, exotic "James Bond" style of this great hotel restaurant hidden away upstairs. In any case, you will soon feel at home. The great virtues here are the superb service run by Mauro Croese (previously with Guy Savoy), the excellent wines, with advice on the long wine list provided by Emmanuel Petit, and of course the fine cuisine, which is solid and traditional, but forging ahead in the hands of Christian Moine, one of Paris's least known great chefs. This veteran of Le Meurice and Le Ritz, formerly with Ducloux at Tournus, showcases the finest produce with a rare precision and unfailing aptness of tone. His latest creations are crabmeat served in the crab's claw with a foamy, sweet mustard dressing, a terrine of foie gras, veal sweetbreads and tongue served with arugula salad dressed in red currant juice, sea bass pan-fried on one side with carrot juice served with buttered baby arugula and herbed ravioli and whole roasted John Dory on a bed of fennel with turmeric. He also offers more carnivorous delights, such as grilled Angus beef with marrow French toast and Colman's mustard, served with a ratte potato purée, or "Monsieur Miéral's" Bresse pigeon roasted like a woodcock and served with creamed fresh peas. The desserts—puff pastry fingers with summer fruit, whipped light cream and red fruit jus,

nougat ice cream or lemon-basil tartlet, cotton candy and gin-fizz sorbet—are droll and successful. The cheese board is always admirable. Although the a la carte prices are less than friendly, the lunchtime prix fixe is a fabulous bargain. Remember that.

GOOD RESTAURANTS & OTHERS

● L'Amuse-Bouche 🐟 SIM

186, rue du Château
Métro: Mouton-Duvernet, Pernety
Tel. 01 43 35 31 61. Fax 01 45 38 96 60
Closed Sunday, Monday, August.
Open until 10:30 PM.
Prix fixe: 24,50€, 30,50€.
A la carte: 40€.

In this brightly colored restaurant, Gilles Lambert delights his crowd of faithful guests with fresh, market-based dishes. We fondly remember the langoustine ravioli with tarragon, fresh crab in rémoulade sauce with Granny Smith apples, tuna steak with cracked black pepper and soy sauce and the calf's liver with a ginger-bread crust. The local wines unearthed more or less throughout France and the aptly crafted desserts, such as apple crumble with salted-butter caramel ice cream, certainly hit the mark.

● Apollo COM

3, place Denfert-Rochereau
Métro: Denfert-Rochereau
Tel. 01 45 38 76 77. Fax 01 43 22 02 15
reservation@restaurant-apollo.fr
www.restaurant-apollo.com
Open daily until midnight.
Prix fixe: 15€ (lunch on weekdays),
18€ (lunch on weekdays). A la carte: 50€.
Terrace. Valet parking.

There is not much left of the former luggage room of Denfert-Rochereau station: just this vast, determinedly pop rock dining room offering trendy world cuisine and relaxed service. Two Pascals—Mousset at the helm and Taperest at the stove—have taken over from the old team. We enjoy the guacamole served in a glass with shrimp and crayfish, the sea bream filet with bell pepper confit and pesto, chicken tagine with olives and preserved lemon, wok-fried noodles in Indonesian sauce and orange salad with honey-gingerbread ice cream. A marvelous terrace and activities for children at lunchtime on Sunday.

● L'Assiette　　　🏠 SIM

181, rue du Château
Métro: Mouton-Duvernet, Pernety
Tel. 01 43 22 64 86
www.chezlulu.fr
Open daily until 11 PM.
Closed lunch (except Saturday, Sunday).
Prix fixe: 50€ (dinner, wine included).
A la carte: 50–100€.

Lulu livens up the atmosphere with her earthy humor in this former delicatessen turned bistro. The dishes are generous here, as are the prices, more sensible than in the past. We never tire of her mackerel rillettes, homemade pork pâté, skate in lemon butter, blood pudding parmentier and Poitou-style salt-cured duck stew with vegetables. And her chocolate fondant and floating island are just as good. As a bonus, guests can play at recognizing the TV and radio celebrities who call on the legendary, brash Lulu.

● L'Atelier 102　　　● SIM

102, rue du Château
Métro: Gaîté, Pernety, Mouton-Duvernet
Tel. 01 43 21 86 16
Closed Sunday, August. Open until 11 PM.
Prix fixe: 12,50€ (lunch), 17€ (dinner), 21€ (wine included). A la carte: 27€.

The frescos on the walls (the work of the proprietor's nephew) offer a reminder of days when this was a haunt for local artists. Abdelkader Bouzouane regales his regulars with sound, regional dishes, typically duck terrine, grilled vegetables, Mediterranean-style red mullet, roasted duck breast with sour cherries. The produce is fresh and the moderate prices only add to our enjoyment. A fine assortment of homemade pastries.

● L'Atelier d'Antan　　　Ⓝ SIM

9, rue Léopold-Robert
Métro: Vavin, Raspail
Tel. 01 43 21 36 19
Closed Saturday lunch, Sunday,
2 weeks in August. Open until 10 PM.
Prix fixe: 15€ (lunch), 18€ (lunch).
A la carte: 38€.

Farewell Da Gigy la Romana. This is now a cozy gourmet workshop. Pascal Molto, formerly at the Oeillade in the seventh arrondissement, hurries from stove to table, serving reliable, fresh, typically French dishes. Fine homemade pâtés, grouper stewed in red wine, a melt-in-your-mouth veal sauté, seasonal fruit crumble and coffee crème brûlée have the satisfying flavor of good old-fashioned cooking.

● Auberge du Petit Tonneau　　　SIM

51, rue Hallé
Métro: Mouton-Duvernet
Tel. 01 43 27 55 85
Closed Saturday, Sunday,
Bank Holidays, 3 weeks in August.
Open until 10:30 PM.
Prix fixe: 21€ (lunch), 27,50€.
A la carte: 40–60€.
Private dining room.

This Fifties' bistro with its fresh new paint and woodwork offers a simple, cheerful atmosphere and excellent traditional cuisine. The homemade rabbit terrine with its jelly is very tasty, as are the deliciously warm asparagus vinaigrette, red mullet filets with sautéed zucchini, a warm, velvety Lyonnaise sausage studded with pistachios and the profiteroles served with an unctuous chocolate sauce. Nice roast prime rib for two.

● Aux Iles Marquises　　　COM

15, rue de la Gaîté
Métro: Edgar-Quinet, Gaîté
Tel.-Fax 01 43 20 93 58
aux.iles-marquises@laposte.net
Closed Saturday lunch, Sunday, August.
Open until 11 PM.
Prix fixe: 26€, 45€. A la carte: 60–65€.
Private dining room.

The freshly painted salmon and burgundy facade and the marine decor, with its painted woodwork, frescos and engravings of old ships, set the tone. Mathias Théry, a veteran of Rostang and Vergé, prepares immaculately fresh dishes with a masterly hand. In this typical Montparnasse street blighted by emporia of a dubious nature, we are surprised to find a restaurant of this quality. The set menu at 26€ is a bargain. The rabbit in basil aspic jelly, monkfish steak with citrus, sautéed calf's liver with balsamic vinegar, rhubarb turnover and the mistress of the house's friendly oenological recommendations are just the ticket.

● Bar à Huîtres   `SIM`

112, bd du Montparnasse
Métro: Vavin
Tel. 01 43 20 71 01. Fax 01 43 20 52 04
www.lebarahuitre.fr
Open daily noon–1 AM. Cont. service.
Prix fixe: 20€, 24€, 32€, 42€.
A la carte: 36–50€.
Air cond. Terrace. Valet parking.

Jean-Pierre Chedal has enthusiastically taken over this marine brasserie offering various types of oysters, shellfish and line-caught fish. Freshness is guaranteed in this temple of seafood, where the platters are generous, the service efficient and the decor designed by Garcia. The squid and monkfish sautéed with Espelette chili pepper, mixed rock fish soup, turbot or skate in lemon butter and sautéed seasonal fruit with salted caramel sauce are just the thing for a light, fresh supper.

● Bel Canto   `COM`

88, rue de la Tombe-Issoire
Métro: Alésia
Tel. 01 43 22 96 15. Fax 01 43 27 09 88
lebelcanto2@wanadoo.fr
www.lebelcanto.fr
Closed Sunday, Monday, August.
Open until 10:30 PM.
Prix fixe: 75€ (wine included).
Air cond. Terrace. Private dining room.
Valet parking.

Comic opera for lovers of lyrical art and Italian cuisine. Like its brothers on Quai de l'Hôtel de Ville and in Neuilly, this Bel Canto offers a package that its patrons love. The program includes Don Juan (baby artichokes roasted with smoked bacon and served with arugula), Carmen (sautéed sea bream, leek butter sauce and basmati rice), Rigoletto (braised lamb shank with skewered baby potatoes and roasted figs), La Tosca (sorbets and fresh fruit coulis). The waiters dart from table to piano, where they perform between two courses. All are apprentice singers at the conservatories of Paris, and this is their first public engagement. Opera, aperitif, wine, water, starter, main course, cheese, dessert and coffee: The whole thing comes to 75€, whatever you do.

● Le Bis du Severo   `SIM`

16, rue des Plantes
Métro: Alésia, Mouton-Duvernet
Tel. 01 40 44 73 09
lebis@cegetel.net
Closed Sunday, Monday, 1 week
Christmas–New Year's, August.
Open until 10:30 PM.
Prix fixe: 18€ (lunch), 22€ (lunch).
A la carte: 32–40€.

Severo's piscine adjunct run by Marie-Magdalein Gaël (dispatched there by William Bernet) lives up to its promises. The Japanese chef, Shigeno Makoto, deftly prepares boudin noir and rosette d'Auvergne (Auvergne dried sausage), scallops, red tuna and steaks. Directly supplied by the parent restaurant, the meat is excellent. Chocolate mousse or tea-flavored blanc-manger to finish, and a moderate tab.

● Bistrot des Pingouins   `€` `SIM`

79, rue Daguerre
Métro: Denfert-Rochereau, Gaîté
Tel. 01 43 21 92 29. Fax 01 45 88 79 09
Closed Saturday lunch, Sunday, August.
Open until 12:30 AM.
Prix fixe: 12,50€ (lunch), 14€ (dinner).
A la carte: 25–30€.
Terrace.

In their sober beige, brown and yellow bistro, Sylvie Demathieu and Michel Cos serve up a cuisine that is graceful enough not to take itself seriously. The fresh tomato and basil tartine, codfish sautéed with thyme and olive oil potato purée, orange and grapefruit salad and chocolate crêpes are unpretentious. The welcome is as friendly as the prices.

● Le Bistrot du Dôme　　　SIM
1, rue Delambre
Métro: Vavin
Tel. 01 43 35 32 00
Closed Saturday, Sunday in August.
Open until 11 PM.
A la carte: 40–50€.
Air cond.

Things have improved at Maxime Bras's. His maritime bistro, a spin off of the neighboring Dôme, offers reasonably priced ocean produce that will not leave you at sea. The salad of langoustines and foie gras, grilled squid, scallops sautéed with spices, small Dover sole sautéed in butter are at the peak of their form, served by staff whose technique is improving. The short wine list features some fine bottles at sensible prices.

● Bistrot Montsouris　　　COM
27, av Reille
Métro: Porte-d'Orléans, Cité-Universitaire
Tel. 01 45 89 17 05. Fax 01 45 80 19 38
Closed Sunday evening, Monday, New Year's,
3 weeks in August. Open until 10:30 PM.
A la carte: 35–42€.
Terrace.

We could be in the countryside in this provincial inn beside the park. Its stone walls, old-fashioned woodwork and friendly atmosphere set the tone. Predominantly Breton and oceanic, the prix fixe does not disappoint. The homemade salmon terrine, the "affinity" salad of lobster and foie gras, scallops brochette, veal kidneys with Port wine and cherry clafoutis or lemon tart gratify the regular customers here.

● A La Bonne Table　　　SIM
42, rue Friant
Métro: Porte-d'Orléans, Cité-Universitaire
Tel. 01 45 39 74 91. Fax 01 45 43 66 92
Closed Saturday lunch, Sunday, 1 week
Christmas–New Year's, 1 week in February,
3 weeks in July. Open until 10:30 PM.
Prix fixe: 25€ (lunch), 29€.
A la carte: 35–45€.
Air cond.

This cozy, soothing restaurant subtly reworks French classics. Japanese chef Yoshitaka Kawamoto, formerly with Guy Savoy, subtly prepares goat cheese croustillant with olive oil, herbed shrimp salad, arctic char filet, andouillette from Troyes and a hot Grand Marnier soufflé: attractive, gratifying dishes at moderate prices.

● Au Bretzel　　　SIM
1, rue Léopold-Robert
Métro: Vavin, Raspail
Tel. 01 40 47 82 37
www.aubretzel.free.fr
Closed Monday, Thursday evening,
3 weeks in August. Open until 10:30 PM.
Prix fixe: 23€. A la carte: 33–40€.
Air cond. Terrace.

No-nonsense and amiably priced, this Weinstübe in wood and off-white shades offers salade vigneronne (a salad of cold sausage and emmental cheese), smoked trout filet, choucroute, flammeküeche (a typical Alsatian pizza-like tart with bacon, onions and cream) and iced vacherin worthy of the better taverns of Strasbourg. In the dining room and kitchen, respectively, Pascale and Renée Kaelbel ensure high standards of quality. The Tokay Pinot Gris and Rieslings are well chosen.

● La Cagouille　　　SIM
10, pl Constantin-Brancusi
Métro: Gaîté
Tel. 01 43 22 09 01. Fax 01 45 38 57 29
la-cagouille@wanadoo.fr
www.la-cagouille.fr
Open daily until 10:30 PM.
Prix fixe: 26€, 42€ (wine included).
A la carte: 55€.
Terrace. Private dining room.

Away from the traffic on a small, unobtrusive square, this seafood eatery is fitted out with woodwork like that in boat frames. In the kitchen, Freddy Amy has taken over from the restaurant's founding chef, Gérard Allemandou, and serves up warm cockles, small fried filets of sole, grilled tuna steak with smoked bacon, grilled John Dory fish, all served with mashed potatoes and regularly featured on the blackboard. We cannot resist the parfait with honey, pinenuts and cognac. A fine shady terrace in the summer.

● **Les Caves Solignac**　🏠 SIM

9, rue Decrès
Métro: Plaisance, Pernety
Tel.-Fax 01 45 45 58 59
Closed Saturday, Sunday, 1 week
Christmas–New Year's, 3 weeks in August.
Open until 10 PM.
Prix fixe: 18€ (lunch), 28€ (dinner).
A la carte: 38€.

Pascal and Philippe Moisant have taken over the reins of this Thirties' decor wine bar, with its old clock on the wall and Magimix espresso machine, and offer a tremendously fresh, market-based cuisine. Asparagus and polenta, croustillant of mackerel with rhubarb, fish of the day, slow-cooked beef cheeks in red wine and roasted apricots with vanilla ice cream suitably accompany the 70 growers' vintages. A few good Calvados apple brandies and a moderate tab pleasantly conclude the proceedings.

● **La Cerisaie**　🔔 SIM

70, bd Edgar-Quinet
Métro: Edgar-Quinet,
Montparnasse-Bienvenüe
Tel.-Fax 01 43 20 98 98
Closed Saturday, Sunday, Christmas–New Year's, August. Open until 10 PM.
A la carte: 38€.

The Lalannes manage beautifully in their mini bistro with its twenty places, serving up generous dishes inspired by Southwestern France, at friendly prices. At the stove, Cyril from the Ariège, who learned his

trade in Paris at Le Bascou and Le Louis XIII and in Toulouse with Garrigues and Vanel, skillfully concocts subtle, charming fare. The sardines in phyllo pastry with cumin and wild arugula, duck confit terrine, grilled tuna steak with piperade, grilled Landais goose breast and spiced roasted peaches and Armagnac-soaked baba will make you melt. Maryse from the Aveyron provides a wonderfully attentive, friendly welcome. No smoking.

● **La Chopotte**　SIM

168, rue d'Alésia
Métro: Plaisance
Tel. 01 45 43 16 16
Open daily until 10:30 PM.
A la carte: 25–33€.
Terrace.

Sébastien Felgines, formerly of Lenôtre and La Tour d'Argent, continues to appeal with his ardent cellar and the beautiful terrines, excellent charcuterie and pâtés and the famous AAAAA andouillette that distinguish this solid local eatery. The products, such as the superb Salers beef top rump steak, come directly from the farm. The warm soft chocolate cake and cherry clafoutis measure up, and the check is held down to a reasonable level.

● **Contre-Allée**　SIM

83, av Denfert-Rochereau
Métro: Denfert-Rochereau
Tel. 01 43 54 99 86. Fax 01 43 25 05 28
www.contre-allee.com
Closed Saturday lunch, Sunday
Open until 11 PM.
Prix fixe: 25€ (lunch), 35€.
A la carte: 40–55€.
Air cond. Terrace. Private dining room.
Valet parking.

A new breeze is blowing through this restaurant renovated by Yannick Huard and Philippe Kukurudz. The Havana brown and beige walls decorated with vintage and curious views of Paris provide a suitable showcase for Sylvain Pinault's meticulous cuisine. The baby spinach salad, duck foie gras terrine, wok-fried vegetables with soy sauce, pig's foot and foie gras crispy cake, minted strawberry soup and pineapple carpaccio with aged rum are all highly polished.

● La Coupole 🏠 COM

102, bd du Montparnasse
Métro: Vavin
Tel. 01 43 20 14 20. Fax 01 43 35 46 14
jtosi@groupeflo.fr
www.flobrasseries.com
Open daily until 1 AM.
Prix fixe: 15€ (lunch), 22,90€, 29,90€.
A la carte: 40–55€.
Air cond. Private dining room. Valet parking.

This historic brasserie has a new management and chef. Jean-Paul Bucher may have relinquished control of the Flo group, but no one seems to have noticed, and the Coupole is doing very well. The seafood platter, salmon rillettes, grilled codfish, generous choucroute, superb grilled rib-eye steak served with thick-cut French fries, the ever-present Indian-style lamb curry and warm soft chocolate cake and roasted pineapple are splendid, served (despite the sea of tables) with promptness and a smile. The Twenties' setting with its fresco-embellished column capitals continues to hold a strong appeal.

● De Bouche à Oreille COM

34, rue Gassendi
Métro: Denfert-Rochereau, Gaîté
Tel.-Fax 01 43 27 73 14
sammian2@hotmail.fr
Closed Saturday lunch, Sunday,
Monday lunch, August. Open until 11 PM.
A la carte: 38–45€.
Terrace.

With Benoît Chagny, disciple of Jean-Pierre Vigato, at the helm and stove, this charming bistro in pastel colors is the pride of its neighborhood. The foie gras roasted with spices and honey, monkfish with preserved lemon and basil, tender braised pork cheeks in vinaigrette and the sugar-roasted brioche in caramel sauce with homemade caramel ice cream are all highly appropriate and sun drenched.

● Le Dôme 🏠 ○ COM

108, bd du Montparnasse
Métro: Vavin
Tel. 01 43 35 25 81. Fax 01 42 79 01 19
Open daily until 12:30 AM.
A la carte: 72–100€.
Air cond. Terrace. Private dining room.

Things have improved in this circa-1920 brasserie, with its refurbished Seventies' decor designed by Slavik. Chef Franck Graux has taken the kitchen firmly in hand and the service, closely supervised by the exacting Madame Bras, is of a very high standard. There are tuna carpaccio, sea bream tartare and marinated raw salmon, lobster salad with slow-roasted tomatoes and radishes in rémoulade sauce, authentic Marseilles bouillabaise, grilled tiny red mullet and large Dover sole fried in butter from the île d'Yeu served with mashed potatoes worthy of Robuchon. All offer undiluted pleasure. There is even a fine chop, from traditionally raised veal, for the carnivorous. We conclude with a splendid rum and vanilla millefeuille. The wine list is rich in divine surprises.

● Le Duc ○ V.COM

243, bd Raspail
Métro: Raspail
Tel. 01 43 20 96 30. Fax 01 43 20 46 73
Closed Saturday lunch, Sunday, Monday,
3 weeks in August. Open until 10:30 PM.
Prix fixe: 46€ (lunch). A la carte: 120€.
Air cond.

This celebrated restaurant has built its reputation on fresh fish. It has been following its star for more than three decades now, and the yacht decor designed by Slavik long ago still wields a dated charm. The service is well timed and customers pour in, filling the place at noon despite prices verging on the piratical. In fact, the best deal is the splendid lunchtime set menu, offering salmon with two peppers or other fish tartare, oysters or fried smelt, scallops simply cooked in their shells or provençal-style monkfish, not to mention the chocolate cake and baba au rhum. The raw sea bass, garlic-sautéed squid, fried strips of Dover sole filets and steamed turbot filet

(62€ when we last visited!) are washed down pleasantly with a good Muscadet.

● Face au Square — SIM

53, rue Didot
Métro: Pernety, Plaisance
Tel.-Fax 01 45 43 18 87
Closed Saturday, Sunday, 1 week
Christmas–New Year's, August.
Open until 10:30 PM.
A la carte: 38€.

Christiane Bordas handles business with a smile from season to season, offering changing dishes of the day at very reasonable prices. The surf and turf salad, vanilla foie gras terrine, sea bass with fennel, sautéed red mullet, beef or veal rib chop, country-style pineapple and coconut clafoutis with aged rum and a mango tarte Tatin: There is always plenty of choice and the wine list is promising with its 50 items.

● Les Fils de la Ferme — ● ● SIM

5, rue Mouton-Duvernet
Métro: Mouton-Duvernet
Tel.-Fax 01 45 39 39 61
www.lesfilsdelaferme.com
Closed Sunday evening, Monday,
3 weeks in August. Open until 10:30 PM.
Prix fixe: 17€ (lunch), 26€.
Private dining room.

Our Special Favorite of 2006 continues to gratify with enticing fare and reasonable prices. The codfish crumble with orange peel and creamy young garlic broth reflect the fine ideas of Stéphane Dutter, who worked with Georges Blanc and Christian Morisset at Le Juana and has settled here with his brother Jean-Christophe, who handles the service. The skate fried in red bell pepper butter, tender slow-roasted leg of suckling pig, rhubarb floating island and red fruit macerated in balsamic vinegar and served with fromage blanc are also magnificent.

● Giufeli — ● SIM

129, rue du Château
Métro: Pernety
Tel.-Fax 01 43 27 32 56
www.giufeli.com
Closed lunch, 3 weeks in August.
Open until 11 PM.
Prix fixe: 22€.
Air cond. Terrace.

This unobtrusive eatery keeps its promises. The prix fixe is a challenge, offering a range of delights. The avocado profiteroles with a carrot and cumin coulis, sea bass with New Zealand spinach sprouts, osso buco in orange sauce, banana spring rolls and tea-infused tropical fruit served in a glass have an easy charm. The wines are well chosen, the service irreproachable and the surroundings cozy, with floor and paintwork refurbished as new.

● La Maison Courtine — V.COM

157, av du Maine
Métro: Mouton-Duvernet, Gaîté
Tel. 01 45 43 08 04. Fax 01 45 45 91 35
Closed Saturday lunch, Sunday, Monday lunch, Christmas–New Year's, August.
Open until 11 PM.
Prix fixe: 32€, 36€.
Air cond. Terrace. Private dining room.

Yves Charles serves up appetizing dishes with gusto: cold cream of spider crab soup, langoustine ravioli with stewed leeks, and grilled foie gras with grapes, sautéed milk-fed veal steak with yellow Planèze lentils and Armagnac-flavored apple pastry topped with crispy phyllo. With its 350 items, the wine list is full of possibilities.

● La Mère Agitée — ● SIM

21, rue Campagne-Première
Métro: Raspail
Tel.-Fax 01 43 35 56 64
www.lamereagitee.com
Closed Sunday, Monday, 2 weeks in August.
Open until 11 PM.
Prix fixe: 19€ (lunch, wine included).
A la carte: 28€.

Within these walls covered in postcards, posters and pictures, Valérie Delahaye wins her customers' hearts with her cordiality and generous cuisine. The poached eggs with lentils, duck rillettes, sea bass with fennel, veal blanquette, roasted leg of suckling pig and apple or raspberry tarts are simply a delight. The fine assortment of farmhouse cheeses is accompanied by select wines.

A SPECIAL FAVORITE

● **Millésime 62**   **N** **COM**
13-15, pl de Catalogne
Métro: Gaîté, Montparnasse-Bienvenüe
Tel. 01 43 35 34 35. Fax 01 43 20 26 21
www.millesimes62.com
Closed Saturday lunch, Sunday,
Bank Holidays, 2 weeks in August.
Open until 10:30 PM.
Prix fixe: 24€ (lunch), 26€.

Elegant and charming, flavorsome and vinic, this "lounge" is perfect for both business and private meals. Close to the Montparnasse rail station on a square planned by Boffil, it has an easy charm. The cuisine is a wonderful surprise, with its lively, fresh dishes escorted by a stream of selected vintages, served by the glass or in bottles of every size. Under the supervision of Pascal Noizet, a veteran of the Flo group, the spring roll of duck confit with meat and balsamic vinegar jus, whole foie gras terrine, goat cheese and fresh sardine filet on grilled bread, grilled codfish with wok-fried vegetables and tender roasted duck breast with basmati rice are first rate. The desserts—baba au rhum, lemon tart, chocolate fondant a la mode, served with an amusing tomato syrup—are up to the same high standards.

● **Monsieur Lapin**   **COM**
11, rue Raymond-Losserand
Métro: Gaîté, Pernety
Tel. 01 43 20 21 39. Fax 01 43 21 84 86
www.monsieur-lapin.fr
Closed Saturday lunch, Monday, August.
Open until 10:30 PM.
Prix fixe: 25€ (lunch on weekdays), 34€,
45€. A la carte: 50–65€.
Air cond.

Franck Enée has taken over this restaurant. Although he admits to a weakness for fish, he has stuck to the name—"Mr. Rabbit"—unchanged for a quarter century. We are tempted by the different possibilities: jellied rabbit terrine or crab appetizer with red onion marmalade? Grilled tuna steak with fingerling potatoes fried in olive oil or rabbit croustillant with dried fruit, nuts and mushrooms? The grilled Salers beef tenderloin offers a compromise solution and the hot praliné soufflé wins unanimous approval.

● **Natacha**   **SIM**
17 bis, rue Campagne-Première
Métro: Raspail
Tel. 01 43 20 79 27. Fax 01 43 22 00 90
restaurantnatacha@wanadoo.fr
Closed Sunday, Saturday lunch, Monday,
3 weeks in August. Open until 11:30 PM.
Prix fixe: 19€ (lunch), 26€ (lunch),
A la carte: 36–44€.
Air cond. Terrace. Private dining room.

Alain Cirelli, a veteran of L'Ambroisie, has breathed new life into this legendary Montparnasse eatery. The changing prix fixe reflects current fashions, but not exclusively. We have happy memories of the steamed baby leeks with poached egg and truffle oil, warm calf's head terrine, John Dory roasted on one side served with asparagus and New Zealand spinach, shepherd's pie, country cherry clafoutis and chocolate fondant with cracked pistachios. A timeless bistro setting, revamped in saffron yellow, white and red.

● **L'O à la Bouche**   **SIM**
124, bd du Montparnasse
Métro: Vavin
Tel. 01 56 54 01 55. Fax 01 43 21 07 87
loalabouche2@wanadoo.fr
Closed Sunday, Monday evening, 2 weeks in
August. Open until 11 PM.
Prix fixe: 20,80€ (lunch), 32€ (dinner).
Air cond. Terrace. Valet parking.

Franck Paquier has his sights set firmly on the South of France. With sobriety and precision, this veteran of Troisgros and Guy

Savoy tries out some interesting combinations, serving a warm crab salad with tomato and bell pepper sauce and a pan-seared duck foie gras with wild berries and young spinach. While the monkfish with Bayonne ham and saffron risotto with piquillo peppers is a classic, duck breast with peaches and nectarines, served with a salad of crisp lettuce and dried fruit provides an original touch. For dessert, cherry gratin with licorice served with vanilla ice cream and pistachio-stuffed roasted apricots with almond ice cream are deliciously unexpected. The selection of wines is good, but a little pricey.

● L'Opportun   SIM

62, bd Edgar-Quinet
Métro: Edgar-Quinet,
Montparnasse-Bienvenüe
Tel. 01 43 20 26 89. Fax 01 43 21 61 88
lopportun@wanadoo.fr
Closed Sunday. Open until 11:30 PM.
Prix fixe: 21€. A la carte: 45€.
Air cond. Terrace. Private dining room.
Valet parking.

This yellow-walled Lyonnaise *bouchon*-style restaurant with its charcuterie (good), Beaujolais and lively atmosphere is pleasant and quite popular. Originally from Roanne, Serge Alzerat has earthy humor, experience and a well-chosen cellar on his side. The plates are piled with salade Lyonnaise (chicory salad with poached egg and bacon) and andouillette, poached eggs in red wine and bacon sauce and Royans ravioli, cod with potatoes and grilled calf's liver, baba au rhum and paris-brest . . . everything that makes life worth living, in fact.

● La Panetière   ⊜ SIM

9, rue Maison-Dieu
Métro: Gaîté, Pernety
Tel. 01 43 22 04 02
Closed Sunday, Monday, 2 weeks in August.
Open until 10 PM.
Prix fixe: 11€ (lunch), 18€.
A la carte: 25€.

Bertrand Gondlach has handed his apron in and his bistro over to Madame Suraud,

who has modernized the decor, but (whew!) not the prices, so regulars from the neighborhood can continue to enjoy the foie gras salad, scallops in broth, cod filet in vermouth sauce, filet mignon with garlic cream, warm apple tart or tiramisu, all meticulously prepared. A fine establishment in a small, out-of-the-way street.

● Chez Papa   SIM

6, rue Gassendi
Métro: Denfert-Rochereau
Tel. 01 43 22 41 19. Fax 01 40 47 55 73
www.chezpapa.fr
Closed Christmas–New Year's.
Open until 1 AM.
Prix fixe: 19,55€ (lunch on weekdays).
A la carte: 25–36€.
Air cond. Terrace.

With its Espelette peppers on the walls, good-natured ambience (half farmhouse, half canteen) and sensible prices, this Parisian institution is proud to fly the flag of Southwest France. Bruno Druilhe, Papa for the occasion and former rugby player, runs his business with brisk efficiency, while chef Anis pleasantly regales his guests with chicken liver salad, poached egg in sheep's milk, sautéed duck breast with peaches, cassoulet or tarte Tatin. We never tire of this amiable eatery.

A SPECIAL FAVORITE

● Parnasse 138   ⌂ ⊜ SIM

138, bd du Montparnasse
Métro: Vavin, Port-Royal
Tel. 01 43 20 47 87. Fax 01 43 22 44 85
Open daily until 11:30 PM.
Prix fixe: 11,50€ (lunch on weekdays),
13,50€, 17,50€. A la carte: 25–30€.
Air cond. Terrace.

Caroula and Nelson Da Rosa have taken over this friendly restaurant. With an eye for fresh produce, the couple has carried off a tour de force, presenting a choice of at least ten starters, entrees and desserts on each prix fixe menu, with a few additional daily specials. Duck terrine with green peppercorns, homemade duck foie gras, sautéed oyster mushrooms, grilled fresh sardines and many more pleasant dishes and flavors. Grilled duck breast with honey, authentic pot-au-feu with marrowbone, veal kidneys, stuffed chicken breast, trout fried in butter with almonds, rack of lamb with thyme blossoms: With this kind of Prévert-style inventory, the only problem is choosing. The desserts are generous: sorbet in a crispy pastry cup, apple millefeuille, vanilla crème brûlée. The cellar is small but well chosen, and the prices are sensible. Why so many dishes on this very reasonably priced set menu? Caroula and Nelson's philanthropy must be partly genetic: Pantelakis Charidemou ran this restaurant for many years before handing it down to his daughter and son-in-law.

● Pavillon Montsouris   V.COM

20, rue Gazan
Métro: Cité-Universitaire
Tel. 01 43 13 29 00. Fax 01 43 13 29 02
www.pavillon-montsouris.fr
Open daily until 10:30 PM.
Prix fixe: 49€.
Terrace. Private dining room. Valet parking.

Located in one of the most beautiful parks in Paris, this pretty, Universal Exhibition–style pavillion has a strong appeal. Looking out at the trees, bathed in the generous light that pours through the glass roof, we give in to the temptation of Stéphane Lemarchand's meticulous cuisine under the attentive eye of proprietor Yvan Courault. The shredded crabmeat with tarragon, fennel purée and slow-roasted tomato jus, shrimp, scorpion fish and clam risotto or the roasted pork served with potato purée with truffle oil charm us effortlessly. They are accompanied by one of the 300 vintages in the cellar, with a citrus fruit salad to conclude.

● Le Petit Baigneur   ●SIM

10, rue de la Sablière
Métro: Pernety, Mouton-Duvernet
Tel. 01 45 45 47 12
Closed Saturday lunch, Sunday,
July 20th–August 20th. Open until 10:30 PM.
Prix fixe: 13€ (lunch), 18€ (dinner).
A la carte: 26€.
Air cond. Terrace. Private dining room.
Valet parking.

How well we remember those Sunday lunches at grandma's: her rabbit stew with prunes, her beef bouguignon, her lamb stew with vegetables. . . . Well, things are just the same here. Regional cuisine has found a home among the bric-a-brac of this old-fashioned bistro. After ordering a Bordeaux or Burgundy from the cellar, we begin by helping ourselves to generous (in fact, unlimited) quantities of a country pâté brought to table in its terrine. Then we move on to the cod brandade or the steak tartare and, if we still have a little room, the soft chocolate cake does the trick. The prices are very modest.

● Les Petites Sorcières   ●SIM

12, rue Liancourt
Métro: Denfert-Rochereau
Tel.-Fax 01 43 21 95 68
lespetitessorcières@wanadoo.fr
Closed Saturday lunch, Sunday, Monday lunch,
mid-July–mid-August. Open until 10:30 PM.
A la carte: 38€.
Private dining room.

The "Little Witches" the restaurant is named after take the form of puppets that watch over Christian Teule's cauldron. A disciple of Joël Robuchon, Christian concocts subtle, precise, seasonal dishes. With a wave of his magic wand, he produces a zucchini and mozzarella clafoutis, tomato stuffed with eggplant caviar and served with olive-anchovy vinaigrette, sautéed jumbo shrimp and chorizo with Espelette chili risotto, roasted duck steak with olives and fingerling potatoes. With iced raspberry and watermelon gazpacho served with melon sorbet, we end on a cool note. The tab is very civilized.

● Le Plomb du Cantal   SIM

3, rue de la Gaîté
Métro: Edgar-Quinet
Tel.-Fax 01 43 35 16 92
Closed August. Open until midnight.
Prix fixe: 19€ (lunch). A la carte: 35€.
Terrace.

Patrons flock to this innocent-looking Parisian café–style bistro for the charcuterie and pâtés, grilled sausage, truffade (potato and cured ham gratin), aligot (cheese and potato purée) and nice omelets. All are lavishly served and accompanied by delightful local wines. Baked by the mistress of the house, Marinette Alric, the chestnut flan is strictly for the healthiest of appetites. Who's worrying about indigestion?

● Le 14 Juillet, Il y a   SIM
   Toujours des Lampions

99, rue Didot
Métro: Plaisance
Tel. 01 40 44 91 19. Fax 01 40 44 41 49
montigny.f@wanadoo.fr
Open daily until 11 PM.
Prix fixe: 12€ (lunch). A la carte: 30–40€.
Air cond.

Franck Montigny provides a warm welcome in this friendly den. His bistro has heart, and the dishes concocted by the shrewd Olivier Padin are unpretentious. The sautéed lamb sweetbreads served with arugula salad, parsleyed oyster mushrooms and young spinach, the marinated grilled swordfish steak with olive oil potato purée, sautéed baby cuttlefish with fingerling potatoes, sliced duck breast with a prune sauce and lamb shank with thyme jus and white haricot beans are not bad. The lemon mousse with apricot coulis goes down easily.

● La Régalade   SIM

49, av Jean-Moulin
Métro: Alésia, Porte-d'Orléans
Tel. 01 45 45 68 58
Closed Saturday, Sunday, Monday lunch,
1 week at the end of July–the end of August.
Open until 11 PM.
Prix fixe: 32€.

Yes, this is where it all began: the fashion for bistros serving deftly prepared dishes at low prices. Bruno Doucet, heir to Yves Camdeborde and veteran of L'Apicius, knows his trade. We enjoy the convivial, noisy, but amiable atmosphere, and we love his prix fixe, with all the delicious, subtle fare it has to offer. For example? The foie gras flan in a creamy chanterelle mushroom broth, Breton cod filet roasted with olive oil, pigeon breast roasted on the bone offer undiluted pleasure, as do the rice pudding with vanilla and salted-butter caramel and the wines, chosen with tremendous flair. It is vital to reserve.

● Aux Rendez-Vous   ⓔ SIM
   des Camionneurs

34, rue des Plantes
Métro: Alésia
Tel. 01 45 40 43 36
Closed Sunday, August.
Open until 10:30 PM.
Prix fixe: 14,50€. A la carte: 28€.
Terrace.

We receive a warm welcome and eat well for a moderate sum in Christian Sochas's congenial den. The place does not look like much, but we happily treat ourselves to Basque pâté, codfish, grilled rib-eye steak with roquefort sauce or duck breast before ending with chocolate cake or a seasonal fruit tart

● Le Severo   🕭 SIM

8, rue des Plantes
Métro: Alésia, Mouton-Duvernet
Tel. 01 45 40 40 91
Closed Saturday, Sunday,
1 week Christmas–New Year's, 1 week at Easter, August. Open until 10:30 PM.
A la carte: 40€.

William Bernet, a conscientious butcher who worked at the Nivernaises and has now turned restaurateur, has made this ordinary looking corner bistro into a gourmet headquarters. His secret? Excellent meat, good food, a very impressive wine list up on the wall next to the blackboard and a cordial welcome. Johnny Béguin, the modest chef, assiduously prepares boned pig's feet, farmhouse blood pudding, steak tartare or grilled rib-eye steak with (real) French fries and chocolate mousse, all of them delightful. Fish is served in neighboring adjunct Le Bis du Severo.

● La Table et la Forme `V.COM`

Marriot Paris Rive Gauche,
17, bd Saint-Jacques
Métro: Glacière, St-Jacques
Tel. 01 40 78 79 60. Fax 01 40 78 79 11
Closed Saturday, Sunday, Christmas–New Year's, 1 week at the end of July, August.
Open until 10:30 PM.
Prix fixe: 30€, 36€, 39€ (lunch, wine included), 48€ (wine included).
A la carte: 45€.
Air cond. Private dining room. Valet parking.

This vast hotel restaurant is not short on charm with its bay windows and marine decor. In the kitchen, Louis-José Bangard provides healthy sustenance in the form of fresh, light dishes that reflect fashion and the season. The scallop ravioli in a foamy satay cream, sautéed monkfish with sage leaves and Paimpol navy beans with bacon or grilled duck breast with spices, water chestnuts and chanterelle mushrooms are finely crafted. The desserts, such as the caramelized midget banana served with thyme sorbet, are up to standard, as is the cellar with its hundred wines.

● Les Tontons `● SIM`

38, rue Raymond-Losserand
Métro: Pernety
Tel. 01 43 21 69 45
Closed Sunday, 2 weeks in August.
Open until 11 PM.
Prix fixe: 12€ (lunch), 14,50€ (dinner), 18,50€ (dinner). A la carte: 30€.

The Tontons' tartares are perfect. We begin with a copious salad with warm goat cheese and smoked duck magret or a plate of Serrano ham later followed by penne with crayfish or steak tartare with foie gras and porcini mushrooms. We are not daunted by crème brûlée with red fruit or the carafe of chilled wine. Or indeed the modest check.

● Les Vendanges `COM`

40, rue Friant
Métro: Porte-d'Orléans
Tel. 01 45 39 59 98. Fax 01 45 39 74 13
guy.tardif@wanadoo.fr
www.lesvendanges-paris.com
Closed Saturday, Sunday.
Open until 10:30 PM.
Prix fixe: 25€, 35€, 12,50€ (children).
Private dining room.

This winegrower's restaurant is an address to remember. Surrounded by bunches of grapes painted on the walls, our glass filled with one of the 300 or so hand-picked vintages in Guy Tardif's cellar, we begin to dream: sautéed Burgundy snails, smoked beef brisket or braised oxtail and porcini mushroom pie, oven-roasted pike-perch filet with creamy watercress sauce, roasted pigeon with salted butter, apple cider, apples and almonds, raspberry soufflé or raspberry and wild strawberry waffle. The prix fixe is copious and the dishes, meticulously prepared by the two Philippes, Joubin and Leroux, are generously served. Our head may be spinning, but with the prix fixes, we need no mental arithmetic to work out the bill, which in any case is not excessive.

● Vin et Marée `COM`

108, av du Maine
Métro: Gaîté, Mouton-Duvernet
Tel. 01 43 20 29 50. Fax 01 43 27 84 11
vin-et-maree@wanadoo.fr
www.vin-et-maree.com
Open daily until 11:30 PM.
Prix fixe: 18,50€, 24,50€.
A la carte: 43–50€.
Air cond. Private dining room. Valet parking.

Valérie Normand has taken over this good seafood establishment with great gusto. The produce is as fresh as ever and the cooking does it justice. At the stove, Christophe Rousseau continues to prepare sweet and sour sautéed shrimp, grilled brill, gilthead bream and tenderloin steak with care and talent. Not to mention the Zanzibar baba, superb!

● Le Zeyer `COM`

234, av du Maine, at 62, rue d'Alésia
Métro: Alésia
Tel. 01 45 40 43 88. Fax 01 45 40 64 51
Open daily until 12:30 AM.
Prix fixe: 18,50€ (lunch).
A la carte: 40–55€.
Air cond. Terrace. Private dining room.

Refurbished two years ago, the Slavik decor is looking good. This eatery continues to gratify its regular locals, lovers of seafood platters and sauerkraut. Two new chefs, Marc Tahon and Bernard Latour, busy themselves with the sautéed jumbo shrimp tails with vermicelli, roasted sea bream from Brittany with fresh fennel and anise sauce, grandmother-style sautéed veal kidneys. The rhubarb crumble is a treat.

INTERNATIONAL RESTAURANTS

● Ban Som Tam `N` `SIM`

5, rue Raymond-Losserand.
Métro: Gaîté, Montparnasse-Bienvenüe
Tel. 01 43 22 65 72. Fax 01 43 22 26 40
www.restoaparis.com, www.e-quartier.com
Closed Sunday, August. Open until 11 PM.
Prix fixe: 15€ (weekday lunch), 25€, 35€ (wine included), 45€. A la carte: 30–40€.

An excellent match here between a French oenologist and a Thai cook. The partnership is highly successful, especially since Franck Poré has built up a carefully composed wine list to flatter the dishes presented by his wife Phannee. We marvel at this festival of flame and flavor: beignets stuffed with red bell pepper, lemongrass or coconut milk soup, raw diced spicey shrimp, scallops with oyster sauce, fish steamed in banana leaves with thai curry sauce, refreshing chilled desserts and sticky rice cake with banana. The choice is impressive, the prices moderate, the decor refined Thai with its white walls and yellow fabric and the atmosphere relaxing.

▼ | SHOPS

BREAD & BAKED GOODS

▼ La Fournée d'Augustine

96, rue Raymond-Losserand
Métro: Pernety
Tel. 01 45 43 42 45. Fax 01 45 43 42 49
7:30 AM–8 PM.
Closed Sunday, 2 weeks in August.
Pierre Thilloux, who was our 2005 Baker of the Year, continues to draw the crowds, who wait in line outside his little store for one of his nine daily breads (rye, wholegrain, country-style . . .) or the traditional-style baguette, which won him the Best Parisian Baguette award in 2004. No magic formula, no special effects, just top quality flours from the Viron mill and the simplicity of skills learnt with Mulot and at the Pétrin d'Antan. His "*coups de cœur du samedi*" (Saturday favorites) offer a chance to taste pistachio Genoa cake, flaky brioche or red fruit clafoutis.

▼ Le Moulin de la Vierge

105, rue Vercingétorix / 82, rue Daguerre
Métro: Plaisance, Gaîté, Denfert-Rochereau
Tel. 01 45 43 09 84 / 01 43 22 50 55
www.lemoulindelavierge.com
7:30 AM–8 PM.
Closed Sunday, Bank Holidays.
At Monsieur Kamir's, everything is cooked in a wood-fired oven: The organic sourdough breads, six-grain bread, focaccia-style olive or anchovy bread and soft and crusty baguettes are delicious. Charentaise shortbread, coconut macarons, mille-feuille, cannelés (small ridged cakes from Bordeaux) or palmiers will have you melting on the spot.

▼ Le Pain au Naturel

4, av du Gal-Leclerc
Métro: Denfert-Rochereau
Tel. 01 43 22 34 13
7 AM–8 PM. Closed Monday.
Michel Moisan, who has opened stores in other parts of Paris, has turned this old-fashioned store into a temple to his thirty types of organic bread: baguette, thin

baguette, yeast bread, wholegrain bread, *marchand de vin* loaves, rustic bread, crown-shaped bread, bougnat wheat-and-rye bread, bacon bread, raisin bread, basil bread. Try them all.

WINE

▼ Bootlegger

82, rue de l'Ouest
Métro: Pernety
Tel.-Fax 01 43 27 94 02
10:30 AM–1 PM, 4–8:30 PM.
Closed Sunday, Monday, Bank Holidays,
3 weeks in August.

What you will find here is beer in its every guise: sweet Faro, aromatic chouffe, Czech Pilsner, Guinness, Belgian Trappist beers, German Weissbieren and French artisanal beers. Christian Boutroux serves them in large or small glasses.

▼ Caves des Papilles

35, rue Daguerre
Métro: Denfert-Rochereau
Tel. 01 43 20 05 74. Fax 01 43 20 22 31
9:30 AM–1:30 PM, 3:30–8:30 PM
(Saturday 10 AM–8:30 PM,
Sunday 10 AM–1:30 PM).
Closed Sunday afternoon, Monday.

This fine cellar pays tribute to natural wines vinified without sulfur. Schueller Alsaces, Thierry Allemand Cornas and Barral Faugères are all to be found here, as well as a wide range of whiskeys, cognacs and Armagnacs. The shrewd advice from the masters of the house is a bonus.

▼ Le Repaire de Bacchus

104, rue Raymond-Losserand
Métro: Pernety
Tel.-Fax 01 40 44 87 37
10 AM–1 PM, 4–8 PM.
Closed Sunday, Monday morning.

Alain-Jérôme Lefèvre presents a broad selection of wines from every region, with a preference for Languedoc, Bordeaux, Burgundy and the Rhône Valley. Also Belgian beers, flavored pastis, whiskeys, cognacs, Armagnacs and Calvados.

CANDY & SWEETS

▼ La Maison des Bonbons

14, rue Mouton-Duvernet
Métro: Mouton-Duvernet
Tel.-Fax 01 45 41 25 55
aldalloz@club-internet.fr
10:30 AM–7:30 PM.
Closed Sunday, Monday, August.

Anne-Laurence Dalloz's store is candy heaven. Her marshmallows, mints, candied rose petals, licorice strings, red poppy candy, licorice, aniseed candy, bergamot-flavored drops from Nancy, almond macarons from Amiens, Quiberon salted-butter caramel, Montargis pralinés, Orléans quince paste and sugar-coated almond and candied fruit lozenges from Aix are exquisite confections.

CHEESE

▼ Fromagerie Boursault

71, av du Gal-Leclerc
Métro: Alésia
Tel. 01 43 27 93 30. Fax 01 45 38 59 56
9 AM–1 PM, 4:30–7:30 PM.
Closed Sunday afternoon, Monday.

Véronique Msaddak selects and ages roquefort, bleu de Termignon, farm-made goat cheeses, mountain reblochon, tignes with parsley, pérail from Causses, camemberts from Normandy and beaufort, at the peak of their form.

▼ Vacroux

5, rue Daguerre
Métro: Denfert-Rochereau
Tel.-Fax 01 43 22 09 04
8:30 AM–7:30 PM.
Closed Sunday afternoon, Monday.

Pascale and Jean-Jacques Vacroux select ash-coated goat cheeses, fruity comtés, beaufort from the Alps and saint-nectaire according to season and maturity. Fontainebleau (whipped cream mixed with fresh cheese) and sainte-suzanne (a local goat cheese) are well worth trying.

PASTRIES

▼ Le Palais d'Or

71, rue de la Tombe-Issoire
Métro: Alésia
Tel. 01 43 27 66 26
8 AM–1 PM, 3:30–7:30 PM. Closed Sunday
afternoon, Monday, Tuesday, July, August.
Michel Gerstenmeyer delights us with his
famous croissants, vanilla millefeuille and
apricot soufflé. His strawberry tart, Saint-
Honoré, chocolate mousse, and flaky
frangipane galette are delicious.

REGIONAL PRODUCTS

▼ Famille Mary

11, rue Daguerre
Métro: Denfert-Rochereau
Tel. 01 53 63 00 60
10 AM–1:30 PM, 3:30–7:30 PM (Saturday
10 AM–7:30 PM). Closed Sunday afternoon
(all day Sunday June–July), Monday,
3 weeks in August.
The Mary family are beekeepers, with
more than 200 hives in the west of France.
Here you will find honey with ginseng,
buckthorn, broom, rhododendron and
lime blossom honeys, pure pollen, jam-
filled gingerbread cakes, gingerbreads,
honey cereals, infusions and organic teas.

◆ RENDEZVOUS

BARS

◆ Kriza Bar

9, rue Vandamme
Métro: Gaîté, Montparnasse-Bienvenüe
Tel.-Fax 01 43 21 57 58
contact@krizabar.com
4 PM–2 AM (Sunday 5 PM–midnight).
Closed Monday, Christmas, 2 weeks in August.
Terrace. Private dining room.
The range of cocktails, wines by the glass,
foie gras, goat cheeses from Barthélemy
and homemade desserts, including
Toblerone chocolate fondue, set the tone
in Isabelle Martel's and Christelle Ben
Hadj's bar. Theatergoers can eat there late.

◆ Le Petit Journal Montparnasse

13, rue du Cdt-René-Mouchotte
Métro: Gaîté
Tel. 01 43 21 56 70. Fax 01 43 21 58 89
info@petitjournal-montparnasse.com
www.petitjournal-montparnasse.com
7 AM–7:30 PM (jazz nights: 2 AM except
August 10–20). Closed Sunday.
Air cond. Terrace.
A step away from the Montparnasse Tower,
this jazz café presents musical evenings, a
variety of cocktails and simple, polished
dishes: marinated salmon, grilled andouillette, grilled duck breast and crème brûlée.

◆ Rosebud   🏠

11 bis, rue Delambre
Métro: Vavin
Tel. 01 43 35 38 54
7 PM–2 AM. Closed Christmas Eve,
New Year's Eve, August.
Air cond.
A Thirties'-style decor, jazzy atmosphere
and waiters in white tuxedos, along with a
lot of cocktails (more than 50, in fact). Pa-
trons also enjoy the beer and whiskey.

PUBS

◆ Le Falstaff

42, rue du Montparnasse
Métro: Edgar-Quinet, Vavin
Tel.-Fax 01 43 35 38 29
7:30 AM–4:30 AM (Friday,
Saturday 5 AM). Cont. service.
Closed Christmas Eve.
Air cond. Private dining room.
House cocktails and beers from every
country—flambéed, green, with cognac or
juniper, Adelscott, Leffe, Bellevue, Linde-
mans, Pilsen—are the specialties of this
old-style pub. Enjoy the mussels stewed in
white wine, sauerkraut, grilled steak with
roquefort cheese sauce and crème brûlée,
served all day.

WINE BARS

◆ Les Crus du Soleil

146, rue du Château
Métro: Pernety
Tel. 01 45 39 78 99. Fax 01 45 39 14 28
10 AM–1 PM, 3:30–8:30 PM (Saturday
10 AM–8:30 PM). Closed Sunday afternoon.
Air cond.

Serge Lacombe champions the regions of
Languedoc and Roussillon with their natural sweet, white, red and rosé wines. They
accompany plates of assorted charcuterie
and pâtés or copious salads. (Other address: 21, rue d'Aligre, 75012)

◆ Le Rallye

6, rue Daguerre
Métro: Denfert-Rochereau
Tel. 01 43 22 57 05. Fax 01 40 47 54 38
9 AM–11:30 PM (Sunday 8 PM).
Closed 1 week from Christmas–New Year's,
3 weeks in August.
Terrace.

Eric Péret offers a warm welcome out on
the terrace or in his cozy bistro. The escargots, warm poached sausages, lamb tripe
sausage stew and pork hocks are washed
down with all the cheerful vintages of the
Beaujolais region.

◆ Le Vin des Rues

21, rue Boulard
Métro: Denfert-Rochereau, Mouton-Duvernet
Tel. 01 43 22 19 78
Noon–3 PM, 6:30–11:30 PM (Sunday
7 PM–11 PM). Closed Sunday lunch.
Terrace.

In this old-fashioned bar, Laurent Cazaux
presents his favorite wines, country-style
dishes and beautiful assorted platters of
cured meats or aged cheeses. Cod brandade, sautéed lamb sweetbreads, whole
veal kidney and the soft chocolate cake are
splendid.

CAFES

◆ Le Café de la Place

23, rue d'Odessa
Métro: Edgar-Quinet
Tel. 01 42 18 01 55. Fax 01 43 35 19 75
7 AM–2 AM (Sunday 8 AM–midnight). Open
daily.
Terrace.

With its neo-1900s' look, this bistro is an
excellent place to meet for a drink at any
time, or to enjoy a foie gras and cured duck
breast salad, Salers beef rib-eye steak or
croque-madame, along with delicious
wines by the glass. A shady terrace when
the weather is fine.

◆ Chez Félicie

174, av du Maine
Métro: Mouton-Duvernet
Tel. 01 45 41 05 75
www.felicie.info
7 AM–2 AM. Open daily.
Terrace.

This old-fashioned café provides a warm
welcome and offers some very appealing
domestic dishes (curried sautéed pork or
steak tartare) along with growers' wines.

○	Very good restaurant
◌◌	Excellent restaurant
◌◌◌	One of the best restaurants in Paris
⑤	Disappointing restaurant
☻	Good value for money
⊜	Meals for less than 30 euros
STM	Simple
COM	Comfortable
V.COM	Very comfortable
LUX	Luxurious
V.LUX	Very luxurious

Red indicates a particularly charming establishment

♠	Historical significance
⚑	Promotion *(higher rating than last year)*
⚜	New to the guide

●	Restaurant
▼	Shop
◆	Rendezvous

15TH ARRONDISSEMENT
A GHOST TOWN

This vast district is a ghost town. Writer and critic Roger Caillois once suggested a "Short Guide to the 15th for Phantoms." Indeed, this gentle giant of an arrondissement is short on landmarks, monuments and beacons, if not gastronomy. An anonymous abode, it is in search of an identity. The riverside is a miniature Manhattan. The "villages" of Javel and Grenelle have been built over. Rue de la Convention is like the main street of a provincial town, while in Vaugirard, where they used to slaughter horses, the abattoirs have been replaced by Georges Brassens Park, a breath of fresh green air for the neighborhood. The Convention Métro station is now the center of the universe in this part of Paris. Pont Mirabeau and place Balard on one side, Montparnasse and its tower on the other, mark the district's frontiers. And the local population? Parishioners as anonymous as the crowds that surge around the trade fairs at Porte de Versailles. They live, stroll and eat here. In fact, the fifteenth arrondissement is rich as a provincial city, with its many restaurants of every kind: international eateries and local bistros. "Embassies" of Italy, India, Spain, Thailand and Vietnam find a home here. Terraces look to the Seine, and welcoming haunts are everywhere. In all, the fifteenth, a gentle giant, is something of a gray area. Yet despite its vastness, it still offers the lively welcome of Old Paris.

RESTAURANTS

GOOD RESTAURANTS & OTHERS

● L'Alchimie ■SIM

34, rue Lettelier
Métro: La Motte-Picquet–Grenelle,
Emile-Zola
Tel. 01 45 75 55 95. Fax 01 45 78 94 66
eric.rogoff@voila.fr
Closed Sunday, Monday.
Open until 10:30 PM.
Prix fixe: 22€, 27€. A la carte: 35€.

Eric Rogoff cultivates flavors from afar, rich blends and just the right degree of cooking. Crab soup with crab quenelles, and shallot-seasoned potatoes, grouper filet with coconut milk sauce and sautéed vegetables, braised beef cheek with orange and a carrot fondant, strawberry rhubarb marmalade with bourbon vanilla ice cream impress us favorably. The welcome is pleasant, the wines intelligently selected and the check reasonable.

● L'Amaryllis ■SIM ●

13, bd Garibaldi
Métro: Cambronne
Tel. 01 47 34 05 98
lamaryllis2@wanadoo.fr
Open daily until 9:30 PM.
Prix fixe: 15€ (wine included).
A la carte: 30–35€.

Everything is going wonderfully for the Sébastien Neveux and Jérôme Mousset partnership. The former welcomes guests and looks after the wine list, while the latter continues to delight a clientele of regular customers who never tire of his bistro cuisine. The charcuterie platter, duck confit and rice pudding slip down smoothly.

● L'Ami Marcel ■SIM

33, rue Georges-Pitard
Métro: Plaisance, Convention
Tel.-Fax 01 48 56 62 06
lamimarcel@lamimarcel.com
www.lamimarcel.com
Closed Sunday, Monday,
3 weeks in August.
Open until 10:30 PM.
Prix fixe: 19€ (lunch), 25€ (lunch),
30€ (dinner). A la carte: 30–35€.
Air cond.

This was last year's great event. Eric Martins, formerly at Ledoyen and Hélène Darroze, has kept up the good work. He has hired a new chef, Pascal Bataillé, formerly with Lloyd's and L'Estaminet Gaya, and the market-based cuisine here has lost none of its charm. White asparagus flan with marinated salmon, roasted sea bass with sautéed Basque peppers and country bacon, roasted veal with celery root gratin and, for dessert, Armagnac-marinated prune beignets and licorice ice cream have a pleasing sense of intelligent modernity. Diners can avoid insolvency by opting for the prix fixe menu.

● L'Antre Amis ■COM

9, rue Bouchut
Métro: Sèvres-Lecourbe, Ségur
Tel.-Fax 01 45 67 15 65
contact@lantreamis.fr
www.lantreamis.fr
Closed Saturday, Sunday, Bank Holidays,
1 week Christmas–New Year's.
Open until 10:30 PM.
Prix fixe: 27€, 33€. A la carte: 40€.
Air cond. Terrace.

The bistro dining room refurbished in designer style has a contemporary chic. Stéphane Pion offers a smiling welcome and advice on the choice of wine and presents the dishes adeptly prepared by Baptiste Anguerin, who is now alone in the kitchen. The menu is well balanced. We enjoy the crisp layered phyllo with marinated jumbo shrimp, tabouli with curried mussels, pan-seared sea bass with vegetables and roasted veal with country ham.

The wines are well chosen and the tab by no means outrageous.

● **L'Archelle**   ⓝ SIM

83, av de Ségur
Métro: Ségur, Cambronne
Tel. 01 40 65 99 10. Fax 01 45 26 33 94
Closed Sunday, Monday, Bank Holidays,
1 week Christmas–New Year's, 3 weeks in
August. Open until 10:15 PM.
Prix fixe: 20€ (lunch, wine included),
25€ (lunch), 30€ (lunch). A la carte: 50€.
Terrace.

Exit De La Garde. Bernard Gauzy, a veteran of Marius et Janette, has opened a restaurant serving lively, subtle dishes. In its all-wood setting, we quietly savor a tartare of three tomatoes with red onions and sardines, cod with ratatouille, Salers sirloin steak with violet mustard butter and cherry clafoutis. All classics, neatly done and at reasonable prices.

● **L'Atelier Aubrac**   ⓝ SIM

51, bd Garibaldi
Métro: Sèvres-Lecourbe, Ségur
Tel. 01 45 66 96 78
Closed Saturday lunch, Sunday,
2 weeks in August. Open until 10:30 PM.
Prix fixe:15€ (lunch). A la carte: 30–35€.

Three friends, Antoine, Paul and Jérôme, have audaciously replaced a good Lebanese restaurant with this new, very French establishment. The charcuterie plate, salads with ham and cheese, boneless rib and rump steak are simple and enjoyable. The degree of cooking is just right, but the accompaniments are a little less successful. The strawberry cream cake provides an acceptable conclusion.

● **Autour du Mont**   SIM

58, rue Vasco-de-Gama
Métro: Porte-de-Versailles, Lourmel
Tel.-Fax 01 42 50 55 63
Closed Saturday lunch, Sunday, Monday,
2 weeks in August. Open until 10:30 PM.
Prix fixe: 18€ (lunch, wine included),
22€ (lunch, wine included), 30€.
A la carte: 30–35€.
Terrace.

In his navy-blue bistro, Philippe Bonne is very much in his element with seafood, as shown by the sea bream tartare with spices and lime, the pan-seared shrimp and squid with Provençal spices and Dover sole with camembert. The chocolate tart is remarkable, as are the prix fixe menus, which include wine.

● **L'Avel**   COM

65, bd Pasteur
Métro: Pasteur
Tel. 01 43 20 21 22. Fax 01 43 20 22 00
Open daily until 11 PM.
Prix fixe: 18€, 22€, 12€ (children).
A la carte: 41–58€.
Air cond. Terrace.

Laurent Debus, formerly at La Guirlande de Julie in place des Vosges, has taken over the kitchen of this chic brasserie, but left the bouillabaisse, roasted sea bass with fork-mashed potatoes and duck breast with raspberry vinegar. Carefully crafted dishes to which he has added a personal touch include lobster salad with jumbo shrimp and lemongrass, not to mention the soft chocolate cake, an additional reason to drop in.

● **Le Bayadère**   SIM

51, rue du Théâtre
Métro: Dupleix, Emile-Zola
Tel. 01 45 77 08 18. Fax 01 45 77 28 44
Closed Sunday. Open until 10:30 PM.
Prix fixe: 12€ (lunch), 15€ (lunch).
A la carte: 35–45€.
Terrace. Private dining room.

The team has changed at this unobtrusive establishment. The gourmet crab meat composition, sea bass cooked skin side up with fennel and calf's liver with honey vinegar don't miss a beat. For dessert, gingerbread millefeuille with fresh mango and nougat ice cream is deservedly popular. The service is efficient and the prices are not too high.

● Le Beau Violet   SIM

92, rue des Entrepreneurs
Métro: Commerce, Félix-Faure
Tel. 01 45 78 93 44
Closed Sunday, August. Open until 11 PM.
Prix fixe: 10€ (lunch). A la carte: 35–40€.
Air cond.

In the tiniest (five tables at most) of Paris's Corsican restaurants, Roger Hébert spares no effort. He does not take orders, but decides for himself. We have no regrets, though, since his produce, brought directly from the Island of Beauty, is remarkable. So we leave in his capable hands scrambled eggs with brocciu (a Corsican ewe's cheese), wood fire–grilled sardines with brocciu, rice with seafood, charcuterie and, for dessert, fresh cheese with figs and walnuts. The wines are Corsican, robust and sunny. With a lunchtime set menu at 10€, this is a place to celebrate.

● Le Bec Rouge   SIM

46 bis, bd du Montparnasse / 1, rue d'Alençon
Métro: Falguière
Tel. 01 42 22 45 54. Fax 01 45 44 22 60
maurice.jean@neufbusiness.fr
Open daily until 11 PM.
Prix fixe: 16€ (lunch on weekdays),
18€ (lunch on weekdays), 20€, 24€.
A la carte: 35–40€.
Air cond. Terrace.

The Alsace we love is right here in Jean-Luc Maurice's eatery. The foie gras, seafood choucroute, the jumbo shrimp flambéed with beer, the rotisserie platter, the thin-crusted Alsatian tart topped with cream, and bacon and the chocolate truffle are all splendid. Riesling and beer are the beverages of choice. The service is fast and friendly, the check moderate.

● Le Bélisaire   ◎ SIM

2, rue Marmontel
Métro: Convention, Vaugirard
Tel.-Fax 01 48 28 62 24
m.garrel@wanadoo.fr
Closed Saturday lunch, Sunday, 1 week
Christmas–New Year's, 1 week at Easter,
3 weeks in August. Open until 10:30 PM.
Prix fixe: 20€ (lunch), 30€ (dinner),
40€, 15€ (children).
Terrace. Private dining room.

Matthieu Garrel continues to astonish us. It comes as no surprise that for both lunch and dinner it is now impossible to get a table without a reservation. This staunchly traditional Breton and his associate, Thierry Duchassaing, produce a highly colorful cuisine with a very seasonal taste, constantly focused on market produce. A glance at the blackboard, presented and commented on by Evelyne, and we settle down to feast on marinated wild mushrooms with beefsteak tomato coulis, scorpion fish in pastry crust with basil and tagine-roasted baby vegetables, beef cheeks braised in red wine and foie gras confit. Proust would have loved the warm madeleines made with salted butter. The wine list is shrewd and continually updated, and the set menus are great bargains.

● Le Beurre Noisette   ● SIM

68, rue Vasco-de-Gama
Métro: Lourmel, Porte-de-Versailles
Tel. 01 48 56 82 49
Closed Sunday, Monday, 3 weeks in August.
Open until 10:30 PM.
Prix fixe: 18€ (lunch), 22€ (lunch),
32€ (dinner).
Terrace.

The simplicity of the decor reflects the nature of the proprietor, Thierry Blanqui, who is quietly continuing his career in this arrondissement after a few years spent with Christian Le Squer at Ledoyen. Featured in set menus at friendly prices, the foie gras cooked in red wine and spices, the fresh fish of the day, the slow-roasted lamb shoulder with lemon confit and cumin and the house baba au rhum are right on target. When the weather is fine, the terrace provides a further attraction.

● Bistro 121   `COM`

121, rue de la Convention
Métro: Boucicaut
Tel. 01 45 57 52 90. Fax 01 45 57 14 69
mousset.stephane@wanadoo.fr
www.bistro121.com
Open daily until 11:30 PM.
Prix fixe: 28€. A la carte: 54–75€.
Air cond. Valet parking.

Run by Stéphane Mousset, this old bistro redesigned by Slavik in the Seventies can always be relied upon. Guy Vitour still concentrates on the great classics: Duck foie gras, Dover sole meunière with steamed potatoes, boneless rib steak with béarnaise sauce, veal kidney grilled with herbed butter and the raspberry financiers are fine examples. The judicious wine list is presented enthusiastically by Sébastien Carridroit.

● Le Bistro Champêtre   `SIM`

107, rue Saint-Charles
Métro: Charles-Michels
Tel. 01 45 77 85 06. Fax 01 45 77 85 27
sofrabif@wanadoo.fr
www.bistro-et-cie.fr
Open daily until 11 PM.
Prix fixe: 16,90€, 33€.
A la carte: 35–40€.
Air cond. Terrace. Private dining room.

Willy Dorr, who has acquired a large number of Parisian bistros, has turned this establishment into one of his honest rustic eateries. The foie gras, pan-seared jumbo shrimp, scallops with seafood broth, thyme-seasoned rack of lamb, flambéed apple tart with Calvados and crisp layered pastry with chocolate are not bad. Assiduous service and no surprises in store when the check arrives (the set menu includes wine and coffee).

● Le Bistrot d'André   `€` `SIM`

232, rue Saint-Charles
Métro: Balard
Tel. 01 45 57 89 14. Fax 01 45 57 97 15
bistrot-andre@wanadoo.fr
Closed Sunday, Christmas–New Year's.
Open until 10:30 PM.
Prix fixe: 13,50€ (lunch on weekdays),
8€ (children). A la carte: 25–30€.
Terrace.

Hubert Gloaguen, brother of Le Routard's proprietor, now has his own good-natured bistro at the far end of the arrondissement. It is worth the trip, if only for Jean-Marc Wambre's very pleasant traditional dishes. The pan-seared foie gras, pike-perch with spinach, classic beef bourguignon and tarte Tatin are fine efforts. The service is efficient and there are no (unpleasant) surprises with the tab.

● Le Bistrot de Cancale   `€` `SIM`

30–32, bd de Vaugirard
Métro: Montparnasse-Bienvenüe
Tel. 01 43 22 30 25. Fax 01 43 22 45 13
Closed Saturday lunch, Sunday, Monday
evening, 2 weeks in August.
Open until 10:30 PM.
Prix fixe: 19€ (lunch, wine included), 23€.
A la carte: 30€.
Terrace. Private dining room.

The seafood here is reliably prepared by chef Victor Bride, who also invites us to join him on his inland peregrinations. The langoustine ravioli, foie gras turnovers with applesauce, cod with olive oil–enriched mashed potatoes and the tender lamb tagine with prunes are well prepared, as is the succulent mango tarte Tatin with sorbet. An amusing seaside hut decor.

● Le Bistrot du Cap   `SIM`

30, rue Péclet
Métro: Vaugirard
Tel.-Fax 01 40 43 02 18
Open daily until 11:30 PM.
Prix fixe: 16,50€, 19,50€,
32€ (wine included).
Air cond. Terrace.

Enthusiastic to a fault, Yves Quintard has turned his bistro into one of the neighborhood's most popular eateries. His terrine of red mullet with saffron and herbs, shelled jumbo shrimp brochette with rice and the generous portion of house pork ribs—the favorite (copious) dish of the chefs—are brilliantly successful. The baba au rhum is splendid as always and there is nothing daunting about the tab. When the weather is fine, there is a terrace, another bonus.

● Le Bistrot d'en Face   SIM

24, rue du Dr-Finlay
Métro: Dupleix
Tel. 01 45 77 14 59. Fax 01 45 77 74 13
mador@distelcom.fr
www.lebistrotdenface.com
Closed 1 week at the end of December,
2 weeks in August. Open until 11 PM.
Prix fixe: 15€ (lunch), 28€.
Terrace.

This is *the* hip address in the west fifteenth arrondissement. In partnership with Julien Doria, the Madamour brothers have found the perfect formula: traditional cuisine adapted to current tastes. The house terrine with red onions, the perch filet with shallot Tatin, and chicken stuffed with goat cheese and pesto are not bad at all. We love the chocolate soufflé. The wine list is attractively composed, the prices reasonable and the terrace very pleasant.

● Bistrot d'Hélène   SIM

40, rue du Colonel-Pierre-Avia
Métro: Corentin-Celton
Tel.-Fax 01 46 48 39 40
Closed Saturday, Sunday, Bank Holidays,
1 week Christmas–New Year's, 3 weeks in
August. Open until 9:45 PM.
Prix fixe: 22€, 16€, 28€.
A la carte: 35–40€.
Terrace. Private dining room.

It takes a little effort to find this bistro on the edge of Paris, near the suburb of Issy-les-Moulineaux. The journalists who work in the area have made it their refectory. They prize Jérôme Barbier's market-based cuisine and, when the lunchtime rush is

on, they go for the dishes of the day—shredded cod with citrus fruits or pork filet with gingerbread sauce—before ending with the marvelous coffee eclair. The selection of wines shows a great deal of imagination. Hélène and Thierry Mauduit's service is remarkably efficient and the prices of the set menus raise no difficulties. In the evening, the place is quieter; it's more of a family restaurant, and much nicer.

● Le Bistrot d'Hubert   COM

41, bd Pasteur
Métro: Pasteur
Tel. 01 47 34 15 50. Fax 01 45 67 03 09
message@bistrodhubert.com
www.bistrodhubert.com
Closed Saturday lunch, Sunday, Monday
lunch, Christmas. Open until 10:30 PM.
Prix fixe: 34€, 26€, 15€ (children).
A la carte: 45–55€.
Terrace.

The three tables on the street soon fill when the sun begins to shine, but we are glad to be inside as soon as the first frosts make their appearance. We run an eye over the kitchen that opens onto the dining room and order from a short menu inspired by the Southwest of France. Arnaud Baertschi concocts a soft-cooked duck leg, red peppers stuffed with brandade, pork medallion with vanilla-scented salt accompanied by fava beans simmered with pork belly. All are all delightful. The desserts, including a salted-butter caramel cake with apple mousse and walnut pralinés, are skillfully prepared. Hubert's daughter Maryline holds sway over the dining room.

● Blacherne   COM

73, rue Brancion
Métro: Porte-de-Vanves
Tel. 01 48 28 24 08. Fax 01 48 56 28 33
contact@blancherne.com
www.leblancherne.com
Closed Sunday, Monday.
Open until 10:30 PM.
Prix fixe: 19,50€, 25€. A la carte: 38€.
Air cond. Terrace.

Opposite Georges Brassens Park and the book market, in his kitchen that opens onto the dining room, Jean-Louis Combalie continues to whip up classic dishes, such as Royans ravioli with herbed cream, pike-perch roasted with spices and braised lamb shank with rosemary. Sandra's charming smile encourages us to prolong our gastronomic experience in the company of roasted pineapple with exotic spices or an all-chocolate volcano. The prices are as friendly as the welcome.

● Blanchette ·· SIM

83, rue Leblanc
Métro: Balard
Tel. 01 45 58 16 00. Fax 01 46 12 05 50
Closed Saturday lunch, Sunday, 2 weeks in beginning of August. Open until 10:30 PM.
A la carte: 28–40€.
Air cond. Terrace.

Christelle Spring is our congenial hostess in this noisy corner bistro, where the customers sit shoulder to shoulder. There is nothing surprising about the salmon tartare, salad with goat cheese on toast, spicy marinated red mullet or boneless rib-eye steak with béarnaise sauce, and that is what they like. The pastry platter (millefeuille, religieuses, eclairs) will keep you at the table a little longer.

● La Cabane à Huîtres ·· SIM

4, rue Antoine-Bourdelle
Métro: Montparnasse-Bienvenüe
Tel. 01 45 49 47 27
Closed Sunday, Monday, August.
Open until 10:30 PM.
Prix fixe: 18€ (wine included).
A la carte: 30€.
Terrace.

For ages now, Francis Dubourg has been making the trip up from Arcachon in Southwest France every week to bring us the oysters his son Frédéric produces. While he opens them, we whet our appetite with a slice of foie gras or smoked duck breast. The vanilla cake baked in a fluted mold provides a sweet conclusion. Reservations are strongly recommended.

● Le Café 117 ·· Ⓝ Ⓔ SIM

117, rue de Vaugirard
Métro: Falguière
Tel. 01 47 34 96 12
www.perso.wanadoo.fr/cafe117
Closed Saturday lunch, Sunday, 2 weeks in August. Open until 10:30 PM.
Prix fixe: 15€ (lunch). A la carte: 25–30€.
Air cond.

There have been changes at the former Grande Rue, now renamed. Its bistro spirit lives on under Thomas Barjau, but with a more modest, less creative approach. In this convivial corridor, a salad of chicory with warm goat cheese and bacon, papilotte of spicy sea bream with ratatouille, steak with béarnaise sauce and the apple tart impress us favorably at honest prices. The shrewd wine list has made room for Chilean and Italian vintages.

● Le Café du Commerce ·· 🏠 SIM

51, rue du Commerce
Métro: Emile-Zola, La Motte-Picquet–Grenelle
Tel. 01 45 75 03 27. Fax 01 45 75 27 40
commercial@lecafeducommerce.com
www.lecafeducommerce.com
Closed Christmas. Open until midnight.
Prix fixe: 14€ (lunch on weekdays), 26€.
A la carte: 30–40€.
Air cond. Private dining room.

We had an unfortunate experience at Etienne Guerraud's establishment not so long ago, with dried-out fries and tasteless calf's head, but this son of a Limousin butcher, who turned this huge Twenties' café with its floors and galleries into a temple to red meat, has put it back on its feet. The pig's ear salad, tuna steak and vegetables with horseradish vinaigrette and baba au rhum are good, but it is his boneless rib steak, back steak and rib-eye that make it all worthwhile. The service is not always attentive.

● **Café Lucas**   SIM

1, pl Etienne-Pernet
Métro: Commerce, Félix-Faure
Tel. 01 48 28 06 06. Fax 01 48 28 36 44
cafelucas@wanadoo.fr
Closed Sunday evening. Open until 11 PM.
Prix fixe: 14,50€ (lunch), 32€ (dinner).
A la carte: 40–50€.
Air cond. Terrace. Private dining room.

The colonial decor has survived, but the cuisine is not quite as good as before. The Reunion Island specialties are carefully prepared though, and sausage with spicy chutney is a very authentic dish. We are also tempted by rabbit terrine with prune compote, scorpion fish with aïoli, braised veal shank with creamy polenta and, for dessert, brioche pain perdu with strawberry and rhubarb compote.

A SPECIAL FAVORITE

● **Le Casier à Vin**   🅿 🍴 SIM

51-53, rue Olivier-de-Serres
Métro: Convention
Tel.-Fax 01 45 33 36 80
Closed Saturday lunch, Sunday, 2 weeks in beginning of August. Open until 10:30 PM.
A la carte: 32–35€.
Air cond.

This wine cellar, grocery store and restaurant is a rising star, making a name for itself on the arrondissement's gourmet scene. Why this success? Simply because the customers feel at home, free to enjoy its culinary delights in their own way. There are those who call in simply to buy a bottle of wine recommended by Henri and Ingrid, others who come to purchase cured meats, pâtés and cheeses to enjoy at home, and then there are the epicures who sit down to savor Iza Guyot's cuisine. Her cooking is lively, cheerful, high in color and never stales, especially since the dishes on the blackboard change almost daily. Why bother telling you that the tartine of ricotta with thin slices of bresaola was perfect, and that the tuna wrapped in pancetta with arugula and virgin oil was magnificent and that the citrus terrine with orange caramel was to die for?

● **La Cave de l'Os à Moelle**   ⓔ SIM

181, rue de Lourmel
Métro: Lourmel
Tel. 01 45 57 28 28. Fax 01 45 57 28 00
Closed Monday, August.
Open until 10:30 PM.
Prix fixe: 20€.
Air cond. Terrace.

Thierry Faucher can pride himself on being one of the first to update the concept of the table d'hôte. His cellar restaurant has been packed for years. Of course, you have to do things for yourself, much as at home: Get up and fetch the soup heating on the warmer or the dish of the day, and pass the bread or terrine to your neighbor. Everyone knows how it works and there are no complaints. The latest offer from the house: a bicycle hire plus picnic-hamper package, as always at unbeatable prices.

● **Les Cévennes**   COM

55, rue des Cévennes
Métro: Javel
Tel.-Fax 01 45 54 33 76
www.restaurant-les-cevennes.com
Closed Sunday, Monday evening, August.
Open until 10 PM.
Prix fixe: 15€, 19,50€.
A la carte: 28–43€.
Air cond.

How good it is to be back at the Carluets'! The lady of the house is in the kitchen and the husband is in the dining room, proudly eulogizing his wife's dishes, such as a roulade of fresh white mushrooms, cod with champagne sauce and beef tenderloin with foie gras and truffles. We conclude delightfully with profiteroles with chocolate sauce. Among the 80 items on the wine list, you will find excellent bottles at prices that do not pump up the tab excessively.

● Le Ciel de Paris   `V.COM`

Tour Montparnasse (56th floor)
33, av du Maine,
Métro: Montparnasse-Bienvenüe
Tel. 01 40 64 77 64 / 01 40 64 77 67.
Fax 01 43 21 48 37
ciel-de-paris.rv@elior.com
www.cieldeparis.com
Open daily until 11 PM.
Prix fixe: 33€ (lunch), 56€ (dinner).
A la carte: 75–90€.
Air cond. Private dining room.

Despite the asbestos controversy these last few years, we climb to the 56th floor in record time (with the help of the elevator) and find Paris spread at our feet. The service is assiduous and Jean-François Oyon's cuisine offers an inspired take on seasonal produce. Lobster salad with crunchy vegetables and herbs, sea bream with zucchini and eggplant chutney, and pan-seared veal kidneys and sweetbreads with horseradish and capers are among his successes. The wine list is worthy and the meal less expensive than an hour over the capital in a helicopter.

● Le Clos Morillons   `SIM`

50, rue des Morillons
Métro: Convention
Tel. 01 48 28 04 37. Fax 01 48 28 70 77
Closed Sunday evening, Monday,
2 weeks in August. Open until 11 PM.
Prix fixe: 18€ (lunch, wine included),
21€ (dinner), 26€, 15€ (children).
A la carte: 36€.
Air cond. Terrace.

A new start for Le Clos Morillons under the supervision of Gaël Allais, a former pupil of Roellinger in Cancale. After a little renovation work, Gaël has turned his attention to the menu, overhauling it completely. Although the shrimp with foie gras and balsamic vinegar and the Alsatian seafood choucroute with beurre blanc does not fully convince us, the bitter chocolate dessert provides an appealing conclusion. With a little effort, success should follow. A friendly welcome.

● La Dînée   `COM`

85, rue Leblanc
Métro: Balard
Tel. 01 45 54 20 49. Fax 01 40 60 73 76
www.restaurant-ladinee.com
Closed Saturday, Sunday.
Open until 10:30 PM.
Prix fixe: 32€, 34€, 36€.
Air cond. Private dining room.

Christophe Recouvreur in the dining room and Nicolas Angebault in the kitchen are our hosts in this restaurant made fashionable by Christophe Chabanel. The cuisine is contemporary. The pan-fried squid with lemon and tomato confit, small flounder baked in a clay pot with tender cardamomseasoned cabbage and lamb tangine with marinated vegetables are not bad. The chocolate fondant tart will delight the most demanding of gourmets. A restaurant to watch.

● Le Dirigeable   `SIM`

37, rue d'Alleray
Métro: Vaugirard
Tel. 01 45 32 01 54
Closed Sunday, Monday, Christmas–New Year's, 3 weeks in August.
Prix fixe: 16,50€, 19€.
A la carte: 30–40€.

A bistro ambience and precise, flavorsome traditional food. At Franck Arif's place, satisfaction is guaranteed for the local customers, who can sit down to pig's foot galette, John Dory fish with shellfish broth or a Landes pigeon with giblet galette without too much damage to their pocket. Some prefer to end with fromage blanc sorbet with citrus sauce, while others go for the upside-down cappuccino. Guy Jeu offers a friendly welcome, and the tab is uncontentious, as long as you stick to the wines served by the glass or small bottle.

● Le Dix Vins ⓔ SIM

57, rue Falguière
Métro: Falguière, Pasteur
Tel.-Fax 01 43 20 91 77
www.le-dix-vins.com
Closed Saturday, Sunday,
2 weeks in beginning of August.
Open until 11 PM.
New owners M. and Ms. Bazin.
Prix fixe: 24€. A la carte: 30€.

This pocket bistro never empties. Hervé Leroux's traditional cuisine is irreproachable and the wines presented by Jean-Philippe Burgeat are perfectly selected. Wander willingly with him down the paths of France's vineyards to find an accompaniment for the pan-seared veal sweetbreads or the pike-perch with tomato, garlic and onion sauce, unless you opt for the veal kidneys with grainy mustard. The lavender-flavored pain perdu is inevitably preceded by a slice of camembert. Sometimes you come across a restaurant like this one, where you want cheese *and* dessert.

● L'Enclos du Temps SIM

31, av du Maine
Métro: Montparnasse-Bienvenüe
Tel. 01 45 44 52 38. Fax 01 42 71 34 93
www.cafeine.com
Closed Sunday. Open until 10:30 PM.
A la carte: 25–35€.
Air cond. Terrace.

In this Thirties' bistro, where crowds flock at lunchtime, the dishes of the day are all the rage. We are in the presence of quality whether we choose the simple tomato mozzarella salad, paprika-seasoned monkfish medallions or veal tenderloin with saffron. The cheese cake and especially the selection of wines are worth the visit. The check is reasonable.

● Fleur de Sel SIM

32, bd du Montparnasse
Métro: Falguière, Duroc
Tel. 01 45 48 52 03. Fax 01 45 48 52 17
restaurant.fleurdesel@wanadoo.fr
www.fleur-de-sel.fr
Closed Saturday lunch, Sunday.
Open until 11 PM.
Prix fixe: 16€ (lunch), 20€, 25€.
A la carte: 35–40€.
Terrace.

At the corner of rue du Cherche-Midi, this restaurant is still on course. With Alain Pecqueur below decks, Captain Pascal Gaulet keeps a steady hand on the helm. The creamy foie gras risotto, roasted scallops with chorizo rice pilaf, red meat served with thick-cut fries, the beef slowly simmered in wine and the Tatin-style apple cookies are gratifying. The wines are carefully selected and the prices restrained. A pleasant terrace.

● Le Gastroquet ⓞ COM

10, rue Desnouettes
Métro: Convention, Porte-de-Versailles
Tel. 01 48 28 60 91. Fax 01 45 33 23 70
Closed Saturday lunch (July–August),
Sunday, Christmas, New Year's,
3 weeks in August. Open until 11:30 PM.
Prix fixe: 19,50€ (lunch), 29€.
A la carte: 55€.

Dany and Madeleine Bulot are adorable people. Whether you are a regular customer or a first timer, they take you in hand and pamper you as if you were their grandchild. Madeleine welcomes the guests, while Dany works in the kitchen, popping out into the dining room from time to time to make sure everything is going well. A genuine, traditional chef, he serves up food in a fine classical vein, tempered to suit current tastes. Leeks in Sauternes aspic, ham and foie gras, de-boned pig's foot with lentils, lamb shoulder with oriental spices and calf's liver with lemon confit are polished dishes indeed. The apple crème brûlée with Calvados is mouthwatering. The wine list has plenty of appeal. Given the quality, the prices are not in the least excessive.

● La Gauloise   🏠 COM

59, av de La Motte-Picquet
Métro: La Motte-Picquet–Grenelle
Tel. 01 47 34 11 64 / 01 47 34 49 78.
Fax 01 40 61 09 70
Open daily until 11 PM.
Prix fixe: 22€, 24€. A la carte: 55€.
Air cond. Terrace.

Open every day, this institution near Ecole Militaire has a certain charm, with its 1880s' stucco ceiling and a terrace for when the weather is fine. No strokes of genius in the kitchen, just reliable dishes such as the salmon carpaccio, goat cheese tartare, langoustine risotto and caramel almond floating island. The service has the sure touch of experience, and the Brouilly almost drinks itself.

● La Giberne   SIM

42 bis, av de Suffren
Métro: La Motte-Picquet–Grenelle,
Champ-de-Mars–Tour-Eiffel
Tel. 01 47 34 82 18 / 01 47 34 62 22.
Fax 01 45 67 28 08
lagiberne@wanadoo.fr
Open daily noon–10:30 PM. Cont. service.
Prix fixe: 23€, 27€. A la carte: 55€.
Air cond. Terrace.

The ever-attentive Dominique Hélard watches over this classical setting, where we can easily imagine the politicians of France's prewar Third Republic feasting in mustachioed splendor. They would have enjoyed the succulent game, which is admirably prepared here, and would not have turned their noses up at the duck foie gras terrine with fig compote, the steamed salmon with seasonal vegetables, duck breast with orange or foie gras sauce or the indispensable baba au rhum.

● La Gitane   ⊜ SIM

53 bis, av de La Motte-Picquet
Métro: La Motte-Picquet–Grenelle
Tel. 01 47 34 62 92. Fax 01 40 65 94 01
www.la-gitane.com
Closed Sunday, Christmas, New Year's.
Open until 11 PM.
Prix fixe: 19€ (lunch). A la carte: 30€.
Air cond. Terrace.

This brasserie has a terrace for sunny days and provides standard, but well-prepared, dishes. We have no complaints about the scallop tartare with arugula salad, skate wing with vinaigrette nor the rich cassoulet with Tarbais beans, perfect in winter. The chocolate profiteroles bring back memories of childhood. The check is humane.

● Harmonies Mets et Vins   COM

Mercure Tour Eiffel,
21-23, rue de la Fédération
Métro: Bir-Hakeim
Tel. 01 45 78 55 41. Fax 01 45 78 42 42
h2175@accor.com
www.mercure.com
Open daily until 10:30 PM.
A la carte: 45€.
Air cond. Terrace. Private dining room.

Christophe Collet at the stove and Sébastien Brot in the dining room add a personal dimension to a hotel restaurant that could otherwise be lacking in character. The quality of the tomato and avocado gazpacho, scallop and leek tart, sea bass filet with grilled vegetables, boneless Salers rib-eye steak and strawberry soup seasoned with thyme and lemon is consistently high. Great vintages available at bargain prices.

● Harumi   COM

99, rue Blomet
Métro: Vaugirard
Tel. 01 42 50 22 27. Fax 01 42 50 22 27
contactharumi@wanadoo.fr
www.harumi.fr
Closed Sunday evening, Monday, mid-July–mid-August. Open until 10:30 PM.
Prix fixe: 25€ (lunch, wine included), 38€.
A la carte: 49€.
Air cond. Valet parking.

Harumi, a Japanese woman, and Fabien Béhal from Burgundy are a match made in heaven. She works in the kitchen; he in the dining room. Their union is reflected in the dishes, where two cultures merge. We drift away on the scents of Asia that rise from the langoustines with herbed breadcrumbs, steamed cod in banana leaf with spring onion and shiitake mushroom fondue, not to forget the lemongrass-seasoned shellfish next to a baby pork chop. The incomparable harmony continues as the dessert arrives, with pineapple tempura with lime cream and pineapple vanilla sorbet. Fabien's welcome is equaled only by his partner's talent. A place to watch.

● Je Thé . . . Me ⛩ SIM

4, rue d'Alleray
Métro: Vaugirard
Tel. 01 48 42 48 30. Fax 01 48 42 70 66
www.restaurantjethemeparis.com
Closed Sunday, Monday, 2 weeks
Christmas–New Year's, August.
Open until 10 PM.
Prix fixe: 33€.
Terrace. Private dining room.

Jacky Larsonneur continues to assuage our appetite with his single prix fixe menu, which we enjoy in this very beautiful late-19th-century setting. The crayfish fricassée with aromatic herbs, spiced tuna tartare, veal kidneys with coarse mustard are perfectly prepared and adapted to current tastes. The house baba au rhum concludes the festival of flavor. This is the kind of restaurant we love.

● Marie-Edith SIM

34, rue du Laos
Métro: Cambronne
Tel.-Fax 01 45 66 44 60
Open daily until 10 PM.
Prix fixe: 24€, 28€. A la carte: 45–50€.
Air cond. Terrace.

Marie-Edith Thibeaud is a local personality. She knows her customers and greets them like old friends. The menu drawn up by the faithful Frédéric Martin changes every day, or almost. He is obviously enjoying himself when he prepares the toast topped with caramelized veal sweetbreads served on salad, and he is in his element with John Dory fish with beurre blanc and classic whole veal kidney *à l'ancienne*. Chaud-froid with apples and whiskey is a fiery dessert. The mistress of the house has turned herself into a wine expert and offers great and small vintages at reasonable prices.

● Le Minzingue Ⓝ SIM

5, pl Etienne-Pernet
Métro: Félix-Faure, Commerce
Tel. 01 45 32 48 54
Closed Sunday, dinner Monday, Tuesday,
Wednesday. Open until 10:30 PM.
A la carte: 29–35€.
Air cond. Private dining room.

Exit the Quinson. This institution, formerly frequented by lovers of bouillabaisse, is now a bastion of regional dishes and wines. With Jean-Louis Piqueronies from Aurillac at the helm, the house terrine, the hand-chopped beef tartare, duck medallions with olive oil potato purée and the beef chop with potato gratin are appealing indeed. The Fleurie, Morgon, Juliénas and Pommard served by the glass are recommended by the master of the house and savored with the contents of the Auvergne cheeseboard prominently displayed on a barrel in the center of the dining room. If you have a little room left, try the millefeuille with berries.

● Le Moulin SIM

70, rue de Vouillé
Métro: Plaisance
Tel.-Fax 01 48 28 81 61
Closed Saturday lunch, Sunday.
Open until 10 PM.
Prix fixe: 23€, 26€, 33€ (wine included).
A la carte: 40–50€.
Air cond. Terrace. Private dining room.

This Moulin (Mill) still turns smoothly, and Roger Buhagiar carries on, indefatigable. His domestic cuisine is a delight: The produce is excellent, the preparation precise and the flavors intact. He serves up honest, tasty dishes such as lightly marinated salmon tart, halibut with vanilla sauce and asparagus and beef tenderloin with foie gras and truffles. We are fond of the apple tart, and we can be sure that the wine list will always provide the right bottle to suit both our tastes and pockets.

● Le Mûrier   €SIM

42, rue Olivier-de-Serres
Métro: Convention
Tel.-Fax 01 45 32 81 88
lepimpecmartin@yahoo.fr
Closed Saturday, Sunday, Christmas,
New Year's, 3 weeks in August.
Open until 10:30 PM (Friday 11 PM).
Prix fixe: 15,50€ (lunch), 18,50€ (lunch),
20,50€ (dinner), 24,50€. A la carte: 30€.

Christophe Le Pimpec and Eric Chau-
meny form a solid team in the dining
room and kitchen, respectively. The latter
dreams up new takes on domestic dishes:
salt and herb–marinated salmon, quick-
seared salmon, simmered veal stew with
Provençal vegetables, crêpes with caramelized apples. The wines are carefully selected and generously served by the glass.

● Oh ! Duo   €SIM

54, av Emile-Zola
Métro: Charles-Michels, Javel
Tel. 01 45 77 28 82. Fax 01 45 75 09 31
Closed Saturday lunch, Sunday, Monday
evening, Christmas–New Year's, 3 weeks in
August. Open until 10:15 PM.
Prix fixe: 25€, 29€.
Air cond. Terrace. Private dining room.

The Valéros make a fine pair, the lady in the
dining room and her husband at the stove.
Their infectious good humor and professionalism are such that no one leaves their
attractive restaurant disappointed. With
three dishes fresh as the morning dew—
minced veal tongue with beets and lamb's
lettuce, Scottish salmon with peppers and
onions and the rhubarb soup with strawberries—Joël charms every palate, and for
less than 30€—which deserves a round of
applause.

● L'Os à Moelle   SIM

3, rue Vasco-de-Gama
Métro: Lourmel
Tel. 01 45 57 27 27. Fax 01 45 57 28 00
th.faucher@laposte.net
Closed Sunday, Monday. Open until 11:30 PM.
Prix fixe: 32€, 38€. A la carte: 55€.
Terrace. Private dining room.

There is no stopping Thierry Faucher: After
opening a basement table d'hôte offshoot,
he has taken over La Maison Trévier in Issy
with his dining room manager, Charles
Madeira, and turned it into Les Symples de
l'Os à Moelle. He is still in residence in this
restaurant though, offering creative market-based dishes at affordable prices. We
have happy memories of the poached eggs
in red wine with bacon, chanterelle mushrooms and green beans, cod with carrot
and fennel mousse and beef braised with
small potatoes and black trumpet mushrooms, as well as the Guanaja chocolate
marquise. This Crillon veteran has not lost
his touch.

● L'Ostréade   SIM

11, bd de Vaugirard
Métro: Montparnasse-Bienvenüe
Tel. 01 43 21 87 41. Fax 01 43 21 55 09
Closed Saturday, Sunday, Bank Holidays,
August. Open until 10:15 PM
(Friday 10:30 PM).
A la carte: 35–40€.
Air cond. Terrace. Private dining room.

The service is rapid if you have a train to
catch, or more relaxed if you have come for
the seafood. This modern brasserie in Gare
Montparnasse rail station hedges its bets
without losing its soul. There is no meat on
the menu, but freshly caught fish features
on the blackboard. The grilled squid, tuna
steak with olive oil and whole roasted trout
are impeccable. The gingerbread tiramisu
is pleasant. Excellent oysters at reasonable
prices.

● Pacific Eiffel   ⑤COM

Hilton Paris, 18, av de Suffren
Métro: Bir-Hakeim,
Champ-de-Mars–Tour-Eiffel
Tel. 01 44 38 56 00. Fax 01 44 38 56 81
irene.asmar@hilton.com
www.hilton.com
Open daily until 11:30 PM.
Prix fixe: 33€ (lunch).
Air cond. Terrace. Private dining room.
Valet parking.

The Hilton deserves a better quality restaurant. This one takes all the easy options for

a clientele of tourists awed by an mediocre phyllo layered with jumbo shrimp, bland Dover sole pan fried in butter, parsley, and lemon, uninspiring Provençal-style rack of lamb or an acceptable crème brûlée. Everything is terribly lacking in character. Having reached the Pacific, we can only wonder what happened to the glories of California, present only on the wine list. The terrace is pleasant, the bar quiet and convivial.

● Chez Papa   €ᴱ SIM

101, rue de la Croix-Nivert
Métro: Commerce, Félix-Faure
Tel. 01 48 28 31 88. Fax 01 56 36 19 06
Closed Christmas–New Year's.
Open until 1 AM.
Prix fixe: 9,55€ (lunch). A la carte: 26–36€.
Air cond.

Homesick natives of Southwest France have only to step inside to be reunited with a cuisine that tastes sweetly of Gers and the Landes. The good-natured Bruno Druilhe brings chicken liver salad, boneless duck filets with peaches and the indispensable cassoulet. The Armagnac is not only served in your still-warm coffee cup, it also features in the Baked Alaska.

● Le Passage   SIM

126, rue de l'Abbé-Groult
Métro: Convention
Tel.-Fax 01 48 42 40 60
Open daily until 10 PM.
Prix fixe: 33€, 16€ (lunch), 19€ (lunch).
A la carte: 46€.
Air cond. Terrace. Private dining room.

A change of chef in this restaurant hidden away in a quiet part of the arrondissement. While some are fascinated by the outmoded decor of the dining room, we very much prefer the terrace bordering an alley given over to pedestrians. In this peaceful spot, we enjoy dishes that are simpler than before, but honest. Bell pepper tart, grilled sea bream with eggplant blossom and passion fruit soufflé slip down delightfully.

● Le Père Claude   COM

51, av de La Motte-Picquet
Métro: La Motte-Picquet–Grenelle
Tel. 01 47 34 03 05. Fax 01 40 56 97 84
lepereclaude@wanadoo.fr
Open daily until 11 PM.
Prix fixe: 27€, 32€. A la carte: 38–55€.
Air cond. Terrace. Private dining room.

Claude Perraudin's fans continue to swear allegiance to this bon vivant who helped to put this place on the map. When he told them he was handing Le Père Claude over to his children Ludovic and Laetitia, and that nothing would change, they remained loyal, and we understand why. The house still boasts its terrines, red meats and rotisserie chicken, while fish lovers delight in sesame-grilled tuna or the house fish stew. Strawberry rhubarb compote with vanilla ice cream provides a refreshing conclusion.

● Le Pétel   SIM

4, rue Pétel
Métro: Vaugirard
Tel.-Fax 01 45 32 58 76
www.restaurant.lepetel.oneline.fr
Closed Sunday, Monday, 1 week at the end of July, 2 weeks in beginning of August.
Open until 10 PM.
Prix fixe: 18€ (lunch), 29,90€.
A la carte: 36€.
Air cond.

Michel Marie is still running this restaurant. It is splendidly reliable, and that is what makes it one of the arrondissement's most popular haunts in the bistro category. We have moving memories of the asparagus ravioli, lamb shanks with risotto and iced nougat with gingerbread, but the emotion would probably have been just as strong if we had opted for crayfish mango salad, veal kidneys with whole-grain mustard sauce or apple gratin with cider butter. A trusted eatery that never lets us down and is easy on the pocket, too.

● Le Petit Champenois   € SIM

6, rue Fourcade
Métro: Convention
Tel. 01 48 28 67 93
Closed Saturday lunch, Sunday, Monday,
1 week in February, August.
Open until 10:30 PM.
Prix fixe: 14,50€ (lunch), 17€ (dinner).
A la carte: 28–30€.
Terrace.

Vincent Deglin has taken up residence in the kitchen of this local bistro. In just a few months he has won the affections of a local clientele that comes to savor the asparagus flan with shellfish and crayfish sauce and spicy Basque tuna steak, not to mention the herbed grilled lamb. Vanilla cream and fresh fruit provide a happy ending. Corinne Broux's charming service makes up for the extras charged on top of the set menu price.

● La Petite Auberge   € SIM

13, rue du Hameau
Métro: Porte-de-Versailles
Tel.-Fax 01 45 32 75 71
Closed Sunday, Christmas–New Year's,
1 week at Easter, 3 weeks in August.
Open until 10 PM.
A la carte: 30€.

Everything is delicious and free of frills in this restaurant where rugby fans gather. Guy Lonlas works with fresh produce exclusively and serves fish, but only on Wednesday and Friday. Warmed individual goat cheese is a first-rate starter. The generous portions of osso bucco and beef tartare accompanied by large homemade fries deserve a round of applause, and the seasonal fruit tarts are brilliant. The prices keep their heads down.

● Le Petit Mâchon   SIM

123, rue de la Convention
Métro: Boucicaut
Tel. 01 45 54 08 62. Fax 01 45 57 35 95
Closed Saturday lunch, Sunday, 1 week
Christmas–New Year's, mid-July–mid-August.
Open until 10:30 PM.
Prix fixe: 16€ (lunch), 19€ (lunch),
28€ (dinner). A la carte: 40–50€.
Air cond.

To the connoisseur, the name says it all: This is Lyon country. The menu is more eclectic though, and in this neo-1900s' decor designed by Slavik, the classic French onion soup, beef tenderloin with morel sauce and tarte Tatin are prepared by the book. But keep a count: The tab tends to climb higher than it should.

● La Plage Parisienne   N ① COM

Port de Javel-Haut
Métro: Javel
Tel. 01 40 59 41 00. Fax 01 40 59 81 50
www.laplage-parisienne.com
Open daily until 10:30 PM.
A la carte: 30–50€.
Terrace. Valet parking.

The sea bream with vegetable julienne is drowned in oil, the penne with foie gras is dull and the jumbo shrimp terrine with olive oil potato purée is insipid, although the desserts (panna cotta with a raspberry coulis and pear and sour cherry clafoutis) are well prepared. The list of wines is forgettable and too few are served by the glass. But who really comes here to eat or drink? The dining room is chic and social, the veranda seems to be hovering over the Seine and the pleasant terrace is the greatest attraction of all.

● Le Pot-au-Feu   € SIM

59, bd Pasteur
Métro: Pasteur
Tel.-Fax 01 43 20 79 80
Closed Sunday evening, Christmas,
New Year's, August 15th. Open until 11 PM.
Prix fixe: 17,50€, 22,50€.
Terrace.

This restaurant has been delighting locals for quarter of a century or close to it, now. The Fifties' decor has been freshened up, but the cuisine has aged a little. The pot-au-feu (beef and vegetable stew served with bone marrow in winter, cold in salad in the summer) is a model of its kind. The chocolate parfait is perfect. With a coffee and a glass of wine, we spend no more than we have to.

● **Le Quinzième Cuisine Attitude** `COM`

14, rue Cauchy
Métro: Javel
Tel. 01 45 54 43 43
resa@lequinzieme.com
www.lequinzieme.com
Closed Saturday lunch, Sunday, Christmas, New Year's, 1 week in August.
Open until 10:30 PM.
Prix fixe: 30€ (lunch), 35€ (lunch), 95€.
A la carte: 75–80€.
Terrace. Private dining room. Valet parking.

We come here because the chef, Cyril Lignac, is a well-known TV personality, and because of the guests, who seem to have stepped out of a TV series. The cuisine has improved, including foie gras and porcini ravioli with white truffle sauce and crunchy potatoes, red mullet with paella-style risotto and saffron broth, and spiced beef tenderloin with Thai-style slow-cooked tomatoes. We finish our visit with a Guanaja chocolate cookie and praliné, rose and passion fruit ice cream. Sadly, the check is steep.

● **Le Relais de Sèvres** `P` `O` `V.COM`

Sofitel Porte de Sèvres,
8-12, rue Louis-Armand
Métro: Balard
Tel. 01 40 60 33 66. Fax 01 40 60 30 00
h0572-fb10@accor.com
www.sofitel.com
Closed Friday evening, Saturday, Sunday, Bank Holidays, August. Open until 10 PM.
Prix fixe: 55€, 70€ (wine included).
Air cond. Private dining room. Valet parking.

The restaurant of the Sofitel Sèvres hotel is in safe hands with Philippe Pentecôte, who attunes his menu to the changing seasons with the focus on market produce. A modest, reliable technician, he adds his own very personal touch, rejecting more facile options. The quick-seared tuna served with rillettes, tomato marmalade and sautéed peppers are proof of his fertile imagination. Sea bass with a truffle crust (first poached, then seared) and served with celery root shellfish ravioli is admirably original and, despite its classical

flavor, the simmered veal sweetbreads with truffled cabbage compote served in a yellow wine sauce is a genuinely modern dish. The desserts are very tasteful, among them pineapple slow cooked in bourbon vanilla with cream. The service is appropriate to a great restaurant, as are the prices (although they are not excessive given the quality). In the brasserie the dishes are simpler and the checks more amenable to reason. Brunch on Sunday.

● **Le Restaurant du Marché** `■``SIM`

59, rue de Dantzig
Métro: Porte-de-Versailles, Porte-de-Vanves
Tel. 01 48 28 31 55. Fax 01 48 28 18 31
Closed Saturday lunch, Sunday, Monday lunch, 3 weeks in August. Open until 10 PM (Saturday, Sunday 11 PM).
Prix fixe: 15€ (weekday lunch, wine included), 23€, 29€. A la carte: 30–35€.

This place had its moment of glory in the Seventies and Eighties, in the days of the Massias, ambassadors of Landes cuisine in Paris. The wooden tables have been stripped of their white cloths and the prices lowered (significantly). With his inexpensive options and the *complète* set menu at 29€, Francis Lévêque (who trained with Lorain and Vigato) could compete in the "best value for money in Paris" category. Not content with taking over this legendary bistro, he has changed its style, introducing a fresh, eloquent, market-based cuisine chalked up on the blackboard. When we visited, pig's foot tartine, salt and herb–marinated salmon presented *en bocal*, scallops with celery root purée, spiced and roasted monkfish with simmered vegetables *en cocotte* and pain perdu with caramel ice cream were godsends—nothing more, nothing less.

● **Le Rond de Serviette** `N` `⊖` `SIM`

19, rue Duranton
Métro: Boucicaut, Lourmel
Tel.-Fax 01 45 58 43 17
Closed Saturday lunch, Sunday evening, Monday evening. Open until 10:30 PM.
Prix fixe: 16,50€, 21€.
Terrace.

The yellow facade of the former Charles Victor, now refurbished and renamed, is explosively cheerful. "Rond de Serviette" means "napkin ring," and we would love to have our own here, marking our personal place where we could savor the minced sweetbreads cooked in Port, pike-perch in a red wine and butter sauce and strawberry sabayon. This is bistro cuisine, but who is complaining, especially when the prices are good as gold?

● Le Saint-Vincent   SIM

26, rue de la Croix-Nivert
Métro: Cambronne
Tel. 01 47 34 14 94. Fax 01 47 67 30 82
lesaint.vincent@wanadoo.fr
www.lesaint-vincent.fr
Closed Sunday, Christmas, New Year's,
2 weeks in August. Open until 11 PM.
Prix fixe: 17€ (lunch). A la carte: 35€.
Air cond. Private dining room.

The ten Beaujolais vintages (at 20€ or by the glass) are bargains, and Pierre Cade promotes them enthusiastically. Stage right, the bistro; stage left, the more classical restaurant. The menu changes twice a year, but each day brings its range of new dishes. The quail salad with raspberry reduction sauce, veal kidney with mustard sauce and the fontainebleau are persuasive. The welcome is friendly, the service cheerful and the prices competitive.

● Le Sept Quinze   SIM

29, av de Lowendal
Métro: Cambronne
Tel. 01 43 06 23 06
Closed Saturday lunch, Sunday, 1 week
Christmas–New Year's, 3 weeks in August.
Open until 11 PM.
Prix fixe: 18€ (lunch). A la carte: 35–40€.
Terrace.

The lunchtime crowd competes for places in this restaurant just a step away from UNESCO headquarters. The diplomats from this UN organization appreciate Catherine Allswang's quintessentially French cuisine. The baby artichokes with grapefruit, grilled tuna with arugula, phyllo-wrapped tenderloin with tapenade,

small goat cheese with Espelette pepper aspic and the house lemon dessert are delights. The wine list offers libations from all the world's wine growing regions. At lunchtime, the prix fixe menu is a bargain.

● Stéphane Martin   SIM

67, rue des Entrepreneurs
Métro: Charles-Michels, Commerce
Tel. 01 45 79 03 31. Fax 01 45 79 44 69
restau.stephanemartin@free.fr
Closed Sunday, Monday, Christmas–New
Year's, 1 week at Easter, 3 weeks in August.
Open until 11 PM.
Prix fixe: 32€. A la carte: 35–40€.
Air cond. Private dining room.

This street corner restaurant is popular with the local inhabitants. Even the firefighters from the station opposite come to eat here. Marie-Lucile's welcome is affable, and in the kitchen, Stéphane Martin (who worked with Alain Dutournier) is an inventive chef. He adds his personal touch, bringing a new flavor to each traditional dish. White asparagus fricassée with parmesan and country bacon, tuna steak with crisp fennel and sorrel, pan-seared foie gras with lamb's lettuce salad and papaya give a good idea of his unusual cuisine. Strawberry tiramisu with strawberry biscuits and flavored with rose is light and airy.

● La Table d'Othe   SIM

281, rue Lecourbe
Métro: Boucicaut, Convention
Tel.-Fax 01 45 58 19 29
Closed Sunday, Monday, August.
Open until 10 PM.
Prix fixe: 26€. A la carte: 35€.

Josette Renaud is everywhere at once: through the dining room, talking to the customers, then back in the kitchen. She adapts her dishes to whatever fresh produce is at hand. Smoked salmon spring rolls with eggplant caviar, scallops cooked in white vermouth and slow-roasted lamb shoulder with tarragon reduction sauce are just some of her successful preparations, along with apples in phyllo pastry served with vanilla ice cream. We indulge ourselves with a few unpretentious, selected wines. The genuine value for money here provides an incentive to visit on a regular basis.

● Thierry Burlot   🏠 ○ COM

8, rue Nicolas-Charlet
Métro: Pasteur
Tel. 01 42 19 08 59
Closed Saturday lunch, Sunday.
Open until 10 PM
(Saturday, Sunday 11 PM).
Prix fixe: 26€, 32€, 59€.
Air cond. Private dining room.

Back to better things this year. Thierry Burlot has put together a more dynamic and efficient team that maintains the same high standards when the master's away. The dishes are light, the cooking keeps all the flavor intact and the compositions are unexpected and always tasteful. Jumbo shrimp with coriander and wild lime set the tone, and the other dishes also display that touch of originality that makes all the difference. Dover sole braised with bacon is served with lemon confit and slow-cooked apples, mint and cumin–roasted lamb shoulder with carrots and orange flower scented semolina. The desserts, such as the caramel and fleur de sel ice cream, are acrobatic. Aurélie Frazier handles the service amiably, playing the role of sommelier on occasion when there is wine to be chosen. The prices are what they are . . . which is quite acceptable when lunch or dinner is a success from start to finish.

● Le Tire-Bouchon   SIM

62, rue des Entrepreneurs
Métro: Charles-Michels
Tel.-Fax 01 40 59 09 27
Closed Saturday lunch, Sunday, Monday lunch, 1 week Christmas–New Year's, 3 weeks in August–beginning of September.
Open until 10 PM.
Prix fixe: 22€ (on weekdays), 32€, 37€.
A la carte: 35–40€.
Air cond.

Laurent and Isabelle Houry spare no efforts in gratifying their guests. She provides the right advice, he enchants with strawberry and foie gras spring roll (!), swordfish with slow-cooked tomatoes and grilled veal sweetbreads with potato cakes and rosemary jus. The menu as a whole changes every month and a half, but a different dish each day reflects the chef's mood and the vagaries of the market. Fine selected vintages.

● Le Troquet   🎒 SIM

21, rue François-Bonvin
Métro: Sèvres-Lecourbe, Cambronne, Volontaires
Tel. 01 45 66 89 00. Fax 01 45 66 89 83
Closed Sunday, Monday, 1 week Christmas–New Year's, 1 week in May, 3 weeks in August. Open until 11 PM.
Prix fixe: 24€ (lunch), 28€ (lunch), 30€ (lunch), 38€.
Terrace.

Make sure you are not ten minutes late for your reservation or you will find your table taken and will have to look for somewhere else to eat. That would be a shame, because Christian Etchebest is a very good chef. Cumin-seasoned eggplant spread, mussels and sea snails in vinaigrette is a fine invention and, with a little luck (he only works with fresh produce and there is sometimes a shortage), you will be able to feast on salt and pepper red tuna with beef bone marrow, unless you prefer a rural dish and opt for suckling pig shoulder. The vanilla soufflé with black cherry jam is mouthwatering. The service, supervised by Patricia Etchebest, is prompt, but you have to vacate your table punctually, because the customers who have reserved it for the second sitting have begun to arrive. The meal does not come cheap, but in the end, there is very little to grumble about.

● Uitr   SIM

1, pl Falguière
Métro: Volontaires, Vaugirard, Pernety
Tel. 01 47 34 12 24. Fax 01 47 34 12 34
Open daily until 10:30 PM.
Prix fixe: 15€, 19€. A la carte: 28–32€.
Terrace.

We love this marine bistro in the style of an oyster hut with its focus on seafood. Hervé Paris makes no concessions to the fresh fish, shellfish and crustaceans that form a large part of the menu, which changes according to the catch. Although there is also prime rib or duck leg with herbed jus, we come here mainly for oysters from Bouzigues, Marennes, or l'aber Benoît, the salad of raw tuna and parmesan, the sea bream grilled with thyme and the squid with parsley and garlic. The apple crumble adds a handsome, sweet note in this temple to the sea.

● La Villa Corse `COM`

164, bd de Grenelle
Métro: La Motte-Picquet–Grenelle, Cambronne
Tel. 01 53 86 70 81. Fax 01 53 86 90 73
lavillacorse@wanadoo.fr
Closed Sunday. Open until 11:30 PM.
Prix fixe: 23€ (lunch, wine included).
A la carte: 55€.
Air cond. Private dining room. Valet parking.

Dedicated entirely to the Island of Beauty, this restaurant is in the original Corsican. Augustin Grisoni's accent is authentic, and the produce comes from his native isle. The millefeuille with Corsican brocciu cheese and slow-cooked vegetables, the Corsican sea bass accompanied by a "fondue" of slow-cooked fennel and three peppers, and thick, tender farm-raised black pork chops en cocotte are splendid. For dessert, the same is true of the warm soft chestnut cake. The wine list offers a wide range of the island's top vintages.

● Le Volant `SIM`

13, rue Béatrix-Dussane
Métro: Dupleix
Tel. 01 45 75 27 67
Closed Saturday lunch, Sunday, Monday lunch, 1 week the end of July, 3 weeks in August. Open until 10:30 PM.
Prix fixe: 22,50€ (lunch).
A la carte: 35–40€.

Race car fanatic and former rugby player with the Stade Français team, Georges Houel, aged 93, continues to look in on each sitting. Seconded by Daniel and Marie in the dining room and Omar in the kitchen, he loves to watch his guests enjoying the mushroom fricassée, grilled sea bass, beef bourguignon and soft chocolate cake. At the end of the meal, we join Georges with our coffee and he tells us tales of his athletic achievements. An engaging man and an appealing restaurant.

INTERNATIONAL RESTAURANTS

● Arti `SIM`

173, rue Lecourbe
Métro: Vaugirard
Tel. 01 48 28 66 68. Fax 01 45 54 50 15
arunparis@hotmail.com
Daily. Open until 11:30 PM.
A la carte: 35€
Air cond. Terrace.

Arun Sachdeva introduces us to the cuisine of Northern India. The tandoori shrimp, chicken tikka, shrimp massala and lamb bhuna ghost are local dishes high in flavor and fresh on the palate. The setting is restful with its woodwork, statuettes and jewelry collection. The prices remain honest, especially if you accompany your meal from start to dessert—kulfi, (a creamy pistachio and almond ice cream flavored with rose)—with tea or a lassi.

● Chen
"Le Soleil d'Est" `V.COM`

15, rue du Théâtre
Métro: Charles-Michels, Bir-Hakeim
Tel. 01 45 79 34 34. Fax 01 45 79 07 53
Closed Sunday, May 1st, August.
Open until 10:30 PM.
Prix fixe: 40€ (weekend lunch), 75€, 15€ (children). A la carte: 80–100€.
Air cond. Private dining room. Valet parking.
Patriarch Fung Chin Chen is now in paradise and the family is assiduously carrying on his work. The faithful Jean Le Gloanec, who has been running the dining room for so long, is assisted by Véronique Chen today. In the half-Chinese, half-contemporary decor of the second floor and in the first floor dining room with its historic woodwork, they recommend sautéed frog's legs with herbs, fresh ginger and

Szechuan pepper, small turbot with exotic spices, broccoli and Cantonese-style sautéed rice—a magical delicacy!—or mountain-style oxtail served with pan juices and slow roasted caramelized egg-plant, a dash of Chinese vinaigrette, black mushrooms and steamed tiger lily flowers. The hot and cold green apple dessert should not be missed. Tea can be chosen to the exclusion of any other beverage and we have no complaints when the check arrives, since quality has its price.

▼ | SHOPS

BREAD & BAKED GOODS

▼ Le Bon Panneton

105, rue Saint-Charles
Métro: Charles-Michels
Tel. 01 40 59 84 70
7 AM–9 PM (Saturday 8:30 PM).
Closed Sunday, Monday

Eric and Valérie Brunet boast the best of the baker's art. Bread with brie, old-fashioned baguette, small cheese breads, bacon and rye rolls, whole-grain and the famous chorizo breads are first rate. We love the fine fruit tarts, chocolate ganache, apple turnover, savory pies and quiches and crunchy roquefort bread, which are a great hit.

▼ Max Poilâne   🏠

87, rue Brançon
Métro: Porte-de-Vanves
Tel. 01 48 28 45 90. Fax 01 48 28 87 88
www.max-poilane.fr
7:30 AM–8 PM
(Sunday and Bank Holidays: 9 AM–7 PM).
Closed Christmas, New Year's Day.

At Max Poilâne's, raisin, rye, nut, whole-grain and white breads favorably impress. The sugar cookies, butter brioche and individual tarts are irresistibly tempting.

▼ Poilâne

49, bd de Grenelle
Métro: Dupleix
Tel. 01 45 79 11 49
7:15 AM–8:15 PM.
Closed Monday

The second Poilâne store is not as famous as the one in rue du Cherche-Midi, but the goods are identical: Poilâne loaves (1.9 kg), rye, nut, butter brioche, apple turnovers, apple tarts and sugar cookies called *punitions* ("punishments") are works of art.

CHARCUTERIE

▼ Charcuterie Mas

25, bd de Grenelle
Métro: Bir-Hakeim
Tel.-Fax 01 45 71 07 78
8 AM–1 PM, 2:30 PM–7 PM.
Closed Sunday, Monday,
Bank Holidays, August.

Roland Mas boasts quality traditional cured meats and pâtés: terrines, stuffed duck necks, seasoned mutton tripe, Auvergne hams, sausages, dried sausages and cassoulet with duck confit. He also supplies Salers meat, but ordered in advance.

▼ Au Cochon Rose

137, rue Saint-Charles
Métro: Charles-Michels, Javel, Boucicaut
9 AM–1:30 PM, 3:30–7:30 PM (Saturday 9 AM–7:30 PM, Sunday 9 AM–1 PM).
Closed Sunday afternoon, Monday,
3 weeks in August.

The dynamic Dominique and Christine Bignon have taken in hand this famous store devoted to pork in all its diversity. White ham (parsley-rolled or on the bone), boudin (Mortagne gold medal in 2006), head cheese, terrines, foie gras and pâté in a pastry crust are some of the delicacies.

▼ Duval

171, rue de la Convention
Métro: Convention
Tel. 01 45 30 14 08. Fax 01 48 32 55 27
10 AM–1 PM, 3:30–7:30 PM.
Closed Saturday, Sunday, August.

Duval's products are home produced in the family workshop in Drancy. We love the andouillette, boudin, artisan-made terrines, tripe, parsleyed ham, stuffed meat bundles and Lyonnaise sausages.

ESCARGOTS

▼ La Maison de l'Escargot

79, rue Fondary
Métro: Emile-Zola, La Motte-Picquet–Grenelle
Tel. 01 45 75 31 09. Fax 01 45 75 33 11
www.maison-escargot.com
9:30 AM–7 PM.
Closed Sunday, Monday, Bank Holidays
This hundred-year-old establishment offers a wide range of snails of all grades and sizes. In the delicatessen section are foie gras, onion jam, and, for accessories, escargot forks and plates. At lunchtime, you can enjoy these specialties in the store and end your meal with a delicious sorbet from Ardèche. Some amazing flavors can be ordered in advance (dill, basil, garlic, pepper).

CHEESE

▼ Laurent Dubois

2, rue de Lourmel
Métro: Dupleix
Tel. 01 45 78 70 58. Fax 01 45 75 10 00
9 AM–1 PM, 4–7:45 PM (Friday and Saturday 9AM–7 :45 PM September–April).
Closed Sunday afternoon, Monday, August.
Laurent Dubois selects and ages French regional cheeses: livarot, beaufort d'alpage, comté d'herbage, fourme d'ambert with Sauternes, saint-nectaire, camembert and pélardon of premier quality.

▼ La Ferme du Hameau

223, rue de la Croix-Nivert
Métro: Porte-de-Versailles
Tel. 01 45 32 88 70. Fax 01 45 32 88 54
lafermeduhameau@wanadoo.fr
8:30 AM–1 PM, 3:30–8 PM. Closed Sunday afternoon, Monday, mid-July–mid-August.
Vincent Pélisson has taken over this store, which mainly promotes products from Normandy. Livarot, pavé d'Auge, pont-l'évêque, beaufort d'alpage, aged comté and crottin de Chavignol go hand in hand. The house specialties are Mortagne sausages, foie gras, wines direct from the winery, farm cider. All delicious.

PASTRIES

▼ Pierre Hermé

185, rue de Vaugirard
Métro: Pasteur
Tel. 01 47 83 89 96. Fax 01 47 83 89 90
www.pierreherme.com
10 AM–7 PM.
Closed Monday, end of July–end of August.
The former Hellegouarch has become the Macaron King's second store (see the sixth arrondissement). His confections—coffee, salted-butter caramel, chocolate, passion fruit and milk chocolate macarons—are marvels. Having achieved great things with Fauchon, then Ladurée, this fashion designer of the cake and pastry world has become a world-renowned crafter of confectionery. His two millefeuilles and his chocolate creations are grand indeed.

▼ Lecoq

120, rue Saint-Charles
Métro: Charles-Michels
Tel. 01 45 77 72 56. Fax 01 45 79 05 06
8:30 AM–7:45 PM.
Closed Monday, 1 week in winter, August.
Chocolate-raspberry, chocolate tart with nougatine, Breton shortbread with pistachio, strawberry or raspberry cream, macaron biscuit with chocolate, Carré Marigny and quality ganaches are Christian Lecoq's sweet treasure. The house jams change from season to season.

REGIONAL PRODUCTS

▼ Comptoir Corrézien du Foie Gras

8, rue des Volontaires
Métro: Volontaires
Tel. 01 47 83 52 97. Fax 01 45 67 88 42
9:30 AM–1:30 PM, 3–8 PM. Closed Sunday, Monday morning, Bank Holidays, August.
Chantal Larnaudie wins our vote with her confits, duck pâté, goose or duck foie gras, cassoulet, mushrooms (correze, mousserons, lactarius and chanterelle) and truffles, not to mention her exquisite baba au rhum.

◆ RENDEZVOUS

This small retro café faithfully run by François Walczak takes you on a tour of yesterday's boxing world. We come for a drink or to enjoy the meticulously prepared good-quality meals.

WINE BARS

◆ Couleurs de Vigne
2, rue Marmontel
Métro: Vaugirard, Convention
Tel.-Fax 01 45 33 32 96   *
alain.touchard@club-internet.fr
9:30 AM–11 PM.
Closed Saturday, Sunday,
Bank Holidays, mid-July–mid-August.
Air cond.

In this tiny barroom, Alain Touchard presents his finds from every wine-growing region, accompanied by tartines, cheese plates, Burgundian stews and delicious lentils with salt pork.

CAFES

◆ Au Métro
18, bd Pasteur
Métro: Pasteur, Sèvres-Lecourbe
Tel. 01 47 34 21 24. Fax 01 45 66 06 13
6 AM–2 AM. Closed Sunday, August.
Terrace.

This café is packed with rugby fans who delight in its Southwestern French specialties: duck breast or cassoulet. The atmosphere is convivial to a fault.

◆ Au Roi du Café
59, rue Lecourbe
Métro: Volontaires, Sèvres-Lecourbe
Tel. 01 47 34 48 50
7 AM–2 AM. Closed Christmas.
Terrace.

This fine traditional café is a cheerful haunt where regulars meet. Charcuterie from the Auvergne, smoked herring with potatoes and olive oil, prime rib, calf's liver and artisanal ice creams are savored in a congenial atmosphere. A heated terrace in winter.

◆ Aux Sportifs Réunis
75, rue Brancion
Métro: Convention, Porte-de-Vanves
Tel. 01 48 28 61 00
11 AM–10 PM. Closed Monday, August.

◆ Le Square
139, bd de Grenelle
Métro: Cambronne, La Motte-Picquet–Grenelle
Tel.-Fax 01 43 06 80 84.
7 AM–2 AM. Closed Christmas.
Terrace.

Christian Sanchez and Rolando Enriques have taken over this modern café, where we savor polished dishes of the day, generous salads and miscellaneous drinks. When the weather is fine, there is a terrace on the sidewalk, and the place hosts pop or rock shows every two weeks.

◆ Le Terminus Balard
1, pl Balard
Métro: Balard
Tel. 01 45 57 81 61. Fax 01 45 54 04 13
7 AM–10 PM.
Closed Sunday, Bank Holidays.
Air cond. Terrace.

A step away from Balard Métro station and André Citroën park, this pleasant brasserie regales us with andouillette, choucroute, steamed mussels, rotisserie chicken and spare ribs, all cheerfully served.

TEA SALONS

◆ Infinithé
8, rue Desnouettes
Métro: Convention
Tel. 01 40 43 14 23
sandrine.letestu@libertysurf.fr
www.infinithe.com
Lunch: noon–3:30 PM, tea: 2–6:30 PM
(Saturday noon–6:30 PM). Closed August.

This Thirties' nonsmoking tearoom serves homemade cakes, savory tarts, composed salads, crumble, cheesecake, soft chocolate cake and delicious jams. In the Infinithé store, you can browse through products of the day and tea-based gift ideas (8 rue Dombasle, Tel. +33 01 48 28 31 42, Tuesday–Saturday, 1–7 p.m.).

◆ Laura Todd Cookies & Bio

81, av de Breteuil
Métro: Sèvres-Lecourbe
Tel. 01 45 67 92 25
10:30 AM–5:30 PM. Closed Saturday,
Sunday, 2 weeks in August.
Terrace.

Enjoy salads, sandwiches and cookies
(cocoa, milk, coconut granola, or hazelnut), along with compotes and brownies in
a good-natured atmosphere, beneath the
low ceiling of this small, sober lair.

◆ Tour Eiffel Café   🔕

Novotel Paris Tour Eiffel
61, quai de Grenelle,
Métro: Bir-Hakeim, Charles-Michels
Tel. 01 40 58 20 75. Fax 01 40 58 21 50
h3546-fb3@accor.com
6–9:30 AM (10:30 AM Saturday, Sunday,
and school vacations), noon–10:30 PM.
Open daily.
Air cond.

Opposite the Seine, this designer tearoom welcomes patrons for a bite in pleasant surroundings. The lemon-marinated
shrimp, celery root and green apple
rémoulade, citrus-grilled swordfish and
soft chocolate cake are all appealing.

○	Very good restaurant
◯◯	Excellent restaurant
◯◯◯	One of the best restaurants in Paris
⑤	Disappointing restaurant
🍖	Good value for money
€	Meals for less than 30 euros
SIM	Simple
COM	Comfortable
V.COM	Very comfortable
LUX	Luxurious
V.LUX	Very luxurious

Red indicates a particularly charming establishment

🏛	Historical significance
🅿	Promotion *(higher rating than last year)*
🆕	New to the guide

●	Restaurant
▼	Shop
◆	Rendezvous

16TH ARRONDISSEMENT
ARE YOU AUTEUIL OR PASSY?

The sixteenth arrondissement has its two communities. "Auteuil is like Passy's countryside," wrote poet and essayist Léon-Paul Fargue. "The people of Passy go to Auteuil like the people of rue Etienne-Marcel go to Brunoy on a Sunday. They almost seem tempted to take their own food." So has the sixteenth arrondissement changed? The Auteuil viaduct has gone. The rail stations have been converted into chic eating spots (La Gare, Le Flandrin). L'Auberge du Mouton Blanc, where France's great 17th-century playwrights Molière and Racine once met, has been resurrected. But despite its Parisian upper crust status, this arrondissement is enormously provincial. Rue de Passy, the epitome of the kind of local main street we might expect to see in Rouen, Dijon or Toulouse, parades its window displays and stores. Auteuil is still a village, with Lenôtre its main grocery. On avenue Victor-Hugo, Le Stella has been refurbished. Grand restaurants proliferate; the local bistros remain. La Table de Joël Robuchon, La Grande Cascade, Le Pré Catelan and Hiramatsu (now at the address of the former Faugeron) are open for business. Among the new stars, L'Astrance and (with a more voguish chic) 6 New York continue to strive for quality. You can eat in every language and style here. From Oum El Banine to the Pavillon Noura, from Auteuil to Passy, the sixteenth arrondissement plays its fashion card with an elegance that is definitely its hallmark.

RESTAURANTS

GRAND RESTAURANTS

● **L'Astrance** ⬭⬭ COM
4, rue Beethoven
Métro: Passy
Tel. 01 40 50 84 40
Closed Saturday, Sunday, Monday, 1 week in
November, Christmas–New Year's, 1 week in
February, August. Open until 9:15 PM.
Prix fixe: 70€ (lunch), 120€ (lunch),
250€ (dinner, wine included).
A la carte: 150€.
Air cond.

The *astrance* (or masterwort), a small plant
native to the Auvergne, can pride itself on
being adopted as the symbol of this great
establishment run by Christophe Rohat,
our Discovery of 2002. L'Astrance's
achievement, its *surprise du chef*, is its ongoing fresh approach to French cuisine
with no place for the commonplace. Pascal
Barbot, the man behind its everyday miracles, is a talented disciple of master Alain
Passard. He brings us light, spirited, im-
pertinent, ingenious, sometimes explosive
but always personal, flawlessly polished
dishes, such as his celebrated slivered avocado with crabmeat, mushroom pancake
with foie gras, sumptuous turbot with a
lemon, ginger and mallow-leaf coulis, the
impish sautéed pigeon with potatoes au
gratin and the staggering soft chocolate
cake with a cookie and milk sorbet. It is
quite a struggle to secure a place among
the mere twenty-five available here (a
three-week wait!) and you can only dream
of sitting down without a reservation. In
the small contemporary dining room in
gray and yellow shades, the talented, good-
natured and indeed indispensable
Christophe Rohat senses our needs, antic-
ipates our expectations, finds the words to
describe his colleague's creations and recommends the right wine from among the
500 in the cellar. Spurred on by the trumpet
blast of Fame, the check naturally scales
new heights.

● **Le Pré Catelan** ⬭⬭ LUX
Rte de Suresnes, Bois de Boulogne
Métro: Porte-Maillot, Porte-Dauphine
Tel. 01 44 14 41 14. Fax 01 45 24 43 25
www.lenotre.fr
Closed Sunday, Monday, 3 weeks in February.
Open until 10 PM.
Prix fixe: 75€ (lunch), 140€ (dinner),
180€ (dinner). A la carte: 180–205€.
Terrace. Private dining room. Valet parking.

In a Belle Epoque style, with pastel shades
and Caran d'Ache frescos, this Napoleon
III lodge in the Bois de Boulogne is a natural, chic destination for the businesspeople and lovers who come together in
Frédéric Anton's remarkable establishment. This hard-working native of the Vosges (a semantic redundancy), formerly
with Boyer at Les Crayères, Bardot at Le
Flambard and Robuchon at Jamin (for
seven years), prepares a refined, highly
meticulous cuisine. Hardly has roasted
Breton lobster begun to whet your appetite
with its garlic snow peas, capers, mushrooms and crispy lobster claw, than you
find yourself swept out to sea by variations
on the theme of the sardine and steamed
seaweed-wrapped turbot served with
shellfish and white wine stew. The lamb—
grilled chops sautéed with fresh green
peas, morel mushrooms and lamb
sausage—melts deliciously in the mouth.
The desserts, light yet intense (caramelized apple with chocolate cream, green
apple sorbet, baked apple and apple tartlet), live up to our expectations, as does the
cellar, which offers no fewer than 950
French and world vintages under the informed supervision of David Rivière. The
service is, of course, perfect.

● **La Table de** ⬭⬭ COM
Joël Robuchon
16, av Bugeaud
Métro: Victor-Hugo
Tel. 01 56 28 16 16. Fax 01 56 28 16 78
latabledejoelrobuchon@wanadoo.fr
Open daily until 11 PM.
Prix fixe: 55€ (lunch, wine included), 150€.
A la carte: 150€.
Air cond. Valet parking.

He has opened restaurants in Las Vegas and New York, and is still doing business in rue Montalembert in Paris, as well as in Tokyo, Macao and Monaco. In this hushed, nonsmoking gourmet club where the dishes are served in gold surroundings on bare tables of precious wood, Joël the First, king of cooks, delegates authority, ideas and talent to his dedicated lieutenants. Brought in from the seventh arrondissement, Antoine Hernandez in the dining room, and range-top virtuosi Philippe Braun and Eric Lecerf, are dedicated soldiers of fortune. The kitchen is run by Frédéric Simonin, who, like pastry chef François Benot, previously worked with Ghislaine Arabian. Everything served here is characterized by an insistence on supreme quality and a love of fine produce. Spider crab and delicate broccoli cream in seawater jelly, red-leg crayfish stewed in white wine with vegetables, whole fried whiting in herbed butter, John Dory fish with southern aromatics and virgin olive oil, sautéed veal chop with olives, young fava beans and baby artichokes, caramelized foie gras-stuffed quail served with truffled potato purée, "secrets of the woods" (iced wild strawberries with red poppy candy, yogurt-ginger cream) or "chocolate sensation" (velvety Araguani chocolate cream, chocolate and Oreo ice cream) all are part of the latest Robuchon collection. This highly refined restaurant is a work of gastronomic *haute couture*, designed by a chef who, not content with defining his era, has also proved to be a precursor of fashion. Explosive!

GOOD RESTAURANTS & OTHERS

● L'Acajou   COM

35 bis, rue Jean-de-La-Fontaine
Métro: Jasmin
Tel. 01 42 88 04 47. Fax 01 42 88 95 12
www.l-acajou.com
Closed Saturday lunch, Sunday, August.
Open until 10 PM.
Prix fixe: 28€, 35€, 40€ (wine included).
A la carte: 70–80€.
Air cond. Terrace. Private dining room.

"For well born souls, value does not wait upon age." The young Jean Imbert is "El Cid" at the age of 24, chef and proprietor (not to mention sports fan) of this comfortable, muted establishment, the former Fontaine d'Auteuil. Decorated with mahogany woodwork, it boasts a fine, inventive cuisine and vibrant service in the hands of René-Louis Arthur. A subtle sommelier, he recommends highly appropriate bottles to accompany the Aquitaine caviar, crab and John Dory stewed with green asparagus and wild mushrooms, the Bellac lamb shoulder slow-roasted with spices and the chocolate soufflé. Sweet flirts with savory; crisp with tender. The prices a la carte are steep, but the set menus are splendid and the welcome excellent. Of course, this means it is essential to reserve!

● Aéro-Club de France   COM

6, rue Galilée
Métro: Boissière
Tel. 01 47 20 88 04. Fax 01 47 20 68 35
v.tahon@sodexho-prestige.fr
www.sodexho-prestige.fr
Closed dinner (except for private parties), Saturday, Sunday, 1 week Christmas–New Year's, August.
A la carte: 55–60€.
Air cond. Private dining room.

Through the dark entrance hall where a huge propeller from Dassault aeronautics is enshrined and our taste buds are ready to taxi. In this private club open to the public, our captain is a lady, Véronique Tahon. In this urbane, pleasant decor of warm tones and woodwork, we are in for a very epicurean passage thanks to the talent of high-flying chef Gaby Martinnon, from takeoff (roasted langoustine in vanilla vinaigrette) to cruising altitude (steamed fish stew with green vegetables or roasted beef prime rib with caramelized shallots) to landing (mango juice and tapioca in coconut milk). The flight goes all the more smoothly since Jean-Michel Groult points us toward the correct French or foreign (Australian, Chilean and Argentinian) wines to aptly accompany this gourmet feast and take us up to seventh heaven.

● A & M `COM`

136, bd Murat
Métro: Porte-de-St-Cloud
Tel. 01 45 27 39 60. Fax 01 45 27 69 71
Closed Saturday lunch, Sunday, August.
Open until 10:30 PM.
Prix fixe: 30€. A la carte: 55€.
Terrace. Valet parking.

For their first offshoot, whose fine, contemporary dining room leads onto a terrace, Jean-Pierre Vigato and Frédéric Grandjean from Apicius and Marius have found a fine exponent of their ideas in the person of Tsukasa Fukuyama. With rapid delicacy, this discreet French-Japanese chef prepares layered terrine of calf's head and foie gras, sautéed red tuna, roasted cod and cod brandade, beef cheeks parmentier, rib-eye steak with fleur de sel, iced caramelized fennel mousse and warm soft chocolate cake. All these dishes are well made, served with a smile and none too expensive.

● Alfred `N` `SIM`

38, av de Versailles
Métro: Mirabeau
Tel. 01 45 25 51 15
Closed Sunday evening, Monday,
Christmas–beginning of January,
end of July–end of August.
Open until 10:45 PM.
Prix fixe: 19,50€ (lunch), 21€ (brunch,
Sunday lunch). A la carte: 35–40€.
Terrace. Valet parking.

This new establishment a step away from Pont Mirabeau has the sweet smell of youth. Alfred Bernardin has opened a bistro inspired by his globetrotting rites of passage: a little of New York in the "trendy" dishes and a touch of St. Barthelemy on the boardwalk terrace, where you can almost hear the waves. The tuna tartare is honest, the crunchy vegetable and crab appetizer a great success. We have no objections to the breaded veal medallions in lemon-honey sauce on a bed of spinach, sautéed sea bream with pesto sauce or cold poached salmon with lemon cream, either, not to mention "my best" chocolate cake, a classic of its kind. The wine list

is concise but first rate. The tab is moderate and the service friendly.

● L'Apropos `N` `SIM`

37, rue Poussin
Métro: Porte-d'Auteuil
Tel. 01 47 43 90 11. Fax 01 46 51 76 79
Closed Saturday lunch, Sunday, 1 week in
August. Open until 10:30 PM.
Prix fixe: 23€. A la carte: 55–60€.
Air cond. Terrace.

This contemporary bistro (the former Escrouzailles) with its pale woodwork, now undergoing renovation, pays tribute to Southwest France with its musical accent, friendly welcome, cheerful ambience and generous dishes. This seasonal homage comes in the form of the homemade foie gras and fig compote, peeled jumbo shrimp on a bed of fresh pasta, beef tenderloin with truffle jus and prunes soaked in Armagnac, a winning combination (especially since the prices keep a low profile).

● Les Arts `V.COM`

9 bis, av d'Iéna
Métro: Iéna
Tel. 01 40 69 27 53. Fax 01 40 69 27 08
maison.des.arts@sodexho-prestige.fr
www.sodexho-prestige.fr
Closed Saturday, Sunday, Bank Holidays,
Christmas–New Year's, August.
Open until 10 PM.
Prix fixe: 38€. A la carte: 75–80€.
Terrace. Private dining room.

In this handsome, impeccably comfortable town house, with tables set well apart, cozy rooms and garden open in the season, we savor the reliable cuisine of the resident Ritz, La Marée and Tante Jeanne veteran. Thierry Chevalier produces fresh, polished dishes, including roasted langoustine tails with shredded leeks in truffle vinaigrette, Dover sole fried in butter with morel mushrooms and fried red onions, diced lamb with coriander and Provençal-style artichoke stew and chocolate pudding with strawberry candy sauce. Afterward we head on to the neighboring Guimet museum, where the arts are less expensive.

● **Auberge Dab** COM

161, av de Malakoff
Métro: Porte-Maillot
Tel. 01 45 00 32 22. Fax 01 45 00 58 50
restaurant@auberge-dab.com
www.rest-gj.com
Open daily until 2 AM.
Prix fixe: 38€. A la carte: 50–60€.
Air cond. Terrace. Private dining room.
Valet parking.

Run by Philippe Grandremy, this elegant brasserie with its paneled decor attracts local patrons and visitors from farther afield, particularly fish fans. Its air conditioning, terrace, private dining room and valet parking cater to their higher needs, while the assorted seafood platter, scallop and sea bream carpaccio, gilthead bream filet with pesto, roasted beef prime rib for two and the giant baba au rhum prepared by new chef Cédric Poncet offer more physical gratification.

● **L'Auberge du Bonheur** SIM

Carrefour de Longchamp, Bois de Boulogne
Métro: Porte-Maillot
Tel. 01 42 24 10 17. Fax 01 42 88 99 06
lagrandecascade@wanadoo.fr
Closed lunch (except in winter), dinner
(except for groups from October–April),
February. Open until 10:45 PM.
A la carte: 47–65€.
Terrace. Private dining room. Valet parking.

A warrior's haven? This former hunting lodge, with its huge terrace in summer, fireplace in winter and fully restored bar, is certainly a perfect rustic retreat, offering the fresh, flavorsome cuisine of new chef Franck Birette. The plates placed before us hold tomato cream with olive oil, balsamic vinegar and tapenade croutons, chicken and jumbo shrimp with chopped garlic and parsley, roasted lamb shank with slow-roasted mixed vegetables, orange and grapefruit salad with fresh mint leaves or authentic crème caramel, all flawless. Pure pleasure.

● **L'Aventure** COM

4, av Victor-Hugo
Métro: Charles-de-Gaulle–Etoile
Tel. 01 45 00 45 11. Fax 01 45 01 55 11
sarlmangel@wanadoo.fr
www.laventure-leclub.com
Closed Saturday evening, Sunday,
2 weeks in August. Open until 2 AM.
Prix fixe: 26€ (lunch). A la carte: 65–70€.
Air cond. Terrace. Private dining room.
Valet parking.

If we found adventure in this comfortable restaurant run by Bruno and Agnès Mandel on the corner of avenue Victor Hugo, would it lie in the contemporary red and gold tones of the refurbished dining room? Or in the tomato tartare, roasted turbot, sautéed beef tenderloin, the croquant de fraises Cardinal (a crisp pastry with strawberries and raspberry coulis) prepared by the chef, Stéphane Lucas? No, there could be little danger in such honest preparations of fine produce. Sommelier Sylvain Gandon's service and advice? No, he is reliable as clockwork. What about the neo-Asian decor, concealing the occasional socialite when night falls? Or perhaps after dinner, when the restaurant turns into a club and discotheque again. . . .

● **Le Beaujolais d'Auteuil** SIM

99, bd de Montmorency
Métro: Porte-d'Auteuil
Tel. 01 47 43 03 56. Fax 01 46 51 27 81
Closed 2 weeks in beginning of August.
Open until 11 PM.
Prix fixe: 25€ (wine included),
27€ (wine included). A la carte: 45–55€.
Air cond. Terrace.

This good old traditional eatery carries on the art of inexpensively feeding the villagers of Auteuil, who like to loosen up with a drop of Beaujolais, take the air on the terrace and taste the simple pleasures of a zucchini millefeuille, salmon tartare, Salers beef rib-eye steak or chocolate fondant prepared by Franck Metinger and Bernard Desfontaine.

● Bon `COM`

25, rue de la Pompe
Métro: La Muette
Tel. 01 40 72 70 00. Fax 01 40 72 68 30
Closed Saturday lunch, Sunday evening,
August. Open until 11:30 PM.
Prix fixe: 25€ (lunch), 30€ (lunch).
A la carte: 55–60€.
Air cond. Private dining room. Valet parking.

Will it work out this time? Many managers have thrown in the towel at this Starck-designed restaurant with its baroque decor, stubbornly run by Philippe Amzalack today. Bruce Meritte is gone and a new chapter has begun with chef Bruno Brangea, who whips up plain fresh crab-meat with broccoli vinaigrette, spice-rubbed codfish with tomato, beef tenderloin with an anchovy and olive jus, thin-crust mango tart with mango sorbet, dishes to be enjoyed with French, Chilean, Spanish or California wines by the glass. Friendlier service, more moderate prices, a more restrained cuisine, a fine chef and a young, good-natured team: This new deal should finally win over the gentlefolk of Passy.

● Le Brandevin `SIM`

29, rue du Dr-Blanche
Métro: Jasmin
Tel. 01 42 24 19 33. Fax 01 40 50 77 47
Closed Sunday, Christmas, New Year's,
August. Open until 11 PM.
A la carte: 40€.
Air cond. Terrace.

Refurbishment is under way at Le Brandevin, a traditional burgundy-colored wine bar with checked tablecloths, posters and oak tables, where we drink and lunch at moderate prices. Mélanie Chauvin amiably serves up oxtail terrine with onion marmalade, smoked haddock filet with lemon butter, calf's liver with sherry vinegar and raspberry tart, all signed by chef Hervé Guillois. Ah, the delightful taste of simple, generous fare!

● La Brasserie de la Poste `SIM`

54, rue de Longchamp
Métro: Trocadéro, Boissière
Tel.-Fax 01 47 55 01 31
Closed Saturday, Sunday, 2 weeks in August.
Open until 10 PM.
Prix fixe: 17€ (wine included), 20€ (wine
included), 30€, 10€ (children).
A la carte: 45–50€.
Air cond. Terrace.

A pleasant Thirties' brasserie in sunny shades, with a neo–art deco setting and alert service. Under the watchful eye of Jérôme Blancard, the vivacious Juliette Fleurot-Beausire serves David Ceheux's sturdy dishes. The herbed foie gras tartare, a creamy spiced-ginger appetizer, cod with caramelized tomatoes, pork tenderloin and potato purée with chorizo and strawberry gazpacho with maple syrup and cookies are new takes on bistro classics. They display culinary daring and slip down smoothly.

● La Butte Chaillot `COM`

110 bis, av Kléber
Métro: Trocadéro
Tel. 01 47 27 88 88. Fax 01 47 27 41 46
buttechaillot@guysavoy.com
www.buttechaillot.com
Closed Saturday lunch, August.
Open until 11 PM.
Prix fixe: 33€. A la carte: 53–63€.
Air cond. Private dining room.

In his Trocadéro eatery, Guy Savoy sets the tone and leaves the house team Alain Pras and Stéphane La Ruelle, formerly at Le Crillon and Le Grand Véfour, to perform their lyrical double act. We are thrilled by their shrewd, sparkling cuisine. The jumbo shrimp salad is sprinkled with sesame seeds, the homemade foie gras is served with pineapple-mango chutney, the sautéed sea bass filet comes with stewed green vegetables and green asparagus tips with a tangy tomato jus and the lamb shank, slow-roasted with rosemary, comes complete with zucchini and eggplant with roasted garlic. Our favorite touches? A Chinese organic wine and the set menu at 33€.

● Café de l'Homme `COM`

Musée de l'Homme, 17, pl du Trocadéro
Métro: Trocadéro
Tel. 01 44 05 30 15. Fax 01 44 05 30 19
cafedelhomme@wanadoo.fr
www.cafedelhomme.com
Open daily until 10:30 PM.
A la carte: 51–73€.
Air cond. Terrace. Private dining room.
Valet parking.

The former Totem within the walls of the Musée de l'Homme is as opulent as ever, with wood, leather couches, superb chandeliers and ethnic decor. There is a stunning view of the Seine and the Eiffel Tower from the terrace, soon packed in summer. In the kitchen, Achille Sayoutchoubien offers a personal take on French tradition. Lobster medallions and green vegetable salad, a spicy jumbo shrimp stew with basmati rice, a slow-roasted, glazed veal tenderloin with young vegetables, the red fruit millefeuille and the caramel candy tart are not short on inspiration.

● Le Chalet des Iles `COM`

Lac inférieur, Bois de Boulogne,
porte de la Muette
Métro: La Muette
Tel. 01 42 88 04 69. Fax 01 42 88 84 09
contact@lechaletdesiles.net
www.lechaletdesiles.net
Open daily until 10:30 PM.
Prix fixe: 14€ (lunch), 23€ (lunch),
30€ (lunch). A la carte: 40–50€.
Terrace. Private dining room. Valet parking.

Raphaël de Montrémy, the shrewd, socialite proprietor of Le Petit Poucet and the River Café, has successfully lured Paris society onto this island in the Bois de Boulogne and into his Second Empire lodge, with its charming yellow and red decor. Stéphane Trouillard's cuisine is appealing indeed with its soft-boiled egg with fresh green pea cream, the jumbo shrimp curry, Caribbean-style, served with basmati rice, the milk-fed rack of lamb with potatoes au gratin and the cheesecake, all very well done.

● Chaumette `N` `SIM`

7, rue Gros
Métro: Ranelagh
Tel. 01 42 88 29 27
Closed Saturday lunch, Sunday, Christmas, August. Open until 10:45 PM.
Prix fixe: 28€ (lunch, wine included).
A la carte: 40–50€.
Terrace.

You think the sixteenth arrondissement is particularly boring? You will soon realize your mistake when you savor the charm of this old-fashioned, Lyon *bouchon*–style bistro, bright and warm in wood and white, and hosted by a forceful young team. Proprietor Charles-Henri Poisson seats guests in the dining room or on the terrace, helps them choose their wine and brings them the pleasant, half-classic, half-modern dishes prepared by chef Tanguy Le Gall: poached egg in a red wine and bacon sauce, red mullet filets with chorizo, the house pot-au-feu and chocolate charlotte. Each day has a fish special, chalked up on the blackboard. The menu changes every two months.

● Paul Chêne `COM`

123, rue Lauriston
Métro: Trocadéro, Victor-Hugo
Tel. 01 47 27 63 17. Fax 01 47 27 53 18
Closed Saturday, Sunday, December 23rd–beginning of January, 1 week at Easter, August. Open until 10 PM.
Prix fixe: 38€, 48€. A la carte: 65€.
Air cond. Private dining room. Valet parking.

The Fifties' setting of this old-style residence, freshened up with a slap of burgundy paint, has plenty of chic. David Souffir's welcome and Philippe Mercier's cuisine do the rest. Cold mackerel in Muscadet, duck foie gras, whole fried whiting, Dover sole fried in butter, beef stew, Grand Marnier soufflé or crêpes Suzette are reassuringly classical. If Paul Chêne came back today, he would find it all encouragingly familiar.

● Le Congrès Auteuil `COM`

144, bd Exelmans
Métro: Porte-d'Auteuil
Tel. 01 46 51 15 75. Fax 01 46 51 59 09
restaurant@congres-auteuil.com
www.rest-gj.com
Open daily until 1 AM.
Prix fixe: 32€ (wine included).
A la carte: 48–58€.
Air cond. Private dining room. Valet parking.

A step away from the Parc des Princes and Roland Garros stadia, this fine, rounded, corner brasserie with its warm paneling is prized for its quality traditional cuisine, fresh oysters and seafood delivered daily and excellent meats of certified origin. Leek and crab salad with chopped egg, scallops, grilled veal kidneys or rib-eye steak, strawberry millefeuille and raspberry macarons are prepared by the book. You can eat directly at the bar.

● Cristal Room Baccarat `SIM`

11, pl des Etats-Unis
Métro: Boissière, Iéna
Tel. 01 40 22 11 10. Fax 01 40 22 11 99
cristalroom@baccarat.fr
www.baccarat.fr
Closed Sunday. Open until 10 PM.
A la carte: 100–150€.
Air cond. Private dining room.
Valet parking.

Anne de Noailles held her salon in this town house acquired by the Maison Baccarat, so it comes as no surprise that Paris socialites flock to its restaurant, redesigned by Starck in a modern romantic style. Do they come to be seen among the chandeliers, shades, bricks, paneling and gilding, or to head upstairs and taste dishes prepared by Thierry Burlot, formerly at Le Crillon and Armani Caffé, also proprietor of a restaurant in his own name in the fifteenth arrondissement? Once the extended names have been simplified, Landais foie gras, langoustines from Brittany, Mediterranean red tuna, roasted lobster with vanilla, roasted pigeon, calf's liver, strawberries or millefeuille turn deftly from classical to contemporary. The price of style, elegance and flavor? Close-set tables, lost

waiters and absurd checks, all drowned in fine wines.

● L'Escale `N` `S` `COM`

71, av Paul-Doumer
Métro: Passy
Tel. 01 45 04 12 81. Fax 01 45 04 00 50
contact@lescale.net
www.lescale.net
Closed Sunday, Monday.
Open until 10:30 PM.
Prix fixe: 23€, 29€. A la carte: 35–50€.
Terrace. Air cond. Private dining room.
Valet parking.

Yesterday, Le Bistrot du Bigorneau, today, L'Escale; yesterday, Sébastien Cassagnol at the stove, today Sébastien Bertin, former advisor to Grégory Coutanceau of La Rochelle. This comfortable seafood restaurant belonging to the Richard group, which already owns Marius et Janette, has a luxury refectory feel to it. The decor, with its refined nautical lines and red walls, the very modish style and the freshness of the produce win our approval. There remains the disappointing preparation of the tuna tartare (tasteless), asparagus cappuccino with parmesan and Serrano ham (insipid), Dover sole fried in butter (overcooked). Roasted beef prime rib for two with béarnaise sauce is not bad. What is curious for a seafood restaurant is that only the meat passes with flying colors. Of course, the Richards are from the cattle farming Aveyron region. . . .

● Le Flandrin `COM`

80, av Henri-Martin
Métro: Rue-de-la-Pompe
Tel. 01 45 04 34 69. Fax 01 45 04 67 41
Closed 24 December, 31 December.
Open noon–11:15 PM. Cont. service.
A la carte: 50–65€.
Terrace. Valet parking.

Crowds flock to the semicircular art deco dining room and terrace of this former station buffet by the Paris beltway to enjoy dishes proficiently prepared by Olivier Denis, formerly of L'Arpège. Crispy hearts of lettuce and parmesan slivers, langoustine ravioli with tarragon, veal scalloppine and pesto spaghetti and whiskey-flavored millefeuille delight the taste buds. An impressive wine list, professional service supervised by that reliable son of the Aveyron region (to coin a redundancy), Jacques Malafosse, and very up-market, sixteenth arrondissement prices.

● **Frugier**   SIM

137, av de Versailles
Métro: Chardon-Lagache, Exelmans
Tel.-Fax 01 46 47 72 00
Closed Sunday, Monday, 3 weeks in August.
Open until 10:30 PM.
Prix fixe: 24€, 29€.
Air cond.

The strong points of this bistro, just two years old, are its modern, refined, flowery setting, its elegant gray-brown and off-white tones and its direct view of the range, where proprietor Eric Frugier concocts his crisp galette of spicy boudin on a bed of young greens, sliced red tuna marinated with green peppercorns, oxtail and foie gras parmentier, warm chocolate cake with a soft center. Here and there, blackboards, listing regularly changing dishes, decorate the dining room. A choice of seven starters, seven main courses and seven desserts, thirty French wines presented by Hervé Richard, soft music, a smiling welcome and fine ideas.

● **Le Galion**   COM

8-10, allée du Bord-de-l'Eau,
Bois de Boulogne
Métro: Porte-Maillot
Tel. 01 44 14 20 00. Fax 01 44 14 20 07
christelle.galion@free.fr
www.restaurantlegalion.com
Closed Sunday evening, Monday,
Christmas–New Year's, August.
Open until midnight.
Prix fixe: 33€.
Terrace.

A fine opportunity to set sail on this cozy "galleon" in a gourmet neck of the Boulogne woods. On the terrace in the summer and in the refined dining room in winter, we savor mischievous dishes from Cédric Pierre, who plays deftly from a con-

temporary score. Crispy shrimp cake with vegetable chips, beef terrine in herbed aspic jelly, duck foie gras with currants and tuna and salmon sushi and sashimi are readily edible. Then there are the grilled tuna steak with wholegrain mustard, the roasted duck breast with sautéed mushrooms, and finally, for dessert, plum and almond paste tart or a beggar's purse of apple with Calvados, which slip down smoothly.

● **La Gare**   ⊛ 🍴 COM

19, chaussée de la Muette
Métro: La Muette
Tel. 01 42 15 15 31. Fax 01 42 15 15 23
www.restaurantlagare.com
Closed Christmas. Open until 11:30 PM.
Prix fixe: 18€ (lunch), 30€, 35€,
12€ (children). A la carte: 55€.
Air cond. Terrace. Valet parking.

An unusual setting! This restaurant inside the former Passy-La Muette rail station (which was running until 1980) is superb. The dining room still has a station concourse feel to it, with an impressively high ceiling, and the terrace is a garden. On the kitchen side, Yann Morel, formerly with Robuchon, Briffard and Yoshino, has to cater for a crowd of 300. The melon and Italian speck with balsamic vinegar coulis, the pollack with black rice and snow peas, slow-roasted lamb shank served with bulgur wheat, dried fruit and fresh pineapple, the light orange blossom cream and coriander financier cake are not of any great interest, to be honest. But do people come here to eat?

**BISTRO
OF THE YEAR**

● **Chez Géraud**   🏠 ○ COM

31, rue Vital
Métro: La Muette
Tel. 01 45 20 33 00. Fax 01 45 20 46 60
Closed Saturday, Sunday, Bank Holidays,
August. Open until 9:15 PM.
Prix fixe: 30€. A la carte: 65€.

Once he was the loud-mouthed, big-hearted bistro owner of Le Val d'Or in avenue Franklin Roosevelt. Now, Géraud Rongier is a discreet, composed, almost serene restaurateur in a quiet Passy street. He has not given up his Homeric tours of the vineyards of Burgundy and the Rhône Valley, though. The proof is in his divine selection of wines, which delight his guests without leaving them penniless: Mâcon whites, a cheerful red Gevray with a Côtes de Nuits touch and a sumptuous Combier Crozes Hermitage, which blend easily with his rational, authentic, healthy cuisine based on first-rate produce. Scrambled eggs with truffles, the catch of the day (a very nice sautéed fresh cod with vegetables, for instance), splendid chicken with truffles, magnificent calf's head, impeccable braised veal sweetbreads, painstakingly prepared by the faithful Gérard Vacher, are fine works indeed. In passing, we might mention the cheeses at the peak of maturity, such as the crumbly Salers that offers a timely reminder of the proprietor's Cantal roots. Turning to the desserts, we enjoy the ritual paris-brest, a ring of choux pastry filled with a perfect praliné buttercream. This is one of the best bistros in Paris, brightened by ceramics inspired by Steinlen, and it would be unfair not to give it its Plate.

● A la Grande Armée ▢COM

3, av de la Grande-Armée
Métro: Charles-de-Gaulle–Etoile
Tel. 01 45 00 24 77. Fax 01 45 00 95 50
Open daily until 1 AM.
A la carte: 50–65€.
Air cond. Terrace. Valet parking.

For those who wish to see and be seen, the oldest restaurant opened by Costes has just undergone a rapid makeover (paint and carpeting). On the food side, things are satisfactory but very expensive. Fried baby squid, roasted sea bass with young spinach, veal steak alla milanese, trisole with berries and chocolate fondant are honest, but not enough to justify their prices. The wines are good, but what about the Third Empire decor (Garcia period Napoleon)?

● La Grande Cascade ○ ▥ LUX

Allée de Longchamp, Bois de Boulogne
Métro: Porte-Maillot
Tel. 01 45 27 33 51. Fax 01 42 88 99 06
grandecascade@wanadoo.fr
www.lagrandecascade.fr
Closed February. Open until 9:30 PM.
Prix fixe: 70€, 165€. A la carte: 175€.
Terrace. Private dining room. Valet parking.

Changes are underway in this former Belle Epoque pavilion built for the Universal Exhibition of 1900. As we go to press, chef Richard Mebkhout is leaving and is to be replaced by Frédéric Robert, brought in from Senderens. On our annual visit to the restaurant, immaculately run by the Menuts, we sensed a little wobble with foie gras pork pie with oversalted aspic jelly, plus another dish was overcooked and the cream sauce in the foie gras and truffle stuffed macaroni was a bit too assertive. Nothing serious, but enough to suggest we give this fine eatery time to catch its breath. In the dining room, lit by the red glow from the great bay windows, raw and cooked green asparagus with asparagus cream and truffle flan, Breton blue lobster in shellfish jus, bitter-herb pasta with a chutney of fresh and half-dried tomatoes, thinly sliced veal sweetbreads roasted with baby carrots and served with cinnamon jus still win our approval. As do the hundred vintages spiritedly championed by Pierre Ouardes.

● GR 5 ⊜SIM

19, rue Gustave-Courbet
Métro: Rue-de-la-Pompe
Tel. 01 47 27 09 84
Closed Sunday. Open until 11 PM.
Prix fixe: 14€ (lunch), 17€ (dinner), 20€ (dinner). A la carte: 30–35€.
Terrace.

Backpackers from the GR5 hiking trail feel at home in Stéphane Schiebold's relaxed bistro, which clashes with the sixteenth arrondissement's ambient elegance. The honeyed goat cheese salad, salmon with crayfish, creamy vacherin cheese, bacon and potato gratin and chocolate fondue are pleasant dishes, inexpensive for the area.

● Hiramatsu ○ LUX

52, rue de Longchamp
Métro: Trocadéro
Tel. 01 56 81 08 80. Fax 01 56 80 08 81
www.hiramatsu.co.jp
Closed Saturday, Sunday, August.
Open until 9:30 PM.
Prix fixe: 48€ (lunch), 95€ (dinner), 130€
(dinner). A la carte: 140–160€.
Air cond. Private dining room. Valet parking.

Given that Hiroyuki Hiramatsu is now running the former Faugeron, a pocket restaurant on quai de Bourbon that once played so deftly on our taste buds, some might expect the cuisine in this very comfortable beige setting, with its modern, rather cold look, to be Japanese. They would be wrong. There is nothing Japanese about the precise, light lobster medallion with truffles and green asparagus, the half-smoked salmon with orange and artichoke jus, the pigeon breast with foie gras flavored with cocoa and strong coffee, the tropical fruit salad with pineapple granita, except the meticulousness and subtlety of their preparation. In their sober, delicate way, they pay tribute to France, with their retinue of 800 Gallic and foreign wines.

● Hôtel Costes K COM

Hotel Costes K,
81, av Kléber / 11 bis, rue de Magdebourg
Métro: Trocadéro, Boissière
Tel. 01 44 05 75 75. Fax 01 44 05 74 74
resak@hotelcostesk.com
Open daily 11 AM–11:30 PM. Cont. service.
A la carte: 65€.
Air cond. Valet parking.

This designer hotel by Bofill has a refined look, all in smoked glass. The menu reflects the modern brasserie spirit devised by the Costes brothers, who have opened restaurants all over Paris. The traditional-style foie gras, tomato and mozzarella salad, salmon grilled on one side, grilled tuna steak, quickly seared beefsteak, chocolate cake and cheesecake are not bad, but no one will be amused by the prices.

● Ilana N SIM

11, rue Jean-Giraudoux
Métro: Iéna, George-V, Alma-Marceau
Tel. 01 40 70 17 04
Closed Saturday, Sunday (except for group reservations), 1 week Christmas–New Year's, 2 weeks in August. Open until 11 PM.
Prix fixe: 15€ (lunch), 20€ (dinner).
A la carte: 40–50€.
Air cond. Terrace.

Exit Chez Génia, replaced by Ilana, a new air-conditioned restaurant in plum and pale-pink tones, run by Pierre-Eric Vigliermo, who concocts scallop tartare with spinach cream, fresh codfish tangine, Salers beef prime rib, a house special and chocolate soufflé. All these very French dishes are served by Marianne (on the terrace too) and change almost every month.

● Jean Bouin SIM

26, av du Gal-Sarrail, Stadium Jean-Bouin
(av. de la Porte-Molitor)
Métro: Porte-d'Auteuil
Tel. 01 40 71 61 00. Fax 01 40 71 61 63
didier.delu@wanadoo.fr
www.didier-delu.com
Closed Sunday evening, Monday evening (November–April), Tuesday evening (November–April), 1 week Christmas–New Year's. Open until 10:30 PM.
Prix fixe: 14,50€, 21,50€, 27,50€.
Terrace. Private dining room.

Located in the stadium of the same name, this is a gastronomic haunt for local athletes. Sabine and Didier Delu, who trained with Blanc, Troisgros and Lameloise, look after their customers well. With their good humor, sautéed scallops, honeyed langoustine salad, pike-perch with beurre-blanc sauce and glazed carrots, duck breast in orange sauce with potatoes au gratin, all-caramel assorted dessert plate and very friendly prices, they win hands down. We cannot wait for the next game at Roland-Garros or Le Stade Français!

● Le Kiosque ⊜ SIM

1, pl de Mexico
Métro: Trocadéro
Tel. 01 47 27 96 98. Fax 01 45 53 89 79
restaurantlekiosque@wanadoo.fr
Closed Christmas. Open until 11 PM.
Prix fixe: 25,90€, 30,90€.
Air cond. Terrace. Valet parking.

A concept eatery! This restaurant belongs to a former journalist, Philippe Lemoine, now a dynamic, charming restaurateur who welcomes a fairly young, well-heeled clientele. It boasts a contemporary setting with a new, bright, cheerful decor featuring press-related drawings and pictures and a slightly exotic and spicy Southern French cuisine cooked up by Jean-Marc Semur: a small tartare of oysters and Scottish salmon, wild sea bass roasted on a stone, thyme-flambéed top rump steak with large hand-cut French fries, warm Guayaquil chocolate cake with a molten center, all pleasantly concluded with a gourmet coffee. The set menus have imaginative names: "*déjeuner copine volubile mais friande*" (garrulous gourmet girlfriend lunch) or "*déjeuner manager affairé mais gourmet*" (busy but foodie manager lunch) and there are allusions to delicious headlines. The service displays some (good-natured) haste in going to press.

● Le Lory SIM

56, rue Poussin
Métro: Porte-d'Auteuil, Michel-Ange–Auteuil
Tel. 01 46 51 47 99
Closed Monday, 3 weeks in August.
Open until 10:30 PM.
Prix fixe: 27€, 32€. A la carte: 55€.
Air cond.

To every season its domestic dishes. This is the theme of this unobtrusive local bistro run by Annie Martin for her regulars, who all appreciate the sautéed fresh mushrooms, monkfish in tomato and brandy sauce, frog's legs fried with garlic and parsley, veal sweetbreads with morel mushrooms and Baked Alaska.

● La Maison du Pêcheur ⊛ SIM

19, rue Lauriston
Métro: Kléber, Charles-de-Gaulle–Etoile
Tel. 01 40 67 11 16. Fax 01 45 00 99 87
Closed Saturday, Sunday, August 12th–15th.
Open until 11 PM.
Prix fixe: 19€. A la carte: 38–50€.
Air cond.

Exit Le Bistrot de l'Etoile. The Chérifs, also proprietors of the very Hispanic Casa Tina and Casa Paco nearby, have completely renovated this eatery in warm tones (brown, beige, orange). Let the Devil take the tapas: Ali has extended his range to fish but still whips up tasty Catalan-style savory toasts, sautéed squid and various meats grilled on skewers. He always has a few bottles of excellent fruity Spanish wine, and we would cross the Mediterranean for his orange salad with cinnamon.

● Maison Prunier 🏠 V.COM

16, av Victor-Hugo
Métro: Charles-de-Gaulle–Etoile, Victor-Hugo
Tel. 01 44 17 35 85. Fax 01 44 17 90 10
prunier@maison-prunier.fr
Closed Sunday, August. Open until 11 PM.
Prix fixe: 59€ (lunch).
A la carte: 80–150€.
Air cond. Valet parking.

A Thirties' decor featuring ceramics, a sculpture of a Breton sailor, a fine bar, well-set tables and very refined dishes prepared by a new chef, Eric Coisel, brought in from Le Chiberta . . . things have just gotten better again for Prunier. We feared the worst and thought this great fish restaurant might turn into a mere "caviar bar." Admittedly, the new boss, Pierre Bergé, associated with Caviar House, promotes Aquitaine caviar in all its forms here, but the king crab ravioli with parmesan slivers, the fresh cod filet roasted with spices and the "genuine" cod brandade are impressive dishes indeed and not necessarily priced too high. The two set menus, with their "Balik" smoked salmon or "signature dishes" are bargains. The Clos Saint Jean Pinot Noir goes down well, as does the Pennautier Cabardès Chardonnay. Then there are exquisite desserts (a splendid baba au rhum), not to mention the striking raw herring with onions and apples, just like the fare at the Zurich Kronenhalle. Prunier has made a full recovery.

● **Aux Marches du Palais**　SIM

5, rue de la Manutention
Métro: Iéna, Alma-Marceau
Tel. 01 47 23 52 80. Fax 01 47 23 87 20
Open daily until 11:30 PM.
Prix fixe: 21€ (lunch, wine included).
A la carte: 45€.
Terrace.

Judging by Ariel Durand and Julien Rouquette's packed dining room with its neo-realist wood and beige tones, the old-style bistro format has its fans in the chic districts of Paris, too. Armed with sound oenological advice from Julien, the suits who let their hair down inexpensively here have no objections to poached egg in foie gras aspic jelly, fish blanquette or sautéed jumbo shrimp, a duck breast with turnips or a lemon curd tart from new chef Loïc Lobet, who has taken over from Richard Legout.

● **Marius**　COM

82, bd Murat
Métro: Porte-de-St-Cloud
Tel. 01 46 51 67 80. Fax 01 40 71 83 75
Closed Saturday, Sunday, August.
Open until 10:30 PM.
A la carte: 55€
Terrace.

François Grandjean, who has opened several "A & M le Bistrot" restaurants with J.-P. Vigato from Apicius, is still very much present in his own establishment. His Fifties' decor with its red-velvet chairs has a retro chic, the fishmonger approach is not bad and the ambience is pleasant. We have no complaints about the fresh anchovies marinated in vinegar, the herbed fresh crab salad, the sea bream baked in a salt crust and fresh cod with olive oil, onions and peppers or the dark chocolate fondant and apple tart, although the restaurant does not really seem to deserve a Plate these days.

● **Mojito Habana**　COM

19, rue de Presbourg
Métro: Charles-de-Gaulle–Etoile
Tel. 01 45 00 84 84. Fax 01 45 00 60 63
Closed Saturday lunch, Sunday, August.
Open until midnight.
Prix fixe: 22€ (lunch), 32€ (lunch).
A la carte: 55€.
Air cond. Valet parking.

The attractions of this faux private club open to all are its torrid, salsa-style atmosphere, friendly service and polished cuisine. Beef carpaccio, zucchini mousse with quail egg, grilled tuna steak with raw tomato and olive oil sauce, spice-crusted lamb loin chops, honeyed ice nougat with craquelin and red berry coulis are fine, timeless standards. An excellent selection of cigars.

● **L'Auberge du**　🛏 COM
Mouton Blanc

40, rue d'Auteuil
Métro: Michel-Ange–Auteuil
Tel. 01 42 88 02 21. Fax 01 45 24 21 07
www.aubergedumoutonblanc.com
Open daily until 10:30 PM.
Prix fixe: 19,40€ (lunch),
30€ (wine included). A la carte: 35€.
Air cond. Valet parking.

In this gracious abode run by Gérard Joulie and Patrick Senhadji, with its light shades, art nouveau decor and paintings, Antonio Goncalvès elegantly concocts a traditional crayfish gratin with spinach leaves, sea bream filet with tender carrots, grilled duck breast with honey and roasted pears and chocolate fondant. You may be interested to know that 17th-century literary giants Molière and La Fontaine used to dine in this very inn.

● **Le Murat**　COM

1, bd Murat
Métro: Porte-d'Auteuil
Tel. 01 46 51 33 17. Fax 01 46 51 88 54
Open daily until midnight.
A la carte: 50–68€.
Air cond. Terrace. Valet parking.

A trendy Costes eatery (associated with Raphaël de Montrémy here) boasting an imperial red decor by Garcia, this establishment offers simple, tasteful dishes. Gazpacho and avocado, herbed lobster salad, grilled tuna steak with coriander, golden-roasted chicken breast and raspberry macaron have a deliciously fresh flavor. The tab is a little steep.

● **Pam's**   SIM

131, bd Murat
Métro: Porte-de-St-Cloud
Tel. 01 40 71 99 26. Fax 01 49 09 14 89
Closed Saturday, Sunday. Open until 11 PM.
Prix fixe: 24€ (lunch), 28€ (lunch).
A la carte: 45€.
Air cond.

Pam was the TV sobriquet of Catherine Corbineau, who worked with comic Stéphane Collaro on his Eighties' shows and has now opened this pleasant and modern bistro. The domestic cuisine prepared by Fabrice Mangin, formerly at La Maison Blanche, is entertaining too. Baked egg and foie gras in a ramekin, sea bass with fennel, Provençal stuffed vegetables and dark chocolate fondant are simple and good. It is a shame that the wines are not up to their task.

● **Passiflore**   ○ V.COM

33, rue de Longchamp
Métro: Trocadéro
Tel. 01 47 04 96 81. Fax 01 47 04 32 27
passiflore@club-internet.fr
www.restaurantpassiflore.com
Closed Saturday lunch, Sunday, 3 weeks in August. Open until 10:30 PM.
Prix fixe: 35€ (lunch), 38€ (dinner), 58€ (dinner). A la carte: 100€.
Air cond. Valet parking.

As the name (meaning passionflower) suggests, Roland Durand, the former maestro of Le Relais de Sèvres, is well versed in subtle Franco-Asian harmonies based on wild herbs and rare condiments. Although the surroundings offer quintessentially traditional bourgeois comfort, this Auvergnat gourmet's approach, with its colorful, lively and shrewd dishes, is in complete contrast to the setting. Accompanied by one of the 350 wines presented and ami-

ably served by Vincent Tavet, the cream of wild mushrooms with langoustine tails, lobster ravioli in a mulligatawny broth with n'go gaï, black rice and langoustines in satay with lime sauce and pigeon roasted with five spices stir our curiosity. Up to and including the dessert—warmed "*grand cru*" chocolate cake or astonishing green, chili-flavored sorbets—the dishes reveal flavors fit for a true citizen of the world. The welcome could be warmer.

● **Le Pergolèse**   ○ V.COM

40, rue Pergolèse
Métro: Porte-Maillot, Argentine
Tel. 01 45 00 21 40. Fax 01 45 00 81 31
le.pergolese@wanadoo.fr
www.lepergolese.com
Closed Saturday, Sunday, August.
Open until 10:30 PM.
Prix fixe: 38€ (dinner), 48€ (lunch, wine included). A la carte: 100€.
Air cond. Private dining room. Valet parking.

Stéphane Gaborieau, who long presided over the stoves at the Villa Florentine in Lyon, has taken over this elegant establishment concealed in a narrow street near Porte Maillot. The frog's legs and wild garlic in crispy phyllo pastry with truffled celery root and a cream soup of fresh green peas with poppy seeds is a fine prelude. We then hesitate between the cylinder-shaped Dover sole filet with a bunch of fresh greens and tiny chanterelle mushrooms or the Bresse chicken cooked two ways, with mushrooms. To conclude, hot raspberry soufflé and berry and basil dessert soup favorably impress. The chef is an old hand and has won round the former clientele with a combination of his predecessor's traditional domestic style and his own Southern-leaning approach. The assiduous service and selected wines meet the same high standards.

● Le Petit Boileau   SIM

98, rue Boileau
Métro: Porte-de-St-Cloud, Exelmans
Tel. 01 42 88 59 05
Closed Saturday lunch, Sunday, February,
Easter, 2 weeks in August.
Open until 10:30 PM.
Prix fixe: 13€ (lunch). A la carte: 40€.
Air cond.

The bosses change and so do the chefs in this charming bistro done in warm tones, whose fresh, lively, polished domestic dishes and quality regional produce have always made an impact. Viviane Henriques has taken over the establishment and offers a well-prepared avocado, crab and grapefruit salad, sea bass filet with raw tomato and olive oil sauce, veal kidneys with whole-grain mustard and crème brûlée in the flavor of the day.

● Le Petit Défi de Passy   ● SIM

18, av du Président-Kennedy
Métro: Passy
Tel. 01 42 15 06 76
defidepassy@defiorg.com
www.defiorg.com
Closed Sunday evening, Bank Holidays.
Open until 11 PM.
Prix fixe: 10€, 15€, 20€.
A la carte: 30–35€.
Air cond. Terrace. Private dining room.

The journalists from France's national Maison de la Radio broadcasting center like a drop of Bordeaux with the goat cheese and warm apples in crispy phyllo pastry, grilled salmon steak, steak tartare or rib-eye steak with a choice of sauce and the homemade tarte Tatin with almonds: Olivier Demeock, chef and proprietor, has kept the marine decor and taken on the task of adapting the menu of seasonal dishes at moderate prices to suit his customers' expectations.

● La Petite Tour   COM

11, rue de la Tour
Métro: Passy
Tel. 01 45 20 09 97. Fax 01 45 20 09 31
Closed Saturday lunch, Sunday,
Bank Holidays, 1 week in August.
Open until 10 PM.
Prix fixe: 28€. A la carte: 50–65€.
Air cond.

Foie gras, filet of wild bass or the fish of the day, molten chocolate cake and flambéed peaches: There is nothing Italian about Ignazio Lasi's cuisine, which consists exclusively of deftly executed traditional French recipes. Delightful service and selected wines.

● Le Petit Pergolèse   SIM

38, rue Pergolèse
Métro: Porte-Maillot, Argentine
Tel. 01 45 00 23 66. Fax 01 45 00 44 03
le.petit.pergolese@wanadoo.fr
Closed Saturday, Sunday,
1 week from Christmas–New Year's, August.
Open until 10:30 PM.
A la carte: 60€.
Air cond. Valet parking.

Albert Corre is still on duty at what once was the adjunct of Le Pergolèse. His contemporary bistro, decorated with sculptures, paintings and drawings by Warhol, Klein, Arman and Calder, is a stylish haunt for art lovers. Apt pupil Frédéric Lagrange's cuisine is not bad either. Slow-roasted quail salad with green beans and foie gras, thin-crust tomato and mozzarella tart, steamed fresh cod with baby spinach, roasted sea bass in truffle vinaigrette, sautéed veal kidneys and sweetbreads, raspberry millefeuille and chocolate fondant are first rate. The prices, though, have not improved.

● Le Petit Rétro   🏠 SIM

5, rue Mesnil
Métro: Victor-Hugo
Tel. 01 44 05 06 05. Fax 01 47 55 00 48
www.petitretro.fr
Closed Saturday lunch, Sunday,
Bank Holidays, Christmas, New Year's,
2 weeks in August.
Open until 10:30 PM.
Prix fixe: 19,50€ (lunch), 24,50€ (lunch),
27€ (dinner), 33€ (dinner).
A la carte: 45€.
Air cond. Private dining room.

Gilbert Godfroi's bistro wields an easy charm with its 1900s' decor, ceramics, moldings, painted ceilings and mirrors, and its beige, orange and green tones. The polished, old-fashioned cuisine includes a fish dish that changes every day. The escargots and oyster mushrooms baked under a crust, Scottish salmon ravioli with stewed leeks and chive cream, traditional veal blanquette with pearl onions and basmati rice are celebrated in the menu, which changes twice a year. The service is quite out of touch, though.

● Au Petit Victor Hugo   SIM

143, av Victor-Hugo
Métro: Rue-de-la-Pompe, Victor-Hugo, Trocadéro
Tel. 01 45 53 02 68. Fax 01 44 05 13 46
aupetitvictorhugo@wanadoo.fr
www.petitvictorhugo.com
Closed Sunday, Christmas, New Year's,
August. Open until midnight.
A la carte: 55€.
Air cond. Terrace. Private dining room.
Valet parking

This chic establishment all dressed in oak, glass and stainless steel is a welcoming place. Among its other features, the fireplace, opening roof, mezzanine, terrace and private dining room are all persuasive arguments. Françoise Bourgoin is keeping up the good work with her chef, Marcel Coquard. His sautéed foie gras on a bed of green salad, turbot with white butter sauce, strip steak with morel mushroom sauce and assorted mini-dessert plate are fine examples of solid bistro cuisine. The

cellar's excellent selected wines keep the customers happy.

● Le Poivre Rose   COM

191, av de Versailles
Métro: Porte-de-St-Cloud, Exelmans
Tel. 01 42 24 49 28
Closed Sunday, Monday.
Open until 10:30 PM.
Prix fixe: 19€ (lunch). A la carte: 45–60€.
Air cond. Terrace. Valet parking.

A new team has spiced up this comfortable art deco "Pink Pepper," with its bay windows and sunny walls in shades of ochre, saffron and orange. The decoration itself is currently being refurbished. New chef Sacha Pertovick's cuisine is a little rich but does not have much trouble winning over the regulars with foie gras cooked rare with gingerbread, sautéed sea bass with eggplant ratatouille and basil apple jus, calf's liver deglazed with vinegar and served with black-olive polenta and soft chocolate cake a la mode.

● Port-Alma   V.COM

10, av de New-York
Métro: Alma-Marceau
Tel. 01 47 23 75 11. Fax 01 47 20 42 92
Closed Sunday, Monday, Christmas–New Year's, August. Open until 10:30 PM.
Prix fixe: 25€ (lunch), 29€ (lunch), 35€ (dinner), 39€ (dinner), 12€ (children).
A la carte: 60–70€.
Air cond. Private dining room.

A sudden urge for fish? We immediately head for the Port-Alma, a chic, sober, tasteful restaurant moored near the Seine, just a cable's length from the Museum of Modern Art. Sonia and Céline Canal have a firm hand on the helm in this pleasant marine establishment in oceanic hues, with bay windows, fine decorative beams and a view of the Eiffel Tower. Brice Goutret (the son-in-law) concocts crab gazpacho, filet of John Dory, flank steak and Grand Marnier soufflé. All these delights are served in the dining room by the charming Céline, who is also a shrewd sommelier, recommending the Viré white that will complement the dishes perfectly. Fine produce treated with respect, refined preparations and devoted work: all very pleasant, even if some of us do miss Paul's special touch and his extra helping of soul.

● Le Relais du Bois   SIM

1, rue Guy-de-Maupassant
Métro: Rue-de-la-Pompe
Tel.-Fax 01 45 04 27 60
Closed Monday, Christmas–New Year's,
1 week in May, August.
Open until 10:30 PM.
A la carte: 45–50€.
Terrace.

If it ain't broke, don't fix it. For thirty years now, this 1908 rococo English establishment, converted into an old-style bistro under the guidance of Lucien Georgelin, has attracted a loyal following of customers charmed by its tasteful domestic dishes, which are prepared by Michel Mougeot, for the moment. In the dining room, decked out in red, green and blue, Lucien in person serves the chef's foie gras, the gilthead bream grilled with thyme and pain perdu with caramel ice cream. The prices seem to have held steady for the last three years.

● Le Relais d'Auteuil   ○ V.COM

31, bd Murat
Métro: Michel-Ange–Molitor,
Michel-Ange–Auteuil
Tel. 01 46 51 09 54. Fax 01 40 71 05 03
relaisdauteuil@wanadoo.fr
Closed Saturday lunch, Sunday, Monday lunch, Christmas–New Year's, August.
Open until 10:30 PM.
Prix fixe: 50€ (lunch).
A la carte: 125–150€.
Air cond. Valet parking.

For now, they are refurbishing the lighting and banquettes in this very comfortable establishment with its hushed atmosphere and cheerful decor of contemporary paintings and white, green and brown shades. The fish here smells of sea spray and the game has the scent of the countryside. Fortunately, the defiant Laurent Pignol is still running things, both as manager and in the kitchen. Try the langoustines flavored

with lemongrass and marjoram, sea bass filet in a pepper crust, suckling pig with chili pepper and ginger, lime soufflé in a shell with a black pepper and vodka coulis charmingly served by Laurence, his wife and muse, and judge for yourselves. Some may find the menu a little short on change, but others will revel in the dependable joys of dishes whose hallmarks are the quality of their regional produce, the extreme precision of their cooking, the majestic blending of their flavors and the love of cuisine they display. The cellar is dazzling with its 2,500 bottles from France and elsewhere (Hungary, Austria, Chile, South Africa and Spain), enthusiastically presented by Nicolas Lepinay.

● Le Roland Garros   COM

2 bis, av Gordon-Bennett
Métro: Porte-d'Auteuil
Tel. 01 47 43 49 56. Fax 01 40 71 83 24
www.laffiche.fr
Closed Sunday evening, Monday evening (in winter), Christmas–New Year's,
3 weeks in August.
Open until 10 PM (in summer: 11 PM).
Prix fixe: 45€, 60€. A la carte: 75€.
Terrace. Valet parking.

Marc Veyrat and the Sodexho group keep a remote eye on this charming eatery under the foliage of the legendary Roland Garros tennis stadium. The patrons here are more epicurean than athletic, and they delight in the cuisine prepared by loyal disciple Xavier Rousseau. In the clubhouse-style dining room or on the teak terrace, warm foie gras with chocolate and orange vinegar, truffle-studded scallops with Puy green lentils and slow-roasted pork belly, rack of lamb roasted on a spit served with baked potatoes and warm chocolate cake served with thyme ice cream play a pleasantly creative game, set and match.

● **La Salle à Manger** `V.COM`

Hotel Raphael, 17, av Kléber
Métro: Kléber
Tel. 01 53 64 32 11. Fax 01 53 64 32 02
banqueting@raphael-hotel.com
www.raphael-hotel.com
Closed Saturday, Sunday, Bank Holidays,
August. Open until 9:30 PM.
Prix fixe: 48€ (lunch, wine included),
60€ (dinner, wine included).
A la carte: 75–85€.
Air cond. Terrace. Private dining room.
Valet parking.

The Hôtel Raphaël's elegant dining room is
open to all, with its flowery terrace and
Louis XVI rooms carpeted in red and gold.
Philippe Delahaye, disciple of Robuchon
and Ducasse, presents lively compositions: Fresh green peas, lettuce in a roasted
onion cappuccino, duck foie gras and langoustines coated in creamy aspic jelly with
carrots, oranges and mangoes. You must
taste his geometrical dish of turbot and
crayfish, fresh chanterelle mushrooms and
fresh pea mousse or his traditional-style
sautéed veal chop with roasted beef marrow and pork rind with arabica jus. The
sweet rice maki with raspberries, chocolate ice cream and brownie rekindle childhood memories.

● **Le Scheffer** `SIM`

22, rue Scheffer
Métro: Trocadéro
Tel. 01 47 27 81 11
Closed Saturday, Sunday, Bank Holidays,
1 week in May, 2 weeks in August.
Open until 10:30 PM.
A la carte: 32–35€.

They make a fine team, the three Js: managers Joël and Joëlle (Chauvin) and Jacky
(Perronnet) at the stove in this nostalgic,
slightly off-beat bistro (old-fashioned bar,
mosaics on the floor, vintage advertisements on the walls and gingham oilcloth
on the tables) in an up-market district
where executives rub shoulders with artisans in overalls. Among the splendid, timeless bistro classics spiritedly served by Joël
and Joëlle, you can enjoy eggs with mayonnaise, Catalan-style squid, grilled rib-

eye steak with fresh herb butter and a fresh
fruit dessert soup all washed down with
unchauvinistic wines at friendly prices.

● **6 New York** `COM`

6, av de New-York
Métro: Alma-Marceau
Tel. 01 40 70 03 30. Fax 01 40 70 04 77
6newyork@wanadoo.fr
Closed Saturday lunch, Sunday, Christmas,
New Year's, 3 weeks in August. Open until
10:30 PM (Saturday 11 PM).
Prix fixe: 28€ (lunch on weekdays),
30€ (lunch on weekdays). A la carte: 57€.
Air cond. Valet parking.

This chic, modern establishment is one of
the most fashionable places in the area, and
its acoustics have just been redone. Jean-
Pierre Vigato has invited chef Jérôme
Gangneux onto the management team—
rightly, since his talent draws the
customers. This veteran of Apicius has
some excellent surprises in store for us,
such as the raw tuna prepared three ways
with horseradish and ginger sweet-and-
savory dressing, the John Dory grilled in its
skin served with potatoes in red sauce or a
variation on pork. The all-chocolate plate
with cocoa sorbet is enchanting. The cellar
is intelligently put together and offers a
good selection of wines by the glass.

● **Le 70** `SIM`

Parc des Princes Stadium,
24, rue du Cdt-Guilbaud
Métro: Porte-d'Auteuil, Porte-de-St-Cloud
Tel. 01 45 27 05 70. Fax 01 40 50 11 18
le.point70.restaurant@elior.com
www.le-70–restaurant.com
Closed dinner (except game nights),
Saturday, Sunday, 1 week from
Christmas–New Year's, August.
A la carte: 40–45€.
Air cond. Terrace.

Alexandre Davila is the striker at the stoves
of this archetypal Seventies' restaurant
with its geometric forms, steel tones and
grained wood, located in the heart of the
legendary Parc des Princes stadium and
named "70" after the year when its home
team, the PSG soccer club, was founded.

He plays a tactical game, maintaining his unbeaten record of trendy dishes with foie gras cooked rare with red wine, "Riviera" sea bream with Mediterranean vegetables, slow-roasted lamb steak with sage and a slightly undercooked chocolate cake. If you can, enjoy them on the terrace, brilliant in summer.

● Le Stade   `SIM`

Géo-André Stadium, 2, rue du Cdt-Guilbaud
Métro: Porte-de-St-Cloud
Tel. 01 40 71 22 22. Fax 01 40 71 22 23
restaurant.lestade@wanadoo.fr
www.lestade-restaurant.com
Closed Sunday, Monday, Tuesday, Wednesday (dinner), Christmas, 2 weeks in August.
Open until 10 PM.
Prix fixe: 23€. A la carte: 40–50€.
Air cond. Terrace.

Once the game is over, what do supporters of the Stade Français rugby team ask of this restaurant run by three musketeers named De Villiers, Marconet and Baschoeffer? Unpretentious, spicy dishes, such as shrimp tidbits with black radish, steamed monkfish carpaccio, Salers beef rib-eye steak and a chocolate delicacy with cardamom-scented coulis. Unaffectedly served by Grégory Campana, these dishes, accompanied by wines from France or South Africa, do their job.

● Le Stella   `SIM`

133, av Victor-Hugo
Métro: Rue-de-la-Pompe, Victor-Hugo
Tel. 01 56 90 56 00. Fax 01 56 90 56 01
Open daily until 1 AM.
A la carte: 60€.
Terrace.

This highly bourgeois, sixteenth arrondissement Lipp (see the sixth arrondissement) has a very Forties' chic. The place has been beautifully renovated, the service is first-rate and the kitchen does not just serve the classics prepared by any good brasserie but puts a lot of care into its daily menu. Salad of fresh green beans with parmesan, thin-crust tomato tart, grilled tuna steak with pesto, grilled fresh cod filet with olive oil, beef brochette with

diablo sauce, calf's head, iced vacherin with caramel sauce and assorted red fruit plate a la mode are not bad.

● La Table de Babette   `V.COM`

32, rue de Longchamp
Métro: Trocadéro, Boissière, Iéna
Tel. 01 45 53 00 07. Fax 01 45 53 00 15
tabledebabette@wanadoo.fr
Closed Saturday lunch, Sunday, 2 weeks in beginning of August. Open until 9:30 PM (Friday, Saturday 10:30 PM).
Prix fixe: 22€ (lunch on weekdays), 39€.
A la carte: 55€.
Air cond. Private dining room. Valet parking.

Babette de Rozières, black pearl of French West Indian cuisine, has taken over the former Robuchon-era Jamin without changing its decor at all. The vaguely British pink and green candy-box look makes a slightly affected showcase for the colorful, spicy cuisine, but why not? The Caribbean boudin, stuffed crab with Antilles chili pepper, cassolette of assorted seafoods, curried shark steak, diced pork fried golden brown, barbecued chicken, coconut tart and banana flambéed with aged rum, meticulously presented here as high points of the genre, have a delectable flavor of Fort-de-France and Pointe-à-Pitre.

● La Table du Baltimore   `V.COM`

Baltimore Sofitel Demeure Hotel,
1, rue Léo-Delibes
Métro: Boissière
Tel. 01 44 34 54 54. Fax 01 44 34 54 44
h2789@accor-hotels.com
www.sofitel.com
Closed Saturday, Sunday, Bank Holidays, August. Open until 10 PM.
Prix fixe: 48€ (lunch), 50€, 95€ (wine included). A la carte: 80–90€.
Air cond. Private dining room. Valet parking.

In this modern restaurant run by Jacqueline Secchi, with its pale woodwork, chef Jean-Philippe Pérol subtly but surely leads his patrons down roads less traveled. Served by Thierry Beatrix and accompanied by wines selected and presented by Jean-Luc Jamrozik (350 vintages from France and further afield), thin lobster medallions with pressed carrot and cumin terrine, langoustines cooked in lemon balm butter with lightly crumpled romaine lettuce ribs, sautéed lamb saddle and slow-roasted Swiss chard with thyme and fresh raspberies, served with thin almond nougatine slivers and mousseline cream, are fine tricks indeed.

● **La Table Lauriston** `SIM`

129, rue Lauriston
Métro: Trocadéro
Tel.-Fax 01 47 27 00 07
Closed Saturday lunch, Sunday, Christmas, New Year's, 3 weeks in August. Open until 10:30 PM.
Prix fixe: 25€ (lunch). A la carte: 55€.
Air cond.

Serge and Nadia Barbey's splendid and very Parisian bistro—a hunting lodge brightly colored in pink and red, where they are boldly renovating the air conditioning, cuisine and decor—is full both at lunchtime and in the evening. Once a chef in the kitchens of Le Soleil in the Saint-Ouen flea market, the good-natured Serge shakes up the culinary routine of the people of Passy, encouraging them to let their hair down with oxtail and foie gras terrine, scallops with wild chanterelle mushrooms, genuine milk-fed veal chop with crème fraîche and jumbo baba au rhum—cheerful, generous, flavorsome regional dishes.

YOUNG CHEF OF THE YEAR

● **Le Relais du Parc** 🏠⊙ `COM`

Sofitel le Parc, 55/57, av Raymond-Poincaré
Métro: Trocadéro, Victor-Hugo
Tel. 01 44 05 66 10. Fax 01 44 05 66 39
lerelaisduparc@accor-hotels.com
www.sofitel.com
Closed Saturday lunch (in winter),
Sunday (in winter), Monday (in winter),
1 week at Christmas, 2 weeks in August.
Open until 10 PM.
Prix fixe: 45€ (lunch).
A la carte: 75€.
Air cond. Private dining room. Valet parking.

Now you can taste Robuchon and Ducasse all in one at the Sofitel le Parc restaurant, which has received a modern makeover. The luxury experiment of Le 59 and Les Jardins du Parc is over: This is a new (or virtually new) establishment. The dining room team is energetically and cheerfully managed by Gonzague, known to us for twenty years at least, who formerly worked at Le Nikko and in rue de Longchamp in the service of Joël the First. In the kitchen, following instructions handed down by the two great traveling, multiple-menu chefs, the young Romain Corbière (formerly at the Louis XV) labors with precision and maturity, preparing the dishes that have made his masters famous. If you have not tasted pork pie in the manner of Lucien Tendret, copied from Alain Chapel, elbow pasta with truffles and ham, cream of pumpkin soup or fried whiting à la Colbert (a new and absolutely brilliant take on a standard), then do so at once. The same goes for roasted red mullet with Swiss chard (an inspiring preparation worthy of Michel Guérard, who created a similar dish), the pigeon with cabbage and foie gras, crispy pork belly with Dutch-oven-roasted Pompadour potatoes—this is the perfect opportunity to indulge yourself (almost) inexpensively! You may find the surroundings designed by Pierre-Yves Rochon a little new and chilly, despite his amusing contemporary pictures on the theme of seasonal fruits, but the wine list selected by the accomplished Gérard Margeon and the exceptional desserts will warm your heart. Small pots of vanilla and chocolate crème and orange gratin with wild tangerine marmalade alone are worth the visit. Every dish here not only carries the hallmark of the two great chefs, but also the stamp of a young talent who displays amazing skill and who is undoubtedly destined for great things. Remember the name!

● Tokyo Eat   SIM

13, av du Pdt-Wilson
Métro: Alma-Marceau, Iéna
Tel. 01 47 20 00 29. Fax 01 47 20 05 62
tokyoeat@palaisdetokyo.com
Closed Monday. Open until 11:30 PM
(Sunday 10:30 PM).
Prix fixe: 12€ (lunch on weekdays).
A la carte: 50–55€.
Terrace.

Although it is located in the impressive setting of Le Palais de Tokyo, there is nothing Japanese about this chic restaurant, which surprises and delights us with extremely well-prepared contemporary French dishes. Under the appealing globe lighting, we savor gilthead bream tartare with tropical fruit chutney and vanilla-ginger oil, roasted codfish with zucchini and lemon tagliatelle, satay-crusted lamb loin with slow-roasted eggplant and the lemon and spéculos cookie cheesecake, dishes in tune with the modern spirit of the place.

● Le Tournesol   Ⓝ 🍴 SIM

2, av Lamballe
Métro: Passy
Tel. 01 45 25 95 94
Open daily until 11:30 PM.
A la carte: 35€.
Terrace.

This authentic Parisian bistro dating from the start of the last century is located on a corner just a step away from France's national Maison de la Radio broadcasting center. Still with its original decor, it has been snapped up by the Chérifs, who already own the Casa Tina and Al Mounia. Having cleaned it up, they have brought in a young team and are offering a sober menu that showcases timeless standards. Sautéed mushrooms, dandelion salad with poached eggs and lardoons, calf's liver with crispy bacon and olive oil–mashed potatoes and "genuine" steak tartare with French fries are the kind of dishes we love: sincere, flavorsome and uncomplicated. Then there are the crème brûlée, apple crumble and the pleasant Le Coudray Saumur red that goes hand in glove with the cuisine.

● Vin et Marée   SIM

183, bd Murat
Métro: Exelmans
Tel. 01 46 47 91 39. Fax 01 46 47 69 07
vmmurat@wanadoo.fr
www.vin-et-maree.com
Open daily until 10:30 PM.
Prix fixe: 18,50€, 24,50€.
A la carte: 50€.
Terrace. Valet parking.

Frédéric Parade has taken over the helm of this contemporary marine restaurant in blue and white, which offers a simple, fresh celebration of seafood. The valet parking is very practical and the terrace superb. Sheltered from culinary storms, chef Abdel Kouldi engagingly prepares roasted sardines, whole young turbot or sea bass, tenderloin steak and Zanzibar baba au rhum for two, which are assiduously served by Joël Poulain. In their capable hands, we sail on, ready to keel over . . . but from delight only.

● Waknine   Ⓝ SIM

9, av Pierre-Ier-de-Serbie
Métro: Iéna
Tel. 01 47 23 48 18
10 AM–midnight. Closed Saturday, Sunday.
A la carte: 35–40€.
Air cond. Terrace. Valet parking.

Decorated with fine flower arrangements, this cozy restaurant and gallery with brown velvet armchairs and solid mahogany bar has a rather charming Forties' air. Samuel Waknine presents an attractive fusion cuisine: gingered langoustine spring rolls, three-citrus scallop carpaccio, grilled tuna steak, coconut milk chicken curry and, for dessert, mango jellied pudding or crisp apple dessert with dulce de leche to be savored as you admire the exhibition of the day and sip an Haut Médoc. Also a tearoom in the afternoon. Valet parking at lunchtime.

● **Zébra Square** `COM`

3, pl Clément-Ader
Métro: Mirabeau
Tel. 01 44 14 91 91. Fax 01 45 27 18 34
paris@zebrasquare.com
www.zebrasquare.com
Open daily until midnight (Friday, Saturday),
11 PM (Sunday, Monday),
11:30 PM (Tuesday, Wednesday, Thursday).
Prix fixe: 25€ (lunch, wine included).
A la carte: 45–65€.
Air cond. Terrace. Private dining room.
Valet parking.

Who is the zebra? The proprietor, Patrick Derderian? Or this vast restaurant with its striped wood and green decor and air-conditioned wine library nestling in a showcase of futuristic architecture? Both, probably. Fabrice Fourrier, the new chef, prepares herbed tuna tartare, large jumbo shrimp sautéed with salt and pepper served with vegetable tempura, thick rib-eye steak with green sauce and French fries, or strawberry gazpacho with light mascarpone cream, that all appeal equally to the young local crowd and broadcasting stars from La Maison de la Radio just opposite, who cannot resist these chic dishes.

INTERNATIONAL RESTAURANTS

● **Conti** `⊕ ○ COM`

72, rue Lauriston
Métro: Boissière
Tel. 01 47 27 74 67. Fax 01 47 27 37 66
Closed Saturday, Sunday, Bank Holidays,
1 week from Christmas–New Year's,
3 weeks in August. Open until 10:30 PM.
Prix Fixe: 32€ (lunch). A la carte: 70€.
Air cond.

We have been negligent enough to allow this fine Italian restaurant, which deftly defies passing fashion, to remain Plateless. The waiters in their tuxedos display a certain elegance, as does the Fifties' Venetian setting in red tones with its bar at the entrance, stucco ceiling and Murano chandeliers. Michel Ranvier trained with Troisgros and used to travel on the Orient Express between the banks of the Seine and the Laguna. His cuisine is reliably enchanting.

The proof is in the remarkable options—calf's head carpaccio with tomato pesto, tagliatelle with scallops, panettone pain perdu—that embellish the lunchtime set menu. All the pasta, as well as the traditional dishes, from the bollito misto, Modena-style, to the carnaroli risotto à la Milanaise and the calamari with radicchio, Florentine-style soup with foie gras and Vallée d' Aoste lard to the sautéed veal kidney surrounded by artichokes with parsley, lemon and garlic, justify a visit here. The wine list could no doubt use a little more research, but the experience as a whole, especially the desserts (chocolate tartuffo with espresso, sabayon with marsala, apples and pears), would incite us to eat here on a regular basis.

● **Oum El Banine** `○ COM`

16 bis, rue Dufrenoy
Métro: Porte-Dauphine, Rue-de-la-Pompe
Tel. 01 45 04 91 22. Fax 01 45 03 46 26
Closed Sunday. Open until 10:30 PM.
Prix fixe: 29,90€ (lunch).
A la carte: 50–55€.
Air cond. Valet parking.

Just like in a tale ... The car attendant arrives as if by magic, then the carved wooden door opens to reveal the elegant, contemporary setting of a Moroccan restaurant: Ahmed Termidi's establishment (with air conditioning, if you please) where the faithful chef Fouad Elgamari busies himself at the stove, concocting delightful, terribly subtle and light dishes of Morocco—a modern Morocco, but one proud of its traditions. There, the flavors and scents of ancient medinas are conjured up by a simple eggplant caviar, a succulent tagine, fish, lamb (with caramelized tomatoes and almonds) or farm-raised chickens and an airy phyllo pastry with almond milk, which concludes the meal sweetly and beautifully. Then, just like in a tale, the magic continues, woven by the sweet intoxication of French, Moroccan, Algerian and Tunisian libations presented by Ahmed in person. When we leave Oum El Banine (dedicated to the founder of the Al Qarawiyyin university in Fez), we catch ourselves murmuring "hamdulillah"!

● **Pavillon Noura** `V.COM`
21, av Marceau
Métro: Alma-Marceau, Iéna, George-V
Tel. 01 47 20 33 33. Fax 01 47 20 60 31
noura@noura.com
www.noura.com
Open daily until 11:30 PM.
Prix fixe: 30€ (lunch), 45€ (lunch), 50€
(dinner), 65€ (dinner). A la carte: 70€.
Air cond. Terrace. Private dining room.
Valet parking.

Care to dine on Lebanese fare with an international vocation in the high comfort of a modern Middle Eastern setting? Then Jean-Paul Bou Antoun's elegant, refined pavilion with its warm tones is for you. The Beirut diaspora returns to its culinary roots here, as Hanna Namnour concocts an authentic, generous cuisine—rekakat (phyllo pastry with feta, onion and parsley), salmon, sole, mixed grill, chicken kebabs, baklava—served by Jean Khoury and accompanied by surprising French and Lebanese wines. (If you are in a hurry, enjoy a quick shawarma in the adjoining chic snack bar.)

● **Tang** ◯ `V.COM`
125, rue de la Tour
Métro: Rue-de-la-Pompe
Tel. 01 45 04 35 35. Fax 01 45 04 58 19
Closed Sunday, Monday, 1 week
Christmas–New Year's, 3 weeks in August.
Open until 11:30 PM.
Prix fixe: 39€ (lunch), 75€ (lunch),
98€ (dinner). A la carte: 90€.
Air cond. Valet parking.

For more than fifteen years, Chinese Charly Tang's restaurant has remained one of the jealously guarded secrets of Paris society. When captains of business and their elegant partners are racked by Oriental culinary cravings, they head for this refined, classical setting in salmon shades, with its wooden banquettes and shining black lacquer. There, David Laxu's delicate, balanced, airy dishes await them. Summer roll with crab, grilled sea bass with a Thai sauce and black rice, farm-raised chicken with banana, croustillant with pineapple blend the flavors of China, Vietnam and Thailand

in fine concoctions with a modern feel to them. The service is impeccable and the vintages live up to the expectations of a smart clientele of connoisseurs. The tab pulls no punches, but the cost is warranted.

▼ | **SHOPS**

BREAD & BAKED GOODS

▼ **Eude**
14, rue de Longchamp
Métro: Iéna
Tel.-Fax 01 47 27 95 94
7 AM–8 PM (Saturday 7 AM–7:30 PM).
Closed Sunday, Monday,
Bank Holidays, August.
Evelyne and Tony Eude offer sourdough baguettes, raisin rolls, focaccia and walnut, olive or herb breads. For a light bite, sandwiches, pizzas specials of the day make a good impression.

CHOCOLATE

▼ **Régis**
89, rue de Passy
Métro: La Muette, Passy
Tel. 01 45 27 70 00. Fax 01 45 27 81 44
regis@chocolats.net
www.chocolats.net
10:30 AM–7:15 PM.
Closed Sunday afternoon, Monday morning.
Gilles Daumoinx specializes in luxury chocolate. Pear Williams chocolate, almond and milk chocolate bonbons, Ganduja, brandy-flavored chocolate and burnt caramels offer proof of his skills. Candied fruit, cannelés (a regional vanilla cake baked in fluted molds), candied chestnuts, cookies and chocolate cakes delight sweet-toothed customers.

CANDY & SWEETS

▼ **Boissier**
184, av Victor-Hugo
Métro: Rue-de-la-Pompe
Tel. 01 45 03 59 11. Fax 01 45 03 44 10
10 AM–6 PM.
Closed Saturday, Sunday.

This institution founded in 1827 is handsome indeed with its moldings and huge windows. The candied chestnuts, chocolate thins, salted caramels, an 80%-cocoa cake are impressive. And don't overlook the cinnamon, coffee and nougatine cake and macarons of various flavors.

▼ La Marquisane

168, av Victor-Hugo
Métro: Rue-de-la-Pompe
Tel. 01 45 53 97 66. Fax 01 47 27 30 18
lamarquisane@cegetel.net
10–7:30 PM. Closed Sunday, Monday morning, Bank Holidays,
10 days in February, August.
Emmanuelle Prosper has turned this fine store into a little temple of candy. Sweets packaged in glass jars, ginger-flavored chocolate and almond-, orange- or ginger-layered sweets are nicely done.

▼ Mazet

116, av Victor-Hugo
Métro: Victor-Hugo
Tel. 01 44 05 18 08. Fax 01 44 05 07 01
10 AM–1 PM, 2–7 PM. Closed Sunday, Monday (July–August), Bank Holidays,
1 week in mid-August.
A century-old tradition originally from Montargis, mazet are pralinés with a delicious taste of caramelized toasted almond. This chic store in their honor also supplies guayaquil chocolate, marzipan, chocolate-and-nougatine-coated hazelnuts and chocolate-coated caramelized hazelnuts.

▼ Servant 🏠

30, rue d'Auteuil
Métro: Michel-Ange–Auteuil, Eglise-d'Auteuil
Tel.-Fax 01 42 88 49 82
9 AM–7:30 PM (July–August: 10 AM–7 PM except Saturday 9 AM–7:30 PM).
Open daily.
In this elegantly retro store, Dominique Autret presents bergamot-flavored drops, aniseed candy, calissons d'Aix (sugar-coated almond and candied fruit lozenges), forestines de Bourges (soft nougatine drops in a crunchy coating), ardoises d'Angers (slate-colored candy from Angers), berlingots de Carpentras (colored fruit drops), Montélimar nougat and anis

de Flavigny (white sugar and aniseed pearls), not to mention chocolates made on the premises.

CHEESE

▼ La Ferme de Passy

39, rue de l'Annonciation
Métro: La Muette
Tel. 01 42 88 14 93
8:30 AM–7:30 PM (July: 8:30 AM–1 PM, 4–7:30 PM). Closed Sunday afternoon, Monday, August.
This city farm presents a vast range of the best farmhouse cheeses aged by Michel Daho. Reblochon, saint-nectaire, époisses, sainte-maure and camembert with Calvados are of honest quality.

▼ Ferme Sainte-Suzanne

17, rue le Marois
Métro: Exelmans
Tel. 01 42 88 00 66. Fax 01 48 83 28 65
8 AM–1 PM, 4–7:30 PM. Closed Sunday afternoon, Monday.
The best cheeses France's regions have to offer are aged in the cellars of this store. Saint-marcellin, livarot with cider, brie from Melun, tomme d'Abondance, farmhouse reblochon, langres with marc and Provençal banon are all perfect specimens.

▼ La Ferme Saint-Hubert

Galerie Saint-Didier, 14, rue des Sablons and 16, rue des Belles-Feuilles
Métro: Victor-Hugo, Trocadéro
Tel. 01 45 53 15 77. Fax 01 47 27 28 79
9 AM–8 PM.
Closed Sunday, Christmas, New Year's Day.
Paulette Voy, who prospered in rue Vignon, has taken over from her husband (who has retired) and expertly ages the cheeses here. The artisinal roquefort, aged mimolette, a crumbly cantal, dry crottins and farmhouse maroilles are splendid. The store also prepares camembert croquettes, "cheesemonger's" andouillettes, roquefort tarts and creamy tartiflette.

▼ Lillo

35, rue des Belles-Feuilles
Métro: Rue-de-la-Pompe, Victor-Hugo,
Trocadéro
Tel. 01 47 27 69 08
8 AM–1:30 PM, 4–7:30 PM
(Bank Holidays: 8 AM–1 PM).
Closed Sunday, Monday.

François Hombrouck and Thibault de
Saint Laumer present fruity comtés, earthy
saint-nectaire, creamy reblochon or brebis
from the Pyrénées. Their puff pastry
turnovers, fresh pasta, gratins, organic
jams and preserves and cheese tartlets also
make an excellent impression.

ICE CREAM

▼ Pascal le Glacier

17, rue Bois-le-Vent
Métro: La Muette
Tel.-Fax 01 45 27 61 84
10:30 AM–7 PM.
Closed Sunday, Monday, February holidays,
Easter, All Saint's Day, Christmas, August.

The store decorated with engravings has a
certain chic, but it is Pascal Combette's flavors that bring us here: litchi with sake,
gingerbread, burnt caramel, fresh fig. Mar-
garita sorbet—the lime and tequila sorbet
with candied orange peel steeped in Cointreau and the white rum punch with
chopped pineapple are explosive.

PASTRIES

▼ Yamazaki

6, chaussée de la Muette
Métro: La Muette
Tel.-Fax 01 40 50 19 19
9 AM–7 PM.,
Closed New Year's.

Laurent Guérin is this Japanese pastry
cook's French chef. We delight in the
shaved ice topped with strawberry, melon
or lemon syrup, as well as the more traditional caramel dacquoise, vanilla millefeuille, chocolate and praliné macaron
cake and Bing cherry and almond tart. We
also enjoy fresh salads or sandwiches in
the store.

REGIONAL PRODUCTS

▼ Labeyrie

11, rue d'Auteuil
Métro: Michel-Ange–Auteuil, Eglise-d'Auteuil
Tel. 01 42 24 17 62. Fax 01 42 24 65 75
www.labeyrie.com
10 AM–7 PM.
Closed Sunday, Monday, August.

Renowned smoked salmon and foie gras
are presented side by side with caviar, taramasalata, blinis, rillettes, duck confit and
Bayonne cured ham and accompanied by
Sauternes, Pacherenc, Jurançon and Lillet.

COFFEE

▼ Sous l'Equateur

15, rue Le Marois
Métro: Porte-de-St-Cloud
Tel.-Fax 01 42 88 62 79
9 AM–1 PM, 3:30–7:30 PM.
Closed Sunday afternoon, Monday.

Jean-Marie Pinson selects and roasts Gala-
pagos coffees, Harrar mocha, Kenya,
Colombian maragogype and Italian mix. A
fine range of teas to savor.

PREPARED FOOD

▼ Lenôtre

44, rue d'Auteuil
Métro: Michel-Ange–Auteuil, Eglise-d'Auteuil
Tel. 01 45 24 52 52. Fax 01 42 30 79 45
www.lenotre.fr
9 AM–8:30 PM. Open daily.

The first store opened in 1947 in Normandy. Today, Lenôtre is everywhere,
under the Accor name. The establishment
in rue d'Auteuil pioneered its universalist
style. Mini-appetizers, jumbo shrimp with
curried vegetables and citrus fruit, lamb
chop marinated in spices, chicken breast
coated in creamy aspic jelly and splendid
desserts (a tarte Tatin–like delight in a
glass, caramel macaron cake, millefeuille,
Opéra chocolate cake) will break your resolve in an instant.

▼ Potel et Chabot

3, rue de Chaillot
Métro: Iéna
Tel. 01 53 23 15 15. Fax 01 53 23 16 00
accueil@poteletchabot.fr
8:30 AM–7 PM (Saturday 9 AM–4 PM).
Closed Saturday afternoon (July–August),
Sunday.

This great caterer organizes the receptions of Paris society and supplies made-to-measure meals under the supervision of chef Jean-Pierre Biffi. Sea bass baked whole and unscaled, a salmon, celery root and coriander salad, a Guinea-fowl pie and pistachio shortbread cookies are just some of his shrewd tricks.

◆ RENDEZVOUS

BARS

◆ Sir Winston

5, rue de Presbourg
Métro: Kléber, Charles-de-Gaulle–Etoile
Tel. 01 40 67 17 37. Fax 01 45 00 88 12
9 AM–4 AM (Sunday, Monday 2 AM;
Tuesday, Wednesday 3 AM). Open daily.
Air cond. Terrace.

This English pub with its jazz ambience in the evening offers an excellent choice of single malt Scotch, beers and many cocktails to be enjoyed in a convivial atmosphere.

WINE BARS

◆ Les Caves Angevines

2, pl Léon-Deubel
Métro: Porte-de-St-Cloud
Tel. 01 42 88 88 93
www.lescavesangevines.com
8 AM–8 PM (Thursday 11 PM). Closed
Saturday, Sunday, mid-July–mid-August.
Air cond.

Frédéric Foucher hosts this rustic wine bar. Traditional dishes (veal blanquette, pot-au-feu, coq au vin), charcuterie and Cantal cheeses accompany small-producer Beaujolais, Chinon and Sancerre wines.

Rendezvous

CAFES

◆ Comptoir de l'Arc

73, av Marceau
Métro: George-V, Charles-de-Gaulle–Etoile
Tel.-Fax 01 47 20 72 04
7 AM–midnight.
Closed Saturday, Sunday, Bank Holidays.
Air cond. Terrace.

A step away from the Arc de Triomphe, Jacques Maurel's small chic brasserie wields an easy charm. Modern decor and timeless dishes go hand in hand.

◆ Le Passy

2, rue Passy
Métro: Passy
Tel. 01 42 88 31 02. Fax 01 42 88 42 80
lepassy@wanadoo.fr
6:30 AM–2 AM.
Closed Sunday, 1 week in August.
Terrace.

This long, narrow modern café with its U-shaped bar offers an honest welcome and serves drinks, tartines and strong espresso.

◆ La Rotonde de la Muette

12, chaussée de la Muette
Métro: La Muette
Tel. 01 45 24 45 45
7 AM–midnight. Closed Christmas Eve.
Air cond. Terrace.

Opposite the rail station of the same name, this elegant brasserie offers modern drinks and timeless dishes (potato gratin, Dover sole, beef tenderloin from the Cantal). A pleasant terrace in good weather.

TEA SALONS

◆ Carette

4, pl du Trocadéro
Métro: Trocadéro
Tel. 01 47 27 88 56. Fax 01 47 27 26 09
7:30 AM–midnight. Open daily.
Air cond. Terrace.

Tearoom, cake store and ice cream parlor, this large café serves breakfast and gourmet snacks. Dainty open sandwiches, croque-monsieur, macarons, millefeuille, sorbets and ice creams are worth the trip.

in butter, tiramisu) are prepared as the customer looks on. Teas and evening functions on request.

◆ Carton

150, av Victor-Hugo
Métro: Rue-de-la-Pompe
Tel. 01 47 04 66 55. Fax 01 47 55 92 48
7 AM–8 PM.
Closed Monday, 3 weeks in August.
Air cond. Terrace.

This modern tearoom warrants a visit for its "debutante ball" ambiance, the delicate pastries (chocolate puff pastry, millefeuille, eclairs) and the choice of Dammann teas.

◆ Maison Béchu Marceau

118, av Victor-Hugo
Métro: Rue-de-la-Pompe, Victor-Hugo
Tel. 01 47 27 97 79. Fax 01 47 27 18 32
7 AM–8:30 PM. Closed Monday.
Air cond. Terrace.

This fine art deco tearoom with its terrace is worth a visit for its attractively presented standards: strawberry and buttercream filled sponge cake, millefeuille, chocolate macarons and breakfast pastries. A delightful welcome.

◆ Passy Zen

35, rue de l'Annonciation
Métro: La Muette
Tel. 01 45 25 95 55
www.passy.fr
9 AM–6 PM.
Closed Sunday, 2 weeks in August.
Air cond. Terrace.

Zen and gourmet, this little tearoom offers tiramisu, crumble, clafoutis, as well as chicken brochette with honey, grilled sesame tuna, assorted smoked fish platter or al dente pasta, for a mostly female clientele, who rapidly fall under its spell.

◆ Presto Caffe

129, rue de la Pompe
Métro: Victor-Hugo, Rue-de-la-Pompe
Tel. 01 56 26 66 66. Fax 01 56 26 61 61
www.prestocaffe.fr
11 AM–7 PM.
Closed Sunday, 2 weeks in August.
Air cond.

Stéphanie Artinian and Yann Lamare have come up with an original Italian fast food and takeaway sales concept. The dishes (grilled vegetables, breaded veal steak fried

○	Very good restaurant
◐	Excellent restaurant
◑	One of the best restaurants in Paris
◈	Disappointing restaurant
⚬	Good value for money
◉	Meals for less than 30 euros
SIM	Simple
COM	Comfortable
V.COM	Very comfortable
LUX	Luxurious
V.LUX	Very luxurious

Red indicates a particularly charming establishment

🏛	Historical significance
🏮	Promotion *(higher rating than last year)*
🏵	New to the guide

●	Restaurant
▼	Shop
◆	Rendezvous

17TH ARRONDISSEMENT
THE CENTER OF THE WORLD

"Place Péreire is the center of the world," observed novelist Roger Nimier. Indeed, you will find everything here in the seventeenth: the elegant buildings of Plaine Monceau, the "working class" neighborhoods of Porte de Saint-Ouen, and districts bordering on place de l'Etoile and place de Clichy. Restaurants flourish on its fringes, which teem with brasseries, bistros, wine bars and fashionable terraces, looking out across the Paris beltway to the suburbs or toward l'Etoile, something of the capital's backbone. The seventeenth is boldly conservative and could easily aspire to self sufficiency. Favoring tasteful, unobtrusive variety, it is a green, flowery, peaceful arrondissement. The Batignolles quarter is its village; Monceau park its green lung; rues de Tocqueville, Lévis, Poncelet and Legendre its markets. The local bistros are remarkable and not to be missed. Like a Meccano set, the seventeenth fits together piece by piece. It has its stars (Guy Savoy), sharp purveyors of international cuisine (Sormani's shrewd Pascal Fayet or the low-key Rocco Anfuso of Il Ristorante), seafood restaurants, second fiddles of vast vitality, elite cheese-mongers (Alléosse, Dubois, Gicquel) and fine stores offering regional or foreign foodstuffs (do you know Le Stübli?). In other words, the seventeenth is a microcosm of Paris. You could live here exclusively, in this city of a thousand faces, never fully revealed.

RESTAURANTS

GRAND RESTAURANTS

● **Guy Savoy** ⓒⓞ **LUX**

18, rue Troyon
Métro: Charles-de-Gaulle–Etoile
Tel. 01 43 80 36 22. Fax 01 46 22 43 09
reserv@guysavoy.com
www.guysavoy.com
Closed Saturday lunch, Sunday, Monday,
1 week from Christmas–New Year's, August.
Open until 10:30 PM.
Prix fixe: 230€, 285€. A la carte: 200€.
Air cond. Private dining room. Valet parking.

The man is in the image of his restaurant: charming and never boastful. At Guy Savoy's, the contemporary decor designed by Wilmotte, the Bram Van Velde and Daniel Humair paintings and the African statuettes seem to have stepped from the pages of a glossy magazine. However, the service (unusually affable for such a superior establishment), the wines presented by Eric Mancio, the head sommelier (who has written a number of guides on the subject), and above all the brilliant, appealing cuisine will soon have you feeling at home. Behind the apparent simplicity lies a love—a passion—for shrewdly prepared produce. This results in short preparations with precise flavors: sharp, absolutely flawless and always surprisingly authentic. Whether this is your first or umpteenth visit, the signature dishes are extraordinary creations. The truffled artichoke soup with mushroom and truffle-seasoned brioche, oysters over an iced seafood broth, foie gras with salt, grilled sea bass seasoned with mild spices and turbot in egg salad and in soup express the qualities of the vegetable, shellfish or fish, refusing to allow themselves to be sidetracked. These examples of a true taste and its hidden qualities are also expressed by the pan-fried veal sweetbreads with truffled potato turnovers and Bresse chicken with lemongrass cream sauce and lightly grilled vegetables. The subtle, precise desserts play from the

same score, like the *déclinaison de fraises* (variations on the strawberry theme), the fabulous crème "minute", served with green apple jus, a masterpiece we found perfectly copied in the restaurant of three-star Londoner Gordon Ramsay, or chocolate spiced with tonka beans. Brilliant! What more can we add? Guy Savoy is clearly one of the subtle maestros of our day.

GOOD RESTAURANTS & OTHERS

● **L'Abadache** 🍴 **SIM**

89, rue Lemercier
Métro: Brochant
Tel.-Fax 01 42 26 37 33
Closed Saturday (except for group reservations), Sunday (except for group reservations), August. Open until 11 PM.
Prix fixe: 15€ (lunch), 19€ (lunch), 26€ (dinner), 10€ (children). A la carte: 36€.
Air cond. Terrace. Private dining room.

With its open kitchen, woodwork, green plants and ceramic floor, Yann Piton and Emma Hauser's bistro is a haven of relaxation and conviviality. Yann comes to us from the world of theater, and his present role suits him perfectly. His training at L'Atelier Berger probably has a lot to do with it. In any case, we delight in the brochette of langoustines with a salad of crunchy vegetables, whole roasted sea bream, grilled vegetable millefeuille with pesto, hand-cut beef tartare with basil, a parmesan, apple and romaine salad and a cherry financier with cocoa sorbet. A fine selection of wines by the glass.

● **L'Ampère** **SIM**

1, rue Ampère
Métro: Wagram
Tel. 01 47 63 72 05. Fax 01 47 63 37 33
Closed Saturday, Sunday, August.
Open until 10 PM.
Prix fixe: 19,50€, 24,50€. A la carte: 50€.
Air cond. Terrace.

After some ups and downs, Philippe Detourbe returns to the bistro stage with this gourmet establishment, which offers infectious good humor and roguish dishes chalked up on the blackboard. The snail fricassée with gnocchi and roquefort sauce, the roasted salmon, green beans and peas, the gingerbread-crusted calf's liver with stewed carrots and the apricot clafoutis meet with unanimous approval, especially since the prices have been whittled down.

● **Aristide** 🏠 SIM

121, rue de Rome
Métro: Rome
Tel. 01 47 63 17 83. Fax 01 47 54 97 55
restaurantaristide@free.fr
Closed Saturday noon, Sunday, 2 weeks in August. Open until 10:30 PM.
Prix fixe: 22€. A la carte: 45€.
Terrace.

This bistro from the turn of the last century has many regular local customers. We cheerfully take our place on a faux-leather banquette to enjoy the dishes concocted by Jean-Philippe Siegrist, inventively listed on the mirrors covering the dining room walls. The salad of crayfish tails, sea bream with aromatic herbs, the duck confit and sautéed potatoes and house millefeuille are all splendid.

● **L'Atelier Gourmand** COM

20, rue de Tocqueville
Métro: Malesherbes, Villiers
Tel.-Fax 01 42 27 03 71
www.ateliergourmand.fr
Closed Saturday noon, Sunday, 3 weeks in August. Open until 10 PM.
Prix fixe: 29€ (lunch), 30€ (lunch), 36€.
A la carte: 48€.
Air cond. Private dining room.

Connoisseurs of the culinary arts meet in this former artist's studio dating from the 19th century to discover its broad palette of tastefully classical flavors. In a series of light touches, Guy-Antoine Fontana's preparations outline what promises to be an excellent meal. We successively savor foie gras cake with gingerbread, steamed pike-perch with sautéed potatoes and red wine sauce, wild boar stew and chocolate walnut cookies. We are still sighing in contentment.

● **Augusta** V.COM

98, rue de Tocqueville
Métro: Malesherbes, Villiers
Tel.-Fax 01 47 63 39 97
Closed Saturday, Sunday, 1 week from Christmas–New Year's, August.
Open until 10 PM.
A la carte: 90€.
Air cond.

Didier Berton celebrates the ocean in this eatery. His cook, Guillaume Capelle, formerly of Le Bas Bréau and La Grande Cascade, bases his elaborate preparations from here and farther afield on supremely fresh fish and shellfish. The quick-sautéed langoustine tails with poppy seeds, smoked wild salmon seasoned with dill and lemon confit, seaweed-steamed cod filet with fois gras mousse, roasted turbot with green and white asparagus all feature on the lively, meticulous menu, and only the prices make waves. When the time comes for dessert, strawberry shortbread cookies offer a refreshing conclusion.

● **L'Azalée** V.COM

78, av des Ternes
Métro: Ternes, Porte-Maillot
Tel. 01 40 68 01 01. Fax 01 40 68 91 88
Closed Saturday, Sunday, Bank Holidays, December 23rd–beginning of January, August. Open until 10 PM.
Prix fixe: 37€ (lunch). A la carte: 55€.
Air cond. Terrace. Private dining room.
Valet parking.

Frédérique Sébag's L'Azalée has replaced L'Amphyclès and is doing well. In its contemporary decor in mauve and gray, we enjoy a subtle, mainly seafood-based, cuisine. Langoustine tart with slow-roasted caramelized tomatoes and a ginger vinaigrette, crab salad with mashed fingerling potatoes, sea bass with fennel and a raw tomato sauce, as well as center-cut tenderloin with a tomato crumble are some of the fine tricks performed by Yoann Chave, who trained with Rostang and at A & M Marée. The grapefruit soup with sweet spices punctuates the meal with a fresh, exotic note.

● Le Ballon des Ternes `COM`

103, av des Ternes
Métro: Porte-Maillot
Tel. 01 45 74 17 98. Fax 01 45 72 18 84
leballondesternes@fr.oleane.com
Closed July 28th–August 22nd.
Open until midnight.
A la carte: 50€.
Air cond. Terrace. Private dining room.

Le Ballon des Ternes is doing well in these timeless, circa 1900 brasserie surroundings, with red velvet banquettes and neatly set tables. We eagerly pick out classics from the menu, such as the goat cheese on toast with salad, cod with garlic mayonnaise, classic simmered veal kidneys and vanilla millefeuille. A glass of Marionnet Gamay, and there you have it!

● Ballon et Coquillages `SIM`

71, bd Gouvion-Saint-Cyr
Métro: Porte-Maillot
Tel. 01 45 74 17 98. Fax 01 45 72 18 84
leballondesternes@oleane.com
Closed August. Open until midnight.
A la carte: 50€.
Air cond.

This oyster bar is a seafood adjunct to Le Ballon des Ternes. The setting is tiny, paneled and refined. After the Andalusian gazpacho and cured salmon come a half-dozen Gillardeau No. 3 oysters or a seafood platter. The millefeuille and the baba au rhum are the same delicious desserts they serve in avenue des Ternes. As a bonus, there is a free glass of wine for each guest.

● Balthazar `COM`

73, av Niel
Métro: Ternes, Pereire
Tel. 01 44 40 28 15. Fax 01 44 40 28 30
www.alexandreizra@aol.com
Open daily. Closed New Year's.
Prix fixe: 24€ (lunch).
A la carte: 40–45€.
Air cond. Terrace. Valet parking.

In designer surroundings and a fashionable atmosphere, Alexandre Izraelewicz provides a first-class welcome and cuisine to match. It is true that the menu scarcely changes, but mixed field greens with crayfish tails, coriander-seasoned jumbo shrimp brochette with sautéed rice and vegetables, calf's liver with balsamic vinegar and house mashed potatoes and molten chocolate cake with almond ice cream are loved by all.

● Baptiste `COM`

51, rue Jouffroy-d'Abbans
Métro: Malesherbes, Wagram
Tel. 01 42 27 20 18. Fax 01 43 80 68 09
Closed Sunday, Monday, Bank Holidays, August. Open until 10:30 PM.
Prix fixe: 24€ (lunch), 30€ (lunch), 32€ (dinner).
Air cond.

This bistro of character with its cozy Thirties' surroundings has plenty of convincing arguments on its side: a creative menu, moderate prices and an extremely friendly welcome. Its success is thanks to Denis Croset, master of the range, and Jean-Baptiste Gay, who looks after the service and cellar. We love the coriander-marinated salmon millefeuille, pan-seared Atlantic cod and mashed fingerling potatoes, lamb shoulder with eggplant caviar and a sesame reduction and the crunchy sugar cookies with strawberries and lemon curd.

● Les Béatilles `COM`

11 bis, rue Villebois-Mareuil
Métro: Charles-de-Gaulle–Etoile, Ternes
Tel. 01 45 74 43 80. Fax 01 45 74 43 81
Closed Saturday, Sunday, 1 week from Christmas–New Year's, August.
Open until 10 PM.
Prix fixe: 35€ (lunch), 45€. A la carte: 100€.
Air cond. Valet parking.

Christian Bochaton, Jacques Manière's pupil, has set his modesty aside in this attractive, modern setting in pale wood and straw yellow. His prices are soaring, but we cannot complain, since the set menus show a certain restraint and there is plenty of talent on display. The wild snail and forest mushroom spring rolls, terrine of duck foie gras and farm-raised poultry, Savoie lake fish (similar to salmon trout) in season, whole John Dory fish with marinated vegetables, farm-raised pork and roasted farm-raised pigeon are very tasteful. For dessert, the all-chocolate platter and crunchy layered apple dessert cannot be faulted. The lively Catherine Bochaton welcomes us warmly and helps us choose wines with the benefit of all her freshly acquired knowledge.

● Le Bistral SIM

80, rue Lemercier
Métro: Brochant, La-Fourche
Tel.-Fax 01 42 63 59 61
Closed Sunday, Monday, 10 days Christmas–New Year's, 2 weeks in beginning of May, 2 weeks in August.
Open until 11:30 PM.
Prix fixe: 29€, 32€. A la carte: 50€.
Terrace.

Alexandre Mathieu energetically welcomes us to this bistro with its trompe-l'œil fresco, where we come as much for the atmosphere as for the shrewd wines and refined set menus. Depending on what produce the market has to offer, Thierry Berland prepares asparagus tart with goat cheese and fig vinaigrette, pan-seared tuna steak with green bean salad and seasoned pepper sauce and rack of lamb with a lovage crust served with olive oil–enriched celery root purée. The melon raspberry soup with chocolate truffles and a lemon verbena mousse look good. A trendy restaurant to watch.

● Bistro Gambas COM

4, rue du Débarcadère
Métro: Porte-Maillot, Argentine
Tel. 01 45 72 22 55. Fax 01 45 72 22 88
bistrogambas@wanadoo.fr
Closed Saturday noon, Sunday, 3 weeks in August. Open until 11 PM.
Prix fixe: 15€ (lunch, wine included), 20€.
A la carte: 35–40€.
Air cond.

Shrimp (gambas) are the thing here; the rest depends on the season and market but shows a penchant for flavors of the South of France. We indulge ourselves with the thin-sliced cured San Daniele ham with pickle and melon tartare, Marseilles-style jumbo shrimp in the shell, grilled beef and fresh fruit carpaccio, especially since the tab is very reasonable. The lunchtime prix fixe menu is a steal.

● Le Bistrot d'à Côté Flaubert SIM

10, rue Gustave-Flaubert
Métro: Ternes, Courcelles, Pereire
Tel. 01 42 67 05 81. Fax 01 47 63 82 75
bistrotrostang@wanadoo.fr
www.michelrostang.com
Closed Saturday lunch, Sunday, Monday, May 1st, 2 weeks in August.
Open until 11 PM.
Prix fixe: 29€ (lunch). A la carte: 60€.
Air cond. Terrace. Valet parking.

The first offshoot of Michel Rostang's neighboring establishment offers a fine solution for those who would like a less expensive introduction to the master's cuisine. Apt pupil Cédric Tessier dynamically concocts duck and foie gras terrine in a pastry crust, with sweet and sour fruit, lake perch filet in brown butter and capers with mashed fingerling potatoes and sorrel or half of a trussed and roasted Bresse chicken for two with a diablo sauce with mashed potatoes (in two courses). Little chocolate pots de crème take us back to our childhood. A fine old-fashioned bistro/café decor.

● Le Bistrot d'à Côté Villiers SIM

16, av de Villiers
Métro: Villiers
Tel. 01 47 63 25 61. Fax 01 48 88 92 42
www.michelrostang.com
Closed Saturday, Sunday, 3 weeks in August.
Open until 11 PM.
Prix fixe: 34€, 39€.
Terrace.

This other Rostang group bistro is an admirable refectory, where we appreciate the service with its thoughtful touches and the sound nature of the seasonal cuisine. The regional pig's foot and tripe dish with escargots, the house terrine, the macaroni and lobster gratin, pan-seared calf's liver and little chocolate pots de crème feature in the appealing set menus.

● Le Bistrot de l'Etoile Niel   SIM

75, av Niel
Métro: Ternes, Pereire,
Charles-de-Gaulle–Etoile
Tel. 01 42 27 88 44. Fax 01 42 27 32 12
gensdarmesb@aol.com
www.bistrotdeletoile.com
Closed Saturday noon, Sunday.
Open until 10:30 PM.
Prix fixe: 25€ (lunch), 29€ (lunch).
A la carte: 45–55€.
Air cond. Terrace. Private dining room.
Valet parking.

Voguish, relaxed and endlessly revised, Bruno Gensdarmes's bistro has gained a following. Its dishes delight the local clientele, who adore the warm escargot and fingerling potato salad, roasted cod with cumin-seasoned carrots and roasted veal shoulder with seasonal vegetables and are more than happy with the hot and cold vanilla chocolate dessert. At lunchtime, the set menus are splendid and the a la carte prices are reasonable. A restaurant to try (again).

● Le Bistro du 17e   SIM

108, av de Villiers
Métro: Pereire
Tel. 01 47 63 32 77. Fax 01 42 27 67 66
bistrobis@wanadoo.fr
www.bistro-et-cie.fr
Open daily until 11 PM.
Prix fixe: 33€.
Air cond. Terrace.

Joël Laboureau toils at the stoves of this bistro, run with gusto by Sébastien Moulinet. It is one of the links in the chain acquired by Willy Carr, aimed at those on a medium budget. The produce is fresh, the dishes seasonal and the set menu balanced. The avocado tartare with crayfish, cod filet with a garlicky purée of salt cod and potatoes and seared calf's liver with Szechuan peppers and spinach are gratifying. The crunchy orange and strawberry cookies are lightness itself, as is the tab,

based on a prix fixe menu at less than 35€, including wine and a kir royal aperitif.

● Le Bistrot du Passage   Ⓝ SIM

14, passage Geoffroy-Didelot
Métro: Villiers, Rome
Tel. 01 43 87 28 10. Fax 01 43 87 28 16
Closed Saturday noon, Sunday.
Open until 11 PM.
Prix fixe: 10,50€ (lunch), 12€ (lunch),
20€ (dinner). A la carte: 35€.
Private dining room.

A new team has been brought in to this bistro taken over by Marc Darugna, who has entrusted the kitchen to Nicolas Merle. The chef is not taking too many chances for the time being, serving eggplant au gratin as a starter, salmon steak with creamy pepper sauce and veal piccata, with cream and basil. We end with chocolate fondant, wondering if all this will be enough to attract a clientele that is much in demand elsewhere. The ploy? "Little" set menus at competitive prices.

● Le Bistrot Saint-Ferdinand   COM

275, bd Pereire
Métro: Porte-Maillot
Tel. 01 45 74 33 32. Fax 01 45 74 33 12
st.ferdinand@wanadoo.fr
www.bistrobis.fr
Open daily until 11:30 PM.
Prix fixe: 33€ (wine included).
Air cond. Terrace. Private dining room.

Nicolas Szup has taken over at the stove in this pleasant local bistro brought to us by Willy Dorr. The menu has not changed, and we have no objections to the artichoke hearts with poached eggs in a whole-grain mustard vinaigrette, monkfish medallions with stewed baby vegetables, cherry-roasted duck breast with slow-cooked roasted caramelized small potatoes and a vanilla-roasted peach with individual tea cakes.

● La Bleuetière   SIM

68, av des Ternes
Métro: Ternes
Tel. 01 44 09 70 07. Fax 01 44 09 76 75
jp.lableuetiere.@wanadoo.fr
www.lableuetiere.com
Open daily until midnight.
A la carte: 35€.
Air cond. Terrace. Private dining room.

A young pink and fuchsia decor, Plexiglas and leather chairs, videos playing on the walls and a jazz ambience: If all this meets with your approval, we can chalk up a success for James Partouche, who (depending on the hour) serves sandwiches or tapas (or maybe even more) from 10 a.m. to midnight. You can try your luck with the rabbit and foie gras terrine with chutney, tuna carpaccio in a spice crust, whole young spring rotisserie chicken or a warm apple pear compote with olive oil and vanilla ice cream.

● Les Bouchons de   COM
François Clerc

22, rue de la Terrasse
Métro: Villiers
Tel. 01 42 27 31 51. Fax 01 42 27 45 76
david.gaucher@neuf.fr
Open daily until 10:30 PM.
A la carte: 48€.
Air cond. Terrace.

The menu is improving and David Gaucher seems set to restore the image of this restaurant, which had been going downhill. We greatly enjoy foie gras terrine with a celery root millefeuille, roasted perch filet with crushed tomatoes and spicy chorizo sausage, lamb steak with tarragon butter and rhubarb crème brûlée with cactus sorbet.

● La Braisière   ○ COM

54, rue Cardinet
Métro: Malesherbes
Tel. 01 47 63 40 37. Fax 01 47 63 04 76
labraisiere@free.fr
Closed Saturday noon, Sunday, August.
Open until 10:30 PM.
Prix fixe: 33€ (lunch). A la carte: 60€.
Air cond.

The decor is refined, the atmosphere hushed, the cellar well stocked and the menu inventive: These are the attractions of this "little firm" (as Prince of Gastronomy Curnonsky used to say) run by Jacques Faussat, who made a name for himself as Alain Dutournier's lieutenant, then as chef at Au Trou Gascon. Today, he shares his ideas with us here, and approval is forthcoming: We just have to taste the foie gras terrine with apricot, pan-seared tuna steak with a galangal glaze, wild mushrooms and onion-ginger jam, and roasted lamb shoulder with thyme, baby artichoke hearts, peppers and green asparagus. The chayote fruit tart with raspberries, served with a rhubarb and star anise sorbet, is succulent. Francine Praly has a gift for unearthing the right bottle from the wide range of small growers' wines of which her list fondly boasts.

● Chez Bubune   ⌂ SIM

16, rue Jouffroy-d'Abbans
Métro: Wagram
Tel. 01 42 67 60 10
Closed dinner, Saturday, Sunday,
3 weeks in May. Open until 2:30 PM.
A la carte: 40€.
Air cond.

Formerly at Fauchon and the Crillon, Denise Hodeau has made her native Sologne the focus of this Parisian restaurant, from decor to dishes. In a rustically styled dining room with lilac-colored tablecloths and shining brasses on the walls, we make short work of lightly spiced oyster mushrooms in salad with thin slices of parmesan, duo of jumbo shrimp and scallops with a sherry butter and mushroom risotto, pheasant with reinette apples and a slightly acidulated cream sauce and the indispensable chocolate pot noir de Bubune with a crisp lace cookie.

● La Cabane   SIM

96, rue de Lévis
Métro: Malesherbes
Tel. 01 46 22 51 50
Closed Sunday, Monday evening,
2 weeks in August. Open until 10:15 PM.
Prix fixe: 16€ (lunch), 24€ (lunch, wine
included), 31€ (wine included).
A la carte: 40€.
Air cond.

This oyster farmer's cabin in the heart of
Paris is home to Hervé Couderc, who beck-
ons to us with red mullet and eggplant terrine, mussels with cream, chicken breast in
creamy white sauce and chocolate fondant. A magnificent shellfish platter offers
a vast range of sea flavors to enjoy here or
take away.

● Le Café d'Angel   SIM

16, rue Brey
Métro: Charles-de-Gaulle–Etoile
Tel.-Fax 01 47 54 03 33
Closed Saturday, Sunday, Bank Holidays,
Christmas–New Year's, 3 weeks in August.
Open until 10:30 PM.
Prix fixe: 19€ (lunch), 22€ (lunch).
A la carte: 40€.
Air cond.

This bistro just a step away from place de
l'Etoile is a great find with its low prices.
Such a great find, in fact, that you are
strongly advised to make a reservation if
you want a chance to taste the shrewd
dishes concocted by Jean-Marc Gorsy,
Alain Reix's former lieutenant at the Jules
Verne. The pan-seared squid with fresh
herbs, slow-cooked tomatoes and lemongrass, scorpion fish filet with slow simmered vegetables and tomatoes,
Norman-style rib-eye steak with roasted
potatoes and a caramelized garlic and basil
jus, chocolate sundae with salted caramel
sauce, crushed almond brittle and
whipped cream provide a tasty bite as we
sit shoulder to shoulder on the faux-
leather banquettes of this deliciously retro
establishment.

A SPECIAL FAVORITE

● Caïus   COM

6, rue d'Armaillé
Métro: Argentine, Charles-de-Gaulle–Etoile
Tel. 01 42 27 19 20. Fax 01 40 55 00 93
Closed Saturday noon, Sunday,
Bank Holidays. Open until 10 PM.
Prix fixe: 23€ (lunch), 38€.
Air cond. Private dining room.

A step away from place de l'Etoile, Jean-
Marc Notelet's restaurant has finally been
refurbished in a cozy, modern, very well-
lit, chocolate-colored decor of pale woodwork, mirrors and thick, dark brown
velvet. We feel quite at home as we enjoy
the set menu of the day put together by
this young chef, who trained with Boyer
and Meneau and practiced his art at Le
Troyon. The season finds its expression in
spirited dishes from France and elsewhere, in which the spices often have the
last word. Littleneck clam cappuccino,
with whipped celery root and a light savory reduction sauce, the remarkable
pain perdu paired with smoked herring
caviar, crisp layered pastry with swordfish
seasoned with tumeric and ginger, veal
cheeks with ginseng and citron confit
pass the time pleasantly. The desserts,
such as roasted rhubarb with whipped
mascarpone cheese, roasted and poached
quince seasoned with cloves, are up to the
same standard.

● La Cave Lanrezac   COM

3, rue du Gal-Lanrezac
Métro: Charles-de-Gaulle–Etoile
Tel. 01 45 72 27 00. Fax 01 45 72 03 21
Closed Saturday, Sunday,
end of July–mid-August. Open until 10 PM.
Prix fixe: 17€ (wine included), 24€, 30€.
A la carte: 45€.
Air cond.

Exit L'Astrée and its French Japanese cuisine. Formerly at La Brasserie de la Poste in
the sixteenth, Marc Roland has opened a
sober, red, gourmet cellar here. Before taking our seats, we go down to choose our
wine, then head back upstairs to enjoy a
sunny cuisine based on revised recipes. At

the stove, Eloi de Fontenay, a Drouant veteran, subtly concocts a tomato tart with arugula salad, red mullet with asparagus, fava beans with sage, lamb shoulder slow cooked with oriental spices served with bulgur with raisins or chilled frozen strawberry soup with rhubarb.

● Caves Petrissans   🍴 SIM

30 bis, av Niel
Métro: Ternes, Pereire,
Charles-de-Gaulle–Etoile
Tel. 01 42 27 52 03. Fax 01 40 54 87 56
cavespetrissans@noos.fr
Closed Saturday, Sunday, Bank Holidays,
August. Open until 10:15 PM.
Prix fixe: 34€. A la carte: 40€.
Terrace. Private dining room. Valet parking.

Since 1895 (Tristan Bernard located his play *Le Petit Café* here), this establishment has had a long, colorful history, and Marie-Christine and Jean-Marie Allemoz are still writing the latest chapter day after day. Although it is reputed for its excellent cellar, the restaurant is not simply a wine bar. Duck foie gras, smoked salmon with potatoes in oil and skirt steak with shallots, like the chocolate cake with crème anglaise, are beautifully executed. Savoring these dishes, we appreciate the contents of our glass all the more.

● Chez Cédric   SIM

13, rue Denis-Poisson
Métro: Argentine
Tel. 01 44 09 03 30. Fax 01 40 68 93 55
chezcedric@chezcedric.fr
www.chezcedric.fr
Closed Sunday, 3 weeks in August.
Open until 11 PM.
Prix fixe: 23€, 29€. A la carte: 55€.
Air cond. Terrace. Private dining room.
Valet parking.

Formerly at Benoît, the lively Ivan-Paul Cassetari has taken over this bistro near Porte Maillot. Carefully prepared by Thierry Atlan, the swimmer crab soup, Lucien Tendret's pâté in a pastry crust, John Dory fish with shellfish, simmered veal kidneys and delicious pig's foot cakes with whole-grain mustard, are promising. The

Fiumicoli de Sartène (Corsican red wine) is easy to drink and the profiteroles with chocolate sauce conjure up childhood memories.

● Le Cercle du 17e   ◉ SIM

5, rue Labie
Métro: Porte-Maillot, Argentine,
Charles-de-Gaulle–Etoile
Tel. 01 45 74 22 98.
Closed Saturday, Sunday, 2 weeks in August.
Open until 10 PM.
Prix fixe: 14€ (lunch), 18,50€ (lunch),
22,50€ (dinner), 27€ (dinner).
Terrace.

Jean-Baptiste and Catherine Santoni had the bright idea of bringing in talented Japanese chef Sadaki Kajiwara to combine the basics of French tradition with Japanese rigor. The results are quite conclusive, with jumbo shrimp ravioli with lemongrass vegetable consommé, seafood brochette with fish soup, grilled pork ribs with coffee beans, roasted duck breast with cinnamon-seasoned mashed sweet potatoes and green tea tiramisu. The set menus are enticing, and the prices keep a low profile.

● Le Congrès   COM

80, av de la Grande-Armée
Métro: Porte-Maillot
Tel. 01 45 74 17 24. Fax 01 45 72 39 80
jeanclaudeventalon@congres-maillot.com
www.rest-gj.com
Open daily noon–2 AM. Cont. service.
Prix fixe: 34€. A la carte: 55€.
Air cond. Terrace. Private dining room.
Valet parking.

Opposite the Palais des Congrès, this large, half Empire-, half Directoire-style brasserie is the ideal spot for a business lunch or dinner. There are no unpleasant surprises with the menu. The dishes on offer include hickory-smoked Scottish salmon, Dover sole pan fried in butter, garlic and parsley, butcher's choice cut and prunes slow cooked in artisan-produced Armagnac. Friendly, attentive, nonstop service.

● **Dessirier** `COM`

9, pl du Mal-Juin
Métro: Pereire
Tel. 01 42 27 82 14. Fax 01 47 66 82 07
www.michelrostang.com
Open daily until 11 PM.
A la carte: 95€.
Air cond. Private dining room. Valet parking.

Michel Rostang's seafood restaurant is on a par with his other establishments (in other words, excellent). Olivier Fontaine knows how to get the best out of shelled crab, grilled line-caught sea bass, young turbot and John Dory fish, pasta and blue lobster gratin, beef tenderloin with mashed potatoes, calf's liver with braised mushrooms and millefeuille with salted butter caramel sauce. Then, of course, there is the consummately fresh oyster bar. So no nasty surprises, except possibly when the time comes to settle the check, which promises to be steep. A very attractive wine list and service to match.

● **L'Ecrevisse** `N` `COM`

212 bis, bd Pereire
Métro: Porte-Maillot
Tel. 01 45 72 17 60. Fax 01 45 72 56 84
Closed Saturday noon, Sunday,
Bank Holidays. Open until 10:30 PM.
A la carte: 45–55€.
Air cond.

From June to January, the crayfish is king at Jean Diaz's establishment. During the other months of the year, there is still plenty to satisfy our appetite, though, with pan-seared foie gras served on spice bread with honey sauce, fish tartare with cucumber salad, vanilla-seasoned cod, veal sweetbreads with truffles and foie gras, and house desserts according to season. The decor is polished, as is the presentation. Real tablecloths, attractive plates and South American paintings are the house's little extras, along with its well-stocked cellar.

● **L'Entredgeu** `SIM`

83, rue Laugier
Métro: Porte-de-Champerret
Tel. 01 40 54 97 24. Fax 01 40 54 96 62
Closed Sunday, Monday, 3 weeks in August.
Open until 10:30 PM.
Prix fixe: 22€ (lunch), 30€.
Private dining room.

We immediately feel at home in Philippe and Pénélope Tredgeu's restaurant. What do we especially like? The simplicity of the unfussy cuisine, the friendly prices and the attentive service. With all these attractions, it is not easy to find a table, but when you do, you are rewarded with the stuffed squid with squid ink vinaigrette, the Basque-style poached eggs with lamb roast, chorizo and parmesan, a roasted cod with stuffed artichokes, the parsley-seasoned eggplant, tomatoes and parmesan, a suckling pig, milk-fed lamb stuffed with foie gras and pig's feet and a rice pudding with a rhubarb and strawberry compote. A growing success that looks set to continue.

● **Epicure 108** ○ `COM`

108, rue Cardinet
Métro: Malesherbes
Tel. 01 47 63 50 91
Closed Saturday noon, Sunday,
Monday evening, 2 weeks in August.
Open until 10 PM.
Prix fixe: 29€, 43,50€. A la carte: 40€.
Air cond.

When a native of Japan falls in love with France and expresses this passion in the kitchen, the results are never dull. After a career that took him to L'Auberge Saint Barnabé in Murbach, Emile Jung's and the Haeberlin brothers' establishments, Tetsu Goya has a passion for Alsace, but not exclusively. A mosaic of warmed assorted vegetables with tomato coulis, pan-fried squid with jumbo shrimp and lentils, veal sweetbread torte and eels sauteed with garlic and parsley are ingenious indeed, as are his interpretations of rabbit terrine seasoned with Sylvaner wine and duck with sauerkraut. For dessert, fruit cup with carrot syrup is pleasantly surprising, like the moderate tab and Kumiko Goya's smile.

● Chez Fred ⟨S⟩ SIM

190 bis, bd Pereire
Métro: Porte-Maillot, Pereire
Tel. 01 45 74 20 48
Closed Sunday. Open until 11 PM.
Prix fixe: 30€. A la carte: 45€.
Terrace. Valet parking.

If you are looking for a brilliant display of Lyon's culinary tradition, Alain Piazza's restaurant is not the place to go. In the kitchen, Claude Lambolley would do well to take another look at the city's recipes and make a better job of his Lyonnaise-style ham terrine, pike quenelles (insipid), crayfish sauce (watery) and warm Lyonnaise-style braised sausage (shriveled up when we last visited). The desserts have more appeal, though.

● Goupil SIM 🔔

4, rue Claude-Debussy
Métro: Porte-de-Champerret
Tel. 01 45 74 83 25.
Closed Saturday, Sunday, 3 weeks in August.
Open until 10:30 PM.
A la carte: 40€.
Terrace.

Our 2006 Special Favorite is still riding high. Eric Mayot, formerly of Maxim's, has turned this likable bistro near Porte de Champerret into an excellent eatery indeed. Admittedly, he stacked the odds in his favor by bringing in the young, talented Guillaume Monjuré, who trained with Vigato, to prepare a very lively market-based cuisine. We delight in his beet carpaccio, lamb's lettuce and crumbled boiled eggs, the Basque-style squid, quick-seared tuna with celery root rémoulade, pan-seared rib-eye for two with sautéed potatoes, juicy pork chop, grilled veal kidneys with béarnaise sauce, baba au rhum and chocolate millefeuille. Fine, thirst-quenching wines, including an amiable Corbières.

● Graindorge COM

15, rue de l'Arc-de-Triomphe
Métro: Charles-de-Gaulle–Etoile
Tel. 01 47 54 00 28.
le.graindgorge@wanadoo.fr
Closed Saturday noon, Sunday,
2 weeks in beginning of August.
Open until 10:30 PM.
Prix fixe: 24€ (lunch), 28€ (lunch),
32€ (dinner). A la carte: 54€.
Air cond. Private dining room.

In his art deco–style restaurant near place de l'Etoile, Bernard Broux makes it a point of honor to introduce his guests to the tastes of his native Flanders. The Maatjes herring filet, roasted langoustine tails with citrus vinaigrette, eel, brasserie-style poultry fricassée, pain perdu and simmered Burla cherries pay keen tribute to the cuisine of the North. Cold beer and fine wines from the cellar.

● L'Hébertard ⊖ SIM

1, rue de Chéroy
Métro: Villiers, Rome
Tel. 01 42 94 80 42
Closed Saturday noon, Sunday, August.
Open until midnight.
Prix fixe: 9,20€ (lunch), 11,80€ (lunch).
A la carte: 30€.
Air cond. Private dining room.

Carlos da Silva Francisco's restaurant pays homage to the cuisine of the South of France. His new chef, Mr. Brahim, reliably prepares tomato carpaccio, salmon pastilla, chicken curry and gingerbread crème brûlée, sunny dishes washed down with carefully selected Portuguese wines.

Good Restaurants & Others

are splendid (paris-brest filled with praliné cream, fluffy baba au rhum using St. James rum). We wash it all down with some delicious wines, often priced under 20€, like the Saint Chinian, which rolls over the tongue like velvet. A fine establishment indeed!

● Hier et Aujourd'hui   Ⓝ 🍴 Ⓔ SIM

145, rue de Saussure
Métro: Villiers
Tel. 01 42 27 35 55
Closed Saturday, Sunday, 2 weeks in August.
Open until 10:30 PM
Prix fixe: 17€ (lunch), 26€.

The location is a changing area of Paris by the Périphérique beltway, near Porte d'Asnières and not far from Porte de Clichy. The restaurant is amusing, modern, tasty, pleasant and inexpensive. In fact, it has everything going for it, despite the background noise. Running it is a keen young duo: Karin Ouet, a petite blonde who provides a smiling welcome and prompt service, and Franck Dervin, a chef full of energy, putting on a one-man show in his kitchen behind glass. The loft-style premises have their charm, with bricks, slate and gray walls. It was a crêperie before, but is now a restaurant to be reckoned with. Franck paid his dues with Guy Savoy and Alain Dutournier and knows plenty about buying quality produce at the right price. What we like here are his freshness, sharpness and precision, and his amusing way of concocting combinations of flavors that work (asparagus salad with mozzarella, tomatoes and pesto, daily vegetable specials, spiced country terrine, for instance). The fish and shellfish (the cod, with a translucent quality that flakes when touched with a fork, served with tomato-seasoned potatoes and the quick-seared scallops with mashed potatoes) plunge us into a world of sea spray and flavor. Turning to the meats, a layered lamb and potato dish with eggplant or tender blade steak with pickles are domestic dishes that take us back to our childhood. As good as grandma's? Better than grandma's! Franck, who does it all on its own and presents an easily adaptable 26€ set menu of the day on the blackboard (starters at 6€, main courses at 15€, desserts at 5€) has the gift. The desserts

● Les Hortensias   COM

4, pl du Mal-Juin
Métro: Pereire
Tel. 01 47 63 43 39. Fax 01 47 22 17 37
Open daily until 11:30 PM.
Prix fixe: 19,50€. A la carte: 37€.
Terrace. Valet parking.

This charmless brasserie could almost pass unnoticed, but it would be a pity to miss out on its tastefully classical menu. The Hortensia or nicoise salads, cod, rib-eye, beef tartare and chocolate mousse are perfectly done, with no surprises and no false notes.

● L'Huîtrier   SIM

16, rue Saussier-Leroy
Métro: Ternes
Tel. 01 40 54 83 44. Fax 01 40 54 83 86
Closed Sunday, Monday.
Open until 10:30 PM.
A la carte: 55€.
Air cond. Private dining room.

This is the second establishment run by Alain Bunel, who is already the proprietor of Côté Phare in Cap-Ferret, in the Bordeaux region. Thanks to his efforts, Parisians can now afford the luxury of remarkably fresh seafood, with a dozen Papillon no. 5 oysters on the half shell, crab salad, sea bream and pan-seared langoustines. Meat lovers will be delighted with pan-seared beef tenderloin and steak tartare. The desserts, such as baba au rhum and orange crêpe, are equally good.

● **Il était une Oie** SIM
dans le Sud-Ouest

8, rue Gustave-Flaubert
Métro: Ternes, Courcelles, Wagram
Tel. 01 43 80 18 30. Fax 01 43 80 99 50
sarlleyrome@wanadoo.fr
Closed Sunday, Monday, 3 weeks in August.
Open until 10:30 PM.
Prix fixe: 18,50€ (lunch), 27,50€.
A la carte: 30–40€.
Terrace. Valet parking.

Damien Rommel has taken over this restaurant to the glory of Southwest France, with Manuel Moreno in the kitchen. They continue to serve the relaxed bistro's trademark classics. Duck foie gras terrine, quick-seared tuna with piperade, the house cassoulet and duck breast slip down smoothly. With the coffee, the Bordeaux-style vanilla cakes take on another dimension. The service is efficient and the prices are inoffensive. A good cellar of Southwestern vintages.

● **L'Improviste** SIM

21, rue Médéric
Métro: Courcelles, Wagram
Tel.-Fax 01 42 27 86 67
pro.pagesjaunes.fr/alimproviste
Closed Sunday. Open until 10:30 PM.
Prix fixe: 30€. A la carte: 40€.
Air cond. Terrace. Valet parking.

In their pleasantly refurbished Thirties' decor, Yvon Mezou and François Desgrees du Loup serve sober bistro standards. The monkfish medallion with lemon and white wine butter sauce, the veal blanquette and the tarte Tatin go down smoothly. Everything is in a delightfully classical vein.

● **Le Jardin d'Ampère** COM

Hotel Ampère, 102, av de Villiers
Métro: Pereire
Tel. 01 44 29 16 54. Fax 01 44 29 16 50
contact@hotelampere.com
www. hotelampere.com
Closed Sunday evening, Bank Holidays
(evening), 3 weeks in August.
Open until 10 PM.
Prix fixe: 30€, 34€. A la carte: 57€.
Air cond. Terrace. Private dining room.
Valet parking.

The Hôtel Ampère has a garden conducive to a relaxing meal, both for the hotel's guests and for passing gourmets. When the sun shines, the flowery terrace is a genuine haven of peace, leaving us plenty of time to immerse ourselves in the pleasures of the table, with colorful, Provence-inspired dishes prepared by François-Régis Cartier, previously at the Martinez in Cannes. The trio of surf and turf tartares with mixed baby greens, the saffron-poached monkfish, brochette of lamb tenderloin served with a chanterelle and basil risotto as well as the hibiscus-flavored peach and a melon minestrone offer a festival of flavors.

● **Le Jardin d'Isa** SIM

1, pl Charles-Fillion
Métro: Rome
Tel. 01 46 27 33 37. Fax 01 42 28 15 75
www.clos-ste-marie.com
Closed Sunday evening, Monday,
end of November–end of January.
Open until 10:30 PM.
A la carte: 40–45€.
Terrace. Valet parking.

With its hushed atmosphere and beige and pink decor, this trim establishment makes a virtue of restraint. The cuisine is flawless and soothingly classical. The mussels in cream sauce served with pan-fried shrimp flambéed with pastis, grilled sea bass with fennel as well as the beefsteak with crushed peppercorns flambéed with cognac have a Southern French accent. An excellent house tart.

● Leclou   🛏 SIM

132, rue Cardinel
Métro: Malesherbes, Villiers
Tel. 01 42 27 36 78. Fax 01 42 27 89 96
le.clou@wanadoo.fr
www.restaurant-leclou.fr
Closed Saturday, Sunday, 1 week from
Christmas–New Year's, 1 week in May, 3
weeks in August. Open until 10:30 PM.
Prix fixe: 21€ (lunch), 30€ (dinner).
A la carte: 40€.
Terrace. Valet parking.

Do not be fooled by this bistro's modern
appearance: The food here is pure tradition. Unaffected by ephemeral trends and
culinary experiments, Christian Leclou is
as delighted as ever to concoct duck foie
gras terrine, cod with olive oil–enriched
mashed potatoes, cooked lamb shoulder
slow roasted for five hours and nougat
glacé. With Isabelle Lamare's smile as an
added bonus, how could you forgo the
pleasure of eating here?

● Chez Léon   SIM

32, rue Legendre
Métro: Villiers
Tel. 01 42 27 06 82. Fax 01 46 22 63 67
chezleon32@wanadoo.fr.
Closed Saturday, Sunday, Bank Holidays,
1 week from Christmas–New Year's, August.
Open until 10 PM.
Prix fixe: 26€. A la carte: 40€.
Private dining room.

The band of regulars at this excellent address in the Batignolles quarter reliably
pack this pleasant Fifties' bistro with its
vintage zinc counter. They come as much
for the convivial, good-natured atmosphere as for the copious gourmet dishes.
Pure tradition exclusively, but the food is
so well prepared that it never stales. Our
thanks go to Emmanuel Klein for the
parsley-marbled ham terrine, simmered
monkfish and chanterelles, classic calf's
head, cheeses from Virginie and layered
crisp pastry with apple, caramel sauce
and vanilla ice cream.

● Le Lutin   SIM

2 bis, rue Fourcroy
Métro: Ternes
Tel. 01 47 63 76 10 / 01 47 63 59 50.
Fax 01 43 80 51 19
angejimbert@hotmail.fr
Closed Saturday, Sunday, mid-August–end of
August. Open until 11:30 PM.
Prix fixe: 38€ (wine included).
Air cond. Terrace.

The merits of Ange Jimbert's rustic establishment lie in its selection of wines and
proficiently prepared, quintessentially
French classics. In the kitchen, Didier Colis
faultlessly concocts foie gras in puff pastry,
Dover sole pan fried in butter, garlic and
parsley, duck leg cooked with olives and
soft chocolate cake.

● M comme Martine   Ⓝ SIM

33, rue Cardinel
Métro: Wagram, Courcelles
Tel.-Fax 01 43 80 63 60
Closed Saturday, Sunday, 2 weeks in August.
Open until 10:15 PM.
Prix fixe: 18€ (lunch), 23€ (lunch).
A la carte: 35€.
Air cond. Terrace.

Exit Le Bacello. In its place, Martine Engel-
hard has just opened this Mediterranean
snack bar and grocery with its refined designer decor. At any time of day you can join
the local epicures here in savoring a sausage
au chocolat, summer sardine compote,
tuna steak with spice crust, pan-seared
veal hangar steak and lime crème brûlée.

● Meating   V.COM

122, av de Villiers
Métro: Pereire
Tel. 01 43 80 10 10
chezmichelpereire@wanadoo.fr
Closed Saturday noon, Sunday, Monday.
Open until 11 PM (Friday,
Saturday midnight).
A la carte: 65 -75€.
Air cond. Private dining room. Valet parking.

For what the format is worth, it has acquired a following. After the starters of the
day at 5€, you can move on to a premium

Angus steak or 500g of prime Irish Hereford beef, unless you prefer the only fish dish, red tuna steak grilled on a wood fire. The desserts are "sweet," as they say these days, in particular the Tanzanian chocolate soup with warm tea cakes. The check is not so sweet, but fans of red meat will have few regrets about indulging their weakness. Forget the Romanian wines, go for California or Spanish.

● **Miss Betsy** ⬛ SIM

23, rue Guillaume-Tell
Métro: Porte-de-Champerret, Pereire
Tel.-Fax 01 42 67 12 67
infos@missbetsy.fr
www.missbetsy.fr
Closed Saturday noon, Sunday, 1 week from Christmas–New Year's, 3 weeks in August.
Open until 10 PM.
Prix fixe: 16€ (lunch, wine included), 27€, 31€, 35€.
Terrace. Private dining room.

Jean-Thomas Lopez and Emmanuelle Redaud are not yet up to cruising speed. We will give them another year to make the veal, cabbage and potatoes with poached egg and wine sauce a little more spirited and ensure that the pan-fried sea bass with sweet potatoes is not overcooked by at least three minutes. The veal sweetbread pastilla with soft-cooked leeks and the pineapple canneloni show that all is not lost. There are no problems at all with the check.

● **L'Orénoc** ⬛ COM

Méridien Etoile, 81, bd Gouvion-Saint-Cyr
Métro: Porte-Maillot
Tel. 01 40 68 30 40. Fax 01 40 68 30 81/94
yves.dannequin@lemeridien.com
www.lemeridien-etoile.com
www.lorenoc.com
Closed Sunday, Monday, end of July–end of August.
Open until 11 PM.
Prix fixe: 38€ (lunch on weekdays).
A la carte: 70€.
Air cond. Private dining room. Valet parking.

Terracotta tones and rare varieties of wood reflect the spicy flavors from the four corners of the world that enliven the regional produce showcased by Pierrick Cizeron, under the guidance of Michel Rostang. Guests of Le Méridien and passing gourmets find themselves whisked away to foreign climes. We yield to the surprises of the warm lobster salad with citrus emulsion and malaguetta pepper, the tuna tataki served warm with wasabi-infused oil, the Indian spiced lamb roast with cashew rice and the roasted thyme-seasoned peaches served with ice cream and red fruit coulis. Wines from all over, a jazz ambience and attentive service.

● **Le Petit Champerret** ⬛ SIM

30, rue Vernier
Métro: Porte-de-Champerret
Tel. 01 43 80 01 39
joellehoutmann@lepetitchamperret.com
Closed Saturday, Sunday, August.
Open until 10:30 PM.
Prix fixe: 19,50€, 27€. A la carte: 35–40€.
Terrace.

Previously at Le Petit Verdot in the sixth, Joëlle Houtmann has turned this old bistro into a convivial haunt. We love her seasonal home-style Lyonnaise cuisine and marvel at the classic gouda cheese tarte, the fish pot-au-feu, the duck breast with potato purée and the baba au rhum. Wines are available by partial bottle, and this tends to lighten the check.

● **Au Petit Chavignol** ⬛ SIM

78, rue de Tocqueville
Métro: Villiers, Malesherbes
Tel. 01 42 27 95 97
Closed Sunday, Bank Holidays.
Open until 11:30 PM.
A la carte: 30€.
Terrace.

A relaxed, family atmosphere in Bernard Roques-Bouges's wine bar. His wife Laurence works at the stove, concocting attractive market based dishes: foie gras terrine, rump steak with vegetables, fresh fish of the day and amazing desserts such as the soft chocolate cake. Everything is simple, good and inexpensive, so naturally you have to reserve.

● Le Petit Colombier `COM`

42, rue des Acacias
Métro: Charles-de-Gaulle–Etoile,
Ternes, Argentine
Tel. 01 43 80 28 54. Fax 01 44 40 04 29
le.petit.colombier@wanadoo.fr
www.lepetitcolombier.com
Closed Saturday noon, Sunday, Christmas,
New Year's Day, August.
Open until 10:30 PM.
Prix fixe: 38€. A la carte: 70–80€.
Air cond. Private dining room.

Francis and Laurence Borel have kept up
the high standards in this establishment.
First of all, the exemplary welcome, then
the cuisine, which takes as long as is necessary. At the stove, Pascal Pineau inno-
vates cautiously, producing successes such
as warm slice of foie gras served warm with
gingerbread and raspberries and roasted
langoustines served with lightly cooked
vegetables. The rest of the menu is more
traditional, but always prepared with genuine skill, as evinced by the stuffed pigeon
with green peas or, for dessert, profiteroles
with cream, vanilla ice cream and warm
chocolate sauce. In season, the game
dishes are remarkable. There are discoveries to be made on the wine list and in the
end, the tab is lower than you might have
expected.

● Le Petit Salé `SIM`

99, av des Ternes
Métro: Porte-Maillot
Tel. 01 45 74 10 57. Fax 01 40 68 95 09
petitsale@wanadoo.fr
Closed Christmas. Open until 11:30 PM.
A la carte: 38€.
Terrace. Private dining room.

As the name suggests, the house specialty
is petit salé (pork belly with lentils), but the
menu has many pleasant surprises in store,
starting with the house terrine and head
cheese. Then come the salmon tagliatelle
and duck confit, and finally crème brûlée
and tarte Tatin.

● Petrus `COM`

12, pl du Mal-Juin
Métro: Pereire
Tel. 01 43 80 15 95. Fax 01 47 66 49 86
Closed 10 days in August. Open until 11 PM.
A la carte: 60€.
Air cond. Terrace. Private dining room.
Valet parking.

Gilles Malafosse, whose father runs Le
Flandrin in the sixteenth, has enthusiastically taken over this marine establishment,
refurbishing it in a sober, contemporary
style and providing it with a new fashionable, deluxe brasserie-style identity. A
young Passard veteran is at the stoves, very
deftly concocting tomato mozzarella tart,
baby romaine lettuce hearts with olive oil,
whole sea bream, cod with peas, Dover
sole simply pan fried, seasoned with garlic
and parsley, and skate with capers. All
these dishes are clear, sharp and fresh, and
the desserts (vanilla millefeuille, dacquoise with white chocolate mousse) impress us very favorably.

● Le P'tit Bougnat `SIM`

118, bd de Courcelles
Métro: Ternes
Tel. 01 47 63 97 11. Fax 01 40 53 87 29
www.tablesdumonde.com
Closed Sunday, August.
Open until 11:30 PM.
Prix fixe: 17€, 28€. A la carte: 35–45€.
Air cond. Terrace. Valet parking.

The food here is not exactly cheap unless
you order the prix fixe menus, but the
quality is excellent, and that is what
counts. A house terrine (depending on the
chef's inspiration and the season), pan-
fried scallops (when they are fresh, of
course), braised pork shank and a tart of
the day are not short on refinement. Quite
the contrary.

● **Rech** `COM`

62, av des Ternes
Métro: Ternes, Charles-de-Gaulle–Etoile,
Argentine
Tel. 01 45 72 29 47 / 01 45 72 28 91.
Fax 01 45 72 41 60
www.rech.fr
Closed Saturday noon, Sunday, August.
Open until 11 PM.
Prix fixe: 22,50€, 27€. A la carte: 55€.
Air cond. Terrace. Private dining room.
Valet parking.

Tradition has survived intact in this genuine institution on avenue des Ternes, a celebrated establishment founded in 1925 by August Rech. In the hushed ambience of its authentic setting, we enjoy classics meticulously maintained by Xavier Grégoire. Oysters, of course, but also mackerel with Muscadet and a citrus reduction sauce with aromatic herbs, poached skate wing with garlic, parsley and caper butter, roasted veal kidneys, camembert prepared in the house style and baba made with aged Antilles rum.

● **Ripaille** `N` `SIM`

69, rue des Dames
Métro: Rome
Tel. 01 45 22 03 03. Fax 01 45 22 04 26
Closed Saturday noon, Sunday noon.
Open until 10 PM
(Saturday, Sunday 10:30 PM).
Prix fixe: 11€ (lunch, wine included),
15€ (lunch), 23€, 29€.
A la carte: 30–35€.
Terrace.

Philippe Favré, previously Gérard Faucher's sommelier, invites you to join him at the former Vent d'Ouest, in the company of chef Antoine Butez, Van Laer's ex-lieutenant at Le Maxence, who went on to work with Gilles Choukroun and then at Le Casual. The setting is simple with exposed stone walls and unfussy wooden tables. Pumpkin soup with bleu d'Auvergne cheese, roasted vegetables seasoned with sea salt flakes and smoked tea, pan-seared scallops with broccoli purée, roasted sea bass with olive-oil mashed potatoes, slow-cooked pork cheeks with fennel, cumin

and polenta are tasteful dishes with that gratifying extra touch. Soft chocolate cake with pepper ice cream and a frozen whiskey parfait with chestnut shortbread and Bailey's meet with unanimous approval. The list of wines chosen by Philippe Favré is a little short and needs to be extended, but the choices are excellent. The atmosphere is friendly and the convivial service will keep Ripaille's already loyal customers coming back. A fine future on the horizon.

● **Michel Rostang** ○ `LUX`

20, rue Rennequin (at rue Gustave-Flaubert)
Métro: Ternes
Tel. 01 47 63 40 77. Fax 01 47 63 82 75
rostang@relaischateaux.fr
www.michelrostang.com
Closed Saturday noon, Sunday, Monday noon,
3 weeks in August. Open until 11 PM.
Prix fixe: 70€ (lunch on weekdays), 95€
(wine included with lunch on weekdays),
175€. A la carte: 170€.
Air cond. Private dining room. Valet parking.

There are some classic restaurants that we are always pleased to visit again and Michel Rostang's is one of them. The noble, paneled setting with its art deco allusions and impressive collection of Robj porcelain, the exuberant Marie-Claude's kind welcome and the extremely friendly service put us at our ease. Then the maestro's cuisine takes over with a display of skillfully modernized dishes in the grand tradition. Atlantic blue lobster with tomato chutney and rice vinegar, sea bass with crunchy skin and creamy macaroni gratin and the duck with blood sauce served in two courses play dazzlingly on contrasting flavors and textures. When the time comes for dessert, the crunchy "cigar" with La Havane tobacco and cognac mousse add a touch of originality that bodes well, although even we traditionalists are starting to think this rich style has had its day. In any case, the selection of wines and Alain Ronzatti's advice cannot be faulted, leaving us in need of a good postprandial nap later on.

● La Soupière   COM

154, av de Wagram
Métro: Wagram
Tel. 01 42 27 00 73. Fax 01 46 22 27 09
Closed Saturday noon, Sunday,
Bank Holidays, 3 weeks in August.
Open until 10:30 PM.
Prix fixe: 30€. A la carte: 46€.
Air cond. Terrace.

We take to Christian Thuillart's restaurant immediately, with its smiling welcome, friendly atmosphere and small, long, narrow dining room ending in trompe-l'œil. We like the dishes too: poached eggs in a glass with rosemary garlic cream, basil-seasoned red mullet with fennel-mashed potatoes, milk-fed Pyrénées lamb with roasted garlic and puff pastry with rhubarb and a red fruit coulis. In season, you can try the all-mushroom menu.

● Le Sud   COM

91, bd Gouvion-Saint-Cyr
Métro: Porte-Maillot
Tel. 01 45 74 02 77. Fax 01 45 74 35 36
www.lesud.fr
Closed Sunday, 3 weeks in August.
Open until 11 PM.
A la carte: 55€.
Air cond. Terrace. Private dining room.
Valet parking.

A step away from Porte Maillot, you can almost hear the song of the cicadas in this elegant Southern French establishment. Michaëla Driguès provides an extremely friendly welcome, and Emmanuel Mussart's range of Côtes de Provence wines is intelligently chosen. In the kitchen, the reliable François Lucchesi-Palli prepares extremely fresh Mediterranean dishes. The rock fish soup, pepper spread, bourride (a Provençal fish soup), eggplant parmesan and apple pastry warm our hearts.

● Sud-Ouest Monceau   SIM

8, rue Meissonnier
Métro: Wagram
Tel. 01 47 63 15 07. Fax 01 43 80 98 42
Closed Sunday, Monday, August.
Open until 10 PM.
A la carte: 40–50€.
Air cond. Terrace

Why change a winning concept? That was what Marjorie and Jacques Moreau thought when they took over this restaurant. As before, the three variations of foie gras terrine (natural, with Sauternes, and with basil), the grilled salmon served with baby vegetables, the beef medallions stacked with foie gras and truffles and the large (34-cm) chocolate or coffee eclair delights the local clientele (business at lunchtime, family in the evening). The food is copious and none too expensive.

● La Table des Oliviers   SIM

38, rue Laugier
Métro: Ternes, Pereire
Tel. 01 47 63 85 51. Fax 01 47 63 85 81
ww.tabledesoliviers.fr
Closed Saturday noon, Sunday, 3 weeks in August. Open until 11 PM.
Prix fixe: 20€ (lunch), 28€.
A la carte: 51€.
Air cond. Private dining room.

The name hints at the content of the dishes prepared by Thierry Olivier. For example? Sea bass carpaccio with Mediterranean spices, langoustine risotto with reduction sauce, Marseilles-style bouillabaisse, veal sweetbreads with wild mushrooms and strawberry carpaccio with balsamic vinegar and an almond milk sorbet. We are already on vacation and can almost hear the song of the cicadas.

● Taïra   ○ COM

10, rue des Acacias
Métro: Argentine
Tel.-Fax 01 47 66 74 14
Closed Saturday lunch, Sunday,
mid-August–end of August. Open until 10 PM.
Prix fixe: 35€, 65€ (dinner). A la carte: 55€
Air cond.

Taira Kurihata, former chef at Prunier, has also worked at Jamin, Le Véfour, Besson and Cagna. He knows exactly how to prepare and serve seafood without any surplus frills. The skills he has acquired here and there are complemented by his delicacy of touch and natural Japanese precision. We succumb to the charms of the red tuna tataki, fresh buffalo milk cheese with pan-fried langoustines, squid and basil fricassée, steamed scopion fish and jumbo shrimp with a herb reduction sauce and vegetables and the fresh fruits served with shisho sorbet. One long succession of treats! If only the surroundings were more cheerful, Paris society (which is partial to seafood) would be in the front row here.

● La Toque SIM

16, rue de Tocqueville
Métro: Villiers
Tel. 01 42 27 97 75. Fax 01 47 63 97 69
latoque16@yahoo.fr
Closed Saturday evening (May-September), Sunday, Christmas–New Year's, August.
Open until 9:30 PM.
Prix fixe: 28€, 32€. A la carte: 35–40€.
Air cond.

The Jouberts have only one aim: to please—she in the dining room, he at the stove. Jacky, who was previously with Guérard, concocts some very sunny dishes. His cold ratatouille with basil-seasoned red mullet, the tagliatelle with pesto and seasonal fish and the calf's liver with cider vinegar are all a success. We finish happily with millefeuille with vanilla ice cream and strawberries. If anything, the prices have fallen, yet another reason to pay a visit to our friends the Jouberts.

● Le Verre-Bouteille SIM

85, av des Ternes
Métro: Porte-de-Champerret
Tel.-Fax 01 45 74 01 02 / 01 47 63 39 99
ameline@leverrebouteille.com
www.leverrebouteille.com
Open daily until 5 AM
(Sunday, Monday 3 AM).
Prix fixe: 14,50€ (lunch), 20€, 25€, 7€ (children). A la carte: 35€.
Air cond.

The food here is fresh, well prepared and served seven days a week, virtually day and night. The chicken liver terrine, crunchy sea bream filet with cold ratatouille and beef hangar steak with shallots and served with scalloped potatoes are first rate, as are the caramelized tuile and the almond milk ice cream with pistachio, lemon and honey. The check is not at all too steep and the wines are well chosen.

● Why Not N COM

123, av de Wagram
Métro: Wagram, Ternes
Tel. 01 42 27 61 50. Fax 01 46 22 25 72
Closed Saturday, Sunday.
Open until 10:30 PM.
Prix fixe: 34€. A la carte: 55€.
Terrace. Valet parking.

Philippe Collin, still at La Table d'Anvers, has eagerly taken over Gérard Faucher's eatery. The atmosphere is very cheerful and convivial, and the cuisine is subtle, fresh and shrewd without taking itself too seriously. At the tables (a little too close together) or the counter of this sober, contemporary haunt, we savor a fine quick-seared tuna, an excellent pig's foot carpaccio and variations on a Grand Marnier theme, all part of a very tempting prix fixe menu.

INTERNATIONAL RESTAURANTS

● La Maison de Charly ○ V.COM

97, bd Gouvion-Saint-Cyr
Métro: Porte-Maillot
Tel. 01 45 74 34 62. Fax 01 45 74 35 36
www.lamaisondecharly.com
Closed Monday, August.
Prix fixe: 29€, 33€. A la carte: 40–50€.
Air cond. Terrace.

Beautiful as a Marrakech palace, Claude and Melvin Drigues's establishment is as warm as its Moroccan counterparts. The recipes pay tribute to the tradition of Greater Maghreb. The eggplant or pepper salad, the grilled fish served with chakchouka (a colorful and spicy vegetable and egg dish), the fish tagine with couscous spiced with harissa, the grilled whole sea bream or European bass (prepared in the same simple, appetizing way), the royal couscous or roasted leg of lamb, featured on the generous set menu, like the orange salad and homemade sorbet, are subtle, flavorsome and successful. The patio, cellar bar, private dining rooms, soft chairs and relaxed ambience incite us to remain a little longer and prolong the pleasure.

● Paolo Petrini   ○ COM

6, rue du Débarcadère
Métro: Argentine, Porte-Maillot
Tel. 01 45 74 25 95. Fax 01 45 74 12 95
resinfo@paolo-petrini.fr
www.paolo-petrini.fr
Closed Saturday lunch, Sunday, 3 weeks in August. Open until 10:15 PM.
Prix fixe: 27€, 29€, 34€. A la carte: 60€.
Air cond.

Talented, self-taught maestro Paolo Petrini has trained many good chefs now working all over Paris. He is never short of imagination, even when he prepares simple, market-based dishes. We like the beef carpaccio, which he naturally serves with arugula with shaved parmesan, the Roman-style artichokes, the red mullet filets with tapenade and fennel and the penne with green asparagus and jumbo shrimp. His recipe for profiteroles is unique. The wines from every region of Italy go wonderfully with the food, but to avoid any chance of a mishap, we can follow Jean-Pierre Mullatier's recommendations.

● La Rucola   SIM

198, bd Malesherbes
Métro: Wagram, Malesherbes
Tel. 01 44 40 04 50. Fax 01 47 63 13 20
rucola@wanadoo.fr
Closed Saturday lunch, Sunday, 3 weeks in August. Open until 11:00 PM.
Prix fixe: 15€ (lunch). A la carte: 40€.
Air cond. Terrace.

The alliance of two great culinary traditions—French and Italian—makes this unique restaurant a favorite for gourmets of every kind. They come here to enjoy wild asparagus, arugula and shaved parmesan

salad, Venetian-style scallops, Dover sole with pesto, veal saltimbocca, Parma ham and scarmozza and a homemade sabayon. Our thanks go to Michel Lukin and Sergio Païs, the men behind this fine concept.

● Sormani   ○ V.COM

4, rue du Gal-Lanrezac.
Métro: Charles-de-Gaulle–Etoile
Tel. 01 43 80 13 91. Fax 01 40 55 07 37
Closed Saturday, Sunday, 3 weeks in August.
Open until 10:15 PM.
Prix fixe: 44€ (lunch). A la carte: 60–90€.
Air cond. Private dining room. Valet parking.

Jean-Pascal Fayet, wine buff, actor and herald of Italian cuisine, is everywhere at once, in the dining room and at the stove. He has turned this establishment close to place de l'Etoile (the Venetian room with its Murano chandeliers has been refurbished in red shades) into a place where elegance and quality are very much the thing. He is unsurpassed at the art of concocting dishes based on summer or winter truffles (ah, his tortellini and black truffle fritto misto!). If we are determined to be sensible, we can still enjoy his vitello tonnato and his caponata, the delicious fritto misto, the sauté of shellfish and crustaceans, the lobster ravioli with tarragon and, for dessert, the house tiramisu set off by coffee ice cream and sabayon do the trick. As for the wine, we can leave everything in the capable hands of sommelier Franck Potier!

▼ | SHOPS

KITCHENWARE & TABLETOP

▼ L'Esprit et le Vin

81, av des Ternes
Métro: Porte-Maillot
Tel. 01 45 74 80 99. Fax 01 45 72 03 32
dsa.espritetlevin@tiscali.fr
www.espritetlevin.com
10 AM–1 PM, 2–7 PM. Closed Sunday, Monday, Bank Holidays, 3 weeks in August.
Corkscrews, cellar books, tasting glasses, strainers, decanters, funnels, buckets

equipped with thermometers, vinegar makers and wine coolers will delight all enthusiasts.

BREAD & BAKED GOODS

▼ La Fournée d'Augustine 🔘

31, rue des Batignolles
Métro: Place-de-Clichy, Rome
Tel. 01 43 87 88 41
7:30 AM–8 PM.
Closed Sunday, 2 weeks in August.

Pierre Thilloux, who was our 2005 Baker of the Year in the fourteenth arrondissement, has opened this spirited store where he sells daily breads (rye, whole grain, country) or the famous traditional baguette. We also love his puff pastry brioche, breakfast pastries and Danishes, and the bread made with pistcachios.

▼ Le Moulin de la Vierge

6, rue de Lévis
Métro: Villiers
Tel. 01 43 87 42 42. Fax 01 43 87 28 54
7:30 AM–8 PM. Closed Wednesday.

Basile Kamir is the Ace of wood-fire-baked breads. The country bread, rye, with bacon or organic sourdough, are remarkable. We also love the savory cakes, financier, pound cake, brownie, and apple tart.

▼ Raoul Maeder

158, bd Berthier
Métro: Pereire, Porte-de-Champerret
Tel. 01 46 22 50 73
7 AM–2 PM, 4–8 PM
(Saturday 7 AM–1:30 PM, 4–8 PM; Sunday 7 AM–1:30 PM).
Closed Sunday afternoon, Monday

Raoul Maeder, winner of the Best Parisian Baguette award in 2000 and 2002, continues to delight his customers with fig bread, whole grain, walnut hazelnut, special house breads, linzertorte, raisin braids, kugelhopf, almond tarte—all delicious.

▼ Schaefer

20, bd des Batignolles
Métro: Place-de-Clichy
Tel. 01 42 93 15 03
7:30 AM–8 PM.
Closed Monday, 1 month July–August.

Serge Schaefer bakes whole-grain rye, dried fruit, whole wheat and country breads, as well as classic baguettes. The mushroom soy loaf with flaxseed or sunflower is highly digestible.

CHARCUTERIE

▼ Bouvier

8, rue de Levis
Métro: Villiers
Tel. 01 43 87 25 85. Fax 01 42 93 92 50
traiteur@noos.fr
8:30 AM–1:30 PM, 3:30–7:30 PM (Friday, Saturday 8:30 AM–8 PM). Closed Sunday afternoon, Monday.

Gérard Kouris, cooked-meat maestro, prepares blood pudding and white veal sausages, foie gras, parsley-marbled ham, andouillette, country terrines and pâtés, prepared entrees to go as well as gold medal winning head cheese.

▼ Léautey

83, av de Saint-Ouen
Métro: Guy-Môquet
Tel. 01 46 27 34 20. Fax 01 46 27 70 50
leautey@aol.com
www.leautey.fr
8:30 AM–1:30 PM, 3:30–8 PM.
Closed Sunday afternoon, Monday.

Christophe Léautey selects his raw materials carefully and offers a wide range of flavorsome products. We adore his scallop terrine, head cheese and garlic sausage. He also organizes receptions and can deliver meals to go on request. Cheese store and delicatessen at 81, avenue de Saint-Ouen.

▼ Maison Pou 🔔

16, av des Ternes
Métro: Ternes
Tel. 01 43 80 19 24. Fax 01 46 22 66 97
9:30 AM (Saturday 9 AM)–7:15 PM. Closed Sunday, Bank Holidays in the afternoon.

Created in 1830 and totally renovated this year, this store is as pretty as a picture. Apart from looking good, it supplies duck and goose foie gras, Parma ham, great pikefish quenelles, impeccable pâté en croûte, smoked salmon and truffled sausages. Of course, all that comes at a price.

CHOCOLATE

▼ Christian Rizzotto

14, rue Brochant
Métro: Brochant
Tel.-Fax 01 42 63 18 70
9 AM–7 PM. Closed Sunday, Bank Holidays,
August.

Watched by curious gourmets, Christian Rizzotto prepares his assorted ganaches: green tea, orange, curry, basil, tarragon, peppered mint, ginger, soft caramel. The lemon or cinnamon praliné and pure fruit sorbets are equally delightful.

CANDY & SWEETS

▼ A la Mère de Famille

107, rue Jouffroy-d'Abbans
Métro: Ternes, Courcelles, Wagram
Tel.-Fax 01 47 63 15 15
www.lameredefamille.com
10 AM–7:30 PM. Closed Sunday,
Monday morning, 2 weeks in August.

Calissons, négus, bergamotes, nougats, house chocolates, jellied fruits and salted butter caramels are all present and correct in this fine store. The jams (guava, mango, watermelon or lemon) are mouthwatering.

GROCERIES

▼ Epicerie Léautey Ⓝ

81, av de Saint-Ouen
Tel. 01 46 27 59 68
leautey@aol.com
www.leautey.fr
8:30 AM–1:30 PM, 3:30–8 PM.
Closed Sunday afternoon, Monday.

Christophe Léautey, quality charcutier for thirty years at number 83 av de Saint-Ouen, has just opened this delicatessen and cheese store that pays tribute to quality regional produce in all its forms. Fine ranges of various goat cheeses from the Loire and mountain cheeses, but also quality olive oil direct from the producer in Arles, unpasteurized milk, condiments, and jams.

CHEESE

▼ Alléosse

13, rue Poncelet
Métro: Ternes
Tel. 01 46 22 50 45. Fax 01 42 29 07 64
www.fromage-alleosse.com
9 AM–1 PM, 3–7 PM. (Friday, Saturday
9 AM–1 PM, 3:30–7 PM, Sunday: 9 AM–
1 PM. Closed Sunday afternoon, Monday,
Christmas, New Year's, August 15th.

Philippe Alléosse, who has taken over from his father Roger, ages the same French regional cheeses in his cellars: crumbly cantal, saint-nectaire with herbs, abbaye de cîteaux, fruity comté, mountain beaufort, camembert with Calvados and creamy reblochon.

▼ Dubois et Fils

80, rue de Tocqueville
Métro: Malesherbes, Villiers
Tel. 01 42 27 11 38. Fax 01 42 27 35 26
9 AM–1 PM, 4–7:45 PM (Saturday
9 AM–7:30 PM). Closed Sunday afternoon,
Monday, 2 weeks in August.

Martine Dubois enthusiastically presents comté, fribourg, saint-marcellin, camembert and fifty artisanal cheeses all stocked in her fine store.

▼ Fromagerie des Moines

47, rue des Moines
Métro: Brochant
Tel. 01 46 27 69 24
8:30 AM–1 PM, 4–7:30 PM. Closed Sunday
afternoon, Monday, mid-July–mid-August.

Jacques and Evelyne Gicquel, advanced cheese-ageing champions, supply camemberts, reblochon, pont-l'évêque, époisses and strongly scented maroilles, always a delight.

ICE CREAM

▼ La Marquisette

31-33, av de Saint-Ouen
Métro: La-Fourche
Tel. 01 45 22 91 65
2–9 PM. Closed Monday, beginning of
November–end of February.

Robert Zannettin is the king of Italian ice cream and has surprised us with his cinnamon, licorice, After Eight mint, banana chocolate, mint tea and rose flower flavors. Do not forget to try the mango and blueberry sorbet, and the famous Bulgarian yogurt.

REGIONAL PRODUCTS

▼ Jean-Claude et Nanou
46, rue Legendre
Métro: Villiers
Tel.-Fax 01 42 27 15 08
9 AM–1 PM, 4–7:30 PM.
Closed Sunday, Monday,
mid-July–end of August.

Nanou and Jean-Claude Clément are pleased to present the Auvergne's gourmet products: Parlan sausage, brioche, rosette de Salers, tripe, fourme d'ambert and boudin sausages with chestnuts will delight all Cantalous at heart.

▼ Oliviers & Co
8, rue de Lévis
Métro: Villiers
Tel. 01 53 42 18 04
www.oliviers-co.com
10 AM–7:30 PM (Friday, Saturday
10 AM–8 PM, Sunday 10 AM–2 PM).
Closed dinner (Sunday, Monday),
Sunday afternoon, August.

This famous store specializes in olive oil and Mediterranean products. Its pasta, rice, antipasti, tapenade, sauces, savory (taralli, ciappe, crostinis) and sweet (canistrelli, navettes, tortas) biscuits are appealing indeed. It has a tasting area.

COFFEE

▼ Brûlerie des Ternes
10, rue Poncelet /
28, rue de l'Annonciation, Paris 16e
Métro: Ternes
Tel. 01 46 22 52 79 / 01 42 88 99 90.
Fax 01 45 25 15 08
9 AM–2 PM, 3:30–7 PM.
Closed Sunday afternoon, Monday.

A hundred loose teas from India, Sri Lanka and China and fine coffees from Guatemala, Colombia and Zimbabwe coexist harmoniously in Sylvie Christian's store. The irresistible scent of roasting coffee and the superb espresso machines and wrought-iron teapots from Japan are a bonus.

PREPARED FOOD

▼ Gastronomia
37, rue Ampère
Métro: Wagram
Tel. 01 47 66 19 30. Fax 01 42 27 62 52
9 AM–1 PM, 2–6:30 PM (Monday 6 PM).
Closed Sunday, Bank Holidays,
3 weeks in August.

This store celebrates flavors of the world: Mexican, West Indian, Lebanese, Italian, Greek and Scandinavian. Poultry with cajun spices, guacamole, curry shrimp or salt cod fritters incite us to travel.

▼ La Rucola
198, bd Malesherbes
Métro: Malesherbes
Tel. 01 44 40 04 50
rucola@wanadoo.fr
Noon–2:30 PM, 7:30 PM–10:30 PM. Closed
Saturday noon, Sunday, 2 weeks in August.

This little Italian-style bistro is also a chic delicatessen, selling Venetian-style tuna carpaccio, vegetable lasagna, antipasti, crab ravioli, individual tiramisu, soft chocolate cake to take away, with fine Alpine wines to wash it all down.

◆ RENDEZVOUS

BARS

◆ Bidou-Bar 🏠
12, rue Anatole-de-la-Forge
Métro: Argentine
Tel. 01 43 80 09 18. Fax 01 53 96 05 94
Noon–2 AM. Closed Saturday, Sunday,
August.

This musical bar with its Thirties' decor and cozy jazz ambience serves all kinds of selected cocktails and robust dishes (kidneys, cutlets, tartare, hamburgers, crêpes Suzette).

PUBS

◆ James Joyce

71, bd Gouvion-Saint-Cyr
Métro: Porte-Maillot
Tel. 01 44 09 70 32
11 AM–2 AM. Open daily.
Air cond.

This Irish pub is paneled and relaxed. Guinness, Kilkenny, Irish stew and Irish coffee are the house specialties. On the second floor you can enjoy splendid smoked salmon with cucumber sauce, Irish toasted open-faced sandwiches and apple crumble.

WINE BARS

◆ Au Petit Chavignol   🄽

78, rue de Tocqueville
Métro: Villiers, Malesherbes
Tel. 01 42 27 95 97
7:30 AM–2 AM.
Closed Sunday, Bank Holidays.

Laurence and Bernard Roques-Bouges enthusiastically run this amiable café and bar where you eat generously, or drink Sancerre, Minervois and Côtes de Blaye at the counter while nibbling on cheeses from Berry or the Auvergne and charcuterie from the Aveyron. (Also see Restaurants.)

◆ Le Petit Verdot

9, rue Fourcroy
Métro: Ternes, Pereire
Tel. 01 42 27 47 42
7:30 AM–6 PM (Thursday and Friday evening 11:30 PM). Closed Saturday, Sunday, Christmas–New Year's.

Jean-François Fontaine cheerfully serves pork rillettes, parsleyed ham terrine, potato pâté or sausage from the Auvergne, accompanied by Loire, Rhône and Beaujolais vintages, at a table or the bar.

◆ Le Tastevin   🄽

14, rue Descombes
Métro: Porte-de-Champerret
Tel. 01 43 80 57 50
7:30 AM–9 PM (Thursday 10:30 PM).
Closed Saturday, Sunday.

Winners of the 1999 Bouteille d'Or award and rugby buffs (he is a supporter of Brive;

Rendezvous

her team is the Stade Toulousain), Jean-Michel Frenkel and Danièle Nougarède offer a warm welcome in this old-style bar. We sip favorite wines at a table or the bar and enjoy Danièle's dishes of the day (pot-au-feu, cassoulet, poule au pot, pork belly simmered with lentils) that change with the weather.

CAFES

◆ Café Monceau

4, av de Villiers
Métro: Villiers
Tel. 01 43 87 28 34. Fax 01 43 87 19 82
7 AM–1 AM. Closed Christmas.
Terrace.

This café, with its modern decor reminiscent of a Right Bank version of Café Flore, serves chic beverages and fashionable dishes (tagine, spicy tandoori chicken, cannelloni). The terrace is packed when the sun shines.

◆ Au Père Pouchet   🄽

55, rue Navier
Métro: Guy-Môquet
Tel. 01 42 63 16 73
7 AM (Sunday 10 AM)–2 AM. Open daily.

Pleasant and trendy, this old-style café has a timeless Parisian chic. All day, the young team serves wines by the glass, dishes chosen from the blackboard and snacks at the counter.

◆ Le Petit Acacia

58, rue des Acacias
Métro: Argentine, Ternes
Tel. 01 45 74 12 28. Fax 01 40 55 01 33
8:30 AM–2 AM. Closed Sunday, August.

A short walk from FNAC place de l'Etoile, this Aveyron brasserie offers aligot (a potato purée), pounti (pork meatloaf with Swiss chard and prunes), braised veal sweetbreads in sweet white wine in an intimate setting decorated with vine leaves. Before lunch or dinner, try the kir auvergnat (chestnut liqueur and sparkling white wine).

◆ Royal Villiers

4, pl de la Porte-de-Champerret
Métro: Porte-de-Champerret
Tel. 01 43 80 85 14. Fax 01 43 80 11 54
7 AM–midnight. Closed 2 weeks in August.
Terrace.

Refurbished in a modern style, this Parisian brasserie has lost nothing of its Southwestern French accent. Guy and Joëlle Maysounave serve up dishes that delight rugby fans.

TEA SALONS

◆ Aux Enfants Gâtés

7, rue Cardinet
Métro: Courcelles
Tel. 01 47 63 55 70. Fax 01 47 64 59 81
nathaliesoudan@wanadoo.fr
8 AM–2 PM, 3:30–7:30 PM.
Closed Sunday afternoon, Monday, August,
1 week in February.

Benoît and Nathalie Soudan serve fresh fruit juice (such as Le Hugo: apple, orange, carrot and ginger), selected teas and quality cakes and pastries in their very attractive tearoom. Caramel mousse, marble cake, macarons, but also goat cheese on toast (made from fresh cheese with eggplant and zucchini), make superb snacks.

◆ Gilda   ℕ

73 bis, av Niel
Tel. 01 42 27 42 20
Noon–midnight. Closed 2 weeks in August.
Air cond. Terrace.

This chic tearoom with its refined setting and gracious welcome serves appealing toasted open-faced sandwiches, or tartines (for example the Nordic, with smoked salmon and scrambled eggs), tuna tataki, ice creams and sorbets from Martine Lambert, not to mention quality house pastries such as crumble and cheesecake.

◆ Le Stübli

11, rue Poncelet
Métro: Ternes, Charles-de-Gaulle–Etoile
Tel. 01 42 27 81 86. Fax 01 42 67 61 69
9 AM–6:30 PM. Closed Sunday afternoon,
Monday, 3 weeks in August.
Air cond. Terrace.

Mouthwatering apple streudel, trüffli, Sacher torte, tartes berlinoises, but also the golden butter-browned walnut and almond tarts delight sweet-toothed patrons here. Customers also come at lunchtime for the wurst brunch, the choucroute, or the salmon koulibiac, meticulously prepared by Gerhard and Sylvie Weber.

○	Very good restaurant
⊚	Excellent restaurant
⊛	One of the best restaurants in Paris
⊘	Disappointing restaurant
♜	Good value for money
⊜	Meals for less than 30 euros
SIM	Simple
COM	Comfortable
V.COM	Very comfortable
LUX	Luxurious
V.LUX	Very luxurious

Red indicates a particularly charming establishment

🏛	Historical significance
☖	Promotion *(higher rating than last year)*
⊕	New to the guide
●	Restaurant
▼	Shop
◆	Rendezvous

18TH ARRONDISSEMENT
A DREAMING VILLAGE

This idyllic, poetic quarter with its steep streets is still one of the proudest symbols of timeless Paris. The choice of the district and its Aux 2 Moulins as the location of the movie *Amélie* was no accident. On either side of Le Lux-Bar (frequented by Bernard Dimey, poet and songwriter), the stores of rue Lepic still display all the charm of Old Paris. In fact, this goes for the whole of the eighteenth, cherished by the great poet and novelist Blaise Cendrars, who wrote *The Prose of the Transsiberian* here, and came to the Lapin Agile to remember his lost youth. Novelist Patrick Modiano held court in Elyette's bar, Au Rêve, while Jacques Prévert and Marcel Aymé rubbed shoulders with the painters in the Bateau Lavoir. Writers Claude Klotz (pen name Patrick Cauvin) and Serge Lentz (author of *The Sandwich Years*) are regular visitors to the market between rue des Abbesses and rue Caulaincourt. Novelist Olivier Châteauneuf (a.k.a. Robert Sabatier) hops down the steps of the butte de Montmartre to taste the nostalgic air of rue Labat and raise a glass at Aux Négociants, Jean Navier's place in rue Lambert. Montmartre is still an artists' village and its inhabitants unsuspecting poets, including its artisans of edibles and old-fashioned innkeepers, who are figures of Parisian tradition whatever their age.

RESTAURANTS

GOOD RESTAURANTS & OTHERS

● A. Beauvilliers ○ V.COM

52, rue Lamarck
Métro: Lamarck-Caulaincourt
Tel. 01 42 55 05 42. Fax 01 42 55 05 87
www.abeauvilliers.com
Closed Sunday lunch, Christmas.
Open until 10:30 PM.
Prix fixe: 25€ (lunch), 35€ (lunch),
45€ (dinner), 63€. A la carte: 65€.
Air cond. Terrace. Private dining room.
Valet parking.

This restaurant, named after Antoine de Beauvilliers, steward of the Count of Provence, was founded in 1974 by Edouard Carlier, who made it the hub of Paris society in Montmartre. A very picturesque establishment, it needs a young chef with audacity and talent to spare. Now it has found one, in the shape of Yohann Paran, trained by Alain Passard and the Conticini brothers, and formerly at Le Restaurant de la Garde in the fifteenth arrondissement. In a refined setting that still displays touches of the past, we let the enthusiastic young dining room staff guide us through the wonderfully fresh menu, a blend of tradition and innovation. The crunchy crab appetizer with cumin, celery and black radish in rémoulade sauce with smoked egg vinaigrette, the grilled scallops in Indian vaduvan spices served with risotto-style rice, the sautéed farm-raised veal chop with stewed winter vegetables and a brioche pain perdu with apples and spices served with baked-apple ice cream all live up to their promises.

● La Bonne Table ⓝ SIM

94, rue des Martyrs
Métro: Abbesses, Pigalle
Tel. 01 46 06 50 73
Closed lunch, Tuesday, 2 weeks in beginning of August. Open until 11:30 PM.
Prix fixe: 15€ (lunch), 19,50€.
A la carte: 55€.

Jean-Louis Huclin, an old acquaintance from Paris's Left Bank who once trained with Manière, paid a lightning visit to the kitchen of this amiable local bistro. Now that he has left again for L'Oeillade, La Bonne Table's future seems uncertain. A pity, since Aline Monselet's welcome and the deftly prepared domestic dishes were highly appealing. Will the steamed foie gras, salmon carpaccio, sea bream baked in a salt crust, Michou's stuffed tomatoes (named after a famous food-loving neighbor) and grilled duck breast with peaches still be there next season? We shall see.

● Le Bouclard SIM

1, rue Cavalotti
Métro: Place-de-Clichy
Tel.-Fax 01 45 22 60 01
michel.bouclard@wanadoo.fr
www.bouclard.com
Closed Sunday, Monday, Christmas, August.
Open until 10:30 PM.
Prix fixe: 20€ (lunch), 45€.
A la carte: 60€.
Air cond.

Cooking is a family business for the Bonnemorts. Rosalie, Michel's great grandmother, was an incomparable cook. Now he carries on the tradition in this old-fashioned restaurant, which brings a touch of the countryside to the back street where it stands, not far from place de Clichy. His frankness and love of fine produce lend the place character. We succumb to the delights of the homemade foie gras with small potatoes and truffle oil, gratin of crayfish tails with white Macon wine, farm-raised chicken with tarragon and a dark chocolate fondant, all accompanied by selected wines.

● Au Clair de la Lune COM

9, rue Poulbot
Métro: Abbesses
Tel. 01 42 58 97 03. Fax 01 42 55 64 74
Closed Sunday, Monday lunch, mid-August–mid-September. Open until 10:30 PM.
Prix fixe: 30€. A la carte: 50€.

We visit Alain Kerfant's establishment as much for the Montmartre ambience as for the reliable, traditional menu. Tourists and local inhabitants enjoy their visit here under the eye of Poulbot, the Montmartre street urchin, star of this antique bistro's wall frescos. We never tire of the quick-seared sliced foie gras, fresh mackerel marinated in muscadet, salmon in champagne sauce, grilled beef tenderloin with truffle and foie gras, and iced nougat with raspberry coulis.

● **Le Cottage Marcadet**   `COM`

151 bis, rue Marcadet
Métro: Lamarck-Caulaincourt
Tel. 01 42 57 71 22
www.cottagemarcadet.com
Closed Sunday, Monday, Easter, August.
Open until 10 PM.
Prix fixe: 24,50€ (lunch), 32€.
A la carte: 75€.
Air cond.

This is one of the coziest restaurants at the foot of the butte de Montmartre, with its twenty seats and warm decor. In both dining room and kitchen, Cyril Choisne steers a course between regional cuisine and gastronomy. Fried frog's legs with creamy risotto and parsley mousse, oven-roasted lobster served with large-grain couscous and spring vegetables, sea-salt-rubbed rack of lamb served with a sweetbread and salsify ragout in a smoky jus or, finally, millefeuille with delicate apple cream and green apple sorbet are polished works indeed. The two set menus are well chosen.

● **Le Diapason**   `N` `V.COM`

Terrass Hotel, 12/14, rue Joseph-de-Maistre
Métro: Abbesses, Blanche, Place-de-Clichy
Tel. 01 44 92 34 00. Fax 01 44 92 34 30
seminaire@terrass-hotel.com
www.terrass-hotel.com
Closed Saturday lunch, Sunday evening, August. Open until 10:30 PM.
Prix fixe: 28€ (lunch). A la carte: 55€.
Air cond. Terrace. Private dining room.

There have been changes at this opulent hotel opposite Montmartre cemetery. The house restaurant has been modernized and now boasts a refined, modern decor, all in sand, gray and black. The new chef,

Julien Roucheteau (who studied under Philippe Legendre, then Michel Troisgros at the Lancaster), has taken over the kitchen with gusto. Crispy Oriental-style kebab, vegetables from Joël Thiébaut's market in a warm tapenade and olive oil dip, fish cooked in a Staub Dutch oven with crunchy fresh peas, glazed pork chop and well-made desserts (rhubarb and mango tartlet, berries and lemon verbena sorbet) make an excellent impression. All these earn full points and mean a quality restaurant in this neighborhood spot at the foot of the butte de Montmartre once again.

● **La Divette du Moulin**   `SIM`

98, rue Lepic
Métro: Abbesses, Lamarck-Caulaincourt
Tel. 01 46 06 34 84
Open daily until 11:30 PM.
A la carte: 45€.
Private dining room.

This bistro institution opposite Le Moulin de la Galette carries on dependably in the hands of the Duplan brothers. Its paneled setting has a nautical flavor. At the stove, Cyrille Van Denawaelle keeps everything on an even keel with his assorted antipasti, grilled swordfish steak with guacamole, Provençal calf's liver with onions, tomatoes and peppers and soft chocolate cake all served in a warm, relaxed ambience.

● **Le Doudingue**   `N` `SIM`

24, rue Durantin
Métro: Abbesses
Tel. 01 42 54 88 08
doudingue@chiello.fr
Closed lunch (except on weekends), Christmas, 3 weeks in August.
Open until 2 AM (Sunday 8 PM).
Prix fixe: 22€ (on weekdays), 28€ (dinner), 32€ (dinner).
Air cond. Private dining room.

A cozy, lounge-style atmosphere, plump cushions and soft music set the tone in this hushed establishment. The passably deft cuisine includes layered terrine of foie gras and artichoke hearts, Provençal-style red mullet filet, chicken breast with honey and red berry cheesecake, accompanied by wines from the New World (a pleasant Merlot from Chile). The Sunday brunch has its aficionados.

● L'Entracte
Chez Sonia et Carlos   SIM

44, rue d'Orsel
Métro: Anvers, Abbesses
Tel. 01 46 06 93 41
chiriaux@aol.com
Closed Sunday evening, Monday, Tuesday, Christmas, Easter, August.
Open until 10:30 PM.
A la carte: 40–50€.
Terrace.

Legendary drag cabaret owner Michou is the star guest in this local bistro, where he pays neighborly visits to Gilles Chiriaux, who officiates in the dining room and at the stove. This is a popular address for lovers of fine cuisine, so remember to reserve. The products are first rate and delicately prepared. Head cheese, mackerel in white wine, skate in brown butter, rack of lamb, Norman-style veal kidneys, fresh fruit tart and chocolate mousse are classics that never stale.

● L'Eté en Pente Douce   SIM

23, rue Muller
Métro: Anvers
Tel. 01 42 64 02 67. Fax 01 46 06 37 08
leteenpentedouce@wanadoo.fr
www.parisrestos.com
Open daily until 11:30 PM.
A la carte: 30–35€.
Terrace.

On the edge of the Montmartre village, just at the foot of the butte de Montmartre, this bistro lives up to its promises. The terrace is very pleasant when the weather is fine. We could spend hours there in the shade of its canopy, or warm as toast in winter within the restaurant's anise green walls. In any season, we enjoy the cured ham on the bone, John Dory fish with fresh figs and the chocolate walnut fondant.

● L'Etrier   SIM

154, rue Lamarck
Métro: Guy-Môquet (exit Lamarck)
Tel. 01 42 29 14 01. Fax 01 46 27 19 15
Closed Monday, 3 weeks in August.
Open until 10 PM.
Prix fixe: 18€ (lunch), 20€ (lunch), 35€ (dinner). A la carte: 40€.
Air cond.

If you come by Métro and take the right exit (rue Lamarck), you cannot miss stumbling over L'Etrier. You will be enchanted by Jean-Philippe Colin's welcome and his invaluable advice on the choice of wine. Thierry Facheaux's cuisine, dedicated to market produce, charms us with its sautéed snails and white cabbage with roasted garlic, scorpion fish parmentier with fresh tomato and chive sauce and veal piccata with mushrooms and basil. The blanc-manger, served with vanilla caramel, is to die for.

● La Famille   SIM

41, rue des Trois-Frères
Métro: Abbesses
Tel.-Fax 01 42 52 11 12
Closed Sunday (except for first Sunday of each month), Monday, last 3 weeks in August. Open until 11 PM.
Prix fixe: 29€, 35€, 50€.
A la carte: 30–35€.
Air cond.

This hip establishment in the Abbesses quarter now has a "ping-pong" evening on the first Sunday of each month. This amusing concept involves bringing in a guest chef to work with La Famille's in a gripping exercise of culinary creativity. On the other days of the week, the daring menu here features combinations that sometimes work and sometimes do not. The oyster cakes with crispy vegetables, nori seaweed and coriander "cappuccino," the special mackerel dish, the terrine of duck confit topped with a light purple purée and a deconstructed lemon tart with lemon verbena jus leave us rather cold.

● **La Galère des Rois**   SIM

8, rue Cavallotti
Métro: Place-de-Clichy, La Fourche
Tel. 01 42 93 34 58
Closed Saturday lunch, Sunday lunch,
August. Open until 11 PM.
Prix fixe: 12,50€ (lunch), 15€ (lunch).
A la carte: 38€.
Terrace. Private dining room.

Samy Khidas has just taken over this restaurant. He is following in his predecessors' footsteps, as is new chef François Torino. The decor is still rustic and the menu is built around trusted standards, such as foie gras and egg baked in a ramekin, country-style salad, salmon grilled on one side, Duval andouillette baked in parchment served with garlicky potatoes fried in duck fat and a pear charlotte with raspberry coulis and crème anglais.

● **Chez Grisette**   SIM

14, rue Houdon
Métro: Abbesses, Pigalle
Tel.-Fax 01 42 62 04 80
Closed lunch, Saturday, Sunday, New Year's,
May 1st, August. Open until 11:30 PM.
Prix fixe: 23€, 29€. A la carte: 35–40€.

Régine Dumas, a.k.a. Grisette, favors the bistro manner. The decor with its wine racks goes hand in hand with the family cuisine. We enjoy the pounti du Cantal (a spinach, prune and bacon terrine), boudin with applesauce and potato purée, veal hanger steak in shallot and white wine sauce with a side of potato gratin and rice pudding with salted-butter caramel. The dishes on the blackboard change with the seasons and market, and the wines will bring roses to your cheeks.

● **Histoire de . . .**   SIM

14, rue Ferdinand-Flocon
Métro: Jules-Joffrin
Tel. 01 42 52 24 60
Closed lunch, 1 week in August.
Open until 11 PM.
A la carte: 38€.

Alain Bourrouilhou has taken over this lively bistro just a stone's throw from the Mairie of the eighteenth arrondissement. The cuisine is domestic but updated and light, the prices well behaved and the atmosphere snug. At dinner only, we come to savor the marinated sea bream escabeche, delicate ratatouille and fried salmon cake, quickly seared beef tartare with shrimp tartare, braised andouillet parmentier and raspberry spring rolls with chocolate, black pepper and ginger coulis. In brief, a variety of amusing dishes that do you a world of good.

● **Kokolion**   €SIM

62, rue d'Orsel
Métro: Abbesses, Pigalle
Tel. 01 42 58 24 41
Closed lunch, Sunday, Monday.
Open until 12:30 PM.
Prix fixe: 24€. A la carte: 40–50€.
Air cond.

Very close to the Théâtre de l'Atelier, Kokolion welcomes diners until late. Red drapes and woodwork set the scene and the food is on a par with the decor. Foie gras with Armagnac and Espelette chili pepper, monkfish in a tomato and brandy sauce, herb-crusted rack of lamb and a warm thin-crust apple tart flambéed with rum and served with Malaga wine ice cream is good to the last bite. The wine list lives up to its promises.

● **Le Maquis**   SIM

69, rue Caulaincourt
Métro: Lamarck-Caulaincourt
Tel.-Fax 01 42 59 76 07
www.lemaquis-montmartre.com
Closed Sunday. Open until 10 PM.
Prix fixe: 15€ (lunch), 20€ (dinner),
30€ (dinner). A la carte: 38€.
Terrace.

This local bistro takes its name from the rag pickers' camp that once stood on the spot now occupied by the neighboring avenue Junot. Since 1981, the Lesages have been running it with modesty and diligence. The dishes are refined and domestic. We savor the roquefort turnover, homemade foie gras, sauteed scallops and a divine cod brandade. The chocolate charlotte and caramelized cream-filled cream puffs are childhood delights. The terrace fills up as soon as the sun shows its face.

● La Mascotte Ⓢ 🏠 SIM

52, rue des Abbesses
Métro: Abbesses, Blanche
Tel. 01 46 06 28 15. Fax 01 42 23 93 83
mascotte.montmartre@wanadoo.fr
www.la-mascotte-montmartre.com
Open daily until 11:30 PM.
Prix fixe: 17,50€ (lunch on weekdays),
29€. A la carte: 37€.
Terrace.

No luck this year in this rue des Abbesses institution, which has been serving food and drink since 1889. Dried-out snails, overcooked pistachio-studded poached sausage, limp sea bass baked in salt and braised lamb shank served with sticky mashed potatoes were quite unappetizing on our last visit. A pity. We still like the workingmen's brasserie setting with its art deco inlay and mirrors, zinc bar, oysters, appealing ambience and Berthillon ice cream.

● Le Moulin de la Galette COM

83, rue Lepic
Métro: Abbesses, Blanche
Tel. 01 46 06 84 77. Fax 01 46 06 84 78
Closed Sunday, Monday. Open until 11 PM.
Prix fixe: 25€ (lunch, wine included).
A la carte: 55–60€.
Air cond. Terrace. Valet parking.

Lured by the strains of accordion music, we eagerly enter this sunny rejuvenated windmill. The goat cheese and bell pepper appetizer, sea bream filet with slow-cooked vegetables, rack of Pyrénées lamb with blackcurrant mustard and sage-flavored wheat risotto and roasted banana with aged rum syrup and ginger sorbet find their inspiration in the South of France, which also provides the wines, which can be enjoyed by the glass.

● No Problemo SIM

21, rue André-del-Sarte
Métro: Anvers, Château-Rouge
Tel.-Fax 01 42 54 39 38
Closed Sunday. Open until 11 PM.
A la carte: 35€.
Terrace.

Far from the crowds of tourists scaling the butte de Montmartre, this little bistro offers a tasty, market-based cuisine orchestrated by the discreet, efficient Nathalie Villard. We have no complaints about the foie gras, skate with capers, hand-chopped beef tartare, big steak (450 g), crème brûlée nor the soft chocolate cake, suitable sustenance for patrons about to take on the flight of steps leading up to Sacré Cœur.

● Le Perroquet Vert COM

7, rue Cavallotti
Métro: Place-de-Clichy, La-Fourche
Tel. 01 45 22 49 16
www.perroquet-vert.com
Closed Saturday lunch, Sunday.
Open until 10:30 PM.
Prix fixe: 12,50€ (lunch), 15€ (lunch),
25€. A la carte: 35€.
Terrace.

This "Green Parrot", where Didier Guy looks after the kitchen and Laurent Teboul the dining room, has had a facelift. The decor, with its light wood shades and fireplace, has been renovated. As for the cuisine, the menu tends toward deft tradition. The baked saint-marcellin cheese on an apple and potato cake, snail ravioli with piperade (a bell pepper and egg stew), roasted red mullet with herbed jus, a thick steak with béarnaise sauce and hand-cut French fries, the pears poached in red wine and orange and the rosemary crackling with fromage blanc sorbet fail to disappoint, especially since the prices have come down.

● A la Pomponnette 🏠 SIM
42, rue Lepic
Métro: Blanche, Abbesses
Tel. 01 46 06 08 36. Fax 01 42 52 95 44
alapomponnette@hotmail.com
Closed Sunday, Monday lunch, August.
Open until midnight.
Prix fixe: 18€ (lunch), 32€.
A la carte: 45€.
Terrace.

This Montmartre institution has barely changed since it was founded by Arthur Delcroix in 1909. Three generations later, Arthur's descendants are still very much in evidence, led by the founder's grand-daughter, Claude Moureau. In a changeless decor of marble, banquettes, pillars and pictures, including some by Poulbot, who was a friend of the house, we enjoy spirited dishes including the rabbit terrine in tar-ragon jelly, house-style hot marrow bones on toast, grenadier filet baked in parch-ment with diced vegetables, Armagnac-flambéed veal kidneys and sweetbreads and a crispy millefeuille.

● Au Poulbot Gourmet 🏠 SIM
39, rue Lamarck
Métro: Lamarck-Caulaincourt
Tel. 01 46 06 86 00. Fax 01 46 06 63 14
Closed Sunday, 3 weeks in August.
Open until 10 PM.
Prix fixe: 18€ (lunch), 36€ (wine included).
A la carte: 50–55€.

Jean-Paul Langevin, long the master of this authentic bistro with its 19th-century stucco, has handed over to Renaud Laudi-geois. The place remains reliable, even if the prices have risen slightly, and there can be no complaints about the skate salad in pesto dressing, asparagus in mousseline sauce, monkfish with honey and lime, nor the veal tenderloin with Banyuls wine and raisins. The raspberry macaron and tarte Bourdaloue (pear and marzipan) deserve a special mention.

● Le Square ● SIM
227 bis, rue Marcadet
Métro: Guy-Môquet
Tel. 01 53 11 08 41. Fax 01 42 81 17 14
Closed Sunday, Monday, weekend of August 15th. Open until 10:30 PM.
Prix fixe: 17€ (lunch), 13€ (lunch).
A la carte: 30€.
Terrace.

This little bistro's interior courtyard and garden, well-chosen produce and enthusi-astic welcome make it a restaurant to re-member. The Swiss chard and cantal cheese spring rolls, mackerel with pre-served lemon, Sicilian eggplant stew and caramelized tomatoes, top rump steak with oyster mushrooms and organic po-tato gratin with tonka beans and the tapi-oca and coconut milk pudding with spiced mangoes are very affordable delights. The lunchtime set menus are a steal.

● La Table d'Hélène SIM
14, rue Duc
Métro: Jules-Joffrin
Tel. 01 46 06 49 68
Closed Sunday, Monday, mid-July–beginning of August. Open until 10 PM.
Prix fixe: 13€ (lunch), 27€.
A la carte: 30–40€.

Hélène Poitevin, a native of Saumur who trained with Ferrandi, is hospitable to a fault. She also has a gift for concocting ap-petizing dishes using the freshest pro-duce. We are soon persuaded by her foie gras with oyster mushrooms, assorted seafood baked under a crust and sautéed beefsteak. A special mention for the cheeses from Virginie's shop next door, on the rue Damrémont, including an amaz-ing apple-cider-marinated camembert served with plum chutney. The chocolate pudding with crème anglaise provides a sweet conclusion.

● Wepler `COM`

14, pl de Clichy
Métro: Place-de-Clichy
Tel. 01 45 22 53 24. Fax 01 44 70 07 50
wepler@wepler.com
www.wepler.com
Open daily noon–1 AM. Cont. service.
Prix fixe: 25€. A la carte: 35–65€.
Air cond. Terrace.

Admittedly, the decor of this historic brasserie has little remaining character, but the place is useful with its continuous service, pleasant welcome and, if not attentive, then at least efficient service. We have no complaints about the wide choice of seafood platters, beautiful oysters, homemade duck foie gras, sautéed scallops, Salers beef tenderloin and crème brûlée. The 25€ set menu is splendid.

INTERNATIONAL RESTAURANTS

● Taka `SIM`

1, rue Véron
Métro: Abbesses
Tel. 01 42 23 74 16
Closed lunch, Sunday, Monday, New Year's, mid-July–mid-August. Open until 10 PM.
Prix fixe: 20€. A la carte: 30–40€.

Japanese from the walls to the dishes, Okamoto Taka's restaurant is as charming as ever. Red tables, screens and kite lanterns set the scene. On the menu are squid with sea urchin cream and fermented soybeans, shrimp and vegetable tempura, smoked eel maki, a Japanese-style fondue with thinly sliced beef, chicken and vegetables cooked tableside in hot duck stock flavored with seaweed, as well as sushi, sashimi and red beans with green tea ice cream. Mouthwatering!

● Le Village Kabyle `COM`

4, rue Aimé-Lavy (at rue du Mont-Cenis).
Métro: Jules-Joffrin
Tel. 01 42 55 03 34. Fax 01 45 86 08 35
Closed Sunday, Monday.
Open until 10:30 PM.
Prix fixe: 30€. A la carte: 35€.
Air cond.

Shops

Here, Wally Chouaki expresses the very essence of his native Kabylia. The former Foucauld company camel driver offers a friendly welcome and puts all his heart into an authentic, domestic cuisine in the shape of onion confit and tomatoes, spiced carrots, couscous served with farm-raised chicken, Algerian spicy beans and salted meat, couscous with tripe, and lamb ragout with olives and lemon, not to mention the final touch: the indispensable house pastries and mint tea.

▼ SHOPS

BREAD & BAKED GOODS

▼ Jacques Laurent

63, rue Caulaincourt
Métro: Lamarck-Caulaincourt
Tel. 01 42 64 56 11
7:45 AM–8:30 PM. Closed Thursday, Friday.
This reliable craftsman bakes a baguette made from twice-fermented dough along with traditional-style breads. The "villageoise" baguette is based on a mix of wheat and rye flour. We love the organic fig, hazelnut or apricot bread, as well as the splendid Viennese pastries.

▼ Au Pain d'Antan

2, rue Eugène-Sue
Métro: Jules-Joffrin
Tel. 01 42 64 71 78
7 AM–1 PM, 3:30–8 PM
(Saturday 7 AM–7 PM). Closed Sunday,
1 month July–August.
In this 1900s' bakery where the baking is done in a Roman oven, Sylvain Hary supplies bread with bacon, olive focaccia, poppy seed, sesame, cumin, rye and multigrain breads, country-style apple tart and prune turnovers.

▼ Au Pétrin d'Antan

174, rue Ordener
Métro: Porte-de-St-Ouen, Guy-Môquet
Tel. 01 46 27 01 46. Fax 01 42 29 09 67
7:30 AM–8 PM (Sunday 7:45 AM–1:30 PM,
4–8 PM). Closed Monday, 3 weeks in
July–August.

Customers can watch Michel Galloyer and Benjamin Vardanega at work in their store. The window in the wall and open oven provide an excellent view as they bake their crusty baguettes and rustic loaves. Sandwiches and fruit tarts are first rate.

BAKED GOODS & PASTRIES

▼ Arnaud Delmontel

57, rue Damrémont
Métro: N.-D.-de-Lorette
Tel. 01 42 64 59 63
7 AM–8:30 PM. Closed Sunday afternoon, Monday, 2 weeks in August.

Arnaud Delmontel, star baker on the ninth arrondissement side of rue des Martyrs, has carefully renovated this store, which offers a "Renaissance" baguette with coarse sea salt, focaccia, kugelhopf, jam beignets and puff pastry lemon cake.

WINE

▼ Caves Dargent   🅝

176, rue Ordener
Métro: Guy-Môquet, Jules-Joffrin
Tel. 01 42 28 80 79
www.cavesdargent.com
10 AM–1 PM, 3:30–8 PM
(Saturday 10 AM–8 PM).
Closed Sunday afternoon, Monday.

Jean-Luc Dargent and Dominique Tissier run this cellar with gusto. Low prices with reliable quality is the house motto, applied throughout a range of more than 600 organic and natural wines. There is a tasting every month on a Saturday morning, hosted by Cyril Sagot.

▼ Les Caves du Roy

31, rue Simart
Métro: Marcadet-Poissonniers
Tel. 01 42 23 99 11
10 AM–1:30 PM. 3–8:30 PM
(Saturday 10 AM– 8:30 PM).
Closed Sunday, Monday morning.

In this delightful cellar, Jean-Luc Tucoulat presents his favorite vintages, which have a charming scent of the South of France. Fifty whiskeys and a hundred vodkas complete the selection. Seasonal tastings with the growers.

CHARCUTERIE

▼ Michel Langlois

20, rue Lepic
Métro: Blanche
Tel. 01 46 06 73 63
8 AM–1 PM, 4–8 PM.
Closed Sunday afternoon, August.

Charcuterie king of the steep rue Lepic, Michel Langlois supplies mouthwatering pig liver pâté from Berry, parsleyed ham terrine or cured ham on the bone, boudin and duck liver mousse. His rabbit or goose rillettes are splendid.

CHEESE

▼ Fromagerie Lepic

20, rue Lepic
Métro: Blanche
Tel. 01 46 06 90 97
8 AM–1 PM, 3:30–8 PM
(Saturday 8 AM–8 PM).
Closed Sunday afternoon, Monday.

Jean Sanles and Bruno Borel enthusiastically present cheeses from every region of France. Fruity beaufort, aged comté, brebis and chèvres, époisses, Mont-d'Or vacherin and artisinal roquefort, not to mention a superb camembert.

▼ Fromagerie de Montmartre

9, rue du Poteau
Métro: Jules-Joffrin
Tel. 01 46 06 26 03
8:30 AM–1 PM, 4–7:45 PM
(Saturday 1:30 PM–7:45 PM).
Closed Sunday afternoon, Monday.

The ubiquitous Marie and Alain Quatrehomme of rue du Cherche-Midi are behind this spirited store, which offers brebis and chèvres, langres, camembert, Alpine beaufort, cantal and tomme aged to the peak of perfection.

▼ Chez Virginie

54, rue Damrémont
Métro: Lamarck-Caulaincourt
Tel. 01 46 06 76 54. Fax 01 42 52 85 69
9 AM–1 PM, 4–8 PM
(Sunday 10 AM–1 PM).
Closed Sunday afternoon,
Monday morning, August.

Virginie Boularouah, who was our Cheesemonger of the Year, presents the best farmhouse quality cheeses in her store. This charming craftswoman is fond of goat cheese (but not exclusively). She offers a fine selection of cheeses from all over France: Her coulommiers with sage, Termignon bleu, mountain tomme, aged comté, Alpine beaufort and herbed saint-nectaire are all mouthwatering.

ICE CREAM

▼ La Butte Glacée

14, rue Norvins
Métro: Lamarck-Caulaincourt, Abbesses
Tel. 01 42 23 91 58
10 AM–7 PM (Friday, Saturday, Sunday
10 AM–midnight). Summer: 10 AM–11 PM.
Closed mid-November–end of December,
beginning of January–beginning of February.
Pascal Vezinet runs this apparently unremarkable store offering exquisite flavors Praliné chocolate "rocks", vanilla ice cream with shaved chocolate, wild fruit sabayon and tiramisu provide a taste of delight.

PASTRIES

▼ Arnaud Larher

53, rue Caulaincourt
Métro: Lamarck-Caulaincourt
Tel. 01 42 57 68 08. Fax 01 42 57 68 22
www.arnaud-larher.com
10 AM–7:30 PM. Closed Sunday, Monday,
1 week in February, August.
Arnaud Larher's cakes and pastries combine innovation and tradition. His praliné eclairs, caramelized pineapple tart, gingerbread, fruit tea loaves, jams, savory petits fours, "pains surprises" (a round, hollowed-out loaf of bread filled with layered sandwiches) and pretty orange blossom cookies are all splendid.

▼ Les Petits Mitrons

26, rue Lepic
Métro: Blanche
Tel. 01 46 06 10 29. Fax 01 46 06 96 00
7:30 AM–1:30 PM, 3–8 PM.
Closed Wednesday, 1 week in February,
2 weeks in August.

Rendezvous

This cutesy store offers classic cakes and pastries with a childhood flavor. We adore the orange, pear, raspberry or rhubarb tarts, as well as the savory basil, spinach, cantal cheese or leek and smoked salmon tarts. The financiers, coffee- or chocolate-cream puffs and millefeuilles will have you melting.

COFFEE

▼ Brûlerie de Montmartre

66, rue Damremont
Métro: Lamarck-Caulaincourt
Tel. 01 42 54 26 29
9:45 AM–1 PM, 3:30–8 PM (Sunday
10:30 AM–1 PM). Closed Monday.
Frédéric Dorbusth supplies no less than 120 types of tea and more than twenty coffees, including Ethiopian Moka Sidamo and Jamaican Blue Mountain. You will also find honeys, jams, cookies and madeleines here. On Sunday, between 11 a.m. and 1 p.m., the tasting area puts on shows of poetic song, fashion and even calligraphy.

◆ RENDEZVOUS

BARS

◆ Chào Bà Café

22, bd de Clichy
Métro: Pigalle
Tel. 01 46 06 72 90. Fax 01 42 51 81 02
8:30 AM–2 AM (Thursday, Friday, Saturday
9 AM–5 AM). Open daily.
Chào Bà means "Hello, Madam" in Vietnamese, but men are just as welcome in this café with its neo-colonial decor. The atmosphere is convivial, the exotic dishes are flavorsome (Peking duck, spring rolls, pancakes) and there is a wide variety of drinks.

◆ Terrass Hôtel

12-14, rue Joseph-de-Maistre
Métro: Place-de-Clichy
Tel. 01 46 06 72 85. Fax 01 42 52 29 11
5 PM–1 AM (Sunday midnight).
Air cond.

At the foot of the butte de Montmartre and a step away from Sacré Coeur, this hotel offers an unobstructed view of Paris from its 7th floor. On the first floor, the Diapason serves fine market-based dishes. (Also see "Restaurants").

PUBS

◆ Le Carolus

130, bd de Clichy (ground floor)
Métro: Place-de-Clichy
Tel. 01 45 22 34 20
7 AM–4 AM. Open daily.

This modern pub serves a wide range of beers to accompany mussels with French fries and various snacks at any hour of the night. Very practical between two movie shows at the neighboring Wepler.

WINE BARS

◆ Au Bon Coin

49, rue des Cloys
Métro: Jules-Joffrin
Tel. 01 46 06 91 36
7:30 AM–11 PM (Saturday 7 AM–6 PM).
Closed Sunday, August.

The capable Jean-Louis Bras runs this typical local bistro where the menu is pinned up next to the bar. Some dishes are marked up regularly: shepherd's pie, veal blanquette, beef bourguignon. To wash them down, he serves delicious Corbières, Saint Véran and Côtes de Blaye.

◆ Café Burq

6, rue Burq
Métro: Abbesses
Tel. 01 42 52 81 27
6 PM–2 AM. Closed Sunday,
Christmas–New Year's.

A delicious haunt with its selected wines, contemporary setting and cheerful dishes. Patrick Bouin is inspired by Mediterranean cuisine. His tapas, sardine rillettes and grilled calamari are appetizing indeed.

◆ La Cave des Abbesses

43, rue des Abbesses
Métro: Abbesses
Tel. 01 42 52 81 54
5:30–9:30 PM (Saturday, Sunday noon–
9:30 PM). Closed Monday.

We drop in to try new wines and find ourselves sampling a glass and nibbling on a plate of assorted cheeses or foie gras. The proprietor provides invaluable advice and we are delighted as we set off again with a bottle in our hand.

◆ La Cave à Jojo

26, rue des Trois-Frères
Métro: Abbesses
Tel. 01 42 62 58 54
5 PM–2 AM. Closed Sunday.

Jojo is Joël Thibaut, who offers a warm welcome in his quiet café. Cured ham on the bone, toasted croque-monsieur on Poilâne bread or a daily special—calf's head, for instance —provide a wonderful accompaniment for a Domaine des Lauribert Côtes du Rhône or a Château Petit Boyer Côtes de Blaye.

◆ Le Colibri

35, rue Véron
Métro: Abbesses
Tel. 01 46 06 07 90
10 AM–1:30 AM (Tuesday 7 PM).
Closed Monday.

Thierry Campion, who runs the neighboring Mascotte, has turned the Colibri into his own special establishment. The place is snug, the choice of wines level headed (an exquisite Domaine du Vissoux Beaujolais) and tartines or dishes from Auvergne (stuffed veal brisket, stuffed cabbage) go down without a hitch.

◆ Aux Négociants

27, rue Lambert
Métro: Lamarck-Caulaincourt, Jules-Joffrin,
Château-Rouge
Tel. 01 46 06 15 11. Fax 01 42 62 97 35
Noon–2:30 PM, 7 PM–10:30 PM.
Closed Saturday, Sunday, August.

This little bistro with its horseshoe-shaped zinc counter has plenty of character. Jean Navier, a native of the Sarthe, presents his Jasnières, along with duck rillettes, pâtés and terrines, boned and stuffed pig's foot and apple tart.

Le Sancerre

35, rue des Abbesses
Métro: Abbesses
Tel. 01 42 58 08 20 / 01 42 58 47 05
7 AM–2 AM. Open daily.

This appealing café near Montmartre is always packed. Patrons drink wines by the glass (and not only Sancerre) and nibble salads, grilled duck breast, duck confit, tartines on Poilâne bread or apple crumble.

CAFES

◆ Au Rêve   🏠

89, rue Caulaincourt
Métro: Lamarck-Caulaincourt
Tel. 01 46 06 20 87
Noon–2 AM. Closed Sunday, Monday,
All Saint's Day, Christmas–New Year's,
end of July–end of August.

Writers Simenon, Céline, Cendrars and Marcel Aymé were regular visitors in this bar, with its engraved glass, stucco and ceramics. A favorite haunt of cartoonist Claire Brétécher, it has lost none of its character in the hands of Elyette. The assorted cheese and charcuterie plates are washed down with Preis Sauvignon, Marionnet Gamay and Trocard Bordeaux

◆ Aux 2 Moulins   🏠

15, rue Lepic
Métro: Abbesses, Blanche
Tel. 01 42 54 90 50
cafedes2moulins@wanadoo.fr
7 AM–2 AM. Open daily.

This café became a legend when it featured in hit French movie *Amélie*. Director Jean-Paul Jeunet is a neighbor and drops in from time to time. The food is plain (steak tartare, toasted ham and cheese sandwich, omelet and veal blanquette).

◆ Francis Labutte

122, rue Caulaincourt
Métro: Lamarck-Caulaincourt
Tel. 01 42 23 58 26. Fax 01 42 52 94 06
8 AM–2 AM. Open daily.

Not far from Abbesses, this is an amiable establishment indeed. After an exhausting climb, we feel we have earned a thirst-quenching drink. We like the tartines and generous salads.

◆ Le Lux-Bar   🏠

12, rue Lepic
Métro: Blanche
Tel. 01 46 06 05 15
7 AM–2 AM.
Closed Sunday evening, Monday.

Its ceramics hidden under a cloak of souvenir photos, the Lux-Bar still has a touch of its former magic from the days when Bernard Dimey, author of *Syracuse*, was a regular. Patrons enjoy tartines on Poilâne bread and grilled meats under the attentive eye of new proprietor Laurent Lopez.

TEA SALONS

◆ Drôle d'Endroit pour   🅝
une Rencontre

46, rue Caulaincourt
Métro: Lamarck-Caulaincourt
10 AM–1:30 AM.
Closed Monday, 3 weeks in August.

The team at this tearoom full of bric-a-brac can be proud. Attracted by its welcoming atmosphere, customers come to read a book, play cards or chat. The menu ranges from bizarre cocktails to a grilled Guinea-fowl sausage—in other words, something for everyone.

19TH ARRONDISSEMENT
LA VILLETTE NOSTALGIA

So what remains of La Villette and its butchers, its carcasses bloodying white aprons and its restaurants for heroic appetites, all part of a vanished heritage (with the exception of Au Boeuf Couronné, revived by Gérard Joulie)? Where the slaughterhouses once stood, a futuristic citadel devoted to science, music and games for the children of today has been raised. Further down, the Buttes-Chaumont park (the green lung of East Paris) has lost none of its rustic poetry. Neither has avenue Simon-Bolivar or rue Botzaris, offering an approach to true provincial France. In short, this is the perfect place to get some air, stroll, daydream and generally recharge your batteries. Around quai de la Seine, the Canal Saint-Martin has enjoyed a makeover, suggesting a now modern, but still multifarious, charming and deceptive nineteenth. The new La Villette is lined with futuristic hotels. Here, the best way to familiarize yourself with the arrondissement is to stroll around it. The few cafés with terraces (Café de la Musique, Rendez-Vous des Quais) warrant a visit when the sun shines, and there are plenty of first-rate artisans worth inspecting (do you know Véronique Mauclair's bakery, Couderc's cakes and pastries and the Duthil delicatessen?). The few good restaurants here (La Cave Gourmande, La Chaumière, Le Relais des Buttes) are opportunities to be grasped. The nineteenth is an oasis ripe for exploration.

● RESTAURANTS

GOOD RESTAURANTS & OTHERS

● Au Bœuf Couronné

188, av Jean-Jaurès
Métro: Porte-de-Pantin
Tel. 01 42 39 44 44. Fax 01 42 39 17 30
au.bœuf.couronne@laposte.net
www.rest-gj.com
Open daily until 10:30 PM.
Pris fixe: 32€ (wine included).
A la carte: 45–60€.
Air cond. Private dining room. Valet parking.

Bone marrow on toast to whet your appetite? Then the prime rib of beef "Villette" for two or the grilled steak with béarnaise sauce for just one? Pan-seared hanger steak or rib-eye steak with red wine and shallots, a strip steak or a thick cut of grilled beef? If there were just a single restaurant keeping our memories of the former La Villette meat market alive, it would be Au Bœuf Couronné in the hands of Gérard Joulie. He is still to be found in this rather elegant art deco setting with its air conditioning, private dining room, veranda and burgundy red and chestnut brown shades—a temple esteemed by the carnivorous. Now all that remains is to refresh ourselves with a pineapple carpaccio or crêpes with orange liqueur, and, under the spell of a great vintage, sing a verse or two of writer, poet and musician Boris Vian's *Les Joyeux Bouchers*: *"C'est le tango, des bouchers d'la Villette"* (It's the tango of La Villette's butchers).

● Brasserie de l'Auditorium SIM

Holiday Inn Paris La Villette,
216, av Jean-Jaurès
Métro: Porte-de-Pantin
Tel. 01 44 84 18 18. Fax 01 44 84 18 00
hilavillette.manager-alliance-hospitality.com
www.holidayinn-parisvillette.com
Closed Saturday, Sunday, Bank Holidays.
Open until 10:30 PM.
Prix fixe: lunch 16–26€, dinner 19–26€.
A la carte: 50€.
Air cond. Terrace.

This hotel restaurant is an oasis in the culinary desert that is the Cité de la Musique. First, because it has recently been renovated in honey-colored shades; second (and above all) because the assiduous service, reasonably priced set menus, fine wines by the glass, terrace in the summer and cuisine are more than honest. Terrine of fresh cheese with figs and cured ham, sea bream roasted with fennel, a trio of kebabs with three sauces, and crème brûlée may not be anything to write home about but will certainly deserve a mention when you get back.

● La Cave Gourmande Restaurant de Mark Singer ○ SIM

10, rue du Gal-Brunet
Métro: Botzaris
Tel.-Fax 01 40 40 03 30
lacavegourmande@wanadoo.fr
Closed Saturday, Sunday (except for group reservations), 1 week in February, 3 weeks in August. Open until 10:30 PM.
Prix fixe: 31€ (lunch), 36€.
Air cond. Private dining room.

American in Paris Mark Singer is the chef and boss of this gourmet cellar, a Special Favorite of ours last year. Does that sound strange? Well, not to worry: Mark Singer studied his rudiments and theory with some great gastronomical names—Robuchon, Coffe, Vergé, Jacques Manière—before setting up here in this delightful back street in the La Mouzaïa quarter, where he is seconded in the dining room by his wife Dominique. Creative and subtle, based on the vagaries of the market and accompanied by a French, Corsican or Chilean vintage, here are smoked haddock roll with tomato ice and oysters, cod crumble with sage and tomato, wild duck served three ways with saffron potatoes and Swiss chard, crispy banana with almond cream and carambar candies. . . . We have just one little reservation: Given the prices a la carte (you can anticipate spending 50€ a head without going wild), the service can be patchy. Does this depend on whether or not you are a "somebody"?

● **Chapeau Melon** ⓔ SIM

92, rue Rébeval
Métro: Pyrénées
Tel. 01 42 02 68 60
Closed Sunday lunch, Monday.
Open until 9 PM.
Prix fixe: 25€ (dinner). A la carte: 25–30€.

From Wednesday to Saturday and in the evening alone, with one seating at 8:30 p.m. by reservation only, Olivier Camus presides as chef, proprietor and sommelier over this friendly, rustic table d'hôte, where the surrounding wood and shades of red warm the heart, and the single set menu (two or three starters and main courses) the stomach: Japanese-style oysters from Normandy, scallop ragoût, Puy lentils with pan-seared fresh foie gras. . . . There is no dessert, except by request, but with prices this friendly, we are willing to keep our sweet tooth in check.

● **La Chaumière** COM

46, av Secrétan
Métro: Bolivar
Tel. 01 42 06 54 69. Fax 01 42 06 28 12
lachaumiere3@wanadoo.fr
Closed Friday evening, Saturday,
mid-October–end of October, 1 week at the end of July. Open until 10:30 PM.
Prix fixe: 30€ (lunch). A la carte: 60–80€.
Air cond. Terrace. Private dining room.

Guy Sassi, who serves in the dining room, has opted for contemporary elegance in this cottage (with its air conditioning, terrace and private dining room) dressed out in burgundy shades and decorated with mirrors and a barrel-shaped bar. Variations of foie gras, fish stew, beef filet medallions with foie gras and truffles and crisp layered pastry with berries and strawberry coulis are the dishes concocted by Thierry Jack-Roch, formerly in the ninth. These lively, fresh, stout offerings are expensive a la carte and deftly chosen for the set menu.

● **La Guinguette à Vapeurs** Ⓝ ⓔ SIM

211, avenue Jean-Jaurès
Métro: Porte-de-Pantin
Tel. 01 40 03 72 21. Fax 01 40 03 76 58
Open daily until 11 PM.
Prix fixe: 18€, 24€, 9€ (children).
Terrace. Private dining room.

In the heart of new wave La Villette, this *guinguette* has the wind in its sails, with its terrace by the water, attentive service, well-behaved prices and quietly modest dishes. Fried smelts, grilled tuna, leg of lamb and rabbit brochette impress us favorably. Beautiful old-fashioned desserts (shortbread fig tart, lemon meringue tart) and Loire wines that almost drink themselves.

● **Millenium Café** ⓔ COM

35, av Corentin-Cariou
Métro: Porte-de-la-Villette, Corentin-Cariou
Tel.-Fax 01 40 36 74 26
Closed dinner (except for group reservations), Sunday (except in summer).
8 AM–2 AM. Cont. service.
Prix fixe: 13,70€ (lunch). A la carte: 30€.
Terrace. Private dining room.

Nicolas Lalsingue in the galley and Cristelle Carrion at the helm: This modern bistro in yellow and burgundy has acquired a new team. When not catering to occasional group reservations, this hushed, cozy restaurant serves dishes from astute a la carte and set menus: tomato and mozzarella salad and cured Parma ham, salmon filet, penne with shrimp and garlic butter, roast prime rib, and tiramisu. We can be sure that the aficionados sipping a charming Côtes du Rhône or unusual pirate cocktail will remain loyal to the place.

● Pena Festayre   Ⓝ SIM

83, bd MacDonald
(in the courtyard of la Cité des sciences)
Métro: Porte-de-la-Villette
Tel. 01 40 05 01 38
www.festayre.com
Closed Sunday, Monday, Tuesday evening.
Open until midnight
(Friday, Saturday 2 AM).
Prix fixe: 12,90€ (lunch), 19€ (dinner),
25€ (dinner), 29€ (dinner).
A la carte: 35€.
Air cond. Terrace.

Over two floors, a bodega just as in Bayonne or Pamplona, serving tapas, squid and codfish, grilled jumbo shrimp and paella, all generously prepared and served. The place as a whole looks good. The premises are vast, the message eloquent and the wines from Southwest France. The yellow and Toulouse brick shades go well together and, for dessert, Basque cake or caramelized vanilla cake baked in fluted molds are just the thing. Unusual and flavorsome to a fault.

● La Pièce de Bœuf   SIM

7, av Corentin-Cariou
Métro: Corentin-Cariou
Tel. 01 40 05 95 95. Fax 01 40 34 67 78
lapiecedeboeuf@club-internet.fr
Closed Saturday (except for group reservations), Sunday, Bank Holidays, 1 week in February, August. Open until 10 PM.
Prix fixe: 33€. A la carte: 60€.
Air cond. Terrace.

Assisted by his wife Fabienne, Bernard Villemont has taken over this meat-eaters' establishment, whose considerable assets include a covered terrace, air conditioning, fine materials, wood and stone decor and burgundy chairs. Bernard shops at the market in Rungis, welcomes guests and takes orders, while Fabienne serves in the dining room and suggests the right wines to match the solid dishes prepared by chef Joël Dumonteil. After the sautéed oyster mushrooms, you will certainly choose the renowned chop, unless the Breton sole or the beef tenderloin with a peppercorn sauce, served with vegetables and steamed

potatoes, prove more to your taste, before a light conclusion in the form of mango carpaccio.

● Au Relais des Buttes   COM

86, rue Compans
Métro: Botzaris
Tel. 01 42 08 24 70. Fax 01 42 03 20 44
Closed Saturday lunch, Sunday,
Bank Holidays (long weekends), New Year's,
August. Open until 10 PM.
Prix fixe: 30€. A la carte: 55–70€.
Terrace. Private dining room. Valet parking.

If it were not for the valet parking, we could imagine we were in the provinces: private dining room, fireplace in the winter, veranda in the summer . . . the peace is permanent here, a step away from Buttes-Chaumont park. Marc and Marie-Ange Gautron have not gone in for high fashion. In ochre and red tones, and furnished with rattan, their inn serves fairly classical dishes at friendly prices, based on fresh produce and washed down with shrewd libations from wine-growing friends. We begin with stuffed crab with morels, followed by John Dory fish with saffron or sautéed sweetbreads with morels and concluding with a croustillant of pears and chocolate. The preparations are fresh and sharp. There you have it.

● Au Rendez-Vous de la Marine   SIM

14, quai de la Loire
Métro: Jaurès, Stalingrad
Tel. 01 42 49 33 40
Closed Sunday, Monday, New Year's,
May 1st, 1 week in August.
A la carte: 38€.
Terrace.

Things buzz and bustle in this virtually essential haunt on quai de la Seine by the Canal de la Villette, just a step or two from the new MK2 cinema. The Auvergnat café frequented by comedian Pierre Desproges has become a bohemian middle class bistro where, among the pictures of movie stars on the walls, we are welcomed by Raymond Ortiz's melodious voice and Raymond de Bergue's pleasant chow. Here, washed down with a little French wine, we find familiar homemade foie gras terrine, striped catfish with green peppercorns, a nice paella, lively apple tart flambéed with cognac. . . . Fairly friendly prices, a generous cuisine, Marcel Carné and Jacques Prévert on our minds . . . and all swift and deft enough to make it necessary to reserve!

● Zoe Bouillon
66, rue Rébeval
Métro: Pyrénées, Belleville
Tel. 01 42 02 02 83. Fax 01 42 02 02 23
www.zoebouillon.fr
Closed Sunday, Monday evening, New Year's, August. Open until 10:30 PM.
Prix fixe: 10€ (lunch), 18€ (dinner).
A la carte: 26€.
Terrace.

An ode to soup in this small, contemporary restaurant currently being renovated (this summer, the paint . . . !), where brown, vanilla and orange delight the eye and taste buds. Then in the evening, a main course and dessert too. For a few euros, your eager plate is filled with soup, fish baked in parchment paper, sautéed veal Italian style with risotto, fontainebleau (fresh cheese enhanced with whipped cream and fresh strawberries). In the hands of Frédéric Clavelle, chef and proprietor, assisted by Thierry Bourbonnais, how could this eatery fail to be a success?

▼ SHOPS

BREAD & BAKED GOODS

BAKER OF THE YEAR

▼ La Boulangerie par Véronique Mauclerc
83, rue de Crimée
Métro: Botzaris
Tel. 01 42 40 64 55. Fax 01 48 03 24 94
8 AM–8 PM. Closed Tuesday, Wednesday.
She acquired a master baker's diploma (unusual for a woman) before taking over this local store and running it with great energy. Véronique Mauclair, who bakes her bread in a wood-fired oven, uses organic flour. Apart from a brilliant crispy light baguette (some varieties made with onions and bacon), she also presents splendid Auvergnat brioches with saffron and licorice rolls, not to mention a bread with Madagascan pepper and a superb country sourdough loaf. Finally, she offers a first-rate range of fine cakes and pastries: caramelized millefeuille, a lemon tart with strawberries in a shortbread crust, a kugelhopf with orange water and at last the "Buttes Chaumont", an almond-cookie cake with bitter chocolate and a crème brûlée center. If this is not an event (and not simply in female terms) we will eat our hat . . . or even go over to the Michelin guide.

WINE

▼ Ma Cave
105, rue de Belleville
Métro: Pyrénées
Tel. 01 42 08 62 95. Fax 01 42 02 38 06
macave@wanadoo.fr
9:30 AM–1 PM, 4–7:30 PM. Closed Sunday afternoon, Monday, 1 week in February, 1 week at Easter, 3 weeks in August.
Stéphane Corazza has taken over this cellar and is carrying on the work begun by Philippe Ansot. He seeks out the finest vintages from every vineyard and promotes them vigorously. Eaux de vie and fine liqueurs also available at every price.

PASTRIES

▼ Pierre Couderc
102, av de Flandre
Métro: Crimée
Tel. 01 40 36 36 24
7:30 AM–7:30 PM (Sunday 8 AM–7 PM).
Open daily.
Pierre Couderc defends the cake- and pastry-making tradition with gusto and delights us with his tarts with chocolate and pears, golden yellow mirabelle or dark purple plums, vanilla or seasonal-fruit millefeuilles, strawberry-pistachio macarons, Valrhona guanaja chocolate, brioches, vanilla cake baked in fluted

molds as well as his splendid chocolates and exquisite candies.

▼ La Vieille France

5, av de Laumière
Métro: Laumière
Tel. 01 40 40 08 31
9 AM–8 PM (Sunday 7 PM).
Closed Monday, August.

Modeled on mom and pop's place in rue de Buci, this little store offering a thousand treats is a must for food lovers. Its Montmorency (chocolate cherry cake), dauphinois with cognac ganache and walnuts, mirliton (flaky pastry with almond cream), chocolate biscuit, lemon tart, linzertorte, "Mona Lisa" chocolate mousse, cakes and shortbread pastries are enchanting.

REGIONAL PRODUCTS

▼ Mon Oncle le Vigneron

2, rue Pradier / 71, rue Rébeval
Métro: Belleville, Pyrénées
Tel. 01 42 00 43 30
11 AM–2:30 PM, reopening at 6 PM.
Closed Sunday, Monday.

This pleasant bric-a-brac style grocery store enthusiastically promotes products from the Basque country. Artisanal charcuteries, liqueurs, eaux de vie and fine local vintages go well together. You can taste products in the store at a communal table d'hôte.

PREPARED FOOD

● Duthil

44, rue de Meaux
Métro: Bolivar, Jaurès
Tel. 01 42 02 11 13. Fax 01 42 49 19 54
8:30 AM–7:30 PM (Saturday 8 AM–
7:30 PM, Sunday 8 AM–1:30 PM).
Closed Sunday afternoon, Monday,
2 weeks in beginning of August.

Mr. Indriéri has taken over this prominent establishment with no change whatsoever to the quality or house products. The supremely fresh dishes (duck with cherries, puff pastry with lobster), pastries and desserts (chocolate ganache with caramelized apples) are harmonious indeed.

RENDEZVOUS

WINE BARS

◆ Le Bar Fleuri   ⓝ

1, rue du Plateau
Métro: Buttes-Chaumont
Tel. 01 42 08 13 38
6:30 AM–8:30 PM. Open daily.

Formica tables, wooden chairs, zinc counter and tiling set the tone in this old-fashioned bar. Joëlle and Martial, brother and sister, offer a warm welcome and serve Beaujolais and Saint Pourçain, stuffed cabbage and Morteau sausage with lentils, choice charcuterie, aged cheeses and Poilâne bread.

CAFES

◆ Café de la Musique

Cité de la Musique, 213, av Jean-Jaurès
Métro: Porte-de-Pantin
Tel. 01 48 03 15 91. Fax 01 48 03 15 18
8 AM–2 AM (Sunday, Monday 1 AM).
Open daily.

Founded by the Costes and managed by their associate Alain Boudou, this contemporary café has an elegant, timeless decor and offers fashionable cuisine. We settle in for a cocktail, a coffee, carpaccio, club sandwich, steak tartare, lamb shank, mille-feuille or profiteroles.

◆ Kaskad Café

2, pl Armand-Carrel
Métro: Bolivar, Laumière
Tel. 01 40 40 08 10
7:30 AM–2 AM. Open daily.

Opposite the Buttes-Chaumont park, we like to take our time breakfasting on beautiful toasts or savoring great drinks, fresh salads or lentils with salt pork. In the evening, we enjoy the gospel music, the piano and even the magician.

◆ Le Rendez-Vous des Quais

10, quai de la Seine
Métro: Stalingrad
Tel. 01 40 37 02 81. Fax 01 40 37 03 18
Noon–midnight. Open daily.

We are favorably impressed by this gourmet café by the La Villette basin in the MK2 cinema complex. It has a large terrace in summer and serves pleasant little dishes: The chicken curry, Aubrac sausage, Argentinean rib-eye are not badly prepared. Brunch on Sunday.

○	Very good restaurant
ⓒⓞ	Excellent restaurant
ⓒⓒⓞ	One of the best restaurants in Paris
⑤	Disappointing restaurant
☗	Good value for money
€	Meals for less than 30 euros
SIM	Simple
COM	Comfortable
V.COM	Very comfortable
LUX	Luxurious
V.LUX	Very luxurious

Red indicates a particularly charming establishment

⚑	Historical significance
⌂	Promotion *(higher rating than last year)*
Ⓝ	New to the guide

●	Restaurant
▼	Shop
◆	Rendezvous

20TH ARRONDISSEMENT
THE VILLAGERS OF BELLEVILLE

Are you a villager of Belleville, Charonne or Ménilmontant? Take a stroll through the Secrétan market, go window shopping in rue des Pyrénées or amble unhurriedly down the rustic lanes of the Saint-Blaise quarter. The delightful Charonne church has a bell tower reminiscent of those that rise over small towns in the French Vexin region. During our wanderings, we find an unusual train station buffet (La Flèche d'Or) and small whitewashed houses and welcoming terraces, a reminder of the quarter's country air. Père Lachaise cemetery is the largest aviary in the capital. Although Maurice Chevalier might fail to recognize his "Ménilmuche" (or Ménilmontant quarter), the neon signs of Belleville flirt with the lights of Tunis or Canton, bringing a touch of exoticism to the district. Place Gambetta is the kind of crossroads you might expect to find in the provincial towns of Châteauroux or Vierzon. Belleville park overlooks Paris from the end of rue des Envierges. Then, between rue Vitruve and Villa Faucheur, the poet Jacques Réda, tireless pedestrian of modern Paris, imagined how the ruins of the capital might look. The twentieth is not Rome or the Forum, but something of a fallow area: eloquent, green, uneven, hilly and rickety. A square, a market, an avenue, a boulevard, a bar with its patrons...a while ago, the twentieth almost faded into anonymity, but now it is back again, an arrondissement like a jigsaw—sinusoidal, colorful and motley.

● RESTAURANTS

GOOD RESTAURANTS & OTHERS

● Les Allobroges COM

71, rue des Grands-Champs
Métro: Maraîchers
Tel. 01 43 73 40 00. Fax 01 40 09 23 22
Closed Sunday, Monday, Bank Holidays,
1st week of November, 1 week at Easter,
end of July–end of August. Open until 10 PM.
Prix fixe: 20€, 29€, 33€.

Olivier Pateyron and his cheerful wife Annette celebrate the Allobroges, a tribe of ancient Gaul, in this East Paris village. The middle class bohemians who pack its two dining rooms in pastel tones (decor designed by Pierre-Yves Rochon, antique engravings from Granville) are right to stray from their more usual haunts. With style and refinement, the set menu presents recipes that reflect current tastes and the changing seasons: terrine of duck foie gras, smoked haddock brandade with basil, roasted duck with Banyuls wine, rum ganache-filled "cigar" pastry. The French wines are a little expensive, but the precise preparations, reliable produce and attention to degree of cooking rarely give cause for criticism.

A SPECIAL FAVORITE

● Le Baratin SIM

3, rue Jouye-Rouve
Métro: Belleville, Pyrénées
Tel. 01 43 49 39 70
Closed Saturday lunch, Sunday, 1 week in February, 1 week in May, 3 weeks in August. Open until 11 PM.
Prix fixe: 14€ (lunch). A la carte: 35€.

From Argentina and France, respectively, Raquel Carena and Philippe Pinoteau bring us lasting pleasure. No, we are not just saying that, we are still as crazy as ever about this wine bar on the slopes of Belleville, where Carena—with smoldering gaze and sure hand—cooks monkfish and galanga

Good Restaurants & Others

broth, sautéed brill with green asparagus, Breton potatoes with ginger and spring vegetables, as well as a remarkable hazelnut pudding. The wines on the blackboard scarcely begin to reflect the 200 items that Philippe Pinoteau tends to in his cellar. Make sure you reserve a table: Le Baratin has been fashionable for a long time now.

● Bistrot des Soupirs SIM

49, rue de la Chine
Métro: Gambetta
Tel. 01 44 62 93 31. Fax 01 44 62 77 83
Closed Sunday, Monday, New Year's, 10 days in the beginning of May, 3 weeks in August. Open until 10:30 PM.
Prix fixe: 17€ (lunch, except Bank Holidays). A la carte: 45€.

Those nostalgic for vintage bistros should pay a visit to this supremely kitschy blue-collar eatery, with its paneling, roughcast plaster surfaces and floor tiles standing in the heart of old Ménilmontant. Here everything is homemade to order and according to the season: lamb sweetbreads in phyllo pastry and sherry sauce, Dover sole fried in butter or line-caught sea bass roasted with fennel, roast prime rib with chanterelle mushrooms and hand-cut French fries, fromage blanc sorbet with homemade liqueur. The talented team is made up of Laurent Baujon, the demanding, perfectionist chef assisted at the stove by Gérard Gauthier, and Rudy Marton, the proprietor, who also serves in the dining room. A sigh of pleasure escapes us as we admire the fresh, generous, flavorsome produce and splendid wine list.

● Le Bœuf Gros Sel ● SIM

120, rue des Grands-Champs
Métro: Maraîchers
Tel. 01 43 73 96 58
Closed Sunday, Monday, Bank Holidays, August. Open until 10 PM.
Prix fixe: 11€ (lunch), 22€ (dinner). A la carte: 25–30€.
Terrace.

Only authentic food finds its way onto the plates in this old-style bistro, which offers true domestic cuisine: reliable, solid and faultless. Accompanied by a selected wine, all-you-can-eat salad buffet, beef pot-au-feu served with coarse salt, rib-eye steak with roquefort cheese or black peppercorn sauce and the pear and chocolate charlotte provide a generous meal. What does the decor and the bric-a-brac matter, as long as its giddy delights, affectionate prices and hospitality remain?

● **La Boulangerie**　　　　🇪SIM

15, rue des Panoyaux
Métro: Ménilmontant
Tel. 01 43 58 45 45. Fax 01 43 58 45 46
Closed Saturday lunch, Sunday,
Christmas–New Year's. Open until 11 PM.
Prix fixe: 13€ (lunch), 16€ (lunch), 30€.

Hassan at the stove, Noureddine in charge of the wines and Fabienne in the dining room have brought new life to this patinated bistro. The reliable cuisine includes pan-seared duck foie gras, pollack filet and asparagus risotto, rack of lamb roasted in a mustard crust, chocolate dessert and homemade sorbet. We should also mention the fine floor mosaic offering a view of the past, the pale woodwork on the walls (following recent renovation), the excellent selection of wines by the glass, the superb cheeses and the remarkable vegetables. What further encouragement do we need to come and take our place here one evening soon, at the foot of "Ménilmuche"?

● **Le Colimaçon (Ma Pomme)**　🇪SIM

107, rue de Ménilmontant
Métro: Ménilmontant, Gambetta
Tel. 01 40 33 10 40. Fax 01 40 33 11 50
www.encolimaçon.com
Closed Sunday. Open until midnight.
Prix fixe: 10€ (lunch). 21€ (dinner).
A la carte: 25–30€.

Climb rue de Ménilmontant and there you are, surrounded by its oak tables and chairs, warm tones and cozy lounge bar area. Each month brings its concerts and exhibition of an artist's work; each day its dishes marked up on the blackboard: salmon tartare, cod brandade, monkfish in tomato and brandy sauce, kangaroo steak in a sauce, a dark chocolate fondant with

basil, all recipes subtly concocted by Anix Amigorena and duly washed down with unpretentious wines by the glass.

● **L'Echappée**　　　　　🇪SIM

38, rue Boyer
Métro: Ménilmontant, Gambetta
Tel. 01 47 97 44 58
lechappee@hotmail.com
Closed Friday evening, Monday, Wednesday evening, August. Open until 11 PM.
Prix fixe: 11€ (lunch), 15€ (lunch), 17,50€ (dinner). A la carte: 28€.
Terrace.

As its name suggests, this place offers an escape from hostile prices and characterless menus. Managed by Gaetan Du Pasquier and Bruno Commergnat with Boly at the stove, this bistro and terrace provides charm and good humor (music on Saturday!), with its sociable canteen air and simple but good recipes, such as pear and blue cheese croustillant with stewed leeks, red mullet and vegetables on a bed of tomato confit, lamb curry with toasted almonds, and finally, the orange and Cointreau soufflé providing a light conclusion.

● **La Mer à Boire**　　　Ⓝ🇪SIM

1-3, rue des Envierges
Métro: Pyrénées
Tel.-Fax 01 43 58 29 43
contact@la.meraboire.com
www.la.meraboire.com
Closed Sunday evening, Christmas,
New Year's, 2 weeks in August.
Open until midnight.
A la carte: 20€.
Terrace.

Devoted to comic books and newspaper cartoons, this pleasant, inexpensive bistro offers various tapas, hummus, cold or hot soups, open sandwiches, charcuterie, cheeses and assorted Oriental plates for customers seeking an inexpensive break from routine. Exquisite chocolate cake. Concerts on Friday evenings and exhibitions all year round.

Good Restaurants & Others

● Le Saint Amour · SIM

2, av Gambetta (at 32, bd Ménilmontant)
Métro: Père-Lachaise
Tel.-Fax 01 47 97 20 15
le-saint-amour@wanadoo.fr
Open daily until 11 PM.
Prix fixe: 10€, 12,50€. A la carte: 35€.
Air cond. Terrace. Private dining room.

Renovation has brought a more modern feel to Jean-Louis and Nathalie Rouchet's corner café, with its air conditioning, terrace, private dining room and meeting rooms upstairs. The surroundings are changing, and the good, old-fashioned recipes no longer allude solely to the Auvergne: goat cheese and apricots in crisp phyllo pastry, Dover sole fried in butter, beef tenderloin with morel mushrooms, diplomate with candied fruit and brandy. The house wines are always a delight.

● Aux Tables du Père Lachaise · COM

44, bd de Ménilmontant
Métro: Père-Lachaise
Tel.-Fax 01 47 97 51 52
Closed Sunday (in winter).
Open until 10:30 PM.
Prix fixe: 12€ (lunch), 17€ (dinner), 10€ (children). A la carte: 35–40€.
Air cond. Terrace.

A pleasantly full, but not bloated stomach? A range of suggestions to suit the season? Stop in at this fashionable but relaxed restaurant run by Annick and Alain Pinna. Salad of lentils and duck gizzard confit, roasted mahi-mahi with mixed vegetables, grilled duck breast and floating island work their charms in the paneled dining room in ochre and burgundy tones.

● Vin Chai Moi · Ⓝ SIM

33, rue de la Chine
Métro: Gambetta
Tel. 01 40 33 48 01
Closed Sunday, Monday, 2 weeks in beginning of April, 2 weeks in beginning of August.
Open until 11:30 PM.
Prix fixe: 10€ (lunch, wine included), 12,80€ (lunch). A la carte: 38€.
Air cond.

Former Guy Savoy sommelier Luc Menier and Delphine Siaud offer a comfortable welcome in this gourmet wine bar. The silk paintings on the walls and open kitchen are easy on the eye. Presented in two set menus (one simple, the other more impressive), the duck foie gras, spiced sea bass in phyllo pastry with herbed potato purée, sautéed duck with vegetable crumble, soft chocolate cake and sorbet with toasted hazelnuts have a natural charm. (Also see Rendezvous.)

● Le Zéphyr · Ⓢ 🏠 SIM

1, rue du Jourdain
Métro: Jourdain
Tel. 01 46 36 65 81. Fax 01 40 33 10 89
luenee@wanadoo.fr
www.lezephyrcafe.com
Open daily until 11:30 PM.
Prix fixe: 13,50€ (lunch on weekdays), 28€ (dinner on weekdays).
A la carte: 40–50€.
Terrace.

We always enjoy the art deco look in burgundy shades here, with faux leather banquettes, mirrors and large windows opening onto a shady terrace. However, on the kitchen front, ambition often rhymes with inattention and affectation. At the risk of upsetting chef and proprietor Ludovic Enée, we feel obliged to suggest he take a more rigorous approach toward the flavors, seasoning, marinades and cooking times of the asparagus carpaccio with roquefort cheese (insipid), roasted sea bass stuffed with vegetables (limp), slow-roasted lamb shank with thyme (overcooked) and the crunchy—actually not that crunchy—strawberry dessert with crushed Montélimar nougat. The price to be paid? The check is fairly high for the area, except at noon, when the set menu combines quality with economy. The downside? The welcome and service (several readers have informed us of serious problems in this area).

▼ SHOPS

BREAD & BAKED GOODS

▼ La Boulange d'Antan ⚙

150, rue de Ménilmontant
Métro: St-Fargeau
Tel. 01 46 36 13 82
7:30 AM–8 PM.
Closed Sunday afternoon, Monday.

The former Ganachaud bakery, later the Pierre bakery, has now been taken over by Mr. Hecht. Its star product is still the Flûte Gana, but its traditional-style loaf, organic bread and prune turnover are also worth the visit.

▼ La Flûte Gana

226, rue des Pyrénées
Métro: Gambetta
Tel. 01 43 58 42 62. Fax 01 43 58 70 57
7:30 AM–8 PM.
Closed Sunday, Monday, August.

Isabelle and Valérie Ganachaud have followed in their father's footsteps, while the eldest, Marianne, handles the Flûte Gana bread franchise. The attractive storefront window looks in on the bakery. Wholegrain bread, thin baguettes, organic bread, hazelnut bread and rye and raisin bread are all high quality, as are the prune turnovers, Landais apple pie with a crisp phyllo topping, Vendée brioche, kouign-amann (a Breton flaky buttered cake), soft apple cake, rice pudding and Norman-style apple tart.

▼ Jean-Claude Rubin

7, rue de Bagnolet
Métro: Alexandre-Dumas
Tel. 01 43 70 27 53
6 AM–8:45 PM (Saturday 2 PM). Closed Saturday afternoon, Sunday, Christmas–New Year's, 2 weeks in July.

Jean-Claude Rubin continues to impress us with his "Grand Siècle" baguette, without additives, made from wheat flour and gluten. It has remained compact and delicate, its taste unchanged over sixty years, and it keeps well. In addition, his multigrain baguette, country-style round loaf, various breads (with olives or bacon, all rye or corn), homemade cookies filled with apples and prunes and fruit tarts are always very commendable.

WINE

▼ Au Bon Plaisir

104, rue des Pyrénées
Métro: Maraîchers
Tel. 01 43 71 98 68. Fax 01 43 71 98 68
10 AM–1 PM, 4–8 PM (Saturday
10 AM–8 PM, Sunday 10 AM–1:30 PM).
Closed Sunday afternoon, Monday,
2 weeks in mid-August.

Here, Didier Lefort presents a fine selection of wines from the Bordeaux region, Languedoc, the Rhône Valley and Provence. His choice of regional products (foie gras, terrines, cheeses, pickles or Corsican charcuterie) is also appealing.

CHOCOLATE

▼ Sucré Cacao

89, av Gambetta
Métro: Gambetta
Tel.-Fax 01 46 36 87 11
9 AM–1:30 PM, 2:30 PM–7:30 PM (Sunday
6 PM), 3 weeks in August.

James and Sophie Berthier took advantage of the opportunity last summer to completely renovate their store. Pistachio clafoutis, Christmas fruitcake, almond cakes, ganaches, filled chocolates (milk or dark), iced cookies and catered foods are still just as appetizing.

CANDY & SWEETS

▼ La Campagne à Paris ⛫

210, rue des Pyrénées
Métro: Gambetta
Tel.-Fax 01 46 36 88 57
9:30 AM–12:45 PM, 3:45–7:45 PM
(Saturday 9:30 AM–1:30 PM,
3:45–7:45 PM). Closed Monday morning.

This exquisite Thirties' boutique presents some of France's provincial delicacies (Montargis pralinés, almond biscotti from Cordes, mountain honeys), as well as a sound range of growers' wines and champagnes.

CHEESE

▼ La Cave aux Fromages

1, rue du Retrait
Métro: Gambetta
Tel. 01 43 66 64 60. Fax 01 47 97 03 99
8 AM–1 PM, 3–7:45 PM
(Saturday 8 AM–7:45 PM). Closed Sunday
afternoon, Monday.

Christian Le Lann, star local butcher, reveals a second string to his bow with this fine cheese store, which also has a 17th-century stone cellar. Goat cheeses from the Loire, Manche camembert, persillé des Aravis (a blue cheese from Savoie), Corsican brocciu, Alpine beaufort and mountain brebis are remarkable.

▼ François Priet

214, rue des Pyrénées
Métro: Gambetta
Tel. 01 46 36 88 90. Fax 01 46 36 10 25
8 AM–1 PM, 4–8 PM
(Saturday 7:30 AM–1:30 PM, 3:30–8 PM).
Closed Sunday afternoon, Monday.

François Priet carefully ages his gruyère, fruity comté, Corsican brebis, artisanal roquefort, genuine Vosgian munster and tomme from Savoie, all meticulously selected.

PASTRIES

▼ Le Triomphe

95, rue d'Avron
Métro: Maraîchers
Tel. 01 43 73 24 50. Fax 01 43 73 23 50
7:30 AM–7:30 PM. Closed Monday, 1 week
in winter, mid-July–end of August.

Alain Clouet and Jean-Pierre Thuillier offer the finest classic cakes and pastries in their excellent store. Various puddings, tarts (cocktail, passion fruit and coconut), filled chocolates (cherry, brandy, truffles, chopped nuts and dried fruit), as well as fruitcakes, brownies, butter cookies and raisin cookies, irresistibly tempt the sweet tooth.

FRUIT & VEGETABLES

▼ Aux Halles Gâtines

216, rue des Pyrénées
Métro: Gambetta
Tel. 01 46 36 87 34
8:30 AM–7:45 PM.
Closed Sunday afternoon, Monday.

This welcoming grocery store is a temple to the finest produce of the vegetable gardens and orchards of France. Beans from Bourgueil, peaches from Estagel, melons from Provence, wild strawberries, raspberries, wild mushrooms, lovely salad greens and various types of potatoes are all hits here.

REGIONAL PRODUCTS

▼ La Gastronomie du Terroir

222, rue des Pyrénées
Métro: Gambetta
Tel. 01 46 36 36 21
8 AM–8 PM.
Closed Sunday afternoon, August.

Marc Fermin, who refurbished his store completely last summer, sells country-style terrine, onion boudin, Alsatian hams and dried sausages, cured ox tongue from Auvergne, Rouergue pâté—all very enticing.

◆ RENDEZVOUS

BARS

◆ La Flèche d'Or

102 bis, rue de Bagnolet
Métro: Alexandre-Dumas
Tel. 01 43 72 04 23
6:30 PM–2 AM
(Saturday, Sunday 10 AM–2 AM).
Closed Monday.

This convivial spot offers a range of musical styles in the former Charonne rail station. Jazz, rock, Latin, and electro concerts enliven its nights. On Sunday afternoon, there is traditional French music (*guinguette*) and a show for the kids.

WINE BARS

◆ Le Baratin

3, rue Jouye-Rouve
Métro: Belleville, Pyrénées
Tel. 01 43 49 39 70
Noon (Saturday 6 PM)–1 AM.
Closed Saturday lunch, Sunday, Monday,
3 weeks in August.

You can come here any time until late to enjoy the generous traditional cuisine. More than 250 wines, accompanied by rabbit in orange sauce or herbed mahi-mahi. (Also see Restaurants.)

◆ L'Escargot d'Or

53, rue de Bagnolet
Métro: Alexandre-Dumas
Tel. 01 43 73 85 69
10 AM–2 AM. Closed Monday.

We like this convivial bar where customers enjoy plates of cheeses or charcuterie, veal stew or duck confit, and we finally succumb to the lure of delicious crème brûlée or soft and moist chocolate cake. Fine wines by the glass.

● Vin Chai Moi   Ⓝ

33, rue de la Chine
Tel. 01 40 33 48 01
10 AM–2 AM. Closed Sunday, Monday,
2 weeks in beginning of April, 2 weeks in
beginning of August.

Delphine Siaud and Luc Menier, formerly at Chai 33 in the new Bercy district, have scored a hit with this chic, refined, flavorsome wine bar. The Bordeaux and Rhône Valley vintages are first rate and the solid fare is just as good as the liquid. (Also see Restaurants.)

CAFES

◆ La Cagnotte de Belleville   🛉

13, rue Jean-Baptiste-Dumay (where it intersects 114, rue de Belleville)
Métro: Jourdain
Tel. 01 46 36 65 40
7 AM–1 AM. Closed Sunday afternoon,
3 weeks in August.

This little bistro with its antique charm presents tartines made with Poilâne bread topped with quality charcuterie and cheese. The food is washed down with a Loire, Beaujolais or Rhône Valley wine.

◆ Lou Pascalou   🛉

14, rue des Panoyaux
Métro: Ménilmontant
Tel. 01 46 36 78 10
9 AM–2 AM. Open daily.

Followers of the hip and fashionable are drawn by the discussions, exhibitions and concerts here. Wines by the glass and assorted sandwiches are enjoyed in a lively atmosphere.

◆ La Maroquinerie

23, rue Boyer
Métro: Gambetta
Tel. 01 40 33 30 60. Fax 01 40 33 35 06
infos@lamar.fr
www.lamaroquinerie.fr
4:30–1 AM. Closed Sunday, August.

On the premises of a former tannery, this literary café has a reading room, a small concert room and a movie theater. Guests snack on green asparagus and goat cheese terrine, porgy with cuttlefish ink risotto, gratin of cardoons and foie gras.

◆ La Mère Lachaise

78, bd de Ménilmontant
Métro: Père-Lachaise
Tel. 01 47 97 61 60
9 AM–2 AM. Closed Christmas, New Year's.

This fashionable café a stone's throw from Père Lachaise cemetery has a lot of charm with its old-style paintings. Patrons enjoy well-garnished salads, tuna with parmesan, honey-braised lamb shank and delicious tiramisu.

◆ Le Piston Pélican   🛉

15, rue de Bagnolet
Métro: Alexandre-Dumas
Tel.-Fax 01 43 70 35 00
8 AM (Saturday, Sunday 10 AM)–2 AM.
Open daily.

This 1900s' café still has its vintage vats, stucco on the ceiling and fine zinc bar. Customers enjoy the innocuous wines, beers on tap and domestic fare. On Friday and Saturday there are blues concerts late in the evening.

TEA SALONS

◆ Le Damier

29, rue Saint-Blaise
Métro: Porte-de-Bagnolet, Maraîchers
Tel. 01 43 72 16 95
9:30 AM–7:30 PM. Closed Saturday,
Sunday, 1 week in Christmas,
3 weeks in August.

The attractions of this fine, convivial tea-room are Jean-Marie and Catherine Féret's smiles and the appealing dishes: cassoulet, couscous, tandoori brochettes, Alsatian tart, chocolate fondant, fruit crumble.

◆ Le Rayan   ◉

80, bd de Belleville
Métro: Belleville
Tel. 01 43 15 64 40
10 AM–2 AM. Open daily.

Customers come to watch sports on the flat screen near the bar, smoke a hookah as they do in Cairo, drink a mint tea and eat a Tunisian "gazelle horn" in this Moorish tearoom, which looks out onto a very ethnic boulevard.

🌱 Restaurant has a Garden or Terrace   ⏰ Open past 11PM   🅂 Open on Sundays

🍽 Restaurant has a Garden or Terrace   ⏲ Open past 11PM   🆂 Open on Sundays

🌿 Restaurant has a Garden or Terrace   🕐 Open past 11PM   S Open on Sundays

🍴 Restaurant has a Garden or Terrace ⏰ Open past 11PM S Open on Sundays

🌿 Restaurant has a Garden or Terrace   🕐 Open past 11PM   🆂 Open on Sundays

🌳 Restaurant has a Garden or Terrace   ⏱ Open past 11PM   S Open on Sundays

🌿 Restaurant has a Garden or Terrace ⏱ Open past 11PM 🅂 Open on Sundays

🍽 Restaurant has a Garden or Terrace   ⏰ Open past 11PM   S Open on Sundays

🌳 Restaurant has a Garden or Terrace   ⏰ Open past 11PM   S Open on Sundays

🍽 Restaurant has a Garden or Terrace   ⏱ Open past 11PM   Ⓢ Open on Sundays

♣ Restaurant has a Garden or Terrace ⏱ Open past 11PM Ⓢ Open on Sundays

🍽 Restaurant has a Garden or Terrace   ⏲ Open past 11PM   S Open on Sundays

🌡 Restaurant has a Garden or Terrace   ⏱ Open past 11PM   S Open on Sundays

🌳 Restaurant has a Garden or Terrace   ◷ Open past 11PM   🅂 Open on Sundays

🌿 Restaurant has a Garden or Terrace   🕐 Open past 11PM   S Open on Sundays

♥ Restaurant has a Garden or Terrace　⊙ Open past 11PM　S Open on Sundays

♣ Restaurant has a Garden or Terrace　◷ Open past 11PM　S Open on Sundays